New York City

THE ROUGH GUIDE

There are more than one hundred Rough Guide titles
covering destinations from Amsterdam to Zimbabwe

Forthcoming titles include
Bangkok • Barbados • Japan • Jordan • Syria

Rough Guide Reference Series
Classical Music • The Internet • European Football • Jazz
Opera • Reggae • Rock Music • World Music

Rough Guide Phrasebooks
Czech • French • German • Greek • Hindi & Urdu • Indonesian • Italian
Mandarin Chinese • Mexican Spanish • Polish • Portuguese • Russian
Spanish • Thai • Turkish • Vietnamese

Rough Guides on the Internet
http://www.roughguides.com

Rough Guide Credits

Text Editor:	Andrew Rosenberg
Series Editor:	Mark Ellingham
Editorial:	Martin Dunford, Jonathan Buckley, Samantha Cook, Jo Mead, Kate Berens, Amanda Tomlin, Ann-Marie Shaw, Paul Gray, Sarah Dallas, Chris Schüler, Helena Smith, Julia Kelly, Caroline Osborne, Judith Bamber, Kieran Falconer, Olivia Eccleshall
Online Editors:	Alan Spicer (UK); Geronimo Madrid (US)
Production:	Susanne Hillen, Andy Hilliard, Judy Pang, Link Hall, Nicola Williamson, Helen Ostick
Cartography:	Melissa Flack, Maxine Burke
Finance:	John Fisher, Celia Crowley, Catherine Gillespie
Marketing & Publicity:	Richard Trillo, Simon Carloss, Niki Smith (UK); Jean-Marie Kelly, SoRelle Braun (US)
Administration:	Tania Hummel, Alexander Mark Rogers

Acknowledgements

Biggest thanks on this new edition go to everyone at both Rough Guides offices, especially Geronimo Madrid for fact-checking and research; Jean Marie Kelly and SoRelle Braun for ideas and good cheer; Susanne Hillen, Helen Ostick, Judy Pang and Nicola Williamson for patient production work; and Melissa Flack for great and speedy mapmaking. Also Greg Ward and Narrell Leffman for Brit and Oz basics; Mel and Martin D for inspiration and guidance; Ty Thomas for top indexing and general error-spotting; Margaret Doyle for proof-reading; and last but not least the inimitable Darren Colby, for all the usual things.

Many thanks are also due to those who wrote in with comments and corrections for the previous edition – see the list on p.iv. Keep the letters coming!

This sixth edition published January 1998 by Rough Guides Ltd, 1 Mercer Street, London WC2H 9QJ.

Distributed by the Penguin Group:

Penguin Books Ltd, 27 Wrights Lane, London W8 5TZ.

Penguin Books USA Inc, 375 Hudson Street, New York 10014, USA.

Penguin Books Australia Ltd, 487 Maroondah Highway, PO Box 257, Ringwood, Victoria 3134, Australia.

Penguin Books Canada Ltd, 10 Alcorn Avenue, Toronto, Ontario, Canada M4V 1E4.

Penguin Books (NZ) Ltd, 182–190 Wairau Road, Auckland 10, New Zealand.

Printed in England by Clays Ltd, St Ives PLC

Typography and **original design** by Jonathan Dear and The Crowd Roars.

Illustrations throughout by Edward Briant.

A catalogue record for this book is available from the British Library.

ISBN 1-85828-296-9

New York City

THE ROUGH GUIDE

Written and researched by
Martin Dunford and Jack Holland

with additional contributions by
Adrian Curry, Anngel Delaney, Lenore Person,
Andrew Rosenberg, Melanie Ross, Julie Taraska
and Andy Young

THE ROUGH GUIDES

Help us update

We've gone to a lot of effort to ensure that this edition of the Rough Guide to New York City is completely up to date and accurate. However, things do change – in New York more rapidly than anywhere – and if you feel that there's something we've missed, or that you'd like to see included, please write and let us know. We'll credit all contributions, and send a copy of the new book (or any other Rough Guide, if you prefer) for the best letters.

Please mark letters "Rough Guide to New York City" and send to:
Rough Guides, 1 Mercer St, London WC2H 9QJ or
Rough Guides, 375 Hudson St, 9th floor, New York, NY 10014.

Email should be sent to:
mail@roughguides.co.uk

Online updates about Rough Guide titles can be found on our Web site at http://www.roughguides.com

The Authors

Martin Dunford and **Jack Holland** first met at the University of Kent at Canterbury. Following jobs as diverse as insurance collection, beer-barrel rolling and EFL teaching in Greece, they co-founded the Rough Guides in the mid-1980s. After co-authoring several other titles, Martin is now editorial director of Rough Guides while Jack recently escaped from Berlin, where he lived for four years.

Readers' letters

We'd like to thank all the readers who wrote in with comments and updates to the previous edition: Neil Abbott, Frances Bate, Leslie Bergin, Jamie "Dipso" Brown, Mark Carroll, Patricia Collins, Dr Gillian Cookson, Simon Crutchley, Angela Easterling, Ian Fletcher, Paul Grove, Paul Fenwick, Fernando Ferrer, Christopher and Helena Hilton, Will Lamson, Jon Melnick, Marion Morton, Tim Passey, Susan Pemberton, Toby Pyle (of Hostelling International), Philip and Karen Rayner, Timothy Riley, Charlie Roberts, Shauna Sampson, L. J. Scott, Jean Wallington, Andrew Whitman, Susan Wilkins, and all the folks who contacted us via email but preferred to remain anonymous.

Our apologies to anyone whose name has been omitted or misspelt.

Rough Guides

Travel Guides • Phrasebooks • Music and Reference Guides

We set out to do something different when the first Rough Guide was published in 1982. Mark Ellingham, just out of University, was travelling in Greece. He brought along the popular guides of the day, but found they were all lacking in some way. They were either strong on ruins and museums but went on for pages without mentioning a beach or taverna. Or they were so conscious of the need to save money that they lost sight of Greece's cultural and historical significance. Also, none of the books told him anything about Greece's contemporary life – its politics, its culture, its people, and how they lived.

So with no job in prospect, Mark decided to write his own guidebook, one which aimed to provide practical information that was second to none, detailing the best beaches and the hottest clubs and restaurants, while also giving hard hitting accounts of every sight, both famous and obscure, and providing up-to-the-minute information on contemporary culture. It was a guide that encouraged independent travellers to find the best of Greece, and was a great success, getting shortlisted for the Thomas Cook travel guide award, and encouraging Mark, along with three friends, to expand the series.

The Rough Guide list grew rapidly and the letters flooded in, indicating a much broader readership than had been anticipated, but one which uniformly appreciated the Rough Guides' mix of practical detail and humour, irreverence and enthusiasm. Things haven't changed. The same four friends who began the series are still the caretakers of the Rough Guide mission today: to provide the most reliable, up-to-date and entertaining information to independent-minded travellers of all ages, on all budgets.

We now publish 100 titles and have offices in London and New York. The travel guides are written and researched by a dedicated team of more than 100 authors, based in Britain, Europe, the USA and Australia. We have also created a unique series of phrasebooks to accompany the travel series, along with the acclaimed series of music guides, and a best-selling pocket guide to the Internet and World Wide Web. We also publish comprehensive travel information on our two websites: http://www.hotwired.com/rough and http://www.roughguides.com

Contents

Part Three Listings 277

Part Four Contexts 439

Index 473

List of maps

MAP SYMBOLS

⊂⊐	Interstate		(i)	Information Centre
– – –	Ferry route		⊠	Post Office
⊏ ⊏ ⊏	Tunnel		♠	Buddhist Temple
——	Waterway		✡	Synagogue
▬▬▬	Chapter division boundary		⊞	Church
Ⓜ	Metro Station		■	Building
✗	Airport		▨	Park
			▨	Beach

Introduction

New York City is the most beguiling place there is. You may not think so at first – for the city is admittedly mad, the epitome in many ways of all that is wrong in modern America. But spend even a week here and it happens – the pace, the adrenaline take hold, and the shock gives way to myth. Walking through the city streets *is* an experience, the buildings like icons to the modern age, and above all to the power of money. Despite all the hype, the movie-image sentimentalism, **Manhattan** – the central island and the city's real core – has massive romance: whether it's the flickering lights of the midtown skyscrapers as you speed across the Queensboro bridge, the 4am half-life in Greenwich Village, or just wasting the morning on the Staten Island ferry, you really would have to be made of stone not to be moved by it all.

None of which is to suggest that New York is a conventionally pleasing city. Take a walk in Manhattan beside Central Park, notably its east side, past the city's richest apartments and best museums, and keep walking: within a dozen or so blocks you find yourself in the lower reaches of Spanish Harlem. The shock could hardly be more extreme. The city is constantly like this, with glaring, in-your-face wealth juxtaposed with urban problems – poverty, the drug trade, homelessness – that have a predictably high profile. Things have definitely changed during the nineties, especially in the recent, Mayor Guiliani years. Crime figures are at their lowest in years and are still dropping (statistically, New York is now one of the country's safest big cities), and renewal plans have finally begun to undo years of urban neglect. But for all its new clean-cut image New York remains a unique place – one you'll want to return to again and again.

The city also has more straightforward pleasures. There are the different **ethnic neighborhoods** of Lower Manhattan, from Chinatown to the Jewish Lower East Side and ever diminishing Little Italy; and the artsy concentrations in SoHo, TriBeCa, and the East and West Village. There is the **architecture** of corporate

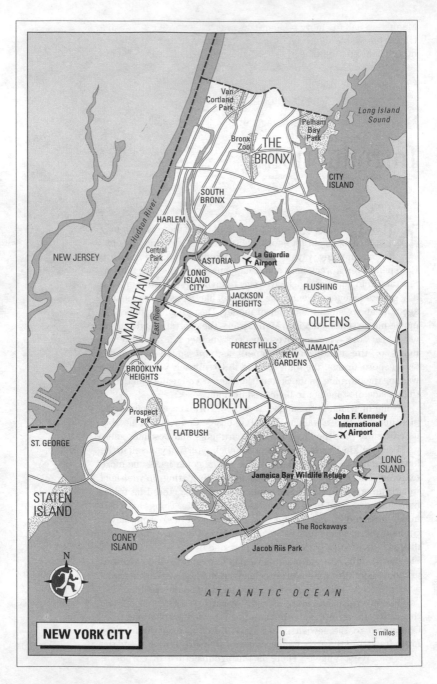

Van
Cortland
Park

Long Island
Sound

Pelham
Bay
Park

Bronx
Zoo

THE
BRONX

CITY
ISLAND

SOUTH
BRONX

HARLEM

Hudson River

NEW JERSEY

Central
Park

ASTORIA

La Guardia
Airport

MANHATTAN

LONG
ISLAND
CITY

East River

JACKSON
HEIGHTS

FLUSHING

QUEENS

FOREST HILLS

JAMAICA

KEW
GARDENS

BROOKLYN
HEIGHTS

Prospect
Park

BROOKLYN

John F. Kennedy
International
Airport

FLATBUSH

ST. GEORGE

Jamaica Bay Wildlife Refuge

LONG
ISLAND

STATEN
ISLAND

CONEY
ISLAND

The Rockaways

Jacob Riis Park

N

ATLANTIC OCEAN

NEW YORK CITY

0   5 miles

Manhattan and the more residential Upper East and West Side districts (the whole city reads like an illustrated history of modern design); and there is the **art**, which affords weeks of wandering in the Metropolitan and Modern Art Museums and countless smaller collections. You can **eat** anything, at any time, cooked in any style; **drink** in any kind of company; sit through any number of obscure **movies**. The established arts – **dance, theater, music** – are superbly catered for, and although the contemporary **music scene** is perhaps not as vital or original as in, say, London or Los Angeles, New York's **clubs** are varied and exciting, if rarely inexpensive. And for the avid consumer, the choice of **shops** is vast, almost numbingly exhaustive in this heartland of the great capitalist dream.

Costs

Perhaps your biggest single problem in New York is going to be **money**, or rather how to hold on to what you have. The exchange rate for foreign visitors is fairly good these days – around $1.60 to the pound sterling at time of writing – and the city, as long as you're not renting an apartment, is as cheap as it has been for some time. Still, it's an expensive place to spend time, and far pricier than most of the rest of the US. **Accommodation** will be your biggest day-to-day expense, with rock-bottom double hotel rooms in Manhattan costing around $80, much more for anywhere in the mid-range, and even a basic YMCA double room going for over $50 – though there are options that work out cheaper (see our recommendations in Chapter 16). The **bottom line** for staying alive – *after this* – is around $30 a day, a figure which will of course skyrocket the more you dine out and party, although it is possible to eat out both well and inexpensively. There are bargain **restaurants** – see Chapter 17 for listings – where you'll be well-fed for $10 or less, while the all-American breakfast will set you up for the day, and ubiquitous delis, pizza places and felafel stands provide the cheapest snacks for just a couple of dollars. Foreign visitors should note that in restaurants of all kinds you're expected to tip no less than fifteen percent, and tipping bartenders around ten percent is customary, too.

Climate and when to go

New York's **climate** ranges from the stickily hot and humid in midsummer to well below freezing in January and February: winter and high summer (most people claim the city is unbearable in July and August) are much the worst time you could come. Spring is gentle, if unpredictable, and usually wet, while autumn is perhaps the best season: come at either time and you'll find it easier to get things done and the people more welcoming. Bring a warm coat, wool sweaters, gloves and thermal underwear in mid-winter (plus boots, stout hats and earmuffs to combat the blizzards), and T-shirts, shorts and the like in summer months. Whatever time of year you come, dress in layers: buildings tend to be overheated during winter months and air-conditioned to the point of iciness in summer. Also bring comfortable and sturdy shoes – you're going to be doing a lot of walking.

	Average New York Temperatures											
	Jan	Feb	Mar	Apr	May	Jun	Jul	Aug	Sep	Oct	Nov	Dec
Max °F	39	40	48	61	71	81	85	83	77	67	54	41
Max °C	4	5	8	16	21	27	29	28	25	19	12	5
Min °F	26	27	34	44	53	63	68	66	60	51	41	30
Min °C	-3	-3	1	6	11	17	18	19	16	10	5	-1

For a full and up-to-the-minute rundown on weather conditions in NYC phone ☎ 212/976-0001.

Part 1

The Basics

Getting there from Britain and Ireland

Unless you're in no hurry and can afford the QE2, the only way to get to New York from Britain and Ireland is **to fly**. A wide range of airlines serve the London–New York route, so competition is intense, and the choice of tickets and fares can be bewildering. For the best current offers, it pays to shop around. Check the travel ads in the Sunday papers – and, in London, *Time Out* and the *Evening Standard* – or consult one of the agents detailed on p.4. Treat our comments as a general guide only, and one that's likely to have undergone at least subtle alterations by the time you read it.

From Britain

Flights tend to **leave** Britain in the morning or afternoon and **arrive** in New York in the afternoon or early evening; flying time is seven to eight hours. Coming back, most flights depart in the evening to arrive in Britain early next morning; flying time, due to the prevailing winds, is shorter – six to seven hours.

Airlines

Of the nine airlines that currently fly between Britain and New York, the major operators are *British Airways*, who offers five nonstop services each day from London Heathrow to JFK, another

from Heathrow to Newark, and one daily flight to JFK from each of London Gatwick, Manchester, and Glasgow. *American Airlines* has six daily flights from Heathrow to JFK, *Continental* has two daily flights to Newark from Gatwick, and one each from Manchester and Birmingham, and *United* has three daily flights from Heathrow, of which two go to JFK and one to Newark. *Virgin Atlantic* flies twice daily Heathrow to Newark and once from Gatwick to Newark, while *Delta* has one or two daily flights from Heathrow to JFK, plus one daily service between Manchester and JFK. *Air India* flies once daily from Heathrow to JFK, *Kuwait Airways* flies the same route three times weekly, and finally *El Al* flies two or three times weekly between London Stansted and Newark.

Fares and agents

Fares vary according to season, availability and the current level of inter-airline competition. There are three main fare seasons: low season (October to March, excluding Christmas and New Year); mid season (April to mid-June); and high season (mid-June to September and three weeks or so around Christmas and New Year). If you contact any of the airlines directly, you may learn of some special cut-price deal (particularly in winter), but they're more likely to offer you an **Apex** ticket. The conditions on these are pretty standard whoever you fly with: seats must be booked 21 days or more in advance, and you must stay for a minimum of seven nights, a maximum of one month; they're also usually nonrefundable and can't be changed without incurring a hefty penalty fee. Prices are pretty much the same across the board: low-season midweek rates start at just under £300 return, rising to around £375 in spring, and over £450 in high season.

> To choose whether you'd rather fly into JFK or Newark airports, and details on how to reach Manhattan from either, see "Points of arrival" on p.13.

Airlines in Britain

Air India	☎ 0181/745 1000	El Al	☎ 0171/957 4100
American Airlines	☎ 0345/789789	Kuwait Airways	☎ 0171/412 0007
British Airways	☎ 0345/222111	United Airlines	☎ 0181/990 9900
Continental Airlines	☎ 0800/776464	Virgin Atlantic	☎ 01293/747747
Delta Airlines	☎ 0800/414767		

Travel agents in Britain

Campus Travel		**STA Travel**	
London	☎ 0171/730 2101	London	☎ 0171/361 6262
Birmingham	☎ 0121/414 1848	Bristol	☎ 0117/929 4399
Brighton	☎ 01273/570226	Cambridge	☎ 01223/366966
Bristol	☎ 0117/929 2494	Manchester	☎ 0161/834 0668
Cambridge	☎ 01223/324283	Leeds	☎ 0113/244 9212
Edinburgh	☎ 0131/668 3303	Oxford	☎ 01865/792800
Manchester	☎ 0161/833 2046	**Trailfinders**	
Oxford	☎ 01865/242067	London	☎ 0171/938 3366
Council Travel		Birmingham	☎ 0121/236 123
London	☎ 0171/437 7767	Bristol	☎ 0117/929 9000
Nouvelles Frontières		Glasgow	☎ 0141/353 2224
London	☎ 0171/629 7772	Manchester	☎ 0161/839 6969
		Travel Bug	
		Manchester	☎ 0161/721 4000

Tour operators in Britain

Bon Voyage		**Trans Atlantic Vacations**	
Southampton	☎ 01703/330332	Horley	☎ 01293/774441
British Airways Holidays		**United Vacations**	
Crawley	☎ 01293/722727	Heathrow Airport	☎ 0181/750 9648
Destination USA		**Virgin Holidays**	
London	☎ 0171/253 2000	Crawley	☎ 01293/617181

Tax of about £30 is added to all fares, and flying at the weekend costs an extra £30 or so.

However, if you're keen to find the cheapest possible fare, it makes more sense to contact an **agent** that specializes in low-cost flights, as listed above. Especially if you're under 26 or a student, these can knock up to fifty percent off the fares quoted by the airlines, bringing prices down to £200 return or less off season, and around £300 return during the mid to high seasons. The best deals are generally with the less popular airlines like *Kuwait Airways* or *Air India*. You might also call one of the **American specialists** we've listed in the box above, who often have access to the very cheapest transatlantic seats as well as summer charters. Their brochures are available in most high street travel agents, or you can contact them direct at the numbers given above.

If you're on a really tight budget you may want to consider flying as a **courier**, although during the off season at least you may find it's not worth the hassle given the variety of low fares available. Most of the major courier firms offer opportunities to travel cheaply in return for delivering a package, at rates of around £150–200 return. Normally, though, you're required to sacrifice your baggage allowance (only hand baggage is allowed) and fit in with some tight restrictions on when you travel – stays of much more than a fortnight are rare. For addresses look in the Yellow Pages.

From Ireland

The only nonstop scheduled services to New York from Ireland are provided by *Aer Lingus*, which flies once to JFK and twice to Newark from

Airlines in Ireland

Aer Lingus	☎ 01/844 4777	Delta Airlines	☎ 01/676 8080
British Airways	☎ 1-800/626747	Virgin Atlantic	☎ 01/873 3388

Travel agents in Ireland

Discount Travel		Student & Group Travel	
Dublin	☎ 01/679 5888	Dublin	☎ 01/677 7834
Flight Finders International		USIT	
Dublin	☎ 01/676 8326	Belfast	☎ 01232/324073
Inflight Travel		Cork	☎ 021/270900
Belfast	☎ 01232/740187	Dublin	☎ 01/679 8833
Joe Walsh Tours			
Dublin	☎ 01/676 3053		

Tour Operators in Ireland

American Holidays			
Belfast	☎ 01232/238762	Dublin	☎ 01/679 8800

Dublin each day, and also once daily from Shannon to JFK, at a cost of up to IR£500 for an Apex ticket. As usual, though, the best plan is to approach an **agent** direct, preferably one specializing in under-26 or student travel, which can bring the price down to as little as IR£315 for a round-trip ticket in low season, around IR£50 more during the summer.

Inclusive tours

All-in deals – flights plus hotel accommodation in New York City – can be a good idea if you're only planning a short stay. Low-season prices per person for a return flight plus three nights staying in a middle-range midtown hotel start at £400–500 and rise to more like £600–700 at peak periods; seven nights would cost from £600 up to around £900 per person, again depending on the time of year. Most high street travel agents have the full range of brochures and can advise on the best deals, or contact the operators listed above.

Entry requirements

Citizens of Britain, Ireland and most European countries in possession of full **passports** (which must remain valid for six months after your trip) do not require visas for visits to the United States of less than ninety days. Instead you are simply asked to fill in the **visa waiver form** handed out on incoming planes. Immigration control takes place on arrival in New York, when you're expect-

For advice on staying on in New York, see p.47.

ed to provide details of where you are staying on your first night.

For further details, contact the American embassies in Britain (24/31 Grosvenor Square, London W1A 1AE; ☎ 0171/499 9000) or Ireland (42 Elgin Rd, Ballsbridge, Dublin; ☎ 1/668 7122). British and Irish consulates in New York are listed on p.437.

Insurance

Though not compulsory, **travel insurance** including medical coverage is essential in view of the high costs of health care in the US. Credit cards (particularly American Express) often have certain levels of medical or other insurance included, especially if you use them to pay for your trip; in addition, if you have a good "all risks" home insurance policy it may well cover your possessions against loss or theft even when overseas, and many private medical schemes also cover you while abroad. If you plan to participate in potentially dangerous activities such as watersports or skiing, you'll almost certainly have to pay an extra premium; check carefully that your policy will cover you in case of an accident.

Most travel agents and tour operators sell travel insurance – policies offered by *Campus Travel* or *STA* in the UK and *USIT* in Ireland are usually reasonable value. If you feel the cover is inadequate, or you want to compare prices, any insurance broker, bank or specialist travel insurance company should be able to help: call *Columbus*

Travel Insurance (☎0171/375 0011), *Endsleigh Insurance* (☎0171/436 4451), or *Frizzell Insurance* (☎01202/292 333). Two weeks' coverage for a trip to the US should cost around £30, a month more like £50.

Getting there from Australia and New Zealand

The **high season** for airfares to the US is mid-May to August and December to January; **low season** is mid-January through February, and October through November; shoulder season is the rest of the year. Tickets purchased directly from the airlines tend to be expensive, and travel agents offer much better deals on fares and have the latest information on fly-drive packages and stopover specials. The best discounts are through **Flight Centres** and **STA**, who can also advise on visa regulations. Fares from eastern Australian capitals are generally the same (airlines offer a free connecting service between these cities), whereas fares from Perth and Darwin are about Aus$400 more.

Not surprisingly, given the distances involved, there is very little in the way of direct scheduled flights and packages to New York **from Australia** or **New Zealand**, and most people reach the

eastern United States by way of the West Coast gateway cities of Los Angeles and San Francisco. You can do this by either buying an **all-in ticket** via LA or San Francisco, or simply flying to LA and using one of the domestic flight coupons you can buy with your international ticket. The latter can work out to be cheaper than opting for a straight-through fare, especially if you intend to take in other US cities besides New York. For example, a low-season straight return ticket to LA costs around Aus$1640/NZ$2000 with *Air New Zealand*, with domestic flight coupons costing around Aus$390 (for a minimum of three), making it one of the cheapest ways to get to New York. In comparison an add-on return fare will cost you in the region of Aus$450/NZ$500. Another option worth consideration if New York is part of a wider US trip – and you have plenty of time – is to travel overland by car, train or bus from your West Coast point of entry.

Traveling from Australia and New Zealand the best onward flight connections, via LA or San Francisco, are with *United Airlines, Air New Zealand and Qantas*, all of which have daily services from Sydney, Melbourne and Auckland via LA or San Francisco for around Aus$2120/NZ$2450 in low season up to Aus$2599/NZ$2899 in high season. The lowest fares to New York, however, are with *JAL*, with daily flights from Sydney, Brisbane and Cairns via Tokyo or Osaka for around Aus$1750–2050, based on the season, and several times a week from Auckland, NZ$1950–2699, also based on season. *Korean Airlines* flies from Sydney and Brisbane via Seoul several times a week from

Airlines and agents in Australia and New Zealand

Accent on Travel, 545 Queen St, Brisbane ☎07/3832 1777.

Air New Zealand, 5 Elizabeth St, Sydney ☎02/9223 4666; corner of Customs and Queen streets, Auckland ☎09/366 2424.

Anywhere Travel, 345 Anzac Parade, Kingsford, Sydney ☎02/663 0411.

Brisbane Discount Travel, 360 Queen St, Brisbane ☎07/3229 9211.

Budget Travel, PO Box 505, Auckland ☎09/309 4313.

Discount Travel Specialists, Shop 53, Forrest Chase, Perth ☎08/9221 1400.

Flight Centres, Australia: Circular Quay, Sydney ☎02/9241 2422; Bourke St, Melbourne ☎03/9650 2899; plus branches nationwide. New Zealand: National Bank Towers, 205–225 Queen St, Auckland ☎09/309 6171; Shop 1M, National Mutual Arcade, 152 Hereford St, Christchurch ☎09/379 7145; 50–52 Willis St, Wellington ☎04/472 8101; other branches countrywide.

JAL, Floor 14, Darlington Park, 201 Sussex St, Sydney ☎02/9283 1111; Floor 12, Westpac Tower, 120 Albert St, Auckland ☎09/379 9906.

Korean Airlines, 36, Carrington St, Sydney ☎02/9262 6000; 7–9 Falcon St, Parnell, Auckland ☎09/307 3687.

Passport Travel, 320b Glenferrie Rd, Malvern, Melbourne ☎03/9824 7183.

Qantas, International Square, Jamison St, Sydney ☎02/9236 3636; Qantas House, 154 Queen St, Auckland ☎09/303 2506.

STA Travel, Australia: 732 Harris St, Ultimo, Sydney ☎02/212 1255 or 281 9866; ☎02/9212 1255 or 9281 9866; 256 Flinders St, Melbourne ☎03/9347 4711; other offices in Townsville, Cairns and state capitals. New Zealand: Traveler's Centre, 10 High St, Auckland ☎09/309 4058; 233 Cuba St, Wellington ☎04/385 0561; 223 High St, Christchurch ☎03/379 9098.

United Airlines, 10 Barrack St, Sydney ☎02/9237 8888; 7 City Rd, Auckland ☎09/307 9500.

Aus$2110–2350 and from Auckland for NZ$2350–2650.

Round-the-world and air passes

If you intend to take in New York as part of a world trip a **round-the-world** ticket offers the best value for money, working out just a little more than an all-in ticket. *Cathay Pacific–UA's* "Globetrotter," *Air New Zealand–KLM–Northwest's* "World Navigator" and *Qantas–BA's* "Global Explorer" all offer six stopovers worldwide, limited backtracking, and additional stopovers (around $120 each), from AUS$2499/$3199–NZ$3089/$3599. More US-oriented, but only available in Australia, is *Singapore–TWA's* "Easyworld" fare, allowing unlimited stopovers worldwide with a maximum of 8 within the US, and limited backtracking within the US (flat rate AUS$3023).

Air passes or coupons valid for single flights in continental US are offered by various domestic airlines. These can only be purchased with your international ticket and all cost about AUS$390 for a minimum of three with each additional coupon costing around AUS$120.

Entry requirements

Australian and New Zealand **passport** holders staying less than 90 days do not require a visa, providing they arrive on a commercial flight with an onward or return ticket. For longer stays a US multiple-entry visa costs AUS$26. You'll need an application form, available from the US visa information service (☎1902/262 682), one signed passport photo and your passport. You must either mail it or personally lodge it at one of the American embassy or consulate addresses – in Australia, 21 Moonah Place, Canberra ACT 2600 (☎2/6270-5000), and in New Zealand, 29 Fitzherbert Terrace, Thorndon, Wellington (☎4/472 2068). For postal applications in Australia, payment can be made at any post office; you'll also need to include the receipt of payment and an SAE. Processing takes about ten working days for postal applications; personal lodgements take two days – but check details with the consulate first. Restrictions still apply to communists and communist sympathizers. Visas are denied to convicted criminals.

Travel insurance

Travel insurance is definitely recommended and is available from most travel agents or direct from insurance companies. Most policies are fairly similar in premium and coverage. A typical policy covering New York will cost around Aus$130/ NZ$145 for two weeks; Aus$190/NZ$210 for one month; and Aus$280/NZ$310 for two months. Companies worth trying are *Cover More* (☎02/9202 8000 or 1-800/251 881) and *Ready Plan* (☎03/9791 5077 or 1-800/337 462; in Auckland ☎09/379 3208).

Getting there from the United States and Canada

For information on how to reach Manhattan from its three **airports** (although most domestic flights come into La Guardia), see "Points of arrival" on p.13. All **Amtrak services**, including trains from Canada, arrive at **Penn Station** at 32nd St and 7th and 8th aves; only local Metro-North commuter trains use Grand Central Station at 42nd St and Park Ave. By **bus**, you arrive in New York at the **Port Authority Bus Terminal**, 8th Ave and 42nd St.

By air

From most places in North America, **flying** is the fastest and easiest way to reach New York. It can also be the cheapest – but finding that cheap fare won't always be easy. Fares fluctuate so wildly that it doesn't make sense to try to quote them here. Even the shuttles – flights used mainly by business people during the week – from nearby Boston and Washington, DC, can vary from month to month.

New York is the hub of most North American traffic so fares are very competitive. Prices depend more on passenger volume than anything else, so you'll do better (if you have a choice) flying from one of the larger cities. Your best bet is to start calling the major airlines (see the box opposite for toll-free numbers) as early as possible – even earlier if you'll be traveling at Thanksgiving or Christmas – because cheap fares usually account for only a portion of the seats available on a given flight, and they fill up fast. It's not impossible to get a last-minute deal, but on the major airlines good fares usually require you to purchase your ticket 14 days (sometimes 21 days) in advance and stay a Saturday night. Try the smaller airlines, too, since they often pitch in with cheaper deals. Travel agents won't necessarily find you a better fare so much as save you the trouble of making the phone calls yourself. As a guideline, round-trip **fares** from the West Coast average $450–500 (though they can be as low as $300), around $100 or so less for the Midwest or Florida. From Canada, reckon on paying Can$300 or so from Toronto or Montréal, around Can$450 from Vancouver – though again, it's quite possible to get flights for much less.

Besides student travel offices, bargain-basement **travel agents, consolidators** and **courier services** (often found in small ads in the backs of newspapers) can be the best place to find last-

Major airline toll-free numbers

Aero California ☎ 1-800/237-6225

Air Canada US ☎ 1-800/776-3000; in British Columbia 1-800/663-3721; in Alberta, Saskatchewan and Manitoba 1-800/542-8940; in eastern Canada 1-800/268-7240

Alaska Airlines ☎ 1-800/426-0333

Aloha Airlines ☎ 1-800/367-5250

American Airlines ☎ 1-800/433-7300

America West Airlines ☎ 1-800/235-9292

Canadian Airlines US ☎ 1-800/426-7000; in Canada ☎ 1-800/665-1177

Continental Airlines ☎ 1-800/525-0280

Delta Airlines ☎ 1-800/221-1212; in Canada call directory inquiries, ☎ 1-800/555-1212, for local toll-free number

Hawaiian Airlines ☎ 1-800/367-5320

Northwest Airlines ☎ 1-800/225-2525

Southwest Airlines ☎ 1-800/435-9792

Tower Air ☎ 1-800/221-2500

TWA ☎ 1-800/221-2000

United Airlines ☎ 1-800/241-6522

US Air ☎ 1-800/428-4322

Discount flight agents

Council Travel, 205 E 42nd St, New York, NY 10017 ☎ 1-800/226-8624 or 212/822-2700, and branches in many other US cities. Student/budget travel agency.

STA Travel, 10 Downing St, New York, NY 10014 ☎ 1-800/777-0112 or 212/627-3111, and other branches in the Los Angeles, San Francisco and Boston areas. Worldwide discount travel firm specializing in student/youth fares; also student IDs, travel insurance, car rental, rail passes, etc.

Travel Avenue, 10 S Riverside, Suite 1404, Chicago, IL 60606 ☎ 1-800/333-3335 or 312/876-6866. Full-service travel agent that offers discounts in the form of rebates.

Travel CUTS, 187 College St, Toronto, ON M5T 1P7 ☎ 416/979-2406, and other branches all over Canada. Organization specializing in student fares, IDs and other travel services.

UniTravel, 1177 N Warson Rd, St Louis, MO 63132 ☎ 1-800/325-2222 or 314/569-2501. Consolidator.

Tour operators

American Airlines Fly Away Vacations ☎ 1-800/321-2121

American Express Vacations ☎ 1-800/241-1700

Broadway Theatours, 1350 Broadway, New York, NY 10018 ☎ 1-800/843-7469.

Delta's Dream Vacations, PO Box 1525, Fort Lauderdale, FL 33302 ☎ 1-800/872-7786.

Smithsonian Study Tours & Seminars, 1100 Jefferson Drive SW, Room 3045, Washington DC 20560 ☎ 800/258-5885.

minute options; they're also good for **one-way tickets**, which can be ridiculously expensive on the big airlines. It's worth checking out their round-trip offers, too, but since these tickets tend to be very restrictive (for example, leave on a Tuesday, return on a Tuesday, stay two weeks only), you'll need to shop around. If you're a nervous flier, bear in mind that these agents often book flights on small, no-name airlines; that's how they get them so cheap.

Inclusive tours

Many operators run **all-inclusive vacations**, combining plane tickets and hotel accommodation

with (for example) sightseeing, wining and dining, or admission to Broadway shows. Even if the "package" aspect doesn't thrill you to pieces, these deals can still be more convenient and sometimes even more economical than arranging the same thing yourself, providing you don't mind losing a little flexibility. With such a vast range of packages available, it's impossible to give an overview – major travel agents will have brochures detailing what's on offer.

By train

For those heading to New York City from within the same radius as the shuttle flights noted on p.8, travel **by train** is a viable alternative, though not likely to be much cheaper. The most frequent services are along the New England–New York–Washington DC corridor; fares from Washington and Boston are around $120 round-trip, $220 for Metroliner tickets. There is also one daily train linking Montréal and Toronto with New York; fares on this service start at around Can$160 return. Train fares are often based on availability; book as early as possible to get the cheapest rates.

Although in theory it's possible to haul yourself **long-distance** from the West Coast, the Midwest or the South, it's a slow trip (three days plus from California). One-way tickets from the West Coast will be downright expensive as well, as much as $325 in peak season, although some tickets do allow **stopoffs** and round-trip fares can be competitive. An "All Aboard" cross-country fare, for example, lets you make the round trip in 45 days with three stopovers, for $378 during the peak season, $318 off-peak. (For *Amtrak*, the off-season is roughly September through June, with the Christmas–New Year rush excluded.) There are also occasional specials, basic nonrefundable tickets with certain restrictions and unlimited stopovers that can be had for as little as $259. Ask your travel agent for more information, or call *Amtrak's* information and reservations number: ☎1-800/USA-RAIL.

By bus

This is the most time-consuming and least comfortable mode of travel, and by the time you've kept yourself alive on the trip it's rarely the most economical. The only way in which buses are more useful than trains is that they serve a much larger portion of the country – so if New York is just one stop on an eclectic back-country tour, check out **Greyhound's** *Ameripass*, though it is (like *Amtrak's USA Railpass*) open to foreign citizens only and as such can only be bought overseas or in New York. It offers unlimited travel on the network for 7 days ($179), 15 days ($289), 30 days ($399) or 60 days ($599). Where you can find bus bargains is within the northeast corridor; in this busy region, bus competition can be as fierce as airline competition, sending prices up and down within days, if not hours. One-way from either DC or Boston to New York can go for as little as $20, though it is usually closer to $30. Call *Greyhound* (☎1-800/231-2222), *Trailways*

(☎1-800/343-9999) or *Bonanza* (☎1-800/556-3815) for up-to-the-minute information.

One alternative to bus hell is the famous, slightly alternative **Green Tortoise** bus, which connects **San Francisco** with New York every couple of weeks between May and October. Not the best choice if your idea of hell tends towards Sartre (the Tortoise is full of "other people"), but more gregarious types can look forward to a laid-back journey with generally like-minded souls through some of America's most beautiful spots. There are plenty of stops for hiking, river-rafting, hot springs and more, and the buses themselves are comfortable and congenial, with tape-deck systems and ample mattresses to sack out on.

The 10-day **northern route** (via Reno, Idaho, Montana, Wyoming, South Dakota, Minnesota, Chicago, Indiana and Pennsylvania) runs mostly in the hottest part of the summer and costs around $300 plus $80 for food, while the 14-day **southern route** (generally via Los Angeles, the Mojave Desert, Arizona, New Mexico, Texas, New Orleans and Appalachia) costs $380 plus $90 for food. From outside the San Francisco Bay area call ☎1-800/TORTOIS for more information (☎415/956-7500 if you're local), or write to 494 Broadway, San Francisco, CA 94133.

Driveaways

Potentially the cheapest legitimate way of getting to New York is to arrange for a **driveaway**, in which you deliver a car cross-country for its owner, paying only fuel costs. Look in your local Yellow Pages under "Automobile Transporters." Cars are not always available – especially to a popular destination like New York – so it helps if you have some flexibility and time to hang around and wait for one.

The usual **requirements** stipulate that you have to be over 21, have a valid driver's license (and sometimes a clean record printout from your local DMV), and have between $100 and $200 and/or a credit card handy as a deposit. The deposit is refundable on arrival and theoretically there's nothing to pay on the way except gas and motel bills. But keep in mind that while it's accepted that you may want to see a bit of the country on the way, there are generally tight delivery deadlines – 2 to 3 weeks coast to coast is the norm – and if you're late without good reason you'll forfeit the deposit. Try to hit the company up for extra days and mileage when you take the job: if on a journey from Chicago to New York you invent a sick auntie who needs to be visited in Atlanta, you might get an official extension right off the bat . . . although you could alternatively find yourself en route to Atlanta and no further while some other eager driver takes your car on to New York.

Entry requirements for Canadians

Canadian travelers will find crossing into the states quite easy. All you need is a **photo ID**, though you'd be wise, as always, to carry your passport, too – and make sure that both are valid. The **US embassy** in Canada is located at 100 Wellington Street, Ottawa, Ontario K1P 5T1 (☎613/238-5335), if you have any questions about visitor status. Other US consulates are in Calgary (☎403/266-8962); Halifax (☎902/429-2480); Montréal (☎514/398-9695); Toronto (☎416/595-1700); and Vancouver (☎604/685-4311).

Insurance

American travelers should find that their health insurance covers any charges or costs – but certain insurers require you to notify them in advance that you'll be on the road, so call. Several of the major **credit cards** offer automatic coverage for various aspects of traveling, and they may also offer their own additional policies; while most **Canadians** are covered for medical mishaps abroad by their provincial health plans. If you only need trip cancellation/interruption coverage (to supplement your homeowner's/credit card/student health plan), this is generally available at around $6 per $100. In this case, however, it could be cheaper to purchase a short-term policy through your travel agent. *Council Travel*, for example (see p.9 for address and phone numbers), charges $25.50 a month for medical coverage, with an additional $37 for baggage insurance, and you're covered anywhere more than a few hundred miles from your home. You could also try *Access America* (☎1-800/283-8300); they also offer a fairly inexpensive and complete plan. If you are unable to use a phone or if the practitioner requires immediate payment, save all forms to support a claim for subsequent reimbursal. Remember also that time limits may apply when making claims, so promptness in contacting your insurer is highly advisable. Few, if any, American health insurance plans cover against theft while traveling, but, taking into account high deductibles, most renter's or homeowner's insurance policies will cover you while traveling – usually for about 10 percent of your regular coverage – if you carry "off-premises theft" as part of your policy.

Health

Coming from Europe, you don't require any inoculations to enter the States. What you do need is insurance (see p.5), as medical bills for the most minor accident can be astronomical – and there's no way they can be escaped.

If you need to see a **doctor**, lists can be found in the Yellow Pages under "Clinics" or "Physicians and Surgeons." Your consulate (see chapter 25, "Directory," for listings) will also have selected names. A basic consultancy fee can be upwards of $125 before you even start talking, and medicines – either prescribed or over the counter – don't come cheap either; keep receipts for all you spend and claim on your insurance when you return.

Minor ailments can be remedied at a **drug-store**. These sell a fabulous array of lotions and potions designed to allay the fears of the most neurotic New Yorkers, but foreign visitors should bear in mind that many pills available over the counter at home are by **prescription only** here (for example, any codeine-based painkillers) and brand names can be confusing. If in doubt, ask at a pharmacy, where prescription drugs are dispensed (for addresses, see p.429).

Should you be in an accident, don't worry about dying on the sidewalk – medical services will pick you up and charge later. For minor accidents, there are emergency rooms, open 24 hours, at the following Manhattan hospitals: *Bellevue Hospital,* 1st Ave and E 27th St (☎562-4141); *St Vincent's Hospital,* 7th Ave at 11th St (☎604-7997); *New York Hospital,* E 70th St at York Ave (☎746-5050); *Mount Sinai Hospital,* Madison Ave at 100th St (☎241-7171). For emergency dental treatment, the number to ring is ☎679-3966.

Alternative and natural medicine

If alternatives to conventional medicine are what you're after, you'll find plenty – just don't expect them to be any cheaper than the standard kind. *C.O. Bigelow Apothecaries* at 414 6th Ave between 8th and 9th sts (☎473-7324) has the largest selection of **homeopathic products** in the city, with a knowledgeable staff who can assist you or recommend a naturopathic doctor. The *New York Open Center,* 83 Spring St, between Broadway and Crosby (☎219-2527), has a small bookstore and a good selection of free publica-

---

Playing safe

HIV/AIDS is one health risk which unfortunately needs its own mention. While much of the hysteria that surrounded the early years of AIDS awareness has died down, the dangers are as real as ever, and not just within the gay community. New York City has one of the highest concentrations of HIV-positive people in the world. You've heard it all before, but we make no apologies for saying it all again: take the obvious precautions. If you choose to use drugs intravenously, on no account share needles; it's best if you bring your own. If you choose to have penetrative sex of any kind, use condoms, which you'll find readily available at supermarkets, 24-hour delis and drugstores. For more information and advice about HIV and AIDS, call the **GMHC Hotline** (run by Gay Men's Health Crisis, an organization not exclusively for gay men) at ☎807-6655.

---

tions having to do with (among other things) health and natural living; you'll be able to find acupuncture, massage therapy, Chinese herbology, Bach flower remedies, and a whole range of other options through them. You'll also find listings in the Yellow Pages and on the bulletin boards of health food stores and natural food restaurants. Keep in mind, however, that many insurers are reluctant to recognize alternative treatments; check your policy carefully before you open your wallet.

Points of arrival

Airports

Three major airports serve New York. **International flights** are handled at **John F Kennedy (JFK)** (☎718/656-4520), in the borough of Queens, and **Newark** (☎908/961-2000), in northern New Jersey; **La Guardia** (☎718/533-3400), also in Queens, handles **domestic flights**.

Wherever you arrive, the cheapest way into Manhattan is **by bus**. In the following sections we've outlined the bus connections from each airport, along with their public transit alternatives. The two Manhattan **bus terminals**, used by all airport buses, are Grand Central Station and the Port Authority Bus Terminal. For most hotels, **Grand Central** (at Park Ave and 42nd St) is the more convenient: well poised for taxis to midtown Manhattan and with a subway station for routes towards the east of the city. Bear in mind also that some of the larger Midtown hotels – the *Marriott Marquis, Hilton,* etc – operate a free shuttle service to and from Grand Central. The **Port Authority Terminal** at 8th Ave and 42nd St (☎564-8484) isn't as good a bet for Manhattan (there's a lot of humping luggage from bus to street level, though you may find it handy if you're heading for the west side of the city (via the #A train) or out to New Jersey (by bus). Some airport buses also stop off at **Pennsylvania Station** on 7th and 8th avenues at 32nd St, where you can catch *Amtrak* long-distance trains on to other parts of America, and at the **World Trade Center** at the bottom of Manhattan – good for downtown/Brooklyn subways and connections to New Jersey.

Taxis are the easiest option if you are in a group or are arriving at an antisocial hour, but are otherwise an unnecessary expense: reckon on paying upwards of $20 from La Guardia, $30 from JFK and $40 or more from Newark; and you'll be responsible for paying the turnpike and tunnel tolls – an extra $5 or so. If you do decide to splurge on a cab, ignore the individual drivers vying for your attention as you exit the baggage claim; these **"gypsy cab"** operators are notorious for ripping off tourists. Ask any airport official to direct you to the taxi stand, where you'll be sure to get into an official New York City yellow taxi.

> For **general information** on getting to and from the airports, call ☎1-800/AIR-RIDE.

There are also a few **car services**, which have direct phones near the exits; they're competitive in price with taxis (they charge set rates), sometimes even lower.

A newer option is the **Gray Line Air Shuttle**, a minibus you can pick up at any of the three airports (check with the ground transportation desk) or arrange by phone (☎1-800/451-0455). These shuttles are giving the older airport buses (see below) a run for their money, since for only a few dollars more they'll take you straight to your hotel – at least if you're staying in Midtown. The shuttles operate from the airport between 7am and 11pm, and from the hotels between 6am and 7pm; the cost is $14 per person to La Guardia, $16.50 to JFK, and $18.50 to Newark. Ask about discounts if you're traveling in a group of three or more.

JFK

Carey Buses. Buses leave JFK for Grand Central Station and Port Authority Bus Terminal every thirty minutes between 6am and midnight; between 6am and 6pm there are also drop offs at Penn Station. In the other direction, they run from Grand Central and Port Authority every twenty to thirty minutes between 5am and 1am (and from Penn Station every hour between 8am and 8pm). Journeys take from 45 to 60 minutes, depending on time of day and traffic conditions; the fare is $13 one-way, with discounts available to students, senior citizens, the disabled, and children when you travel from (not to) Grand Central. For details on services, call ☎718/632-0500 or 1-800/678-1569; for discount information, call ☎1-800/284-0909.

> When you come to **catch your flight home**, remember that JFK is large and very spread out: if your terminal is last on the bus route (like *British Airways*) you should allow a further fifteen minutes or so to get there.

Airline offices in New York City

Many of these airlines have additional offices throughout the city.

Aer Lingus	☎557-1110	**Delta**	☎1-800/221-1212
122 E 42nd St		100 E 42nd St	
Air Canada	☎1-800/776-3000	**El Al**	☎768-9200
1166 Ave of the Americas	or ☎869-8840	Call for offices	
(6th Ave)		**Kuwait**	☎308-5454
Air India	☎751-6200	430 Park Ave	
400 Park Ave	or ☎407-1460	**Northwest**	☎1-800/225-2525
American	☎1-800/433-7300	100 E 42nd St	
100 E 42nd St		**TWA**	☎1-800/892-4141 (domestic)
British Airways	☎1-800/247-9297	1 E 59th St	
530 5th Ave		**United**	☎1-800/241-6522
Continental Airlines	☎319-9494	1 E 59th St	
One World Trade Center Airline Lobby		**Virgin Atlantic**	☎1-800/862-8621
		96 Morton St	or ☎242-1330

Public transit. Free shuttle buses run from all terminals at JFK to the Howard Beach/JFK subway stop on the #A train; from there, one subway token ($1.50) will take you anywhere in the city you want to go. Late at night, this might not be your best choice, since trains run infrequently and can be rather deserted, but in the daytime or early evening, it's a very viable, if tedious (travel time is at least an hour to Midtown) option. Alternatively, you can take the #Q10 green bus (subway token or $1.50, exact change and no paper money) to its last stop, right by the subway in Kew Gardens, Queens, and pick up the #E or #F train (for an additional token) to Manhattan. Travel time is about the same, but avoid this route like the plague at rush hour, since it's the most over-crowded line in the whole transit system. See the subway map (color map at back) to determine which is the most convenient route to your particular destination. For more information on subway and bus options, call ☎718/330-1234 between 6am and 9pm any day of the week.

Newark

New Jersey Transit. Buses run to the Port Authority Terminal once an hour, 24 hours a day. Journey time is about 30 to 45, and the fare is only $3.25, making it your best bet. Details on ☎201/762-5100.

Olympia Trails Airport Express. Buses leave for Manhattan every fifteen to twenty minutes (6.15am–midnight), stopping at the World Trade Center, Grand Central, Penn Station and Port Authority; going the other way, they run just as frequently, with the first bus leaving Grand Central at 5am. The buses leave Port Authority 24 hours a day. In either direction, the journey takes 30 to 45 minutes depending on the traffic, and the fare is $10. Details on ☎908/354-3330 or 718/622-7700.

PATH Rapid Transit. Involves a shuttle *Airlink* bus to Newark's Penn Station, where *PATH* trains run to stations in Manhattan; the fare is $4 for the bus, $1 for the train. Note that while the *PATH* train runs 24 hours a day, the *Airlink* buses only run from approximately 6am to 1.30am the next morning. Call ☎718 330-1234.

La Guardia

Carey Buses. Between 6.45am and midnight, buses leave every twenty to thirty minutes for Grand Central and Port Authority, and between 6am and 6pm for Penn Station as well. In the other direction, buses run between 7am and 1am (8am and 8pm for Penn Station). Journey time is 45 to 60 minutes, depending on traffic, and the fare is $10 one-way. For details on services, call ☎718/632-0500 or 1-800/678-1569; for discount information (from Grand Central only), call ☎1-800/284-0909.

Public transit. The best (and least-known) bargain in New York airport transit is the #M60 bus, which for $1.50 will take you into Manhattan, across 125th Street, and down Broadway to 106th Street. Ask the driver for a transfer when you get on the bus and you can get practically anywhere (for an explanation of transfers, see p.18). If you're heading for the youth hostel, it's an easy four-block walk from the #M60's last stop. Journey time can range from 20 minutes late at night to an hour in rush-hour traffic.

If the Upper West Side is not your destination, you might want to consider taking the #Q33 bus ($1.50) from La Guardia to Jackson Heights, Queens, where for another $1.50 you can get the #7, #E, #F or #R subway to Manhattan. Total travel time is approximately 40 minutes to Midtown.

JFK to La Guardia

Carey Buses. There's a service that links JFK and La Guardia airports between 5.40am and 11pm. Buses leave, on average, every thirty minutes (though it varies depending on your direction and the time of day) and take 45 to 60 minutes; at select times they make one stop along the way. The fare is $10 one way; call ☎1-800/678-8000.

Arriving by bus or train

If you're coming to New York by *Greyhound*, *Trailways*, *Bonanza* or any of the other long-distance **bus lines**, you'll arrive at the Port Authority Bus Terminal at 42nd St and 8th Ave (see p.13 for details of both terminals). By *Amtrak* **train**, you'll be coming in at Penn Station, 32nd St and 7th and 8th aves.

Getting around the city

The subway

The New York **subway** is dirty, noisy, intimidating and initially incomprehensible. It's also the fastest and most efficient method of getting from A to B throughout Manhattan and the Outer Boroughs, and it is a great deal safer and more user-friendly than it used to be. Put aside your qualms: an average of 3.6 million people ride the subway every day, quite a few for the very first time.

One way to make yourself feel better right at the start is to **familiarize yourself** with the sys-

tem when you first arrive. Read over the map inserted at the back of this book, or pick up a free subway plan at any subway station (also at the information booth on the concourse at Grand Central, the New York Convention and Visitors Bureau at Columbus Circle, or any of the Visitors Information Centers listed on p.21). The following basic guidelines will make more sense when you combine them with visual information.

The basics

• Broadly speaking, **train routes** in Manhattan run uptown or downtown, following the great avenues and converging, as the island itself does, in the downtown financial district. Crosstown routes are limited.

• Trains and their routes are generally identified by a **number or letter**. Though the subway is open 24 hours a day, some routes operate at certain times of day only; read your map carefully for the details. In the interest of safety, some entrances to stations are only open during certain hours – look for the green globe outside the entrance to signal it's staffed around the clock.

• There are two types of train: the **express**, which stops only at major stations, and the **local**, which stops at every station. If your destination is an express stop, the quickest way to get there is to change from local to express at the first express station, either by walking across the platform or taking the stairs to another level.

• Any subway journey costs a **flat fare of $1.50**. The most common way to pay your fare is with a **subway token**, available from any token booth, some delis and pharmacies, and any *McDonald's* (also useful when you need a token for the bus). There's no discount for buying several, but stocking up means no waiting in line, and they can be used for buses too. The best way to do this is to ask for a "ten-pak," which costs $15.

• The **MetroCard**, a multitrip card with an electronic strip, is the newest way to pay for your trip. It's available in pre-packaged denominations of $3, $6 and $15, or you can purchase it at the token booth and put up to $80 on it. But while it looks similar to discount cards you might find in other cities, the only discount that the MetroCard offers is a free transfer from a subway to certain bus lines – and vice versa – within a two-hour period. Other than that, its main advantage is that it weighs less in your pocket than a ten-pak and that you can reuse it, unlike a token. Unfortunately, MetroCards can only be used in new turnstiles; a growing number – though still not all – of the system's 469 stations are equipped with them. In other words, in the course of your New York explorations, you will probably need a regular token at some point.

• **Service changes** due to track repairs and other maintenance work are frequent (especially after midnight and on weekends) and confusing even to the most proficient subway rider. To keep abreast of the situation, read every Service Notice you see – they're the red-and-white posters plastered on bulletin boards and posts throughout the system – and don't be afraid to ask other passengers what's going on.

• Again, don't be afraid to **ask directions** or **look at a map** on the train or in the station. You may draw attention, but not the threatening kind you're thinking of – you're more likely to get ten people all talking at once, offering you ten pieces of contradictory advice. Obviously, if you're traveling late at night you should be sure of your route before you set out – knowing it will enable you

to travel much easier and with more confidence, and prevent the appearance of the "TOURIST - PLEASE MUG" sign that hangs around the necks of all those who peer at maps or look lost. But, if you follow common-sense safety rules (see the box opposite and the "Police and trouble" section, p.39), there's nothing wrong with admitting you're new at any of this.

• If you're starting to panic, or are lost, phone ☎718/330-1234. State your location and your destination and the operator will tell you the most direct route by subway or bus. Unfortunately, this service is only in operation between 6am and 9pm.

Lines and directions

Perhaps the main source of confusion for visitors is the multiplicity of **line/train names**. The letters and numbers on the subway map will be recognized by everyone, but the old line names – the IRT, the IND and the BMT – are still very much in use (even though they ceased to exist as separate compa-

Safety on the subway

Everyone has different views on **subway safety**, and everyone, too, has their horror stories. Many are exaggerated – and the subway definitely *feels* more dangerous than it actually is – but it's as well to follow a few established rules.

At night, always try to use the **center cars**, since they are more crowded. Yellow signs on the platform saying "During off hours train stops here" indicate where the conductor's car will stop. While you're waiting, keep to the **"Off-Hour Waiting Area"** (marked in yellow), where you can be seen by the token booth attendants; in cases where this area is on a different level, there will be a sign (accompanied by a chirping sound) to let you know a train is arriving, so don't worry about missing your train.

By day the whole train is theoretically safe, but don't go into empty cars if you can help it. If you do find yourself in an empty or nearly empty car, move into a fuller one at the next station. Some trains have doors that connect between cars, but do not use them other than in an emergency, since this is both dangerous and illegal.

Keep an eye on **bags** at all times, especially when sitting or standing near the doors. With all the jostling in the crowds near the doors, this is a favorite snatching spot.

For more information on safety, see "Police and trouble," p.39.

---

nies in 1940), as are popular "direction names." Just to give one example: the West Side IRT, Broadway Local, 7th Avenue Local and Number 1 train are all the same thing. One way in which New Yorkers do *not* refer to trains is by color: if you're looking for the #2 or #3 train, the red line, you'll probably be met with a blank stare.

The main lines and directions in Manhattan are outlined below.

• The local #1 and #9 and express #2 and #3 trains run north and south along Broadway and 7th Ave. This is the West Side IRT (for Interborough Rapid Transit, the company that opened New York's first subway line) and is also known as the Broadway line or the 7th Avenue line. Pay close attention north of 96th St and south of Chambers St, where the local and express trains diverge.

• The local #6 and express #4 and #5 trains run north and south along Lexington and Park avenues, diverging north of 125th St and south of Brooklyn Bridge. This is the East Side IRT, and is often called the Lexington Avenue line.

• The #7 train runs east and west along 42nd St from Times Square (Broadway/7th Ave) to Grand Central (Park Ave) and then out to Queens. This is also an IRT train, known commonly as the Flushing line.

• The express #A and local #C and #E trains run north and south along 8th Ave in midtown Manhattan, with the #E branching off south of Canal Street (to go to the World Trade Center) and north of 50th St (where it heads crosstown out to Queens). The #A and #C diverge north of 145th St. These IND trains (named after the Independent subway line, the first to be owned by the city rather than a private company) are often known collectively as the 8th Avenue line.

• The local #F and express #B, #D and #Q trains run north and south along 6th Ave in Midtown, turning east at W 4th St to provide something of a crosstown connection in lower Manhattan. North of the 47–50 St stop (Rockefeller Center), the #F, the #Q, and sometimes the #B branch off to go crosstown to Queens; check your map for details, since this line can be confusing. IND trains all, they're collectively known as the 6th Avenue line.

• The #N and #R trains succeed in connecting east and west several times, running along Broadway from lower Manhattan and then cutting east again after 57th St. These were originally BMT (Brooklyn–Manhattan Transit) trains, and are still referred to as such.

• The **Grand Central–Times Square Shuttle** connects the east and west sides of the IRT by running under 42nd St. It's marked on maps as the #**S** train.

• The #**L** is another useful crosstown line, running east and west along 14th St between 8th and 1st avenues. East of 1st Ave, the #L (a BMT train) runs out to Brooklyn.

Buses

New York's **bus system** is a lot simpler than the subway, and you can also see where you're going and hop off if you pass anything interesting. It also features many more crosstown routes, which are especially useful if you're going from the Upper West Side to the Upper East Side or vice versa. The major disadvantage of the bus system is that it can be extremely **slow** – in peak hours almost down to walking pace. **Bus maps**, like subway maps, can be obtained from the main concourse of Grand Central or the Convention and Visitors Bureau at Columbus Circle. We've printed a small Manhattan bus map, located at the back of the book, to tide you over.

A quick glance at the **routes** will reveal that they run along all the avenues and across major streets. There are three **types of bus**: **regular**, which stop every two or three blocks at five- to ten-minute intervals; **limited stop**, which travel the same routes, though stop at only about a quarter of the regular stops; and **express**, which cost extra and stop hardly anywhere, shuttling commuters in and out of the Outer Boroughs and suburbs. In addition, you'll find small private buses running in from New Jersey. Buses display their **number, origin and destination** up front.

Bus stops are marked by yellow curbstones and a blue, white and red sign that often (but by no means always) indicates which buses stop there. In addition, there will sometimes be a sign showing routes, times (rarely accurate) and intersections. To signal that you want **to get off** a bus, press the black strip on the wall. The "Stop Requested" sign at the front of the bus will come on, and the driver will stop at the next official bus stop. After midnight, you can request to get off on any block along the route the bus travels, regardless of whether it's a regular stop or not.

Fares and transfers

Anywhere in Manhattan the **fare** is $1.50, payable on entry with either a subway token (the most convenient way) or with the correct change – no pennies. And although there are now fareboxes that accept MetroCards, you still can't pay with a dollar bill.

If you're going to be using buses a lot, it pays to understand the **transfer system**. Transfers were designed to let a single fare take you, one way, anywhere in Manhattan. Since few buses go both up and down *and* across, you can trans-

Bus and subway information
☎ 718/330-1234 (daily 6am–9pm)
Lost and found ☎ 718/625-6200

fer from any bus to almost any other that continues your trip. (You can't use transfers for return trips.) They're given free on demand when you pay your fare, although if you use a transfer to get on a bus, you can't then ask for another one. The top of the transfer will tell you how much time you have in which to use it – usually around two hours. If you're not sure of where to get off to transfer, just ask the driver for some help.

Private bus companies

The lack (and disruption) of bus services in lower-income areas both in and out of Manhattan has been a major source of controversy over the years. It seems that whenever the city feels the need to cut back on services, those who need them the most end up losing out. In Queens, **private bus companies** pick up the slack (you'll find their routes marked, without additional information, on the regular Queens Bus Map), and in outer regions of most of the Outer Boroughs, small vans pick up and drop off passengers along old bus routes, generally for $1 or $1.50. While these vans are not strictly legal, they serve a definite purpose, and if you ask the driver or another passenger, you may be able to figure out how to use them.

Taxis

Taxis are worth considering if you're in a hurry, in a group, or if it's late at night.

In Manhattan, there are two types: **medallion cabs**, immediately recognizable by their yellow paintwork and medallion up top, and **gypsy cabs**, unlicensed, uninsured operators who tout for business wherever tourists arrive. Avoid gypsy cabs like the plague as they're rip-off merchants – their main hunting grounds are outside usual tourist arrival points like Grand Central.

Up to **four people** can travel in an ordinary medallion cab – **five** if the driver's in a particularly good mood or if you're lucky enough to grab one of the last-remaining, old-fashioned Checker cabs. **Fares** are $2 for the first eighth of a mile, 30¢ for each fifth of a mile thereafter. Basic charges rise by 50¢ after 8pm, and by 100 percent if you're rich or foolish enough to take a cab outside the New York City limits (eg to Newark airport). Trips outside Manhattan can additionally incur toll fees; not all of the crossings cost money, however, and the driver should ask you which route you wish to take.

The **tip** should be ten to twenty percent of the fare; you'll get a dirty look if you offer less. Also likely to cause a problem is change: drivers don't like splitting anything bigger than a $10 bill, and anything bigger than a $20 will produce invective.

Before you hail a cab, it's always a good idea to work out exactly where you're going and if possible the quickest route there – a surprising number of cabbies are new to the job and some speak little English. If you feel the driver doesn't seem to know your destination, don't hesitate to point it out on a map. An **illuminated sign** on top of the taxi indicates its availability; if the small lights on the side of the sign are lit, it means the cab is off duty or on radio call and won't pick you up.

Officially there are certain **regulations** governing taxi operators. A driver can ask your destination only when you're seated – and must transport you (within the five boroughs), however undesirable your destination may be. You may face some problems, though, if it's late and you want to go to an outer borough. Also, if you request it, a driver must pick up or drop off other passengers, open or close the windows, and stop smoking (they can also ask you to stop). If you have any **problems** with a driver, get the license number from the right-hand side of the dashboard, or medallion number from the rooftop sign or from the print-out receipt for the fare, and phone the *NYC Taxis and Limousine Commission* on ☎302-8294. This is also the number to call if you realize you've **left something** in a cab.

Driving

In a word, don't. Even if you're brave enough to take responsibility for dodging lunatic cab drivers, car rental is expensive, parking lots almost laughably so, and street parking hard to find. There's not much else to compare it to in the States, and if you're from abroad, better to keep your American driving fantasies to upstate excursions.

If you do need to drive, bear in mind a number of **rules. Seatbelts** are compulsory for everyone in front and for children in back. The **speed limit** is 35mph within the city, and you can be pulled over and given a breathalyzer test (known as the *alcotest*) at a police officer's discretion. (You're within your rights to refuse, but you'll then have to go to police headquarters.) Unlike most of the rest of the country, within city limits it's illegal to make a **right turn** at a red light.

Read signs carefully to figure out where to **park** – if the sign says "No Standing," "No Stopping," or "Don't Even THINK of Parking Here" (yes, really), that's a no. Also watch for street-cleaning hours (when an entire side of a street will be off-limits for parking), and don't park in a bus stop or in front of a fire hydrant. Private parking is expensive, extremely so at peak periods, but it makes sense to leave your car somewhere legitimate: if it's towed away you'll need to liberate it from the **car pound** (☎971-0770) – expect to pay around $150 in cash ($15 for each additional day they store it for you) and waste the best part of a day.

Car **theft and vandalism** are also problems, although more so in less-traveled parts of the city where vandals won't be seen working on your car. If you're going to have a car in the city for a while you should utilize some form of obvious deterrent to would-be thieves – the long yellow bars that lock between steering wheel and windscreen are a popular choice, as is the "Club." Avoid leaving valuables in your car at any time.

Cycling

Pulling away from the lights on a bike in Manhattan can mean a replay of the Monaco Grand Prix, and it's just about as dangerous. To enjoy it – and it can be a viable form of transportation once you're confident enough – do as the locals do and go for all possible rentable safety equipment: pads, a helmet, goggles and a whistle to move straying pedestrians. When you stop, be sure to chain, lock, and chain again your machine to something totally immovable if you'd like it to be there when you return.

Bike **rental** starts at about $6 an hour or $25 a day – which means opening to closing, so ask about 24-hour rates. You'll need one or two pieces of ID (passport and credit card will be sufficient) and, in some cases, a deposit (usually $150), though some firms will take your credit card details instead. Rates and deposits are generally more for racing models and mountain bikes.

The **Yellow Pages** have full listings of **bike rental firms** but among good-value, central suppliers are:

Bikes in the Park, Loeb Boathouse, Central Park (☎861-4137). The best place to rent bikes to tour the park.

Metro Bicycles, 1311 Lexington Ave at 88th St (☎427-4450); 546 6th Ave at 15th St (☎255-5100); and other branches in Manhattan. One of the city's largest bike stores.

Midtown Bicycles, 360 W 47th St at 9th Ave (☎581-4500). Standard at $6 an hour and $25 a day – but ask if they still have their "$24 for 24 hours" deal, a great bargain.

West Side Bikes, 231 W 96th St between Broadway and Amsterdam (☎663-7531). Upper West Side store, again handy for Central Park.

Walking

Few cities equal New York for sheer street-level stimulation, and getting around **on foot** is often the most exciting – and exhausting – method of exploring. Count on around fifteen minutes to walk ten north–south blocks – rather more at rush hour. And keep in mind that however you plan your wanderings you're going to spend much of your time slogging it out on the streets. **Footwear** is important (sneakers are good for spring/summer; winter needs something water-proof). So is **safety**: a lot more people are injured in New York carelessly crossing the road than are mugged. Pedestrian crossings don't give you automatic right of way unless the WALK sign is on – and, even then, cars may be turning, so be prudent. A good rule of thumb is to make eye contact with the driver, giving him or her your best "don't mess with me" New York look; if you can't make eye contact, run.

Rollerblading

While **rollerblading** is still a popular form of recreation, more and more people are using it as a speedy way to get around the city. If you're not proficient, the streets of Manhattan aren't really the place to learn; get some practice in Central Park or one of the other traffic-free skating spots (see

City address finder

Deciphering **avenue addresses** without knowing the cross streets is, for the most part, fairly easy. In general, drop the last figure, divide by two, then add or subtract according to the table below:

Avenues A, B, C and D	add 3
1st and 2nd avenues	add 3
3rd Avenue	add 10
4th Avenue	add 8
5th Avenue	up to 200 add 13
	up to 400 add 16
	up to 600 add 18
	up to 775 add 20
	from 777 to 1286 drop
	last figure and
	subtract 18
	up to 1500 add 45
	up to 2000 add 24
6th Avenue	subtract 12
7th Avenue	add 12; above
	110th St add 20
8th Avenue	add 10
9th Avenue	add 13
10th Avenue	add 14
Amsterdam Avenue	add 60
Audubon Avenue	add 165
Broadway	754 to 858
	subtract 29
	858 to 958
	subtract 25
	over 1000 subtract 31
Central Park West	divide number by 10
	and add 60
Columbus Avenue	add 60
Convent Avenue	add 127
Edgecombe Avenue	add 134
Fort Washington Avenue	add 158
Lenox Avenue	add 110
Lexington Avenue	add 22
Madison Avenue	add 26
Manhattan Avenue	add 100
Park Avenue	add 35
Pleasant Avenue	add 101
Riverside Drive	below 165th Street
	divide number by 10
	and add 72
St Nicholas Avenue	add 110
Wadsworth Avenue	add 173
West End Avenue	add 60

"Sports and Outdoor Activities," p.377, for details), though, and you're away. You'll find rentals, once again, in the Yellow Pages, or try one of the popular *Blades* stores (120 W 72nd St between Central Park West and Columbus, ☎787-3911; 1414 2nd Ave between 73rd and 74th streets, ☎249-3178). A credit card should be deposit enough, and prices run the gamut, ranging from $16 for 2 hours on weekends to $16 for 24 hours during the week. If after a day or two you find that you're hooked, some places give you a discount off the purchase price for having rented first.

Information, maps and tours

Once in New York, the best place to head for all kinds of information is the **New York Convention and Visitors Bureau** at 2 Columbus Circle, where 59th St, 8th Ave and Broadway meet (Mon–Fri 9am–5pm, Sat & Sun 10am–3pm; or call their "New York by Phone" recording at ☎397-8222). Going to the office is worthwhile: they have up-to-date leaflets on what's going on in the arts and elsewhere plus bus and subway maps and information on hotels and accommodation – though they can't actually book anything for you. Their high-gloss *Big Apple Guide* is good too, though the kind of information it gives – on restaurants, hotels, shopping and sights – is also available in the various free tourist magazines and guidettes you'll find in hotels and elsewhere. These include complete (if superficial) rundowns on what's on in the (more mainstream) arts, eating out, shops, etc and a host of ads that might just point you in the right direction.

The state-run **I Love New York** organization also has a good stock of free booklets and maps. They have offices in Times Square at 1515 Broadway, New York, NY 10036 (☎827-6251), and at 1 Commerce Plaza, Albany, NY 12245 (☎518/474-4116). Much of their information concentrates on New York State, though; if you're

---

You'll find other small **tourist information centers** and kiosks all over the city, starting with the airports, Grand Central and Penn stations, and Port Authority Bus Terminal. You'll probably come across others without trying, but the following list should help:

Bloomingdale's International Visitors' Center, Lexington Ave (at 59th St) ☎705-2098.

Fashion BID Visitors' Center, kiosk at the corner of 39th St and 7th Ave ☎398-7943.

Harlem Visitors' Bureau, 1 W 125th St (at 5th Ave) ☎283-3315.

NYU Information Center, 50 W 4th St (at Greene St/Washington Square) ☎998-4636.

Saks Fifth Avenue Ambassador Concierge Desk, 611 5th Ave (at 49th St) ☎940-4141.

Times Square Visitor and Transit Information Center, The Selwyn Theater, 229 W 42nd St (between 6th and 7th avenues) ☎869-5453.

Travelers' Aid/Victim Services, 2 Lafayette St (at Canal St) ☎577-7700.

New York on the Internet

There are countless **Web sites** that contain travel information about New York; if you have access to the **Internet**, you may want to do some extra research before (or during) your trip. What follows is a short list of both fun and informative sites for travelers. Here you'll find what's on around town, a sampling of local media and Woody Allen's given name (Allen Konigsberg). Be sure, too, to check out our own Web Site at *http://www.roughguides.com*

CitySearch NY
http://www.citysearchnyc.com/nyc/index.html
A solid search engine, weekly updated listings and tame features all on this comprehensive site.

Data Lounge
http://www.datalounge.com/
Where gay travelers can peruse community news, glance at the city's social calendar, or simply test the matchmaking skills of Edwina.

NYC Beer Guide
http://www.nycbeer.org/toc.html
The Beer Guide serves up the suds, from microbreweries to well-stocked bodegas.

PaperMag
http://www.papermag.com/
Updated daily and covering the cultural gamut, this hip guide has been on the cutting-edge of every trend to hit the streets.

Total NY
http://www.totalny.com/
One of few guides sporting real New York attitude, Total's quirky features and eclectic listings will tell you where to go and what to do.

The Village Voice
http://www.villagevoice.com/
The best thing here, from the elder (some say out-of-touch) alternative weekly, is the paper's witty listings section, "Choices."

Webtunes
http://webtunes.com/
Loaded with RealAudio samples and venue listings, this site has the lowdown on the city's music scene.

Woody Allen
http://www.media.uio.no/studentene/ ragnhild.paalsrud/woody/Woody.html
Everything you ever wanted to know about Woody but were afraid to ask.

---

at all interested in exploring beyond the five boroughs, it's worth getting their comprehensive state-wide map and regional guides. They do also have specifically New York City-oriented information, not least restaurant and hotel lists and maps.

Maps

We reckon our maps of the city should be fine for most purposes; **commercial maps**, like the *Rand McNally* "Plan of the City and all Five Boroughs" ($2.95), fill in the gaps. Others include the tiny laminated *Streetwise* maps – neatly laid-out and not expensive at around $5–6 from most book stores. Street atlases of all five boroughs cost about $8–9; if you're after a map of one of the individual Outer Boroughs, try those produced by *Geographia* at $3.50, again on sale in bookstores. For fun, try the surprisingly useful *New York City Unfolds* – a glossy, gimmicky pop-up map for $6.95. For more options, or if you have

trouble finding any of these, the *Complete Traveler* is a good map and guide shop; see p.425 for details.

Tours

One way of getting a hold on New York is simply to climb up to the **observation deck** of one of its tallest buildings, most obviously the Empire State Building or the World Trade Center. Of the two, the Empire State's position in the heart of Manhattan gives it the edge; see p.124 for more details. You can enjoy the view of lower Manhattan for free by simply walking across the Brooklyn Bridge (see p.193), or almost for free by taking the Staten Island Ferry (see p.24 and p.229). However, if you want more detailed background than this, or you have a specific interest in the city, there are all kinds of **tours** you can join, taking in the city from just about every angle and by just about every means available.

Big Apple Greeter

If you're at all nervous about exploring New York, or even just overwhelmed by the possibilities the city offers, look into **Big Apple Greeter**. One of the best – and certainly cheapest – ways to see the city from a native's viewpoint, it's a nonprofit organization run out of the Manhattan Borough President's office that matches up visitors with trained, volunteer "greeters." You can specify the part of the city you'd like to see, indicate an aspect of New York life you'd like to explore, or plead for general orientation – whatever your interests, the chances are that they will find someone to take you around. Tours, if they can be called that, have a friendly, informal feel, and generally last a few hours (although some have been known to go on all day). Best of all, the service is free. While you can call once you're in New York, it's strongly recommended that you contact the organization as far in advance as possible to ensure greeter availability. Write to: Big Apple Greeter, 1 Centre St, New York, NY 10007 (☎669-8159, fax 669-4900), or email *cstone@bigapplegreeter.org*

Bus tours

Apart from equipping yourself with a decent map, perhaps the most obvious way of orienting yourself to the city is to take a **bus tour** – something that's extremely popular, though frankly you'll find yourself swept around so quickly as to scarcely see anything. Still, the tops of double deckers are a great place to figure out what's where for later explorations – and in recent years, there has been an explosion of these, with the deals getting better (and the routes more comprehensive) each year as the three biggest companies – *Gray Line, New York Apple* and *New York Double Decker* – clamor for your business. In all three cases, the basics are the same: you purchase a ticket from the bus terminal, your hotel, or the bus itself at one of its many stops, and you can hop on and off the bus anywhere along its route. The more you spend, the more of the city you're entitled to see, and the longer time you have for seeing it – in general, an all-city tour over two days will cost $30, while you can also have two-hour or half-day tours for under $20. All tours have discounts for children under 12. Buses run seven days a week, from (approximately) 9am to 6pm, with special rates and times for evening tours.

Double decker bus tours

Gray Line Sightseeing Terminal
Port Authority at 42nd St and 8th Ave
New York, NY 10019   ☎397-2600

New York Apple Tours
1040 6th Ave
New York, NY 10018   ☎944-9200
Terminal: 8th Ave and 50th St

New York Double Decker Tours
Empire State Building
350 5th Ave, #4503
New York, NY 10118   ☎967-6008

Both *Gray Line* and *New York Apple* offer a wide range of other tours as well – stop by their terminals or pick up their leaflets at a Visitor Center or your hotel for up-to-date specifics.

Helicopter tours

If you have the money, a better and certainly more exciting option is to take a look at the city from the air, by taking a ride in a **helicopter**. This is expensive, but it's an experience you won't easily forget. *Island Helicopter*, at the far eastern end of E 34th St (☎683-4575), and *Liberty Helicopter Tours*, at the western end of 30th St or from the Wall St heliport at Pier 6 (☎967-6464), offer flights from $44 upwards – buy your ticket ahead of time (at a hotel or tour operator) to avoid a $5 surcharge. Helicopters take off regularly between 9am and 9pm, every day unless winds and visibility are too bad; you don't need to make a reservation (sometimes they won't let you), but in high season (and nice weather) you may have quite a wait if you just show up. One decision to make is whether to go by day or night; after doing one, you'll probably want to do the other.

Tours on water

New York is an island city, and a great way to see it from that standpoint is to take the **Circle Line boat** (☎563-3200). True to its name, it sails all the way around Manhattan, taking in everything from the classic soaring views of downtown Manhattan to the bleaker stretches of Harlem and the industrially blighted Bronx – complete with a live wisecracking commentary and on-board bar. Boats leave from Pier 83 at the far west end of 42nd Street between March and

December, running roughly twice a day in low season, almost hourly in midsummer, and the three-hour voyage costs $20 ($10 for children under 12). The two-hour evening cruise is superb in summer.

An alternative is the **Seaport Liberty Cruise**, Pier 16 at the South Street Seaport (☎630-8888), which for $12 ($6 for children under 12) spends an hour cruising around New York Harbor, offering views of lower Manhattan and the outlying islands. A slightly expanded version of this is offered by *NY Waterway* (☎1-800/533-3779), with 90-minute tours leaving the far west end of 38th Street several times daily; $14 for adults, $7 for children 6–12, and free for children under 6. *NY Waterway* also offers Hudson Valley tours to historic spots further up the river; call for details.

The bargain that still can't be beaten, even more so now that the fare has been obliterated, is the free **Staten Island Ferry** (☎806-6940), which leaves from its own terminal in lower Manhattan's Battery Park. It's a commuter boat, so avoid crowded rush hours if you can; at other times, grab a spot at the back (going out) and watch the skyline shrink away. Departures are every 15–20 minutes at rush hours, every 30 minutes mid-day and evenings, and every hour late at night – weekend services are less frequent. (Few visitors spend any time on Staten Island itself; it's easy to just turn around and get back on the ferry. For information on what's outside the terminal, see p.227.)

Walking tours

Options for **walking tours** of parts of Manhattan or the Outer Boroughs are many and varied. Usually led by experts, these tours offer fact-filled wanders through particular areas or focus on particular subjects. You'll find fliers for some of them at the various Visitor Centers; for what's happening in a particular week, check the *New York Times* (Friday or Sunday), the weekly *Village Voice* (which comes out Wednesdays), or any of the free weekly papers around town. Detailed below are some of the more interesting tours we've encountered: note that they don't all operate year-round, the more esoteric only setting up for a couple of outings at specific times of year. If you're interested, phone ahead for the full schedules.

Art Tours of Manhattan (☎609/921-2647). Much the best people to go with if you're interested in first-hand accounts of the city's art scene, establishment and fringe. The custom-designed tours include the galleries of SoHo, 57th St and Madison Ave, as well as "hospitality" visits to an artist's studio, all guided by qualified – and entertaining – art historians. All this individual attention doesn't come cheap. Tours for up to four people cost around $225.

Big Onion Walking Tours (☎439-1090; email: sik2@columbia.edu). Founded by two Columbia University graduate students, Big Onion specializes in tours with an ethnic and historical focus: pick one particular group, or take the "Immigrant New York" tour and learn about everyone. Cost is $9, $7 for students and seniors; $12 for the food-included "Multi-Ethnic Eating Tour."

Bronx County Historical Society, 3309 Bainbridge Ave, Bronx (☎718/881-8900). According to its fans, there really is enough in the Bronx to warrant neighborhood tours, ranging from strolls through suburban Riverdale to furtive hikes across the desolate wastes of the South Bronx. Excellent value at about $5 per person, though the least frequent of any of the tours listed here.

Brooklyn Center for the Urban Environment, Tennis House, Prospect Park, Brooklyn (☎718/788-8500). Focusing on the architectural as well as the natural environment, this organization specializes in summertime neighborhood "noshing" tours that give you a flavor – literally – of Brooklyn's distinct ethnic neighborhoods. Other frequent tours focus on historic Greenwood Cemetery (see p.204); all walking tours cost $8, $5 for students and seniors. Ask about $25 ecology boat tours around Jamaica Bay or the oddly fluorescent Gowanus Canal, too.

Brooklyn Historical Society, 128 Pierrepont St, Brooklyn Heights (☎718/624-0890). Walking tours of various Brooklyn neighborhoods, including Brooklyn Heights itself. Around $12 (discounts for children and seniors); call ahead for information.

Harlem Spirituals Gospel and Jazz Tours, 890 8th Ave, 2nd floor (☎757-0425). Various tours of Harlem, the Bronx, and Brooklyn, ranging from Sunday-morning church visits to night-time affairs taking in dinner and a club. Professionally run and excellent value, with prices in the range of $15–75 per person (discounts for children).

Joyce Gold, 141 W 17th St (☎242-5762; email: *nyctours@aol.com*). Twenty different weekend tours of all Manhattan neighborhoods by an informed local author and historian; $12 per person. Her areas of expertise include Greenwich Village and the Financial District, and books of her tours are also available.

Lower East Side Tenement Museum, 97 Orchard St (☎431-0233). This museum organizes Saturday and Sunday walking tours of the Lower East Side, focusing on the heritage of the various ethnic groups present, community rebuilding, and relations among different groups. Prices are $12, $10 for students and seniors, with combination tickets available for museum admission and tour together.

Municipal Arts Society, 457 Madison Ave (☎439-1049 or 935-3960). Opinionated tours taking a look at New York neighborhoods from an architectural, cultural, historical and often political perspective. On occasion, these tours visit spots not otherwise open to the public – look out for "hard hat" jaunts around construction sites – so it's worth calling for a schedule. Free (donations requested) Wednesday lunchtime tours of Grand Central Station start at 12.30pm from the information booth. Most other tours also start at 12.30pm, last for 90 minutes, and cost from $10 to $15, with discounts for students and seniors.

Museum of the City of New York, 5th Ave at 103rd St (☎534-1672, ext 206). Walking tours the first and last Saturday of the month between April and October. First Saturday tours start at the museum and concentrate on East Harlem. Last Saturday tours complement current exhibitions. Call for meeting place. Prices are $9, $7 for students and seniors; no advance reservations needed.

The 92nd Street Y, 1395 Lexington Ave (☎996-1100). None better, offering a mixed bag of walking tours ranging from straight explorations of specific New York neighborhoods to art tours, walking tours of political New York, or a pre-dawn visit to the city's wholesale meat and fish markets. Average costs are $15–20 per person, and specific tours can be organized to accommodate groups with special interests. Look out, too, for the Y's day excursions by bus to accessible parts of the Tri-State area: New York, New Jersey and Connecticut. Commentary is almost always guaranteed to be erudite and informative, and the organization, which sponsors concerts, readings and other events, is well worth checking out in any case.

The Penny Sightseeing Company, 1565 Park Ave (☎410-0080). A Harlem-based company that claims to give an "honest view of Harlem as it is." Walking tours run on Tuesdays, Thursdays and Saturdays at 11am and cost $18 per person; gospel tours that take in the rousing spiritual singing of a Sunday service start at 10.30am and cost $20. Reservations are needed a day in advance for all tours.

Queens Historical Society, 143-35 37th Ave, Flushing, Queens (☎718/939-0647). No actual guided walking tours, but if you stop by their headquarters in historic Kingsland Homestead (see Chapter 14 for more information), they'll give you a free do-it-yourself walking tour of "historic" Flushing. Can you resist?

River to River Downtown Tours, 375 South End Ave (☎321-2823). Individual and small group tours of lower Manhattan by New York aficionado Ruth Alscher-Green. Individual prices are $35, or $50 for two people, for a unique two-hour tour spiced with gossip and anecdotal tidbits.

The Urban Park Rangers. A varied selection of free educational walks in all five boroughs throughout the year, focusing on nature and sometimes history in the city's parks. Manhattan ☎427-4040; Brooklyn ☎718/438-0100; Queens ☎718/217-6034; Bronx ☎718/548 0912; Staten Island ☎718/667-6042.

The media

Newspapers and magazines

The 1990s have not been good to the New York print media, and the days are gone when New York could support twenty different **daily newspapers**. Today, only three remain: the broadsheet *The New York Times* and the tabloids *The Daily News* and *The New York Post* – with the recent demise of a fourth, the semi-tabloid *Newsday* (still available in the city, but in Queens and Long Island editions), reminding both readers and publishers of the precarious standing of the rest. The tabloids, especially, seem to take turns battling for survival: in 1990, the *Daily News* became embroiled in a dispute that saw the circulation of the paper drop by two-thirds, as it was boycotted by newsstands and sold by homeless hawkers on the subway. In July 1993 the *New York Post* almost closed down after a succession of owners and a deal in which the staff accepted a pay cut of twenty percent to recover debts of some $25 million. Only by bending the federal anti-trust laws was the paper's future secured. The general feeling is that New York's readership won't be able to support two such similar papers indefinitely, but for now both are managing to hold steady.

The New York Times (60¢) is an American institution: it prides itself on being the "paper of record" and is the closest thing America's got to a quality national paper. It has solid, sometimes stolid, international coverage, and places much emphasis on its news analysis; significant recent improvements in its coverage of local issues are largely a legacy of the fierce competition offered by its defunct rival *Newsday*. Each weekday there's a special section, such as a sports section on Monday and a good weekend section on Friday. The Sunday edition ($2.50), available from early Saturday night in most parts of the city, is a thumping bundle of newsprint divided into eight or nine different supplements that could take you the whole day (or the whole week) to read; it's traditionally enjoyed over coffee and bagels. The paper's legendary crossword puzzles, which increase in difficulty throughout the week, culminate in Sunday's *New York Times Magazine*'s puzzle, which should keep you occupied all weekend.

It takes serious coordination to read the *Times* on the subway (just watch the way the commuters fold it), one reason (but a minor one) why many turn to the *Post* and the *Daily News*. Tabloids in format and style, these arch-rivals concentrate on local news, usually screamed out in banner headlines. Pre-strike, the **Daily News** (50¢) was far and away the better of the two, renowned as a picture newspaper but with a fresh, energetic – and serious – style that put its British equivalents to shame, with intelligent features and many racy headlines, most famous of which was its succinct summary of the president's attitude to New York during the crisis of the mid-1970s: "FORD TO CITY – DROP DEAD." Five months after the strike began, the paper's owners, the *Chicago Tribune*, paid Robert Maxwell $60 million to take the paper (with all its pension and severance liabilities) off their hands, and the unions agreed to return to work. However, crippled by enormous debts and having lost most of its star writers, the general feeling was that "New York's Hometown Newspaper," as it likes to call itself, was about to go down the pan. After Maxwell's death, one Mortimer Zuckerman stepped in as the new owner, but the *News* still can't seem to get back on the rails – as the 1997 departure of respected editor Pete Hamill attested.

The **New York Post** (50¢; 35¢ in Brooklyn) is the city's oldest newspaper, started in 1801 by Alexander Hamilton, though it's been in decline for the last twenty years. Known for its solid city news reporting, not to mention consistent conservative-slanted sermonizing, it's perhaps renowned most for its sensational approach to stories: "HEADLESS WOMAN FOUND IN TOPLESS BAR" was one of its more memorable headlines from the 1980s. The *Post* came close to ceasing publication after a sorry series of long-running wrangles that came to a head when real-estate broker Abraham Hirschfeld attempted a takeover of the paper early in 1993. The *Post* devoted four extraordinary issues to vilifying Hirschfeld, dishing the dirt on his business affairs. This had the desired effect, and he backed off, letting News International mogul Rupert Murdoch into the bidding: his company has run the paper from March 1993, but has had problems concerning his ownership of other areas of the media. Rather than force the *Post* into bankruptcy, the laws governing media monopolies were relaxed in Murdoch's favor – and since then, the paper has managed to continue its precarious existence.

The other New York-based daily newspaper is the **Wall Street Journal** (75¢), in fact a national financial paper that also has strong national and international news coverage (with a decidedly conservative bent) – despite an old-fashioned design that eschews the use of photographs. The USA's only other national daily newspaper is *USA Today* (50¢), a color broadsheet that places its emphasis on weather and news roundups rather than in-depth reporting – all in all an exceptionally dull read. It was the original model for the now defunct British tabloid *Today*, and you'll see it on sale throughout New York – though it's less frequently read than the local papers.

The weeklies and monthlies

Of the **weekly papers**, the **Village Voice** (Wednesdays, free in Manhattan, $1.25 elsewhere) is the most widely read, mainly for its comprehensive arts coverage and investigative features. Originating in Greenwich Village, it made its name as a youthful, intelligent, vaguely left-leaning journal – the nearest the city ever got to "alternative" journalism. After a brief flirtation in the 1980s with Rupert Murdoch's News International group, the paper is now owned by pet-food mogul Leonard Stern, and many would say its decline into the mainstream is just a matter of time. In 1995 the *Voice* saw the controversial firing of some of its longest-standing and most popular columnists (including the entire sports department) – despite vocal criticism from their colleagues who remained. Nonetheless, the *Voice* is still a good read, offering vocal and opinionated news stories with sharp focus on the media, gay issues and civil rights. It's also one of the best pointers to what's on around town. Catch it early enough on Wednesday morning (or late Tuesday night at the newsstand on Astor Place) and you could grab yourself a free pass to a new movie the following week; look out for the full-page ad that tells you where and when to wait in line.

The other leading weeklies include glossy **New York** magazine ($2.95), which has reasonably comprehensive listings and is more of an entertainment journal than the harder-hitting *Voice*, and **Time Out New York** ($1.95) – a clone of its London original, combining the city's most comprehensive what's on listings with New York-slanted new stories and entertainment and lifestyle features. Look out also for the free weekly **New York Press**, which has news, listings and opinions on all aspects of city life, with a major focus on restaurant coverage. Then there's the long-established **New Yorker** ($2.95). British editor Tina Brown was brought in to rid the magazine of its conservative, fuddy-duddy image, and although she was initially decried by fans, the general consensus seems to be that Brown has taken the magazine back to its smart, sophisticated, irreverent and urbane roots of the 1930s; certainly the theatre and gallery reviews remain the best available. The late Andy Warhol's **Interview** ($2.95) is, as the name suggests, mainly given over to interviews, as well as fashion. Perhaps the best, certainly the wackiest, most downtown-oriented alternative to the *Voice* is **Paper** magazine ($3.50), a monthly that carries witty and well-written rundowns on New York City nightlife and restaurants and all the current news and gossip.

International publications

British and European newspapers are widely available throughout the city, usually the day after publication – except for the *Financial Times*, which is printed (via satellite) in the US and sold on most newsstands. If you're after a specific paper or magazine, there are a number of outlets worth trying: *Eastern News* in the MetLife (formerly PanAm) building, just up the escalator from Grand Central (☎687-1462); *The Magazine Store*, 30 Lincoln Plaza, at 63rd St and Broadway (☎246-4766), where you can also pick up most UK periodicals; *Hotalings*, 142 W 42nd (☎840-1868); the kiosks on 42nd St between 5th and 6th aves, and at Union Square (14th St and Broadway); or *Nico's*, on the corner of 6th Ave and 11th St (☎255-9175) – one of the best sources in the city of general and specialist magazines, with a huge worldwide stock. In addition, the *Barnes & Noble Superstores* (see Chapter 24 for addresses) stock a wide selection of magazines and some international newspapers, which you can peruse for free over coffee.

TICKETS TO TV SHOW TAPINGS

If you want to experience the excitement, horror, boredom and surprise of American TV up close, there are always **free tickets** on offer for various shows. While some of the more popular require written requests months in advance, almost all have standby lines where you can try your luck on a particular day. Keep in mind that for most shows you must be over 16 and sometimes 18 to be in the audience; if you're underage or traveling with children, call ahead to be sure. Listed here are some of the more popular shows:

Late-night shows

David Letterman. Still everyone's top choice even after his move to CBS and the Ed Sullivan Theater. Send a postcard request as far in advance as possible to Letterman Tickets, 1697 Broadway, New York, NY 10019. The limit is two tickets per postcard. Alternatively, standby tickets are given away at noon at the same address (between 53rd and 54th sts); get there no later than 9.30am or forget it. Information: ☎975-4321.

Late Night with Conan O'Brien. Letterman's replacement on NBC is fun in a harmless sort of way; his studio audience tends to be made up of people who couldn't get tickets to Letterman. Write to NBC Tickets, "Late Night with Conan O'Brien," 30 Rockefeller Plaza, New York, NY 10112, or go to the Page Desk at that address before 9.15am, Monday to Friday, to pick up a same-day ticket. Information: ☎664-3056.

Saturday Night Live. Despite this comedy show's decline, audience members keep coming, so the policy of an annual ticket lottery still stands. Not very convenient unless you're willing to plan your trip around the date they give you, but you can send a postcard – which must arrive in August – to NBC Tickets, "Saturday Night Live," 30 Rockefeller Plaza, New York, NY 10112, and see what happens. They hand out standby tickets at the 49th St side of the GE Building at 30 Rockefeller Plaza at 9.15am any Saturday that there's a show (call ☎664-4444 to make sure, since some Saturdays are reruns), and you might get lucky if you get there early enough.

Daytime shows

Geraldo Rivera. One of the longer-established talk show hosts, whose reputation tends to the

Television

For foreign travelers to understand the many facets of the American psyche, they should find TV with cable and surf through the 70-plus stations. Chaos reigns, and it's easy to get addicted – morbid curiosity about home shopping networks, psychic hotlines, Spanish soap operas, and public access proselytizing can get the best of even the most devout television snob. Even if your hotel only gets the regular broadcast stations, start watching the morning line-up of tabloid talk shows or the evening run of sitcoms and you're in danger of forgetting to see the New York sights altogether. In almost all cases, programs are interrupted by frequent, blaring commercials, which you may find fascinating until they become downright annoying.

If after this warning you're still brave enough to take the plunge, here's a brief guide to help you sort through some of what's available: for more

complete listings, grab a copy of *TV Guide* (99¢) or check the newspaper listings – the *New York Times* has the most comprehensive ones.

Broadcast TV

Broadcast TV is what you automatically get (with reception variations, of course) when you plug a TV into the wall; on most hotel TV sets, you'll be able to get some or all of the channels listed below.

Perhaps the most noticeable trend in American broadcast TV in recent years has been the explosion of **daytime talk shows**, which have all but obliterated the game shows and soap operas that once dominated the mornings and afternoons respectively. Generally devoted to exploring and exploiting the more bizarre weaknesses of everyday people, these shows feature confrontational and/or sympathetic hosts who interrogate on-stage guests with the help of vocal controversial, if not downright tacky. He tackles more serious topics than some of the newcomers, and is good for celebrity gossip whenever possible. Write to Geraldo Tickets, 524 W 57th St, New York, NY 10019, or try for standby at least an hour before a scheduled taping (Tues–Thurs at 1pm and 4pm) by going to the CBS Broadcast Center at 530 W 57th St between 10th and 11th aves. More information: ☎265-1283.

Montel Williams. Possibly the least tacky of the daytime hosts, aimed at both young and old and focusing on finding resolutions to problems. Inter-racial topics feature prominently, too. Call the Montel Williams Show ☎830-0300; or go to 433 W 53th St (between 9th and 10th aves) at 8.45am on Thursday or Friday.

Regis and Kathie Lee. The show itself is almost a throwback to the earlier days of American talk TV with a variety of topics aimed at a family audience. Kathie Lee Gifford is equally well known for her problems with the tabloids. There's more than a year's wait, but if you want to try, write to Live Tickets, PO Box 777 Ansonia Station, New York, NY 10023, or stop by the ABC studios at 67th St and Columbus Ave at 8am to pick up a standby

number which might get you in. More information ☎456-1000.

Ricki Lake. The younger, fresher face of talk; her shows are known for being fun, hip, and much less likely to make you feel like you're spying on the miseries of people less fortunate than you. Write to Ricki Lake, 401 5th Ave, New York, NY 10016, or go to that address (at the corner of 37th St) at least an hour before a taping (Tues–Thurs 4pm and 6pm) for standby. More information: ☎889-6767.

Rosie O'Donnell. This comedian/actress is a relative newcomer in the talk show game, but her show is immensely popular and not really at all trashy. The show's reps claim that there's more than a year's wait for tickets, but you could try writing The Rosie O'Donnell Show, 30 Rockefeller Plaza, Suite 800, New York, NY 10012. More information: ☎506-3200.

Sally Jessy Raphael. Another big name who tackles the trashy; her shows tend to be more sedate, however, than some others. Tapings are Monday to Thursday, and you can make reservations up to a day in advance by calling ☎582-1722. Same-day standby tickets are also available at 9.45am from NBC at 515 W 57th St between 10th and 11th aves.

audience participants. Competition has seen the topics of each show become more and more sensational, and it's become common practice to tell guests they're on stage for one reason and then spring the real topic on them. The frenzy came to a terrible – and some would say inevitable – conclusion in 1995, when one guest on the *Jenny Jones Show*, outraged at discovering on national TV that the person who had a secret crush on him was, in fact, a man, went out after the show and shot his unfortunate admirer dead. Yet despite the obvious connection between this outburst of violence and the tactics that predicated it, tabloid talk shows continue to flourish on all networks.

Something else you'll probably notice is the amount of **scheduled news** shown every evening. Despite all the offerings, you can still find yourself uninformed, since most of the news is local, much time is devoted to sports and weather, and sensational stories dominate as the

various networks battle for the attention of the talk-show-happy public. The only truly **national news coverage** is at 6.30pm on ABC, CBS and NBC. *Sixty Minutes* (CBS, Sunday at 7pm) is prob-

Broadcast TV channels
2 WCBS (CBS)
4 WNBC (NBC)
5 WNYW (Fox)
7 WABC (ABC)
9 WWOR (independent)
11 WPIX (independent)
13 WNET (PBS)
21 WLIW (PBS)
25 WNYE (educational)
31 WNYC (PBS)
41 WXTV (Spanish language)
47 WNJU (religious/Spanish language)
50 WNJN (PBS)
55 WLIG (independent)

FM radio stations

88.3 (WBGO) Jazz*
89.1 (WFDU/WNYU) College (two stations share one frequency) – grunge/alternative or folk traditions
89.5 (WSOU) College – hard rock and heavy metal
89.9 (WKCR) College – jazz
90.7 (WFUV) Contemporary folk/Celtic/international*
91.1 (WFMU) College – eclectic
91.5 (WNYE) Educational/community
92.3 (WXRK) Classic rock/Howard Stern in the morning
92.7 (WDRE) "Modern" rock (alternative/80s new wave)
93.1 (WPAT) Adult contemporary
93.5 (WRTN) Nostalgia
93.9 (WNYC) Classical*
95.5 (WPLJ) Top 40
96.3 (WQXR) Classical

96.7 (WKHL) Oldies
97.1 (WBLS) Hip-hop
97.5 (WALK) Adult contemporary
97.9 (WSKQ) Hispanic
98.7 (WRKS) Urban classics
99.1 (WAWZ) Christian
99.9 (WEZN) Adult contemporary
100.3 (WHTZ) Alternative/top 40
101.1 (WCBS) Oldies
101.5 (WPDH) Album rock
101.9 (WQCD) Contemporary jazz
102.7 (WNEW) Rock/alternative
103.5 (WKTU) Dance/techno
103.9 (WFAS) Adult contemporary
104.3 (WAXQ) Hard rock
105.1 (WMXV) Adult contemporary
105.9 (WNWK) Multi-ethnic
106.7 (WLTW) Adult contemporary
107.5 (WBLS) Urban contemporary

AM radio stations

570 (WMCA) Christian/talk
620 (WSKQ) Hispanic
660 (WFAN) Sports/Imus in the Morning
710 (WOR) News/talk
770 (WABC) Talk/Rush Limbaugh
820 (WNYC) News/talk*
880 (WCBS) News
930 (WPAT) Adult contemporary
970 (WWDJ) Contemporary Christian

1010 (WINS) News
1050 (WEVD) News/sports/talk
1130 (WBBR) News/business
1190 (WLIB) Afro-Caribbean news/talk
1280 (WADO) Hispanic
1380 (WKDM) Multi-ethnic
1480 (WZRC) Korean
1560 (WQEW) Nostalgia
1600 (WWRL) Gospel/black

Indicates national public radio (NPR), often with syndicated programs

ably the best news analysis show, and an American institution, with top-quality investigative reporting. *Nightline* (ABC, 11.30pm Monday to Friday), anchored by leading journalist Ted Koppel, is also worth catching, a decent forum for debate on the major stories that day.

As for entertainment, the mid- and late 1990s have seen a pronounced decline in the quality of sketch comedy television, something that was pioneered in New York in the 1970s by the brash and daring *Saturday Night Live* (NBC, Saturday 11.30pm). Most of the clones the show inspired have come and gone, and *SNL* itself, which made its reputation when it launched the careers of Dan Ackroyd, Eddie Murphy and John Belushi

and showed a resurgence in the early 1990s with the likes of Mike Myers and Dana Carvey, is now a pale imitation of its former self, though a few apologists labeled the 1996–97 season yet another comeback.

Channels 13, 21 and 31 are given over to **PBS (Public Broadcasting Service)**, and are a different planet from the other stations as far as quality is concerned – for now, at any rate. With the Republican majority in Congress actively targeting public broadcasting, this haven for drama, documentaries, educational programs and the arts could be slashed or forced to air commercials to generate revenue at any moment. Certain to remain, however, are the endless repeats of both the best and the worst that British TV has to export. If you missed the best episodes of *Fawlty Towers* or *Are You Being Served?*, now is your chance to make up for it.

Cable TV

Cable TV is also available in many hotels: the number of channels received depends on how much the subscriber pays; to watch a recently released film on one of the movie channels usually adds about $5 to your hotel bill. Cable networks appear on different channels in different parts of New York; if the back of the remote control (a fixture no cable box is without) doesn't list them, ask the hotel desk or simply channel-surf.

As with broadcast TV, you'll find quite a bit of trash, but high-quality programming does exist. There are various movie channels, including **HBO** (Home Box Office), which has repeated schedules of recently released and popular movies; endless sports channels showcasing international as well as American games (look for British Premier League soccer on Monday afternoons on **SportsChannel**); and again plenty of news. **CNN** (Cable News Network), already well known in Europe, offers around-the-clock news; **C-SPAN** does much the same but concentrates on news from Congress and the Supreme Court, including live sessions from both, as well as the British

House of Commons. On a lighter note, **MTV** offers a thoroughly addictive, mindless mix of rock/pop/new wave videos, concerts and interviews. Several stations offer **public access** slots – these provide, amidst much dross, some of the most bizarre viewing on the planet, with the city's most deranged weirdos exercising their right to twenty minutes' air time.

Radio

The **FM** dial is crammed with local stations of highly varying quality and content. If you possess a Walkman radio, bring it, as skipping through the channels is a pleasure. Stations are constantly chopping and changing formats, opening up and closing down, but we've tried to give a current listing of some of what's on offer. **AM** stations aren't nearly so interesting, although two good all-news stations provide 22-minute capsules of information; the rest is a sea of lobotomized easy listening, with a sprinkling of good talk shows and special-interest shows. The *New York Times* lists highlights on a daily basis; explore on your own, however, and you're sure to come across something interesting.

Incidentally, it's possible to tune into the **BBC World Service** on the 49-meter shortwave band, or just the World Service news, broadcast on a number of the public radio stations.

Money and banks

New York is an expensive place to visit pretty much any way you slice it. Though there's plenty to do and see that's fairly inexpensive, or even free, inevitably the costs will catch up to you – most likely in the form of accommodation and food and drink. See the Introduction (p.xi), for an overview of costs.

Taking, changing and accessing money

Expect to pay most of your major expenses by **credit card**; hotels and car rental agencies usually demand a credit card imprint as security, even if you intend to settle the bill in cash, and you'll be at a serious disadvantage if you don't have one. *Visa, Mastercard, Diners Club, American Express* and *Discover* are the most widely used.

You'll also need to carry a certain amount of **cash**. If you have a *Mastercard* or *Visa*, or a cash-dispensing card linked to an international network such as **Cirrus** or **Plus** – check with your home bank before you set off – you can withdraw cash from appropriate **automatic teller machines** (ATMs). For both American and foreign visitors, US dollar **travelers' checks** are a better way to carry money than ordinary bills; they offer the great security of knowing that lost or stolen checks will be replaced. Checks such as *American Express, Visa* and *Thomas Cook* are universally accepted as cash in stores, restaurants and gas stations. You'll get your change in dollars, so remember to order a good number of $10 and $20 checks: few places like to hand over all their spare change in return for a check. Additionally, almost all 24-hour Korean greengrocers will cash small checks – a lifesaver if you run out of cash at 4am. Foreign travelers should not bring travelers' checks issued in their own currencies; it can be hard to find a bank prepared to change them, no other business is likely to accept them, and you will probably lose some money in exchange fees to the bank if they do choose to help you out.

Emergencies

All else has failed. You're broke and 3500 miles from home. Before you jump off the Brooklyn Bridge, weigh up the alternatives.

Assuming you know someone who is prepared to send you money in a crisis, the quickest way is to have them take the cash to the nearest *American Express Moneygram* (☎1-800/543-4080) office and have it instantaneously wired to the office nearest you, subject to the deduction of ten percent commission. In the US this process should take no longer than ten minutes. They charge according to the amount sent (ranging from $13 to wire $100, to $49 for $1000). Western Union offers a similar service, at slightly higher rates (US ☎1-800/325-6000; UK ☎0800/833833); if credit cards are involved they charge an extra $10.

If you have a few days' leeway, it's cheaper to mail a postal money order, which is exchangeable at any post office. The equivalent for foreign travelers is the international money order, for which you need to allow up to seven days in the mail before arrival. An ordinary check sent from overseas takes two to three weeks to clear.

Should you have literally no cash nor access to any, the alternatives include selling blood or working illegally (see "Staying on," p.47. Foreign travelers have the final option of throwing themselves on the mercy of their nearest national consulate (see chapter 25, "Directory"), who will – in worst cases only – repatriate you, but will never, under any circumstances, lend money.

Banks and exchange

Banking hours are usually (with some variation) Monday–Friday 9am–3pm: some banks stay open later on Thursdays or Fridays, and a few have limited Saturday hours. Major banks – such as **Citibank** and **Chemical** – will exchange travelers' checks and currency at a standard rate. Outside banking hours, you're dependent on a limited number of private exchange offices in Manhattan (listed below), as well as offices at the international airports. All will change travelers' checks and exchange currency, although they may have disadvantageous rates and/or commission charges, the cost of which it's wise to ask about first.

Money: a note for foreign travelers

US currency comes in bills of $1, $5, $10, $20, $50 and $100, plus various larger (and rarer) denominations. All are the same size and same green color, making it necessary to check each bill carefully. The dollar is made up of 100 cents (¢) in coins of 1 cent (known as a penny), 5 cents (a nickel), 10 cents (a dime) and 25 cents (a quarter). Change – especially quarters – is needed for buses, vending machines and telephones, so always carry plenty.

Generally speaking, one pound sterling will buy between $1.50 and $1.70; one Canadian dollar is worth between 70¢ and 90¢; one Australian dollar is worth between 70¢ and 90¢; and one New Zealand dollar is worth between 60¢ and 75¢.

Exchange offices

The following offices are all open outside banking hours, and handle wire transfers and money orders as well as straightforward transactions.

Avis Currency Exchange, 200 Park Ave at 44th St (Met Life Building, formerly the PanAm Building), Third Floor East, Room 332 (Mon–Fri 8am–4pm; ☎ 1-800/258-0456 or 661-0826). Also on the main concourse at Grand Central (Mon–Fri 7am–7pm, Sat & Sun 8am–3pm; ☎ 661-0826), and in Stern's Department Store, 33rd St and 6th Ave (Mon–Sat 10am–6pm, Sun 11am–6pm; ☎ 268-8517).

Chequepoint, 609 Madison Ave at 58th St (daily 9am–7pm; ☎ 1-800/544-9898 and 750-

2255). Also 22 Central Park South (daily 9am–7pm; ☎ 544-9898).

Thomas Cook, Grand Central Station, 317 Madison Ave at 42nd St (Mon–Fri 8.30am–6pm, Sat 10am–6pm; ☎ 883-0400). Also 511 Madison Ave at 52nd St (Mon-Sat 9am–5pm; ☎ 757-6915), 1590 Broadway at 48th St in Times Square (Mon–Sat 9am–7pm, Sun 9am–5pm; ☎ 265-6049), 1271 Broadway at 32nd St (Mon–Sat 10am–6pm; ☎ 679-4365), 29 Broadway at Morris St (Mon–Fri 9am–5pm; ☎ 363-6208), and at the International Arrivals Building, JFK Airport (daily 8am–7.30pm; ☎ 718/656-8444).

Numbers to ring for lost credit cards or travelers' checks

American Express checks	☎ 1-800/221-7282	*Mastercard*	☎ 1-800/826-2181
American Express cards	☎ 1-800/528-4800	*Thomas Cook/Mastercard*	☎ 1-800/223-9920
Citicorp	☎ 1-800/645-6556	*Visa* cards	☎ 1-800/336-8472
Diners Club	☎ 1-800/234-6377	*Visa* checks	☎ 1-800/227-6811

Communications: telephones and the post

The New York **telephone system** is reliable if expensive, especially when dialing long distance, though the **postal system** doesn't quite match the efficiency European visitors may expect.

Phone calls

Public telephones are easily found – you'll see them on street corners as well as in hotel lobbies, bars and restaurants, although you may have to look for one that actually works. With the decentralization of the American phone system, rival phone companies are free to set up pay phones; they all look alike at first glance, but most New Yorkers will tell you to look for the more reliable **NYNEX** phones, since the others don't always give the same value for money. All pay phones take 25¢, 10¢ and 5¢ coins, and

Rasps, squeaks and blips

If it's your first time in the USA, the various **tones** used by the phone system need a little explanation. The **dial tone** is a low, continuous rasp or a single low drone; the **ringing tone** a long nasal squawk with short gaps; the **busy signal** (engaged tone) a series of rapid blips; **number unobtainable** is a single high-pitched squeak or an extremely rapid busy signal.

the cost of a local call – ie one within the 212 and 718 area codes covering the five boroughs – is 25¢ (slightly more to or from really remote parts of 718). If your pay phone won't accept your quarter, it means the change box is full. It's nothing personal, you'll just have to keep trying other phones. On a NYNEX phone, 25¢ will give you three minutes. After that, you won't be cut off; you'll probably hear a click or a voice instructing you to put in more money. If you hang up without paying the extra charge, the phone will ring and an operator will demand cash; if you ignore the call or don't pay up, the outstanding amount will be billed to the person you were calling.

Recently making a debut on the streets of New York are America's first **cardphones** – yellow NYNEX phones that take NYNEX "change cards." Cardphones now are steadily springing up everywhere, and can be a useful way to make local or long-distance calls at regular NYNEX/AT&T rates. Look for them in grocery stores and newsstands – though they are still not overly widespread – and expect them to become more readily available as the system increases in popularity. Cards are available for $5, $10 and $20; call ☎1-800/545-EASY for more information.

Making **telephone calls from your hotel room** will cost considerably more than from a payphone and should be avoided if possible (you'll usually find pay phones in the lobby). On the other hand, some budget hotels offer free local calls from rooms – ask when you check in.

Long-distance and international calls

All **long-distance** and **international calls** can be dialed direct from any private or public phone; the problem has always been coming up with the copious amounts of change necessary to call anywhere for any length of time. A number

of new options have sprung up recently to help solve this problem, however, including the yellow cardphones mentioned above, and **long-distance phone cards**, which you can purchase at many drugstores and supermarkets. These are issued by the major phone companies as well as countless regional companies, and give you a prepaid dollar amount of long-distance time, which you access by punching in numbers (instructions are on the card) at any public phone. There are also **telephone offices**, which charge you for making long-distance calls on their phones, which are showing up all over the place these days. Rarely associated with any particular phone company, these offices find their homes in storefronts; they'll let you call anywhere in the world, but since they market to primarily South American and Asian populations, you tend to see them in primarily heavily ethnic neighborhoods under awnings labeled "Llamadas Internacionales." Check the rates before you call, though.

An increasing number of phones accept **credit cards** – simply swipe the card through the slot and dial; international rates are usually competitive. Beware of using your *BT* or *Mercury* **charge cards** – their international rates can be staggeringly expensive. **Reversed-charge** calls (or "collect calls") can also prove costly: it's always best to use a collect call to give your number to the person you are calling – and then get them to call you back. To make a collect call through a US phone company, dial ☎0, then ☎1-800/COLLECT or ☎1-800/CALLATT – the last two numbers both claim to be the cheapest. It's also possible to make a collect call by **calling an operator** in your own country: see the box opposite for the relevant numbers.

Within the US, **rates** are generally cheapest between 11pm and 8am weekdays, all day on weekends; the next cheapest time is between 6pm and 11pm weekdays. For overseas, the best times vary depending on the time difference; a general rule is that if it's a convenient time for the person you're trying to reach, it's an expensive time for you to make the call. Another factor making it difficult to predict the cost of your call is that the three big long-distance companies – *AT&T*, *Sprint* and *MCI* – are constantly warring to offer the better deal to customers. Their rates are generally within a penny of each other – if they're not, they will be when you call back an hour later. But before you make a call using any of the

Area codes around New York

Bronx, Brooklyn, Queens and Staten Island (1) **718**
Long Island (1) **516**
Other nearby areas of New York State (1) **914**

New Jersey (north) (1) **201** or **908**
New Jersey (south) (1) **609**
To phone into Manhattan from these areas or anywhere else (1) **212**

Service numbers

Emergencies **911** for police, ambulance and fire
Operator **0**

Directory assistance **411** (New York City) **1** + **(area code)** + **555-1212** (numbers in other area codes)

Useful telephone codes

The telephone code to dial **to the US** from the outside world is **1**.

To make international calls **from the US**, dial **011** followed by the country code:
Australia 61
Denmark 45
Germany 49

Ireland 353
Netherlands 31
New Zealand 64
Sweden 46
United Kingdom 44

For codes not listed here, dial the operator or check the front of the local White Pages.

Overseas operator numbers

To call an operator in your own country from the US, dial the following numbers:

Australia ☎1-800/682-2878; ☎1-800/937-6822; ☎1-800/676-0061 (☎008/032 032 in Australia for information).

Ireland ☎1-800/562-6262 (☎1800/250 250 in Ireland for information).

New Zealand ☎1-800/248-0064 (☎123 or ☎126 in New Zealand for information).

United Kingdom ☎1-800/445-5667 (☎0800/345 144 in the UK for information).

Telephone services and helplines

Al-Anon (for families of alcoholics) ☎254-7230
Alateen (for teenage drinkers) ☎254-7230
Alcoholics Anonymous ☎647-1680
AIDS Hotline ☎447-8200
Crime Victims Hotline ☎577-7777 (24 hours)
Herpes Advice Line ☎213-6150
Missing Persons Bureau ☎374-6913
Movies ☎777-FILM
Narcotics Anonymous ☎929-6262
New York City On Stage ☎768-1818
NYC Gay and Lesbian Anti-Violence Project ☎807-0197
Overeaters Anonymous ☎206-7859
Pills Anonymous ☎874-0700
Sex Crimes Hotline ☎267-7273
Suicide Hotline ☎1-800/673-3000, ☎543-3638
Suicide Prevention Hotline ☎718/389-9608.

Any number with **800** in place of the area code is "toll-free," which means it costs nothing to call. Many national firms, government agencies, inquiry numbers, hotels and car rental firms have a central toll-free number. To find it look in the Yellow Pages or dial ☎**1-800/555-1212** for toll-free directory inquiries.

A so-far purely American phenomenon is using **letters** as part of a phone number – the idea is that it'll be easier for you to remember that way, and whether it's a toll-free information number (such as ☎1-800/AIR RIDE for airport transport) or a chicken delivery service (in Brooklyn's Cobble Hill, a sign says simply "DIAL HOT BIRD"), it actually seems to work. Take a look at the keypad of any push-button phone and you'll get the hang of it in no time.

options listed above – and this includes reversed-charge calls – it pays to dial the operator to check the rate.

Yellow Pages

Unbelievably useful (if hardly the sort of things you'll want to lug around) are the **NYNEX White** and **Yellow Pages** phone books. The first is an alphabetical list of private numbers and businesses (with the **Blue Pages** at the end containing government agencies); the second details every consumer-oriented business and service in the city, listing delicatessens, grocers, liquor stores, pharmacies, physicians and surgeons by location, and restaurants by location and cuisine. It's also handy for finding bike and car rental firms – and just about anything legal that can be paid for. Look for it in most bars, hotel rooms and lobbies and the larger post offices. Additionally, the phone center on the main concourse at Grand Central has phone books for all over the country.

Area codes

Normally, **telephone numbers** are in the form of ☎123/456-7890. The first three digits are the **area code** and are needed only when dialling a different area. In New York City, the **212** code covers Manhattan; the **718** code covers the Outer Boroughs of Brooklyn, the Bronx, Queens, and Staten Island. Phoning within any area code, simply dial the last seven digits of the number. Outside the area, dial **1** first, then the **area code** and **number**.

Where we've given phone numbers for places outside Manhattan, you'll find codes are included. To check codes elsewhere, consult the phone book or call the operator (see box on p.35).

Letters and post restante

In terms of efficiency the New York (and American) **postal service** comes a very poor second to its phone system. New Yorkers will tell you stories about postcards arriving thirty years after they were sent – legends, mostly, but ones with a basis in truth. The service is rarely atrocious, but it is unpredictable and unreliable – even within Manhattan mail can take a few days to arrive, and a letter to LA might take a week. Overseas airmail can take anything between five and fourteen days, and sending mail abroad by surface post consigns it to anywhere from four to eight weeks' disappearance.

Letters

Ordinary mail **within the US** costs 32¢ for letters weighing up to an ounce, 20¢ for postcards; any "G" stamps you come across are left over from the recent rate changes, with the white ones equivalent to 32¢ and the yellow equivalent to 20¢. (Keep in mind these are only valid for post within the US, however.) Letters to Canada are 46¢ for the first half-ounce or 50¢ for up to an ounce; for Mexico, they're 40¢ for the first half-ounce and 46¢ for up to an ounce. Postcards to Canada are 40¢, and to Mexico 35¢.

Airmail service is the same price for anywhere else in the world. Postcards and aerograms are cheapest at 50¢; letters are 60¢ for the first half-ounce and staggering after that. If you're a long-winded letter-writer, buy your stamps from the post office window to make sure you put enough postage on – the US postal service doesn't take kindly to being shortchanged.

Envelopes in the US must include the sender's address and the recipient's zip code: without the code, letters can end up terminally lost, and certainly delayed. If you're unsure of a Manhattan zip use the guide we've printed opposite or phone ☎967-8585; elsewhere ask for the relevant zip-code directory at the post office.

You can **buy stamps** in shops, some supermarkets and delis, and from (usually nonfunctioning) vending machines, though these cost around three times the face value. The best place is, unsurprisingly, a **post office**: these are open Monday–Friday 9am–5pm, Saturday 9am–noon, and there are a lot around. In Manhattan, the massive main **General Post Office** at Eighth Ave between W 31st and W 33rd streets is open seven days a week, around-the-clock, for important services; see for yourself by going there at 11.30pm on April 15 (tax day in the US), when the television news crews gather to capture the procrastinators' frantic last-minute rush. Letters posted from this or other large post offices seem to arrive soonest, whereas the blue bin-like **mailboxes** on street corners tend to take a while.

Packages

Packages. Packages cost a lot to send however you decide to do it, with the price increasing in direct proportion to the size of the package, the

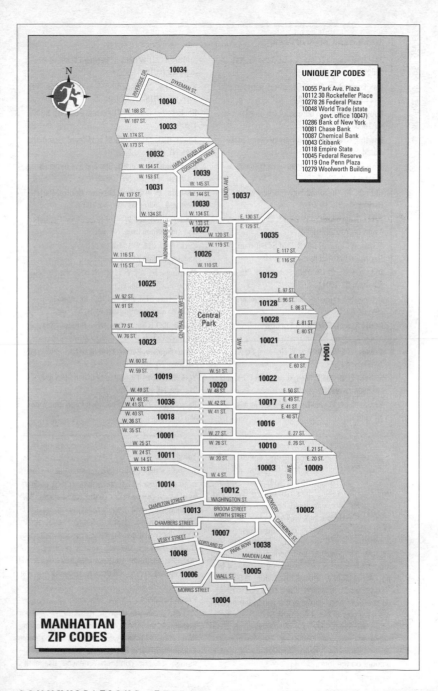

UNIQUE ZIP CODES

10055 Park Ave. Plaza
10112 30 Rockefeller Place
10278 26 Federal Plaza
10048 World Trade (state
      govt. office 10047)
10286 Bank of New York
10081 Chase Bank
10087 Chemical Bank
10043 Citibank
10118 Empire State
10045 Federal Reserve
10119 One Penn Plaza
10279 Woolworth Building

**MANHATTAN
ZIP CODES**

Manhattan post offices

JAF Building, 421 8th Ave at 33rd St, NY 10001.

Knickerbocker, 130 E Broadway between Pike and Essex sts, NY 10002.

Cooper, 93 4th Ave between 11th and 12th sts, NY 10003.

Bowling Green, 25 Broadway between State and Morris sts, NY 10004.

Wall Street, 73 Pine St between Williams and Pearl sts, NY 10005.

Church, 90 Church St between Vesey and Barkley sts, NY 10007.

Peter Stuyvesant, 432 E 14th St between Ave A and 1st Ave, NY 10009.

Madison Square, 149 E 23rd St between Lexington and 3rd aves, NY 10010.

Old Chelsea, 217 W 18th St between 7th and 8th aves, NY 10011.

Prince, 103 Prince St between Greene and Mercer sts, NY 10012.

Canal Street, 350 Canal St between Broadway and Church St, NY 10013.

Village, 201 Varick St at W Houston St, NY 10014.

Murray Hill, 205 E 36th St between Park and Lexington aves, NY 10016.

Grand Central, 450 Lexington Ave at 45th St, NY 10017.

Midtown, 221 W 38th St between 7th and 8th aves, NY 10018.

Radio City, 322 W 52nd St between 8th and 9th aves, NY 10019.

Rockefeller Center, 610 5th Ave at 49th St, NY 10020.

Lenox Hill, 221 E 70th St between 2nd and 3rd aves, NY 10021.

Franklin D Roosevelt, 909 3rd Ave between 54th and 55th sts, NY 10022.

Ansonia, 40 W 66th St between Central Park West and Columbus Ave, NY 10023.

Planetarium, 131 W 83rd St between Columbus and Amsterdam aves, NY 10024.

Cathedral, 215 W 104th St between Broadway and Amsterdam Ave, NY 10025.

Morningside, 232 W 116th St between 7th and 8th aves, NY 10026.

Manhattanville, 365 W 125th St between St Nicholas and Morningside aves, NY 10027.

Gracie, 229 E 85th St between 2nd and 3rd aves, NY 10028.

Times Square, 340 W 42nd St between 8th and 9th aves, NY 10036.

Yorkville, 1619 Third Ave between 90th and 91st sts, NY 10128.

Peck Slip, 1 Peck Slip between Pearl and Water sts, NY 10038.

---

distance of the location, and the speed of the service. The post office sells boxes in different sizes, or you can come up with your own by scouring the streets; just make sure it's clean enough for your writing to be read when you address it. Seal your box well with tape, but don't tie it with string, which can cause disaster in automated postal equipment. Mark both the address it's going to and your return address (General Delivery is OK) on the same side of the package, clearly indicating (with "TO" and "FROM") which is which. If the package is headed overseas, once you're at the window the clerk will have you fill out a Customs Declaration form, which is straightforward – if all you're sending home is smelly old clothes, it's fine to put NCV (No Commercial Value) instead of a dollar amount on the form.

Telegrams

To send a **telegram** – also called a cable – you'll need to go to a telegraph company office, addresses of which can be found in the Yellow Pages. With a credit card you can simply phone up (☎1-800/325-6000 or 1-800/835-4723) and dictate. Prices for international telegrams are marginally cheaper than the shortest possible phone call. For domestic telegrams ask for a **mailgram**, which will be delivered to any address the following morning.

Poste restante

You can receive mail **poste restante** by having it addressed to you c/o General Delivery, General Post Office, 421 8th Ave, NY 10001. (Don't panic if your friends and family write "poste restante" – though it's not common American usage, it's unlikely to confuse anyone.) To collect letters, go to the window (☎330-3099) between 10am and 1pm, Monday to Saturday; you'll need to show your passport or some other photo ID. Check regularly, as mail is kept for only ten days before being returned to sender – so tell your correspondents to make sure there's a return address on the envelope. General Delivery will not forward mail to a new address once you leave. **Receiving mail at someone else's address**, be sure your correspondent puts "c/o" that person's name on the envelope, since without that you risk your mail being returned to sender by an over-zealous letter carrier.

The Internet

This is everyone's new favorite way of staying in touch, and when you travel, it doesn't need to be different. You can send your findings about New York to us: our **email address** is *newyork@ roughguides.co.uk* You can also visit **our own Web site** at *http://roughguides.com* as a starting point for travel information (and many other resources).

If you're traveling without your own computer and modem, accessing the Internet is possible at a number of locations, such as the **Cyber Café**, 273A Lafayette St at Prince St (☎334-5140; Web site: *http://www.cyber-cafe.com*); and **alt.coffee**, 139 Ave A (☎529-2233; Web site: *http://www .altdotcoffee.com*). These places charge you for computer use, usually an average of $10 per hour, during which you can telnet to your email account back home, enabling you to pick up and send mail as if you'd never left. You can also surf the net to your heart's content, fiddle around with CD-ROMS, scan, print, or just drink coffee; if you're new at this whole game, the staff will gladly help you figure things out.

Police and trouble

The **New York City Police** – the NYPD, aka "New York's Finest" – are for the most part approachable, helpful and overworked. This means that asking directions gets a friendly response, reporting a theft a weary "Whaddya want me to do about it" – and any smile is greatly appreciated. Unfortunately, in this realm of New York life as in others, race can play a part in the response you get, especially in light of recent media attention (here as elsewhere in the US). Wary of strained relations between police and minority communities, officers – even those from minority communities themselves – may be a little more reserved with you if your skin is any color but white. This is not to say that they'll refrain from helping you if you're in trouble, however.

Each area of New York has its own **police precinct**; to find the nearest station to you, call ☎374-5000 (during business hours only) or check the phone book or directory inquiries (☎411). In **emergencies phone ☎911** or use one of the outdoor posts that give you a direct line to the emergency services. Out of the city you may have to tangle with the **State Police**, who operate the Highway Patrol – and do so quite ruthlessly.

Staying out of trouble

Irrespective of how dangerous New York really is – and it is considerably safer than it was, say, a decade ago – it can sometimes *feel* dangerous.

Perhaps more than in any other city in the world, a sense of nervy self-preservation is rife here: people make studied efforts to avoid eye contact, and any unusual behavior clears a space immediately: the atmosphere of impending violence is sometimes sniffable.

The reality is somewhat different. There is a great deal of crime in New York, some of it violent. But keep in mind that more than eight million people live in the city, and, as far as per capita crime rates go, Boston is more dangerous, as are New Orleans, Dallas, Washington DC, and, believe it or not, one hundred and some odd other US cities. Even considering New York on its own, it's pleasing (and not misleading) to note that in 1997 the city boasted its lowest crime rate – violent crimes included – since 1968. And it's still on its way down. This is due in part to periodic gun amnesties and increased gun confiscation: anyone taken into custody for even the most petty crime can be searched for weapons, so the police have simply started cracking down on the minor offenses, like shoplifting, even public urination, which they used to overlook. A less inspiring contributing factor is the shift in focus of the criminal drug culture; where crack, a stimulant that inspired violence in its addicts, once ruled, heroin, a depressant that causes sluggishness more than anything, is now much more prevalent.

New York's tension doesn't automatically mean violence; it's largely due to the frenetic pace at which most of the city operates. Take several million people, pump them full of caffeine, make them believe that they have to get where they're going five minutes faster than is actually humanly possible, and pack them onto a tiny island – there's bound to be an edge in the air. Which is not to say you should discount the possibility of danger altogether. Do as the locals do and keep it in the back of your consciousness, not at the forefront. As with any big city, the main thing is to walk with confidence and remember the few places and/or times that you really should avoid. Throughout the guide, we've outlined places where you should be careful and those few best skirted altogether, but really it's a case of using your common sense; it doesn't take long to figure out that you're somewhere unsavory.

The hard and fast rule that will best enable you to travel around New York safely and confidently is simple to remember: **be aware of your surroundings at all times**. Contrary to the warnings of the folks back home, it's OK to let on you're a visitor – if you follow rules of paranoia and never look up, you'll miss a lot of what's striking about New York. Looking up and around, reading this guidebook, and pulling out your camera can make you more of a target, but only because the assumption is that tourists are careless. You are much more likely to have your pocket picked while you're looking at your map than you are to encounter something more violent. So carry bags closed and across your body, don't let cameras dangle, keep wallets in front – not back – pockets, and don't flash money or your Oyster Rolex around. Avoid crowds, especially around rip-off merchants like street gamblers, where half the con is played on the participants and the other half on the spectators. Never be afraid to move away if you feel someone is standing too close to you.

It is, of course, the murders that make the headlines: reassure yourself that ninety percent of victims are known to their killers, which is to say most killings are personal disputes rather than random attacks. **Mugging**, on the other hand, can and does happen. It's impossible to give hard and fast rules on what to do should you meet up with a mugger: whether to run or scream or fight depends on you and the situation. Most New Yorkers would hand over the money every time, and that's probably what you should do – in fact, some people always carry a spare $20 or so as "mug money," lest their attacker turn nasty at finding empty pockets. Having a spare $20 should be your common practice anyway; if you find yourself somewhere you'd rather not be, you want to be able to jump in a cab.

Of course the best tactic is to **avoid being mugged**, and following the "awareness" rules outlined above is a good start. Some good late-night points are worth adding to that: even if you are terrified, or drunk (or both), don't appear so; never walk down a dark side street, especially one you can't see the end of, or through a deserted park; walk in the street itself, stick to the roadside edge of the sidewalk or where it's easier for you to run into the road if necessary and attract the attention that muggers hate.

If the worst happens and your assailant is toting a gun or (more likely) a knife, play it calmly. Remember that he (for this is generally a male pursuit) is probably almost as scared as you and has run off, hail a cab and ask to be taken to the nearest police station: taxis rarely charge for this, but if they do the police are supposed to pay. Standing around on the street in a shocked condition is inviting more trouble, though you'd be pleasantly surprised at the number of people who would sincerely come to your aid. At the station, you'll get sympathy and little else; file the theft and take the reference to claim your insurance back home.

just as jumpy; keep still, don't make any sudden movements – and do what he says. When he

Women's New York: problems and contacts

Newcomers to the city, whether male or female, face the fact that New York is a huge, overwhelming and potentially violent place. On a first visit, it will probably take a few days to mentally adjust to the city and its culture, and this is the time when you'll be feeling (and appearing) at your most vulnerable. Affecting an attitude of knowing where you're going (even if you don't) protects you from trouble, as will some basic tips in survival psychology.

The first – and fundamental – step is to avoid being seen as an easy target: female New Yorkers project a tough, streetwise image through their body language and dress, even when they're all glammed up and ready to party. If this play-acting sounds exhausting, the pay-off is that there's nothing unusual in women traveling in the city alone or with other women, at pretty much any time of day or night, so you won't be the focus of attention that you might be in other parts of the world. People gravitate to New York from the rest of America whether to study, further their careers or just hang out – so it's easy to move around, make friends and plug into New York's networks. Also on the positive side, the women's movement of the 1960s and 1970s has had a much more dynamic effect in New York (indeed throughout East and West Coast America) than in Europe. Women are much more visible in business, politics and the professions

than you may be used to, and the attitudes around can equally well be more progressive and sophisticated.

All this progress has had a somewhat paradoxical effect, however, with successful mainstreaming eliminating the impetus, if not the need, for a strong women's community. New York's last feminist bookstore closed its doors in 1994, and while women's work still flourishes in all aspects of the arts, there's no central source for information on what's going on. Nowadays, most if not all feminist activism centres around reproductive rights, which you'll find to be one of the most volatile issues in American politics. If you want to see the political side of New York feminism, you'll find it outside an abortion clinic. In addition, check out the lesbian listings in "Gay and lesbian New York", on p.43 and throughout the guide.

Feeling safe

It must be safe to travel around New York; American women do it all the time. So runs the thinking, but New York does throw up unique and definite problems for women – and especially for women traveling alone and just getting to know the city. If you feel and look like a visitor, not quite knowing which direction to ride the subway, for instance, it's little comfort to know that New York women routinely use it on their own and late in the evening. What follows are a few points to bear in mind when beginning your explorations of the city: if they duplicate, in part, the comments in "Staying out of trouble, p.39," no apologies.

The truth is you're more likely to feel unsafe than *be* unsafe – something that can lead to problems in itself, for part of the technique in surviving (and enjoying) New York is to look as if you know what you're doing and where you're going. Maintain the facade and you should find a lot of the aggravation fades away, though bear in mind that for Americans subtle hints aren't the order of the day: if someone's bugging you, let them know your feelings loudly and firmly. Some women carry whistles; many more carry their keys between their fingers when walking home at night. These tactics, while not much good in the event of real trouble, can lend you confidence, which in turn wards off creeps. Much more powerful are **chemical repellents** such as CS gas or OC Pepper sprays, available from sporting goods stores. If you do carry one of these, make sure you know how and when to use it, and what its effects will be. Properly used they are extremely effective at disabling your attacker long enough for you to make good your escape, and they do not cause any lasting injury to the attacker.

Harassment in the city is certainly worse for women than men – and it can be a lot scarier. But it's not always that different, at least in intent. You're far, far less likely to be raped than you are **mugged**. For a few ground rules on lessening chances of mugging, see p.40, but above all be wary about any display of wealth in the wrong place – if you wear jewelry (or a flash-looking watch), think about where you're walking before setting out for the day; in general, it's a good idea to tuck necklaces inside your clothing and turn rings around so the stones don't show, at least when you're out on the street or riding the subway. If you are **being followed**, turn around and look at the person following you, and step off the sidewalk and into the street; attackers hate the open, and they'll lose confidence knowing you've seen them. Never let yourself be pushed into a building or alley and never turn off down an unlit, empty-looking street; listen to your instincts when they tell you to take the long way around. If you're unsure about the area where you're staying, don't hold back from asking other women's advice. They'll tell you when they walk and when they take a bus so as to avoid walk-

ing more than a block; which bars and parks they feel free to walk in with confidence; and what times they don't go anywhere without a cab. Listen to this advice and merge it into your own experience. However, don't avoid parts of the city just through hearsay – you might miss out on what's most of interest – and learn to expect New Yorkers (Manhattanites in particular) to sound alarmist; it's part of the culture.

If you don't have much money, **accommodation** is important: it can be very unnerving to end up in a hotel with a bottom-of-the-heap clientele. Make sure that your hotel has a lobby that's well lit, the door locks on your room are secure and the night porters seem reliable. If you feel uneasy, move. If you're staying for a couple of weeks or more, you might try one of the city's women-only long-term residences; for addresses of these, see "Staying on," p.50.

Crisis/support centers

There are competent and solid **support systems** for women in crisis, or in need of medical or emotional support. At the following you can be assured of finding skilled, compassionate staff.

Women's Care Clinic, 654 Madison Ave at 60th St, 5th floor (☎319-5535). Handles all women's health needs for reasonable fees.

Women's Healthline ☎230-1111. Provides a broad range of information on women's health problems (such as birth control, abortion, sexually transmitted diseases) and can refer callers to specific hospitals and medical practices.

Sex Crimes Hotline ☎267-7273 or 267-RAPE. Staffed by specially trained female detectives of the New York City Police Department who will take your statement and conduct an investigation, referring you to counseling organizations if you wish. If you don't want to go to the police, then the **Bellevue Hospital Rape Crisis Program**, 1st Ave and 27th St (☎562-3755or 3435), provides free and confidential counseling as well as referrals for medical treatment and follow-up counseling and referral. See also the Victim Services phone line, p.41.

Other contacts

Barnard College Women's Center, Barnard College, 117th St and Broadway (☎854-2067). A friendly but primarily academic resource which maintains an extensive research library collection of books, articles and periodicals.

See also the lesbian listings in "Gay and lesbian New York" below, and the women's/lesbian bars and clubs fully detailed in Chapters 18 and 19.

Ceres, 584 Broadway, Suite 306 (☎226-4725). Art gallery run by an all-women cooperative. Exhibits mainly – though not exclusively – women's work.

Eve's Garden, 119 W 57th St (between 6th and 7th aves), Suite 1201 (☎757-8651). This "sexuality boutique for women and their partners" stocks erotic accessories, books and videos. Occasional events and a flier-full bulletin board make this the closest thing to a women's bookstore New York's got these days. Open to women (men only when accompanied by a woman) Mon–Sat, noon–7.00pm.

Minoan Sisterhood, at *Enchantments*, 341 E 9th St (☎228-4394). Spiritual group of witches-in-training meets in the back garden of *Enchantments* (May–Oct) to celebrate festivals, learn and enjoy. Primarily a lesbian group, but all women are welcome.

NARAL (National Abortion Rights Action League), 462 Broadway, Suite 540 (☎343-0114). A good source of information on current legal issues; they'll also refer you to reliable providers of reproductive services.

National Organization for Women, 105 E 22nd St, Suite 307 ☎260-4422. The largest feminist organization in the US.

National Council of Jewish Women, 9 E 69th St, ☎535-5900. Organization focused primarily on community service. Occasionally sponsors lectures, discussion groups and other events.

New York Clinic Defense Task Force ☎967-7711, ext. 3564. Arranges escorts for women at clinics targeted by anti-choice groups; organizes full-scale defense, city-wide, when necessary.

WOW (Women's One World Theater), 59 E 4th St ☎777-4280. Feminist/lesbian theatre collective with meetings open to all women on Tuesdays at 6.30pm. Call for information on upcoming events.

Gay and lesbian New York

There are few places in America – indeed in the world – where **gay culture** thrives as it does in New York. A glance at the pages of the *Village Voice*, where gay theater, gossip and politics share space with more mainstream goings-on, is enough to show how proudly the gay and lesbian community shows its many faces. It's estimated that around twenty percent of New Yorkers are lesbian or gay; and when you extend that category to include bisexuals and transgender individuals, the numbers climb even further – as they do when you take into account the numbers of gay-identified newcomers who come to New York each day for the welcome refuge the city can offer them.

Until recently, the liberal face of New York politics has been good to the gay community, with tremendous strides having been made for gay rights since the catalyst of the Stonewall Riots 25 years ago. The passage of the **Gay Rights Bill** contributed significantly to the high visibility of lesbians and gay men in local government; until recently, the New York State governor, the mayor, the City Council president and controller, and the Manhattan borough president all employed full-time liaison officers to work with gay and lesbian groups. Unfortunately, the election of both a Republican governor and a Republican mayor have seen cutbacks in this area and a move away from officially sanctioned support for gay-oriented initiatives. While the gay community has enough of a widespread political base to resist any onslaught on the battles already won, negative effects are definitely being felt in the most time-sensitive areas of gay activism: HIV/AIDS legislation and research. The urgency of this devastating epidemic – which still affects the gay community more than any other – is one reason the outspoken New York gay community will not lapse into complacency.

Socially, lesbians and gay men are fairly visible, and while it's not recommended that you and your partner hold hands in public before checking out the territory, there are **neighborhoods** in the city where you'll find yourself in a comfortable majority. Chelsea (centered around 8th Ave between 14th and 23rd sts) and the East Village are the largest of these, and have largely replaced the West Village as the hub of gay New York. There's still a strong presence centered around Christopher Street, but it's in Chelsea and the East Village that gay socializing is most out and open. The other haven is Brooklyn's Park Slope, though perhaps more for women than for men; it's primarily a residential area and so a little harder to get to know, but talk to enough of the Chelsea regulars and you're bound to find a bunch who call Park Slope home.

There are several **free newspapers** that serve New York's gay community: *Metro Source*, *Next*, and *Homo Xtra* (*HX*) primarily for men, and *HX for Her* for women. You'll find all three available at the Center (see below), at bars, lesbian and gay bookshops, and occasionally at newsstands along with glossy national mags such as *Out*. Below are some of the other resources we think you'll find helpful. In addition, we've listed gay-run (and gay-friendly) hotels opposite; and gay bars and nightclubs in Chapters 18 and 19 respectively.

Lesbian and gay resources

The Lesbian and Gay Community Services Center, 208 W 13th St (☎620-7310). More than 5,000 people a day come into the Center, which is on the verge of a multimillion-dollar renovation. This should give you an idea of how it's grown in the twelve years since it opened in an abandoned school. Home now to more than 400 diverse organizations (pick up a free listing), including Act-Up and, for the time being, the Community Health Project, a low-cost, volunteer-staffed clinic open to anyone, the Center also sponsors dances, movie nights, guest speakers, youth services, programs for parents and kids, an archive and library, and lots more that we don't have room to list here. Even the bulletin boards are fascinating. All in all, you really can't beat it as a place to start.

Shades of Lavender, 470 Bergen St at Flatbush Ave, Brooklyn ☎718/622-2910. Regular events, social and support groups. A small but friendly operation popular with the Park Slope crowd.

New York Area Bisexual Network ☎459-4784. Call for information on bisexual support groups, discussions, social events and other activities.

Lambda Legal Defense and Education Fund, 120 Wall St, 15th floor, NY 10005 ☎809-8585. Active against discrimination affecting people with AIDS and the lesbian, gay, bisexual and transgender community. Publications, speakers and newsletter.

GLAAD-NY (Gay and Lesbian Alliance Against Defamation), 150 W 26th St at 7th Ave, Suite 503 ☎807-1700. Monitors the portrayal of gays, lesbians and bisexuals in the media, and organizes caucuses and discussion groups on media topics. Volunteers and visitors welcome.

Gay and Lesbian Switchboard ☎777-1800 (daily 10am–midnight). Help and what's-on information. Staffed by volunteers, so hours can be erratic.

Bookshops

The Oscar Wilde Memorial Bookshop, 15 Christopher St near 6th Ave (☎255-8097). The first gay bookstore in America. Unbeatable.

A Different Light, 151 W 19th St (☎989-4850). Excellent selections of books and publications from around the country. Open late throughout the week; often hosts book signings and readings.

Health and well-being

Center Mental Health and Social Services, at the Center, 208 W 13th St (☎620-7310). Free confidential counseling and referrals.

Community Health Project, at the Center, 208 W 13th St, 2nd floor (☎675-3559). Low-priced clinic which can either treat or refer you. Walk-ins Mon–Thurs, 7–9pm.

Gay Men's Health Crisis (GMHC), 129 W 20th St (☎807-6664). Despite the name, this organization – the oldest and largest not-for-profit AIDS organization in the world – provides information and referrals to everyone.

Identity House, 39 W 14th St, Suite 205 (☎243-8181). Psychological assistance and counseling for the lesbian, gay and bisexual community.

SAGE: Senior Action in a Gay Environment, at the Center, 208 W 13th St (☎741-2247). Advice and numerous activities for gay seniors.

Arts and media

There's always a fair amount of gay theater going on in New York: check the listings in the Village Voice and the free papers noted above.

Dyke TV. A half-hour show Tuesday nights at 8pm on Manhattan Cable Channel 34. Magazine format covering news, arts, politics, sports and other features – including current issues in lesbian activism. More info (on non-Manhattan channels too) on ☎343-9335.

Gay Cable Network. A variety of programs featuring news, interviews, entertainment reviews and more, mainly for men. Broadcast on Manhattan Cable Channel 35 and on other cable networks in the city; call ☎727-8825 for times and channels.

Heritage of Pride. 154 Christopher St, Suite 1D, NY 10014 (☎80-PRIDE). The group that organizes the bulk of city-wide events for June, Gay Pride Month.

Leslie-Loman Gay Art Foundation, 127 Prince St between Wooster and W Broadway (in the basement) (☎673-7007). The foundation maintains an archive and permanent collection of lesbian and gay art, with galleries open to the public from September to June.

New Festival (formerly the New York Lesbian and Gay Film Festival). Annually in the month of June; details on ☎254-7228.

WBAI 99.5FM. A number of lesbian, gay and bisexual programs. Programming schedule is changing as we go to press; call ☎279-0707 for an up-to-date listing.

Accommodation

A few suggestions if you're looking for a place to rest your head that is specifically friendly to gays and lesbians and convenient for the scene. These hotels also welcome straight guests.

Chelsea Mews Guest House, 344 W 15th St (☎255-9174). The oldest gay guest house in New York, with 8 reasonably priced rooms, although most share bathrooms. Local calls are included.

Chelsea Pines Inn, 317 W 14th St (☎929-1023). Well-priced hotel housed in an old brownstone on the Greenwich Village/Chelsea borders that offers clean, comfortable, attractively furnished rooms. Best to book in advance.

Colonial House Inn, 318 W 22nd St (☎243-9669). Economical, 20-room bed-and-breakfast in the heart of Chelsea. Boasts a clothing-optional roofdeck.

Incentra Village House, 32 8th Ave between 12th and Jane sts (☎206-0007). Twelve-room town house, some rooms with kitchenette. Two-night minimum stay at weekends.

Religion

There are numerous gay religious organizations in New York.

Congregation Beth Simchat Torah, 57 Bethune St, NY 10014 (☎929-9498). Lesbian and gay synagogue with Friday night services at 8.30pm.

Dignity/Big Apple ☎818-1309. Catholic liturgy and social each Saturday at 8pm at the Center.

Metropolitan Community Church, 446 W 36th St, NY 10018 (☎629-7440). Ecumenical.

Exclusively for women

Lesbian Switchboard, (☎741-2610 Mon–Fri 6–10pm). Because no lesbian organizations receive any centralized funding, the community relies on the commitment of small groups of volunteers. One such group is the Switchboard – the place to phone for information on events, happenings and contacts in the New York community.

Astraea, 116 E 16th, 7th floor, NY 10003, #520 (☎529-8021). National lesbian action foundation offering information and networking service.

Lesbian Herstory Archives, PO Box 1258, NY 10116 (☎718/768-DYKE; fax 718/768-4663). Celebrated and unmissable. Call or write for an appointment.

See also "Women's New York," p.41.

Disabled access in the city

> Knowing the rolling topography of New York City under my wheels is like downloading some ancient guidebook directly into the soul.
>
> John Hockenberry in The New York Times, August 26, 1995.

With an introduction like that, how could you miss it? For disabled travelers, New York presents challenges, to be sure, but the rewards almost always outweigh the difficulties.

New York City has had recent, wide-ranging disabled access regulations imposed on an aggressively disabled-unfriendly system. The Americans with Disabilities Act, a landmark achievement essentially guaranteeing the rights of the disabled in the US, stipulated that public buildings (and this includes hotels) built after 1993 must be accessible. Buildings built before that time must be modified – to the extent that this is possible – although this is open to some interpretation. The reality in New York is that there are wide variations in accessibility, making navigation a tricky business. At the same time, you'll find New Yorkers surprisingly willing to go out of their way to help you. If you're having trouble and you feel that passers-by are ignoring you, it's most likely out of respect for your privacy – if you need assistance, never hesitate to ask.

In an effort to make up for the limitations to the city's accessibility, city agencies offer a considerable amount of information and advice. New York is also home to many of the country's largest disabled services and advocacy groups, so you can be almost certain to find the support you need to overcome initial obstacles. The key is to be informed before you arrive. To that end, we've listed the most useful contacts below.

Getting around

For wheelchair users, getting around on the **subway** is next to impossible without someone to help you, and extremely difficult at most stations even then. The New York City Mass Transit Authority is working to make the majority of stations accessible, but at the rate they're going (and the state the subway is in), it won't happen soon.

Buses are another story, and are the first choice of many disabled New Yorkers themselves. (For a detailed explanation of the bus system, see "Getting around the city," p.18.) All MTA buses are equipped with wheelchair lifts and locks. To get on a bus, wait at the bus stop to signal the driver you need to board; when he or she has seen you, move to the back door, where he or she will assist you. For travelers with other mobility difficulties, the driver will "kneel" the bus to allow you easier access. Wheelchair users may also be eligible for the MTA's Access-a-Ride bus service, though probably not if you're staying a very short time. For more information, including a Braille subway map and a free publication called Accessible Travel, contact the MTA by calling ☎718/330-1234 or 718/596-8585; TDD 718/596-8273; or writing to 370 Jay St, Brooklyn, NY 11201.

Taxis are a viable option for visitors with visual and hearing impairments and minor mobility difficulties; for wheelchair users, however, the disappearance of all but a handful of the big Checker cabs has made taxi travel pretty impossible. If you have a collapsible wheelchair, drivers are required to store it and assist you; the unfortunate reality is that most drivers won't stop if they see you waiting. If you're refused, try to get the cab's medallion number and report the driver to the Taxi and Limousine Commission at ☎221-8294.

Aside from the bus, the best way to travel New York by wheelchair is still the **sidewalk**. Watch out for uneven curbs and cobblestones, especially on smaller streets, but overall you shouldn't have a problem.

General advice and information

Big Apple Greeter, 1 Center St, New York, NY 10007 (accessibility info on ☎669-3602, fax 669-3685, TTY 669-8273, or email cstone@big applegreeter.org). One of the few city offices to employ a full-time access coordinator, Big Apple Greeter is accepted by many as the main authority on New York accessibility. The free service (described in more detail on p.23) matches you with a volunteer who spends a few hours showing you the city. Big Apple Greeter has also compiled a resource list especially for travelers with disabilities, and they'll be happy to supply you with this on request.

The Lighthouse, 111 E 59th St, New York, NY 10022 (☎821-9200). General services for the visually impaired. They also have Braille and large-print guides to New York.

The Mayor's Office for People with Disabilities, 52 Chambers St, Room 206, New York, NY 10007 (☎788-2830; TDD 788-2838). General information on access.

New York Society for the Deaf, 817 Broadway, 7th floor, New York, NY 10003 and (☎ and TDD

777-3900). A good source of information on interpreter services.

The New York State Travel Information Center, 1 Commercial Plaza, Albany, NY 12245 (☎1-800/225-5697). Publishes the *I Love New York Travel Guide*, a general booklet to the state and city that includes accessibility ratings.

Finally, **Access for All** is a comprehensive guide to cultural resources for the disabled. A copy is available for $5; write to Hospital Audiences, Inc, 220 W 42nd St, New York, NY 10036 (☎1-888/424-4685, ☎575-7663; TDD 575-7673).

Staying on

Nobody ever says it's easy to **live and work** in New York City, New Yorkers especially – most of whom, when you broach the subject of prolonged residence, will talk obsessively about their jobs and salaries (assuming they have them), and where they live, or will live, or won't be living any more. When the movie *Single White Female* came out, New Yorkers didn't question its credibility on artistic levels: they knew it was make-believe because there was no way Bridget Fonda could have found, let alone afforded, that apartment in the Ansonia building. You know you're somebody if you've got access to the *New York Times* real estate section before it hits the newsstands; everyone else can be found lining up in

Cooper Square to pick up the *Voice* the minute it comes out on Tuesday night – even though the new listings are available on their website earlier in the day (see p.27). Basically, finding a place to live that's safe, clean and affordable is a challenge at best and torture at worst. And once you've got that, you still have to get a job to pay for it.

If you're a **foreigner**, you naturally start at a disadvantage, at least as far as contacts go. If you have an English accent it may help, but don't count too heavily on it. The British Consulate claims that each year an alarming number of Britons wind up in New York City in need of shelter, sustenance and sympathy. Both work and rooms, however, are there, if you've got the energy, imagination or plain foolhardiness to pursue them. Below are the basic ground rules and those matters of bureaucracy which, even if you choose to ignore them, you should certainly be aware of.

Legal (and illegal) work: information for foreigners

For **extended, legal stays** in the US it helps if you have relatives (parents, or children over 21) who can sponsor you. Alternatively, a firm offer of work from a US company or, less promisingly, an individual, will do. Armed with a letter specifying this

Overstaying your welcome; advice for foreign travelers

For visitors granted admission to the US under the **visa waiver scheme** (see p.5), the date stamped in your passport is the latest you're legally entitled to stay. Leaving a few days after may not matter, especially if you're heading home, but more than a week or so can result in a protracted – and generally unpleasant –interrogation from officials: it's been known for immigration control to question overstayers deliberately long enough to miss their flights. Additionally, you may well find that you are denied entry to the US in the future, and that your American hosts and/or employers face legal proceedings.

If you do want to stay on, the best option is to get an **extension** before your time is up. You do this by applying to the US Immigration and Naturalization Service for an Issuance or Extension of Permit to Re-Enter the USA. In New York you'll find the office at **26 Federal Plaza** (at Worth St between Lafayette and Centre sts), open for in-person visits Monday to Friday between 7.30am and 3.30pm; you can also speak to an officer by phone (☎206-6500) between 8am and 5.30pm. Brace yourself – you're plunging, voluntarily, into a side of American bureaucracy that's known for being frustrating, unpleasant and, above all, suspi-

cious. Your application must be submitted not fewer than 15 and not more than 60 days before you're meant to leave, and it costs a hefty – and nonrefundable – $75, so think carefully about what you're doing. Think, too, about how you'll answer any questions, as it will automatically be assumed that you are working illegally; it's up to you to furnish convincing proof that you can support yourself financially. Taking along an upstanding US citizen to vouch for you is a good idea. You'll also need to think up a good reason to explain why you didn't allow the extra time initially: well-worn but effective excuses include saying your money lasted longer than you planned, or that your parents/husband/wife have decided to come over for a while. Should you need a further extension, apply for it at a different office, and keep your fingers crossed.

Your only other option is to **leave the country** and **come back in**. From New York, Montréal is a short flight or a long train/bus ride away; and you don't need a visa to get in. You can apply for a new visa there, or, if you came in on a visa waiver, just turn around and come back. Keep in mind that the longer you spend in Canada, the less obvious your return to New York State will be.

---

you can apply for a **special working visa** from any American embassy or consulate abroad *before* you set off for the States.

There are a whole range of these visas, depending on your skills, projected length of stay, etc – but with a couple of exceptions they're extremely hard to get. The **easiest** tend to be for academic posts or other jobs (in the computer field, for instance) which the US feels it particularly needs to fill. For **students** (and occasionally non-students) there are a limited number of Exchange Visitor Programs (EVPs), whose participants are given a **J-1** visa that entitles them to accept paid summer employment and to apply for a **social security number** (an identification for tax purposes which virtually no American citizen is without). Most J-1 visas are issued for positions in American summer camps through schemes like BUNAC: information is available from their office at 16 Bowling Green Lane, London EC1R 0BD (☎0171/251 3472).

Should all this seem too far-fetched, you could, like thousands of others each year, forget regulations completely and hunt out **work on your own**. To do this you'll have to pound the streets, check the bulletin boards (see the "Directory" on p.439) and the media, and in most cases lie about your social security number to satisfy your prospective boss. If you're already in New York and decide you want to stay and work, this will most likely be your only choice: employment visas can't realistically be obtained in the city. Be advised, though, that for anyone with only a standard tourist visa, **any kind of work is totally illegal**. If you're caught, you could be liable for deportation, and your employer for a $10,000 fine – something that has virtually destroyed the market for casual labor.

Of more immediate concern for temporary workers is the business of finding out exactly what people do in New York – and how you can fit in. For ideas (and positions) check the employment ads in *The New York Times* and *Village Voice* and in the plethora of smaller, free neighborhood tabloids available throughout the city. Other papers to try are the ethnic weeklies that crowd every newsstand: the *Irish Voice* and *Irish Echo* can be particularly useful for Irish travelers if you want to get in touch with the large immigrant population who came before you.

Possibilities obviously depend on your own personal skills and inventiveness, but among the more general or obvious you might look at some of the following suggestions.

• **Restaurant and bar work**. With more than 25,000 restaurants in the city, this is perhaps the best bet, especially since 15% of the bill (see "Tipping," p.439) can add up to a lot of extra take-home pay at the end of the night. For the reasons mentioned above, however, restaurateurs are much more wary than they were about taking on someone who doesn't have (or who has obviously made up) a social security number, and jobs are no longer assured in this field. Experience helps, as does dropping by in person, since most restaurants won't deal with you over the phone. This is one area in which a "refined" British accent is a plus, since many owners and managers will appreciate the positive effect it may have on customers.

• **Child-care, house-cleaning, dog-walking**. New Yorkers frequently advertise these tasks on notices posted in supermarkets and corner drugstores, healthfood shops, bus shelters, and on university and college bulletin boards.

• **Telemarketing/market research**. Often not too choosy about whom they employ – and sometimes impressed (especially the market research people) with very English English.

• **Music teacher**. If you can teach guitar, saxophone or keyboards there's lots of scope among wannabe band members in the East Village.

• **Painting and decorating**. Hard work but good rates. Some agencies offer this kind of work – or you can hunt privately through friends.

• **Foreign language lessons**. If you've a language or two, try advertising on a bulletin board or in the weeklies. Rates can be good.

• **Artist's model**. Pass your name and a contact number around to the various independent studios or artist hangouts in SoHo or TriBeCa. Or try to reach the model-booking directors at the art schools themselves.

• **Nightclub bouncer**. For those with physique – and a liking for the hours.

• **Blood donation**. A final, if slightly desperate, option for quick emergency cash. Check Yellow Pages for agencies or hospitals.

Whatever you do (or try to do), proceed with caution at all times. Remember, as an illegal worker you have *no* rights, and some potential employers will be eager to exploit this. Be selective, if you can. And don't enter into any slave labor type set-up if you're at all suspicious.

Finding an apartment or long-stay room

If work can be hard to find, wait till you start **apartment hunting**. Costs are outrageous. A studio apartment – one room with bathroom and kitchenette – in a reasonably safe Manhattan neighborhood can rent for upwards of $1000 a month, and even in traditionally undesirable parts of the city – **the Lower East Side** and **Hell's Kitchen** being the most recent and extreme examples – gentrification (and property rentals) are proceeding apace. Many newcomers to the city settle for sharing studios and one-bedrooms among far too many people; the alternative, not a bad one, is to look in the Outer Boroughs or the nearby New Jersey towns of Jersey City or Hoboken. With everyone else following that example, however, even those neighborhoods are becoming expensive, and to find a real deal you have to hunt hard and check out even the most unlikely possibilities.

The best source for actually hearing about an apartment or room is, as anywhere, word of mouth. On the media front, keep an eye on the ads in the *Voice*, *The New York Times* and the smaller ethnic papers mentioned above; and if you're reading this before setting out for New York, consider advertising yourself, particularly if you have a flat in London to exchange. Try the **commercial and campus bulletin boards**, too, where you might secure a temporary apartment-sit or sublet while the regular tenant is away.

Some of the city's many **universities and colleges** also provide vacancies, especially in the summertime. For instance, Barnard College (Columbia University, 3009 Broadway, NY 10027; ☎854-8021) offers a variety of dormitory facilities from the end of May to mid-August for upwards of $600 a month: write well in advance, as they're "selective" about who gets a room, and be prepared to show that you've got a temporary job, internship, or course of study that requires you to be in the city. New York University Summer Housing (14A Washington Place, NY 10003; ☎998-4621) charges a weekly rate that varies according to the room's amenities and your enrollment status (if you are not a student, plan on paying between $150 and $210 per week, with mandatory and optional meal plan). There's a three-week minimum stay, and priority is given to students in NYU programs; once again, write well in advance.

Less satisfactory perhaps, but a common fallback option, are **long-stay hotels**. A number of these cater specifically to single women on long stays: *Allerton House*, 130 E 57th St, NY 10022 (☎753-8841); the *Martha Washington Hotel*, 29 E 29th St, NY 10016 (☎689-1900); *Webster Apartments*, 419 W 34th St, NY 10001 (☎967-9000); *Parkside Evangeline Residence*, 18 Gramercy Park South (☎677-6200); and *Katherine House*, 118 W 13th St (☎242-6566). The last two are by far the nicest, though each usually has a long waiting list – call ahead. Others, open to both women and men, include: the *West Side Y*, 5 W 63rd St, NY 10023 (☎787-4400); the *International Student Hostel*, 154 E 33rd St, NY 10016 (☎228-7470) - students only; the *Chelsea Center*, 313 W 29th St, NY 10011 (☎243-4922); and the *International Student Center*, 38 W 88th St, NY 10024 (☎787-7706). At most of these, prices vary depending on the facilities available; though bear in mind that most of the cheaper hotels offer reduced weekly rates. Contact the respective reservations managers for full details.

The **New York Convention and Visitors Bureau** at 2 Columbus Circle (☎397-8222) can also be worth a call. They dole out a leaflet listing all reduced hotel rates. As a last resort, call **Travelers' Aid** at the Port Authority Bus Terminal (☎944-0013). Although they mostly deal with crime victims and (US) travelers stranded without funds, they may refer you to low-budget (or even free) temporary accommodation; city shelters, however, are notoriously dangerous and unsavory, so don't end up there if you can at all avoid it.

Just possibly (and only if you can afford a couple hundred dollars' fee), you might find it to your advantage to resort to one of the city's several roommate-finding agencies. Oldest and most reliable is **Roommate Finders**, 250 W 57th St (☎489-6942), a nondiscriminatory but discriminating company. If you use one of the other agencies – the *Voice* carries all their names, numbers and descriptions – make sure you read the contract before money changes hands or papers are signed.

Lastly, for the really organized, other viable accommodation alternatives include **homesteading, co-op** and **mutual housing associations**. These revolve around low-rent group occupation and renovation of often abandoned, city-owned buildings. It's the group element – and the commitment this entails - that mark this system as different from squatting. Each individual tenant contributes the particular skills at his or her disposal, as well as monthly dues that collectively support normal operating, maintenance and repair costs. Various agencies designed to assist and protect co-op groups and tenant associations have sprung up, providing legal assistance, rehabilitation and repair loan pools, architectural services, tool lending and so on: all very urban grass roots, community-oriented stuff. As for getting involved: in the words of one young British homesteader, it's a matter of "being in the street and seeing what's happening." Sound advice in any case, but for more direct information call the *Urban Homestead Assistance Board* at 120 Wall St, NY 10005 (☎479-3300), and inquire about *Self-Help Work Consumer Cooperative*. And good luck.

The City

Chapter 1

Introducing the City

New York City comprises the central island of Manhattan along with four Outer Boroughs – Brooklyn, Queens, the Bronx and Staten Island. **Manhattan**, to many, is New York. Certainly, whatever your interest in the city it's here that you'll spend the most time, and, unless you have friends elsewhere, are likely to stay. Understanding the intricacies of Manhattan's layout, and above all getting some grasp on its subway and bus system (for which see *Basics*), should be your first priority. If at all possible, try to master at least some of the following before arrival – on your flight, train trip or bus ride if need be.

A guide to the Guide

New York is very much a city of **neighborhoods**, and the chapters of our guide reflect this: each chapter covers a large area, and even the shortest will require at least a day of wandering, even if you intend to take in only the salient parts of what there is to see. The neighborhoods may be ethnic, geographic or historic: in some cases the name is more of a convenient label than an accurate description. For an overview of each neighborhood, turn to the introduction of each chapter.

The chapters

The guide starts at the southern tip of the island and moves north: **Chapter 2**, "The Harbor Islands," comprises the first parts of New York (and America) that nineteenth-century immigrants would have seen – the Statue of Liberty and Ellis Island, the latter recalling its history in an excellent Museum of Immigration. **Chapter 3**, "The Financial District and the Civic Center," takes in the skyscrapers and historic buildings of Manhattan's southern reaches – the famous silhouette seen on a thousand and one posters, with icons like the World Trade Center and the Woolworth Building prominent. North of the Civic Center are the first of the ethnic

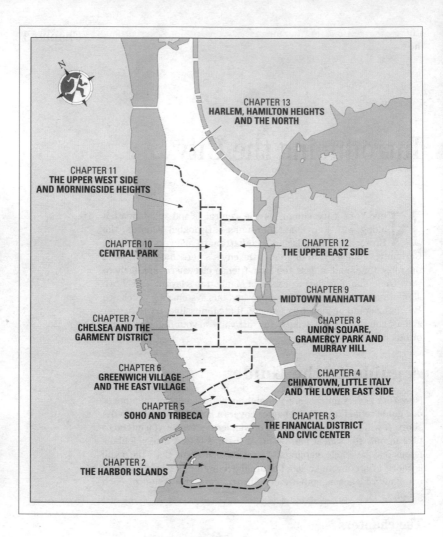

neighborhoods: Chinatown is perhaps the city's most homoge-
neous ethnic area, a vibrant locale that's great for Chinese food and
ethnic shopping; Little Italy, on the other hand, has few traces of
the once-strong immigrant presence. These two, along with the
Lower East Side, a traditionally Jewish – though now strongly
Hispanic as well – neighborhood that's scattered with some interesting low-life bars and clubs, plus a few trendy ones, form
Chapter 4. SoHo was once an area of light industry and office
buildings, but when the industry went into decline, artists moved
into the buildings: their open-plan design made them perfect for

THE CITY: CHAPTER 1

studios, and SoHo is now the number-one district for galleries and
the commercial art scene. TriBeCa is catching some of the fallout of SoHo's art dealing and is now similarly happening; read about both neighborhoods in **Chapter 5**. Greenwich Village has long been a cool place to hang out (at least in name), the jazz clubs and cafés forming a focus for the area's students and would-be bohemians. In the East Village the radicalism is a little more real; you'll find both described in **Chapter 6**. **Chapter 7** covers Chelsea and the Garment District: Chelsea is a mostly residential neighborhood, but it has been working hard to redefine itself via a growing arts scene, a vibrant shopping strip and some tourist attractions; the Garment District gets its name from the clothes production that goes on here, though you're only likely to notice it from the racks of clothes you'll see being trundled along the street. **Chapter 8**, "Union Square, Gramercy Park and Murray Hill," covers an area that was once the most fashionable in town, the birthplace of presidents and home to the Morgan banking dynasty. Today its greatest claim to fame is that enduring symbol of the city and skyscraper extraordinaire, the Empire State Building.

Chapter 9, "Midtown Manhattan," covers the stretch that runs from 42nd Street to Central Park. Here the great avenues – Fifth, Park, Madison and Third – reach their wealthiest: for years this has been a showcase for corporate building, and you'll find some of New York's most awe-inspiring, neck-cricking architecture here (the Chrysler Building, the Rockefeller Center), along with some superb museums (the Museum of Modern Art, the Museum of TV and Radio) and opulent shops. **Chapter 10** covers Central Park, a supreme piece of nineteenth-century landscaping without which life in Manhattan would be unthinkable – and certainly unlivable. Flanking the park, the Upper West Side – **Chapter 11** – is mostly residential, with the Lincoln Center, Manhattan's temple to the performing arts, the main focus. This chapter also contains descriptions of Columbia University, Morningside Heights and the Cathedral of St John the Divine, the largest Gothic building in the world. On the other side of the park, the Upper East Side (**Chapter 12**) is decidedly grander, the nineteenth-century millionaires' mansions now transformed into a string of magnificent museums known as the "Museum Mile." Alongside is a patrician residential neighborhood that boasts some of the swankiest addresses in Manhattan.

Above Central Park lie several distinct neighborhoods: Harlem, the historic black city-within-a-city whose name was for a long time synonymous with racial tension and urban deprivation, but today has a healthy sense of an improving go-ahead community; Hamilton Heights, a comparatively affluent area that feels too rural to be part of Manhattan; and Washington Heights, a mixed neighborhood far from the downtown attractions, one that few visitors ever venture to visit. Inwood, at the very northern tip of Manhattan island, has an unusual draw in the Cloisters, a nineteenth-century mock-up of a medieval monastery, packed with the finest European Romanesque and Gothic art and (transplanted) architecture. These areas are all described in **Chapter 13**.

It's a fact that few visitors, especially those with limited time, bother to venture off Manhattan island and out to the Outer Boroughs – covered in **Chapter 14**. This is a pity, because each of the Boroughs – Brooklyn, the Bronx, Queens and Staten Island – has points of interest even if, as in the South Bronx, it's an example of a neighborhood struggling to overcome years of urban blight and neglect. But elsewhere, in the picturesque streets of Brooklyn Heights, the nature sanctuaries of Queens or the atmospheric charm of Coney Island and nearby Brighton Beach, there's much to see.

Transport, terminology and the layout of the city

As mentioned above, each of the chapters covers a large area: you'll need to have at least a basic knowledge of New York's public transit system in order to get around what are often distances too long to tackle on foot. For a complete guide to the city's transit networks, see "Getting around the city" in *Basics*.

Despite its grid-pattern arrangement, Manhattan can seem a wearyingly complicated place to get around: blocks of streets and avenues, apparently straightforward on the map, can be uniquely confusing on foot and the psychedelic squiggles of the subway impenetrably arcane. Don't let subways and buses overawe you, though, since with a little know-how you'll find them efficient and fast. And if you're at all unsure, just ask – New Yorkers are the most helpful and accurate of direction givers and have seemingly infinite interest in initiating visitors into the great mysteries of their city.

You should also bear in mind that you'll hear the terms "lower Manhattan," "Midtown" and "upper Manhattan": roughly speaking, **lower Manhattan** runs from the southern tip of the island to around 14th Street; **midtown Manhattan** stretches from 14th Street to the southern tip of Central Park; and **upper Manhattan** contains the Park itself, the neighborhoods on either side of it, and the whole area to the north.

From north to south the island of Manhattan is about thirteen miles long and from east to west around two miles wide. Whatever is north of where you're standing is **uptown**; whatever south, **downtown**. East or west is **crosstown**. The **southern (downtown) part of Manhattan** was first to be settled, which means that its streets have names and that they're somewhat randomly arranged; similarly, the tangle of Greenwich Village is difficult to navigate, and you can waste much time wondering how West 4th and West 11th streets could possibly intersect. **Uptown, above Houston Street on the east side, 14th Street on the west,** the streets are numbered and follow a strict grid pattern. The numbers of these streets increase as you move north. Downtown, the main **points of reference** are buildings: the World Trade Center and the Woolworth Building are unmistakable landmarks. Uptown, just look for the big north–south **avenues. Fifth Avenue**, the greatest of these, cuts along the east side of Central Park and serves as a dividing line between east streets (the **"East Side"**) and west streets (the **"West Side"**). **House numbers** increase as you walk away from either side of Fifth Avenue; numbers on avenues increase as you move north. For a key to deciphering Manhattan addresses, see *Basics*, p.20.

Chapter 2

The Harbor Islands

T he tip of Manhattan island and the enclosing shores of New Jersey, Staten Island and Brooklyn form the broad expanse of **New York Harbor**, one of the finest natural harbors in the world and one of the things that persuaded the first immigrants to settle here several centuries ago. The harbor is an almost landlocked body of water, divided into the Upper and Lower Bay, some hundred miles square in total and stretching as far as the Verrazano Narrows – the narrow neck of land between Staten Island and Long Island. It's possible to appreciate Manhattan by simply gazing out from the promenade on Battery Park. But to get a proper sense of New York's specialness, and to get the best views of the classic skyline, you should really take

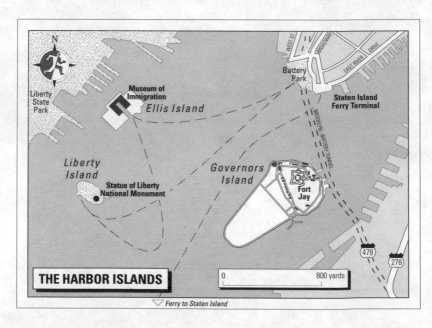

THE HARBOR ISLANDS

0   800 yards

▽ Ferry to Staten Island

to the water. You can do this either by taking a ride on the Staten Island ferry, or by taking the *Circle Line* ferry out to the Statue of Liberty and Ellis Island: two far more compelling targets for a trip.

Practicalities

Ferries, run by *Circle Line*, go to both the Statue of Liberty and Ellis Island and leave from the pier in Battery Park, every half-hour in summer roughly between 9.15am and 3.30pm during the week, 4.30pm at weekends. The fare is $7 for the full round-trip, and half that price for children (tickets from Castle Clinton in Battery Park). If you took the last ferry, it wouldn't be possible to see both islands, so it's best to try and leave as early as possible, thereby avoiding the lines (which can be long in high season, especially on weekends) and giving yourself enough time to explore both islands thoroughly. Liberty Island needs a good couple of hours, especially if the weather's fine and there aren't too many people; Ellis Island, too, demands at least two hours if you want to see everything. There are no admission fees for either Ellis Island or the Statue of Liberty.

The Statue of Liberty

MANHATTAN

Out of all of America's symbols, none has proved more enduring or evocative than the **Statue of Liberty**. This giant figure, torch in hand and clutching a stone tablet, has for a century acted as a figurehead for the American Dream; indeed there is probably no more immediately recognizable profile in existence. It's worth remembering that the statue is – for Americans at least – a potent reminder that the USA is a land of immigrants: it was New York Harbor where the first big waves of European immigrants arrived, their ships entering through the Verrazano Narrows to round the bend of the bay and catch a first glimpse of "Liberty Enlightening the World" – an end of their journey into the unknown, and the symbolic beginning of a new life.

These days, although only the very wealthy can afford to arrive here by sea, and a would-be immigrant's first (and possibly last) view of the States is more likely to be the customs check at JFK Airport, Liberty remains a stirring sight, with Emma Lazarus's poem, *The New Colossus*, written originally to raise funds for the statue's base, no less quotable than when it was written . . .

> *Here at our sea-washed, sunset gates shall stand*
> *A mighty woman with a torch, whose flame*
> *Is the imprisoned lightning, and her name*
> *Mother of Exiles. From her beacon-hand*
> *Glows world-wide welcome; her mild eyes command*
> *The air-bridged harbor that twin cities frame.*
> *'Keep ancient lands, your storied pomp!' cries she*
> *With silent lips. 'Give me your tired, your poor,*
> *Your huddled masses yearning to breathe free,*

The Statue of Liberty

The wretched refuse to your teeming shore.
Send these, the homeless, tempest-tost to me,
I lift my lamp beside the golden door.'

The statue, which depicts Liberty throwing off her shackles and holding a beacon to light the world, was the creation of the French sculptor Frédéric Auguste Bartholdi, who crafted it a hundred years after the American Revolution in recognition of solidarity between the French and American people (though it's fair to add that Bartholdi originally intended the statue for Alexandria in Egypt). Bartholdi built Liberty in Paris between 1874 and 1884, starting with a terracotta model and enlarging it through four successive versions to its present size, a construction of thin copper sheets bolted together and supported by an iron framework designed by Gustave Eiffel. The arm carrying the torch was exhibited in Madison Square Park for seven years, but the whole statue wasn't officially accepted on behalf of the American people until 1884, after which it was taken apart, crated up and shipped to New York.

It was to be another two years before it could be properly unveiled: money had to be collected to fund the construction of the base, and for some reason Americans were unwilling – or unable – to dip into their pockets. Only through the campaigning efforts of newspaper magnate Joseph Pulitzer, a keen supporter of the statue, did it all come together in the end. Richard Morris Hunt built a pedestal around the existing star-shaped Fort Wood, and Liberty was formally dedicated by President Cleveland on October 28, 1886, in a flag-waving shindig that has never really stopped. The statue was closed for a few years in the mid-1980s for extensive renovation and, in 1986, fifteen million people descended on Manhattan for the statue's centennial celebrations.

Today you can climb steps up to the crown, but the cramped stairway though the torch sadly remains closed to the public. Don't be surprised if there's an hour-long wait to ascend. Even if there is, Liberty Park's views of the lower Manhattan skyline, the twin towers of the World Trade Center lording it over the jutting teeth of New York's financial quarter, are spectacular enough.

Ellis Island

Just across the water, and just a few minutes on by ferry, sits **Ellis Island,** the first stop for over twelve million immigrants hoping to settle in the USA. The island, originally known as Gibbet Island by the English (who used it for punishing unfortunate pirates), became an immigration station in 1894, a necessary processing point for the massive influx of mostly southern and eastern European immigrants. It remained open until 1954, when it was abandoned and left to fall into atmospheric ruin.

The immigration process

Up until the 1850s, there was no official **immigration process** in New York. Then, the surge of Irish, German and Scandinavian immigrants escaping the great famines of 1846 and failed revolutions of 1848 forced authorities to open an immigration center at Castle Clinton in Battery Park. By the 1880s, widespread hardship in eastern and southern Europe, the pogroms in Russia and the massive economic failure in southern Italy forced thousands to flee the Continent. At the same time, America was experiencing the first successes of its industrial revolution, and more and more people started to move to the cities from the country. Ellis Island opened in 1894, just as America came out of a depression and began to assert itself as a world power. News spread through Europe of the opportunities in the New World, and immigrants left their homelands by the thousands.

The immigrants who arrived at Ellis Island were all steerage-class passengers; richer immigrants were processed at their leisure onboard ship. The scenes on the island were horribly confused: most families arrived hungry, filthy and penniless, rarely speaking English and invariably awed by the beckoning metropolis across the water. Immigrants were numbered and forced to wait for up to a day while Ellis Island officials frantically tried to process them; the center had been designed to accommodate 500,000 immigrants a year, but double that number came during the early part of the century. Con men preyed from all sides, stealing immigrants' baggage as it was checked and offering rip-off exchange rates for whatever money they had managed to bring. Each family was split up – men sent to one area, women and children to another – while a series of checks took place to weed out the undesirables and the infirm. The latter were taken to the second floor, where doctors would check for "loathsome and contagious diseases" as well as signs of insanity. Those who failed medical tests were marked with a white cross on their backs and either sent to the hospital or put back on the boat. Steamship carriers had an obligation to return any immigrants not accepted to their original port, though according to official records, only two percent were ever rejected, and many of those jumped into the sea and tried to swim to Manhattan, or committed suicide, rather than face going home.

There was also a legal test, which checked nationality and, very important, political affiliations. The majority of the immigrants were processed in a matter of hours and then headed either to New Jersey and trains to the West, or into New York City to settle in one of the rapidly expanding ethnic neighborhoods.

The Museum of Immigration

By the time of its closure, Ellis Island was a formidable complex. The first building burned down in 1897, the present one was built

Ellis Island   in 1903, and there were various additions built in the ensuing years
– hospitals, outhouses and the like, usually on bits of landfill that
were added to the island in an attempt to contend with the swelling
numbers passing through. The buildings were derelict until the
mid-1980s, since when the main, four-turreted central building has
been completely renovated, reopening in 1990 as the **Museum of
Immigration**. This is an ambitious museum which eloquently
recaptures the spirit of the place, with films, exhibits and tapes
documenting the celebration of America as the immigrant nation. It
also is surprisingly well-done and uncommercial, considering how
easy it would be to pull at heartstrings and make the place a trea-
cly tourist trap. All the same, you can't help but feel that it might
have been more memorable before the authorities got their hands
on the place.

Some 100 million Americans can trace their roots back
through Ellis Island and, for them especially, the museum is an
engaging display. On the first floor, located toward the back, is
the excellent "Peopling of America," which chronicles four centuries of American immigration, offering a statistical portrait of
those who arrived – who they were, where they came from, why
they came.

The huge, vaulted Registry Room on the second floor, scene of
so much trepidation, elation and – occasionally – despair, has been
left bare, with just a couple of inspectors' desks and American
flags. In the side hall, a series of interview rooms recreate step by
step the process that immigrants passed through on their way to
being naturalized; oddly, the white-tiled rooms are more reminiscent of a prison or mental institution than a stepping stone to liberty. Each is illustrated by the recorded voices of those who passed
through Ellis Island, recalling their experience, along with photographs, thoughtful and informative explanatory text, and small
artifacts – train timetables and familiar items brought from home.
There are descriptions of arrival and the subsequent interviews,
and examples of questions asked and medical tests given. One of
the dormitories, used by those kept overnight for further examination, has been left almost intact. On the top floor, there also are
evocative photographs of the building before it was restored, along
with items rescued from the building and rooms devoted to the
peak years of immigration.

Outside, the museum has an eerie, unfinished feel, heightened
by the empty shell of what was once the center's hospital. On the
fortified spurs of the island, names of immigrant families who
passed through the building over the years are engraved in copper; paid for by a minimum donation of $100 from their descen-
dants, this "American Immigrant Wall of Honor" helped fund the
restoration.

Governor's Island

Until recently, **Governor's Island**, the last of the three small islands
that lie just south of Manhattan, was a Coast Guard facility, housing
some 3000 service personnel and their families, and visitable by the
public once a month. On May 15, 1997, the island – the oldest military installation in continuous service in the US, active since 1637 –
was formally closed down and its personnel relocated. The annual
upkeep – estimated at $30 million – was too much to justify in light
of budget cuts and the end of the Cold War. President Clinton offered
to persuade Congress to turn the island over to New York for $1 –
contingent on its redevelopment to include park space accessible to
the public – but Mayor Guiliani and Governor Pataki balked at the
gesture; as a result, the US government has put the property on the
market and anticipates it will fetch $500 million.

"Nowhere in New York is more pastoral," Jan Morris wrote of
Governor's Island; indeed, the new owner of the 174-acre tract of
land will have unobstructed views of lower Manhattan and New York
Harbor. Also included are a handful of colonial and nineteenth-century houses, as well as **Fort Jay** and **Castle Williams** – the latter, the
complement to Castle Clinton, put up in 1789 by zealous and ever-
vigilant volunteers in the Revolution. The buyer will have to decide
the fate of the services that flourished on the island during the Coast
Guard's occupation, including a bank, golf course, bowling alley,
school, *Super 8* motel and library. New York University has shown
some interest in the island, albeit as a storage space; and, perhaps
predictably, Donald Trump's name has come up as well. To get the
latest, best to call the **New York Convention and Visitors Bureau**
(☎397-8222) and ask about visitor (and owner) status.

Chapter 3

The Financial District and the Civic Center

T he skyline of Manhattan's two most southerly neighborhoods – the **Financial District** and **Civic Center** – is the one you see in all the movies, dramatic skyscrapers pushed into the narrow tip of the island and framed by the monumental elegance of the Brooklyn Bridge. Despite its emphasis on business, it's perhaps Manhattan's most historic locale, and as such makes for a neat wander after (or before) visiting the Harbor Islands.

The Financial District

The heart of the nation's wheeler-dealing, the **Financial District** is where Manhattan (and indeed America) began – though precious few buildings remain from those days, having been shunted out by big business eager to boost corporate image with headquarters in the right place. A nascent residential community – housed in converted office space and formerly abandoned buildings along the waterfront – and the accompanying increase in local cultural events have helped the Financial District begin to shed its nine-to-five existence. Still, don't expect too much down here outside of business hours.

Wall Street and the New York Stock Exchange

The Dutch arrived here first, building a wooden wall at the edge of their small settlement to protect themselves from pro-British settlers to the north: hence the narrow canyon of today's **Wall Street** gained its name. It's here, behind the thin Neoclassical mask of the **New York Stock Exchange**, that the purse strings of the capitalist world are pulled. Take a long look at the mythological figures on the building's pediment: when the original stone figures began deteriorating in the Manhattan air, the Exchange clandestinely replaced them with these virtually indestructible sheet-metal copies, for

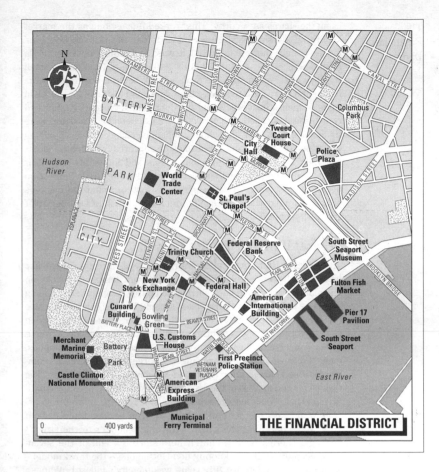

THE FINANCIAL DISTRICT

under no circumstances was any aspect of vulnerability to be associated with the Exchange.

From the Visitors' Gallery (Mon–Fri 9.15am–4pm; free), the Exchange floor appears a mêlée of brokers and buyers, all scrambling for the elusive fractional cent on which to make a megabuck. Sit through the glib introductory film, though, and the hectic scurrying and constantly moving hieroglyphs of the stock prices make more sense. Along with the film, there's a small exhibition on the history of the Exchange – notably quiet on the more spectacular screw-ups. The most disastrous, the notorious "Black Tuesday" of 1929, is mentioned almost in passing, perhaps because it was so obviously caused by the greed and short-sightedness of the money men themselves. In those days, shares could be bought "on margin," which meant the buyer needed to pay only a small part of their total cost, borrowing the rest using the shares as security. This worked fine as long as the market kept rising – as share dividends came in to pay off the loans, investors' money bought more shares. But it was, as Alistair Cooke put it, "a mountain of credit on a molehill of actual money," and only a small scare was needed to start the avalanche. When the market investors had to find more cash to service their debts and make up for the fall in value of their stocks, they sold off their shares cheaply. A panicked chain reaction ensued, and on October 24, sixteen million shares were traded; five days later, the whole Exchange collapsed as $125 million was wiped off stock values. Fortunes disappeared overnight: millions lost their life savings; banks, businesses and industries shut their doors; and unemployment spiraled helplessly. The Great Depression began. It says much for the safety nets that surround the market's operations today that the equally tumultuous crash of October 1987 caused comparatively negligible reverberations.

Federal Hall and Trinity Church

The **Federal Hall National Memorial**, at Wall Street's canyon-like head, can't help but look a little foolish: a Doric temple that woke up one morning and found itself surrounded by skyscrapers. The building was once the Customs House, later a bank, but the exhibition inside (Mon–Fri 9am–5pm; free) relates the headier days of 1789 when George Washington was sworn in as America's first president from a balcony on this site. It was a showy affair for a great, if rather pompous, man: "I fear we may have exchanged George III for George I," commented one senator after observing Washington's affectations. The documents and models of the event repay a wander, as does the daintily rotund hall. Washington's statue stands, very properly, on the steps.

At Wall Street's other end, **Trinity Church** (guided tours daily at 2pm) waits darkly in the wings, an ironic onlooker to the street's dealings. There's been a church here since the end of the seventeenth century, but this knobby neo-Gothic one – the third model – went up in 1846, and for fifty years was the city's tallest building, a reminder of just how recently high-rise Manhattan has sprung up. It has the air of an English church (Richard Upjohn, its architect, came from Dorset in southern England), especially in the sheltered **graveyard**, resting place of early Manhattanites and lunching office workers. A search around the old tombstones rewards with such luminaries as the first secretary to the Treasury, Alexander Hamilton.

Around Wall Street

Trinity Church is an oddity amid its office-building neighbors, several of which are worth nosing into. **One Wall Street**, immediately opposite the church, is among the best, with an Art Deco lobby in sumptuous red and gold that naggingly suggests a bankers' bordello. East down Wall Street, the **Morgan Guaranty Trust Building**, at no.

23, bears the scars of a weird happening on September 16, 1920: a horse-drawn cart pulled up outside and its driver jumped off and disappeared down a side street. A few seconds later, the cart blew up in a devastating explosion, knocking out windows half a mile away. Thirty-three people were killed and hundreds injured, but the explosion remains unexplained. One theory holds that it was a premeditated attack on Morgan and his vast financial empire; another claims that the cart belonged to an explosives company and was illegally traveling through the city. Curiously, or perhaps deliberately, the pockmark scars on the building's wall have never been healed.

A most impressive leftover of the confident days before the Wall Street Crash is the old **Cunard Building** at 25 Broadway. Its marble walls and high dome once housed a steamship's booking office – hence the elaborate, whimsical murals of sea travel and nautical gods splashed around the ceiling. As the large liners gave way to jet travel, Cunard could no longer afford such an extravagant shop window. Alas, its sorry fate is to house nowadays a post office – one that's been fitted out with little feeling for the exuberant space it occupies.

Bowling Green and around

Broadway comes to a gentle end at the **Bowling Green,** an oval of turf used for the game by eighteenth-century colonial Brits on a lease of "one peppercorn per year." The encircling iron fence is an original of 1771, though the crowns that once topped the stakes were removed in later revolutionary fervor, as was a statue of George III, which was melted down into some 42,088 musket balls – little bits of the monarch that were fired at his troops during the Revolutionary War. In 1783, the green was one of the last areas to be evacuated by the British, and it was the site of celebration when New York ratified the Constitution in 1788.

Earlier, the green was the location of one of Manhattan's more memorable business deals, when Peter Minuit, first director general of the Dutch colony of New Amsterdam, bought the whole island from the Indians for a handful of baubles worth sixty guilders (about $25). The other side of the story (the part you never hear) was that these Indians didn't actually own the island; no doubt both parties went home smiling. Today, the green is a spot for office people picnicking in the shadow of Cass Gilbert's **US Customs House,** an heroic monument to the Port of New York and home of the **National Museum of the American Indian.** The House, built in 1907, was intended to pay homage to the booming maritime market, and the four statues (sculpted by Daniel Chester French, who also created the Lincoln Memorial in Washington, DC) at the front of the building represent the four continents; the twelve scenes on the facade personify the world's commercial centers; and the head of Mercury – Roman god of commerce – adorns the top of each exterior column for good measure. As if French foresaw the House's current use, the

For an
account of the
museum of the
American
Indian see
chapter 15,
Museums and
Galleries.

sculptor blatantly comments on the mistreatment of Indians in his statues: most striking is the work on the left side of the front main staircase, which depicts a Native American in full headdress timidly peering over the shoulder of "America," who sits grandly on her throne and holds an oversized ear of corn on her lap – a symbol of Indian prosperity and contribution to world culture. Equally telling is the sculpture on the opposite side of the stairs, in which "America," this time her throne decorated with Mayan glyphs, has her foot on the head of Quetzalcoatl, the plumed serpent.

Inside the House, on the rotunda, are blue, gray and brown murals of bustling ships, painted by Reginald Marsh. In these renditions, steamers bring cargo, people and prosperity to the New York harbor side, all under the approving eye of Liberty herself. Portraits of explorers who played a critical role in establishing the US's frontiers – Cabot, Hudson, Columbus, Gomez – are interspersed between the scenes. Considering how the adjacent Indian Museum reminds one how poorly indigenous people on "discovered" lands were treated, these homages read, ironically, like a rogues' gallery.

Battery Park and Castle Clinton

Beyond the Customs House, lower Manhattan lets out its breath in **Battery Park**, a bright and breezy space with **Castle Clinton** at one side. Before landfill closed the gap, this nineteenth-century fort was an island, protecting Manhattan's southern tip, with its battery of cannons providing its name. Later, it found new life as a prestigious concert venue – in 1850, the enterprising P.T. Barnum threw a hugely hyped concert by soprano Jenny Lind, the "Swedish Nightingale," with tickets at $225 a throw – before doing service (pre-Ellis Island) as the dropoff point for arriving immigrants. Today, the squat castle isn't that interesting, though if you're curious it's open to the public (daily 9am–5pm); bear in mind that it's also the place to buy ferry tickets to the Statue of Liberty and Ellis Island.

South of Castle Clinton stands the **East Coast Memorial**, a series of granite slabs inscribed with the names of all the American seamen who were killed in World War II; to the castle's north, perched ten feet into the harbor, is the Merchant Marine Memorial, an eerie depiction of a marine futilely reaching for the hand of man sinking underneath the waves. Fittingly, both these memorials look out across New York Harbor; they also offer tremendous views of the Statue of Liberty and Ellis Island.

Back on State Street, a dapper Georgian facade identifies the **Shrine of Elizabeth Ann Seton**, the first native-born American to be canonized. St Elizabeth lived here briefly before moving to found a religious community in Maryland. The shrine – small, hushed and illustrated by pious and tearful pictures of the saint's life – is one of a few old houses that have survived the modern onslaught. Another one of these houses is **Fraunces Tavern**, located on the corner of

Pearl and Broad streets. Set dramatically against a backdrop of sky-scrapers, the three-story Georgian brick house has been almost total-ly reconstructed to mimic its appearance in December 4, 1783, the day of the incident that ensured its survival: it was then, after the British had been conclusively beaten, that a weeping George Washington took leave of his assembled officers, intent on returning to rural life in Virginia: "I am not only retiring from all public employ-ments," he wrote, "but am retiring within myself." With hindsight, it was a hasty statement, for six years later he was to return as the new nation's president. The Tavern's second floor recreates the simple colonial dining room where this took place – all probably as genuine as the relics of Washington's teeth and hair in the adjacent museum (Mon–Fri 10am–4.45pm, Sat noon–4pm; $2.50, $1 students).

Along Water Street

Turn a corner by the Tavern and you're on **Water Street**, in its south-ern reaches an attenuated agglomeration of skyscrapers developed in the early 1960s. At that time, the powers-that-were thought that Manhattan's economy was stagnating because of lack of room for growth, so they widened throughways like Water Street by razing many of the Victorian brownstones and warehouses that lined the waterfront. By doing so, they missed a vital chance to allow the old to give context to the new; ironically, a decent chunk of the office buildings they ambitiously built have since been converted to con-dos. With their streamline steel, glass, and concrete facades, the buildings are rather faceless: if you stand in the barren plaza of the nearby **American Express Building** at 2 New York Plaza and look up, it's hard to feel anything but dwarfed and insignificant.

Not all of Water Street's development is so depressing: turn east down Old Slip and a pocket-size palazzo that was once the **First Precinct Police Station** slots good-naturedly into the narrow strip, a cheerful throwback to a different era. A little to the south, off Water Street, is the **Vietnam Veterans' Memorial**, an assembly of glass blocks etched with troops' letters home. The mementos are sad and often haunting, but the memorial is disrespectfully shabby.

Cross Water Street, take the next left to Pine Street and you'll find one of Manhattan's most joyful skyscrapers. In 1916, the authorities became worried that the massive buildings looming up around town would shield light from the streets, and turn the Lower and Midtown areas into grim passages between soaring monoliths. The result of their fears was the first zoning ordinance, which ruled that a build-ing's total floor space couldn't be any more than twelve times the area of its site. This led to the "setback" style of skyscraper, and the **American International Building** at 70 Pine Street is the ultimate wedge of Art Deco wedding cake: light, zestful and with one of the best Deco interiors. As with other lobbies, no one minds you going in, and you can get a good view of the whole building – which might have been almost as well known as the Empire State or Chrysler had it been more visible. Almost opposite, I.M. Pei's gridiron **88 Pine Street** stands coolly formal in white: a self-contained and confident modern descendant.

Around the South Street Seaport

At the eastern end of Fulton Street the **South Street Seaport** comes girded with the sort of praise and publicity that generally augurs a commercial bland-out. In reality it's a mixed bag: a fair slice of commercial gentrification was necessary to woo developers and tourists, but the presence of a working fish market has kept things real in a way that should be a lesson for the likes of London's Covent Garden.

For a hundred years, this stretch of the waterside was New York's sailship port: it began when Robert Fulton started a ferry service from here to Brooklyn and left his name on the street and then its market. The harbor lapped up the trade brought by the opening of the Erie Canal and by the end of the nineteenth century was sending cargo ships on regular runs to California, Japan and Liverpool. Trade eventually moved elsewhere though, and the blocks of warehouses and ship's chandlers that had been gradually and secretively bought by property speculators were left to rot. Their rescue – by a historical monument order – was probably just in time.

Regular guided tours of the Seaport run from the **Visitors' Center**, an immaculate brick-terraced house located at 12–14 Fulton Street. An assemblage of upmarket chain shops like *Ann Taylor*, *Coach*, and *Guess?* line Fulton and the adjacent Front Street: such bland boutiques are a typical element of US waterfront refurbishment projects. 203 Front Street – now a store for mail-order monopoly *J. Crew* – is worth a look, however: in the 1880s, the building was a hotel that catered to unmarried laborers on the dock.

Nestled among this shopping district is the **New Fulton Market**, constructed in 1983. Recently refurbished, it's essentially a craft emporium, with a few cafés and fast-food eateries on the second floor. Across the way, the cleaned-up **Schermerhorn's Row** has the "English" *North Star Pub* at one end and the pricey *Sloppy Louie's* at the other; for food, it's better to wander down Front Street, past the formerly derelict residences, to *Jeremy's Ale House* (254 Front St at Dover St). *Jeremy's* is a brick warehouse that serves tasty yet inexpensive fried clams, calamari, and oysters, and offers the local dockworkers half-price beer from 8 to 10am.

The Fish Market and South Street Seaport Museum

The elevated East Side Highway forms a suitably grimy gateway to the **Fulton Fish Market**, a tatty building that wears its eighty years as the city's wholesale outlet with no pretensions. This enclave generates over a billion dollars in revenues annually, and is a place where one's word of honor still seals business dealings; however, it has recently come under the jurisdiction of municipal authorities, intent upon stemming the corruption and mafia influence in the area. These backroom dealings are of no threat to casual visitors, and by no means should stop you from touring the site.

If you can manage it, the time to be here is around 5am when buyers' trucks park up beneath the highway to collect the catches, the air reeks of salt and scale and there's lots of nasty things to step in. It's invigorating stuff, a twilight world that probably won't be around much longer – the city's regulation of the area, along with the adjacent **Pier 17 Pavilion**, a hypercomplex of restaurants and shops, may be nails in its coffin.

Next door, around piers 15 and 16, is the **South Street Seaport Museum** (April 1–Sept 30 daily 10am–6pm, Thurs 10am–8pm; Oct 1–March 31 Wed–Mon 10am–5pm; $6, admission includes all tours, films and galleries). The Seaport offers a collection of refitted ships and chubby tugboats, plus a handful of maritime art and trades exhibits. In the summer, the schooner *Pioneer* (or, more conventionally, a sightseeing ferry) will coast you around the harbor for an additional consideration. Unless sailing is your passion, it's better to skip the ships and freeload at the numerous **outdoor concerts**, held almost nightly throughout the warmer months.

The Brooklyn Bridge

From just about anywhere in the Seaport you can see one of New York's most celebrated delights, the **Brooklyn Bridge**. One of several spans across the East River (the Manhattan and Williamsburg bridges, respectively, are in sight behind it), the bridge's Gothic gateways are dwarfed by lower Manhattan's skyscrapers. But in its day, the Brooklyn Bridge was a technological quantum leap: it towered over the low brick structures around it and, for twenty years, was the world's largest suspension bridge, the first to use steel cables and – for many more – the longest single span. To New Yorkers it was an object of awe, the massively concrete symbol of the Great American Dream: "All modern New York, heroic New York, started with the Brooklyn Bridge," wrote Kenneth Clark, and indeed its meeting of art and function, of romantic Gothic and daring practicality, became a sort of spiritual model for the next generation's skyscrapers.

It didn't go up without difficulties: John Augustus Roebling, its architect and engineer, crushed his foot taking measurements for the piers and died of gangrene three weeks later; his son Washington took over only to be crippled by the bends from working in an insecure underwater caisson, and subsequently directed the work from his sickbed overlooking the site. Twenty workers died during the construction and, a week after the opening day in 1883, twelve people were crushed to death in a panicked rush on the bridge's footpath. Despite this (and innumerable suicides), New Yorkers still look to the bridge with affection: for the 1983 centennial it was festooned

For more on
Brooklyn see
Chapter 14,
The Outer
Boroughs

with decorations – "Happy Birthday Brooklyn Bridge" ran the signs – and the city organized a party, replete with shiploads of fireworks.

Whether the bridge has a similar effect on you or not, the view from it is undeniably spectacular. Walk across its wooden planks from City Hall Park and don't look back till you're midway: the Financial District's giants clutter shoulder to shoulder through the spidery latticework, the East River pulses below and cars scream to and from Brooklyn. It's a glimpse of the 1990s metropolis, and on no account to be missed.

The Federal Reserve Bank

Back on the island, Fulton Street arcs right across lower Manhattan with **Maiden Lane** as its southern parallel, an august and anonymous rollercoaster of finance houses with **Nassau Street** linking the two in a downbeat area of discount goods and fast food. Where Nassau and Maiden Lane meet, Johnson and Burgee's toybox castle of **Federal Reserve Plaza** resounds like a witless joke over the original **Federal Reserve Bank**, whose fortress-like walls supplied their postmodernist idea. While the loggia of the plaza isn't all bad, the Federal Reserve Plaza proved to be one of Philip Johnson's last projects with John Burgee: he split with the architect soon after, leaving Burgee broke and in the architectural wilderness.

There's good reason for the Reserve Bank proper's iron-barred exterior: stashed eighty feet below the street are most of the "free" world's **gold reserves** – 11,000 tons of them, occasionally shifted from vault to vault as wars break out or international debts are settled. It is possible – but tricky – to tour the piles of gleaming bricks; write to the Public Information Department, Federal Reserve Bank, 33 Liberty St, NY 10045 or phone ☎ 720-6130 at least a week ahead, since tickets have to be mailed.

Upstairs, in the Bank, dirty money and counterfeit currency are weeded out of circulation by automated checkers who shuffle dollar bills like endless packs of cards. Assistants wheelbarrow loads of cash around ("How much there?" I asked one; "$8.5 million," he replied), and, as you'd imagine, the security is just like in the movies.

Around the Federal Reserve Bank

When you've unboggled your mind of high finance's gold, you can see some of its glitter at **1 Chase Manhattan Plaza**, immediately to the south on Pine Street. This, the prestigious New York headquarters of the bank, boasts a boxy international-style tower that was the first of its kind in lower Manhattan, and which brought to downtown the concept of a plaza entrance. Unfortunately, Chase Manhattan's plaza has all the charm of a parking lot, and even Dubuffet's *Four Trees* sculpture can't get things going.

Continue to the end of Cedar Street, and you'll find the **Marine Midland Bank** at 140 Broadway: a smaller, more successful tower by the same design team and decorated with a tiptoeing sculpture by Isamu Noguchi. More sculpture worth catching lies behind Chase Manhattan Plaza on **Louise Nevelson Plaza**. Here, a clutch of Nevelson's works lie like a mass of shrapnel on an island of land: a striking ploy of sculpture that works well in the urban environment.

Go back down Liberty Street to Church Street and at **1 Liberty Plaza** stands the **US Steel Building**, a threatening black mass all the more offensive since the famed **Singer Building** was demolished to make way for it. Ernest Flagg's 1908 construction was one of the most delicate on the New York skyline, a graceful Renaissance-style tower of metal and glass destroyed in 1968 and replaced with what has justly been called a "gloomy, cadaverous hulk." But before you conclude that modern monoliths seem to be all size and no style, double back down John Street to **no. 127**, where you'll see a most playful creation, a bit cutesy but cheekily out of synch with its surroundings. Designed by Emery Roth and Sons, the building struts a blue and red neon exterior that is the antithesis of the Financial District's staid and streamline facades; its interior, featuring brightly colored ducts and pipes wrapped in twinkling Christmas lights, are enough to induce heart attacks in the area's conservative populace. The restaurant adjacent to the property refused to sell to the developer, so architects made its side wall into a giant-size digital clock which keeps accurate time, even down to the second.

The World Trade Center

Wherever you are in lower Manhattan, two buildings dominate the landscape. Critics say the twin Ronson lighters of the **World Trade Center towers** don't relate to their surroundings and aren't especially pleasing in design – and, spirited down to a tenth of their size, they certainly wouldn't get a second glance. But the fact is that they're big, undeniably and frighteningly so, and a walk across the plaza in summer months (closed in winter, as icicles falling from the towers can kill) can make your head reel.

The bombing of the World Trade Center

On February 26, 1993, the World Trade Center complex was rocked by an explosive device left in one of the underground parking lots; six people were killed and over a thousand injured. For a moment, the nightmare scenario of the destruction of one of the world's largest office buildings seemed possible, but apart from some minor structural damage, the building held fast. The evacuation of over 50,000 office workers was swiftly and safely carried out, and the biggest headache for the companies in the Trade Center was the fact that the towers were closed for weeks while structural examinations took place. Blame for the bomb fell upon an Arab terrorist group led by the radical Muslim cleric Shaikh Omar Abdel-Rahman, who was found guilty of involvement by a NYC court in summer 1995.

The TKTS booth on the mezzanine level sells discounted same-day tickets for Broadway shows (Mon–Fri 11am–5.30pm, Sat 11am–3.30pm).

Perhaps the idea of so huge a project similarly affected the judgment of the Port Authority of New York and New Jersey, the Center's chief financier, which for several years found itself expensively stuck with two half-empty white elephants – which were quickly surpassed as the world's tallest building by the Sears Tower in Chicago. Now the Center, whose towers are the best part of a five-building development, is full and successful, and the building has become one of the emblems of the city itself. With courage, a trip to the 107th floor **observation deck** of 2 World Trade Center (June–Sept daily 9.30am–11.30pm; Oct–May daily 9.30am–9.30pm; $10) gives a mind-blowing view from a height of 1350 feet – over a quarter of a mile. From the open-air rooftop promenade (closed during bad weather), the silent panorama is more dramatic still: everything in New York is below you, including the planes gliding into the airports. Even Jersey City looks exciting. As you timidly edge your way around, ponder the fact that one Philippe Petit once walked a tightrope between the two towers: nerve indeed. Best time to ascend is toward sunset, when the tourist crowds thin and Manhattan slowly turns itself into the most spectacular light show this side of the Apocalypse. If you're hungry or thirsty – and willing to shell out – you could also get the view by visiting the refurbished *Windows on the World* restaurant (1 World Trade Center, 107th floor), and its accompanying bar, modestly titled *The Greatest Bar on Earth*.

St Paul's Chapel

Straight across from the World Trade Center, yet coming from a very different order of things, is **St Paul's Chapel**. It's the oldest church in Manhattan, dating from 1766 – eighty years earlier than Trinity Church and almost prehistoric by New York standards. Though the building seems quite American in feel, its architect was from London, and he used St Martin-in-the-Fields in London as his model for this unfussy eighteenth-century space of soap-bar blues and pinks. George Washington worshipped here and his pew, zealously treasured, is much on show.

Battery Park City

The hole dug for the foundations of the World Trade Center's towers threw up a million cubic yards of earth and rock; these excavations were dumped into the Hudson to form the 23-acre base of **Battery Park City**. The Park, a self-sufficient island of office blocks, luxury apartments and chain boutiques bordered by an esplanade over a mile long landscaped as a park, is a paradigm for the Financial District: here the

Big Boys and Girls can be in the heart of things but work in a climate that's less frantic and more nature-oriented than most in Manhattan.

The centerpiece of the Park is the rather ugly **World Finance Center**, coordinated by Olympia and York Co, the Toronto team that was also responsible for London's Canary Wharf disaster. The buildings – four chunky, interconnected granite and glass towers with geometrically shaped tops – look like piles of building blocks. Their interiors are more refined: six acres of marble were used for their lobby floors and walls, while jacquard fabric lines the elevators. **Wintergarden**, a huge, glass-ceiling public plaza, brings light and life into the mall of shops and restaurants. Decorated by sixteen palm trees transplanted from the Mojave Desert, the plaza is an oasis; bask here for a bit, have some lunch, and take in a view of the swanky private boats docked in North Cove.

The Financial District

See chapter 15, Museums and Galleries" for an account of the new Museum of Jewish Heritage.

City Hall Park and the Civic Center

Broadway and Park Row form the apex of **City Hall Park**, a noisy, pigeon-splattered triangle of green with the **Woolworth Building** as a venerable and venerated onlooker. Some think this is New York's definitive skyscraper, and it's hard to disagree – money, ornament and prestige mingle in Cass Gilbert's 1913 "Cathedral of Commerce", whose soaring, graceful lines are fringed with Gothic decoration more for fun than any portentous allusion: if the World Trade Center towers railroad you into wonder by sheer size, then the Woolworth charms with good nature. Frank Woolworth made his fortune from his "five and dime" stores – everything cost either 5¢ or 10¢, strictly no credit. True to his philosophy, he paid cash for his skyscraper, and the whimsical reliefs at each corner of the lobby show him doing just that: counting out the money in nickels and dimes. Facing him in caricature are the architect (medievally clutching a model of his building), renting agent and builder. Within, vaulted ceilings ooze honey-gold mosaics and even the mailboxes are magnificent. The whole building has a well-humored panache more or less extinct in today's architecture – have a look at the *Citibank* next door to see what recent years have come up with.

The Civic Center and City Hall

At the top of the park, marking the beginning of the **Civic Center** and its incoherent jumble of municipal offices and courts, stands **City Hall** (Mon–Fri 10am–4pm). Finished in 1812 to a good-looking design that's a marriage of French Chateau and American Georgian, its first sorry moment of fame came in 1865 when Abraham Lincoln's body lay in state for 120,000 New Yorkers to file past. Later, after the city's 1927 feting of the returned aviator Charles Lindbergh, it

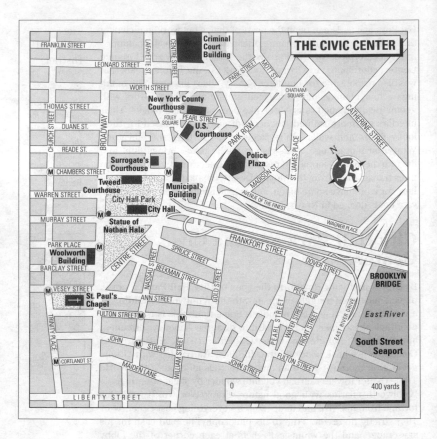

became the traditional finishing point for Broadway tickertape parades given for astronauts, returned hostages and, recently, the city's triumphant baseball team – the NY Yankees. Inside, it's an elegant meeting of arrogance and authority, with the sweeping spiral staircase delivering you to the precise geometry of the Governor's Room and the self-important rooms that formerly contained the **Board of Estimates Chamber**.

The Tweed Courthouse

If City Hall is the acceptable face of municipal bureaucracy, the **Tweed Courthouse** is a reminder of its corruption. Located directly behind City Hall, William Marcy "Boss" Tweed's monument to greed looks more like a gentile mansion than a municipal building: its long windows and sparse ornamentation are, ironically, far less grandiose or ostentatious than many of its peers. The man behind its construction, Boss Tweed, had worked his way from nowhere to become

chairman of the Democratic Central Committee at Tammany Hall in
1856 and, by a series of adroit and illegal moves, had manipulated
the city's revenues into both his own and his supporters' pockets. He
consolidated his position by registering thousands of immigrants as
Democrats in return for a low-level welfare system, and then paid off
the queues of critics.

For a while Tweed's grip strangled all dissent (even over the court
house's budget, which rolled up from $3 million to $12 million, possibly because one carpenter was paid $360,747 for a month's work,
a plasterer $2,870,464 for nine) until a political cartoonist, Thomas
Nast, and the editor of the *New York Times* (who'd refused a half-
million-dollar bribe to keep quiet) turned public opinion against him.
With suitable irony Tweed died in 1878 in Ludlow Street jail – a
prison he'd had built when Commissioner of Public Works.

City Hall Park is dotted with statues of worthier characters, not
least of whom is Horace Greeley, founder of the *New York Tribune*
newspaper, and in front of whose bronzed countenance a farmer's
market – fresh fruits, vegetables and bread – is held each Tuesday
and Friday (April–Dec 8am–6pm). Poll position in the worthy patri-
ot statue league goes to **Nathan Hale**. In 1776 Hale was captured by
the British and hanged for spying, but not before he'd spat out his
gloriously and memorably famous last words: "I regret that I only
have but one life to lose for my country." Those words, and his
swashbuckling statue, were to be his epithet.

The same year and at this same place, **George Washington**
ordered the first reading in the city of the Declaration of
Independence. Thomas Jefferson's eloquent, stirring statement of
the new nation's rights had just been adopted by the Second
Continental Congress in Philadelphia, and it no doubt fired the
hearts and minds of the troops and people assembled.

> *We hold these truths to be self-evident, that all men are created
> equal, that they are endowed by their creator with certain unalien-
> able rights, that among these are Life, Liberty and the pursuit of
> Happiness; that to secure these rights Governments are instituted
> among Men, deriving their just powers from the consent of the gov-
> erned; that whenever any form of Government becomes destructive
> of these ends, it is the Right of the People to alter or abolish it, and to
> institute new Government . . .*

The Municipal Building and around

Back on Centre Street, the **Municipal Building** stands like an oversized chest of drawers, its shoulders straddling Chambers Street in
an attempt to either embrace or engulf City Hall. Atop, an extravagant pile of columns and pinnacles signals a frivolous conclusion to
a no-nonsense building; below, though not apparent, subway cars
travel through its foundation. Walk through the building's arch and
you'll reach **Police Plaza**, a concrete space with the russet-hued

Police Headquarters at one end and a rusty-colored sculpture at its center. One side of the plaza runs down past the anachronistic neo-Georgian Church of St Andrew's to the pompous **United States Courthouse**, and stops at the glum-gray Foley Square, named after the sheriff and saloonkeeper Thomas "Big Tom" Foley. On the northeast edge of the square resides the **New York County courthouse**, a grand though underwhelming building that's much more interesting and accessible, its rotunda decorated with storybook WPA murals illustrating the history of justice. If there's time, take a look too at the Art Deco **Criminal Courts Building** (known as "The Tombs," from a funereal Egyptian-style building that once stood on this site located on Centre Street), and the fortress-like **Family Court**, a Rubik's cube that's been partially twisted, facing it across the way. All courts are open to the public (Mon–Fri 9am–5pm); the Criminal Courts are your best bet for viewing pleasure.

By and large, civic dignity begins to fade north of here, as ramshackle electrical stores and signs offering "Immigrant fingerprinting and photo ID" mark the edge of Chinatown.

Chapter 4

Chinatown, Little Italy and the Lower East Side

W ith more than 100,000 residents, 7 Chinese newspapers, 12 Buddhist temples, around 150 restaurants and over 300 garment factories, **Chinatown** is Manhattan's largest and only truly thriving ethnic neighborhood. Over recent years, it has pushed its boundaries north across Canal Street into Little Italy, now sprawling east into the nether fringes of the Lower East Side.

On the surface, Chinatown is prosperous – a "model slum," some have called it – with the lowest crime rate, highest employment and least juvenile delinquency of any city district. Walk through its crowded streets at any time of day, and every shop is doing a brisk and businesslike trade: restaurant after restaurant is booming; there are storefront displays of shiny squids, clawing crabs and clambering lobster; and street markets offer overflowing piles of exotic green vegetables, garlic and ginger root. Chinatown has the feel of a land of plenty, and the reason why lies with the Chinese themselves: even here, in the very core of downtown Manhattan, they have been careful to preserve their own way of dealing with things, preferring to keep affairs close to the bond of the family and allowing few intrusions into a still-insular culture. There have been several concessions to Westerners – storefront signs now offer English translations, and *Haagen Dazs* and *Baskin Robbins* ice-cream stores have opened on lower Mott Street – but they can't help but seem incongruous. The one time of the year when Chinatown bursts open is during the **Chinese New Year festival**, held each year on the first full moon after January 19, when a giant dragon runs down Mott Street to the accompaniment of firecrackers, and the gutters run with ceremonial dyes.

Beneath the neighborhood's blithely prosperous facade, however, there is a darker underbelly. Sharp practices continue to flourish, with traditional extortion and protection rackets still in business. Non-union sweatshops – their assembly lines grinding from early morning to late into the evening – are still visited by the US

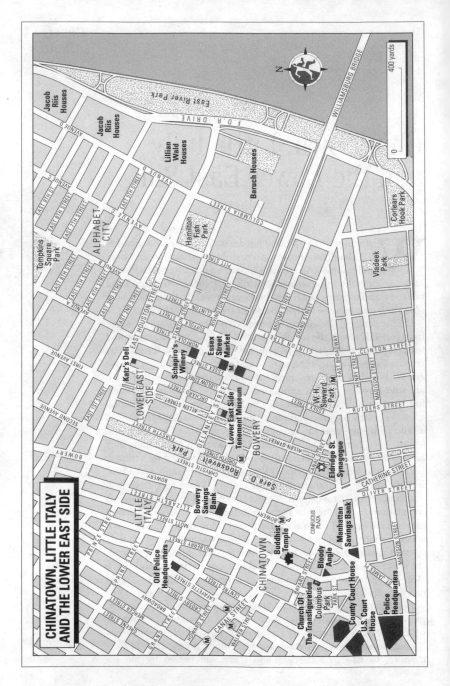

CHINATOWN, LITTLE ITALY
AND THE LOWER EAST SIDE

Jacob Riis Houses

Jacob Riis Houses

Lillian Wald Houses

East River Park

F.D.R. DRIVE

Baruch Houses

Corlears Hook Park

WILLIAMSBURG BRIDGE

N

400 yards

0

Tompkins Square Park

ALPHABET CITY

Hamilton Fish Park

AVENUE D

AVENUE C

AVENUE B

AVENUE A

EAST 8TH STREET

EAST 7TH STREET

EAST 6TH STREET

EAST 5TH STREET

EAST 4TH STREET

EAST 3RD STREET

EAST 2ND STREET

EAST HOUSTON STREET

FIRST AVENUE

EAST 1ST STREET

SECOND AVENUE

Vladeek Park

COLUMBIA STREET

PITT STREET

STANTON STREET

RIVINGTON STREET

CLINTON STREET

SUFFOLK STREET

NORFOLK STREET

ESSEX STREET

LUDLOW STREET

ORCHARD STREET

ALLEN STREET

FORSYTH STREET

CHRYSTIE STREET

BOWERY

Katz's Deli

Schapiro's Winery

Essex Street Market

M

LOWER EAST SIDE

Lower East Side Tenement Museum

Sara D. Roosevelt Park

DELANCEY STREET

BROOME STREET

GRAND STREET

BOWERY

M

ALLEN STREET

CANAL STREET

W. H. Seward Park

M

EAST BROADWAY

HENRY STREET

MADISON STREET

RUTGERS STREET

Eldridge St. Synagogue

CATHERINE STREET

OLIVER STREET

LITTLE ITALY

PRINCE STREET

SPRING STREET

BROADWAY

CROSBY STREET

LAFAYETTE STREET

MOTT STREET

MULBERRY STREET

ELIZABETH STREET

Bowery Savings Bank

Old Police Headquarters

CHINATOWN

Buddhist Temple

CONFUCIUS PLAZA

Bloody Angle

Manhattan Savings Bank

Church Of The Transfiguration

Columbus Park

BAYARD STREET

BOWERY

PARK ST.

JAMES ST.

County Court House

U.S. Court House

Police Headquarters

MERCER STREET

GREENE STREET

GRAND STREET

HOWARD STREET

CANAL STREET

WALKER STREET

CENTRE STREET

BAXTER STREET

M

M

M

Department of Labor, who come to investigate workers' testimonies of being paid below minimum wage for seventy-plus-hour work weeks. Living conditions are abysmal for the poorer Chinese – mostly recent immigrants and the elderly – who reside in small rooms in overcrowded tenements ill-kept by landlords. Yet, because the community has been cloistered for so long and has only just begun to seek help from city officials for its internal problems, you won't detect any hint of difficulties unless you reside in Chinatown for a considerable length of time.

For more on Chinese New Year, see chapter 22, Parades and Festivals.

Chinese immigration

The Chinese began to arrive in the mid-nineteenth century, following in the wake of a trickle of Irish and Italian immigrants. Most of these Chinese had previously worked out West, building railways and digging gold mines, and few intended to stay: their idea was simply to make a nest egg and retire to a life of leisure with their families (99 percent were men) back in China. Some, a few hundred perhaps, did go back, but on the whole the big money took rather longer to accumulate than expected, and so Chinatown became a permanent settlement. The residences were not particularly welcomed by the authorities: the Mafia-style Tong Wars, which occurred toward the end of the nineteenth century, made the quarter's violence notorious. As a result, in 1882, the US government passed an act forbidding entry to any further Chinese workers for ten years.

After the 1965 Immigration Act did away with the 1924 "National Origins" provision, a large number of new immigrants, many of whom were women, began arriving in Chinatown; within a few years, the area's massive male majority had been displaced. Local businessmen took advantage of the declining Midtown garment business and made use of the new, large and unskilled female workforce: they opened garment factories and paid their workers low wages. At the same time, many small restaurants opened up, spurred by the early 1970s Western interest in Chinese food and by the plight of working Chinese women, who, no longer having time to cook, took food from these restaurants home to feed their families. When the Wall Street crowd became interested in the area, fancier restaurants, more money and greater investment flowed into the quarter; that capital soon attracted more Asian money from overseas. In little time, Chinatown had an internal economy unlike any other new immigrant neighborhood in New York.

In the early 1990s, waves of illegal immigrants from the Fujian province of China began to arrive in New York, upsetting the power structure in Chinatown. Unlike the established Cantonese, who had dominated Chinatown's politics for a century or so, these were largely uneducated laborers who spoke Mandarin. The cultural and linguistic differences made it difficult for the Fujianese to find work in Chinatown, and a large number turned to more desperate means.

Fujianese-on-Fujianese violence comprised the majority of Chinatown's crime in 1994, prompting local Fujianese leaders to break Chinatown's traditional bond of silence and call in city officials for help. They also began to construct a network of social agencies and political groups to improve the immigrants' plight. Aided by this, and by the fact that many well-off Cantonese have moved to Queens and the suburbs, the Fujianese have now become the controlling force in Chinatown.

MANHATTAN

Exploring Chinatown

Most New Yorkers come to Chinatown not to get the lowdown on Chinese politics but to eat. Nowhere in this city can you eat so well, and so much, for so little. **Mott Street** is the area's main thoroughfare, and along with the streets around – Canal, Pell, Bayard, Doyers and Bowery – hosts a glut of restaurants, tea and rice shops and grocers. The food is dotted all over; Cantonese cuisine predominates, but there are also many restaurants that specialize in the spicier Szechuan and Hunan cuisines, along with Fukien, Soochow and the spicy Chowchou dishes. Anywhere you walk into is likely to be good, but if you're looking for specific recommendations (especially for lunchtime dim sum), some of the best are detailed in Chapter 17, *Eating*.

Besides eating, the lure of Chinatown lies in wandering amid the exotica of the shops and absorbing the neighborhood's vigorous street life. There are a few interesting routes if you want to set structure to your explorations. Mott Street, again, is the obvious starting point: follow it from Worth Street and there's the **Chinatown Museum** (see Chapter 15, *Museums and Galleries*) at the far end, on the site of the district's first Chinese shop. Further up, a rare building predates the Chinese intake, the early nineteenth-century **Church of the Transfiguration**; to the right, at the corner of Pell and Doyers streets is what was once known as "Bloody Angle," so named for its miserable reputation as a dumping ground for dead bodies during the Tong Wars. Around the Angle there is a lattice of streets and alleys where you'll find shops stocked with Old World trinkets and plastic tourist goods.

Returning to Mott, take a left down Bayard Street and you've arrived at **Columbus Park,** a shady haunt favored by the neighborhood's elderly. At the Park's northernmost tip is an open-air concert hall, topped by a pagoda roof and decorated with fading pictures of a bird and a dragon. Continue on north and you'll arrive at **Canal Street,** at all hours a crowded thoroughfare crammed with jewelry shops and kiosks hawking sunglasses, T-shirts and fake Rolexes. As you approach **Grand Street** – which used to be the city's Main Street in the mid-1800s – outdoor fruit, vegetable and seafood stands line the curbs – offering snow peas, bean curd, fungi, oriental cabbage and brown eggs to the passers-by. Ribs, whole chickens and Peking

ducks glisten in the storefront windows nearby: the sight of them can
put more than a vegetarian off his food. Far more salubrious are the
Chinese herbalists. The roots and powders in their boxes, drawers
and glass are century-old remedies, but, to those accustomed to
Western medicine, may seem like voodoo potions.

Once you've traveled this circuit (or at least a rough approxima-
tion of it), you've seen Chinatown's nucleus. Moving on, stroll over
to **Bowery** and wander the streets leading down to the housing projects that flank the East River, most of which are nowadays inhabited by Fujianese Chinese. Then double back by way of East Broadway
or Henry Street to where the **Manhattan Bridge**, with its grand
Beaux Arts entrance out of place amid the neon signs and Chinese
cinemas, crosses the East River. From here you could head north up
Chrystie Street, which forms the nominal border between Chinatown
and the Lower East Side, or west down Canal Street, past the hubbub
and into the area known as Little Italy, long regarded as the center of
the city's considerable Italian community.

Little Italy

Signs made out of red, green and white tinsel effusively welcome visitors to **Little Italy**, a signal perhaps that Little Italy is light years
away from the solid ethnic enclave of old. It's a lot smaller and more
commercial than it was, and the area settled by New York's huge
nineteenth-century influx of Italian immigrants – who (like their
Jewish and Chinese counterparts) cut themselves off clannishly to
recreate the Old Country – is being encroached upon a little more
each year by Chinatown. Few Italians still live here and the surfeit of
restaurants – some of which pipe the music of NY's favorite Italian
son, Frank Sinatra, onto the street – tend to have valet-parking and
high prices. In fact, it is this quantity of restaurants, more than anything else, that gives Little Italy away: go to the city's true Italian
areas, Belmont in the Bronx or Carroll Gardens in Brooklyn, and
you'll find very few genuine Italian eateries, since Italians prefer to
consume their native food at home. It's significant, too, that when
Martin Scorsese came to make *Mean Streets* it was in Belmont that
he decided to shoot it, even though the film was about Little Italy.

But that's not to advise missing out on Little Italy altogether.
Some original bakeries and *salumerias* (Italian specialty food
stores) do survive, and there, amid the imported cheeses, sausages
and salamis hanging from the ceiling, you can buy sandwiches made
with slabs of mozzarella or eat slices of homemade focaccia. In addition, there still are plenty of places to indulge yourself with a cappuccino and pricey pastry, not least *Ferrara's* on Grand Street, the
oldest and most popular.

If you're here in September, the **Festa di San Gennaro** is a wild,
tacky and typically Italian splurge to celebrate the saint's day, when

Little Italy   Italians from all over the city converge on Mulberry Street, Little Italy's main strip, and the area is transformed by street stalls and numerous Italian fast-snack outlets. None of the restaurants around here really stands out, but the former *Umberto's Clam House*, on the corner of Mulberry and Hester streets, was quite notorious in its time: it was the scene of a vicious gangland murder in 1972, when Joe "Crazy Joey" Gallo was shot dead while celebrating his birthday with his wife and daughter. Gallo, a big talker and ruthless business-man, was keen to protect his business interests in Brooklyn; he was alleged to have offended a rival family and so paid the price.

In striking counterpoint to the clandestine lawlessness of the Italian underworld, the old **Police Headquarters**, a palatial Neoclassical confection meant to cow would-be criminals into obedi-ence with its high-rise dome and lavish ornamentation, is located at the corner of Centre and Broome streets. The police headquarters moved to a bland modern building in the Civic Center in 1973, and the overbearing palace has been converted into upmarket condo-miniums, some of which Steffi Graf, Winona Ryder and Christy Turlington have all called home. Walk beyond Broadway and you're already in **SoHo**, which, like Chinatown, is a booming district burst-ing its borders from the further side of Broadway (see Chapter 5).

The Lower East Side

I don't wanna be buried in Puerto Rico
I don't wanna rest in Long Island cemetery
I wanna be near the stabbing shooting
gambling fighting and unnatural dying
and new birth crying
So please when I die . . .
Keep me nearby
Take my ashes and scatter them thru out
the Lower East Side . . .

Miguel Piñero, *A Lower East Side Poem*

The **Lower East Side** is one of Manhattan's least changed and most unalluring downtown neighborhoods, a little-known quarter which began life toward the end of the last century as an insular slum for over half a million Jewish immigrants. Coming here from eastern Europe via Ellis Island, these refugees were in search of a better life, scratching out a living in a free-for-all of crowded, sweatshop com-petition. Since then, the area has become considerably depopulated, and the slum-dwellers are now largely Puerto Rican or Chinese rather than Jewish; but otherwise, at least on the surface, little has visibly changed.

The area's lank brick tenements, ribbed with blackened fire escapes, must have seemed a bleak kind of destiny for those who arrived here, crammed into a district which daily became more densely populated and where low standards of hygiene and abysmal housing made disease rife and life expectancy low. It was conditions like these that spurred local residents like Jacob Riis and, later, Stephen Crane to record the plight of the city's immigrants in their writings and photographs, thereby spawning not only a whole school of realistic writing but also some notable social reforms. Not for nothing – and not without some degree of success – did the Lower East Side become known as a neighborhood where political battles were fought. Today the Lower East Side splits neatly into two distinct parts. South of East Houston Street is the more intriguing: wholesomely seedy and even a bit trendy, with new nightspots popping up almost weekly. North of East Houston is an area known as "Alphabet City" (avenues A, B, C and D), a former Slavic enclave abutting the East Village that is gentrifying at an alarming rate.

South of Houston

This is the most readily explored part of the Lower East Side – and the most rewarding. In the streets south of Houston, Jewish immigrants indelibly stamped their character with their own shops, delis, restaurants, synagogues and, later, community centers. Even now, with the runover of immigrants from Chinatown having settled in the neighborhood, it still holds the remnants of its Jewish past, such as the area's homemade Kosher cuisine and the Orthodox bathhouse. Some outsiders are drawn to the area for the **bargain shopping**. You can get just about anything at cut-price in the stores: clothes on Orchard Street, lamps and shades on the Bowery, ties and shirts on Allen Street, underwear and hosiery on **Grand Street**, textiles on Eldridge. And, whatever you're buying, people will if necessary haggle down to the last cent. The time to come is Sunday morning, for the **Orchard Street Market**, when you'll catch the vibrancy of the Lower East Side at its best. Weekdays the stores are still there, but far fewer people come to shop and the streets can have a forbidding, desolate feel. The **Lower East Side Tenement Museum**, at 97 Orchard Street, is by far the best place to get the lowdown on the neighborhood's immigrant past and present.

Around East Broadway

Although the top half of **East Broadway** is now almost exclusively Chinese, the street used to be the hub of the Jewish Lower East Side. For the old feel of the quarter – where the synagogues remain active (many in the area have become churches for the Puerto Ricans) – best explore north of here, starting with **Canal Street**. **The Eldridge Street Synagogue** is worth a look in particular. In its day it was one of the neighborhood's most grand, but the main doors of its formidable facade have been sealed shut and only the basement is left open to the public for the sporadic get-togethers of a much-dwindled congregation. Tours are offered on Sundays (hourly noon–4pm; $5).

Carry on east down Canal Street and, at nos. 54–58, look above the row of food and electrical stores and you'll see the shell of **Sender Jarmulovsky's Bank**, founded in 1873 to cater to the financial needs of the influx of non-English-speaking immigrants. Around the turn of the century, as the bank's assets accrued, rumors began circulating about its insolvency. As World War I became an imminent reality, the bank was plagued by runs and riots when panicked patrons tried to withdraw their money to send to relatives back in Europe. Finally, in 1914, the bank collapsed; with its closure, thousands lost what little savings they had.

Continue on east, past the junction of Canal Street and East Broadway, and you'll come to the dilapidated, graffiti-covered **New York Ling Laing Church**, the building that once housed the editorial offices of *Forward*, the foremost Jewish-language newspaper. Nowadays, the Hebrew characters on the facade have been covered over by signs in Chinese: a testament to how each wave of immigrants salvages the precious space and makes it their own by painting over predecessors' history. Move along further, to the intersection of East Broadway and Grand, where, adjacent to the Puerto Rican *bodegas* (grocery stores) and the concrete and glass eyesore Public School 134, proudly stands a cultural anachronism: an operating *mikveh*, or ritual bathhouse, where Orthodox Jewish women must bathe prior to marriage and monthly thereafter.

East down Grand leads through housing projects to the messy **East River Park** – not one of the city's most attractive open spaces. It's better to skip that area and double back up Grand, toward Essex Street, where you'll find more stores and activity. A few blocks on your way you'll pass the **Church of St Mary**, the oldest (1832) neo-Gothic building in the city. The Church is a favorite resting spot of elderly Jewish couples, who sit on the benches outside and watch the world go by.

Essex Street and around

Essex Street leads to **Delancey**, the horizontal axis of the Jewish Lower East Side, and to the **Williamsburg Bridge** – formerly a shelter to New York's homeless and now a makeshift parking lot. On either side of Delancey sprawls the **Essex Street Covered Market**, with *Ratner's Dairy Restaurant*, one of the Lower East Side's most famous dairy restaurants, nearby at 138 Delancey. Incongruously, the back room of *Ratner's* has been converted into a fashionable, somewhat hidden nightspot, *Lansky's Lounge* (the barely marked alley entrance is at 104 Norfolk Street). Back on Essex, at no. 35, is *The Essex Street (Guss') Pickle Products*, where people line up outside the storefront to buy homemade pickles taken fresh from barrels of garlicky brine.

East of Essex Street, the atmosphere changes abruptly. Here the inhabitants are mainly Latino, mostly Puerto Ricans but with a fair

For more on Jewish food in the Lower East Side – and elsewhere in New York – see Chapter 17, Eating, and chapter 18 Drinking.

smattering of immigrants from other Latin and South American countries. Most of the Jews who got richer long ago moved into middle-income housing further Uptown or in the other boroughs, and there's little love lost between those who remain and the new inhabitants. Today, much of the area east of Essex has lost the traditional Sunday bustle of Jewish market shopping and has been replaced by the Saturday afternoon Spanish chatter of the new residents shopping for records, inexpensive clothes and electrical goods. **Clinton Street** – a mass of cheap Latino retailers, restaurants and travel agents – is in many ways the central thoroughfare of the Puerto Rican Lower East Side.

One stalwart from bygone times is **Schapiro's Winery,** at 124 Rivington Street. If you are here on a Sunday, check out the free wine tours and tastings (11am–4pm, on the hour) at this, the neighborhood's – and probably the city's – only kosher wine and spirits warehouse, where wine is made on the premises. A block further east, at 156 Rivington, is the storefront of **ABC No Rio**, a community arts center that best exemplifies the neighborhood's struggle between its recent past and rapidly upmarket future. In 1980, the space was given to a group of artists who had put on a notable exhibit concerning skyrocketing rents; it has gone on to host gallery shows, concerts, installations and the like. The Housing and Preservation Department (HPD) attempted to reclaim the space in June 1995, saying it was a neighborhood blight. It was indeed shabby. Since then, however, a deal has been struck for *ABC* to keep the building, as long as they put in $75,000 worth of improvements.

Ludlow and Orchard streets

Double back west, past Essex, and you'll run into the newly happening **Ludlow Street.** A half-dozen or so bars, such as the popular *Luna Lounge* (171 Ludlow) and *Max Fish* (178 Ludlow), dot the block; a smattering of young designers have boutiques in the area; and there's a number of secondhand stores offering kitsch items and slightly worn treasures. On the corner of Ludlow and Houston you'll find *Katz's Deli*, lauded by locals as one of the best in New York. If it looks familiar, don't be surprised: this was the scene of Meg Ryan's faked orgasm in *When Harry Met Sally*.

Walk west on Houston and you arrive at **Orchard Street**, center of the so-called Bargain District, and best on Sundays when it is filled with stalls and storefronts hawking discounted designer clothes and bags. The rooms above the stores here used to house sweatshops, named so because whatever the weather, a stove had to be kept warm for pressing the clothes that were made there. The garment industry moved uptown ages ago, and the rooms are a bit more salubrious now – often home to pricey apartments.

The Bowery

Walk east from here and it's for the most part burned-out tenements interspersed with a scattering of Spanish-style grocery stores; to the west things aren't much better. Bowery spears north out of Chinatown as far as Cooper Square on the edge of the East Village. This wide thoroughfare has gone through many changes over the years: it took its name from "Bouwerie," the Dutch word for farm, when it was the city's main agricultural supplier; later, in the closing decades of the last century, it was flanked by music halls, theaters, hotels and middle-market restaurants, drawing people from all parts of Manhattan. Though in some sections it is still a skid row for the city's drunk and derelict, such days are limited; as the demand for apartments continues, the tide of gentrification is slowly sweeping its way south through the Lower East Side.

The one – bizarre – focus, certainly a must for any Lower East Side wanderings, is the **Bowery Savings Bank** on the corner of Grand Street. Designed by Stanford White in 1894, it rises out of the neighborhood's debris like a god, as does its sister bank on 42nd Street, a shrine to the virtue of saving money. Inside, the original carved check-writing stands are still in place, and the coffered ceiling, together with White's great gilded fake marble columns, couldn't create a more potent feeling of security. An inscription above the door as you exit leaves you in no doubt: "Your financial welfare is the business of this bank." Quite so, but back on the Bowery, moving between the panhandlers and shabby new businesses, you wonder whose interests they have in mind.

North of Houston

Cross East Houston Street and the Lower East Side takes on another mantle, veering from Tompkins Square and the East Village to one of the most dramatically revitalized areas of the city. Here the island bulges out beyond the city's grid structure, the extra avenues being named A to D, and the area, by its newly acquired devotees, **Alphabet City**. (Its Puerto Rican inhabitants have called it *Loisaida* for decades.) Not many years ago this was a notoriously unsafe corner of town, run by drug pushers and gangsters. People told of cars lining up for fixes in the street, and the burned-out buildings were well-known safehouses for the brisk heroin trade. Most of this was brought to a halt in 1983 with "Operation Pressure Point," a massive police campaign to clean up the area and make it a place where people would want to live. This has been achieved, with crime down and only the area beyond **Avenue B** questionable; the change, though, has wiped away much of the character and made the streets the haunt of well-heeled young bohemians. Go beyond Avenue C and you may get hassled, but – during the day at least – you're unlikely to be mugged. It's worth a quick circuit around this part of the Lower East Side just to see some of the murals and public art (like the church

decorated with mosaics and mirrors on Fifth Street between avenues
C and D) and to witness how bad things can get through lack of effective city money or control.

Walking down **Avenue A** away from Tompkins Square park and
toward Houston Street, there are a number of hip thrift and clothes
shops, with the Beastie Boys' *X-Large*, located at no. 151, the most
famous. There also are plenty of good bars, restaurants, and bohemian cafés in the patch along the park, including *7B's* (Seventh St at
Ave B), *Life Café* (Tenth St at Ave B) and *alt.coffee* (Ninth St at Ave
A). Heading east from there, the mood shifts a bit. **Avenue C**, also
known as "Avenue Loisaida," is the residence of many of the Latinos
in the area; *salsa* and *merengue* boom from open windows, and old
men gather in storefront social clubs to sip drinks and play dominos.
Some communal gardens – such as the one that spans Avenue C
between East 9th and East 10th streets – have sprung up, but the
spate of new construction threatens to destroy such local charms.
Already the infamous *Gas Station* (Second St at Ave B), a bizarre
outdoor gallery of recycled junk turned into art, has been leveled, to
make way for a planned high-rise. Further over, past **Avenue D**, are
the East River housing projects, a good bet if you are a drug dealer,
but not recommended otherwise.

Chapter 5

SoHo and TriBeCa

S ince the mid-1960s, **SoHo**, the grid of streets that runs *So*uth of *Ho*uston Street, has meant art. The midland between the Financial District and Greenwich Village, it had been, for most of the twentieth century, a raggedy, gray wasteland of manufacturers and wholesalers. But as the Village increased in price and declined in hipness, artists moved into the loft spaces and cheap-rental studios. Galleries were established, which quickly attracted the city's art crowd, as well as boutiques and restaurants. Like in the Village, gentrification soon followed, and what remains is a mix of chichi antique, art and clothes shops, earthy industry and high living. Yet although SoHo now carries the veneer of the establishment – a loft in the area means money (and lots of it) – no amount of gloss can cover up SoHo's quintessential appearance, its dark alleys of paint-peeled former garment factories fronted by some of the best cast-iron facades in the country.

Some history

Even up to the late 1960s, SoHo was a slum. It had experienced a bit of a vogue in the mid-nineteenth century when it fringed New York's then-liveliest and most fashionable street, Broadway, but quickly became a seamier backdrop of industrial and red-light areas – cheerfully known as "Hell's Hundred Acres" – when 14th Street replaced Broadway as the commercial and entertainment center. At the turn of the century, SoHo – now nicknamed "The Valley" because of its low industrial buildings – was scandalized by the **Triangle Shirtwaist Factory Fire** of 1911, when a sweatshop's young, mostly immigrant female workforce burned to death because they were locked inside the building during their shift hours and had no means to escape when fire broke out.

In the 1940s, costs drove artists from Greenwich Village: they began moving into SoHo, converting the large, cheap and light-filled factories into lofts and work spaces. One hindrance plagued them, however: the buildings were zoned exclusively for small industry, shipping and

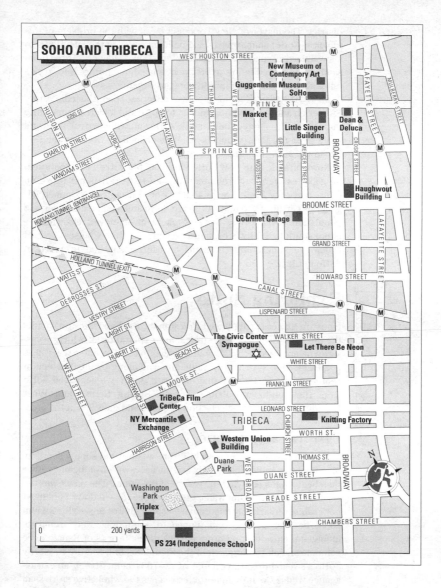

SOHO AND TRIBECA

WEST HOUSTON STREET

New Museum of
Contempory Art
Guggenheim Museum
SoHo

PRINCE ST.

Market

Little Singer
Building

Dean &
Deluca

SPRING STREET

Haughwout
Building

BROOME STREET

Gourmet Garage

GRAND STREET

HOLLAND TUNNEL (ENTRANCE)

HOWARD STREET

HOLLAND TUNNEL (EXIT)

CANAL STREET

LISPENARD STREET

The Civic Center
Synagogue

WALKER STREET

Let There Be Neon

WHITE STREET

FRANKLIN STREET

TriBeCa Film
Center

LEONARD STREET

NY Mercantile
Exchange

TRIBECA

Knitting Factory

WORTH ST.

Western Union
Building

THOMAS ST.

Duane
Park

DUANE STREET

Washington
Park

READE STREET

Triplex

CHAMBERS STREET

0   200 yards

PS 234 (Independence School)

HUDSON ST.
KING ST.
CHARLTON STREET
VARICK STREET
VANDAM STREET
SIXTH AVENUE
SULLIVANT STREET
THOMPSON STREET
WEST BROADWAY
GREENE STREET
WOOSTER STREET
MERCER STREET
BROADWAY
CROSBY STREET
LAFAYETTE STREET
MULBERRY STREET
WATTS ST.
DESROSSES ST.
VESTRY STREET
LAIGHT ST.
HUBERT ST.
BEACH ST.
N. MOORE ST.
GREENWICH ST.
HARRISON STREET
WEST STREET
CHURCH STREET
WEST BROADWAY

warehouses; residence in them was illegal. Pestered by these law-
breakers, the city government attempted to raze parts of SoHo in the
early 1960s. Joining forces with the conservationist movement, the
wily artists trumpeted SoHo's formidable cast-iron architecture –
indeed, some of the most impressive in America – and saved the quarter (and their accommodation) by having the area declared an **historic**

district. The mayor of New York, still faced with the problem of this (albeit historic) slum, revised the building codes in the late 1960s to allow industrial spaces to be open to "artists in residence." Three thousand artists moved in in the first year, and contemporary New York's full-scale intertwining of industry and art began.

In 1970, several major uptown galleries (Leo Castelli, Andre Emmerich and John Weber) moved to SoHo and injected money into the scene. The Guggenheim marked Downtown's arrival – several years after the fact, though – when it opened its SoHo branch on Broadway at Prince Street in 1992.

Nowadays, despite how SoHo was won, few artists or experimental galleries are left in the area: the late-1980s art boom drove up rents, and only the more established or consciously "commercial" galleries can afford to stay. Although SoHo still has the city's densest population of galleries, the risk-takers have moved elsewhere – either south to TriBeCa or, more recently, north to Chelsea, both of which are undergoing the same transformation that occurred in SoHo in the late 1960s.

MANHATTAN

Exploring SoHo

Houston Street (pronounced *How*ston rather than *Hew*ston) marks the top of SoHo's trellis of streets, any exploration of which necessarily means criss-crossing and doubling back. **Greene Street** is as good a place to start as any, highlighted all along by the nineteenth-century cast-iron facades that, in part if not in whole, saved SoHo from the bulldozers. **Prince Street**, **Spring Street** and **West Broadway** hold the best selection of shops and galleries in the area.

Cast-iron architecture

The technique of cast-iron architecture was utilized simply as a way of assembling buildings quickly and cheaply, with iron beams rather than heavy walls carrying the weight of the floors. The result was the removal of load-bearing walls, greater space for windows and, most noticeable, remarkably decorative facades. Almost any style or whim could be cast in iron and pinned to a building, and architects indulged themselves in Baroque balustrades, forests of Renaissance columns and all the effusion of the French Second Empire to glorify SoHo's sweatshops. Have a look at **72–76 Greene Street**, an extravagance whose Corinthian portico stretches the whole five stories, all in painted metal, and at the strongly composed elaborations of its sister building at **no. 28–30**. These are the best, but from Broome to Canal streets, most of the fronts on Greene Street's west side are either real (or mock) cast iron.

Ironically, what began as an engineering trait turned into a purely decorative one as stone copies of cast iron (you'd need a magnet to tell the real from the replicas) came into fashion. At the northeast corner of Broome Street and Broadway is the magnificent **Haughwout Building**, perhaps the ultimate in the cast-iron genre. Rhythmically repeated motifs of colonnaded arches are framed behind taller columns in a thin sliver of a Venetian palace – and it was the first building ever to boast a steam-powered Otis elevator. In 1904, Ernest Flagg took the possibilities of cast iron to their conclusion in his **"Little Singer" Building** at 561 Broadway (at Prince St), a design whose use of wide window frames points the way to the glass curtain wall of the 1950s.

Exploring Soho

Markets and galleries

SoHo celebrates its architecture in Richard Haas's smirky **mural** at 114 Prince Street (corner of Greene St), also the venue of one of SoHo's affordable **markets** (there's another at the meeting of Spring and Wooster streets). Many of the clothes and antique shops around are beyond reasonable budgets, although the *Stussy* store at 104 Prince is a favorite haunt of clubbers from the Continent. Bargain treasures and pure bric-a-brac can also be found at the **Antique Flea Market**, held every weekend on the corner of Grand Street and Broadway. See Chapter 24, *Shops and Markets*, for other suggestions.

What you'll find in the innumerable **galleries** is similarly overpriced but makes for fascinating browsing, with just about every variety of contemporary artistic expression on view. No one minds you looking in for a while, and doing this is also a sure way of bumping into the more visible eccentrics of the area. Most of the **galleries** are concentrated on West Broadway and Prince Street, in a patch that fancies itself as an alternative Madison Avenue (though certainly not lower in price). They're generally open from Labor Day to Memorial Day, Tuesday–Saturday 10/11am–6pm, Saturdays being most lively; for listings of galleries (and details of gallery tours) see Chapter 15, *Museums and Galleries*, and pick up a copy of *Time Out New York* or the more in-depth *Gallery Guide*, the latter available free at galleries upon request. For a view of recent art outside the confines of SoHo, drop in on the **New Museum of Contemporary Art** at 583 Broadway between Prince and Houston streets (again, see Chapter 15).

For something slightly less contemporary, visit the Guggenheim SoHo, p.264.

South to Canal Street

Loosely speaking, SoHo's diversions get grottier as you drop south. Still, **Broome** and **Grand** streets, formerly full of dilapidated storefronts and dusty windows, have recently become home to a small band of boutiques, galleries, cafés and French restaurants. The new development is particularly concentrated around Sixth Avenue, where old warehouses still offer some cheap – though increasingly rare – loft space. Most people come down this way for the clothes places like the **Canal Jean Co** at 504 Broadway (between Spring and Broome streets) or to buy a homemade lunch at *Gourmet Garage* (Broome at Greene Street). Just south is **Canal Street**, which links the Holland Tunnel with the Manhattan Bridge and forms a main thoroughfare between New Jersey and Brooklyn. On the edge of Chinatown is SoHo's open bazaar: brash storefronts loaded with fake designer watches, electrical gear, leather goods, sneakers, and some porn video shops. Sadly, as TriBeCa – SoHo's other southern neighbor – skips up the social ladder, Canal Street is becoming increasingly "cleaned up."

TriBeCa

TriBeCa, the *Tri*angle *Be*low *Ca*nal Street, has caught the fallout of SoHo artists, and is rapidly changing from a wholesale garment district to an upscale community that mixes commercial establishments with loft residences, studios, galleries and chic eateries. Less a triangle than a crumpled rectangle – the area bounded by Canal and Chambers streets, Broadway and the Hudson River – it takes in spacious industrial buildings whose upper layers sprout plants and cats behind tidy glazing: the apartments of TriBeCa's new gentry. Like "SoHo," the name TriBeCa was a late 1960s invention, a semiotic rehaul more suited to the increasingly trendy neighborhood than its former moniker, Washington Market.

In the late 1980s, when the East Village became gentrified and SoHo properties skyrocketed in value, there was a scramble for TriBeCa's warehouses: many of the apartments and lofts were bought abandoned and still resemble the former sweatshops they replaced, with clothes rails running through the rooms. Today, however, living space in TriBeCa is approaching SoHo in status and price. Although pockets of the area are still enclaves for blue-collar folk, the neighborhood is attracting the media elite – John F. Kennedy, Jr. and his wife, Carolyn Bessette, live here, as does supermodel Naomi Campbell – as well as upper-middle-class families. Most of these new residents are smitten by the neighborhood's slower pace – indeed, because it is on the edge of the island, it's not well traveled – and by its sense of community. The low buildings and clean streets make the area seem more suburban than urban.

Despite rising rents, commercial space in TriBeCa is still cheaper than that of any of the other "artistic" neighborhoods, so creative industries have been moving to the area en masse. Galleries, recording studios, computer graphics companies and photo labs are setting up shop in old garment warehouses; avant-garde performance venues like *Franklin Furnace* – a longtime resident of the neighborhood – and *The Knitting Factory* – on Leonard Street – are bringing art out of the closet and into public space. The film industry is also making TriBeCa their home, with the **TriBeCa Film Center** – a film production company owned by, among others, Robert De Niro – paving the way. The Center is located in the same building – 375 Greenwich St – as one of Mr De Niro's restaurants, the *TriBeCa Grill*, whose clientele often includes well-known names and faces from the film world.

In the evening, TriBeCa isn't as deserted as it used to be: as little as five years ago, come nightfall, the sound of footsteps would echo off the cobbled streets and against the cast-iron buildings. TriBeCa used to shut when the Wall Street crowd went home, but the growth of **Battery Park City** has brought smart restaurants into the neighborhood, and some of the traditional after-work bars – like *Puffy's*, an old Prohibition speakeasy at 81 Hudson St – now stay open much later.

TriBeCa

For more on TriBeCa restaurants and nightlife, see chapters 17 and 19.

Exploring TriBeCa

To get a feel of TriBeCa's mix of old and new, go to **Duane Park**, a sliver of green between Hudson and Greenwich streets. Around the Park's perimeter you can see old depots of egg and cheese distributors wedged between new residential apartments; the Art Deco facade of the **Western Union Building** is at the edge of the block, while the World Trade Center and Woolworth and Municipal buildings guard the skyline like soldiers. Off the park's western corner you can also catch a glimpse of *A.L. Bazzini* (339 Greenwich St), the city's largest dried fruit and nut supplier; try out some of the company's homemade delicacies – especially the freshly ground peanut butter – at the adjoining bakery/store.

Walk a few blocks south on Hudson Street to hit **Chambers Street**, home to much of the evidence of the neighborhood's upswing. Freshly scrubbed brick buildings have replaced many of the discount shops, along with bookstores and restaurants. A new public elementary school – **PS 234**, also known as **Independence School** – sits at the intersection of Greenwich and Chambers; built in 1988, it sports a fanciful exterior, with images of boats and ships worked into its iron gates. Across from the school is the verdant and expansive **Washington Market Park**, built on the site where the city's first major fruit and vegetable market was located.

Continuing down Chambers toward West Street, you'll pass the **Triplex** at the Borough of Manhattan Community College (the largest performing arts center in lower Manhattan, it stages over 200 events a year, and finally arrive at the **TriBeCa Bridge**, a futuristic walkway across West Street made of silver steel tubes, white girders and glass. Located across the street, and in the long shadow of the World Trade Center, there is a public recreation center called **Pier 25**, which boasts three beach volleyball courts – built atop 540 cubic yards of sand trucked in from New Jersey – and a miniature golf course.

Alternatively, if you're not in the mood for sports, take a left out of Duane Park and follow Greenwich toward Canal Street. This is the main strip for the area's new clientele, and restaurants from the affordable (*Yaffa's*) to the outrageously expensive (*TriBeCa Grill*) line the street. Because the road is so wide, traffic moves at highway speed, an irksome development that has spurred a plan to reduce the street's lanes from six to two by planting trees where there is now tarmac.

Parallel to Greenwich is Hudson Street, which catches the overflow of fancy restaurants then, in sharp contrast, peters into still-active warehouses, whose denizens do the same work they have for decades. Instead of heading down there, walk east along to White Street where it meets Church Street. Located at 49 White Street is **The Civic Center Synagogue**, a temple whose curving, wave-like facade is quite striking, while at no. 38 is Rudi Stern's *Let There Be Neon*, a gallery boasting signs, chairs, household goods and stage sets all in – you guessed it – neon.

Chapter 6

Greenwich Village and the East Village

C leanly bordered by Houston Street to the south and 14th Street to the north, **Greenwich Village** and its grungier sister, the **East Village**, continue to serve, if in name only, as the Bohemia of New York City. On the west side, Greenwich Village proper makes for a great day of walking through a grid of streets that doesn't even attempt to conform to the rest of the city's established numbered pattern. At least you'll never be bored since, despite a commercialization that has sanitized the neighborhood, there is still a quaintness to Greenwich Village that is genuine and enjoyable. Across the divide of Broadway is the East Village, which despite the encroachment of chain stores like the *Gap* and *K-Mart*, retains its decidedly ethnic mix, down and dirty demeanor, and – much more so than Greenwich Village – a political and anti-establishment edge that endures.

Greenwich Village

If you're a New Yorker, it's fashionable to dismiss **Greenwich Village** (or "the Village" as it's most widely known) as *passé*. And it's true that, while the bohemian image of Greenwich Village endures well enough if you don't actually live in New York, it's a tag that has long since ceased to hold genuine currency. The only writers who can afford to live here nowadays are copywriters, the only actors those who are starring regularly on Broadway, and as for politics – the average Village resident long since scrapped them for the more serious pursuit of making money. Greenwich Village is firmly for those who have Arrived. Not that the Village doesn't have appeal: to a great extent the neighborhood still sports the attractions that brought people here in the first place, and people still clamor for a Greenwich Village address: quaint side streets and

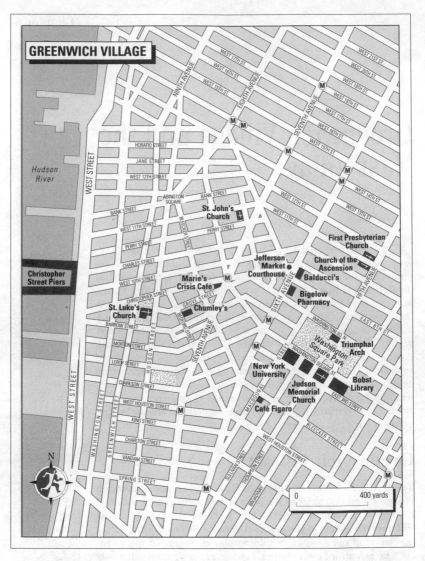

GREENWICH VILLAGE

Hudson River

WEST 21ST ST
WEST 17TH ST
WEST 16TH ST
WEST 20TH ST
WEST 19TH ST
WEST 15TH ST
WEST 18TH ST
NINTH AVENUE
EIGHTH AVENUE
SEVENTH AVENUE
WEST 17TH ST
WEST 16TH ST
WEST 15TH ST
WEST STREET
HORATIO STREET
JANE STREET
WEST 12TH STREET
WEST 14TH ST
WEST 13TH ST
ABINGTON SQUARE
BANK STREET
BANK STREET
WEST 12TH ST
WEST 11TH ST
St. John's Church
WEST 11TH STREET
PERRY STREET
PERRY STREET
BLEECKER STREET
CHARLES STREET
PERRY STREET
First Presbyterian Church
Jefferson Market Courthouse
Church of the Ascension
Balducci's
WEST 10TH STREET
FIFTH AVENUE
SIXTH AVENUE
Marie's Crisis Café
GROVE STREET
Bigelow Pharmacy
CHRISTOPHER STREET
Chumley's
St. Luke's Church
BARROW STREET
WASHINGTON SQ N
EAST 8TH ST
Washington Square Park
Triumphal Arch
MORTON STREET
HUDSON STREET
SEVENTH AVENUE
LEROY STREET
WASHINGTON SQUARE ST
New York University
Bobst Library
CLARKSON STREET
Judson Memorial Church
EAST 3RD STREET
WEST HOUSTON STREET
Café Figaro
WEST STREET
WASHINGTON STREET
GREENWICH STREET
KING STREET
MACDOUGAL ST
CHARLTON STREET
VANDAM STREET
BLEECKER STREET
SPRING STREET
WEST HOUSTON STREET
SULLIVAN STREET
THOMPSON STREET
BROADWAY
N

Christopher Street Piers

0   400 yards

---

stunning historic brownstones that can't be rivaled elsewhere in town. It's quiet, residential, but with a busy street-life that lasts later than in any other part of the city; there are more restaurants per head than anywhere else; and bars, while never cheap, clutter every corner. If interesting people no longer live in the Village, they do hang out here – Washington Square is a hub of aimless activity throughout the year – and as long as you have no illusions about the "alternativeness" of the place there are few better initiations into the city's life, especially at night.

Some history

Greenwich Village grew up as a rural retreat from the early and frenetic nucleus of New York City, first becoming sought after during the yellow fever epidemic of 1822 as a refuge from the infected streets downtown. When the fever was at its height the idea was mooted of moving the entire city center here. It was spared that dubious fate, and left to grow into a wealthy residential neighborhood that sprouted elegant Federal and Greek Revival terraces and lured some of the city's highest society names. Later, once the rich had moved uptown and built themselves a palace or two on Fifth Avenue, these large houses were to prove a fertile hunting ground for struggling artists and intellectuals on the lookout for cheap rents, and by the turn of the century Greenwich Village was well on its way to becoming New York's Left Bank; at the very least it has always been seen this way by outsiders – gentrification actually set in rather quickly. Of early Village characters, one Mabel Dodge was perhaps most influential. Wealthy and radical, she threw parties for the literary and political cognoscenti – parties to which everyone hoped, sooner or later, to be invited. Just about all of the well-known names who lived here during the first two decades of the century spent some time at her house at 23 Fifth Avenue, a little north of Washington Square. Emma Goldman discussed anarchism with Gertrude Stein and Margaret Sanger; Conrad Aiken and T.S. Eliot dropped in from time to time; and John Reed – who went on to write *Ten Days That Shook the World*, the official record of the Russian Revolution – was a frequent guest.

The Village Voice, *NYC's premier listings/ comment/ investigative magazine, began life as a chronicler of Greenwich Village nightlife in the 1060s – see p.27.*

Washington Square and around

The best way to see the Village is to walk, and by far the best place to start is its natural center, **Washington Square**, commemorated as a novel title by Henry James and haunted by most of the Village's illustrious past names. It is not an elegant-looking place – too large to be a square, too small to be a park. But it does retain its northern edging of redbrick row houses – the "solid, honorable dwellings" of Henry James's novel and now home to mostly administrative offices for New York University (NYU) – and more imposingly, Stanford White's famous **Triumphal Arch**, built in 1892 to commemorate the centenary of George Washington's inauguration as president. Marcel Duchamp, along with an agitator going by the name of "Woe," climbed to the top of the arch in 1913 to declare the Free Republic of Greenwich Village. Don't plan on repeating that stunt; the arch has been cordoned off around its perimeter in an effort to ward off graffiti. James wouldn't, however, recognize the south side of the square now: only the fussy **Judson Memorial Church** stands out

amid a messy blend of modern architecture, its interior given over
these days to a mixture of theater and local focus for a wide array of
community-based programs.

Most importantly, though, Washington Square remains the symbolic heart of the Village and its radicalism – so much so that when
Robert Moses, that tarmacker of great chunks of New York City,
wanted to plow a four-lane roadway through the center of the
square there was a storm of protest that resulted not only in the
stopping of the road but also the banning of all traffic from the park,
then used as a turnaround point by buses. And that's how it has
stayed ever since, notwithstanding some battles in the 1960s when
the authorities decided to purge the park of folk singers and nearly
had a riot on their hands. You may find it a little threatening at
times, particularly after dark when the drug dealers seem even more
intimidating as they hawk their wares along the park's many paths.
The park itself is closed after 11pm, a curfew that is strictly
enforced. But, frankly, nothing's likely to happen to you in this part
of town and if things look at all hazardous it's just as easy to walk
around. As soon as the weather gets warm, the park becomes running track, performance venue, chess tournament and social club,
boiling over with life as skateboards flip, dogs run, and acoustic guitar notes crash through the urgent cries of dope peddlers and the
studied patrols of police cars. At times like this, there's no better
square in the city.

Exploring Washington Square

Eugene O'Neill, one of the Village's most acclaimed residents, lived
(and wrote *The Iceman Cometh*) at 38 Washington Square South
and consumed vast quantities of ale at **The Golden Swan Bar**,
which once stood on the corner of Sixth Avenue and West 4th
Street. *The Golden Swan* (variously called *The Hell Hole, Bucket
of Blood* and other enticing nicknames) was best known in O'Neill's
day for the dubious morals of its clientele – a gang of Irish hoodlums
known as the Hudson Dusters – and for the pig in the basement that
ate the customers' trash. O'Neill was great pals with this crowd and
drew many of his characters from the personalities in this bar. It was
nearby, also, that he got his first dramatic break, with a company
called the Provincetown Players who, on the advice of John Reed,
had moved down here from Massachusetts and set up shop on
Macdougal Street, in a theater which still stands (see "Theater" in
Chapter 20, *The Performing Arts and Film*). A basketball court
now fronts the block joining West 4th and West 3rd streets on Sixth
Avenue. Here, some of the best and toughest street basketball you'll
ever see is played out to often large crowds of spectators and the
occasional TV crew.

At Washington Square South and La Guardia Place, where the
NYU Student Center now stands, was once the boarding house

known as Madame Katherine Blanchard's **House of Genius** – Willa Cather, Theodore Dreiser, and O. Henry all called it home at one time or other. Back at the southwest corner of the park, follow **Macdougal Street** south, pausing for a detour down Minetta Lane (once one of the city's most prodigious slums) and you hit **Bleecker Street** – Main Street, Greenwich Village in many ways, with a greater concentration of shops, bars, people and restaurants than any other Village thoroughfare. This junction is also a vibrant corner with mock-European sidewalk cafés that have been literary hangouts since the beginning of this century. The **Café Figaro**, made famous by the Beat writers in the 1950s, is always thronged throughout the day: far from cheap, though still worth the price of a cappuccino to people-watch for an hour or so. Afterwards, you can follow Bleecker Street one of two ways – east toward the solid towers of Washington Square Village, built with typical disregard for history by NYU in 1958, or west right through the hubbub of Greenwich Village life.

West of Sixth Avenue

Sixth Avenue itself is mainly tawdry stores and plastic eating houses, but on the other side, across Father Demo Square and up Bleecker Street (until the 1970s an Italian open marketplace on this stretch, and still lined by a few Italian stores), are some of the Village's prettiest residential streets. Turn left on **Leroy Street** and cross over Seventh Avenue, where, confusingly, Leroy Street becomes St Luke's Place for a block. The houses here, dating from the 1850s, are among the city's most graceful, one of them (recognizable by the two lamps of honor at the bottom of the steps) the ex-residence of **Jimmy Walker**, mayor of New York in the 1920s. Walker was for a time the most popular of mayors, a big-spending, wisecracking man who gave up his work as a songwriter for the world of politics and lived an extravagant lifestyle that rarely kept him out of the gossip columns. Nothing if not shrewd, at a time when America had never been so prosperous, he for a time reflected people's most glamorous, big-living aspirations. He was, however, no match for the hard times to come, and once the 1930s Depression had taken hold he lost touch, and – with it – office.

South of Leroy Street, the Village fades slowly into the warehouse districts of SoHo and TriBeCa, a bleak area where nothing much stirs outside working hours and the buildings are an odd mixture of Federal facades juxtaposed against grubby-gray rolldown-entranced packing houses. There's a neatly preserved row from the 1820s on Charlton Street between Sixth Avenue and Varick; the area just to its north, **Richmond Hill**, was George Washington's headquarters during the Revolution, later the home of Aaron Burr and John Jacob Astor. But those apart, you may just as well continue on Hudson Street up to **St Luke's in the Fields Church** at Barrow Street. The

The excellent White Horse Tavern, 567 Hudson at West 11th St, is where Dylan Thomas had his last drink. See p.103 for details.

church dates back to 1821 and the row of Federal-style brick houses next door, housing for school and church administrators, went up a few years later. Look behind the church for St Luke's **Gardens**, a labyrinthine patchwork of garden, grass and benches open to the public during the day and accessible through the gate between church and school.

Hudson Street north of the church and up to Abington Square (where Hudson bends to become Eighth Avenue and heads for Chelsea) is a good avenue for meandering, with a bevy of unique stores, coffee bars and restaurants. Fans of TV's *Taxi* will notice the garage that posed as the "Sunshine Cab Company" (actually the Dover Cab Company) at West 10th Street.

Around Bedford Street

Directly facing St Luke's, **Grove Street** runs into **Bedford Street**. If you have time, peer into **Grove Court**, one of the neighborhood's most typical and secluded little mews. Along with Barrow and Commerce streets nearby, Bedford Street is one of the quietest and most desirable Village addresses – Edna St Vincent Millay, the young poet and playwright who did much work with the Provincetown Playhouse, lived at no. 75$^{1}/_{2}$ – said to be the narrowest house in the city, nine feet wide and topped with a tiny gable. Another superlative: the clapboard structure next door claims fame as the oldest house in the Village, built in 1799 but much renovated since and probably worth a considerable fortune now.

Further down Bedford Street, the former speakeasy **Chumley's** (see Chapter 18, *Drinking*) is recognizable only by the metal grille on its door – a low profile useful in Prohibition years that makes it hard to find today. Back on Seventh Avenue look out for **Marie's Crisis Café** (see "Gay and lesbian bars" in Chapter 18), now a gay bar but once home to Thomas Paine, English by birth but perhaps *the* most important and radical thinker of the American Revolutionary era, and from whose *Crisis Papers* the café takes its name. Paine was significantly involved in the Revolution, though afterwards regarded with suspicion by the government, especially after his active support for the French Revolution. By the time of his death here, in 1809, he had been condemned as an atheist and stripped of citizenship of the country he helped to found. Grove Street meets Seventh Avenue at one of the Village's busiest junctions, **Sheridan Square** – not in fact a square at all unless you count Christopher Park's slim strip of green, but simply a wide and hazardous meeting ("the Mousetrap," some call it) of several busy streets.

Christopher Street

Christopher Street, main artery of the West Village, leads off from here – traditional heartland of the city's gay community. The square was named after one General Sheridan, cavalry commander in the

Civil War, and holds a pompous-looking statue to his memory, but it's better known as scene of one of the worst and bloodiest of New York's Draft Riots, when a marauding mob assembled here in 1863 and attacked members of the black community. It's said that if it hadn't been for the protestations of local people they would have strung them up and worse; as it was they made off after sating the worst of their blood lust.

Not dissimilar scenes occurred in 1969, when the gay community wasn't as established as it is now. The violence on this occasion was down to the police, who raided the **Stonewall gay bar** and started arresting its occupants – for the local gay community the latest in a long line of harassments from the police. Spontaneously they decided to do something about it: word went around the other bars in the area, and before long the *Stonewall* was surrounded, resulting in a siege that lasted the better part of the night and sparked up again the next two nights. The riot ended with several arrests and a number of injured policemen. Though hardly a victory for their rights, it was the first time that gay men had stood up en masse to the persecutions of the police and, as such, represents a turning point in their struggle, formally instigating the gay rights movement and honored still by the annual **Gay Pride march** (held on the last Sunday in June).

Nowadays, too, the gay community is much more a part of Greenwich Village life, indeed for most the Village would seem odd without it, and from here down to the Hudson is a tight-knit enclave – focusing on Christopher Street – of bars, restaurants and bookstores used specifically, but not exclusively, by gay men. The scene along the Hudson River itself, along and around West Street and the river piers, is considerably raunchier at night; by day, an attractive pedestrian walkway links Battery Park City up to the top of the Village and is bustling with bikers, runners and bladers who come for the river breezes and the view. Once the sun goes down, though, only the really committed or curious should venture (native New Yorkers, gay ones included, warn against going there at all). But on this far east stretch of Christopher, things crack off with the accent less on sex, more on a camp kind of humor. Among the more accessible gay bars, if you're strolling this quarter, are *The Monster* on Sheridan Square itself, *Marie's Crisis* on Grove Street (see opposite), and *Ty's*, further west on Christopher Street; for full gay listings, see "Gay and lesbian bars" in Chapter 18, *Drinking*.

*For more on
gay New York,
see p.43,
Basics.*

North of Washington Square

At the eastern end of Christopher Street is another of those car-buzzing, life-risking Village junctions where Sixth Avenue is met by **Greenwich Avenue**, one of the neighborhood's major shopping streets. Hover for a while at the romantic Gothic bulk of the **Jefferson Market Courthouse**, voted fifth most beautiful building in America in 1885, and built with all the characteristic vigor of the age. It hasn't actually served as a courthouse since 1946; indeed, at one time – like so many buildings in this city – it was branded for demolition. It was saved thanks to the efforts of a few determined Villagers, including e. e. cummings, and now lives out its days as the local library. Walk around behind for a better look, perhaps pondering for a moment on the fact that the adjacent well-tended allotment was, until 1971, the **Women's House of Detention**, a prison known for its abysmal conditions and numbering Angela Davis among its inmates. Look out, also, for **Patchin Place**, a tiny mews whose neat gray row houses are yet another Village literary landmark, home to the reclusive Djuna Barnes for more than forty years. Barnes's longtime neighbor e. e. cummings used to call her "Just to see if she was still alive." Patchin Place was at various times also home to Marlon Brando, John Masefield, the ubiquitous Dreiser and O'Neill, and John Reed (who wrote *Ten Days that Shook the World* here).

Across the road, **Balducci's** forms a downtown alternative to its uptown deli rival, *Zabar's*, its stomach-tingling smells pricey but hard to resist. Nearby, **Bigelow's Pharmacy** is possibly the city's oldest drugstore and apparently little changed; and, south a block and left, **West 8th Street** is an occasionally rewarding strip of brash shoe stores and cut-price clothes stores. Up **West 10th Street** are some of the best-preserved early nineteenth-century townhouses in the Village, and one of particular interest at **no. 18**. The facade of this house, which juts into the street, had to be rebuilt after the terrorist Weathermen had been using the house as a bomb factory and one of their devices exploded. Three of the group were killed in the blast, but two others escaped and remained on the run until a few years ago.

For anyone not yet sated on architecture, a couple of imposing churches are to be found by following 10th Street down as far as the Fifth Avenue stretch of the Village, where the neighborhood's low-slung residential streets lead to some eminently desirable apartment buildings. On the corner stands the nineteenth-century **Church of the Ascension**, a small, light church built by Richard Upjohn (the Trinity Church architect), later redecorated by Stanford White and recently restored outside and in, where a gracefully toned La Farge altarpiece and some fine stained glass are on view. A block away, Joseph Wells's bulky, chocolatey-brown Gothic revival **First Presbyterian Church** is decidedly less attractive than Upjohn's structure, less soaring, heavier, and in every way more sober, with a tower said to have been modeled on the one at Magdalen College Oxford, England. To look inside, you need to enter through the discreetly added Church House (ring the bell for attention if the door's locked). Afterwards you're just a few steps away from the pin-neat prettiness of **Washington Mews**.

The East Village

The **East Village** is quite different in look, feel and tempo from its
western counterpart, Greenwich Village. Once, like the Lower East
Side proper which it abuts, a refuge of immigrants and always a
solidly working-class area, it became home to New York's noncon-
formist fringe in the earlier part of this century when, disenchanted
and impoverished by rising rents and encroaching tourism, they left
the city's traditional Bohemia and set up house here. Today the differences persist: where Greenwich Village is the home of Off-
Broadway, the East Village plays stage to Off-Off; and rents, while

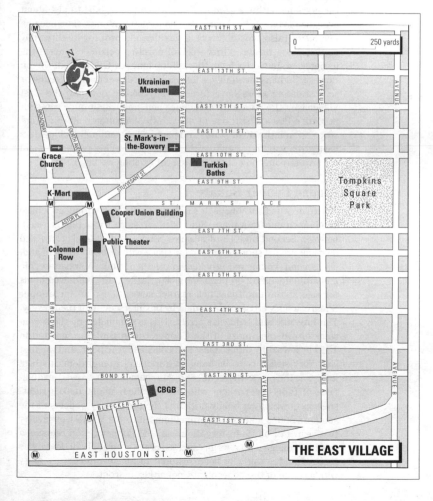

THE EAST VILLAGE

rising fast as the district becomes trendier and more sanitized, are still for the most part less than what you'll pay further west.

The East Village has seen its share of famous artists, politicos and literati: W.H. Auden lived at 77 **St Mark's Place**, the neighborhood's main street, and from the same building the Communist journal *Novy Mir* was run, numbering among its more historic contributors Leon Trotsky, who lived for a brief time in New York. Much later the East Village became the New York haunt of the Beats – Kerouac, Burroughs, Ginsberg et al – who, when not jumping trains across the rest of the country, would get together at Allen Ginsberg's house on East 7th Street for declamatory poetry readings and drunken share-outs of experience. Later, Andy Warhol debuted the Velvet Underground at the *Fillmore East*, which played host to just about every band you've ever heard of – and forgotten about – then became *The Saint* (also now-defunct), a gay disco known for its three-day parties. More recently, Richard Hell noisily proclaimed himself the inventor of punk rock at the still-rocking **CBGB** club down on Bowery. Perhaps inevitably, a lot has changed over the last decade or so. Escalating rents have forced many people out, and the East Village isn't the hotbed of dissidence and creativity it once was. But St Mark's Place is still one of downtown Manhattan's more vibrant strips, even if the thrift stores and panhandlers and political hustlers have given way to a range of ritzy boutiques selling punk chic, and the area remains one of the city's most exciting enclaves.

Around Cooper Square

To explore the East Village, it's best to use **St Mark's Place** as a base and branch out from there. Start at the western, more peopled end, between Second and Third avenues, where radical bookstores and discount record shops compete for space with offbeat clothiers and, just beyond, young self-proclaimed priests of funky Manhattan chic mill around wolfing on pizzas or gazing lazily at the mildewed items for sale at the unofficial flea market across the road on **Cooper Square**, a busy crossroads formed by the intersection of the Bowery, Third Avenue and Lafayette Street. This is dominated by the seven-story brownstone mass of the **Cooper Union Building**, erected in 1859 by a wealthy industrialist as a college for the poor, and the first New York structure to be hung on a frame of iron girders. It's best known as the place where, in 1860, Abraham Lincoln wowed an audience of top New Yorkers with his so-called "might makes right" speech, in which he boldly criticized the pro-slavery policies of the southern states and helped propel himself to the White House later that year. For all its history, however, the Cooper Union remains a working college with a well-respected architecture school, and it has recently and sensitively been restored to nineteenth-century glory with a statue of the benevolent Cooper just in front.

Astor Place and around

Just beyond, feeding through to Broadway, is **Astor Place**, named
after John Jacob Astor and, for a very brief few years, just before
high society moved west to Washington Square, one of the city's
most desirable neighborhoods. In the 1830s Lafayette Street in particular was home to the city's wealthiest names, not least John Jacob,
one of New York's most hideously greedy tycoons, notorious for having won his enormous fortune by deceiving everybody right up to the
president. It's said that when he was old and sick in his house here –
no mean affair by all accounts but long since destroyed – although so
weak he could accept no nourishment except a mother's milk and so
fat he had to be tossed up and down in a blanket for exercise, his
greed for money was such that he lay and dispatched servants daily
to collect his rents. The Astor Place **subway station,** bang in the middle of the junction, discreetly remembers the man on the platforms,
its colored reliefs of beavers recalling Astor's first big killings – in the
fur trade. The giant cube just south of the station is the spinnable
steel sculpture "Alamo" (by Bernard Rosenthal), in place since 1967.
Get some mates to help you spin it around, if you can wade past the
skateboarders who congregate there. More recently, this intersection has been developed not unlike a mall: on the northwest corner,
K-Mart, discount retailer nonpareil, opened its doors in 1997 to the
general horror of city snobs. The *K Café*, on the second floor, behind
the underwear, has a great view of Astor Place and hosts occasional
poetry readings. Really.

Today it's hard to believe that Astor Place was the home to wealth
and influence. **Lafayette Street** is an undistinguished sort of thoroughfare, steering a grimy route through the no-man's land between
the East Village and, further down, SoHo, and all that's left to hint
that this might once have been more than a down-at-heel gathering
of industrial buildings is **Colonnade Row**, a strip of four monumental houses, now home to the Colonnade Theater. Opposite, the
stocky brownstone and brick building is the late Joseph Papp's
Public Theater, something of a legend as forerunner of Off-
Broadway theater and original venue of hit musicals like *Hair* and *A
Chorus Line* and for years run by the man who pioneered
Shakespeare in the Park (see "Theater" in Chapter 20, *The
Performing Arts and Film*). Today, the strip is home to a number
of expensive furniture shops, a fashion designer or two, and the
Village Voice.

From the Public Theater you can either follow Lafayette Street
down to Chinatown, or cut down Astor Place and turn right into
Broadway. Two minutes away, **the corner of Washington Place and
Greene Street** is significant. It was here in 1911 that one of the city's
most notorious sweatshops burned to the ground, killing 125 women
workers and spurring the State to institute laws forcing employers to
take account of their workers' safety. Even now, though, there are

sweatshops in New York in which safety conditions are probably little better. Back on Broadway, look north: filling a bend in the street is the lacy marble of **Grace Church**, built and designed in 1846 by James Renwick (of St Patrick's Cathedral fame) in a delicate neo-Gothic style. Dark and aisled, with a flattened, web-vaulted ceiling, it's one of the city's most successful churches – and, in many ways, one of its most secretive escapes.

Heading east

Walk east from here, cross back over Third Avenue and you come to another, quite different church – **St Mark's-in-the-Bowery**, a box-like structure originally built in 1799 but with a Neoclassical portico added half a century later. In the 1950s the Beat poets gave readings here, and it remains an important literary rendezvous with regular readings, dance performances and music recitals, as well as a traditional gathering point for the city's down-and-outs, desperately hanging on to their can collections (passport to a frugal meal that night) or slumped half-dead on drugs. Cross Second Avenue, on this stretch lined with Polish and Ukrainian restaurants, and you're on **10th Street**, formerly the heart of the East Village art scene, though nowadays very quiet, most of the galleries having moved to SoHo or further uptown; as yet no new center has emerged as a focus for avant-garde, relatively affordable art. Follow 10th Street east, past the old redbrick **Tenth Street Turkish Baths**, its steam and massage services active back into the last century, and you will reach Avenue A, which now buzzes with cool thrift stores and trendy bars, then Tompkins Square Park and what is in effect the eastern fringe of the East Village.

*See chapter 25
Directory, for
the lowdown
on visiting the
10th Street
Turkish Baths.*

Tompkins Square Park

Tompkins Square Park isn't one of the city's most inviting spaces, but has long acted as focus for the Lower East Side/East Village community and has a reputation as the city's center for political demonstrations and home of radical thought. It was here in 1874 that the police massacred a crowd of workers protesting against unemployment, and here too in the 1960s that protests were organized and made themselves heard. The late Yippie leader Abbie Hoffman lived nearby, and residents like him, along with many incidents in the square and on St Mark's Place (which joins the square on its western side), have given the East Village its maverick name.

A few years back Tompkins Square Park became the focus of dissent against the gentrification of the East Village and Lower East Side. From the mid-1980s, large chunks of real estate were bought up, renovated and turned into condominiums, co-ops or high-rent apartments for the new professional classes, much to the derision of the old squatters and new activists. Until the early 1990s, the Square was

more or less a shantytown (known locally as "**Tent City**") for the
homeless, who slept on benches or under makeshift shelters on the
patches of green between the paths. In the winter, only the really
hardy or really desperate lived here, but when the weather got warmer
the numbers swelled, as activists, anarchists and all manner of state-
ment-makers descended upon the former army barracks from around
the country, hoping to rekindle the spirit of 1988. That was the year
of the Tompkins Square **riots**, when in August massive demonstrations led to the police, badge numbers covered up and nightsticks
drawn, attempting to clear the park of people. In the ensuing battle,
many demonstrators were hurt, including a large number of
bystanders, and in the investigation that followed the police were
heavily criticized for the violence that had occurred. In the summer of
1995 another riot erupted as police tried to evict a group of squatters
who had set up house in an empty apartment building. This time, pro-
testers were armed with video cameras and, though heated, the riot
never reached the proportion of the 1988 violence.

The park has been recently overhauled and completely cleaned up,
though a mix of homeless people and leftovers from last night's parties can be found at most hours of the day. One of the few things to
see on the Square is a small **relief** just inside the brick enclosure on
the northern side, which shows a woman and child gazing forlornly
out to sea. It's a commemoration of a disaster of 1904, when the
local community, then mostly made up of German immigrants, was
decimated by the sinking of a cruise ship, the *General Slocum*, in
Long Island Sound, with the death of around a thousand people.

Chapter 7

Chelsea and the Garment District

ew visitors traditionally bother with **Chelsea** and the
Garment District, though the driving reason behind this –
that there's nothing to do – has now been rendered obsolete.
Chelsea is a low-built, sometimes seedy grid of tenements, row
houses, and warehouses of very mixed character, with its heart
between 14th and 23rd streets west of Broadway. It's here that the
neighborhood has become a commercial player, mostly boosted by
spillover from SoHo and the Village: stores, restaurants and a few
notable tourist attractions pepper the scene, along with increasingly upmarket real estate. It then meanders – somewhat uninter-
estingly – up to 30th Street or so, leading to the Garment District,
which muscles in between Sixth and Eighth avenues on 34th to
42nd Streets and takes in the dual monsters of **Penn Station** and
Madison Square Garden. The majority of people who come here
do so for a specific reason – to catch a train or bus, to watch
wrestling or basketball, or to work in factories, and it's only a
wedge of stores between Herald and Greeley squares that attracts
the out-of-towner.

Chelsea

Chelsea took shape in 1830 when its owner, Clement Clarke
Moore, anticipated New York's movement Uptown and laid out his
land for sale in broad lots. Enough remains to indicate Chelsea's
middle-class suburban origins, though in fact the area never quite
made it onto the shortlist of desirable places to be. Stuck between
Fifth Avenue and Hell's Kitchen and caught between the ritziness of
the one and the poverty of the other, Manhattan's chic residential
focus leapfrogged Chelsea to the East 40s and 50s. The arrival of
the slaughterhouses and working-class poor who came to people
the area sealed Chelsea's fate as a rough-and-tumble no-go area for

CHELSEA & THE GARMENT DISTRICT

0   500 yards

decades. For years dreary facades and neglected buildings gave Chelsea its atmosphere of run-down residentialism, with the grid plan seeming too wide, the streets too bare to encourage visitors to linger.

The last few years, however, have seen a new Chelsea emerge and, with it, good reason to visit. This regeneration has been shaped by many forces, not the least of which has been the arrival of a large new gay community, seeking alternatives to the Village's soaring rents. The area's cafés, clubs and gyms teem with so-called "Chelsea Boys": neatly groomed and hypermuscled gay men, often in T-shirts and 501s. Also influential here is New York's peripatetic art scene. In the late 1980s and early 1990s, a number of respected galleries began making use of the large spaces available in the low-rise warehouses of Chelsea's western reaches, bringing a new cultural edge to the once down-and-out west side. And, tak-

For more on the Chelsea gay scene see p.43.

ing advantage of large buildings that had fallen into disuse through the years, a retail boom of superstores along Sixth and Seventh avenues has brought many new shoppers into the neighborhood. Along the Hudson River, *Chelsea Piers*, an ultra-expensive sports complex development, is playing its part in the Chelsea boom. Despite the encroachment of these moneyed forces, many of the long-entrenched Hispanic families are staying put in their rent-controlled apartments, making today's Chelsea a good mix of the old world and the new, as fashionable restaurants, bars and shops catering to all persuasions grow up alongside leftover thrift stores, *bodegas* and grungy liquor stores.

Around Eighth Avenue

If Chelsea has a main drag it's **Eighth Avenue**, where the transformation of the neighborhood is most pronounced. A perfect route to wind your way up from the Village into the heart of Chelsea, Eighth Avenue between 14th and 23rd has a new retail energy to rival the fast-moving traffic in the street. A spate of new bars, restaurants, health food stores, gyms, bookstores and clothes shops have opened in the last five years in response to the new population. Eighth Avenue at 19th Street is home to one of the more important dance theaters in New York, the **Joyce**. The accomplished *Feld Ballet* is in residence here and a host of other touring companies keep this Art Deco style theater (complete with garish pink and purple neon signs) doing brisk business (see Chapter 20, *The Performing Arts and Film*). Even the Salvation Army store at 21st Street seems to have got into the act, with spruced up interiors and a fresh paint job.

If you detour west from Eighth Avenue, the cross streets between Ninth and Tenth avenues, especially 20th, 21st and 22nd, have some attractive houses on display. The great variety of Italianate and Greek Revival row houses date from around the 1890s and serve to demonstrate the faith some early developers had in Chelsea as an up-and-coming New York neighborhood. On Ninth Avenue the block bounded by 20th and 21st streets contains one of Chelsea's oddities, the **General Theological Seminary** on Chelsea Square. Clement Clarke Moore donated an island of land to the institute in which he formerly taught, and today the assembly of ivy-clad Gothicisms surrounding a restive green feels like part of an Ivy League college campus. Though the buildings still house a working seminary, it's possible to explore the park on weekdays and Saturday at lunchtime, as long as you sign in and keep quiet (the entrance is via the modern building on Ninth Avenue). The countrified feel is what makes it special, though, rather than any outstanding architectural feature. When Eighth Avenue reaches West 23rd Street, take a right toward Seventh Avenue to find one of the neighborhood's major claims to fame – the *Chelsea Hotel*.

The Chelsea Hotel

During the nineteenth century this area, especially West 23rd Street, was a center of New York's theater district before it moved uptown. Nothing remains of the theaters now, but the hotel that put up all the actors, writers and bohemian hangers-on remains a New York landmark. The **Chelsea Hotel** has been the undisputed watering hole of the city's harder-up literati for decades: Mark Twain and Tennessee Williams lived here and Brendan Behan and Dylan Thomas staggered in and out during their New York visits. Thomas Wolfe assembled *You Can't Go Home Again* from thousands of pages of manuscript he had stacked in his room, and in 1951 Jack Kerouac, armed with a specially adapted typewriter (and a lot of Benzedrine), typed the first draft of *On the Road* nonstop onto a 120-foot roll of paper. William Burroughs (in a presumably more relaxed state) completed *Naked Lunch* here, and Arthur C. Clarke, Arthur Miller and Paul Bowles all had rooms.

In the 1960s the *Chelsea* took off again when Andy Warhol and his doomed protégés Edie Sedgwick and Candy Darling walled up here and made the film *Chelsea Girls* in (sort of) homage; Nico, Hendrix, Zappa, Pink Floyd and various members of the Dead passed through, Bob Dylan wrote songs in and about it and, more recently, Sid Vicious stabbed Nancy Spungen to death in their suite, a few months before his own pathetic life ended with an overdose of heroin. On a more cheerful note, the hotel inspired Joni Mitchell to write her song *Chelsea Morning* – a song that twanged the heartstrings of the young Bill and Hillary Clinton, who named their daughter after it (though there's no record of Chelsea ever having stayed in her eponymous hotel).

With a pedigree like this it's easy to forget the hotel itself, which has a down-at-heel Edwardian grandeur all of its own, and, incidentally, is also an affordable place to stay; see Chapter 16, *Accommodation*.

West Chelsea

Further west along 23rd Street is one of New York's premier residences for those who believe in understated opulence. The **London Terrace Apartments,** two rows of apartment buildings a full city block long surrounding a private interior garden, had the misfortune of being completed in 1930 at the height of the Great Depression. Despite a swimming pool and doormen dolled out in London police uniforms, London Terrace stood empty for several years. Today, though, it's home to some of New York's trendier names, especially those from the fashion, art and music businesses. It was nicknamed "The Fashion Projects" recently in the *New York Times,* as much for its retinue of big-time designer, photographer and model residents (including Isaac Mizrahi, Annie Leibovitz and Deborah Harry) as for its ironic proximity to Chelsea's real housing projects just to the south and east.

Continue along 23rd Street and brave crossing the West Side Highway, and you'll reach Manhattan's newest waterfront project, the **Chelsea Piers**, a $100 million, 1.7-million-square-foot development along four historic piers on the Hudson River. Opened in 1910 and designed by Warren and Whetmore (who were also at work on Grand Central Terminal at the time), this was the place where the great transatlantic liners would disembark their passengers (it was en route to the Chelsea Piers in 1912 that the *Titanic* sank). By the 1950s, however, the newer passenger ships were docking uptown at larger terminals, and the Piers were only used for freight. In the 1960s, the Piers fell into disuse and decay, and it is only recently that the area has been revived. The heart of the development is a huge sports complex, with two enclosed ice rinks and two open-air roller rinks, and a landscaped golf driving range, all open to the public (see Chapter 21, *Sports and Outdoor Activities*). There is also an impressive (though membership-only) indoor sports center, with basketball courts, batting cages, a rock climbing wall, and more. Perhaps the best part of the development, though, is its emphasis on **public spaces**, including a waterfront walkway of over a mile and a pleasant water's edge park at the end of Pier 62. There's also *Chelsea Brewing* – a microbrewery – along with a few outdoor restaurants along the water. All feel somewhat contrived, but they still offer an away-from-the-city atmosphere and put you as close to the Hudson River as you can (or would want to) get.

The Chelsea Arts Scene

Back over the West Side Highway and along 22nd Street are the galleries and warehouse spaces that house New York's newest **art scene**. The New York commercial art scene is in constant motion, always in search of better rents and the ultimate "cool" place to be and be seen. Galleries and exhibition spaces are already here, and more are on the way: nearly a dozen galleries have opened recently with an especially strong presence along West 22nd Street between Tenth and Eleventh avenues. The **Dia Center for the Arts**, a Chelsea pioneer, with space here since 1987, should be done with converting their 42,000-square-foot warehouse into a museum by summer 1998. Their main exhibition gallery, at 548 West 22nd St, features a dramatic **open-air** space on top where the *Rooftop Urban Park* opened in 1991. The effect of the two-way glass mirror pavilion is remarkable, its impact in constant flux as it works with the changing light and visual effects of the sky. More on the galleries of Chelsea in Chapter 15.

East Chelsea

The eastern edge of Chelsea has become a busy strip of commerce, concentrated mostly along **Sixth Avenue**, where a crush of moder-

ately priced clothing stores, such as *Old Navy* and *Today's Man*,
have driven the likes of local institution *Barney's* to bankruptcy –
although places like *Barney's* seem to have a habit of surviving (see
"Macy's" on p.116). A neighborhood giant that is doing just fine is
the obligatory *Barnes & Noble* superstore, between 21st and 22nd
streets, though more interesting is *A Different Light*, around the
corner on 19th Street, the country's largest gay and lesbian bookstore. Heading north above 23rd Street, away from Chelsea's heart,
the city's largest **antiques market** takes place on weekends in a few
open-air parking lots at the junction of Sixth Avenue and 26th Street:
it's open till 6pm, and it's possible to find bargains amid the piles of
overpriced junk (see Chapter 24, *Shops and Markets*). The area
around 28th Street is also Manhattan's **Flower Market**: not really a
market as such, more the warehouses where potted plants and cut
flowers are stored before brightening offices and atriums across the
city. Nothing marks the strip, and you come across it by chance, the
greenery bursting out of drab blocks, blooms spangling storefronts
and providing a welcome touch of life to an otherwise dull neighborhood. For the record, West 28th Street was the original **Tin Pan
Alley**, where music publishers would peddle songs to artists and producers from the nearby theaters. When the theaters moved, so did
the publishers.

The Garment District and around

A few streets north, Sixth Avenue collides with Broadway at **Greeley
Square**, an overblown name for what is a trashy triangle celebrating
Horace Greeley, founder of the *Tribune* newspaper. Perhaps he
deserves better: known for his rallying call to the youth of the nineteenth century to explore the Continent ("Go West, young man!"), he
also supported the rights of women and trade unions, commissioned
a weekly column from Karl Marx and denounced slavery and capital
punishment. His paper no longer exists (though one of its descendants is the bored traveler's last resort, the *International Herald
Tribune*) and the square named after him is one of those bits of
Manhattan that looks ready to disintegrate at any moment.

Herald Square

Herald Square faces Greeley Square in a headlong replay of the battles between the *Herald* newspaper and its arch rival Horace
Greeley's *Tribune*. During the 1890s this was the Tenderloin area,
with dance halls, brothels and rough bars like *Satan's Circus* and
the *Burnt Rag* thriving beside the elevated railway that ran up Sixth
Avenue. When the *Herald* arrived in 1895 it gave the square a new
name and dignity, but it's perhaps best recognized as the square
George M. Cohan asked to be remembered to in the famous song.

These days it wouldn't fire anyone to sing about it, saved only from unkempt sleaziness by *Macy's* on the corner below.

Macy's

Macy's is the all-American superstore. Until the mid-1970s it contented itself by being the world's largest store (which it remains); then, in response to the needs of the high-rolling 1980s yuppie lifestyle it went fashionably and safely upmarket. When the economy went into a tailspin in 1990 *Macy's* fortunes declined dramatically, burdened by overexpansion and debt: New Yorkers were stunned when word went around that it was near to closure, and the ensuing media coverage was about as intense as if the mayor had sold the Statue of Liberty to Iraq. Fortunately *Macy's* scrambled out of bankruptcy by the skin of its teeth, with a debt restructuring plan that allowed it to continue financing its famed annual Thanksgiving Day Parade, one of the most famous and best-attended Manhattan parades, marked by its giant cartoon-character balloons and the arrival of Santa. Like all great stores *Macy's* is worth exploring – there's an amazing food emporium plus a reconstruction of P.J. Clarke's bar in the basement – though it may be wise to leave all forms of spending power at home. Nearby, the thoroughly unlikable eight floors of the A & S Plaza attempt to add a little gloss to the street scene, though, inside at least, they can't hold a candle to *Macy's*.

Exploring the Garment District

In a way this part of Broadway is the shopfront to the **Garment District**, a loosely defined pool between 34th and 42nd streets and Sixth and Eighth avenues. From this patch three-quarters of all the women's and children's clothes in America are made, though you'd never believe it: outlets are strictly wholesale with no need to woo customers, and the only clues to the industry inside are the racks of clothes shunted around on the street and occasional bins of offcuts that give the area its look of an open-air rummage sale. Every imaginable button, bow, boa and bangle is on display – ideal if you like looking at things you can hardly believe are still manufactured. Anti-fur zealots should steer clear of West 30th Street (though a few blocks down, it's more Garment District than Chelsea), where peeking from industrial-sized barrels in cooled storefronts are the heads and tails of whole minks and foxes, waiting their turn to become winter coats.

One of the benefits of walking through this part of town is to take advantage of the designer's "**sample sales**," where floor samples and models' used castoffs are sold to the public at cheap prices, though if you can't afford a $750 Donna Karan dress, you probably still can't afford it at $450 (more on sample sales in Chapter 24). The Garment District is another New York neighborhood that has undergone a recent resurgence. An energetic Business Improvement District partnership has gone out of its way to splash up a revitalized Garment District that has seen more and more of its industry coming back to New York from overseas for local manufacturing. Brighter street lighting and better security help make the area safer for walking through, especially at night – which, despite the clean-up, is still all you're likely to be doing here.

Around Madison Square Garden

The Garment District is something to see in passing: the most prominent landmark in this part of town is the **Pennsylvania Station and Madison Square Garden complex,** a combined box and drum structure that swallows up millions of commuters in its train station below and accommodates the Knicks basketball and Rangers hockey teams (along with their fans) above. There's nothing memorable about Penn Station: its subterranean levels seem to have all the grime and just about everything else that's wrong with the subway, and to add insult to injury the original Penn Station, demolished to make way for this, is now hailed as a lost masterpiece, one that brought an air of dignity to the neighborhood and created the stage for the ornate **Post Office** and other elaborate Belle Epoch structures that followed. One of McKim, Mead and White's greatest designs, the original Penn Station reworked the ideas of the Roman Baths of Caracalla to awesome effect, its grand arcade lavishly covered with floors of pink marble and walls of pink granite. Glass tiles in its main waiting room allowed the light from the glass roof to flow through to the trains and platforms below: "Through it one entered the city like a god . . . . One scuttles in now like a rat," mourned an observer.

For details of how to get tickets for the Knicks and Rangers games, see p.383.

Photos of the older building can be seen in the Amtrak waiting area of the new Penn Station. And you can walk back in time at the new entryway to the Long Island Railroad ticketing area on 34th Street at Seventh Avenue: one of the old station's four-faced time pieces now hangs from the tall steel-framed glass structure which is itself reminiscent of the original building. Andrew Leicester's *Ghost Series* was commissioned in 1994 and lines the walls of the new corridor: terracotta wall murals saluting the Corinthian and Ionic columns of the old Penn Station, as well as a rendering of *Day & Night*, an ornate statue surrounding a clock that once welcomed passengers at the old station's entrance. Also of note in the Long Island Railroad ticketing area: look above your head for a Maya Lin sculpture depicting the immeasurability of time in a subtly crafted ellipsis with random number patterns.

One further, more whimsical reminder of the old days is the **Penta Hotel** on the corner of Seventh Avenue and 33rd Street: a main venue for Glenn Miller and other big swing bands of the 1940s, it keeps the phone number that made it famous – 736-5000: under the old system, PENNsylvania 6-5000, the title of Miller's affectionate hit.

The General Post Office

Immediately behind Penn Station, the **General Post Office** is a McKim,
Mead and White structure that survived, a relic from an era when munic-
ipal pride was all about making statements – though to say that the Post
Office is monumental in the grandest manner still seems to underplay it.
The old joke is that it had to be this big to fit in the sonorous inscription
above the columns – "Neither snow nor rain nor heat nor gloom of night
stays these couriers from the swift completion of their appointed
rounds" – a claim about as believable as the official one that the
Manhattan postal district handles more mail than Britain, France and
Belgium combined. There's still a working post office branch here,
though the main sorting stations have moved into more modern space
further west. For the last five years a plan has been bandied around to
utilize the building as a new entrance to Penn Station, perhaps as some
sort of expiation for the destruction of the original station. Whether the
scheme will come to anything, time will tell – bureaucracy and money
troubles seem to have tied this plan up indefinitely.

*For full
practical
details on the
Port Authority
Terminal see
p.13.*

The **Port Authority Terminal Building** at 40th Street and Eighth
Avenue is another sink for the area, though its poor reputation as a
haven for down-and-outs is belied by its appearance these days as a
spruced-up and efficiently run modern bus station. *Greyhound*
leaves from here, as do regional services out to the boroughs, and
(should you arrive in the early hours) it's a remarkably safe place, station staff keeping the winos and weirdos in check. Harder to believe
is that the station holds an exceptional **bowling alley**, should you
immediately have the urge upon arrival (see Chapter 21, *Sports and
Outdoor Activities*, for more details). To the west of Port Authority,
at no. 330 42nd Street, is the **McGraw-Hill Building**, a greeny-blue
radiator that architects raved over: "proto-jukebox modern," Vincent
Scully called it. The lobby should definitely be seen.

Chapter 8

Union Square, Gramercy Park and Murray Hill

B roadway forms a dividing line between Chelsea and the Garment District to the west and the area that comprises **Union Square**, **Gramercy Park** and **Murray Hill** to the east. Bounded by 14th Street to the south and 42nd Street to the north, this is a more salubrious, more residential counterpart to its eastern neighbor. It's here, too, between the great avenues – Third, Park and Fifth – that midtown Manhattan's skyscrapers begin to rise from the low-lying buildings, with perhaps the greatest of them all, the **Empire State Building**, marking the junction of 34th Street and Fifth Avenue.

Union Square and around

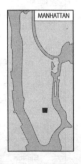

Union Square, where Broadway, Fourth and Park avenues meet, was once the elegant center of the city's theatrical and shopping scene, but has been better known more recently as gathering point for political demonstrations and, up until the mid-1980s, a seedy haunt of dope pushing and street violence. It's much more inviting now, the spill of shallow steps enticing you in to stroll the paths, feed the squirrels and gaze at its array of statuary – something no one would have dared do a few years back. As for the statues, they include an equestrian figure of George Washington, a Lafayette by Bartholdi (more famous for the Statue of Liberty), and, at the center of the park, a massive flagstaff base whose bas-reliefs symbolize the forces of Good and Evil in the Revolution.

On Mondays, Wednesdays, Fridays and Saturdays, the park plays host to the city's best and most popular **greenmarket** on its northern edge. Farmers and other food producers from upstate New York, Long Island, New Jersey and even from Pennsylvania Dutch country sell fresh fruit and vegetables, baked goods, cheeses, eggs, meats, plants and flowers, all of very high quality (an advisory committee sets up and enforces stringent rules on the growers and keeps out

Union Square and around

wholesalers and brokers). During the warmer months (mid-April to mid-Oct), the *Luna Park Café* sets up shop in the beautifully refurbished **Pavilion** at the park's north end. Run by the trendy *Coffee Shop* business across the road, the all-outdoors restaurant makes Union Square nights a touch more swanky with music and twinkling white lights elegantly setting off the darkness.

The square itself is flanked by some good cafés and restaurants and quite a mixture of buildings, not least the **American Savings Bank** on the eastern edge, of which only the grandiose columned exterior survives. The pedimented building just south of here is the former **Tammany Hall**, the once notorious headquarters of the Democratic Party, decorated with a Native American headdress, while the narrow building almost opposite was Andy Warhol's original Factory. The **Consolidated Edison** structure, off the southeast corner, the headquarters of the company responsible for providing the city with ener-

UNION SQUARE,
GRAMERCY PARK
AND MURRAY HILL

gy and those famous steaming sewer access holes, is, with its campanile, an odd premonition of the Metropolitan Life Building a few blocks further north. Inside, there's a museum devoted to the city's power supplies through the ages – strictly for energy buffs.

North of Union Square

North of Union Square, walk the six blocks of **Irving Place** toward Gramercy Park. O. Henry lived along this stretch, at what was once no. 55, and there's also the landmark *Pete's Tavern* (18th St and Irving Place) – one of New York's oldest bars, in business since 1864. The bar propagates itself as the place where O. Henry dreamed up and wrote *Gift of the Magi*. Though that fact is in dispute, the legend serves the place and its atmosphere well.

The stretch of **Broadway** north of here was known once as "Ladies' Mile" for its fancy stores and boutiques (*Lord & Taylor* started trading here), but notwithstanding a few sculpted facades and curvy lintels, it's now hard to imagine it as an upmarket shopping mall. The high-end shopping jumped over to Fifth Avenue around the turn of the century. Turn right on East 20th Street for **Theodore Roosevelt's birthplace** at no. 28 (Wed–Sun 9am–5pm; $2), or at least a reconstruction of it: a rather grim brownstone mansion that's not terribly exciting, just a few rooms with their original furnishings, some of Teddy's hunting trophies and a small gallery documenting the president's life, viewable on an obligatory guided tour.

Gramercy Park

Cross Park Avenue from here and Manhattan's clutter breaks into the ordered open space of **Gramercy Park**, a former swamp reclaimed in 1831. Residential London in spirit, this is one of the city's best squares, its center clean, tidily planted and, most noticeably, completely empty for much of the day – principally because the only people who can gain access are those rich or fortunate enough to live here. Still, stroll around the edge for a walk through a place that was once the center of New York's theater scene. Inside the gates is a statue of the actor Edwin Booth (brother of Lincoln's assassin, John Wilkes Booth), who had a home off the park – 16 Gramercy Park South – until he had it turned into the **Players Club** in 1888 by architect Stanford White. Back then, actors and actresses were still not accepted into regular society, so Booth created the club for play and socializing. At the same time, Booth established a Theater Library in the club to chronicle the history of the American stage. Tours are given now by appointment only (☎228-7610). Along Gramercy Park West, note the row of townhouses sporting ornate wrought-iron work reminiscent of New Orleans's French Quarter.

The NYC Police museum at 235 East 20th St is worth a look if you're interested in the history of New York's Finest – see p.268.

To the east, **Peter Cooper Village** and **Stuyvesant Town** are perhaps the city's most successful examples of dense-packed urban housing, their tall, angled apartment buildings siding peaceful, tree-lined walkways. It's worth knowing, though, that this is private not public housing, and the owners, Metropolitan Life, were accused of operating a color-bar when the projects first opened. Certainly, the contrast with the immigrant slums a little way downtown isn't hard to detect. At the northeast corner of Peter Cooper Village stands the **Asser Levy Recreation Center**, named after the country's first Jewish citizen and kosher butcher, who arrived in 1654. The most notable of the many city-run athletic centers, the Asser Levy building was originally constructed in 1908 as a bathhouse – modeled on the Roman public baths – for the huddled, unwashed masses (the tenements of the East Side supposedly had but one bath for every 79 families). Abandoned in the 1970s, it was reopened as a city gym in 1990; the indoor skylit pool is anchored by a marble dolphin statue that doubles as a fountain. As with all city gyms, membership costs $25 a year (see Chapter 21, *Sports and Outdoor Activities*).

A few blocks west, the land that makes up **Stuyvesant Square** was a gift to the city from its governor and, like Gramercy Park, the park space in the middle was modeled on the squares of London's Bloomsbury. Though partially framed by the buildings of **Beth Israel Medical Center** and cut down the middle by the bustle of Second Avenue, it still retains something of its secluded quality, especially on the western side. Here there's a smatter of elegant terrace, the strangely colonial-looking **Friends' Meeting House**, and, next door, the weighty brownstone **Church of St George** – best known as the place where financier J.P. Morgan used to worship.

Lexington Avenue begins its long journey north from Gramercy Park, past the lumbering 69th Regiment Armory – site in 1913 of the notorious Armory Show which brought modern art to New York for the first time (see "Twentieth-century American art" in *Contexts*) – to Manhattan's most condensed ethnic enclave, **Little India**. Blink, and you might miss this altogether: most of New York's 100,000 Indians live in Queens, and their only trace here is a handful of restaurants and fast-food places – far outnumbered by those down on East Sixth Street – and a pocket of sweet and spice stores.

Madison Square

To the north and west of Gramercy Park, where Broadway and Fifth Avenue meet, is **Madison Square**, by day a maelstrom of dodging cars and cabs, buses and pedestrians but, mainly because of the quality of the buildings and the clever park-space in the middle, possessing a monumentality and neat seclusion that Union Square has long since lost. The **Flatiron Building**, set cheekily on a triangular plot of land on the square's southern side, is another famed city building, one that evokes images of Edwardian New York. Its thin, tapered structure creates unusual wind currents at ground level, and years ago policemen were posted to prevent men gathering to watch the wind raise the skirts of women passing on 23rd Street. The cry they gave to warn off voyeurs – "23 Skidoo!" – has passed into the language. It's hard to believe that this was the city's first true skyscraper, hung on a steel frame in 1902 with its full twenty stories dwarfing all the other structures around. Not for long though: the **Metropolitan Life Company** soon erected its clock tower on the eastern side of the square which, height-wise at least, put the Flatiron to shame.

Next door is the Corinthian-columned marble facade of the **Appellate Division** of the New York State Supreme Court, resolutely righteous with its statues of Justice, Wisdom and Peace turning their weary backs on the ugly black glass New York Life Annexe behind. The grand structure behind that, the **New York Life Building** proper, was the work of Cass Gilbert, creator of the Woolworth Tower downtown. It went up in 1928 on the site of the original **Madison Square Garden** – renowned scene of drunken and debauched revels of high and Broadway society. This was the heart of the theater district in those days and the place where the Garden's architect, **Stanford White**, was murdered by Harry Thaw. White, a partner in the illustrious architectural team of McKim, Mead and White, who designed many of the city's great Beaux Arts buildings, such as the General Post Office, the old Penn Station and Columbia University, was something of a rake by all accounts, with a reputation for womanizing and fast living. His affair with Thaw's wife Evelyn Nesbit, a Broadway showgirl, had been well publicized – even to the extent that the naked statue of the goddess Diana on the top of the building was said to have been modeled on her. Millionaire Thaw was so humiliated by this that one night he burst into the roof garden, found White, surrounded as usual by doting women and admirers, and shot him through the head. Thaw was carted away to spend the rest of his life in mental institutions, and his wife's showbusiness career took a tumble: she resorted to drugs and prostitution, dying in 1961 in Los Angeles.

So ended one of Madison Square's more dramatic episodes. Madison Square Garden has moved twice since then, first to a site on Eighth Avenue and 50th Street, finally to its present location in a hideous drum-shaped eyesore on the corner of 32nd Street and Seventh Avenue. There is, however, one reminder of the time when this was New York's theaterland – the **Episcopal Church of the Transfiguration** just off Fifth Avenue on 29th Street. This, a dinky rusticated church set back from the street, brown brick and topped with copper roofs, has since 1870 been the traditional place of worship of showbiz people. It was tagged with the name "The Little Church Around the Corner" after a devout but understanding priest from a nearby church had refused to marry a theatrical couple and sent them here. It's an intimate building, furnished throughout in warm wood and with the figures of famous actors (most notably Edwin Booth as Hamlet) memorialized in the stained glass.

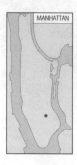
MANHATTAN

The Empire State Building

Further up Fifth Avenue is New York's prime **shopping territory**, home to most of the city's heavyweight department stores. *Macy's* is just a short stroll away on Herald Square; filling the space between 38th and 39th streets are the lavish headquarters of *Lord & Taylor* (see Chapter 24, *Shops and Markets*). The **Empire State Building** – overshadowing by far the lure of such consumer items – occupies what has always been a prime site. Before it appeared this was home to the first *Waldorf Astoria Hotel*, built by William Waldorf Astor as a ruse to humiliate his formidable aunt, Caroline Schermerhorn, into moving uptown. The hotel opened in 1893 and immediately became a focus for the city's rich – in an era, the "Gay Nineties," when "Meet me at the *Waldorf*" was the catchphrase to conjure with.*

However, though the reputation of the *Waldorf* – at least for its prices – endures to this day, it didn't remain in its initial premises for very long, moving in 1929 to its current Art Deco home on Park Avenue.

Few would dispute the elegance of what took its place. The Empire State Building remains easily the most potent and evocative symbol of New York, and has done since its completion in 1931. The ground-breaking took place just three weeks before the stock market crash in October 1929, but despite the Depression, the building proceeded full steam ahead and came in well under budget after just fourteen months in the making. Soon after, King Kong clung to it and distressed squealing damsels while grabbing at passing planes; in 1945 a plane crashed into the building's 79th story (see opposite); while in 1979, two Englishmen parachuted from its summit to the ground, only to be carted off by the NY Police Department for disturbing the peace. More recently came the darkest moment in the building's history: in February 1997 a man opened gunfire on the observation deck, killing one tourist and injuring seven others; as a result there is tighter security upon entrance, with metal detectors, package scanners and the like.

Its 103 stories and 1472 feet – toe to TV mast – make it the world's third tallest building, but the height is deceptive, rising in stately tiers with steady panache. Inside, its basement serves as an underground marbled shopping mall, lined with newsstands, beauty parlors, cafés, even a post office, and is finished everywhere with delicate Deco touches. After wandering around you can visit the **Guinness World of Records Exhibition** – though, frankly, you'd be

---

*It was the consort of Mrs Schermerhorn Astor, Ward Macallister, who coined the label "The Four Hundred" to describe this crowd. "There are only about four hundred people in fashionable New York society," he asserted. "If you go outside that number you strike people who are either not at ease in a ballroom or else make other people not at ease. See the point?"

The plane that hit the Empire State Building

On the morning of Saturday, July 28, 1945, Lieutenant Colonel William Franklin Smith Jr was flying a **B-25 bomber** in thick fog above the Hudson River. A veteran of 34 bombing missions over Germany, he was impatient to get his plane on the ground. Having been told he would have to wait three hours for a landing slot at Newark airport, he falsely declared having "official business" at La Guardia – with the intention of diverting to Newark once he'd been cleared. He'd already strayed into La Guardia's busy airspace, so he was given immediate clearance to land at Newark to get the aircraft out of the way. Realizing this meant his flying across Manhattan, La Guardia air control sent out a warning message: "*At present we can't see the top of the Empire State Building...*".

Neither could Smith. At 9.49am his twelve-ton plane smashed into the side of the 79th floor of the building, killing Smith, his co-pilot and a 20-year- old sailor who had been given permission to fly home on the plane to console his parents, who had learned that his brother had been killed in the Pacific. The Empire State swung back and forth in a two-foot arc as the plane smashed a twenty-foot hole in the wall. Fuel from the ruptured tanks flooded out and set two floors on fire. The port engine smashed straight through the building, exited the south wall and tumbled down to demolish a penthouse apartment on 34th Street. The other engine fell into the Empire State's elevator shaft, severing the cables and plunging the elevator and its attendant, Betty Lou Oliver, 1000 feet down to a subcellar: despite a broken back and legs, she survived. Ten others in the building were killed; had the accident happened on an ordinary working day, many more would undoubtedly have died.

better advised to save your money for the assault on the top of the tower. Also worth missing is the **New York Skyride** on the second floor. The ten-minute simulated flight ($7.95, $5.95 kids and seniors) soars above the skyscrapers, through Times Square, down Coney Island's Cyclone, and among other New York landmarks, but will leave the weak-hearted merely dizzy and the strong-willed wondering why they spent their money on this.

Getting to the top

The first elevators, alarmingly old and rickety if you've previously zoomed to the top of the World Trade Center, take you to the 86th floor, summit of the building before the radio and TV mast was added. The **views** from the outside walkways here are as stunning as you'd expect – better than those from the World Trade Center since Manhattan spreads on all sides. On a clear day visibility is up to eighty miles, but, given the city's pollution, on most it's more likely to be between ten and twenty. If you're feeling brave, and can stand the wait for the tight squeeze in the single elevator, you can go up to the Empire State's last reachable zenith, a small cylinder at the foot of the TV mast which was added as part of a harebrained scheme to erect a mooring post for airships – a plan subsequently abandoned

The Empire State Building

Skyscrapers

Along with Chicago and Hong Kong, Manhattan is one of the best places in the world in which to see **skyscrapers**, its puckered, almost medieval skyline of towers the city's most familiar and striking image. In fact there are only two main clusters of skyscrapers, but they set the tone for the city – the Financial District, where the combination of narrow streets and tall buildings forms slender, lightless canyons, and midtown Manhattan, where the big skyscrapers, flanking the wide central avenues between the 30s and the 60s, have long competed for height and prestige.

The term "skyscraper" was coined in 1890 by one John J. Flinn, describing the evolving style of building in turn-of-the-century Chicago, since when the two cities have always been battling to produce the tallest building. It's uncertain which city actually built the first real skyscraper, but the first generally recognized instance in New York was the Flatiron Building on Madison Square, designed in 1902, not least for the obvious way its triangular shape made the most of the new iron-frame technique of construction that had made such structures possible. A few years later, in 1913, New York clinched the title of the world's tallest building with the sixty-stories Woolworth Building on Broadway, later going on to produce such landmarks as the Chrysler and Empire State buildings, and, more recently, the World Trade Center – though the latter's status as world's tallest building has since been usurped by Chicago's Sears Tower.

Styles have changed over the years and have perhaps been most influenced by the stringency of the city's zoning laws, which early in the century placed restrictions on the types of building permitted. At first skyscrapers were sheer vertical monsters, maximizing the floor space possible from any given site but with no regard to how this affected the neighboring buildings, which more often than not were thrown into shade by the new arrival. In order to stop this happening the city authorities invented the concept of "air rights," putting a restriction on how high a building could be before it had to be set back from its base. This forced skyscrapers to be designed in a series of steps – a law most elegantly adhered to by the Empire State Building, which has no less fewer ten steps in all, but it's a pattern you will see repeated all over the city.

Due to the pressure on space in Manhattan's narrow confines and the price of real estate, which makes speculatively constructing office buildings so lucrative, the skyscrapers continue to rise, and it's always possible to see some slowly rising steel frame somewhere in the city. Traditionally the workers who brave the heights to work on the skyscrapers, lifting the girders into place and bolting them together, often bent into impossible positions, squatting or balancing on thin planks, are Native Americans, due to a supposedly remarkable head for heights. They still make up forty percent of such workers in New York, and even eighty floors up don't wear any kind of safety harness, claiming it restricts their movements too much.

As for the future, there seems to be almost no limit to the heights that are envisaged, the most notable plan being Donald Trump's bid to reclaim the tallest-building title for New York with a new structure on the Upper West Side well over a hundred stories high. Whether or not this comes off, it's certain that even in times of recession skyscrapers remain the "machines for making money" that Le Corbusier originally claimed they were.

after some local VIPs almost got swept away by the wind, and a second attempt at mooring, made by a Navy blimp, resulted in the flooding of 34th Street. Once the wind got ahold of the Navy blimp, they had to drop the water used as ballast to balance, and the "blimp port" was permanently closed. You can't go outside and the extra sixteen stories don't really add much to the view, but you will have been to the top. Try getting there around sunset when most of the crowds have gone and you'll be treated to Manhattan by day *and* night (daily 9.30am–midnight; $4, $2 for under 12s and seniors). The building's management has decided to close the 102nd floor observatory on weekends during the summers, because the crowds make the smallish space unmanageable, so go during the week if you want to hit the very top.

The Empire State Building

Murray Hill

Back down to earth, Fifth Avenue carves its way up the island. East down 34th Street lies **Murray Hill**, a tenuously tagged residential area of statuesque canopy-fronted apartment buildings, but with little apart from its WASPish anonymity to mark it out from the rest of midtown Manhattan. Built on one of the few remaining actual hills in the lower part of Manhattan island, Murray Hill is residential by design – no commercial building was allowed until the 1920s, when greedy real estate interests successfully challenged the rule in court. Like Chelsea further west, it lacks any real center, any sense of community and, unless you work, live or are staying in Murray Hill, there's little reason to go there at all; indeed you're more likely to pass through without even realizing it. Its boundaries are indistinct, but lie somewhere between Fifth Avenue and Third and, very roughly, 32nd to 40th streets, where begins the rather brasher commercialism of the Midtown business district.

When Madison Avenue was on a par with Fifth as the place to live, Murray Hill came to be dominated by the **Morgan family**, the crusty old financier J.P. and his offspring, who at one time owned a clutch of property here. Morgan junior lived in the **brownstone** on the corner of 37th Street and Madison (now headquarters of the American Lutheran Church), his father in a house that was later pulled down to make way for an extension to his **library** next door, the mock but tastefully simple Roman villa that still stands and is commonly mistaken for the old man's house. (If you've read the book or seen the film *Ragtime*, you'll remember that Coalhouse Walker made this fundamental mistake when attempting to hold Pierpoint Morgan hostage.) In fact, Morgan would simply come here to languish among the art treasures he had bought up wholesale on his trips to Europe: manuscripts, paintings, prints and furniture. Here, during a crisis of confidence in the city's banking system in 1907, he entertained New York's richest and most influential men night after night until they agreed to put up the money to save what could have been the entire country from bankruptcy, giving up $30 million himself as an act of good faith. You can visit the library's splendid interior and priceless collection; see Chapter 15, *Museums and Galleries*.

As you continue up Madison Avenue the influence of the Morgans rears its head again in the shape (or at least the name) of **Morgan's Hotel** between 37th and 38th streets – the last word in ostentatious discretion, not even bothering to proclaim its presence with the vulgarity of a sign. Stop in at its elegant bar for a drink if you've got the cash, and for details on how much it costs to sleep here, see Chapter 16, *Accommodation*.

Chapter 9

Midtown Manhattan

Y ou're likely to spend a fair amount of time in **midtown Manhattan**. It's here that most of the city's hotels are situated, here too that you'll arrive – at Penn or Grand Central Station, or the Port Authority. And the area is in many ways the city's center. Cutting through its heart is **Fifth Avenue**, New York's most glamorous (and most expensive) street, with the theater strip of **Broadway** and the razzle-dazzle of **Times Square** to the west.

East of Fifth Avenue are the corporate businesses, a skyward wave that creates Manhattan's rollercoaster appearance. If you have any interest in architecture (or simply sensation) you'll want to stroll this sector, looking in and up at such delights as the **Chrysler**, **Citicorp** and **Seagram** buildings and the magnificent **Rockefeller Center**. Fifth Avenue itself is where to check out New York's most venerable sites of conspicuous consumption. And of course this is also a major museum strip, with the **Museum of Modern Art** and a host of lesser collections grouped together on 53rd Street (see the individual museum accounts in Chapter 15 for more on these).

West of Fifth Avenue, in particular west of Broadway, the area has a distinctly different appeal. Times Square, previously the city's sleaze center, is a jumble of 24-hour neon, old theaters and new megastores – much rehabilitated by Disney, whose efforts have been met with a mixed reception. Further west is Clinton, better known as **Hell's Kitchen**, a bit bereft attraction-wise but with a welcome edge, at least around its main strips, that the Broadway area has now lost.

East along 42nd Street

42nd Street is one of the few streets in the world to have an entire musical named after it. With good reason too, for you *can* do anything on 42nd Street, highbrow or low, and it's also home to some of the city's most characteristic buildings, ranging from great Beaux Arts palaces like **Grand Central Station** to vulgar charge-card traps like the **Grand Hyatt Hotel**. Surrounded by superb architecture and

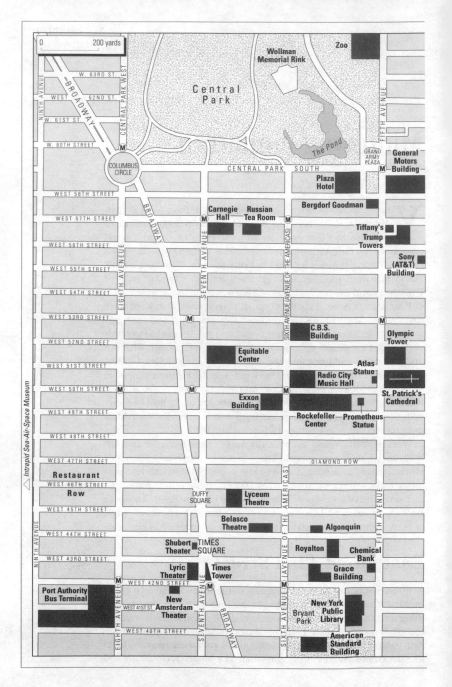

MIDTOWN MANHATTAN

EAST 64TH STREET
EAST 63RD STREET
EAST 62ND STREET
EAST 61ST STREET
EAST 60TH STREET
EAST 59TH STREET
EAST 58TH STREET
EAST 57TH STREET
EAST 56TH STREET
EAST 55TH STREET
EAST 54TH STREET
EAST 53RD STREET
EAST 52ND STREET
EAST 51ST STREET
EAST 50TH STREET
EAST 49TH STREET
EAST 48TH STREET
EAST 47TH STREET
EAST 46TH STREET
EAST 45TH STREET
EAST 44TH STREET
EAST 43RD STREET
EAST 42ND STREET
EAST 41ST ST
EAST 40TH STREET

MADISON AVENUE
PARK AVENUE
LEXINGTON AVENUE
THIRD AVENUE
SECOND AVENUE
FIRST AVENUE
YORK AVENUE
RIVERVIEW TERRACE
SUTTON PLACE
EAST RIVER DRIVE
BEEKMAN PLACE

Lever House
St. Peter's Church
Citicorp Center
Seagram Building
Villiard Houses
General Electric Building
Waldorf-Astoria Hotel
Helmsley Building
TURTLE BAY
United Nations Headquarters
General Assembly Building
Conference Building
MetLife (Pan Am) Building
Grand Central Terminal
Chrysler Building
Secretariat
Phillip Morris Building
Bowery Savings Bank
Chanin Building
Daily News Building
Tudor City

N

breathtaking views down the great avenues, this section of New York is one of the most characterful – and by extension characteristic – parts of the city.

The New York Public Library

The **New York Public Library** (Center for the Humanities) on the corner of 42nd and Fifth Avenue is the first notable building on 42nd Street's eastern reaches: Beaux Arts in style and faced with white marble, its steps act as a meeting point and general hangout for pockets of people throughout the year. To tour the library either walk around yourself or take one of the tours (Mon–Sat 11am & 2pm; free), which last an hour and give a good all-round picture of the building. The traditional highlight of such a tour, or just poking around by yourself, is the large coffered **Reading Room** at the back of the building – though unfortunately it's closed off to the public until summer 1999 while it gets a technological makeover. Trotsky worked here on and off during his brief sojourn in New York just prior to the 1917 Revolution, introduced to the place by his friend Bukharin, who was bowled over by a library you could use so late in the evening. The opening times are considerably less impressive now, but the library still boasts a collection among the five largest in the world: 88 miles of books stored in eight levels of stacks beneath this room and running the length of Bryant Park, which alone covers half an acre.

Grand Central Terminal

Back outside, push through the crush crossing Fifth Avenue and walk east down Manhattan's most congested stretch to where Park Avenue lifts off the ground at Pershing Square to weave its way around the solid bulk of **Grand Central Terminal**. This, for its day, was a masterful piece of urban planning: after the electrification of the railways made it possible to reroute trains underground, the rail lanes behind the existing station were sold off to developers and the profits went towards the building of a new terminal – constructed around a basic iron frame but clothed with a Beaux Arts skin. Since then Grand Central has taken on an almost mythical significance, and though with the insidious eating-away of the country's rail network its major traffic is now mainly commuters speeding out no further than Connecticut or Westchester County, it remains in essence what it was in the nineteenth century – symbolic gateway to an undiscovered continent.

You can either explore Grand Central on your own or take one of the excellent free **tours** run by the *Municipal Arts Society* (see *Basics*). But for the efforts of a few dedicated New Yorkers (and, strangely enough, the late Jackie Onassis, whose voice was no doubt a godsend), Grand Central wouldn't be here at all, or at least it would be much uglified. It was only deemed a National Landmark in 1978, after the railroad's plan to cap the whole thing with an office building was quashed. The most spectacular aspect of the building is its size, now cowed by the soaring airplane wing of the Metropolitan Life building (formerly known as the Pan Am building) behind, but still no less impressive in the main station concourse. This is one of the world's finest and most imposing open spaces, 470 feet long and 150 feet high, the barrel-vaulted ceiling speckled like a Baroque church with a painted representation of the winter night sky, its 2500 stars shown back to front: "As God would have seen them," the painter is reputed to have remarked. Stand in the middle and you realize that Grand Central represents a time when stations were seen as appropriately dwarfing preludes to great cities – "a city within a city," as it has been called.

In 1995 the MTA (Metropolitan Transit Association) embarked on a massive renovation of Grand Central, cleaning the ceiling and restoring faded treasures, such as the massive chandeliers. The plans are not without commercial thrust – there will be four new restaurants that overlook the main concourse – but the terminal's more esoteric reaches remain (thankfully) intact. Search out the **Tennis Club** on the third floor, which used to be a CBS studio but now offers up court-time for a membership fee of several thousand dollars a year; and the **Oyster Bar** (see also p.334) in the vaulted bowels of the station – one of the city's most highly regarded seafood restaurants, serving something like a dozen varieties of oyster and crampacked every lunchtime with the Midtown office crowd. Just outside is something that explains why the *Oyster Bar*'s babble is not solely the result of the big-mouthed business people who eat there: you can stand on opposite sides of any of the vaulted spaces and hold a conversation just by whispering, an acoustic fluke that makes this the loudest eatery in town.

Around the Chrysler Building

Across the street, the **Bowery Savings Bank** echoes Grand Central's grandeur – like its sister branch downtown, extravagantly lauding the twin shibboleths of sound investment and savings. A Roman-style basilica, it has a floor paved with mosaics, the columns are each fashioned from a different kind of marble and, if you take a look at the elevator doors (through a door on the right), you'll see bronze bas-reliefs of bank employees hard at various tasks. But then, this kind of lavish expenditure is typical of the buildings on this stretch of 42nd Street, which is full of lobbies worth popping inside for a glimpse. Start with the **Philip Morris Building**, across from Grand Central on the corner of Park Avenue and 42nd, which contains a small offshoot of the Whitney Museum of American Art (see Chapter 15, *Museums and Galleries*); the immense vaulted-glass atrium-cum-sculpture court is a bit showy but impressive nonetheless. The **Grand Hyatt**

Hotel back on the north side of 42nd Street is another notable instance of excess, perhaps the best example in the city of all that is truly vulgar about contemporary American interior design, its slushing waterfalls, lurking palms and gliding escalators representing plush-carpeted bad taste at its most meretricious.

The **Chrysler Building**, across Lexington Avenue, is a different story, dating from a time (1930) when architects carried off prestige with grace and style. This was for a fleeting moment the world's tallest building – until it was usurped by the Empire State in 1931 – and, since the rediscovery of Art Deco a decade or so ago, has become easily Manhattan's best loved, its car-motif friezes, jutting gargoyles and arched stainless steel pinnacle giving the solemn Midtown skyline a welcome touch of fun. Its designer, William Van Alen, indulged in a feud with an erstwhile partner who was designing a building at 40 Wall Street at the same time. Each were determined to have the higher skyscraper: Alen secretly built a stainless steel spire inside the Chrysler's crown; when 40 Wall Street was finally topped out a few feet higher than the Chrysler, Alen popped the 185-foot spire out through the top of the building, and won the day.

The Chrysler corporation moved out some time ago, and for a while the building was left to degenerate by a company that didn't wholly appreciate its spirited silliness, but now a new owner has pledged to keep it lovingly intact. The **lobby**, once a car showroom, is for the moment all you can see (there's no observation deck), but that's enough in itself, with opulently inlaid elevators, walls covered in African marble and on the ceiling a realistic, if rather faded, study of work and endeavor, showing airplanes, machines and brawny builders who worked on the tower.

Beyond the Chrysler Building

Flanking each side of Lexington Avenue on the southern side of 42nd Street are two more buildings worthy of a studied walk past. The **Chanin Building** on the right is another Art Deco monument, cut with terracotta carvings of leaves, tendrils and sea creatures. More interestingly, the design on the outside of the weighty **Mobil Building** across the street is deliberately folded so as to be cleaned automatically by the movement of the wind.

East of here is the somber yet elegant **Daily News Building**, whose stone facade fronts a surprising Deco interior. The **lobby** is well worth examining: there's a large globe encased in a lighted circular frame, in place since 1923 – as the geography proves; and various bronze measuring devices are displayed on the walls. The marble floor is inlaid with a system of intersecting bronze lines that detail the distances between NY and other major cities. The tabloid paper after which the building is named has recently moved its headquarters a bit further downtown.

Further east still, 42nd Street grows more tranquil. And on the left, between Second and First avenues, is one of the city's most peaceful (if surreal) spaces of all – the **Ford Foundation Building**. Built in 1967, this was the first of the atriums that are now commonplace across Manhattan, and it is certainly the most lush. Structurally, it's a giant greenhouse, gracefully supported by soaring granite columns and edged with two walls of offices visible through the windows. Workers, in turn, can look down on the subtropical garden, which changes naturally with the seasons. This was one of the first attempts at creating a "natural" environment, and it's astonishingly quiet. 42nd Street is no more than a murmur outside, and all you can hear is the burble of water, the echo of voices and the clipped crack of feet on the brick walkways, mingled with the ripe smell of the atrium's considerable vegetation. The indoor/outdoor experience here is one of New York City's great architectural coups.

East to the United Nations Building

At the east end of 42nd Street, steps lead up to **Tudor City**, which rises behind a tree-filled parklet; with its coats of arms, leaded glass and neat neighborhood shops it is the very picture of self-contained dowager respectability. Trip down the steps from here and you're plum opposite the building of the **United Nations**, which rose up after the World War II on the site of what was once known as Turtle Bay. Some see the United Nations complex as one of the major sights of New York; others, usually those who've been there, are not so complimentary. For, whatever the symbolism of the UN, there can be few buildings that are quite so dull to walk around. What's more, as if to rationalize the years of UN impotence in war and hunger zones worldwide, the (obligatory) guided tours emphasize that the UN's main purpose is to promote dialogue and awareness rather than enforcement. So the organization itself moves at a snail's pace – bogged down by regulations and a lack of funds – the general feel of the tour as well.

For the determined, the complex consists of three main buildings – the thin glass-curtained slab of the **Secretariat**, the sweeping curve of the **General Assembly Building** and, just between, the low-rise connecting **Conference Wing**. It went up immediately after World War II and was finished in 1963, the product of a suitably international team of architects which included Le Corbusier – though he pulled out before the building was completed. Daily **tours** leave from the monumental General Assembly lobby (First Avenue at 46th Street; tours leave every 30min, 9.15am–4.45pm; $7.50, $4.50 students; ☎963-7539) and take in the main conference chambers of the UN and its constituent parts, the foremost of which is the General Assembly Chamber itself, expanded a few years back to accommodate up to 179 members' delegations (though there are at present only 159). It's certainly impressive, even given (or perhaps due to) its 1960s feel, though it does seem wasted on a body that meets only three months each year. Other council chambers situated in the Conference Building include the Security Council, the Economic and Social Council and the Trusteeship Council – all similarly retro (note the clunky machinery of the journalists' areas) and sporting some intriguing Marxist murals.

Once you've been whisked around all these, with the odd stop for examples of the many artifacts that have been donated to the UN by its various member states – rugs, sculptures, a garishly colored mosaic based on a Norman Rockwell painting (courtesy of Nancy Reagan) – the tour is more or less over and will leave you in the basement of the General Assembly Building. Here a couple of shops sell ethnic items from around the world and a **post office** will flog you a UN postage stamp to prove that you've been here – though bear in mind it's only valid on mail posted from the UN. There's also a **restaurant** that serves a daily lunch buffet with dishes from different UN member countries, but the food, like the tour, is fairly taste-free.

Fifth Avenue and East Midtown: 42nd Street to Central Park

Fifth Avenue bowls ahead from 42nd Street with all the confidence of the material world. It's been a great strip for as long as New York has been a great city and its name is an automatic image of wealth and opulence. Here that image is very real: all that considers itself suave and cosmopolitan ends up on Fifth, and the shops showcase New York's most opulent consumerism. That the shopping is beyond the power of most people needn't put you off, for Fifth rewards with some of the city's best architecture: the boutiques and stores are just the icing on the cake.

Fifth Avenue

In its lower reaches **Fifth Avenue** isn't really as alluring as the streets off. The only eye-catcher is the **Chemical Bank** on the southwest corner of 43rd, an early glass 'n' gloss box that teasingly displays its safe to passers-by, a reaction against the fortress palaces of earlier banks. Around the next corner, West 44th Street contains three New York institutions. The Georgian-style **Harvard Club** at no. 27, easily spotted of an evening by the paparazzi hanging around outside, has interiors so lavish that lesser mortals aren't allowed to enter. But it's still possible to enjoy the **New York Yacht Club**, its playfully eccentric exterior of bay windows molded as ships' sterns, and with waves and dolphins completing the effect of tipsy Beaux Arts fun. For years this was home of the Americas Cup, a yachting trophy first won by the schooner *America* in 1851 and held here (indeed bolted to the

Fifth Avenue
and East
Midtown:
42nd Street
to Central
Park

table) until lost to the Australians amid much loss of face in 1984. Now though, for the time being at least, it's back in its place.

"Dammit, it was the twenties and we had to be smarty." So said Dorothy Parker of the group known as the Round Table, whose members hung out at the **Algonquin Hotel** at no. 59 and gave it a name as the place for literary visitors to New York – a name that to some extent still endures. The Round Table used to meet regularly here, a kind of American-style Bloomsbury Group of the city's sharpest-tongued wits, and the club had a reputation for being as egotistical as it was exclusive. Times have changed considerably, but over the years the *Algonquin* has continued to attract a steady stream of famous guests, most with some kind of literary bent, not least Noel Coward (whose table someone will point out to you if you ask nicely), Bernard Shaw, Irving Berlin and Boris Karloff. The bar is one of the most civilized in town.

Taking over from the *Algonquin* as the lunch and supper spot for the literary set in the 1990s is the **Royalton** (44 W 44th St), a Philippe Starck-designed hotel whose design, style and Deco atmosphere bring the word "trendy" to new heights. Step into the nearly unmarked hotel for a peek at the lobby, keeping an eye out for Armani-clad doormen, whose snappy appearance belies the fact that behind the padded doors is a hotel, not a private club.

West 47th Street, or Diamond Row (described more fully on p.148), is another surprise off Fifth Avenue, but before hitting that, duck into the **Fred French Building** at 551 Fifth Avenue. The colorfully tiled mosaics on its outside are a mere prelude to the combination of Art Deco and Near Eastern imagery inside. More strking still is the facade of what was once **Charles Scribner & Son's bookstore** at 597 Fifth Avenue. The black and gold iron-and-glass storefront that seems to have fallen from an Edwardian engraving has been given historic landmark status. All the more anachronistic, then, that the building now houses a *United Colors of Benetton*; the lone remnant of its literary history is a basement café-cum-salon that hosts frequent readings.

Rockefeller Center

Central to this stretch of Fifth is a complex of buildings that, more than any other in the city, succeeds in being utterly self-contained and at the same time in complete agreement with its surroundings. Built between 1932 and 1940 by John D. Rockefeller, son of the oil magnate, the **Rockefeller Center** is one of the finest pieces of urban planning anywhere: office space with cafés, a theater, underground concourses and rooftop gardens work together with an intelligence and grace rare in any building then or now. It's a combination that shows every other city-center shopping mall the way, leaving you thinking that Cyril Connolly's snide description – "that sinister Stonehenge of Economic Man" – was way off the mark.

Fifth Avenue
and East
Midtown:
42nd Street
to Central
Park

You're lured into the Center from Fifth Avenue down the gentle slope of the **Channel Gardens** (whimsically named because they divide La Maison Française and the British Empire Building) to the **GE Building** (formerly the RCA Building, but renamed when General Electric took it over a few years ago), focus of the Center. Rising 850 feet, its monumental lines match the scale of Manhattan itself, though softened by symmetrical setbacks to prevent an overpowering expanse of wall. At its foot the **Lower Plaza** holds a sunken restaurant in the summer months, linked visually to the downward flow of the building by Paul Manship's sparkling *Prometheus*; in winter it becomes an ice rink, giving skaters a chance to show off their skills to passing shoppers. More ponderously, a panel on the eastern side relates John D. Rockefeller's priggish credo in gold and black.

Inside, the GE Building is no less impressive. In the lobby José Maria Sert's murals, *American Progress* and *Time*, are faded but eagerly in tune with the 1930s Deco ambience – presumably more so than the original paintings by Diego Rivera, which were removed by John D.'s son Nelson when the artist refused to scrap a panel glorifying Lenin. A leaflet available from the lobby desk details a **self-guided tour** of the Center, and while you can't reach the building's summit, a cocktail in *The Rainbow Room* restaurant on the 65th floor (see p.341) gives you one of Manhattan's best skyscraper views, especially at night, when helicopters hang like fireflies over the Financial District, and Central Park glitters to the north.

Among the many offices in the GE Building are the **NBC Studios**, and it's possible to tour these (one-hour tours leave regularly, daily 9.15am–5pm, reservations from the desk in the GE foyer first; $10; arrive as early as possible since tours fill fast; ☎664-4000). For an early-morning TV thrill, gawk in at NBC's *Today Show*, which broadcasts live from 7am to 9am weekday mornings from glass-enclosed studios in the new NBC News Building on the southwest corner of 49th and Rockefeller Plaza. The TV studios here also hand out free tickets for TV show recordings, which can be a great way of seeing the best and tacky worst of the nation's television.

See pp.28–29
for the full
story on TV
show tapings.

Radio City Music Hall

Just northwest of Rockefeller Center, at Sixth Avenue and 50th Street, is the **Radio City Music Hall**, an Art Deco jewel box that represents the last word in 1930s luxury. The staircase is regally resplendent with the world's largest chandeliers, the murals from the men's toilets are now in the Museum of Modern Art, and the huge auditorium looks like an extravagant scalloped shell or a vast sunset: "Art Deco's true shrine," as Paul Goldberger rightly called it. Believe it or not Radio City was nearly demolished in 1970: the outcry this caused left it designated a national landmark. To explore, take a tour from the lobby (Mon–Sat 10am–5pm, Sun 11am–5pm; $13.75; ☎632-4041).

North toward Central Park

A further bit of sumptuous Deco is the **International Building** on Fifth Avenue, whose black marble and gold leaf give the lobby a sleek, classy feel dramatized by the ritz of escalators and the view across Lee Lawrie's bronze *Atlas* out to **St Patrick's Cathedral**. Designed by James Renwick and completed in 1888, St Patrick's sits bone-white in the sullied streets and seems the result of a painstaking academic tour of the Gothic cathedrals of Europe – perfect in detail, lifeless in spirit. There's something wrong too in the way the cathedral slots ever-so-neatly into Manhattan's grid pattern; on the plus side, the Gothic details are perfect and the Cathedral is certainly striking – and made all the more so by the backing of the sunglass-black **Olympic Tower**.

North of 52nd Street, Fifth Avenue's ground floors quickly shift from airline offices to all-out glitz, with *Cartier*, *Gucci*, and *Tiffany's* among many gilt-edged names. If you're keen to do more than merely window-shop, *Tiffany's* is worth a perusal, its soothing green marble and weathered wood interior best described by Truman Capote's fictional Holly Golightly: "It calms me down right away . . . nothing very bad could happen to you there." Notable too are *Steuben Glass*, 715 Fifth Avenue at 56th Street, a showcase of delicate glass and crystalware perfectly displayed; and Japan's largest department store chain, *Takashimaya*, at no. 683, where East meets West, expensively. Further along, the famed department store *Bergdorf Goodman*, at no. 754, holds a wedding-cake interior, all glossy pastels, chandeliers, pink curtains and the like. Newcomers to this prestigious area are the hardly-needed-but-here-anyway *Coca-Cola Store* at 711 Fifth Avenue, and on the northeast corner of Fifth and 57th, a three-story *Warner Brothers* paraphernalia store (see Chapter 24 for fuller listings).

Just when you thought all the glitter had gone about as far as it could there's the **Trump Tower** at 57th Street, whose outrageously overdone atrium is just short of repellent – perhaps in tune with those who frequent the glamorous designer boutiques here. Perfumed air, polished marble paneling and a five-story waterfall are calculated to knock you senseless with expensive "good" taste: as it is, even some of the security people look faintly embarrassed. But the building is clever, a neat little outdoor garden is squeezed high in a corner, and each of the 230 apartments above the atrium gets views in three directions. Donald Trump, the property developer all New York liberals love to hate, lives here, along with other worthies of the hyper-rich crowd.

The antidote to all this is **F.A.O. Schwarz**, a block north at 745 Fifth Avenue at 58th Street, a colossal emporium of children's toys. Fight the kids off and there's some great stuff to play with – once again, the best money can buy. Across 58th Street, Fifth Avenue broadens to **Grand Army Plaza** and the fringes of Central Park.

For listings of all Fifth Avenue's best stores, see chapter 24, Shops and Markets.

Fifth Avenue
and East
Midtown:
42nd Street
to Central
Park

The other great attractions as you walk north toward the park are the museums – chiefly the **Museum of Modern Art** (11 W 53rd St; see p.248), and also the nearby **Museum of TV & Radio** (25 W 52nd St; p.265) and **American Craft Museum** (40 W 53rd St; p.261). For full accounts of each, see Chapter 15, *Museums and Galleries*.

Looming impressively on the plaza is, aptly enough, the **Plaza Hotel**, recognizable from its many film appearances. Have a wander around to soak in the (slightly faded) gilt-and-brocade grandeur; the inside, including the snazzy **Oak Room** bar, is worth a snoop too. The hotel's reputation was built not just on looks, but on lore: it boasts its own historian, keeper of such bits as when legendary tenor Enrico Caruso, enraged with the loud ticking of the hotel's clocks, stopped them all by throwing a shoe at one (they were calibrated to function together). The Plaza apologized with a magnum of Champagne.

To continue on, go back down to **57th Street** and head east toward Madison – it's an elegant stretch of exclusive shops and art galleries, albeit with the odd superstore. One dubious, though unmissable, attraction at no. 6 is **Nike Town**, an unrestrained celebration of the sneaker that needs be seen to be believed. The overly earnest attempt at a museum, laden with sound-effects, space-age visuals and exhibits inlaid into the floor, walls and special display cases – including one that holds a custom-designed gold-plated athletic shoe worn by Michael Jordan – can't mask that it's a store at heart.

Madison, Park and Lexington avenues

If there is a stretch that is immediately and unmistakably New York it is the area that runs east from Fifth Avenue in the 40s and 50s. The great avenues of **Madison**, **Park**, **Lexington** and **Third** reach their richest heights as the skyscrapers line up in neck-cricking vistas, the streets choke with yellow cabs and office workers, and Con Edison vents belch steam from old heating systems. More than anything else it's buildings that define this part of town, the majority of them housing anonymous corporations and supplying excitement to the skyline in a 1960s build-'em-high glass-box bonanza. Others, like the Sony Building and the Citicorp Center, don't play the game; and enough remains from the pre-box days to keep variety.

Madison Avenue

Madison Avenue shadows Fifth with some of its sweep but less of the excitement. A few good stores sit behind the scenes here, like *Brooks Brothers*, on the corner of East 44th Street, traditional clothiers to the Ivy League and inventors of the button-down collar, but Madison doesn't have quite the prestige of Fifth or Park. Between 50th and 51st streets the **Villard Houses** merit more than a passing glance, a replay of an Italian palazzo (one that didn't quite make it to Fifth Avenue) by McKim, Mead and White. The houses have been surgically incorporated into the *Helmsley Palace Hotel* and the interiors polished up to their original splendor.

Madison's most interesting buildings come in a four-block strip above 53rd Street: **Paley Park**, on the north side of East 53rd between Madison and Fifth, is a tiny vest-pocket park complete with mini-waterfall. Around the corner the **Continental Illinois Center** looks like a cross between a space rocket and a grain silo. But it's the **Sony Building** (formerly the AT&T Building), between 55th and 56th streets, that grabbed all the headlines. A Johnson–Burgee collaboration, it followed the postmodernist theory of eclectic borrowing from historical styles: a Modernist skyscraper sandwiched between a Chippendale top and a Renaissance base – the idea being to quote from great public buildings and simultaneously return to the fantasy of the early part of this century. The building has its fans, but in the main the tower doesn't work, and it's unlikely to stand the test of time. Perhaps Johnson should have followed the advice of his teacher, Mies van der Rohe: "It's better to build a good building than an original one." The first floor is well worth ducking into to soak in the brute grandeur. It now houses a music store and a spate of interactive exhibits on record production and video-game production (ceremoniously named the *Sony Wonder Technology Lab*). There is also the requisite coffee-bar and deli abutting a rather sombre public seating area.

The **IBM Building** next door at 590 Madison has a far more user-friendly plaza. Tinkling music, plants, the ubiquitous coffee bar and comfortable seating area make for a far less ponderous experience. Across 57th Street, as the first of Madison's boutiques appear, the **Fuller Building** is worth catching – black and white Art Deco, with a fine entrance and tiled floor. Cut east down 57th Street to find the **Four Seasons Hotel**, notable for its I.M. Pei-designed foyer and lobby, ostentatious in its sweeping marble.

Park Avenue

"Where wealth is so swollen that it almost bursts," wrote Collinson Owen of **Park Avenue** in 1929, and things aren't much changed: corporate headquarters jostle for prominence in a triumphal procession to capitalism, pushed apart by Park's broad avenue that once carried railtracks. Whatever your feelings, it's one of the city's most awesome sights. Looking south, everything progresses to the high altar of the **New York Central Building** (now rechristened the Helmsley Building), a delicate, energetic construction with a lewdly excessive Rococo lobby. In its day it formed a skilled punctuation mark to the avenue, but had its thunder stolen in 1963 by the **Met Life Building** (formerly the Pan Am Building) that looms behind. Bauhaus guru Walter Gropius had a hand in designing this, and the critical consen-

Fifth Avenue
and East
Midtown:
42nd Street
to Central
Park

sus is that he should have done better. As the headquarters of the now-defunct international airline, the building's profile meant to suggest an aircraft wing, and the blue-gray mass certainly adds drama to the cityscape; though whatever success the Met Life scores, it robs Park Avenue of the views south it deserves and needs, sealing 44th Street and drawing much of the vigor from the buildings all around. Another black mark was the building's rooftop helipad, closed in the 1970s after a helicopter undercarriage collapsed shortly after landing, causing a rotor to sheer off and kill four passengers who had just got off, as well as injuring several people on the ground.

Despite Park Avenue's power, an individual look at most of the skyscrapers reveals the familiar glass box, and the first few buildings to stand out do so exactly because that's what they're not. Wherever you placed the solid mass of the **Waldorf Astoria Hotel** (between 49th and 50th) it would hold its own, a resplendent statement of Art Deco elegance. Duck inside to stroll through a block of vintage Deco grandeur, sweeping marble and hushed plushness. If you're tempted, it's a smidgen cheaper than the comparable competition, with double rooms between $200 and $300. Crouching behind, **St Bartholomew's Church** is a low-slung Byzantine hybrid that by contrast adds immeasurably to the street, giving the lumbering skyscrapers a much-needed sense of scale. That hasn't stopped the church fathers from wanting to sell the valuable air rights to real estate developers; so far landmark preservationists have prevented them from wrecking one of the few remaining bits of individuality in this part of the city. The spiky-topped **General Electric Building** behind seems like a wild extension of the church, its slender shaft rising to a meshed crown of abstract sparks and lightning strokes that symbolizes the radio waves used by its original occupier, RCA. The lobby (entrance at 570 Lexington) is yet another Deco delight.

Among all this it's difficult at first to see the originality of the **Seagram Building** between 52nd and 53rd streets. Designed by Mies van der Rohe with Philip Johnson, and built in 1958, this was the seminal curtain-wall skyscraper, the floors supported internally rather than by the building's walls, allowing a skin of smoky glass and whiskey-bronze metal (*Seagram* is a distiller), now weathered to a dull black. In keeping with the era's vision, every interior detail down to the fixtures and lettering on the mailboxes was specially designed. It was the supreme example of Modernist reason, deceptively simple and cleverly detailed, and its opening caused a wave of approval. The plaza, an open forecourt designed to set the building apart from its neighbors and display it to advantage, was such a success as a public space that the city revised the zoning laws to encourage other high-rise builders to supply plazas. The result was the windswept anti-people places now found all over down- and midtown Manhattan, and a lot of pallid Mies copies, boxes that alienated many people from "faceless" modern architecture.

Across Park Avenue McKim, Mead and White's **Racquet and Squash Club** seems like a Classical continuation of the Seagram Plaza. More interesting is the **Lever House** across the avenue between 53rd and 54th, the building that set the Modernist ball rolling on Park Avenue in 1952. Then, the two right-angled slabs that form a steel and glass bookend seemed revolutionary compared to the traditional buildings that surrounded it. Nowadays it's overlooked and not a little dingy.

Lexington Avenue and east

Lexington Avenue is always active, especially around the mid-40s, where commuters swarm around Grand Central and a well-placed **post office** on the corner of 50th Street. Just as the Chrysler Building dominates these lower stretches, the chisel-topped **Citicorp Center** (between 53rd and 54th streets) has taken the north end as its domain. Finished in 1979, the graph-paper design sheathed in aluminum is architecture mathematics, and the building is now one of New York's most conspicuous landmarks. A story goes that a student of the building's engineer was playing with some of the equations of the just-finished tower's design when he discovered a flaw which placed it, as built, in danger from very strong winds. Though the force of wind required to topple the building was an unlikely occurrence, a secretive mission to reinforce the structure was undertaken. Before the project was completed, the drama of a hurricane warning was played out with not a few architects, engineers and lawyers having a (thankfully unwarranted) sleepless night.

The slanted roof was designed to house solar panels and provide power, but the idea was ahead of the technology and Citicorp had to content itself with adopting the distinctive top as a corporate logo. The atrium of stores known as "The Market" is pleasant enough, with some food options (try a gooey *Cinnabon* pastry), though many of its spaces are now vacant.

Hiding under the Center's skirts is **St Peter's**, a tiny church built to replace one originally demolished to make way for the Citicorp. Part of the deal was that the church had to stand out from the Center – which explains the granite material. Thoroughly modern inside, it's worth peering in for sculptor Louise Nevelson's Erol Beaker Chapel, venue for Wednesday lunchtime jazz concerts (and evening concerts as well).

The Citicorp provided a spur for the development of Third Avenue, though things really took off when the old elevated railway that ran here was dismantled in 1955. Until then Third had been a strip of earthy bars and rundown tenements, in effect a border to the more salubrious Midtown district. After the Citicorp gave it an "official" stamp of approval, office buildings sprouted, revitalizing the flagging fortunes of midtown Manhattan in the late 1970s. The best section is between 44th and 50th streets – look out for the sheer marble mon-

Fifth Avenue
and East
Midtown:
42nd Street
to Central
Park

ument of the **Wang Building** between 48th and 49th, whose cross-patterns reveal the structure within.

All this office space hasn't totally removed interest from the street (there are a few good bars here, notably *P.J. Clarke's* at 55th, a New York institution – see Chapter 18, *Drinking*), but most life, especially at night-time, seems to have shifted across to **Second Avenue** – on the whole lower, quieter, more residential and with any number of singles/Irish bars to crawl between. The area from Third to the East River in the upper 40s is known as **Turtle Bay**, and there's a scattering of brownstones alongside chirpier shops and industry that disappear as you head north. Of course the UN Headquarters Building (see p.135) has had a knock-on effect, producing buildings like **1 UN Plaza** at 44th and First, a futuristic chess piece of a hotel that takes its design hints from the UN Building itself. Inside, its marbled, chrome lobby is about as uninviting as any other modern American luxury hotel. Should this be your cup of tea, a double room will set you back a few hundred dollars; if not, just pray that all New York hotels don't end up like this.

First Avenue has a certain raggy looseness that's a relief after the concrete claustrophobia of Midtown, and **Beekman Place** (49th to 51st streets between First Avenue and the river) is quieter still, a beguiling enclave of garbled styles. Similar, though not quite as intimate, is **Sutton Place**, a long stretch running from 53rd to 59th between First and the river. Originally built for the lordly Morgans and Vanderbilts in 1875, Sutton increases in elegance as you move north and, for today's *crème de la crème*, **Riverview Terrace** (off 58th St) is a (very) private enclave of five brownstones. The Secretary-General of the UN has a place here and the locals are choosy who they let in: late, disgraced ex-President Richard Nixon was refused on the grounds he would be a security risk.

West Midtown: the West 40s and 50s

The area **west of Fifth Avenue** in midtown Manhattan takes Times Square as its center, an exploded version of the east-side's more tight-lipped monuments to capitalism. Though it can't claim to compete with the avenues to the east, the area around this stretch of "naughty, bawdy 42nd Street" is still well worth exploring. Most of the pornography and crime are gone, replaced by products of Disney's imagination; for seediness, keep heading west to Eighth Avenue and beyond. There aren't many tourist attractions in this direction, which may be reason enough to go, though all the way over on the West Side Highway sits the massive *Intrepid Sea, Air and Space Museum* (for an account of which see chapter 15, *Museums and Galleries*).

Around Bryant Park

Forming the backyard of the New York Public Library on 42nd Street, **Bryant Park** is, like Greeley Square to its south, named after a newspaper editor – **William Cullen Bryant** of the erstwhile *New York Post*, also famed as a poet and instigator of Central Park. The park has a rich history – it was the site of the first American World's Fair in 1853, with a Crystal Palace, modeled on the famed London Crystal Palace, on its grounds – and it benefited from a civic cleanup a few years back, regaining some of its former glory. It's an attractive green space, and somewhat of a hotspot, too: there's a rather aggressive singles' scene at the outdoor *Bryant Park Cafe* well into the night, and free outdoor movies, shown Monday evenings during the summer, pack in the crowds.

From here you can't miss the **Grace Building** which swoops down on 42nd Street, breaking the rules by stepping out of line with its neighbors, though with a showiness that rings rather hollow – and which, in any case, is less well finished than its twin, the Solow Building, on West 57th Street. Much more approachable is the **American Radiator Building** (now the American Standard Building) on West 40th, its black Gothic tower topped with honey-colored terracotta that lights up to resemble a glowing coal – appropriate enough for the headquarters of a heating company.

Times Square

West from Bryant Park, 42nd Street meets Broadway at **Times Square**, the center of the theater district, where the pulsating **neon** suggests a heart for the city itself. Since the major cleanup launched by the city and by business interests like Disney, the ambience here has changed dramatically. Traditionally a melting pot of debauch, depravity and fun, the area became increasingly edgy, a place where out-of-towners supplied easy pickings for petty criminals, drug dealers and prostitutes (always, seemingly, a companion to theater districts). Most of the peep shows and sex shops have gone, and Times Square is now a largely sanitized universe of consumption. The neon signs seem to multiply at the same rate as coffee-bars, and Disney rules the roost on the stretch of 42nd between Seventh and Eighth, home to the remaining palatial Broadway "houses" and movie palaces.

Like Greeley and Herald squares, Times Square took its name from a newspaper connection when the *New York Times* built offices here in 1904. While the *Herald* and *Tribune* fought each other in ever more vicious circulation battles, the *NYT* took the sober middle ground under the banner "All the news that's fit to print," a policy that enabled the paper to survive and become one of the country's most respected voices. **Times Tower** at the southernmost edge of the square was its headquarters, originally an elegant building

modeled on Giotto's *Campanile* in Florence. In 1928, the famous
zipper sign displaying the news of the world was added; the building
was "skinned" in 1965 to be covered with the lifeless marble slabs
visible today. It's also here where the alcohol-sozzled masses gather
for New Year's Eve, to witness the giant apple dropping at the top of
the Tower. The paper itself has long since crept off around a corner
to 43rd Street, and today most of the printing goes on in New Jersey.

Dotted around here are some of the great **theaters** (see Chapter
20, *The Performing Arts and Film*), though many have been
destroyed (like the Vaudeville palaces that preceded *them*) to make
way for office buildings. The **New Amsterdam** and the **Victory**, both
on 42nd Street between Seventh and Eighth avenues, have been refurbished by Disney to their original splendor, one of the truly welcome
results of the massive changes here. There are others, too, that add
flavor to the scene: the clock-and-globe-topped **Paramount Theater
Building** at 1501 Broadway, between 43rd and 44th streets, is a
favorite, and the **Lyceum**, **Shubert** and **Lyric** each have their original
facades. Among the oldest is the **Belasco** on 44th Street between
Sixth and Seventh avenues, which was also the first of Broadway's
theaters to incorporate machinery into its stagings. The neon, so
much a signature of the square, originally accompanied the building
of the theaters and spawned the term "the Great White Way"; in 1922,
its lights moved G.K. Chesterton to remark, "What a glorious garden
of wonder this would be, to anyone who was lucky enough to be
unable to read." Today, businesses that rent offices here are actually
required to allow signage on their walls – the city's attempt to retain
the square's traditional feel. The displays, of course, have modernized
– note the steaming Cup of Noodles at the southern end – and even
the **Port Authority Bus Terminal** on 42nd and Eighth, a former sink
of depravity, is to be covered with a skin of metal for ad displays.

Duffy Square is the northernmost island in the heart of Times
Square and offers an excellent panoramic view of the square's lights,
mega-hotels, theme-stores and theme-restaurants metastasizing
daily. The nifty orange-canvas-and-frame stand of the **TKTS booth**,
modest in comparison, sells half-price, same-day tickets for
Broadway shows (whose exorbitant prices these days make a visit to
TKTS a near necessity). A lifelike statue of Broadway's doyen
George M. Cohan looks on – though if you've ever seen the film
Yankee Doodle Dandy it's impossible to think of him other than as
a swaggering Jimmy Cagney. Last word on the scene to Henry Miller
from *Tropic of Capricorn*:

> *It's only a stretch of a few blocks from Times Square to Fiftieth Street,*
> *and when one says Broadway that's all that's really meant and it's*
> *really nothing, just a chicken run and a lousy one at that, but even*
> *at seven in the evening when everyone's rushing for a table there's a*
> *sort of electric crackle in the air and your hair stands on end like an*
> *antenna and if you're receptive you not only get every bash and*
> *flicker but you get the statistical itch, the quid pro quo of the inter-*

active, interstitial, ectoplasmic quantum of bodies jostling in space like the stars which compose the Milky Way, only this is the Gay White Way, the top of the world with no roof and not even a crack or a hole under your feet to fall through and say it's a lie. The absolute impersonality of it brings you to a pitch of warm human delirium which makes you run forward like a blind nag and wag your delirious ears.

West of Times Square: Clinton, aka Hell's Kitchen

To the west of Times Square lies what's famously known as Hell's Kitchen, an area centered on the engaging slash of restaurants, bars and ethnic delis of **Ninth Avenue**. Extending down to the Garment District and up to the low 50s, this was once one of New York's most violent and lurid neighborhoods. Named after a tenement at 54th Street and Tenth Avenue (but a nineteenth-century term for *any* dismal situation), Hell's Kitchen was originally an area of soap and glue factories, slaughterhouses and the like, with sections named "Misery Lane" and "Poverty Row." Irish immigrants were the first inhabitants, soon joined by Greeks, Latinos, Italians and blacks – amidst the overcrowding, tensions rapidly developed between (and within) ethnic groups. Gangs roamed the streets, and though their rule ended in 1910 after a major police counter-offensive, the area remained dangerous until fairly recently (and in truth, it still pays to be wary). Rechristened **Clinton** in 1959 to hide its notorious past, the name hasn't really stuck, though the district has attracted a number of new tenants, mostly musicians and Broadway types.

Head to it from Eighth Avenue (which now houses the porn businesses expelled from the square) down 46th Street – the so-called **Restaurant Row** that is the area's preferred haunt for pre- and post-theater dining. Here you can begin to detect a more pastoral feel, which only increases on many of the side streets around Ninth and Tenth avenues. Also check out the unstuffy **St Clements Episcopal Church** at 423 West 46th: it doubles as a community theater and in its foyer is a picture of Elvis Presley and Jesus, with the caption, "There seems to be a little confusion as to which one of them actually rose from the dead."

Continuing west, there's not too much to see. Ragged Eleventh Avenue is home to the automobile warehouses that used to spice up Times Square's Automobile Row, and past that is the sleazy West Side Highway. These streets are undistinguished, only highlighted by two well-preserved, old-timey restaurants on Eleventh, the *Landmark Tavern* (46th St) and the *Market Diner* (44th St).

North of Times Square

Heading north from Times Square, the **West 50s** between Sixth and Eighth avenues are emphatically tourist territory. Edged by Central Park in the north and the Theater District to the south, and with Fifth Avenue and Rockefeller Center in easy striking distance, the area has been invaded by overpriced restaurants and cheapo souvenir stores: should you want to stock up on "I Love New York" underwear, this could be the place.

One sight worth searching out is the **Equitable Center** at 757 Seventh Avenue. The building itself is dapper if not a little self-important, with Roy Lichtenstein's 68-foot *Mural with Blue Brush Stroke* poking you in the eye as you enter: best of all, look out for Thomas Hart Benton's *America Today* murals (in the left-hand corridor), which dynamically and magnificently portray ordinary American life in the days before the Depression.

Sixth Avenue

Sixth Avenue is properly named **Avenue of the Americas**, though no New Yorker ever calls it this: guidebooks and maps labor the convention, but the only manifestation of the tag are lamppost flags of Central and South American countries which serve as useful landmarks. If nothing else Sixth's distinction is its width, a result of the elevated railway that once ran along here, now replaced by the Sixth Avenue subway. In its day the Sixth Avenue "El" marked the border between respectability to the east and dodgier areas to the west, and in a way it's still a dividing line separating the glamorous strips of Fifth, Madison and Park avenues from the brasher western districts.

Diamond Row

One of the best things about New York City is the small hidden pockets abruptly discovered when you least expect them. West 47th Street between Fifth and Sixth is a perfect example: this is **Diamond Row**, a short strip of shops chock-full with wildly expensive stones and jewelry, managed by ultra-Orthodox Hasidic Jews who seem only to exist in the confines of the street. Maybe they are what gives the street its workaday feel – Diamond Row seems more like the Garment District than Fifth Avenue, and the conversations you overhear on the street or in the nearby delicatessens are memorably Jewish. The Hasidim are followers of a mystical sect of Judaism – the name means "Pious Ones" – and traditionally wear beards, sidelocks and dark, old-fashioned suits. A large contingent live in Williamsburg and Crown Heights in Brooklyn.

Around the Rockefeller Extension

By the time it reaches midtown Manhattan, Sixth Avenue has become a dazzling showcase of corporate wealth. True, there's little of the ground-floor glitter of Fifth or the razzmatazz of Broadway, but what is here, and in a way what defines the stretch from 47th to 51st streets, is the **Rockefeller Center Extension**. Following the earlier **Time & Life Building** at 50th Street, three near-identical blocks went up in the 1970s, and if they don't have the romance of their predecessor they at least possess some of its monumentality. Backing on to Rockefeller Center proper, by day and especially by night, the repeated statement of each block comes over with some power, giving the wide path of Sixth Avenue much of its visual excitement. At street level things can be just as interesting: the broad sidewalks allow peddlers of food and handbills, street musicians, mimics and actors to do their thing.

Across the avenue at 49th Street **Radio City Music Hall** has far greater rewards (for a description, see p.138). Keep an eye open too for the **CBS Building** on the corner of 52nd Street: dark and inscrutable, this has been compared to the monolith from the film *2001* and, like it or not, it certainly forces a mysterious presence on this segment of Sixth Avenue.

West of Fifth Avenue, the rack of streets below Central Park is home to some of the most opulent hotels, apartments and restaurants in America, especially on Central Park South. Also impressive is 57th Street, which has recently overtaken SoHo as the center for upmarket art sales; galleries here are noticeably snootier than their downtown relations, often requiring an appointment for viewing. A couple that usually don't are the **Marlborough Gallery** (2nd floor, 40 W 57th), specializing in famous names both American and European, and the **Kennedy Gallery** (same building, 5th floor), which deals in nineteenth- and twentieth-century American painting.

Carnegie Hall and the Russian Tea Room

Closer to Seventh Avenue than Sixth, and almost on Central Park, **Carnegie Hall**, an overblown and fussy warehouse-like venue for opera and concerts at 154 West 57th Street, is the thing to see (Tchaikovsky conducted the program on opening night and Mahler, Rachmaninov, Toscanini, Frank Sinatra and Judy Garland played here). The superb acoustics ensure full houses most of the year. If you don't want, or can't afford, to attend a performance, sneak in through the stage door on 56th Street for a look – no one minds as long as there's not a rehearsal in progress. Alternatively, catch one of the tours (Mon, Tues, Thurs & Fri, except Summer, 11.30am, 2pm & 3pm; $6, $5 students; ☎903-9790 for more details).

A few doors down at no. 150, the **Russian Tea Room** (see Chapter 17, "Eating") was one of those places to see and be seen at, ever popular with "in" names from the entertainment business. It's been all but demolished, the action of a new owner who promises to restore it to its original glories, and is scheduled to reopen in Fall 1998.

Chapter 10

Central Park

" **A** ll radiant in the magic atmosphere of art and taste." So raved *Harper's* magazine on the opening of **Central Park** in 1876, and though it's hard to be quite so jubilant about the place today, few New Yorkers could imagine life without it. It shows in how much locals use the park: midtown suits walk up to grab hot dogs by the Maine Monument; Latino families descend from El Barrio to picnic by the waters of Harlem Meer; and it's an obvious prime target for every jogger, rollerblader, weekend athlete and nature lover in the city. Over the years the park has seen some hard times, from official neglect to some truly horrible criminal episodes; but New Yorkers still treasure it more than any other city institution (with the possible exception of rent stabilization). Certainly life in New York would be a lot poorer without it.

Some history

Central Park came close to never happening at all. It was the poet and newspaper editor, **William Cullen Bryant**, who had the idea for an open public space back in 1844. He spent seven years trying to persuade City Hall to carry it out, while developers leaned heavily on the authorities not to give up any valuable land. But eventually the city agreed, and an 840-acre space north of the city limits was set aside, a desolate swampy area then occupied by a shantytown of squatters. The two architects commissioned to design the landscape, **Frederick Olmsted** and **Calvert Vaux**, planned to create a rural paradise, "Greensward" as they called it, a complete illusion of the countryside smack in the heart of Manhattan. Greensward was to bring nature to an increasingly congested city thought to be badly in need of its edifying virtues.

The sparseness of the terrain provided Olmsted and Vaux with the perfect opportunity to design the park according to the precepts of English landscape gardening. They designed elegant bridges, each unique, and planned a revolutionary system of sunken transverse roads to segregate different kinds of traffic. Finally, after the nearly twenty years required for its construction, Central Park was unveiled in 1876. It opened with such publicity that Olmsted and Vaux were soon in demand as park architects all over the States. Locally they went on to design the Riverside and Morningside parks in Manhattan, and Prospect Park in Brooklyn. Working alone, Olmsted laid out the campuses of Berkeley and Stanford in California, and had a major hand in that most televised of American artificial landscapes – Capitol Hill in Washington, DC; all admirable, though ultimately paler efforts than the mid-Manhattan masterpiece.

At its opening, Central Park was declared a "people's park" – though most of the impoverished masses it was allegedly built to serve had neither the time nor the carfare to come up from their downtown slums to 59th Street and enjoy it. But as New York grew and workers' leisure time increased, people began flooding in, and the park began to live up to its mission, sometimes in ways that might have scandalized its original builders.

Today, in spite of the advent of motorized traffic, the sense of disorderly nature Olmsted and Vaux intended largely survives, with cars and buses cutting through the park in the sheltered canyons originally meant for horse-drawn carriages. The skyline, of course, has changed, and buildings thrust their way into view, sometimes detracting from the park's original pastoral intention. Robert Moses's grand improvement schemes have also had a deleterious effect, turning large stretches of landscaped open space into asphalted playground. But over the years public opinion has kept damage to a minimum; even the hubristic Moses was finally brought to bay by outraged citizens – when in 1956 the Master Builder tried to tear down a park playground to build a parking lot for *Tavern on the Green*, mothers and children stood in the way of the bulldozers, and the city sheepishly backed off. Today a nonprofit group called the Central Park Conservancy looks out for the park, and the government has earmarked large funds to erase bits of rot, increase the park's policing, and renovate large areas (as with the rehabilitation of the Great Lawn). It may never be as pristine as people would like, but in view of its constant (over)use, it couldn't be much better.

Getting around the park

Central Park is so enormous that it's almost impossible to miss and nearly as impossible to navigate once you've arrived. Nevertheless, the intricate **footpaths** that meander through the park are its greatest success. After all, the point here is to lose yourself . . . or at least to *feel* like you can. Legend has it that you can use the New York City skyline as your guiding compass, but even dyed-in-the-wool New Yorkers aren't completely comfortable with this method.

That said, you can never stray too far from the footpaths, landmarks, or the more route-savvy regulars that blanket the park. To **figure out exactly** where you are, find the nearest **lamppost**: the first

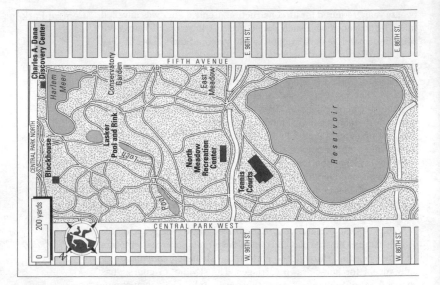

*For more
advice on how
to keep safe,
see pp.39–40.*

two figures signify the number of the nearest street. As for trouble, should you run into anything serious it's best to give up all you've got and make a run for it. You should be all right during the day, though always be careful. After dark, it's more tense, so if you want to look at the buildings of Central Park West lit up, à la Woody Allen's film, *Manhattan*, the best option you have is to fork out for a **buggy**.

Bicycle rental and buggy rides

*For more on
bicycle rental,
see p.388.*

The best way to see the park during the day is to **rent a bicycle** from either the Loeb Boathouse (see p.155) or *Metro Bicycles* (Lexington at 88th St – see p.20). Bikes from the Boathouse start at $8 an hour, from *Metro* at $6 an hour, both much better deals than the famed "romantic" buggy rides (about $40 for a 20min trot; ☎ 246-0520 for more information). Bear in mind that there has been long-standing vocal opposition to the buggy practice being allowed at all, with claims that the incompetence and greed of the buggy drivers lead to great cruelty to the horses used. Care has been improved: according to a law enacted in 1994, the horses must get fifteen-minute rest breaks every two hours, and cannot work more than nine hours a day; they're also not supposed to work at all when the temperature goes above 90°F. Buggy drivers can get their licenses suspended or revoked for disobedience.

Exploring the park

The **Reservoir** divides Central Park neatly in two. The larger and more familiar **southern part** holds most of the attractions (and peo-

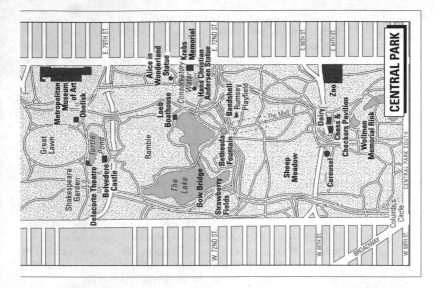

ple), but the **northern part** is well worth a visit for its dramatically different ambience and funkier recreants. Organized walking tours are available, but almost any stroll (formal or informal) will invariably lead to something interesting. To visit Central Park is to begin to understand and catch a glimpse of New York City and its residents – not to mention the fact that the park offers some of the city's most enjoyable and most reasonably priced, if not altogether free, activities.

The southern park

Entering at the most southeasterly point of the park, **Grand Army Plaza**, at Fifth Avenue and East 59th Street, to your left lies the **Pond** and a little further on the **Wollman Memorial Rink** (63rd St at midpark; ☎396-1010). Sit or stand above the rink to watch skaters and contemplate the view of Central Park South's skyline emerging above the trees. Or **rent skates** of your own – $3 for rollerskates and $6 (with credit-card deposit) for rollerblades, the most versatile mode of park transportation if you know how to use them.

To the east of the rink at East 64th Street and Fifth Avenue is the small **Central Park Zoo** (Mon–Fri 10am–5pm, Sat, Sun & holidays 10.30am–5.30pm; $2.50 adults, 50¢ children aged 3–12; ☎439-6500), whose collection is based on three climatic regions – the Tropic Zone, the Temperate Territory and the Polar Circle. It has always tried to keep caging to a minimum and the animals as close to the viewer as possible: the puffins and penguins, for example, swim around at eye-level in plexiglass pools. This complex also boasts a

See also p.384 for information on how to go ice-skating in Central Park.

recently reopened **Children's Petting Zoo**. Still, for a more inclusive look at wildlife, you're better off heading to the **Bronx Zoo** (p.223).

Unless you're attracted to a game of chess at the **Chess and Checkers Pavilion** (playing pieces are available at the Visitors' Center), the next point to head for is the **Dairy** (65th St at mid-park), a kind of dolly-Gothic ranch building originally intended to provide milk for nursing mothers. It now houses the Park's **Visitors' Center** (Tues–Sun 11am–5pm; ☎794-6564), a worthwhile rest stop that distributes free leaflets and maps (and sells better ones), sells books on the history and development of the park, and puts on sporadic exhibitions.

Just west of the Dairy, you will see the octagonal brick building that houses the **Carousel**. Built in 1903 and moved to the park from Coney Island in 1951, this is one of the park's little gems (64th St at mid-park; open Mon–Fri 10.30am–5pm, Sat & Sun 10.30am–6pm, weather permitting; ☎879-0244). One of fewer than 150 left in the country (one of the others is at Coney Island), the Carousel offers a ride on still-magical hand-carved jumping horses accompanied by the music of a military band organ for only 90¢ a pop. (You can also book it for birthday parties; call ☎396-1010, ext. 13).

If you continue straight ahead and north past the Dairy and through the **Mall**, you will witness every manner of street performer. A recent landmark ruling allows minstrels to electronically amplify their music outside of the park's "quiet zones," which the Mall certainly is not. Flanked by statues of an ecstatic-looking Robert Burns and a pensive Sir Walter Scott, the Mall is the park's most formal stretch. To the west lies the **Sheep Meadow** (66th–69th streets, west side), fifteen acres of commons where sheep grazed until 1934; today the area is usually crowded with picnic blankets, sunbathers and frisbee players. Two lawn-bowling and croquet grass courts are maintained on a hill near the Meadow's northwest corner; to the southwest are volleyball courts, one with its own sandpit. (Call ☎360-8133 for information on obtaining a permit.) Near the volleyball courts, rollerbladers frolic to hip-hop and dance music. Further to the west is the once-exclusive, still-expensive, but now-tacky landmark restaurant and finishing point of the annual New York City Marathon, **Tavern on the Green**. If you're not in the mood for pretension, grab a hot dog instead at the **Ballplayers' House** just to the east.

At the northernmost point of the Mall lie the **Bandshell**, the **Bethesda Terrace and Fountain** (72nd St at mid-park), and the **Rumsey Playfield**, site of the free *Summerstage* performance series. The crowning centerpiece of the Bethesda Fountain is the nineteenth-century **Angel of the Waters** sculpture; its earnest puritanical angels (Purity, Health, Peace and Temperance) continue to watch disappointedly over their wicked city. (Theater fans may remember that the last scene of the Pulitzer Prize-winning play *Angels in America* is set at this fountain.) Bethesda Terrace, the only formal element of the original Greensward Plan, overlooks the lake; under it is an **Arcade** that is being fully restored. You can go for a Venetian gondola ride or rent a rowboat from the **Loeb Boathouse** on the lake's eastern bank. (March–Nov Mon–Fri 10am–5pm, Sat & Sun 10am–6pm, weather permitting. Rowboats are $10 for the first hour, $2.50 per hour afterward, with a refundable deposit; gondola rides are given 5–10pm for $30 per 30min per group and require reservations; ☎517-2233 for more information.)

Across the water, by the elegant cast-iron-and-wood **Bow Bridge**, delve into the unruly woods of **The Ramble**, by far the best place in the park for a stroll – and anonymous sex. AIDS and some violent incidents have toned things down a bit, but the business is still very much alive. To your left, **Cherry Hill Fountain** provided a turnaround point for carriages and has deliberately excellent views of the lake, which sprawls a gnarled finger from here across the heart of Central Park. West of here is **Strawberry Fields** (72nd St and Central Park West), a relatively peaceful though unimpressive region of the park dedicated to the memory of John Lennon, who in 1980 was murdered in front of the **Dakota Building**, his home, across the street on Central Park West. Strawberry Fields is invariably crowded with those here to remember Lennon and other doomed cultural icons. Just east of the West 72nd Street entrance to the park is an Italian mosaic spelling the word "Imagine," a memorial donated by Yoko Ono.

Back to the east of Bethesda Terrace is the **Conservatory Water** (East 72nd St and Fifth Ave), a concrete basin where you can watch model boat races and regattas every Saturday (or participate by renting a craft from the cart in front of the **Krebs Memorial Boathouse**, just east of the water; $10 per hour), or climb on the fanciful *Alice in Wonderland* statue at the northern end. During the summer the New York Public Library sponsors Saturday morning storytelling sessions for children at the Hans Christian Andersen Statue across the way (☎340-0906 for more information). If you continue north you will reach the backyard of the Metropolitan Museum of Art (see Chapter 15, *Museums and Galleries*) to the east and the **Obelisk**, a gift from Egypt dating back to 1450 BC, to the west.

Further north lies the **Great Lawn**, the **Police Precinct** and the **Reservoir**. The Lawn has recently reopened after a two-year reconstruction; and features eight ballfields and a refurbished **Turtle Pond** with a so-called nature blind for better viewing of the amphibious wildlife. What's not new, on the southeast corner, is a massive statue of fourteenth-century Polish king **Wladyslaw Jagiello**, a gift of the Polish government. Southwest of the Lawn is the **Delacorte Theater**, the venue of the annual *Shakespeare in the Park* festival. Just below, the placid **Shakespeare Garden** holds, they say, every species of plant or flower mentioned in the Bard's plays.

East of the garden is **Belvedere Castle**, a mock medieval citadel first erected atop **Vista Rock** in 1869 as a lookout, but now the home

Central Park

Seasonal events and activities

• *SummerStage* and *Shakespeare in the Park* are two of the most popular urban summertime programs. Both activities are free and help to take the sting out of New York's infamous hazy, hot and humid summers. In 1986 *SummerStage* presented its inaugural Central Park concert with Sun Ra to an audience of fifty people, but by the time he returned, with Sonic Youth, six years later, the audience had grown to ten thousand. Known for bringing some of the world's most sought-after musicians, *SummerStage*'s popularity has continued to grow steadily ever since. A concert here is an invariably crowded, sticky, but somehow bonding experience; besides which, it's free. Call the *SummerStage* hotline (☎360-2777) for more information.

Tickets for *Shakespeare in the Park* are distributed at the Delacorte and Public theaters daily at 1pm, but you'll probably have to get in line well before. Two plays are performed each summer; Shakespeare is the Festival's meat, but having just completed the whole cycle of plays (*Shakespeare in the Park* has been extant for more than twenty years), the Festival is now trying other works.

• *New York Philharmonic in the Park* (☎875–5709) and *Metropolitan Opera in the Park* (☎362–6000) hold evenings of classical music in the summer.

• *Claremont Riding Academy*, 175 West 89th St ☎724-5100. Open Mon–Fri, 6.30am–10pm; Sat & Sun 8am–5pm. **Horseback riding lessons** and rentals for riders experienced in the English saddle. $38 for 30min lesson, $33 for a ride on Central Park's bridlepaths.

• *Harlem Meer Festival*, 110th St between Fifth and Lenox aves (☎860-1370). Fairly intimate and enjoyable performances of jazz, salsa and funk music outside the Dana Center on Sundays throughout the summer.

• *Moonlight Dancing at Wollman Rink*, 63rd St at mid-park, ☎396-1010. An orchestra plays swing and ballroom music as you glide under the stars; Thurs–Sun, July–Oct. $12 per person, $20 per couple.

General information

• Daily Park Information ☎360-3444.

• Founded in 1980, the Central Park Conservancy (☎315-0385) is a non-profit organization dedicated to preserving and managing the park.

• Manhattan Urban Park Rangers ☎427-4040 (activities information); ☎860-1351 (emergencies). The rangers are there to help; they lead walking tours, give directions and provide first aid in emergencies.

• Restrooms are available at the North Meadow Recreation Center, The Conservatory Garde, Delacorte Theater and Hecksher House.

• Traffic: the East and West drives run just inside the periphery of the park and are closed to motor traffic (and open to joggers, bikers and skaters) on weekdays, 10am–3pm and 7–10pm; weekends, 7pm Friday to 6am Monday; and holidays, 7pm the night before until 6am the day after.

of the Urban Park Rangers and a **Visitors' Center** (Wed–Mon 11am–5pm; ☎772-0210). The highest point in the park, and as such a splendid viewpoint, the Castle also houses the New York Meteorological Observatory's weather center, responsible for providing the daily official Central Park temperature readings, and makes a lovely background prop for the Delacorte's Shakespeare performances. The **Swedish Marionette Theater** (mid-park at 79th St) at the base of Vista Rock holds puppet shows, like *The True Story of Rumpelstilskin*, for children (☎988-9093 for reservations and information).

The northern park

There are fewer attractions, but more open space, above the Great Lawn. Much of it is taken up by the **Reservoir** (around which disciplined New Yorkers faithfully jog). To the east, past a large expanse of tennis courts, ballfields, and open spaces, is the **Conservatory Garden** between East 103rd and 106th streets, a pleasing six-acre display of terraced shrubs, fanciful fountains, and shaded benches. Near the top of the park is the **Charles A. Dana Discovery Center** (110th St, between Fifth and Lenox aves; Tues–Sat 11am–5pm, 4pm in winter; ☎860-1370), an environmental education center and good starting point for exploring the park's scenic northern woodlands; a good path to follow goes along the **Harlem Meer** as it dribbles down through the **Loch** to the **Pool**. The Discovery Center features multicultural exhibits and performances, amid crowds of locals fishing in the Meer, an eleven-acre restored lake stocked with more than 50,000 fish. (The Discovery Center provides bamboo poles and bait free of charge, though you'll have to release your catch of the day.) In summer there are jazz and Latin music performances here as well.

Another space of note is the **Robert Bendleim Playground** for disabled children, at 100th Street near Fifth Avenue. Here physically challenged youngsters play in "accessible" sandboxes or work out their upper bodies on balance beams, all very much in keeping with the inclusive nature of Central Park.

Chapter 11

The Upper West Side and Morningside Heights

T hough dominated by some dazzling turn-of-the-century apartment buildings and the city's most prestigious performance
space, the **Upper West Side** has always had a more unbut-
toned vibe than its counterpart across the park. Rather than a stage
for old wealth – mostly because the area was late to develop – it has
seen its share of struggling actors, writers, opera singers and the like
move into its spaces over the years, somewhat tempered in recent
years by waves of gentrification. This isn't to say it lacks glamour:
there is plenty of money in evidence on the southern fringe, especially along stretches of Central Park West and Riverside Drive and at
Lincoln Center, New York's palace of culture, but this is considerably
less true as you move north. At its top end, marked at the edge by the
monolithic Cathedral of St John the Divine, is **Morningside Heights**,
an area that is the last gasp of Manhattan's wealth before Harlem.

The Upper West Side

North of 59th Street, paralleling the spread of Central Park, midtown
Manhattan's tawdry West Side becomes decidedly less commercial,
less showy and, after the Lincoln Center, fades into a residential area
and urban strip mall of sorts. The Upper West Side is one of the city's
most desirable addresses, and tends to attract what you might call
New York's cultural elite and new-money types – musicians, journalists, curators and the like – though there is also a small but jarringly
visible homeless presence.

First some **orientation**. The Upper West Side is bordered by
Central Park to the east, the Hudson River to the west, Columbus
Circle at 59th Street to the south, and 110th Street (the northernmost point of Central Park and beginning of Morningside Heights) to
the north. The main artery is Broadway and, generally speaking, the
further you stray east or west, the wealthier things become, until you

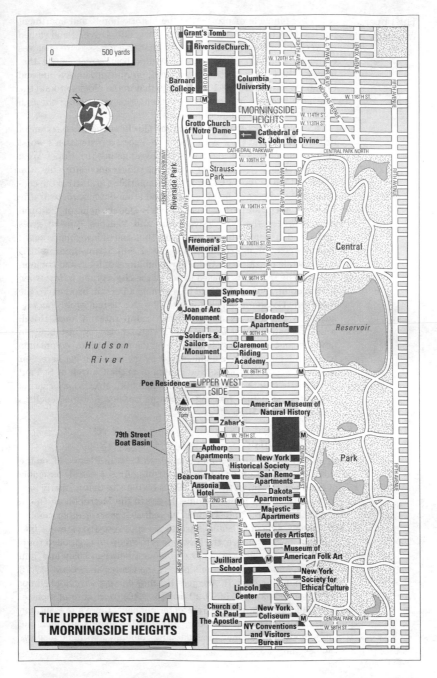

THE UPPER WEST SIDE AND
MORNINGSIDE HEIGHTS

reach the pinnacle of prosperity, the historic hotels and apartment houses of Central Park West and Riverside Drive. Sandwiched between these most prestigious of Manhattan addresses are enclaves of public housing, SRO hotels and downbeat street hustle that increase the further north you go, until, on Amsterdam Avenue and Columbus Avenue in the 100s (streets that in the blocks around the 70s have become irreparably yuppified), you're walking through solidly poor Latino neighborhoods.

To explore, best start at **Columbus Circle** at the intersection of Broadway, Central Park West and 59th Street: a pedestrian's worst nightmare but a good place to start investigating the Upper West Side nonetheless. Christopher Columbus stands uncomfortably atop a lone column (a recent target for anti-Imperialist graffiti) in the center of this odd cast of buildings grouped around a hazardous traffic circle. At the southern end is the city's **Department of Cultural Affairs**, where the **NY Conventions and Visitors Bureau** gives advice and dispenses free leaflets, city, bus and subway maps seven days a week (Mon–Fri 9am–6pm, Sat & Sun 10am–3pm; ☎397-8222), while upstairs is a venue for exhibitions of local and community art. The Bureau is housed in one of the city's grand *folies*; when it went up in 1965, it was said to resemble a Persian brothel. To the west is the **Coliseum**, an exhibition hall with a dismal white concrete facade. A block up is the glittering **Trump International Hotel**, which recently added to the area's visual noise by installing an unwieldy and inelegant golden globe on the facing plaza; complaints from residents may have eliminated it by the time you get here. For relief, go west a few blocks and contemplate the **Church of St Paul the Apostle** (Ninth Ave between 59th and 60th streets), a beautiful Old Gothic structure housing Byzantine basilica features, such as Stanford White's High Altar.

Lincoln Center

Broadway sheers north from the circle to **Lincoln Plaza** and, on the left, the **Lincoln Center for the Performing Arts**, a marble assembly of buildings put up in the early 1960s on the site that formerly held some of the city's poorest slums. Home to the Metropolitan Opera and the New York Philharmonic, as well as a host of other smaller companies, Lincoln Center is worth seeing even if you're not into catching a performance; the best way is to go on an **organized tour**. These leave roughly every hour on the hour between 10am and 5pm each day, and take in the main part of the Center at a cost of $7.75 for an hour-long tour. Be warned that they can get very booked up; best phone ahead (☎769-7020 or 875-5350) to be sure of a place. You could also stop by for free entertainment: there's the Autumn Crafts Fair in early September, folk and jazz bands at lunchtime throughout the summer, and dazzling fountain and light displays each evening.

The New York State Theater and Avery Fisher Hall

The complex itself pulls you in by way of its neat central plaza and fountain, which focuses on the grand classical forms of the Opera House. Of the principal halls, Philip Johnson's **New York State Theater** on the left (home of the New York City Ballet, the New York City Opera and the famed annual performance of *The Nutcracker Suite*) is the most imposing, at least inside. Its foyer is serried with balconies embellished by delicately worked bronze grilles and a ceiling finished in gold leaf.

Johnson also had a hand in the **Avery Fisher Hall** opposite; he was called in to refashion the interior after its acoustics were found to be below par. The seating space here, though, has none of the magnificence of his glittery horseshoe-shaped auditorium across the way, and the most exciting thing about Avery Fisher Hall is its foyer, dominated by a huge hanging sculpture by Richard Lippold, whose distinctive style you may recognize from an atrium or two downtown.

The Metropolitan Opera House

The **Metropolitan Opera House** (aka "the Met") is by contrast overdone, its staircases designed for the gliding evening wear of the city's elite. Behind each of the high windows hang **murals** by Marc Chagall. The artist wanted stained glass, but it was felt these wouldn't last long in an area still less than reverential toward the arts, so paintings were hung behind square-paned glass to give a similar effect. These days they're covered for part of the day to protect them from the morning sun; the rest of the time they're best viewed from the plaza outside.

The mural on the left, *Le Triomphe de la Musique*, is cast with a variety of well-known performers, landmarks snipped from the New York skyline and a portrait of Sir Rudolph Bing, the man who ran the Met for more than three decades – here garbed as a gypsy. The other mural, *Les Sources de la Musique*, is reminiscent of Chagall's renowned Met production of *The Magic Flute*: the god of music strums a lyre while a Tree of Life, Verdi and Wagner all float down the Hudson River.

The opera house, with its elegant interior of African rosewood and red velvety chairs, says opulence pure and simple. The acoustics and the singers make the music here; there is no electronic voice enhancement whatsoever (though the new multilingual titling and translation system is definitely state-of-the-art). As for performances, you'll find full details of what you can listen to and how to do it in Chapter 20, *The Performing Arts and Film*.

The rest of Lincoln Center, and heading north...

Each side of the Met broadens into two further piazzas, one centering on the **Guggenheim Bowl** where you can catch free summer lunchtime concerts, the other faced by the **Vivian Beaumont**, designed by Eero Saarinen in 1965, and the **Mitzi E. Newhouse Theaters**. This latter square is mostly taken up by a pool, around which Manhattan office workers munch their lunch while mid-pond reclines a lazy Henry Moore figure, given counterpoint at the edge by a spidery sculpture by Alexander Calder.

The **New York Public Library for the Performing Arts** (☎870-1630) connects the opera house and the theatre and holds over eight million items. Within this complex is **Alice Tully Hall**, the famed **Juilliard School of Music**, and the **Walter E. Reade Theater**, which features foreign films and retrospectives and, together with the Avery Fisher and Alice Tully halls, hosts the annual New York Film Festival in September. In addition, Lincoln Center hosts a variety of affordable summertime events, including *Mostly Mozart*, the country's first and most popular indoor summer classical music series, and *Midsummer Night Swing*, a summertime dance series that allows you to swing, salsa, hustle and ballroom dance on an outdoor bandstand at the Lincoln Center Plaza Fountain.

Whatever people say about Lincoln Center, there can be little doubt of its impact on an area which before the 1960s was one of the city's most pitiful urban disasters (it was here that the film *West Side Story* was shot in 1960). As well as creating an arts center, the Lincoln scheme was an exercise in urban renewal, a grand plan intended to make this part of the Upper West Side a truly desirable neighborhood – which has succeeded remarkably well, even if in typical New York style it has in effect replaced a poor ghetto with a rich one and dumped the slum dwellers further uptown. Up from Lincoln Plaza roads lead all ways, Broadway curving off north and Ninth Avenue becoming the increasingly sought-after **Columbus Avenue**. Not so long ago this too was run down; now its shops are being upgraded and its restaurants – and there are plenty, especially between the 60s and 80s – battle it out for the upwardly mobile custom of the local residents.

Around Broadway

Across from Lincoln Center is **Dante Park**, a small triangular island with a statue designed in 1921 to commemorate the 600th anniversary of the poet's death, and the **Museum of American Folk Art** (see p.265). Continuing north on Columbus Avenue you will come across the **American Broadcast Company (ABC)** television studios and the Capital Cities/ABC corporate headquarters, an imposing postmodern building that overwhelms some of its less intrusive neighbors (and now features a Disney store, stocked with unattractive ABC logo-identified materials).

Just up the road from Lincoln Center, and smack at the self-avowed forefront of cutting-edge technology, are the imposing **Sony Theaters**, with their huge IMAX 3D screen. This new movie theater makes a nod to the Golden Age of Hollywood in the form of twelve auditoriums that bear the names and design motifs from prestigious movie houses of the past. Not surprisingly, Sony's highly publicized 3D movies so far have been more impressive for their effects than for their plots.

Further up Broadway at West 72nd Street, where several streets meet in a busy, hustly riot of fast-food joints and downgrade bars, is another small island dedicated to an Italian. **Verdi Square** is a good place to take a breather and contemplate the ornate balconies, corner round towers, and cupolas of the **Ansonia Hotel** (2109 Broadway between W 73rd and W 74th streets). Completed in 1904, this dramatic Beaux Arts building is still the artsy grande dame of the Upper West Side. It has welcomed such luminaries as Enrico Caruso, Arturo Toscanini, Lily Pons, Florenz Ziegfeld, Theodore Dreiser, Igor Stravinsky, and even Babe Ruth. **The Beacon Theater** (2124 Broadway, between W 74th and 75th streets; ☎ 496-7070) is nothing particularly special from the outside. But step into the lobby, or better yet the auditorium (a designated landmark) to get the full effect of its extravagant Greco-Deco-Empire interior.

The enormous limestone **Apthorp Apartments** (at 2211 Broadway) occupy an entire block from Broadway to West End and West 78th to West 79th streets. The ornate iron gates of the former carriageway entrance lead into a central courtyard with fountain. Across the street is **Zabar's**, the Upper West Side's principal gourmet shop and area landmark. Here you can find more or less anything connected with food; the ground floor is given over to things edible, the first to cooking implements and kitchenware, a collection which, in the obscurity of some of its items, must be unrivaled anywhere. What kitchen, for example, could do without a duck press? Up at 215 West 84th Street, there's a place marking the one-time address of **Edgar Allen Poe**, now sadly just a faceless condo; if you're a real Poe fan, head over to Riverside Park and sit on the rocky outcropping known as **Mount Tom** at 83rd Street, where Poe was said to have written a few works, such as "To Helene."

If you continue weaving your way through inevitably crowded sidewalks, you will eventually reach the **Symphony Space** (2537 Broadway between W 94th and 95th streets; ☎ 864-5400), one of New York's primary performing arts centers, known for its sophisticated, if slightly quirky, programming. *Symphony Space* regularly sponsors short story readings, classical and world music performances but is perhaps best known for its free, twelve-hour music marathons, like the annual Leonard Bernstein Marathon, and the uninterrupted reading of James Joyce's *Ulysses* every Bloomsday (June 16).

At 107th Street, Broadway and West End Avenue meet at the somber **Strauss Park**, a small vest-pocket space centered on an **Augustus Lukeman statue** of a reclining woman gazing over a water basin. It's a tribute by *Macy's* founder Nathan Strauss to his brother/business part-

ner Isidor and Isidor's wife Ida, both of whom lived nearby, and who
went down with the Titanic in 1912 – legend has it that Ida refused to
leave Isidor for the lifeboats. For better or for worse indeed.

West to the Hudson

A short walk west brings you down to the **Hudson River** and **West
Side Highway**, where you can see the old **Penn Railroad Yards**,
abandoned for close on two decades, though now earmarked for a
new luxury housing project. Local residents, scared of yet another
new influx of people into an already crowded and increasingly gentrified neighborhood, have protested and thus far are winning. North
from here, weaving its way up the western fringe of Manhattan island
is **Riverside Drive**, flanked by palatial townhouses and multistory
apartment buildings put up in the early part of this century by those
not quite rich enough to compete with the folks down on Fifth
Avenue. The **West 105th Street Historic District** (Riverside Drive
between W 105th and 106th streets) consists of turn-of-the-century
French Beaux Arts townhouses, one of which is part of the New York
Buddhist Church and American Buddhist Academy.

Riverside Park follows for fifty blocks or so; landscaped in 1873
by Frederick Olmsted of Central Park fame, it provides a gentle
break before the traffic hum of the Henry Hudson Parkway. The park
has some notable memorials. There's the **Firemen's Memorial** (W
100th St), a large, stately commemorative frieze. Further down, the
Joan of Arc Monument (W 93rd St) sits atop a 1.6-acre cobblestone
and grass park named Joan of Arc Island, and there's also the
Soldiers' and Sailors' Monument (W 89th St), a marble temple
memorial to the Civil War dead.

Several blocks south, through the park and down the steps under
the road, is a place few people know about: the **79th Street Boat
Basin**, where a couple of hundred Manhattanites live on the water.
It's one of the city's most peaceful locations, and while the views
across to New Jersey aren't exactly awesome, they're a tonic after
the congestion of Manhattan proper, especially if seen from the outdoor restaurant that recently opened there.

On and around Central Park West

A block east from Columbus Avenue has always been well-off – and as
long as the monumental apartment buildings that line Central Park
West continue to stand, the area will remain so. Stroll down West 67th
Street past the **Hotel des Artistes**, one-time Manhattan address of the
likes of Noel Coward, Norman Rockwell, Isadora Duncan and
Alexander Woollcott. On the ground floor is the famous **Café des
Artistes**, one of Manhattan's most overpriced Continental restaurants.

The nearby **New York Society for Ethical Culture** (2 W 64th St at
Central Park West; ☎874-5210), "a haven for those who want to share

the high adventure of integrating ethical ideals into daily life," organizes occasional recitals and lectures on community building and social responsibility. Building on the Ethical Culture Movement begun in 1876, this distinguished organization also helped to found the National Association for the Advancement of Colored Peoples and the American Civil Liberties Union. J. Robert Oppenheimer, who directed the development of the first atomic bomb, was a student here.

Follow Central Park West north as far as the junction of 72nd Street. More mammoth apartment buildings loom here, first the **Majestic**, a yellow Art Deco building best known for its roof towers and avant-garde brickwork. Across the street is the more famous **Dakota Building**, so called because at the time of its construction in 1884 its uptown location was considered to be as remote as the Dakota Territory. The grandiose German Renaissance-style mansion was built to persuade wealthy New Yorkers that life in an apartment could be just as luxurious as in a private house. Over the years there have been few residents here not publicly known in some way: big-time tenants included Lauren Bacall and Leonard Bernstein, and in the 1960s the building was used as the setting for Polanski's film *Rosemary's Baby*. But the most famous recent resident of the Dakota was John Lennon – see box on the previous page.

The death of John Lennon

Today most people know the Dakota Building as the former home of **John Lennon** – and present home of his wife Yoko Ono, who owns a number of the apartments. It was outside the Dakota, on the night of December 8, 1980, that Lennon was murdered – shot by a man who professed to be one of his greatest admirers.

His murderer, Mark David Chapman, had been hanging around outside the building all day, clutching a copy of his hero's latest album, *Double Fantasy*, and accosting Lennon for his autograph – which he got. This was nothing unusual in itself – fans often used to loiter outside and hustle for a glimpse of Lennon – but Chapman was still there when the couple returned from a late-night recording session, and pumped five .38 bullets into Lennon as he walked through the Dakota's 72nd Street entrance. Lennon was picked up by the doorman and rushed to the hospital in a taxi, but he died on the way from a massive loss of blood. A distraught Yoko issued a statement immediately: "John loved and prayed for the human race. Please do the same for him."

Why Chapman did this to John Lennon no one really knows; suffice it to say his obsession with the man had obviously unhinged him. Fans may want to light a stick of incense for Lennon across the road in Strawberry Fields, a section of Central Park that has been restored and maintained in his memory through an endowment by Yoko Ono; trees and shrubs were donated by a number of countries as a gesture toward world peace. The gardens are pretty enough, if unspectacular, and it would take a hard-bitten cynic not to be a little bit moved by the *Imagine* mosaic on the pathway and Yoko's handwritten note inviting passers-by to pay their respects.

Nearby museums

Afterward, keep on north up Central Park West, past the dull gray Beaux Arts slab of the **New-York Historical Society**, which has a permanent collection of books, prints, portraits, the 432 original watercolors of Audubon's *Birds of America*, as well as a research library (see Chapter 15, *Museums and Galleries*). Pause to admire some of the beautiful residences (such as the limestone **Kenilworth** at 151 Central Park West and the set-back **San Remo Apartments** at 145-146 Central Park West, familiar to fans of TV's *The Odd Couple* as the home of Oscar and Felix) before taking in the **American Museum of Natural History** between 77th and 81st streets. Said to be the largest museum of any kind in the world, this elegant giant fills four blocks with a strange architectural mélange of heavy Neoclassical and rustic Romanesque styles that was built in several stages, the first by Calvert Vaux and Jacob Wrey Mould in 1872. Its vast front steps are a great reading-and-sunning place, and stand behind an appropriately haughty statue of President Theodore Roosevelt – patron saint of the museum – riding his mount with resolute gaze as a pair of Native Americans march gamely along on either side. For a full account of the museum and its exhibits, again see Chapter 15, *Museums and Galleries*.

Heading North

To the north, the Upper West Side gets rapidly more seedy, merging into poor black and Latino neighborhoods where people hang out listlessly on street corners, hassling for small change. The transformation is sudden, but like so many districts of New York it's not entirely complete, and even here stately apartment buildings rub shoulders with SRO hotels. The multistory **Claremont Riding Academy** (175 W 89th St between Columbus and Amsterdam aves; ☎724-5100), home to the steeds of New York's privileged Upper West Siders, is the oldest functioning commercial stable in Manhattan. You can take a lesson or ride in the bridle paths of Central Park a few blocks away. Finally, the luxury Art Deco **Eldorado Apartments** (300 Central Park West between 90th and 91st Sts), the northernmost of Central Park West's twin-towered apartment buildings, peaks tantalizingly over the skyline.

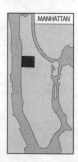

The Cathedral of St John, Columbia University and Morningside Heights

The **Cathedral Church of St John the Divine** (Amsterdam Ave between W 110th and 113th streets) rises out of the tenements of the southern fringes of Harlem with a sure, solid kind of majesty – far from finished but already one of New York's main tourist hotspots, and on the itinerary of a steady stream of tour groups throughout the season. The church was begun in 1892 to the specifications of a Romanesque design that, with a change of architect, became French Gothic. Work progressed quickly but stopped with the outbreak of war in 1939 and has only resumed recently, fraught with funding difficulties and hard questioning by people who consider that, in such an impoverished area of the city, the money might be better spent on something of more obvious benefit.

That said, St John's is very much a community church, housing a soup kitchen and shelter for the homeless, studios for graphics and sculpture, a gymnasium, and (still to be built under the choir) an amphitheatre for the production of drama and concerts. And the building work itself is being undertaken by local African-Americans trained by English stonemasons. Progress is long and slow: still only two-thirds of the cathedral is finished, and completion isn't due until around 2050 – even assuming it goes on uninterrupted. The Portal of Paradise, the Cathedral's entrance on the west face, was recently completed – and a dazzling thing it is, with its 32 biblical figures (as befits the enlightened West Side, both male and female, despite the original men-only design), and such startling images as a mushroom cloud rising apocalyptically over Manhattan, chiselled in limestone and painted with metallic oxide. But this alone took more than ten years and represents a fraction of the work left to do.

Still, if finished, St John the Divine will be the largest cathedral structure in the world, its floor space – at 600 feet long and at the transepts 320 feet wide – big enough to swallow both the cathedrals of Notre Dame and Chartres whole, or, as tour guides are at pains to point out, two full-size football fields.

Walking the length of the nave, these figures seem much more than just another piece of bigger-is-better Americana. Here, too, you can see the welding of the two styles, particularly in the choir, which rises from a heavy arcade of Romanesque columns to high, light Gothic vaulting, the dome of the crossing to be replaced by a tall and delicate Gothic spire. The cathedral appears finished at first glance, but when you gaze up into its huge, uncompleted towers, you realize how much is left to do.

For some idea of how the completed cathedral will look, glance in on the gift shop, housed, for the moment, in the north transept, where there's a scale model of the projected design. Beside the cathedral are the Bestiary Gates, their grillwork adorned with animal imagery (celebrating the annual beast-blessing ceremony held here on the Feast of St Francis), and a **Children's Sculpture Garden** showcasing small bronze sculptures created annually by schoolchildren. Afterward, take a stroll through the cathedral yard and workshop, where you can watch Harlem's apprentice masons tapping away at the stone blocks of the future – and finished – cathedral.

The
Cathedral of
St John,
Columbia
University
and
Morningside
Heights

Columbia University and Morningside Heights

West of the cathedral, Broadway is fringed by a number of cheap restaurants, bars, cafés and bookstores. No. 2911, between 113th and 114th streets, is the **Westend Gate**, formerly the *West End Café* and a hangout of Kerouac, Ginsberg and the Beats in the 1950s; "one of those non-descript places," wrote Joyce Johnson, "before the era of white walls and potted ferns and imitation Tiffany lamps, that for some reason always made the best hangouts." It still serves the student crowd from the nearby university, though stand-up comedy and karaoke have replaced *Howl* as the performances of choice.

Columbia University and around

Columbia University, whose campus fills seven blocks between Amsterdam and Broadway, is one of the most prestigious academic institutions in the country, ranking with the other Ivy League colleges of the northeast and boasting a campus laid out by McKim, Mead and White in grand Beaux Arts style. Of the buildings, the domed and colonnaded **Low Memorial Library** stands center-stage at the top of a wide flight of stone steps, focus for demonstrations during the Vietnam War. Guided tours leave regularly Monday to Friday during the school year from the **information office** on the corner of 116th Street and Broadway. Call ahead (☎854-4900) to schedule a tour or get additional information. For sustenance and great views of Manhattan, eat in the *Terrace* restaurant on the top floor of the **Butler Hall** and gaze out the window at the Tudor glory of **Russell Hall**, among other beautiful vistas.

Across the road **Barnard College** is no less pastoral in feel, but until relatively recently, when Columbia removed their men-only policy, was the place where women had to study for their degrees. Many women still choose to study here, and Barnard retains its status as one of America's elite "Seven Sisters" colleges. Just beyond, **Riverside Church** (Mon–Sat 9am–4.30pm, Sun service 10.45am), has a graceful French Gothic Revival tower, loosely modeled on Chartres and, like St John's, turned over to a mixture of community center and administrative activities for the surrounding parish. Take the elevator to the 20th floor and ascend the steps around the carillon for some classic spreads of Manhattan's jaggy skyline, New Jersey and the hills beyond – and the rest of the city well into the Bronx and Queens. Take a look too at the church, whose open and restrained interior (apart from the apse, which is positively sticky with Gothic ornament) is in stark contrast to the darkened mystery of St John the Divine.

Around the corner from the church is **Grant's Tomb** (daily 9am–5pm; ☎666-1620), a Greek-style memorial and the nation's largest mausoleum in which, the old joke notwithstanding, conquering Civil War hero and blundering eighteenth U.S. president Grant is interred with his wife, in black marble Napoleanic sarcophogi.

The tomb was refurbished in 1996, so current visitors will be spared the graffiti and trash that for some years festooned the resting place of a national hero.

Morningside Heights

The area adjacent is known as **Morningside Heights**, buffer zone for Harlem sprawling below, and with an academic, almost provincial air lent by its abundance of colleges and some swanky properties on Riverside and Morningside drives. **Morningside Park**, stretching from 110th to 123rd streets, was landscaped in 1887 by Frederick Olmsted; its foliage is lush and attractive, but after dark at least, is to be treated with more than a bit of caution. If it's light it's quite feasible to walk north into Harlem, taking in lovely buildings like the **Grotto Church of Notre Dame** at 114th St.

Chapter 12

The Upper East Side

T he defining characteristic of Manhattan's **Upper East Side**, a two-square-mile grid scored with the great avenues of Madison, Park and Lexington, is wealth, and wealth does have its privileges. While other neighborhoods are affected by incursions of immigrant groups, artistic trends, and the like, this remains primarily an enclave of the well-off, with tony shops, clean and relatively safe streets, well-preserved buildings and landmarks, and some of the city's finest museums. It's the western part of this area that sets such a tenor; east of Lexington Avenue was until recently a working-class district of modest houses, though not surprisingly, gentrification quickly changed its character.

The west East Side: Fifth and Madison avenues

Fifth Avenue has been the haughty patrician face of Manhattan since the opening of Central Park in 1876 lured the Carnegies, Astors, Vanderbilts, Whitneys and other capitalists north from lower Fifth Avenue and Gramercy Park to build their fashionable residences on the strip alongside. Once unthinkable, upper Fifth Avenue addresses not only became acceptable but stylish. To this day the address remains so prestigious that buildings with no Fifth Avenue entrance to speak of call themselves by their would-be Fifth Avenue addresses instead of the more accurate side-street address, the latter being much too common. Gazing out over the park, these buildings went up when Neoclassicism was the rage, and hence the surviving originals are cluttered with columns and Classical statues. A great deal of what you see, though, is third- or fourth-generation building: through the latter part of the nineteenth century, fanciful mansions were built at vast expense, to last only ten or fifteen years before being demolished for even wilder extravagances. Rocketing land values made the chance of selling at vast profit irresistible.

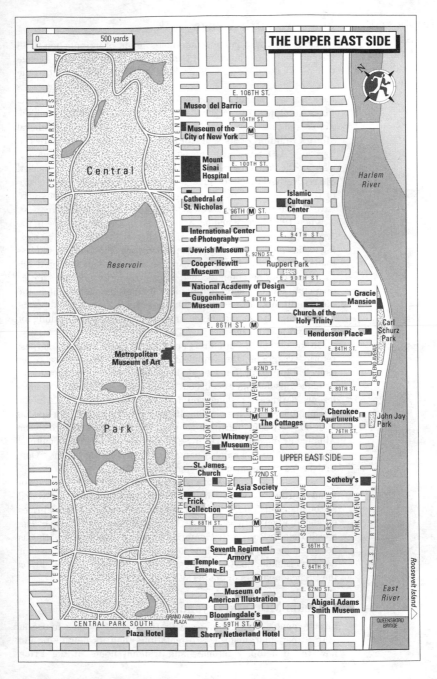

THE UPPER EAST SIDE

Southern Fifth Avenue

Grand Army Plaza is the southernmost point of introduction to all this, an oval at the junction of Central Park South and Fifth Avenue that marks the division between Fifth as a shopping district to the south and a residential boulevard to the north. It's one of the city's most dramatic public spaces, flanked by the extended chateau of the **Plaza Hotel**, with the darkened swoop of the **Solow Building** behind. Across the plaza, no one has a good word to say for the **General Motors Building** or its sunken forecourt, though the six stories of toys at **F.A.O Schwartz**, the building's main commercial tenant, alleviate the grim effect somewhat. Two more hotels, the high-necked **Sherry Netherland** and **Pierre**, luxuriate nearby, mocked by the size of General Motors' marble-clad monolith. Many of the rooms here have permanent guests; needless to say, they're not on welfare.

When **J.P. Morgan** and his pals arrived on the social scene in the 1890s, established society looked askance at "new money" by closing its downtown clubs on Morgan and anyone else it considered less than up to snuff. Morgan's response was the time-honored all-American one: he commissioned Stanford White to design him his own club, bigger, better and grander than all the rest – and so the **Metropolitan Club** at 1 East 60th Street was born, an exuberant confection with a marvelously outrageous gateway. Just the thing for arriving robber barons.

On the corner of 65th Street and Fifth Avenue, America's largest reform synagogue, the **Temple Emanu-El**, strikes a more sober aspect, a brooding Romanesque-Byzantine cavern that manages to be bigger inside than it seems out. The interior melts away into mysterious darkness, making you feel very small indeed (Mon–Fri 10am–5pm, Sat noon–5pm, Sun 10am–5pm; ☎744-1400 for special high holy day schedules). To get your fix of things Gallic go to the **Alliance Française** (22 E 60th St; ☎355-6100), the French cultural institute that hosts a number of noteworthy lectures as well as a Ciné Club series of classic and contemporary French films.

The rest of the East 60s are typical Upper East Side, a trim mix of small apartment houses which, although not as valuable or coveted as the mansions on the avenues, escaped demolition as land prices escalated. Even so they've always been salubrious places to live: **The Sarah Delano Roosevelt Memorial House** at 45–49 East 65th was commissioned by Sarah Delano Roosevelt as a handy townhouse for her son Franklin, no. 142 belonged to Richard Nixon, and no. 115 is the US headquarters of the PLO. Quite a neighborhood.

Museum Mile and beyond

Fifth Avenue's wall continues with Henry Clay Frick's house at 70th Street, marginally less ostentatious than its neighbors and now the deliciously intimate and tranquil home of the **Frick**

Collection, one of the city's musts – even the lush gardens that surround it are a treat. This is the first of many prestigious museums that gives this stretch its name of "Museum Mile." Along the avenue (or just off it) are the **Whitney** (modern American art), the **National Academy of Design**, the **Metropolitan Museum** (the "Met"), the **Guggenheim Collection** (twentieth-century painting housed in Frank Lloyd Wright's helter-skelter mustard pot), the **Cooper-Hewitt Museum of Design**, the **International Center of Photography** and, pushing further north, the **Museum of the City of New York** and **El Museo del Barrio**. There's more than enough to keep you busy for a week at least; for listings see Chapter 15, *Museums and Galleries*.

The west East Side: Fifth and Madison avenues

Take away Fifth Avenue's museums and a resplendent though fairly bloodless strip remains. **Madison Avenue**, especially above 62nd Street, is totally different, lined with top-notch designer clothes stores whose doors are kept locked, with security cameras to check you over before you're allowed to enter. One notable exception is the stately **St James' Church** at 865 Madison Avenue, between 71st and 72nd streets, with its graceful Byzantine altar. **Park Avenue** is less developed and less extravagant yet still as stolidly comfortable – medium-rise apartment buildings in anonymous dark brick with a little ornament at ground level to prove the worth of their owners. The occasional building stands out, like the self-glorifying **Colonial Club** at 62nd Street, as do the **sculptures** on display along the traffic islands, but the best feature is the view as Park Avenue coasts down to the **New York Central** and MetLife (originally Pan Am) buildings.

Another standout landmark is the **Seventh Regiment Armory** (Park Ave between 66th and 67th streets), a Lego fortress bedecked with fairy-tale crenellations – yet just a little sinister all the same. There's some interesting Civil War memorabilia on display here, but call ahead for a tour (☎744-8180), as the Armory still functions as a working military office. The winter antiques fair held at the Armory each January presents a good opportunity to gawk at the enormous drill hall inside, one that drew complaints from the locals not so long ago when it was used as a temporary shelter for the homeless.

The Asia Society (725 Park Ave between E 70th and 71st streets; ☎288-6400) has a permanent display of the Rockefeller Collection of Asian art and often hosts symposia, lectures, performances and film series and has a well-stocked bookstore on the ground floor.

Carnegie Hill

At the northernmost part of this stretch, as the museums keep rolling by, is **Carnegie Hill**, an historic district bounded by 86th and 99th streets and Fifth and Lexington avenues. This well-tended and well-policed area retains the air of a gated community without the gates, and is largely inhabited by the more recently *riche*; you might catch a glimpse of celebrity tenants such as Bette Midler or Michael J. Fox, and their bodyguards, jogging down to Central Park. Aside from art and celebrity-sightings, the highlight here is the **Russian Orthodox Cathedral of St Nicholas** (15 E 97th St), most notable for its polychromatic Victorian body and five onion domes on top. Get too much past here, and the upscale living quickly fades.

The east East Side

Lexington Avenue is Madison without the class; as the west became richer, property developers rushed to slick up real estate in the east. The signs of its 1960s heyday – hot bars like *Maxwell's Plum*, big stores like *Alexander's* – are gone, and this is now one of the cheaper areas for studio apartments. Much of the East 60s and 70s now houses young, unattached and upwardly mobile professionals – as the number of "happening" singles bars on Second and Third avenues will attest.

The southern stretches

On the southern perimeter of the Upper East Side, **Bloomingdale's** at 59th and Third is the celebrated American store for clothes and accessories, skillfully aiming its wares at the stylish and affluent (see Chapter 24, *Shops and Markets*). Nearby, at 421 East 61st St between York and First Avenue, is the **Abigail Adams Smith Museum** (Mon–Fri noon–4pm, Sun 1–5pm; closed in August; adults $3, students and senior citizens $2, children under 12 free; ☎838-6878), another of those eighteenth-century buildings that managed to survive by the skin of its teeth. This wasn't the actual home of Abigail Adams, daughter of President John Quincy Adams, just its stables, restored with Federal-period propriety by the Colonial Dames of America. The furnishings, knick-knacks and the serene little park out back are more engaging than the house itself, but there's an odd sort of pull if you're lucky enough to be guided around by a chattily urbane Colonial Dame.

The house is hemmed in by decidedly unhistoric buildings and overlooked by the **Queensboro Bridge**, which may stir memories as the **59th Street Bridge** of Simon and Garfunkel's *Feeling Groovy* or from the title credits of TV's *Taxi*. This intense profusion of clanging steelwork links Manhattan to Long Island City in Queens but is utterly unlike the suspension bridges that elsewhere lace Manhattan to the boroughs. "My God, it's a blacksmith's shop!" was architect Henry Hornbostel's comment when he first saw the finished item in 1909.

There's not much just north of this way, save a few yuppie strip clubs, until you hit the New York auction gallery of London-based Sotheby's, the oldest fine arts auctioneer in the world, at 1334 York Avenue between East 71st and 72nd streets (☎606-7000). Admission to a few of the largest auctions is by ticket only, but all viewings are open to the public.

Yorkville

It's left to **Yorkville**, originally a German-Hungarian neighborhood that spills out from East 77th to 96th streets between Lexington and the East River, to try to supply the Upper East Side with a tangible ethnicity. Much of New York's German community arrived after the failed revolution of 1848–49, to be quickly assimilated into the area around Tompkins Square. The influx of Italian and Slavic immigrants to the Lower East Side, the tragic sinking of an excursion steamer carrying Tompkins Square residents, and the opening of the Elevated Railway all around the turn of the century hastened their move uptown to Yorkville. Other groups followed not long after, and some splendid little townhouses were built for these newcomers, such as **The Cottages** on Third Avenue between E 77th and 78th streets, whose stylish English Regency facades and courtyard gardens remain intact.

Today, the Teutonic community here is greatly depleted, leaving only the elderly among the German-speaking residents, but the four-or five-block stretch around 86th Street still has traditional German delicatessens like **Schaller and Weber** (1654 Second Ave between 84th and 85th sts) and **Bremen House** (218–220 E 86th between Second and Third aves). Try also the baroque cakes and pastries at **Café Geiger** (206 E 86th St) or a bootful of beer and some liver dumpling soup at the **Heidelburg** (1648 Second Ave).

Beginning on East 76th Street and East End Drive is **John Jay Park**, a nice patch of green centering around a beautiful pool and gym – which you can't use, unfortunately; only New Yorkers with Parks Department passes can ($35 per year). Fronting the park on Cherokee Street between 77th and 78th streets are the **Cherokee Apartments**, originally the Shively Sanitarium Apartments, an understatedly elegant row with a splendid courtyard. Up the block at 81st Street is **John Finley Walk,** a bleak concrete promenade that runs north into the park named after **Carl Schurz**, a nineteenth-century German immigrant who rose to fame as Secretary of the Interior under President Rutherford B. Hayes and as editor of *Harper's Weekly* and the *New York Evening Post*. Winding pathways lead through this small, model park – a breathing space for elderly German speakers and East Siders escaping their postage-stamp apartments. The **FDR Drive** cuts beneath, giving uninterrupted views across the river to Queens and the confluence of dangerous currents where the Harlem River, Long Island Sound and Harbor meet – not for nothing known as **Hell Gate**.

Gracie Mansion and Henderson Place

One of the reasons Schurz Park is so exceptionally well-mani-
cured and maintained is the high-profile security that surrounds
Gracie Mansion at 88th Street nearby. Built in 1799 on the site
of a Revolutionary fort as a country manor house, it is one of the
best-preserved colonial buildings in the city. Roughly contemporary with the Morris–Jumel Mansion (see "Washington Heights,"
p.188) and the Abigail Adams house, Gracie Mansion has been
the official residence of the mayor of New York City since 1942,
when Fiorello LaGuardia, "man of the people" that he was, reluc-
tantly set up house – though "mansion" is a bit overblown for
what was a rather cramped clapboard cottage. The mansion is
open for tours, usually on Wednesday, though you need to book
in advance. (Suggested admission $4, $3 for seniors; ☎570-
4751.)

Across from the park and just below Gracie Mansion at East
86th Street and East End Avenue is **Henderson Place**, a set of
old servants' quarters now transformed into an "historic district"
of luxury cottages. Built in 1882 by John Henderson, a fur
importer and real-estate developer, the small and sprightly
Queen Anne-style wooden and brick dwellings were constructed
to provide close and convenient housing for servants working in
the palatial old East End Avenue mansions, most of which have
now been torn down. Ironically, these servants' quarters now
represent some of the most sought-after real estate in the city,
offering the space, quiet and privacy that most of the city's housing lacks.

Around Yorkville's outskirts

Just west of here is **Ruppert Park**, a shaded and civilized bit of village green between East 90th and 91st streets and Second and Third
avenues. The remainder of the area's attractions consists of two religious centers. The **Church of the Holy Trinity** (316 E 88th St
between First and Second aves) is a picturesque and discreet
Victorian church with an enchanting little garden. On Third Avenue
at East 96th Street is the **Islamic Cultural Center**, New York's first
major mosque, whose orientation toward Mecca was precisely pin-
pointed with a computer. It was here that the funeral of **Betty
Shabazz**, widow of **Malcolm X**, was held in July 1997.

North of here, the mood begins to change rapidly as the bright
turquoise facade of the diagonal housing projects on 97th and First
signal the change as the streets become busier with the offshoots of
El Barrio, the best-known part of New York's significant Latino community. Further west, the elevated tracks of the #4, #5 and #6
Bronx-bound trains surface at Park and 96th, signaling the end of
Park Avenue's old-money dominance, while both Madison and Fifth
retain their grandeur for only a few blocks more.

Roosevelt Island

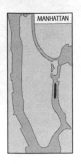

MANHATTAN

An **aerial tramway** near **Queensboro Bridge** connects mainland Manhattan with **Roosevelt Island** across the water. Though the island was connected by tunnel to the subway system a few years back, the tram is more fun (trams run every 15min, Mon–Thurs 6am–2am, Fri–Sat 6am–3.30am, Sun 6am–2am; every 7 1/2min during rush hours; $1.50 one way). Once on the island, you can jump on the bright-red minibus that will shuttle you off to the northern end of the island for 25¢. If you feel like exploring, Roosevelt Island rewards with some imaginative housing and unusual views.

Only two miles long and no more than 800 feet wide, Roosevelt Island was owned, inhabited and farmed by the **Blackwell** family from 1676 to 1826, and the brick paving and narrowness of **Main Street** preserve the small-town feel virtually unavailable in any other part of the city today. **Meditation Steps** and the **East River Walk**, a walking and rollerblading path on the western side of the island, permit uncluttered views of Manhattan's East Side and the rattling grates of Queensboro Bridge's metalwork overhead.

On paper this should long have been an ideal residential spot, but its history as "**Welfare Island**," a gloomy quarantine block of jail, poorhouse, lunatic asylum and smallpox hospital, for years put it out of bounds to Manhattanites. The stigma only started to disappear in the 1970s when Johnson and Burgee's master plan spawned the Eastview, Westwood, island House and Rivercross housing areas. Today these and other residential complexes house deliberately racially and ethnically diverse residents of low-income and market-value housing. The narrow streets, bold signage and modular buildings are locally considered a triumph of urban planning; outsiders may find it reminiscent of the village in the TV series *The Prisoner*.

Grim reminders of Welfare Island remain. There are still two chronic-care hospitals on the island, and the **Octagon Tower**, now off-limits, at the island's north end was once an insane asylum (it briefly housed Mae West after an unpalatably lewd performance in 1927). At the northernmost point of the island the **Lighthouse** affords excellent views of the upper reaches of the East River and the surging waters of Hell Gate, and **Lighthouse Park** is a romantic retreat of grassy knolls and weeping willows.

To the south are the stabilized ruins of what was once the island's **Smallpox Hospital**, now a ghostly Gothic shell, and the **Strecker Laboratory**, the city's premier laboratory for bacteriological research when it opened in 1892. The ruins can be easily spotted from the Manhattan side of the East River but are all but impossible to see from the island itself, as the area surrounding the hospital is boarded up with rows of corrugated metal fencing.

Roosevelt Island seems far away from New York City, a sort of post-Manhattan purgatory before the borough of Queens.

Roosevelt Island

Crossing back over the bridge gives a spine-tingling panorama of the city, the one Nick Carraway described in F. Scott Fitzgerald's *The Great Gatsby*:

> *Over the great bridge, with the sunlight through the girders making a constant flicker upon the moving cars, with the city rising up across the river in white heaps and sugar lumps all built with a wish out of non-olfactory money. The city seen from the Queensboro Bridge is always the city seen for the first time, in its wild promise of all the mystery and the beauty in the world . . . "Anything can happen now that we've slid over this bridge" I thought; "anything at all ..."*

Chapter 13

Harlem, Hamilton Heights and the North

This chapter covers the most northerly stretches of Manhattan island, which comprises a disparate group of localities. **Harlem** has long been synonymous with racial conflict and urban deprivation, though as a visit here will reveal, that's only part of a much bigger picture, one often simplified and jaundiced by media hostile to the black culture here. Though Harlem has its problems, it's a far less dangerous neighborhood than its reputation suggests, especially in light of solid city and neighborhood improvement efforts. Spanish Harlem – **El Barrio** – has an undeniably rougher edge to it, and reasons for visiting are far fewer than for Harlem proper. Further north, **Hamilton Heights** is richer and more residential, an old house and an excellent small museum its only real draws. Continuing up, **Washington Heights** is a patchy neighborhood with little in the way of attractions, though you still may have reason to pass through. Because oddly enough, the most visited site north of Central Park lies very near the top end of the island – the **Cloisters Museum**, a mock medieval castle that holds the Metropolitan Museum's superlative collection of medieval art.

Harlem

"As goes Harlem, so goes Black America."

Langston Hughes

Harlem is a side of Manhattan that few visitors – and only some New Yorkers themselves – bother to see. This is a rather unfortunate byproduct of an enduring legacy: it has languished under a reputation of racial tension and urban decay earned from years of outward neglect and internal strife throughout the 1940s, 1950s and 1960s. Yet Harlem is the most famous African-American community in America, and, arguably, the bedrock of black culture in this century. The Harlem Renaissance of the 1920s and 1930s, where the talents

HARLEM, HAMILTON HEIGHTS AND THE NORTH

Riverside Park

Morris-Jumel Mansion

Hispanic Museum

W. 155TH ST.

MACOMBS BRIDGE

HENRY HUDSON PARKWAY

BROADWAY

AMSTERDAM AVE.

NICHOLAS AVE.

COMVENT AVE.

W. 150TH ST.

W. 145TH ST.

146TH STREET BRIDGE

0   900 yards

Aunt Len's Doll & Toy Museum

Hamilton Grange

Strivers' Row

Abyssinian Baptist Church

HAMILTON HEIGHTS

Nicholas Park

Schomburg Center

MADISON AVENUE BRIDGE

W. 135TH ST.

E. 135TH ST.

THIRD AVENUE BRIDGE

HARLEM RIVER DRIVE

WALLIS AVENUE

Cotton Club

City College

HARLEM

Apollo Theater

Black Fashion Museum

Sylvia's

FIFTH AVENUE

MADISON AVENUE

PARK AVENUE

125TH ST.

TRIBOROUGH BRIDGE

W. 125TH ST.

Grant's Tomb

Theresa Towers

Studio Museum of Harlem

Marcus Garvey Park

Riverside Church

Morningside Park

W. 120TH ST.

E. 120TH ST.

LEXINGTON AVE.

THIRD AVENUE

Columbia University

W. 116TH ST.

E. 116TH ST.

EL BARRIO

MALCOLM X BLVD.

POWELL BLVD.

EIGHTH AVE.

Cathedral

CENTRAL PARK NORTH

W. 109TH ST.

E. 109TH ST.

LA MARQUETA

Central Park

W. 104TH ST.

Museo del Barrio

E. 104TH ST.

See 'Upper West Side' Map

Harlem River

of such icons as Billie Holiday, Paul Robeson and James Weldon
Johnson took root, set the course for the generations of musicians,
writers and performers that followed. Harlem's history is rich and
not a little turbulent. Up until recently, because of its near-total lack
of support from federal and municipal funds Harlem formed a self-
reliant and inward-looking community. For many downtown
Manhattanites, white and black, 125th Street was a physical and
mental border not willingly crossed.

Today, however, the fruits of a cooperative effort involving businesses, residents and City Hall funding are manifest in new housing, retail and community projects. This is not to say that Harlem is
without problems: wander just a bit off the beaten path and poverty – and the dangerous climate it often sadly breeds – is still the
mainstay of large patches. But to understand New York fully, its
problems and its strengths, it is necessary to understand – and
explore – Harlem.

Some hints and history

Practically speaking, Harlem's sights are too spread out to amble
between. You'll do best to make several trips, preferably beginning
with a **guided tour** (see "Information, Maps and Tours" in *Basics*) to
get acquainted with the area and to help you decide what to come
back to see on your own. If you're a white visitor, it should be obvious to you that you *will* stand out in this almost exclusively black
neighborhood. If you intend to tour Harlem on your own, it will serve
you well to feel comfortable about where you're going beforehand,
stick to the well-trodden streets and behave confidently once there.
The predominant feeling among Harlem residents you'll see in the
commercial and historic areas will be warm and inviting: Harlem as
a community is actively seeking the tourist trade.

Harlem's beginnings

As the name suggests, it was the **Dutch** who founded the settlement
of **Nieuw Haarlem**, naming it after a town in Holland. Until the mid-
nineteenth century this was farmland, but when the New York and
Harlem railroad linked the area with Lower Manhattan it attracted
the richer immigrant families (mainly German Jews from the Lower
East Side) to build elegant and fashionable brownstones in the
steadily developing suburb. When work began on the IRT Lenox line
later in the century, property speculators were quick to build good-
quality homes in the expectation of seeing Harlem repeat the success
of the Upper West Side. They were too quick and too ambitious, for
by the time the IRT line opened most of the buildings were still
empty, their would-be takers uneasy at moving so far north. A black
real-estate agent saw his chance, bought the empty houses cheaply
and rented them to blacks from the rundown Midtown districts.

The black community

Very quickly Harlem became black, while remaining home to a mix
of cultural and social communities: the western areas along **Convent
Avenue** and **Sugar Hill** were for years the home of the middle classes and preserve traces of a well-to-do past. In the east, the bulge
between Park Avenue and the East River became **Spanish Harlem**,
now largely peopled by Puerto Ricans and more properly called **El
Barrio** – "the Neighborhood." In between live the descendants of

West Indian, African, Cuban and Haitian immigrants, often crowded into poorly maintained housing.

This cramping together of dissimilar cultures has long caused tensions and problems not easily understood by the city's bureaucracy. Dotted around Harlem are buildings and projects that attest to an uneasy municipal conscience but that have not in any real sense solved the problems of unemployment and urban decay. Sometimes, amid the boarded-up storefronts and vacant lots, it's hard to believe you're but a mile or two away from the cosily patrician Upper East Side.

The 1920s and 1930s: The Harlem Renaissance

There was a brief period when Harlem enjoyed a golden age. In the 1920s whites began to notice the explosion of black culture that had occurred here: jazz musicians like Duke Ellington, Count Basie and Cab Calloway played in nightspots like *The Cotton Club, Savoy Ballroom, Apollo Theater* and *Small's Paradise*; the drink flowed as if Prohibition had never been heard of, and the sophisticated set drove up to Harlem's speakeasies after Downtown had gone to bed. Maybe because these revelers never stayed longer than the last drink, neither they, nor history, recall the poverty then rife in Harlem. One of the most evocative voices heard in the clubs those days was of Ethel Waters, who sang in the *Sugar Cane Club*:

> *Rent man waitin' for his forty dollars,*
> *Ain't got me but a dime and some bad news.*
> *Bartender give me a bracer, double beer chaser,*
> *Cause I got the low-down, mean, rent man blues.*

Equally symbolic, if not more so, of the Harlem Renaissance was the literature of the time – the rich writings of Langston Hughes, Jean Toomer and Zara Neale Hurston, among many others, which caught the fancy of blacks and whites alike. Still, music and literature were not enough to sustain a neighborhood where most were on the economic brink; even before the Depression, it was hard to scrape out a living, and decline drove middle-class blacks out of Harlem.

Harlem today

By the early 1970s, the genesis of redevelopment had begun. Scandalous living conditions had residents finally angry enough to begin pointing fingers at slumlords and absentee landlords. The city, which had become accustomed to letting Harlem implode for decades, was ultimately stirred into long-overdue action. A plethora of urban and community development grants were put into effect for housing, commercial and retail development, and general urban renewal (unlike many so-called "ghettos," the basic quality of the nineteenth-century housing here is excellent and ripe for modernization). Twenty-five years later, the investment is paying off: Harlem's historic areas are well maintained and everywhere you turn, construction seems underway. More than 35,000 housing units have been or are being built, as well 600 or so commercial sites. Harlem residents have taken to saying that a Second Harlem Renaissance is underway: combined with recent figures that show a dramatic drop in crime in the neigborhood and a renewed community spirit, this may not be an overoptimistic view.

Exploring Harlem

125th Street between Broadway and Fifth Avenue is the working center of Harlem, a flattened, shell-shocked expanse, spiked with the occasional skyscraper, that serves as the main commercial and retail drag. The subway throws you up here, and the **New York State Office Building** on the corner of Seventh Avenue provides a looming modern landmark: commissioned after the last serious riots in 1968, it was intended to show the state's commitment to the support of the community, though really it's an intrusion on the earthy goings-on of 125th Street. Walk a little west from here and you reach the **Apollo Theater** at no. 253. Not much from the outside, it was right into the 1960s the center of black entertainment in New York City and northeastern America: almost all the great figures of jazz and blues played here along with singers, comedians and dancers. Past winners of its famous "Amateur Night" have included The Jackson Five, Sarah Vaughan, Marvin and James Brown. Since its heyday it's served as a warehouse, movie theater and radio station, and in its latest incarnation is the venue for a weekly TV show, *Showtime at the Apollo*. Now an official landmark building, the *Apollo* offers daily 45-minute tours (☎749-5838). Across the way at 125th and Seventh Avenue the Theresa Towers office building was until the 1960s the **Theresa Hotel**. Fidel Castro was once a guest here, shunning Midtown luxury in a popular political gesture. The open-market feel of this stretch has dimmed somewhat to make way for chain-store development; indeed, there are even plans in the works for a **Harlem USA** theme-mall nearby the *Apollo*.

125th Street rolls energetically eastward: there's the **Studio Museum of Harlem**, at no. 144 (see Chapter 15, *Museums and Galleries*); after that, turn right (south) at **Lenox Avenue** (officially named Malcolm X Boulevard, though known locally by both names) to enter the **Mount Morris Park Historical District**. At 201 Lenox (at 120th St) stands the **Mount Olivet Church**, an American version of a Roman version of what they thought a Greek temple looked like, and one of literally hundreds of religious buildings dotted around Harlem. The somber, bulky **St Martin's** at the southeast corner of Lenox Avenue and 122nd Street is among them, and both have been fortunate in avoiding falling into decay as church and community declined. Elsewhere the Mount Morris District compris-

Lenox Avenue has been officially renamed Malcolm X Boulevard – but it's still known by the old name.

es some lovely **row houses** that went up in the speculative boom of the 1890s: take a look at the block on Lenox Avenue between 120th and 121st streets or the Romanesque **Mount Morris Park West** for the best. When, a few years back, the city held a lottery to sell a dozen abandoned houses on Mount Morris Park West there was an immediate outcry from the local people, who considered one of the prime slices of Harlem was being raffled off to faceless downtown concerns. A compromise was reached that ensured each prospective buyer who lived in Harlem would be entered three times, guaranteeing a 50:50 chance of a win. For these twelve houses, 2500 applications were received – which is hardly surprising. Looking at Mount Morris Park West you can't help but feel that it too will go the way of Greenwich Village and the Lower East Side – the quality of building is so good, the pressures on Manhattan so great, it seems just a matter of time.

The former Mount Morris Park is now **Marcus Garvey Park**, taking its name from the black leader of the 1920s, and altogether a decidedly odd urban space. Craggy peaks block off views, meaning you never get an idea of the square as a unity, and the jutting outcrops contradict the precise lines of the houses around. At the top an elegant octagonal fire tower of 1856 is a unique example of the early-warning devices once found throughout the city. Spiral your way to the top for a great view.

Continue down Lenox Avenue to 116th Street at no. 102 to find the onion-domed mosque, **Masjid Malcolm Shabazz**, named after Malcolm X who once preached here, and now serving as the East Coast headquarters for the Muslim faith. Diagonally across from – and sponsored by – the mosque is the **Malcolm Shabazz Harlem Market**, the new home for about 175 street vendors recently whisked off 125th Street by the city authorities to make the emerging retail street less bazaar-like. The market's offerings include cloth, T-shirts, jewelry, clothing and more with a distinctly African flavor. The irony here is that these former street vendors who used to run from police and clash with other local merchants now pay taxes, accept credit cards, and take accounting courses at the mosque.

Powell Boulevard

Seventh Avenue becomes **Adam Clayton Powell Jr Boulevard** above 110th Street, a broad sweep pushing north between low-built houses that for once in Manhattan allow the sky to break through. Since its conception Powell Boulevard has been Harlem's main concourse, and it's not difficult to imagine the propriety the shops and side streets had in their late nineteenth-century heyday. As with the rest of Harlem, Powell Boulevard shows years of decline in its graffiti-splattered walls and storefronts punctuated with demolished lots. An **Empowerment Zone Project** has promised a $300 million allocation of federal, state and local funds to redevelop the boulevard and connect it commercially with the now bustling retail streets of 125th and 145th. If this doesn't make some difference, it's hard to see what will.

To look back at past times rather than the uncertain future, it's worth checking out the **Schomburg Center for Research in Black Culture** at 515 Lenox Avenue at 135th Street (Mon–Wed noon–8pm, Fri & Sat 10am–6pm, closed Sun; ☎491-2200) for its exhibitions on the history of black culture in the US: see Chapter 15, "Museums and Galleries". On your way up, at no. 328, is the most renowned soul food restaurant in New York – perhaps anywhere – *Sylvia's*.

The Reverend Adam Clayton Powell Jr

A few streets north at 132 West 138th St (☎862-5959) is another church – though this one, the **Abyssinian Baptist Church**, is special not because it's architecturally interesting, but because of its long-time minister, the **Reverend Adam Clayton Powell Jr**. In the 1930s Powell was instrumental in forcing the mostly white-owned, white-workforce stores of Harlem to begin employing the blacks who ensured their economic survival. Later he became the first black on the city council, then New York's first black representative at Congress – a career which came to an embittered end in 1967, when amid strong rumors of the misuse of public funds he was excluded from Congress by majority vote. This failed to diminish his standing in Harlem, where voters twice re-elected him before his death in 1972. In the church there's a small **museum** to Powell's life, the scandal of course unmentioned, but a more fitting memorial is the boulevard that today bears his name. The museum may or may not be open when you visit: construction in 1997 forced it to be temporarily dismantled. Still, it's worth a trip if you can see the gut-busting **choir** – call the number above, or see "Information, Maps and Tours" for details.

Strivers' Row

Across from the Abyssinian Baptist Church at 138th Street between Powell and Eighth Avenue (aka Frederick Douglass Boulevard) is what many consider the finest, most articulate block of row houses in Manhattan – **Strivers' Row**. Commissioned during the 1890s housing boom, Striver's Row consists of 138th and 139th streets. Three sets of architects were commissioned: James Brown Lord, Bruce Price and Clarence Luce, and the best, McKim, Mead and White's north side of 139th: the results are uniquely harmonious, a dignified Renaissance-derived strip that's an amalgam of simplicity and elegance. Within the burgeoning black community of the turn of the century this came to be the desirable place for ambitious professionals to reside – hence its nickname.

Sunday gospel

Lately it's the incredible **gospel music** that has attracted visitors up to Harlem. And for good reason: the music and the entire revival-style Baptist experience can be both amazing and invigorating. Gospel tours are becoming big business, and churches seem to be jockeying to get the most tourists. Many of the arranged tours (outlined in "Information, Maps and Tours" in *Basics*) are pricey, but they usually offer transportation uptown and brunch afterwards. You can, however, easily go it on your own if you're looking for a more flavorful view. The choir at the Abyssinian Baptist Church is arguably the best in the city, but others of note include **Metropolitan Baptist Church** (151 W 128th St at Adam Clayton Powell Blvd; ☎289-9488), **Mount Moriah** (2050 Fifth Ave at W 127th St; ☎722-9594), and **Mount Nebo** (1883 Seventh Ave at W 114th St; ☎866-7880). Keep in mind, if you do attend one of the services, that this isn't a tourist attraction but an actual church where worship is taken especially seriously. Dress accordingly: jackets for men and skirts or dresses for women.

El Barrio

From Park Avenue to the East River is Spanish Harlem or **El Barrio**, dipping down as far as East 96th Street to collide head on with the affluence of the Upper East Side. The center of a large Puerto Rican community, it is quite different from Harlem. El Barrio was originally a working-class Italian neighborhood (a small pocket of Italian families survives around 116th St and First Ave) and the quality of building here was nowhere as good as that immediately to the west. The result is a more intimidating atmosphere. It has been predominantly Puerto Rican since the early 1950s, when the American government offered Puerto Ricans incentives to emigrate to the US under a policy known as "Operation Bootstrap" (so named in the theory that the scheme would help pull Puerto Rico up "by the straps of its boots" by reducing its overpopulation problem). But the occupants have had little opportunity to evolve Latino culture in any meaningful or noticeable way; the main space where cultural roots are in evidence is **La Marqueta** on Park Avenue between 111th and 116th streets, a five-block **street market** of Spanish products. Originally a line of pushcart street vendors hawking their wares, it's more regulated now, selling everything from tropical fruit and vegetables, jewelry, figurines and clothing to dried herbs and snake oils. To get some background on the whole scene, **El Museo del Barrio** at Fifth Avenue and 104th Street (see Chapter 15, *Museums and Galleries*) is a showcase of Latin American art and culture and also includes **La Casa de la Herencia Cultural Puertorriquena**, a Puerto Rican heritage library. To the northeast, El Barrio's **International Art Gallery** at 309 108th St (between Third and Lexington aves) is an alternative space for local artists of Latin, African-American and Asian origin.

Hamilton Heights

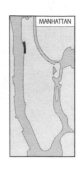

The further uptown you venture, the less like New York it seems. Much of Harlem's western edge is taken up by the area known as **Hamilton Heights**, like Morningside Heights to the south a mixed bag of campus, trash-strewn streets and slender parks on a bluff above Harlem. Just one stretch, the **Hamilton Heights Historic District** that runs down Convent Avenue to City College, pulls Hamilton Heights up from the ranks of the untidily mediocre. Years ago the black professionals who made it up here and to Sugar Hill a little further north could glance down on lesser Harlemites with disdain: it's still a firmly bourgeois residential area – and one of the most attractive uptown.

But even if this mood of shabbiness around a well-heeled neighborhood is to your liking, there's little in the way of specific sights. The 135th Street St Nicholas subway is as good a place to start as any, for up the hill and around the corner is Convent Avenue, containing the Heights's single historic lure – the house of Alexander Hamilton, **Hamilton Grange**, at 287 Convent Avenue, at 142nd Street (daily 9am–5pm; free).

Alexander Hamilton's life is as fascinating as it was flamboyant. He was an early supporter of the Revolution, and his enthusiasm quickly brought him to the attention of George Washington. He became the general's aide-de-camp, later founding the Bank of New York and becoming first Secretary to the Treasury. Hamilton's headlong tackling of problems made him enemies as well as friends: alienating Republican populists led to a clash with their leader Thomas Jefferson, and when Jefferson won the presidency in 1801, Hamilton was left out in the political cold. Temporarily abandoning politics, he moved away from the city to his grange here (or rather near here – the house was moved in 1889) to tend his plantation and conduct a memorably sustained and vicious feud with one **Aaron Burr**, who had beaten Hamilton's father-in-law to a seat in the Senate and then set up the Bank of Manhattan as a direct rival to the Bank of New York. After a few years as vice president under Jefferson, Burr ran for the governorship of New York; Hamilton strenuously opposed his candidature and after an exchange of extraordinarily bitter letters, the two men fought a **duel** in Weehawken, New Jersey, roughly where today's Lincoln Tunnel emerges. Hamilton's eldest son had been killed in a duel on the same field a few years earlier, which may explain why, when pistols were drawn, Hamilton honorably discharged his into the air. Burr, evidently made of lesser stuff, aimed carefully and fatally wounded Hamilton. So died "the most restless, impatient, artful, indefatigable and unprincipled intriguer in the United States," as President John Adams described him. He's only one of two non-presidents to find his way on to US money: you'll find his portrait on the back of a $10 bill.

Hamilton
Heights

All of this is a lot more exciting than the **house**, a Federal-style mansion today uncomfortably transplanted between a fiercely Romanesque church – which actually curls around it in the front – and an apartment building. It's probably only worth dropping in if visiting the wonderful **Aunt Len's Doll and Toy Museum** nearby – for which you'll need an appointment; see Chapter 15, *Museums and Galleries*.

Convent Avenue and City College

If you've just wandered up from Harlem, **Convent Avenue** comes as something of a surprise – and a quite welcome one at that. Its secluded, blossom-lined streets have a garden suburb prettiness that's spangled with Gothic, French and Italian Renaissance hints in the happily eclectic houses of the 1890s. Running south, the feathery span of the **Shepard Archway** announces **City College**, a rustic-feeling campus of Collegiate Gothic halls built from gray Manhattan schist dug up during the excavations for the IRT subway line and mantled with white terracotta fripperies. Founded in 1905, City College made no charge for tuition, so becoming the seat of higher learning for many of New York's poor, and though free education came to an end in the 1970s, 75 percent of the students still come from minority backgrounds to enjoy a campus that's as warmly intimate as Columbia is grandiose.

MANHATTAN

Washington Heights

The change from Convent Avenue to Broadway is almost as abrupt as it is up from Harlem. Broadway here is a once-elegant, now raggy sweep that slowly rises to the northernmost part of Manhattan island, **Washington Heights**. From Morningside Heights, the haul is a long one, though the best stopoffs are easily reached from the #1 train to 157th and Broadway or the A to 155th or 163rd; if you're in Hamilton Heights, just continue north for a largely uneventful walk. **Audubon Terrace** at 155th and Broadway is an Acropolis in a cul-de-sac, a weird, clumsy nineteenth-century attempt to deify 155th Street with museums dolled up as Beaux Arts temples. Officially the **Washington Heights Museum Group**, it was originally built in the vain anticipation of the movement north of New York's elite aristocratic society. Now the complex stands in mocking contrast to its still decrepit area. Included here is the **American Academy of Arts and Letters**, the **American Numismatic Society** and the **Hispanic Society of America**. As you might expect from something so far from the center of town, the complex is little known and little visited, though the Hispanic Museum alone is worth the trip. For a full account of each museum, see Chapter 15, *Museums and Galleries*. One avenue east, at 155th Street and Amsterdam, is the **Trinity**

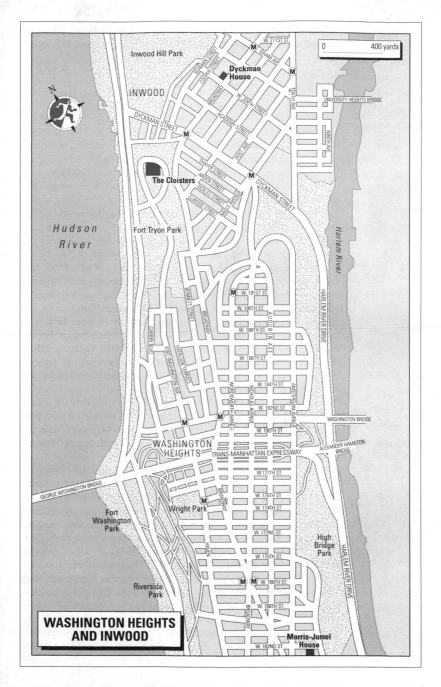

WASHINGTON HEIGHTS
AND INWOOD

Church Cemetery, a large, placid grounds dotted with some fanciful mauselea; the remains of robber baron John Jacob Astor are said to be buried up here.

The Morris–Jumel Mansion

Within easy walking distance of Audubon Terrace and the cemetery, the **Morris–Jumel Mansion** (65 Jumel Terrace at 160th and Edgecombe Ave; ☎923-8008; Wed–Sun 10am–4pm; $3) is another uptown surprise: cornered in its garden, the mansion somehow survived the destruction all around, and today is one of the more successful house museums, its proud Georgian outlines faced with a later Federal portico. Inside, the mansion's rooms reveal some of its engaging history: built as a rural retreat in 1765 by Colonel Roger Morris, it was briefly Washington's headquarters before falling into the hands of the British. A leaflet describes the rooms and their historical connections, but curiously omits much of the later history. Wealthy wine merchant Stephen Jumel bought the derelict mansion in 1801 and refurbished it for his wife Eliza, formerly a prostitute and his mistress. New York society didn't take to such a past, but when Jumel died in 1832, Eliza married ex-vice-president Aaron Burr (the nemesis of Alexander Hamilton) – she for his connections, he for her money. Burr was 78 when they married, twenty years older than Eliza: the marriage lasted for six months before old Burr upped and left, to die on the day of their divorce. Eliza battled on to the age of 91, and on the top floor of the house you'll find her obituary, a magnificently fictionalized account of a "scandalous" life.

Just opposite the entrance to the mansion's grounds is the quaint block of **Sylvan Terrace**, a tiny cobblestone mews lined with yellow and green wooden houses – and seeming impossibly out of place just barely off the wide-open intersection of Amsterdam and St Nicholas avenues.

From most western stretches of Washington Heights you get a glimpse of the **George Washington Bridge** that links Manhattan to New Jersey, and it's arguable that the feeder road to the bridge splits two distinct areas: below is bleakly rundown, the biggest area of illegal drug activity in the city, mainly to New Jersey residents making good use of the bridge; above the streets relax in smaller, more diverse ethnic neighborhoods of old-time Jews, Greeks, Central Europeans and especially Irish, though a major Hispanic community has recently built up. A skillful, dazzling sketch high above the Hudson, the bridge skims across the channel in massive metalwork and graceful lines, a natural successor to the Brooklyn Bridge. "Here, finally, steel architecture seems to laugh," said Le Corbusier of the 1931 construction. To appreciate what he meant, grit your teeth and walk – midtown Manhattan hangs like a visible promise in the distance.

The Cloisters Museum and Inwood

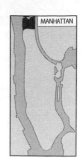

What most visitors pass through Washington Heights to see, though, is **The Cloisters**, the Metropolitan Museum's collection of medieval art housed in a Frankenstein's monster of a castle in Fort Tryon Park. Unequivocally, this is a must (see Chapter 15, "Museums and Galleries", for persuasion), and should you plump for riding up on the subway you'll find an additional reward in the park itself, cleverly landscaped by Frederick Law Olmsted, Jr – son of the famed Central Park and Prospect Park architect – and a comfortable place to get lost for half an hour or so.

Inwood

Fort Tryon Park joins **Inwood Park** by the Hudson River and, despite the presence of the Henry Hudson Parkway running underneath, it is possible to walk across Dyckman Street and into Inwood Park. The path up the side of the river gives a beautiful view of New Jersey, surprisingly hilly and wooded this far upstream. Keep walking and you will reach the very tip of Manhattan, an area known as *Spuyten Duyvil* ("the spitting devil" in Dutch), nowadays Columbia University's Athletic Stadium. Inwood Park itself is wild and rambling, often confusing and a little threatening if you get lost. It was once the stamping ground for Indian cave dwellers, but unfortunately the site of their original settlement is now buried under the Henry Hudson Parkway. Inwood's single tourist attraction is the **Dyckman Farmhouse Museum** (4881 Broadway at 204th St, ☎304-9422; Tues–Sun 11am–4pm; free), an eighteenth-century Dutch farmhouse restored with period bits and pieces – pleasant enough, but hardly worth the journey.

Chapter 14

The Outer Boroughs

Manhattan is a hard act to follow, and the four **Outer Boroughs** – Brooklyn, Queens, the Bronx and **Staten Island** – inevitably pale somewhat in comparison. But while they lack the glamour (and the mass money) of Manhattan, and the life there, essentially residential, is less obviously dynamic, a visit to any or all of the boroughs can offer some unexpected and refreshing perspectives on the city.

Most visitors never step foot off the island, though if you have more than a few days there's much out here to be recommended. The most common places to start are a trip on the **Staten Island ferry** or a walk over the Brooklyn Bridge to the **Brooklyn Heights Promenade**. Other modest attractions abound: in Brooklyn, there's salubrious **Brooklyn Heights** and beautiful **Prospect Park**, along with the rundown seaside resort of **Coney Island**. **Queens**, scarcely visited by outsiders, has the bustling Greek community of **Astoria** and some top-notch museums. As for **Staten Island**, the ferry is its own justification. The **Bronx** is a harder call: it's ordinarily residential at its north end and it has perhaps the country's best zoo, but the south, as many New York stories attest, can be Hard Territory – though definite strides are being made to reverse this label.

Perhaps the Outer Boroughs's most fascinating quality is their rich assortment of ethnic neighborhoods: Orthodox Jews in **Williamsburg**, Russians in **Brighton Beach**, and Poles in **Greenpoint** (all in Brooklyn); Indians and South Americans in **Jackson Heights** (Queens), Italians in **Belmont** (the Bronx); and the list goes on. These towns have been first stops for immigrants for

---

Be warned that the Outer Boroughs are much larger than Manhattan, and to get to some of the highlights you'll have to take various subways and buses in succession – it can be a long haul. Make sure you're familiarized with the transit system by studying "Getting around the city" in *Basics*, plus the maps at the back of the book, before you start.

---

more than two hundred years; as such, much of the best ethnic cuisine can be found here and you can walk long stretches without hearing English spoken.

Brooklyn

THE OUTER BOROUGHS

Maybe he's found out by now dat he'll neveh live long enough to know the whole of Brooklyn. It'd take a guy a lifetime to know Brooklyn t'roo an' t'roo. An' even den, you wouldn't know it at all.

Thomas Wolfe, *Only the Dead Know Brooklyn*

"The Great Mistake." So New York writer Pete Hamill summed up the **Brooklyn** annexation in 1898, and in a way, that's how most long-standing Brooklynites feel even today, traditionally seeing themselves as Brooklyn residents first, inhabitants of New York City a poor second. Maybe this sense of autonomy comes from the strong Brooklyn legacy – the Brooklyn Dodgers, the unmistakable accent, the famed sons and daughters like Woody Allen, Mel Brooks and Barbra Streisand, all of which have become part of the urban folklore that's a common heritage for Brooklynites of vastly different backgrounds.

If it were still a separate city Brooklyn would be the fourth largest in the United States, but until as recently as the early 1800s it was no more than a group of loosely connected towns and villages existing relatively autonomously from already thriving Manhattan across the water. It was with the arrival of Robert Fulton's steamship service, linking the two, that Brooklyn began to take on its present form, starting with the establishment of a leafy retreat at Brooklyn Heights. What really changed the borough was the opening of the **Brooklyn Bridge**, and thereafter development began to spread deeper inland, as housing was needed for the increasingly large workforce necessary to service a more commercialized Manhattan. By the turn of the century, Brooklyn was fully established as part of New York City, and its fate as Manhattan's perennial kid brother was sealed.

You can go to almost any neighborhood and find something worthwhile; the most obvious – and justly the most visited district – is **Brooklyn Heights**. Though many never get past this, the other areas around downtown – **Cobble Hill**, **Carroll Gardens** and **Fort Greene** – offer a lively enough mix. **Park Slope** has some of the city's best-preserved brownstones and is home to many up-and-coming professionals and a large lesbian community; Olmsted and Vaux's **Prospect Park** is for many an improvement on their more famous bit of landscaping in Manhattan. **Williamsburg**'s converted lofts are a favorite for artists; **Coney Island** and **Brighton Beach** are nothing if not unique, and definitely worth the subway ride.

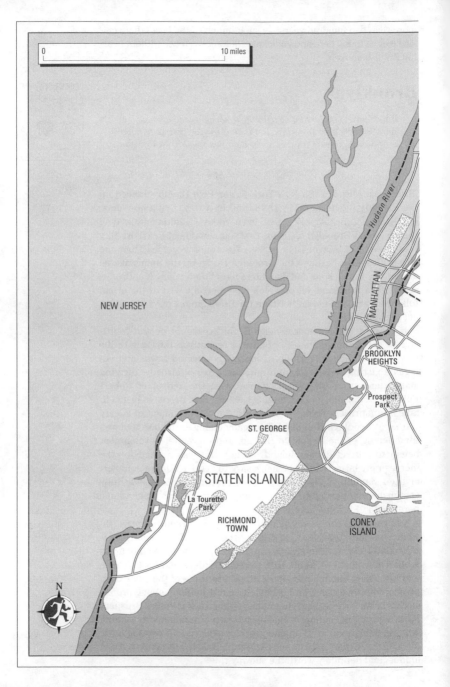

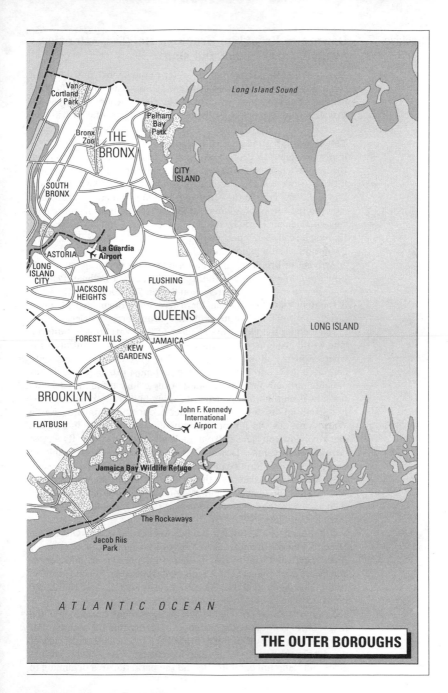

THE OUTER BOROUGHS

Downtown Brooklyn: Brooklyn Heights, Atlantic Avenue, Fort Greene and south

The stretch of Brooklyn from the water to the Brooklyn Academy of Music quickly moves from warehouses to brownstownes to the staid buildings found in most any civic center. Getting there, if you choose to walk, could turn out to be the most exciting part of your trip.

The Brooklyn Bridge and Fulton Ferry District

If you are going to Brooklyn, begin by walking over the **Brooklyn Bridge** – it's not too long (less than a mile across) and it may hold the best views of Manhattan that you will get. The walkway begins at City Hall Park next to the Municipal Building and ends in Brooklyn either at the corner of Adams and Tillary streets or at the more convenient Cadman Plaza East staircase. If you're not up to walking (though it really is the best way), the #2, #3, #4, #5, N, R, A, C and F subways all stop in downtown Brooklyn.

Arriving in Brooklyn from the bridge, walk down the stairs and bear right, following the path through the park at Cadman Plaza. If you cross on to Middagh Street, you'll soon find yourself in the heart of the Heights; follow Cadman Plaza West down the hill to Old Fulton Street, and you'll find yourself in the **Fulton Ferry District**.

Hard under the glowering shadow of the **Watchtower building** (the world headquarters of the Jehovah's Witness organization) is where Robert Fulton's ferry used to put in: during the nineteenth century it grew into Brooklyn's first and most prosperous industrial neighborhood. With the coming of the bridge it fell into decline, but now is on the way up again: its aging buildings are being slowly tarted up as loft spaces (check out the imposing **Eagle Warehouse**, 28 Old Fulton St; its penthouse, with the huge glass clock-window you can see from the bridge, is one of the city's most coveted apartments). Down on the ferry slip itself, a couple of barges-cum-restaurants – most notably the *River Café* – entice die-hard Manhattanites across the bridge by night, as well as Wall Street types for power lunching. Locals are more likely to follow their noses to the brick-oven *Patsy's Pizza* for some of the best pizza in New York.

If it's open, the **Brooklyn Bridge Anchorage** across Old Fulton Street is well worth a visit. A cavernous space, cool and quiet under (inside, actually) the bridge, it's home to sporadic art and performance art happenings. There's no central number to call for information, but a call to ☎212/206-6674 in the summer months should get you a schedule of their events.

Just north of here, reachable by walking through the garden of the *River Café*, is a waterfront warehouse district ripe for renewal. For now, the **Empire Fulton Ferry State Park** offers a beautiful view of the river at river level – something increasingly rare – and occasional art and sculpture exhibits. Behind the park, the area beginning to

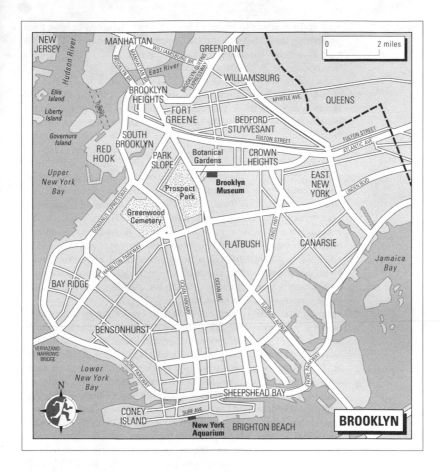

be known as **DUMBO** (Down Under Manhattan Bridge Overpass) is rumored to be the next big thing. So far, it's not – but if you make it over that way by daylight, the warehouse buildings and cobblestone streets are interesting enough.

Brooklyn Heights
Brooklyn Heights is one of New York City's most beautiful and wealthy neighborhoods. From the early eighteenth century on, bankers and financiers from Wall Street could live among its peace and exclusivity and imagine themselves far from the tumult of Manhattan, but still close enough to gaze across to the monied spires. Today the Heights are not far different.

Walking up the hill from Old Fulton Street, you can take Everett or Henry streets into the oldest part of Brooklyn Heights proper. It's

Brooklyn

easy and enjoyable to wander these streets – so many houses have plaques on them that you can take yourself on a self-guided walking tour. One house that doesn't have a plaque is 24 Middagh Street (at the corner of Willow); an unassuming but perfectly preserved Federal-style wooden house dating to 1824, it's the neighborhood's oldest house. Two streets down, on Orange between Hicks and Henry, you'll see the **Plymouth Church of the Pilgrims**, a simple church that went up in the mid-nineteenth century and became famous as the preaching base of **Henry Ward Beecher**, abolitionist and campaigner for women's rights. Beecher was a great orator: he held mock slave auctions here and used the money to buy slaves' freedom, and toured the country persuading the rich to give to charitable institutions. This brought the famous to his church, and Horace Greeley, Mark Twain, even Abraham Lincoln all worshipped here on more than one occasion. Sadly, though, Henry Ward remains less known outside New York than his wife, Harriet Beecher Stowe, author of *Uncle Tom's Cabin*, since his later years were marred by an adultery scandal of which he was acquitted but never finally cleared in public esteem. The church is kept locked most of the time, so the only chance you'll get to see its barn-like interior is when there's a service on. No great loss.

South from here is **Pierrepont Street**; one of the Heights's main arteries, it's studded with delightful – and fantastic – brownstones. At the corner of Henry Street the **Herman Behr House**, a chunky Romanesque Revival mansion, has been, successively, a hotel, brothel, Franciscan monastery (it was the brothers who added the horrific canopy) and, currently, private apartments. Further down Pierrepont, look in if you can on the **Brooklyn Unitarian Church** – originally known as the Church of the Savior – which is notable for its exquisite neo-Gothic interior. Across the road at no. 128 is the **Brooklyn Historical Society**, which guards its treasures somewhat territorially: it costs a hefty $5 to get into the well-stocked research library. A better bargain is the **museum** (Tues–Sat noon–5pm; ☎718/624-0890; $2.50, $1 for children/seniors), which features a fascinating exhibit on the evolution of Brooklyn neighborhoods; see also "Information, maps and tours" in *Basics*. If you can plan your day to coincide with a walking tour or other program, so much the better.

The Promenade, Montague Street and around
Walk west on any of the streets between Clark and Remsen and you'll reach the **Promenade** (aka "the Esplanade"), a boardwalk with one of the most spectacular – and renowned – views in all of New York. It's hard to take your eyes off the skyline, the water and the Statue of Liberty in the distance, but do turn around and notice the creeper-hung palaces set back modestly from the walkway. Norman Mailer lives in one of these, and a few others are weekend homes for the rich and famous: it doesn't hurt to keep your eyes peeled.

Leading off the southern end of the Promenade is **Montague Street,** Brooklyn Heights's lively main thoroughfare, lined with bars and restaurants and, surprisingly for such an exclusive district, with a workaday atmosphere that makes it one of New York's most pleasant thoroughfares. It looks like it could be in Manhattan what with its *Banana Republic* and *Starbucks*, but it's not – and luckily you can feel that. Numerous restaurants have outdoor seating in good weather: try *Caffè Buon Gusto* for delicious Italian food in a prime people-watching spot, or *Ozzie's* for coffee and pastries on their secluded back patio.

South of Montague, the brownstone streets continue, taking you toward Atlantic Avenue and Cobble Hill. Between Remsen and Joralemon, look for **Grace Court Alley** and **Hunts Lane,** two mews tucked away off Hicks and Henry respectively.

Downtown Brooklyn and Fulton Mall

The eastern end of Montague is known as "Bank Row" – downtown Brooklyn's business center – and leads on to what is in effect the borough's Civic Center, with the end of the residential Heights signaled by the tall Art Deco buildings of Court Street. Across the road the sober Greek-style **Borough Hall** is topped with a cupola-ed belfry; further east are the massive State Supreme Court and Romanesque **post office**, next to which stands a bronze of Henry Ward Beecher. There's little to linger for, but your tired feet should know that this is where to find the large Borough Hall subway station.

Beyond the civic grandeur **Fulton Street** leads east, principal shopping street for the borough as a whole and here pedestrianized into a bustling shopping mall. There are some good bargains to be found here, but all in all the streets – lined with fast-food franchises – can be a little depressing. What you will find here is *Gage & Tollner*, Brooklyn's most famous restaurant, which serves seafood and steaks in a setting determinedly left unchanged. However, the food doesn't come cheap. Another neighborhood landmark, and one more affordable, is *Junior's* on the corner of Flatbush and DeKalb avenues; their cheesecake is justly famous and their other dishes aren't far behind.

Just south of Fulton Mall, Adams Street turns into Boerum Place, and at the corner of Schermerhorn you'll see a subway entrance that actually leads to the **New York Transit Museum**, housed in an unused station that hasn't seen a train for over forty years: see p. 269 for details.

Fort Greene and the Brooklyn Academy of Music

To the east of downtown Brooklyn and easily navigated by keeping an eye on the **Williamsburg Savings Bank** – Brooklyn's tallest building (go to the 26th floor for the view) – sits **Fort Greene**, named after Nathaniel Greene, a prominent general in the American Revolution. Long established as a strong multiracial community, Fort Greene is now home to a growing African-American professional contingent, and a number of exciting venues for music and events have opened up: check out *Royston's Rhythms*, a jazz club at 63 Lafayette Avenue (☎718/243-0900); or the Friday night poetry readings at the *Brooklyn Moon Café* (745 Fulton St at S. Portland; ☎718/243-0424). Along with these are several good restaurants such as *Sapodilla* (412 Myrtle Ave between Vanderbilt and Clinton), which dishes up excellent soul and Cajun food; most restaurants and cafés here are located along Fulton Street. Fort Greene also boasts America's oldest performing arts center, the **Brooklyn Academy of Music** (BAM to its fans, who come from all over the city) at 30 Lafayette Avenue (☎718/636-4111). BAM is one of the borough's most hyped institutions, and has played host over the years to a glittering – and innovative – array of artists, albeit at considerably higher prices (and profile) than the newer spots opening up. Another, younger, neighborhood institution that's become a large attraction to visitors from outside the area is **Spike's Joint,** the movie merchandise and clothes store of film director and Fort Greene native Spike Lee, at 1 South Elliot Place, right near Fort Greene Park (☎718/802-1000).

Atlantic Avenue

South of Brooklyn Heights is **Atlantic Avenue,** which runs from the East River all the way to Queens. This stretch – and spilling south into Cobble Hill – is center to a vibrant Middle Eastern community. There are some fine and reasonably priced Yemeni and Lebanese restaurants here and a good sprinkling of Middle Eastern grocers and bakeries. Take a wander through the *Sahadi Importing Co.* at no. 187, known throughout the city for nuts, dried fruit, halva, and more than a dozen varieties of olives along with delicacies from other parts of the world. Next door at no. 185, *Peter's Ice Cream Parlor and Coffeehouse* is a neighborhood institution for both its fabulous homemade ice cream and its friendly atmosphere (☎718/852-3835).

Cobble Hill, Boerum Hill, Carroll Gardens and Red Hook

Across Atlantic Avenue, **Cobble Hill, Boerum Hill,** and **Carroll Gardens** – along with the old wharfing community of **Red Hook** – make up the area once known as South Brooklyn. Court Street holds the most interest here with its restaurants, cafés and shops, but there's not too much of a reason to make a special trip.

Cobble Hill

The main streets of **Cobble Hill** – Congress, Warren and Amity – are a mixture of solid brownstones and colorful redbrick row houses, most of which have long been a haven of the professional classes: rents here are beginning to approximate those of Brooklyn Heights, and signs of the young professional migration can be seen in the cafés springing up in the area. Among the best are *Bagel Pointe Café* (231 Court St), which has good brunch and a nice outdoor patio, and the charming *Roberto Cappuccino Caffe and Tea Room* (221 Court St). The who-was-who tour of Cobble Hill should take you to 197 Amity Street, where **Jenny Jerome,** later Lady Randolph Churchill and mother of Winston, was born – the house is unfortunately disfigured by aluminium windows and a modern rustic facing. **Warren Place** is worth a look as well – easy to miss if you're not looking carefully, this tiny alley of late nineteenth-century workers' cottages is a shelter of quiet on the last block of Warren Street, just a stone's throw from the thunder of the Brooklyn–Queens Expressway. The Bergen stop on the F train will get you to and from this neighborhood, as well as neighboring Boerum Hill.

Boerum Hill

To the east of Cobble Hill, and south of Atlantic Avenue, **Boerum Hill** is scruffier and less architecturally impressive than its neighbors, though it has its share of sober Greek Revival and Italianate buildings. One of the more solidly integrated neighborhoods in Brooklyn, it's home to Italian- and Irish-descended families, Arabs and a long-established Puerto Rican population which has since become part of a more diverse Latino community. They bring salsa music and dancing to the stoops of the neighborhood brownstones, and single-room storefront social clubs are a common sight on Smith Street, the commercial strip of this neighborhood.

Carroll Gardens

Going south along Court Street, Cobble Hill merges into **Carroll Gardens** around De Graw Street (also serviced by the F train; stop at Carroll St). Originally a middle- and upper-class community of many nationalities, this part of South Brooklyn was invaded by a massive influx of Italian dockworking immigrants who came in the early 1900s; the area was later named after Charles Carroll, the only Roman Catholic signee of the Declaration of Independence. Today, as Cobble Hill turns into the next Brooklyn Heights, parts of Carroll Gardens are turning into the next Cobble Hill, and youthful professionals are a new sight coming out of the brownstones. But you'll still find plenty of pizza and pastry on Court Street, and a strong sense of community prevails, as the lower-middle-class, family-oriented, Italian population manages to coexist peacefully with the newcomers. If you are looking for a place to relax, stop by *Shakespeare's Sister* at 270 Court, a gift shop-cum-café.

A real treat is to wander the streets of Carroll Gardens around holidays, particularly Christmas and Easter. Many of the large gardens that give the neighborhood its name are decorated with religious shrines and statues all year-round, but at holidays the residents pull out the stops, outdoing each other with flashing lights, incandescent monuments, and even appropriate music to produce the most all-encompassing display.

Red Hook

After Carroll Gardens, the desolation of **Red Hook** is striking. The growing automatization of the docking industry (vividly portrayed in the film and the notorious novel *Last Exit to Brooklyn*) left Red Hook behind; the building of the Gowanus Expressway shortly thereafter isolated the area, and it's never been able to recover. Today a small Italian contingent remains and shares the now-cheap housing with African Americans and Latinos, many of whom live in the infamous Red Hook housing projects. This is not a place for casual sightseeing.

There are, however, a few things that could point to better days ahead. In 1995, community volunteers presented their own ambitious urban renewal plan, though it has yet to be realized; meanwhile, two arts organizations are contributing to the revitalization of the waterfront area: the **Hudson Waterfront Museum**, housed in a restored barge, now makes its home at Pier 45 (Conover St at Beard St; ☎718/935-9019) and sometimes sponsors concerts; and the **Brooklyn Waterfront Artists Coalition** holds its month-long Spring Show in May (call ☎718/596-2507 for specifics) on the piers as well. Still, change in this neighborhood is slow, and it remains not a highly recommended area to visit.

Prospect Park, Park Slope and Flatbush

Where Brooklyn really asserts itself – architecturally, at any rate – as a city in its own right is Flatbush Avenue leading up to **Grand Army Plaza**: pure classicism, with traffic being funneled around the central open space (best reached by the #2 or #3 train, Grand Army stop). It was laid out in the late nineteenth century by Olmsted and Vaux, who designed it as a dramatic approach to their newly completed Prospect Park just behind. The triumphal **Soldiers and Sailors' Memorial Arch**, which you can climb (spring and autumn weekends only), was added thirty years later and topped with a fiery sculpture of Victory in tribute to the triumph of the north in the Civil War. On the far side of the square the creamy-smooth **Brooklyn Public Library** continues the heroic theme, its facade smothered with stirring declarations to its function as fountain of knowledge, and with an entrance showing the borough's home-grown poet, Walt Whitman. Behind, there's the **Brooklyn Museum** and the **Brooklyn Children's Museum** (see Chapter 15, *Museums and Galleries*) and the **Brooklyn Botanic Garden** (April–Sept Tues–Fri 8am–6pm, Sat & Sun 10am–6pm; Oct–March Tues–Fri 8am–4.30pm, Sat & Sun 10am–4.30pm; ☎718/622-4433).

The Botanic Garden is one of the most enticing park spaces in the city, smaller and more immediately likable than its more celebrated rival in the Bronx, and making for a relaxing place to unwind after a couple of hours in the museum. Sumptuous but not overplanted, it sports a Rose Garden, Japanese Garden, a Shakespeare Garden (laid out with plants mentioned in the Bard's plays), a staircase commemorating famous Brooklynites, and some delightful lawns draped with weeping willows and beds of flowering shrubs. There's also a conservatory, housing among other things the country's largest collection of bonsais, and there's a gift shop that stocks a wide array of exotic plants, bulbs and seeds.

Prospect Park

The Botanic Garden is about as far away from Manhattan's bustle as it's possible to get, but if you can tear yourself away there's also **Prospect Park** itself. Energized by their success with Central Park, Olmsted and Vaux landscaped this in the early 1890s, completing it just as the finishing touches were being put to Grand Army Plaza out-side. In a way it's better than Central Park, having more effectively managed to retain its pastoral quality. Although there have been encroachments over the years – tennis courts, a zoo – and plenty of people use the park for picnics, walks and soccer games, it remains for the most part remarkably bucolic in feel. Focal points include the **Lefferts Homestead**, an eighteenth-century colonial farmhouse shifted here some time ago and now open, free of charge, on week-ends; the **Wildlife Center** (formerly the Zoo), in which the animals have benefited recently from a humane overhaul like that in Central Park, open (for a small charge) every day; a restored carousel; and the lake in the southern half. Many of the various park attractions have been specially geared to children, so if you're traveling with kids, it's definitely worth a trip. And if you're worried about exhaus-tion – it's about 3.5 miles around the park on the main road – there's a free trolley bus (☎718/965-8967) that makes the rounds of the popular spots on weekends. The **boathouse** has maps and informa-tion on events in the park (dance, drama and music are performed in the bandshell most summer weekends), or you can pick up all kinds of park information on ☎718/965-8999.

Park Slope

The western exits of Prospect Park leave you on the fringes of **Park Slope**. Walk down any of the quiet cross-streets (with some of New York's best-preserved brownstones) and you'll reach the trendy shopping street of Seventh Avenue (you can also get here by the F train, 7th Ave stop), where new restaurants and cafés share space with more long-standing businesses and some grandiose churches. This area has become a serious rival to Brooklyn Heights, with some of the city's fastest-soaring property prices. As young professionals and families flock to its amenities, even the more downmarket Fifth Avenue – until recently solidly Hispanic – is showing signs of taking some of Seventh's overflow, though it already owned some of the most favored neighborhood eateries, especially *Aunt Suzie's* at no. 247 and *Cucina* at no. 256, two fine Italian joints.

The Slope is also home to a thriving lesbian and gay population, more famously the former. The action is split between Fifth and Seventh avenues: there's the specialty bookstore *Beyond Words* (Fifth Ave off Sackett St) and its next-door neighbor *Rising Café*; also, down Seventh Avenue is the prime gay lounge in the area, *Sanctuary* (at 15th St).

Walk back down Fifth Avenue, across the Prospect Expressway, and you reach **Greenwood Cemetery**: larger even than Prospect Park and very much the place to be buried in the last century if you could afford an appropriately flashy headstone or, better still, mau-soleum. Among the names buried here: Horace Greeley, politician and campaigning newspaper editor, lies relatively unpretentiously on a hill; William Marcy "Boss" Tweed, nineteenth-century Democratic chief and scoundrel, slumbers deep in the wilds; and the Steinway family, of piano fame, have their very own 119-room mausoleum. Look out also for the tomb of one John Matthews, who made a fortune out of carbonated drinks and had himself a memorial carved with birds and animals, some fierce-looking gargoyles and (rather immodestly) scenes from his own life. You can stroll around the cemetery and find all this for yourself; or try to catch one of the **tours** given by the Brooklyn Center for the Urban Environment (see "Information, maps and tours" in *Basics*).

Flatbush

Southeast of Prospect Park is **Flatbush**, a busy though largely uninteresting residential and shopping area inhabited mostly by West Indians – though that makes it a decent enough place to get food or other wares from that part of the world. There are a couple of other notable highlights. An exclusive (and exhaustively planned) community of large single-family houses developed in 1899, **Prospect Park South** is a surprising haven centered on several quiet secluded streets around Albemarle Road – just walk south from Church Avenue (reachable from the park or the D and Q trains), on either Buckingham Road or Coney Island Avenue. Back on Church, at the corner of Flatbush Avenue, stands the **Reformed Protestant Dutch Church of Flatbush**, which was founded in 1654 by Peter Stuyvesant. This isn't the original building, but it's still attractive: the small graveyard in the back is a jewel. Many of the headstones have sunk into the ground or are hard to read, but if you try to make out the names and inscriptions, you'll see that at least several are in Dutch. The large building across the street, the **Erasmus Hall High School** (founded as a private academy by the church in 1786), gets a mention only because Barbra Streisand went to school there.

Further down Flatbush Avenue (at the end of the #2 and #5 trains) is **Brooklyn College**. There's not much reason to go here, but the campus is a pleasant place to stroll if you happen to be in the neighborhood. One of the best reasons to come is to catch the #Q35 (Queens local bus which originates in Brooklyn at Flatbush by Brooklyn College) to Jacob Riis Park in Rockaway (see p.219 for details).

Central Brooklyn

The areas loosely comprising **Central Brooklyn** are fairly rougher terrain, known mostly these days as pockets of violence and decline, though not without some historical appeal.

Bedford-Stuyvesant

Immediately east of Fort Greene, though quite different in feel, is **Bedford-Stuyvesant**, once one of the most elegant neighborhoods in the city, today one of the most badly neglected. Originally it was two separate areas, populated by both blacks and whites; the opening of the Brooklyn Bridge and later the construction of the A train brought a massive influx of African-Americans into the area. (Duke Ellington's "Take the A Train" commemorates that exodus from Harlem, which many hoped would give them a better life.) This led to increased hostility between the two groups, which in turn led to fighting, and in the 1940s the white population left, taking funding for many important community services with them. This was the start of the economic decline of "Bed-Stuy," as it has become colloquially known, and though the area has suffered the all-too-usual problems of inner-city neglect, today the African-American community here, the second largest in the country after Harlem, is desperately trying to stop Bed-Stuy's rot and take advantage of an architectural legacy of some of the best Romanesque Revival brownstones in the city.

There is a cultural and historical legacy here as well, one which was largely forgotten until the 1960s and which remains unknown to many outside the area still. The nineteenth-century village of **Weeksville** – named after one of the first black landowners to move there – was a community of free blacks which evolved after slavery was abolished in New York State in 1827. Little remains of Weeksville today, but an archaeological dig in 1969 turned up some fascinating artifacts, and community efforts saved several landmark houses on Bergen Street, in what was once the center of Weeksville and is now on the Bed-Stuy/Crown Heights border. **The Society for the Preservation of Weeksville and Bedford-Stuyvesant History** now operates a **museum** of African-American history in these houses and, while its efforts are directed primarily at local school groups, the Society welcomes visitors. It's best to call ahead (☎718/756-5250). To get to Weeksville take the A train to Utica Ave.

East of Bedford-Stuyvesant, there's not a lot to see. The neighborhood of **Brownsville** is notable for historical reasons: in the early part of this century, it was notorious as a hotbed for prominent anarchists, Bolsheviks, and other political free thinkers. Emma Lazarus, author of the spirited inscription on the Statue of Liberty, lived here, and in 1916, with more than 150 prospective clients waiting outside its doors, the first birth control clinic in America opened here – only to be raided and closed nine days later by the vice squad, and its founder, Margaret Sanger, imprisoned for thirty days as a "public nuisance."

Crown Heights

Fulton Street and Atlantic Avenue separate Bedford-Stuyvesant from **Crown Heights**, home to the largest West Indian neighborhood in New York (Brooklyn has the largest African-Caribbean population outside the Caribbean itself), and to an active, established community of Hasidic Jews. Coexistence between these two groups has always been strained and, though things have settled since the death of a black child and the subsequent murder of a Hasidic man set off riots in 1991, relations are far from comfortable: the name "Crown Heights" remains synonymous with racial tension to many New Yorkers. In general, though, it's not dangerous to wander Crown Heights, and the lively atmosphere of Eastern Parkway (reachable by the #2 or #3 to Eastern Parkway/Brooklyn Museum or the #2, #3 or #4 to Franklin Ave) can be extremely enjoyable. If you're in town on Labor Day, too, this is the place to be, when the annual **Mardi Gras Carnival** (aka West Indian Day Parade) bursts into life, (held in September rather than February because of the climate) with music, food, costumes and general revelry.

Coastal Brooklyn

It's possible, in theory, to walk, rollerblade or bike almost the entire southern **coast** of Brooklyn. On occasion, paths disappear, leaving you to share the service road off the highway with cars, but you'll never be on the actual highway itself. In short, it can be done. Even if you're of less sturdy stock it's worth making the trip to at least one of these areas to take in the often breathtaking views.

Bay Ridge

Way down south at the end of the R train is **Bay Ridge**, a traditionally Scandinavian community that's now more Irish and Italian (with a smattering of Russians and Arabs), although the annual Norwegian Independence Day Parade on May 17 still remains. It's a relaxed place, where newcomers and old-timers share space comfortably. Third Avenue is known for the huge proliferation of bars and restaurants; there's a lot to choose from, but for the sheer history of it, go to *Lento's* (at the corner of Ovington St) and ask any of the waiters to explain some of the pictures that cover the wall. One shows the christening – in the back room – of the current owner, the granddaughter of Mr Lento himself, who opened the place in 1926. It's worth the (sometimes long) wait – and the pizza, in the running for the thinnest in New York, isn't bad either.

From the Bay Ridge Avenue (locals call it 69th Street) stop on the R train, walk west – passing the **Shore Belt Cycle Club** (basic bikes for $6 an hour, 25¢ extra for hand brakes) – and keep going until you get to the 69th Street pier, start of the **Shore Road Bike Path**. (Rollerblade enthusiasts should get off the subway at 95th St and detour to *Panda Sport* on Fifth Ave at 92nd, where rentals are $20 for the day. There's an entrance to the Bike Path at 95th St.) Looking north from the shoreline, lower Manhattan seems further away than expected; just to the south of the pier is the shimmering **Verrazano Narrows Bridge**, flashing its minimalist message across the entry to the bay. This slender, beautiful span was, until Britain's Humber Bridge opened, the world's longest at 4260 feet – so long, in fact, that the tops of the towers are visibly an inch or so out of parallel to allow for the curvature of the earth.

The Bike Path, part of a narrow strip of park that follows the coast south and then east, is a lovely stroll, marred only by the roar of the Belt Parkway it runs alongside. Follow it till you get to the larger expanse of **Dyker Beach Park** (named after the beach that still exists underneath the lawn; at low tide, you can see sand at the water's edge), where old and young from the surrounding neighborhood come for sunshine and expert kite-flying. After that, you can turn back, or follow the path to the end, turn left on Bay Parkway, and walk to the end of the B train. The truly determined can continue east to Coney Island.

Coney Island

Accessible to anyone for the price of a subway token, the beachfront amusement spot of **Coney Island** has long given working-class New Yorkers the kind of holiday they just couldn't get otherwise. Look at old movies and black-and-white photos from the earlier part of this century; then take the subway to Stillwell Avenue (last stop on the B, D, F or N) to see for yourself. These days, the music blares louder than it once did, the language of choice on the boardwalk is Spanish as often as English, and the innocence captured in those old snapshots is, as elsewhere in the 1990s, long gone; but step out into the sunshine on a summer Saturday and you'll feel the same excitement that's filled generations of kids about to ride the Cyclone for the very first time.

You do have to be in the right frame of mind. On weekdays, rainy days, and off-season, the festive atmosphere can disappear, making for an experience that's bittersweet, if not downright depressing. The beach can be overwhelmingly crowded on hot days, and it's never the cleanest place in or out of the water. But show up for the annual **Mermaid Parade** on the first Saturday of summer (late June, but check the newspapers to be sure), and you'll get caught up in the fun of what's got to be one of the oddest – certainly glitziest – small-town festivals in the country, where paraders dress in King Neptune and mermaid attire.

On arrival, head for **Nathan's**, the fast-food spot on the corner when you get off the subway. This is the home of the "famous Coney Island hot dog" advertised in *Nathan's* branches elsewhere in the city, and while that delicacy is eminently skippable in Manhattan, only vegetarians have an excuse for missing it here. (*Nathan's* holds an annual "Hot Dog Eating Contest" on July 4th – so far the record is 24$\frac{1}{2}$ hot dogs, with buns, in 12 minutes.) One block from *Nathan's* is the boardwalk, where a leisurely stroll gives you ample opportunity to people-watch as you look for clues to Coney Island's past in the fading paint on the sides of buildings.

Go west to see the overgrown remains of a burned-out **roller coaster** and the landmark parachute jump, now parachute-less and painted orange for no particular reason. In the opposite direction, you come upon the **Coney Island Museum**, maintained by a non-profit organization and home of such long-standing performers as the Human Blockhead, the Illustrated Man and the Snake Woman. Unofficial, somehow more authentic, sideshows (such as the Two-Headed Baby, the Headless Woman and the Giant Killer Rat) abound on the side streets, but don't expect much for your money.

Coney Island's amusement area comprises several amusement parks, none of which are connected. What this means is that the POP (pay-one-price) **tickets** each park offers don't really make a lot of sense unless you have kids (nearly all the children's rides are in *Deno's Wonder Wheel Park*) or plan on riding one ride more than four times. Since individual ticket prices are expensive, make your choices carefully. The **Wonder Wheel** ($2.50) is a must – after 75 years, it's still the tallest ferris wheel in the world, and the *only* one in the world where "swinging" cars shift position as the wheel makes its slow circle twice around. The **Cyclone roller coaster** ($4; $3 for a repeat ride) is another landmark attraction, but if you're used to slick modern loop-coaster rides, be forewarned: this low-tech creaky wooden coaster is not for the faint of heart. Rides to miss are the "Spook-a-rama," which seems promising for kitsch but fails to deliver, and the "Zipper" (affectionately nicknamed "the Vomitorium"), which will get rid of your *Nathan's* hot dog for you, if not bring your day to an end altogether. Further down the boardwalk, halfway to Brighton Beach, is the **New York Aquarium** (see p.401 for details) – well worth a visit if you have the time.

Rather unfortunately, the face of Coney Island may be changing in the next few years – now that Times Square has been spiffed up, some are targeting this as their next agenda. Indeed, a multimillion-dollar sports-and-entertainment complex is in the early planning stages.

Brighton Beach

Further along, **Brighton Beach**, or "Little Odessa," is home to the country's largest community of Russian emigrés who arrived in the 1970s following a relaxation of emigration restrictions on Soviet citizens entering the US. There's also a long-established and now largely elderly Jewish population. You know when you're out of Coney Island – not only have the amusements disappeared, but there's a residential aspect to the place that gives Brighton Beach a greater appeal.

The neighborhood's main drag, **Brighton Beach Avenue**, runs parallel to the boardwalk, underneath the elevated subway until the train swings north (the D and Q stop here). The street is a bustling mixture of **foodshops**, appetizing **restaurants**, and shops selling every type of Russian **souvenir** imaginable. Eating is half the reason to go to Brighton Beach: for a taste of tradition, try the long-established *Mrs Stahl's Knishes* on the corner of Brighton Beach and Coney Island Avenue, right where the train turns. Even more fun is to pick one of the many grocers/deli shops and try ordering yourself a picnic lunch – maybe some caviar or smoked fish as a topping to some heavy black bread. Be brave: the further away from the subway you get, the less English is spoken, and this community is not known for its outward friendliness. Sit-down food is also readily available throughout Brighton Beach, though you'd be better off waiting until evening as it's then the restaurants really heat up, becoming a near-parody of a rowdy Russian night out with loud live music, much glass-clinking and the frenzied knocking back of vodka. The most popular and accessible spots are *National*, *Ocean* and *Odessa*, all on Brighton Beach Avenue at 273, 1029 and 1113 respectively.

Sheepshead Bay

Next stop on the D or Q subway line heading back to Manhattan is **Sheepshead Bay**, which claims distinction as "New York's only working fishing village" (though City Island in the Bronx – see p.226 – might beg to differ). Much quieter than Coney Island or even Brighton Beach, Sheepshead Bay's **Emmons Avenue** maintains a definite charm nonetheless, with locals strolling past the piers of fishing boats and relaxing at outdoor cafés whenever the weather is fine. In early evening, the adventurous can shop the boats themselves for what is undoubtedly the freshest **fish** in the city; all others can sample an earlier catch anywhere along the strip. The city's clean-up efforts have been quite successful and, according to residents, the fishing is better than it has been in years. Truly dedicated fish fanatics can go out on one of the many **boats** that take out visitors – the cost is around $25 per person, and all you have to do is show up at the piers before 7am and see who's around. Many of the fishing boats also do **sunset cruises** to various points of interest in New York Harbor. The cost of these is about $15, and you can either wander the piers after 5pm to see who's going out or check the ads in the *Daily News*. Diving trips are also possible, although you may have to rent equipment in Manhattan. For more information, ask on the boats, or stop in to *Harvey's Ski/Sport Shop* at 3179 Emmons (☎718/743-0054). They in fact only *sell* diving equipment, though will refill your tank if you've got one, and the owner is a wealth of information about Sheepshead Bay in general, not to mention the rest of Brooklyn. He'll point you in the right direction and, if you wish, rent you rollerblades and bikes.

Just across the bridge from Sheepshead Bay is the tiny neighborhood of **Manhattan Beach**, where the beach of the same name is popular with locals and largely unknown to most New Yorkers. It's a very pleasant spot to swim, especially on less-crowded weekday afternoons. Just northeast of Sheepshead Bay (although more easily accessible by bus from Flatbush) are the marshland of **Marine Park** and **Floyd**

Bennett Field – an old airfield that serves as headquarters for the Gateway National Recreation Area in **Jamaica Bay** (see p.219).

Northern Brooklyn: Greenpoint and Williamsburg

Head south from **Newtown Creek**, the sludge-filled separation between Queens and Brooklyn, and you'll see several of the most clear-cut shifts in neighborhood makeup in the city. Between Polish north **Greenpoint** and Hasidic south **Williamsburg** there are worlds of difference.

Greenpoint

Greenpoint (reachable by the G to Greenpoint Ave or L to Bedford Ave) hasn't been green for a long time. The Industrial Revolution was good to the economy here, but the environment bears its legacy: the "Black Arts" – printing, pottery, gas, glass and iron – thrived, creating jobs for a growing community, although the pollution was considerable, and the industries that replaced them – primarily fuel and garbage – haven't really improved matters. That said, it's surprising what a pleasant community Greenpoint really is. And if you can manage to get a glimpse of the Manhattan skyline from between the buildings, so much the better.

To really understand what makes Greenpoint tick, take a look at the imposing **Russian Orthodox Church of the Transfiguration**, south of McCarren Park, at the corner of North 12th and Driggs streets along Bedford and/or Berry Street. The dominant language around here is Polish, and it's a great place to try Polish food.

Continuing south, toward Williamsburg, an artistic community has recently put down its roots, with the attendant new shops and cafés mostly along Bedford Avenue. Among the highlights are *Oznot's* (79 Berry St at N 9th St), a stylish Middle-Eastern restaurant with an outdoor patio; *Two Cats From Brooklyn* (189 Bedford Ave), featuring clothes, jewelry and art made by locals; and the recently opened *Brooklyn Brewery* (118 N 11th St). A century ago there were nearly fifty breweries in Brooklyn, though now the tradition has mostly died out. You can tour this one on Saturdays from noon to 4pm; it's relatively small and makes for a pleasant visit.

Williamsburg

Beyond here, the neighborhood turns completely Hispanic, and you're in **Williamsburg**, where, like many other such enclaves throughout the city, a strong family atmosphere offsets the feeling of menace instilled by rundown buildings – although it's not the city's most welcoming neighborhood. The area's biggest claim to fame is *Peter Luger's Steak House* at 178 Broadway (at Driggs Ave), reputed to have the best steak in the city – for a hefty price (see p.346). South of the Williamsburg Bridge, **Division Avenue** marks the divide between the Hispanic community and the **Hasidic Jewish** part of Williamsburg, where the men wear black suits and long *payess* (curls) hanging from under their hats, and women are conservatively dressed with scarves or wigs. The Jewish community has been prominent here since the **Williamsburg Bridge** linked the area to the Lower East Side in 1903 and many of the Jews from that neighborhood left for the better conditions across the East River (the bridge was unkindly nicknamed the "Jew Plank"). During World War II a further settlement of Hasidim, mainly from the ultra-orthodox Satmar sect, established Williamsburg as a firmly Jewish area, and Puerto Ricans to the north and east began to arrive, since which time the two communities have coexisted in a state of strained tolerance. While tensions have on occasion boiled over, there has never been anything on the scale of what has been seen in Crown Heights. The bridge itself has been undergoing massive renovations recently, though you can still walk over it from the Lower East Side. It's a gritty and somewhat harrowing journey, not necessarily advised.

The best place to start exploring Jewish Williamsburg is **Lee Avenue**, the main shopping street, or the more residential **Bedford Avenue** that runs parallel (take the J, M or Z to Marcy Ave to get there). On both you'll see manifestations of the neighborhood's character: *Glatt Kosher* delicatessens line the streets; signs are written in both Yiddish and Hebrew. Don't take it personally if you're ignored – you may feel like you've dropped in from another planet, and the residents may feel like you have, too. Further south on Lee Avenue, you're far away from any subway – the B44 bus will get you back to the Williamsburg Bridge; the B61 will take you to downtown Brooklyn.

At the southern tip of the neighborhood is the former **Brooklyn Naval Yard**, a crucial World War II construction ground for famous battleships such as the *Iowa*, *New Jersey*, *Arizona* and *Missouri*. Despite great public opposition, the Yard was closed in 1966; the site is now an uninspiring industrial park.

Queens

THE OUTER BOROUGHS

Of New York City's four Outer Boroughs, **Queens**, named after the wife of Charles II, is probably the least visited by outsiders – not counting when they arrive at one of the two airports. In fact, that's as far as most other New Yorkers get. It seems that the diversity of this, the largest borough geographically, works against it somehow: unlike Brooklyn, the Bronx or Staten Island, Queens has no focal point so compelling as to require attention. Queens was never its own city before incorporating into New York in 1898; it was a county of separate towns and villages, a legacy that is seen today in the individuality of its neighborhoods, not to mention their mailing addresses.

With some exceptions, you can see all the highlights by taking the elevated **#7 train**, which cuts through neighborhoods of ever-shifting ethnic diversity. If you're pressed for time, the train itself offers

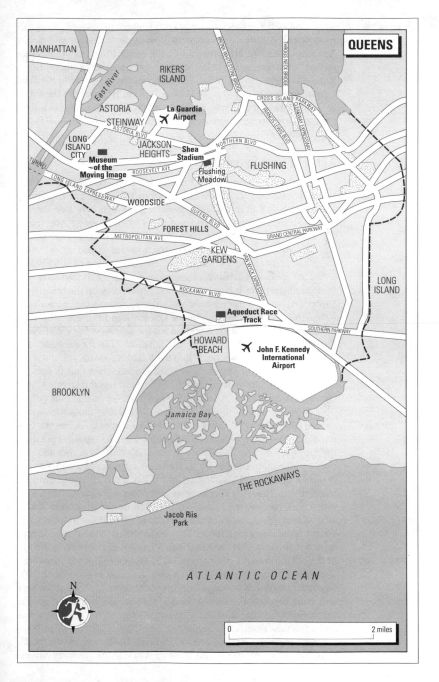

MANHATTAN

RIKERS
ISLAND

East River

ASTORIA

STEINWAY

La Guardia
Airport

ASTORIA BLVD

CROSS ISLAND PARKWAY

BRONX WHITESTONE BRIDGE

THROGS NECK BRIDGE

CLEARVIEW EXPRESSWAY

FRANCIS LEWIS BLVD

LONG
ISLAND
CITY

TUNNEL

JACKSON
HEIGHTS

Museum
of the
Moving Image

Shea
Stadium

NORTHERN BLVD

FLUSHING

ROOSEVELT AVE

Flushing
Meadow

LONG ISLAND EXPRESSWAY

WOODSIDE

QUEENS BLVD

FOREST HILLS

METROPOLITAN AVE

GRAND CENTRAL PARKWAY

KEW
GARDENS

VAN WYCK EXPRESSWAY

LONG
ISLAND

ROCKAWAY BLVD

Aqueduct Race
Track

SOUTHERN PARKWAY

HOWARD
BEACH

John F. Kennedy
International
Airport

BROOKLYN

Jamaica Bay

THE ROCKAWAYS

Jacob Riis
Park

ATLANTIC OCEAN

N

0   2 miles

QUEENS

some view of the urban landscape and excellent people-watching. Go from Greek **Astoria** through Irish **Woodside** to Indian and South American **Jackson Heights** and finally Asian **Flushing**, which can feel as suburban as Long Island some days and as exotic as Hong Kong on others. South of the #7 train, reachable by taking the E or F from Manhattan or even the R from Jackson Heights, are the solidly Jewish neighborhoods of Rego Park, Forest Hills and Kew Gardens, where city and suburbia really do manage to combine in the same locale.

Astoria and around

Bleak, industrial **Long Island City** (which really was a city, and the largest community in Queens county, from 1870 until incorporation) is most people's first view of Queens: it's through here that the #7 and N subway trains cut above ground after crossing over from Manhattan. Unless it's a weekend and you're keen to visit the **Isamu Noguchi museum** (see p.264), there's no point in getting off since there's nothing to see. For years now, the colonization of Long Island City's loft spaces by artists escaping extortionate Manhattan rents has been predicted, but it hasn't happened yet. So stay on the train, or if you've arrived by a more adventurous route (options include walking – though the pedestrian path on the Queensboro Bridge is not a very pleasant or peaceful stroll – and taking the new New York Waterway Ferry from Manhattan's 33rd St; ☎ 1-800/533-3779 for information), get on the train and take the N into the heart of Astoria.

Astoria is one of Queens's original communities and is famous for two things: film-making and the fact that it has the largest single concentration of Greeks outside Greece itself, or so it claims (whatever Melbourne says to the contrary). Until the **movie industry** moved out to the West Coast in the early 1930s, Astoria was the cinematic capital of the world, and Paramount had its studios here until the lure of Hollywood's reliable weather left Astoria empty and disused by all except the US Army. That's how it remained until recently, when Hollywood's stranglehold on the industry weakened and interest – in New York in general and Astoria in particular – was renewed. The new studios here now rank as the country's fourth largest and, encouraged by the success of films done in New York, are set for a major expansion. They're not open to the public at present, but you can visit the **American Museum of the Moving Image** in the old Paramount complex at 34–31 35th Street, near Broadway (near the Broadway stop on the N or the Steinway stop on the R). Newly renovated, it houses a stellar collection of posters, stills, sets and equipment both from Astoria's golden age and more recent times. See Chapter 15, *Museums and Galleries*, for opening times and a full description.

Greek Astoria stretches from Ditmars Boulevard in the north right down to Broadway, and from 31st across to Steinway Street.

Between 80,000 and 100,000 Greeks live here (together with a substantial community of Italians) and the evidence is on display in a sizable quantity of **restaurants** and **patisseries** that require a closer look. There's not a great deal else to see, but check out the restaurant listings in Chapter 17 before you write the area off.

Steinway

East of Astoria lies **Steinway**, a district that was bought up by the piano manufacturers and used as housing for their workers. These were mainly Germans and the area had for a time a distinctly Teutonic feel, but the community has long since gone and, apart from the piano factory (☎718/721-2600 for visits), there is only a long shopping strip to grab your interest.

Next door the noise-trap of **La Guardia Airport** handles domestic flights to and from the city. It's unlikely that you'll find yourself traveling through the **Marine Air Terminal**, but if you're an airplane buff, you might want to leave a little time before your flight to take one of the free **shuttle buses** over. A small exhibit details the history of this stylish building, which was built in the early 1930s for the huge flying boats that took off from the lake outside. Its best feature is the mural depicting the history of flight, uncovered recently after being declared "Socialist" and painted over in the early 1950s. Just offshore, **Riker's Island** holds the city's largest and most overcrowded **prison**. It's very much in use and not for visiting casually. Not surprisingly, this isn't the city's most appealing corner.

Sunnyside and Jackson Heights

From Astoria and Steinway, the R train bypasses the largely Irish communities of **Sunnyside** and **Woodside**, taking you straight to Jackson Heights at the Roosevelt Avenue stop. Architecturally, you're not missing much, although planning enthusiasts may have heard of the **Sunnyside Gardens** development, the first planned "garden city" in the United States. Started in 1924, it's not nearly as impressive to modern eyes, but if you'd like to see what it was all about, get off the #7 at 46 St-Bliss and walk down 46th Street, on the opposite side of Queens Boulevard from the Art Deco "Sunnyside" sign. Other than that, the two neighborhoods are mainly noteworthy for being home to Irish immigrants of several generations. On a Friday or Saturday night, the area's active **bar scene** comes alive.

Jackson Heights

After Sunnyside the #7 train swings away from Queens Boulevard and up narrow Roosevelt Avenue, and the accent of the neighborhood changes. Get off at 74th Street and you'll find yourself in the heart of South American **Jackson Heights**, where at least 150,000 or so Colombians, half as many Ecuadorians, and a good number of

Argentinians and other South American peoples make their home in a self-contained area where English is rarely the language of choice. The neighborhood first turned Hispanic in the 1960s, when huge influxes of people came over – many illegally – to find work and escape from the poverty and uncertain politics of their own countries, and it's now the largest South American contingent in the States. Tighter immigration controls, however, have radically cut the intake, and the community here is now more or less static.

Roosevelt Avenue and, running parallel, 37th Avenue between 82nd Street and Junction Boulevard are the foci for the district, and eating-wise, there's no better part of Queens for exotic, unknown and varied **cuisines**. Along both streets you'll find Argentinian steakhouses, Colombian restaurants, and pungent coffee houses and bakeries stacked high with bread and pastries. But head back down 37th Avenue to 74th Street, and you'll see sudden contrast. With its proliferation of colorful sari shops, this area is known to many as **Little India**, and the word on the street is that the restaurants here far surpass the fare available on well-known 6th Street in Manhattan; there are also plenty of shops for Indian spices and the like. Try the fare at the popular *Jackson Diner* (74th St at 37th Ave), or see Chapter 17 for restaurant listings. If you're into such things, the *Menka Beauty Salon* (74th St between Roosevelt and 37th aves) is a good place to indulge in the henna trend (hands, not hair).

Corona, Shea Stadium and Flushing Meadow Park

East of Jackson Heights you hit **Corona**, its subway yards ringed by menacing barbed wire and patrolled by dogs to deter graffiti artists – no visit required here. A few steps away is **Shea Stadium**, home of the New York Mets. The Beatles, too, played here in 1965 (at that point far more successfully than the Mets – who have since, however, won two World Series), as did the Rolling Stones in 1989. Concerts out here are rare but appreciated; baseball games, on the other hand, are frequent and, attendance-wise, a bit hurting, though the Mets do have a solid fan base. For details on the Mets and when they play, see Chapter 21, *Sports and Outdoor Activities*.

Shea went up as part of the 1964 World Fair, held in adjoining **Flushing Meadow Park**. This is now the site of the US Tennis Open Championships at the end of each summer, and boasts around thirty courts and seating for well over 25,000 people (again see Chapter 21). Even if you can't get tickets to the Open, this is the best time of year to visit the park, since it's the only event for which air traffic is rerouted. At most other times, the roar of the jet engines can be deafening, marring what would otherwise be a truly lovely place to spend a day.

Flushing Meadows Corona Park, as it's officially known, literally rose out of ashes – replacing a dumping ground known to locals as "Mount Corona" and described by F. Scott Fitzgerald in *The Great*

Gatsby as "a fantastic farm where ashes grow like wheat into ridges and hills and grotesque gardens." Begun for the 1939 World's Fair, it took its present shape around the time of the later fair, and today it's a beautifully landscaped park with a couple of key attractions that may make the schlep out here worthwhile.

Queens

From Shea, you'll find your way to the park easily; from the 111th Street stop on the #7 train, it's not as obvious, but if you walk *down* 111th Street itself, you'll come to it, starting with the **New York Hall of Science**. An interactive science museum kids will love, it's fun but exhausting for adults – probably missable except on rainy days. The adjacent **Wildlife Center** (once the zoo) is interesting in that it features exclusively North American animals. But the real reason to come here is the **Queens Museum** and the **Unisphere** in front. Created for the 1964 World's Fair, the Unisphere is a 140-foot-high, stainless-steel globe that weighs 700,000 pounds – probably the main reason why it never left its place in the park. It was finally declared a landmark, to the delight of the borough, and it's now lit at night – you may have seen it when you came in from the airport. Robert Moses intended this park to be the "Versailles of America," and it's from this vantage point that you can see that plan in action: carefully planned pathways connect lawns, small pools and two lakes. On a summer day, the park is swarming with kids on bikes and rollerblades; you can rent a bicycle yourself, or even a boat. The park puts out a good map, which you can pick up free from inside the museum.

See Museums and Galleries, *chapter 15, for more on Queens' museums.*

If the museum has one main jewel (and it really doesn't have much else), it's the **Panorama of the City of New York**. With one inch of model equal to one hundred feet of city, the Panorama (and its 895,000 individual structures) is the world's largest architectural model. It was recently updated, and new remodeling of the space allows you to walk all around (and occasionally over) the parameters of the five boroughs. For $1, you can rent binoculars, which for any kind of close scrutiny are essential. While the model is useful for understanding the geography of the city, the fun really comes when you know what you're looking at – to that end, it's possible (though not easy) to make this your last stop in New York on the way to the airport. Assuming you can haul your luggage back to Roosevelt Avenue, the Q48 bus goes to La Guardia; alternatively, a cab (called from inside the museum) to either airport shouldn't cost more than $10.

Flushing

At the other end of the park (Main Street, last stop on the #7 train) lies **Flushing**, most notable for its status as New York's second Chinatown. In actuality, Flushing is home to immigrants from many different Asian countries – too many cuisines to choose from if you're only going to be there for an hour or so. Chinese, Japanese,

Korean, Malaysian and Vietnamese restaurants, along with pastry shops and ubiquitous fruit stalls selling a variety of surprises, line Roosevelt Avenue and Main Street – although you may not always be able to read the signs to figure out what's what.

The **historical** side of Flushing is interesting, but less so. The town picked up the tag "birthplace of religious freedom in America" for its role as secret Quaker meeting place during the seventeenth century, when anyone who wasn't a Calvinist was persecuted by the Dutch. The Quaker **Bowne House** still stands; one of the oldest houses in the city (it dates from 1661), it's open to the public on Tuesday, Saturday and Sunday afternoons (2.30–4.30pm), and if you're in Flushing you may just as well take a look at the drab little place. (You'll run into Bowne St walking east on Roosevelt; just make a left, and the house will be a few blocks up, between 37th and 38th aves.) You can find out more information (and pick up a map for a do-it-yourself walking tour of the historic sites) by stopping in at the **Queens Historical Society** at the Kingsland Homestead across the way – an historic house in its own right, shifted here from its original site about a mile away and reputedly the first house in Flushing to release its slaves. Truthfully, these houses are quite unimpressive, and unless you have a particular interest in Quaker history or are coming out here for ethnic eats (*Kum Gang San*, a Korean spot on 138-28 Northern Blvd at Union St, is especially recommended), don't make a special trip.

Forest Hills and around

South of Flushing Meadows, the stretch of Queens Boulevard that comprises **Rego Park**, **Forest Hills** and **Kew Gardens** is a comfortable, residential area that's more than sixty percent Jewish, something that's manifest in the abundance of synagogues and Jewish centers, although the area is much more secular than the Orthodox enclaves of Williamsburg and Crown Heights in Brooklyn. The Rego Park stretch isn't much of a draw, and you may as well take the E or F straight to 71st Street – Continental Avenue in the heart of Forest Hills. Incidentally, the name "Rego" comes from the "Real Good Construction Company" – the Queens construction company responsible for much of the original development here.

Forest Hills was for a long time one of the choicest Queens neighborhoods, home to the West Side Tennis Club, which used to host the US Open and still holds important matches. The priciest part of Forest Hills is still largely unchanged: **Forest Hills Gardens**, a mock Tudor village interesting not for what it is but for what it might have been, since it was built originally as housing for the urban poor until the rich grabbed it for themselves. Walk through to see for yourself and, if you do, wend your way to *Eddie's Sweet Shop* on the corner of Metropolitan and 72nd avenues – reckoned by many who've frequented it in its seventy-year history to have the best ice cream in the world.

Further down Queens Boulevard (at the Union Turnpike stop on the E or F) is another "planned" neighborhood, **Kew Gardens**, which extends south from Queens Boulevard and skirts the edge of Forest Park, a pleasant but unspectacular wilderness. At the turn of the century, Kew Gardens was a watering-hole popular with aging New Yorkers, complete with hotels, lakes and a whole tourist infrastructure. That's all gone now, but Kew Gardens remains, in a leafy and dignified kind of way, one of Queens's most visually enticing districts. The Q10 bus to JFK airport gives you a nice view if you don't actually wish to visit.

Jamaica Bay and the Rockaways

What you may have not noticed when you flew into New York for the first time is that JFK airport is situated on the edge of the wild, island-dotted indent of **Jamaica Bay**. At the **Wildlife Refuge**, near Broad Channel on the largest of these islands (take the A train to Broad Channel and walk a half-mile; the Q53 bus from Rockaway or Jackson Heights also stops there), you can observe more than 300 varieties of **birds** for free, seven days a week, including a couple of bona fide endangered species. For more information, you can call the Refuge (☎718/318-4340); or, to find out more about the federally administered **Gateway National Recreation Area** of which it is a part, call ☎718/388-3799.

See pp.13–14 for full details on arrival at JFK.

Partly enclosing the bay, the narrowing spit of the Rockaways is the largest **beach area** in the country, stretching for ten miles back toward Brooklyn – most of it strollable by the boardwalk. The action really centers around Beach 116th Street (a subway stop serviced by the A or the Rockaway Shuttle, depending on the time of day), where the boardwalk bustles and the surfers gather. This is the only place to surf in New York City proper, so it's popular with expat Californians. For more information on surfing and beaches, see Chapter 21.

At the far western end, **Jacob Riis Park** is also part of the Gateway area, but is a quieter beach, much less built-up, mostly because the subway doesn't go there (take the Q22 from Beach 116th or the Q35 from Flatbush in Brooklyn). Named for the crusading journalist who battled for better housing and recreation facilities, it features architecture reminiscent of less accessible beaches created by Robert Moses in later years, including a stately brick bathhouse and an outdoor clock. The country's only all-women lifeguard tournament is held here every summer, a popular athletic event (call Gateway for dates, or ☎1-800/NP8-SWIM for specific info). In the eastern corner of the beach, nude bathing is tolerated (if not officially allowed); it's also an area frequented by predominantly gay male naturists.

The Bronx

The city's northernmost borough, **The Bronx**, was for a long time its toughest and most notoriously crime-ridden district. At one time, most notably in the 1980s, parts were completely off-limits, even, at times, to the police, and there was no other part of the city about which people are so ready to roll out their most gruesome horror stories. Nowadays its poorer reaches still represent some of the most severe examples of urban deprivation you're ever likely to see. But much of the borough has undergone a successful recent transformation (parts were in any case always prime residential territory), and even in the notorious **South Bronx** things are looking up. There were always plenty of attractions, beautiful parks and vistas, a world-class botanical garden and zoo; and there are more improvements on the way, such as a plan for a network of promenades and paths designed for walkers and bikers. Much credit is due to community group efforts, as the **Bronx Tourism Council** (880 River Ave, Suite 2; ☎718/590-3518) will no doubt be glad to tell you. Go there to pick up a visitor's pass which will get you some discounts on your wanderings.

The Bronx is the only mainland borough, and as might be expected it has more in common, geographically, with Westchester County to the north than it does with the island regions of New York City: steep hills, deep valleys and rocky outcroppings to the west, and marshy flatlands along the Long Island Sound to the east. Economically, the Bronx developed – and declined – more quickly than any other part of the city. First settled in the seventeenth century by a Swedish landowner named Jonas Bronck, like Brooklyn and Queens it only became part of the city proper at the turn of the last century. From 1900 onwards things moved fast, and the Bronx became one of the most sought-after parts of the city in which to live, its main thoroughfare, the **Grand Concourse**, becoming edged with increasingly luxurious Art Deco apartment buildings – many of which, though greatly rundown, still stand today. This avenue runs the length of the borough, and many places of interest lie on it or reasonably close by.

Unlike Brooklyn or Queens, the Bronx doesn't lend itself to extensive wandering from neighborhood to neighborhood, perhaps because some of the main attractions (like the **Zoo** and the **Botanical Gardens**) take a long time to explore, while others (like **Wave Hill** or **Orchard Beach**) take a long time to get to. An excellent way to get around is by bus – the Bx12, in particular (which actually begins in Inwood, the northernmost part of Manhattan), winds a useful route past many of the places described on the following pages. Pick up a Bronx bus map (the driver may have one if you don't have time in advance). If you don't mind spending a few tokens to get around, the buses – plus the subways we've indicated – will enable you to do more in one day than you'd be able to otherwise.

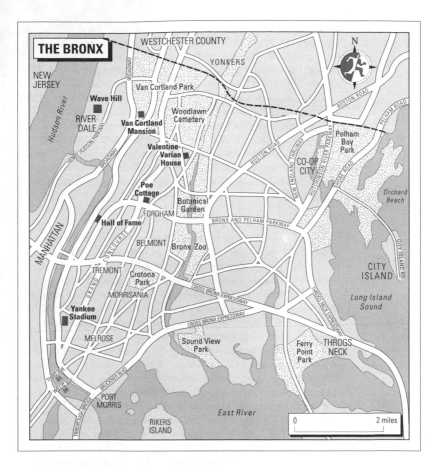

Yankee Stadium and the South Bronx

The first stop on the C and D subways after leaving Manhattan, and the third such stop on the #4, is **Yankee Stadium,** home to the New York Yankees baseball team and holding some of the best facilities for the sport in the country. You can tour the stadium – including the clubhouse and dugout – on Mondays and Wednesdays between 10am and noon, by appointment only (☎718/293-6013; $8, $4 kids and seniors). The Yankees played in north Harlem before moving here in 1923, a move that was in part due to their most famous player ever, **George Herman "Babe" Ruth,** who joined the team in the spring of 1920 and led them for the next fifteen years. It was the star quality of Babe Ruth, the original Bronx Bomber (who lent that nickname to the entire team), that helped pull in the cash to build the current stadium, which for a while was known as the "House that Ruth Built."

The Bronx

Inside, Babe Ruth, Joe di Maggio and a host of other baseball heroes are enshrined by statues, but unless coming here to see a game (or, on occasion, be blessed – the Pope said Mass here in 1965 and 1979 to more than 50,000 New Yorkers), there's little reason to visit. (See Chapter 21, *Sports and Outdoor Activities*, for ticket information.)

If you did disembark at the first rather than the third stop on the #4 train out of Manhattan, you'd be right near the neighborhood of **Port Morris**, a small outpost of antique shops that's a good example of the South Bronx's recent resurgence – though it's only worth the trip if you're hard into antiques. Amid the once-abandoned warehouses is *Gallery 69* (69 Bruckner Blvd; ☎718/665-8132), the first shop of its kind to take advantage of the dirt-cheap rents in the area; they specialize in African and Caribbean art.

The South Bronx

North and west stretches the **South Bronx**, first part of the borough to become properly urbanized, then scarred from the 1960s until fairly recently by huge squares of rubble, leveled apartments sprawling between gaunt-eyed tenements and groups of aimless teenagers. In the late 1990s, however, it has become known as the Bronx Miracle – and though this may be stretching it just a bit, economic revival has taken foot. Abandoned buildings have been renovated into cooperative apartments or cleared to make room for new housing. Backed by federal funds, private investments and a myriad of involved community groups, retailers long missing in this area – basic ones such as *Rite-Aid*, *Pathmark*, *Caldor* and other chains – have reappeared. However, there's still not much for a visitor to see and do, unless you're a student of city planning. If you're seriously interested, a trip on the elevated #4 train down to Yankee Stadium affords a good view.

If you get off, the **Grand Concourse** in its lower reaches is the most alluring – and the safest place to walk. Stray to either side and you're getting into areas that many would consider dangerous, especially at night. The Concourse itself contains the ever-busy **Bronx County Court House**, at 161st Street, where part of *The Bonfire of the Vanities* was filmed, and further along at 1040 Grand Concourse and East 165th Street, the **Bronx Museum of the Arts** (Wed, Thurs and Fri 10am–5pm, Sat & Sun 1–6pm; $3, $2 students, $1 seniors, kids free) with changing displays of temporary exhibits, many oriented toward the Bronx. Carry on, and the junction with Fordham Road marks the beginning of two main **shopping districts**. East Fordham and West Fordham roads are the main department stores and the focus of Saturday afternoon shopping, with Fordham Road boasting every fast-food franchise imaginable, and hundreds of families, street vendors and barbecued-shrimp sellers all vying for space on the crowded sidewalk. This is borderline north–south Bronx, and it's unlikely that you'll feel uncomfortable.

Central Bronx: Belmont, the Zoo and the Botanical Gardens

Beyond 180th Street the Bronx improves radically. Turn north up Arthur Avenue and you're in **Belmont**, a strange mixture of tenements and clapboard houses that is home to by far the largest segment of New York's Italian community. It's a small area, bordered to the east by the **Zoo** and the west by Third Avenue, with 187th Street as its axis. While there has been a small influx of other ethnic groups – most notably Haitian, Yugoslavian and Mexican – the staunch Italian community is still the dominant force. Few tourists come here, but if you're on your way to the zoo, amble through to see its pungent grocery stores, live poultry market, pork butchers, cafés and sweet-smelling bakeries. There's also no better part of the Bronx if you want to eat: choose from swanky *Mario's* (where Al Pacino shot the double-crossing policeman in *The Godfather*) or the pizzas at *Ann & Tony's* or *Gianetto's Brick Oven* – all on Arthur Avenue (see Chapter 17, *Eating*, for more details).

The Bronx Zoo

Follow 187th to the end and you're on the edge of the **Bronx Zoo/Wildlife Conservation Park** (March–Oct Mon–Fri 10am–5pm, Sat & Sun 10am–5.30pm; Nov–Feb daily 10am–4.30pm; $6.75, $3 for seniors and kids, free to all on Wed, parking is $6, rides and some exhibits are an additional charge; ☎718/367-1010), accessible either by its main gate on Fordham Road or by a second entrance on Bronx Park South. (This last is the entrance to use if you come directly here by subway – the East Tremont Ave stop on the #2 or #5.)

The zoo is probably the only reason many New Yorkers from outside the borough ever visit the Bronx. Even if you don't like zoos, it's as good a one as any: it is the largest urban zoo in the United States, and one of the first to realize that animals both looked and felt better out in the open; something that's been done artfully through a variety of simulated natural habitats. Visit in summer to appreciate it at its best; in winter, a surprising number of the animals are kept in indoor enclosures without viewing areas. One of the most interesting parts is the Wild Asia exhibit, an almost forty-acre wilderness through which tigers, elephants and deer roam relatively freely, viewable either by walking or (for $2 extra, and only from May to October) from an elevated monorail train. Look in also on the World of Darkness (a re-creation of night, holding nocturnal species) and a simulation of a Himalayan mountain area, with endangered species like the giant panda and snow leopard. There's a children's section where they can climb spider webs and wriggle through their own groundhog tunnels. As a park, the zoo functions particularly well, too, making for nice strolling. All in all, it's a good focus for a day trip to the Bronx.

New York Botanical Gardens

Across the road from the zoo's main entrance is the back turnstile of the **New York Botanical Gardens** (Tues–Sun 10am–6pm; $3, $1 seniors, students and kids, free to all on Wed; ☎718/817-8500), which in their southernmost reaches are as wild as anything you're likely to see upstate. Further north near the main entrance (the D train to Bedford Park Blvd, or more conveniently, the Metro-North train – from Grand Central or 125th St – ☎532-4900 for costs and package deals) are more cultivated stretches. The Enid A. Haupt Conservatory, a landmark, turn-of-the-century crystal palace, showcases jungle and desert ecosystems, a palm court and a fern forest, among other seasonal displays ($7.50, $3.50 students and seniors). In addition, there are tram tours and plant sales, and the gardens themselves are enormous enough to wander around happily for hours.

The Poe Cottage and the Museum of Bronx History

Leave the gardens by their main entrance and walk west (or take the D or #4 train to Kingsbridge Road) – and you'll come eventually to Grand Concourse and the **Poe Cottage**, in Poe Park. This tiny white clapboard anachronism in the midst of the Bronx's bustle was Edgar Allan Poe's home for the last three years of his life, though it was only moved here recently when threatened with demolition. Never a particularly stable character and dogged by problems, Poe was rarely happy in the cottage, and he didn't write much more than the short, touching poem "Annabel Lee." The house is open to the public on weekends only (Sat 10am–4pm, Sun 1–5pm; $2; ☎718/881-8900); it has displays of memorabilia and manuscripts, but overall tells you little. Still, if you're a fan, or happen to be around on Halloween, when there are readings of his works . . .

A bit north of here (at 3266 Bainbridge Ave and E 208th St; D to 205th St or #4 to Mosholu Parkway) is the Valentine-Varian House, an eighteenth-century Georgian stone farmhouse that now houses the **Museum of Bronx History**. Considering how much the Bronx has changed – it was farm country only fifty years ago – the old photographs and lithographs can be fascinating. Like the Poe Cottage, though, the museum is only open on weekends (Sat 10am–4pm, Sun 1–5pm; $2; ☎718/881-8900).

North Bronx

The North Bronx is the topmost fringe of New York City, and if anyone actually makes it up here it's to see the **Woodlawn Cemetery**, open on Jerome Avenue at Bainbridge (last stop, Woodlawn, on the #4), which is worth a stroll around if only to see how money doesn't necessarily buy good taste. This has for many years been the top people's cemetery, and like Greenwood in Brooklyn (see p.204) boasts some tombs and mausolea that are memorable mainly for their garishness. It's a huge place but there are some tombs that stand out: one Oliver Hazard Belmont, financier and horse dealer, lies in a dripping Gothic fantasy near the entrance, modeled on the resting place of Leonardo da Vinci in Amboise, France; F.W. Woolworth has himself an Egyptian palace guarded by sphinxes; while Jay Gould, not most people's favorite banker when he was alive, takes it easy in a Greek-style temple. And that's not all. Pick up a guide from the office at the entrance and you can discover all kinds of famous names and disgusting mausolea.

Van Cortlandt Park

West of the cemetery lies **Van Cortlandt Park**, a forested and hilly all-purpose recreation space, used in winter by skiers and tobogganists, in fall and spring by high-school cross-country track teams. Apart from the sheer pleasure of hiking through its woods, the best thing here is the **Van Cortlandt Mansion**, nestled in its southwest corner not far from the subway station. This is the Bronx's oldest building, an authentically restored Georgian structure, very pretty, and with its rough-hewn gray stone really rather rustic. During the Revolution it changed hands a number of times, and was used as an operations headquarters by both the British and the Patriots. On the hills above, George Washington had fires lit to dupe the British into thinking that he was still here (he was in fact long gone), and it was in this house that he slept before heading his victory march into Manhattan in 1783. Unfortunately, the condition of the house is deteriorating rapidly, and only two of the rooms are open to the public (Tues–Fri 10am–3pm, Sat & Sun 11am–4pm, closed Mon; ☎718/543-3344). Needless to say, the Society of Colonial Dames of America, who run the place, would welcome donations – especially of the large corporate kind.

Riverdale

Immediately west rise the monied heights of **Riverdale** – one of the most desirable neighborhoods in the city, and so far from the South Bronx in feel and income it might as well be on the moon. This part of the Bronx (and it is part of the Bronx, though residents and real-estate agents prefer to forget that) is extremely hard to get to without a car; Metro-North to Riverdale or the #1 or #9 to West 242nd Street are the closest rail options, and even the buses cover little of the residential streets. If you do make the trip, you'll be rewarded with suburban escape and – when you can get through the trees – spectacular views. Well worth a visit is **Wave Hill**, a small country estate overlooking the Hudson River and Palisade Cliffs which was donated to the city a couple of decades back; in previous years, it was briefly home to Mark Twain and, later, Teddy Roosevelt. The delightful grounds are botanical gardens, the nineteenth-century mansion a forum for temporary art installations, concerts and workshops: a great idea, but a pity it couldn't have been in a part of the city that needed it more badly (Tues–Sun 9am–5.30pm; $4, $2 students and seniors; ☎718/549-3200).

City Island

On the east side of the Bronx, jutting out into the Long Island Sound, **City Island** is, historically, a fishing community and, while much of the industry has gone, the atmosphere remains, despite the proximity of the urban Bronx (a short causeway takes the Bx29 bus – pick it up at the Pelham Bay Park subway stop on the #6 – to and from the mainland). With all the historic house-moving that goes on these days, it's easy to believe that City Island was imported from Maine or Massachusetts by some nautically minded philanthropist.

Most people come here for the **restaurants** – in fact, on a weekend night, it's nearly impossible for the bus to get down the traffic-clogged City Island Avenue, and the restaurants overflow with "off islanders." You're better off making the trip on a weekday; not only will the "clamdiggers" (as the locals, at least the old-timers, call themselves) be more friendly, but you'll stand a better chance of getting something fresh when you order your dinner. One way to avoid disappointment is to go with the maxim (generally true): "The better the view, the worse the food." You do stand a good chance at either the *Lobster House* (691 Bridge St) or *JP Waterside Restaurant* (703 Minneford Ave) for seafood and outdoor seating.

Aside from the restaurants, City Island is interesting primarily for its New England-style houses and its small-town feel. You can easily walk the length of it, and though walking back and forth can be tiring, both the main drag and the back roads deserve a look. On **City Island Avenue**, small **shops** are the rule of the day – stop in at *Mooncurser Antiques* to see one of the largest collections of vinyl **records** assembled anywhere. In the last few years, an **arts community** has begun to thrive here too, led by *CIAO Gallery and Arts Center* (278 City Island Ave; ☎718/885-9316). While there, pick up a brochure listing the twelve other spaces on the island to view and buy arts and handicrafts. There's an annual arts and crafts fair held during the last weekend of May. Heading back toward the causeway, turn right on Fordham Street and then left on King Street. King and Minnieford streets are where the bigger houses on City Island have remained; to make yourself really jealous, look back behind the houses at the private piers and beaches.

Before you head back to the mainland, stop in at the **North Wind Undersea Institute**, 610 City Island Avenue (Mon–Fri 10am–5pm, Sat & Sun noon–5pm; $3; ☎718/885-0701), a quaint museum that, strangely, was co-founded by Woodstock legend Richie Havens. Housed in an old ship captain's retirement home, its exhibits center around an ecological theme, with particular attention to its own role in the rehabilitation and rescue of threatened and stranded marine life. Prowl around to see the collection of old diving gear, whaling artifacts and bones dating back to 1502, a nineteenth-century ship's brig, a blue lobster (still alive, and incredibly rare), and a superb collection of scrimshaw (whalebone etched with intricate designs), which many consider to be the first true American folk art form.

Pelham Bay Park and Orchard Beach

From City Island, it's an easy walk to **Orchard Beach**, the easternmost part of the expansive **Pelham Bay Park** – just make a right after the causeway, and cut across the polluted waterfront area at low tide, or the longer but more scenic park path at high tide. These days, Orchard is known locally as the "Spanish Riviera," and beach and boardwalk pulse constantly with a salsa beat. **Free concerts** in summer are common, and even if nothing is going on, wander long enough and you're bound to hear music: beachgoers often bring their own instruments, and impromptu jam sessions (complete with dancing) spring up all over the place.

At the northernmost end of the boardwalk, a sign for the **Kazimiroff Nature Trail** takes you into a wildlife preserve that's also part of Pelham Bay Park. It's named after Theodore Kazimiroff, the noted naturalist who helped stop these wetlands from being turned into a landfill. The trail winds through meadow, shrubland, forest and marsh, and is serene and peaceful – a stark contrast to much of the rest of the park, which is now criss-crossed by highways that take away from its original charm. Without a car, unfortunately, exploring the further reaches of Pelham Bay Park is difficult.

The **Bartow-Pell Mansion Museum and Gardens** (Wed, Sat & Sun noon–4pm; ☎718/885-1461) is a national landmark worth seeing for its family plot and magnificent formal gardens that overlook Long Island Sound, but to get there you have to go back to the Pelham Bay Park subway station and take bus Bx45 (no service Sunday).

Staten Island

Until just over thirty years ago **Staten Island**, the common name for what's officially Richmond County, was isolated – getting to it meant a ferry trip or long ride through New Jersey, and daily commuting into town was almost an eccentricity. Staten Islanders enjoyed an insular, self-contained life in the state's least populous borough, and the stretch of water to Manhattan marked a cultural as much as physical divide. In 1964 the opening of the **Verrazano Narrows Bridge** changed things; land-hungry Brooklynites found cheap property on the island and swarmed over the bridge to buy their parcel of suburbia. Today Staten Island has swollen into tightly packed residential neighborhoods amid the rambling greenery, forming endless backwaters of tidy, look-don't-touch homes.

THE OUTER BOROUGHS

Map labels (clockwise / by region):

△ New Jersey △ Jersey City Ferry to Manhattan △

N

Snug Harbour Cultural Center
Ferry Terminal
ST. GEORGE
NEW BRIGHTON
The Narrows
STATEN ISLAND EXPRESSWAY
WILLOWBROOK EXPRESSWAY
FOREST AVE
FOREST AVE
VICTORY BLVD
BAY ST
RICHMOND ROAD
Alice Austen House
VERRAZANO-NARROWS BRIDGE
Brooklyn △

VICTORY BLVD
Fresh Kills Landfill
Jaques Marchais Center of Tibetan Art
La Tourette Park
KILL ROAD
RICHMOND AVENUE
HYLAN BLVD
FATHER CAPODANO BLVD
South Beach
Lower Bay

Richmondtown Restoration
RICHMOND PARKWAY
AMBOY ROAD
DRUMGOOLE BLVD
HYLAN BLVD
Great Kills Harbor

△ New Brunswick

ATLANTIC OCEAN

0   2 miles

Conference House Park

STATEN ISLAND

If New Yorkers from other boroughs know anything about Staten Island – and it's not guaranteed that they would – it's limited to two words: garbage and secession. Though recycling efforts have significantly reduced the amount of **garbage** the city produces, more than 75,000 tons a week are dumped in Staten Island's Fresh Kills landfill. This is the largest landfill in the world, holding 2400 million cubic feet of refuse (for lovers of useless facts, that's 25 times the size of the Great Pyramid at Giza), and it's a claim to fame over which residents feel strong resentment, particularly in the light of citywide political reforms that have left Staten Island vulnerable to decisions made by the votes in more populous boroughs. The landfill is, however, scheduled to close on December 31, 2001, with parkland promised in its wake.

Over the years there's been much talk of Staten Island **seceding** from the city, and a recent referendum showed overwhelming sup-

port for the idea; that vote, however, decided nothing more substantial than that the state legislature will look into the feasibility of
the proposal.

With this stellar reputation, it's no wonder that nine out of ten
tourists who take the Staten Island ferry to drool over the view turn
back to Manhattan immediately on arrival. We won't berate them for
that; travel by public transportation on Staten Island can be slow-
going (bicycle may be the best way to get around), and there's nothing so unbeatable there that you should lose any sleep if you miss out
on it. Should you decide to stay, however, your efforts will be rewarded – since each of the few, spread-out attractions here is a worthwhile excursion in itself.

The ferry, St George and the Snug Harbor Cultural Center

The **Staten Island ferry** sails around the clock, with departures
every 15–20 minutes at rush hours, every 30 minutes mid-day and
evenings, and every 60 minutes late at night – weekends less frequently. It is truly New York's best bargain: completely free (a 1997
innovation), with wide-angled views of the city and the Statue of
Liberty becoming more spectacular as you retreat. By the time you
arrive, Manhattan's skyline stands mirage-like, filtered through the
haze as the romantic, heroic city of a thousand and one posters.
Unfortunately, the ferry terminal at the Staten Island end quickly dis-
pels any romance: it's a mundane, disreputable sort of place, which
serves as a mini-training ground for winos on their way to the
Bowery. But if you're exploring the island it's easy enough to escape
to the adjoining **bus station** – have change or a token ready, whatever your plans, since they're unavailable at the terminal. Arm yourself with a bus map, and – if you can find one – a "Staten Island Sites
and Scenes" brochure (both of which are more readily available in
the Manhattan terminal), and you're on your way. For an advance
brochure, call ☎ 800/573-SINY.

The town of **St George** is adjacent to the ferry terminal, and it's a
strange, underutilized place for a spot with such obvious potential. In
an area that should be reaping the benefits of its closeness to
Manhattan, empty storefronts abound, and crowds that should flock
on nice days to hilly streets with fabulous views are nowhere to be
found. There is a landmarked Historic District with a wonderful collection of residential buildings in shingle style, Queen Anne, Greek
Revival and Italianate styles.

In contrast, the **Snug Harbor Cultural Center**, 1000 Richmond
Terrace ☎ 718/448-2500, in nearby New Brighton (take the S40 bus
from the ferry terminal), thrives with signs of cultural growth. This
arts center's 28 buildings are spread out over a campus that once
served as a retirement home for sailors. With galleries and studios
for up-and-coming artists, an annual outdoor Summer Sculpture

Festival, and events and concerts year-round (including summer performances of the Metropolitan Opera and New York Philharmonic – good music in outdoor surroundings more intimate than anywhere in Manhattan), it draws visitors from all over the borough, if not yet from outside. There's also the lively Harmony Street Fair, held annually the second Sunday in June. Also in the same park area are the **Staten Island Children's Museum** and the **Botanical Gardens**. The Snug Harbor grounds are open all the time and are free to the public; tours, also free, are given on weekend afternoons.

The Alice Austen House

If you pack a picnic lunch for your trip to Staten Island (not a bad idea, since there's little guarantee that your necessary bus stop will be near anywhere to eat), enjoy it on the grounds of the **Alice Austen House**, 2 Hylan Boulevard (Thurs–Sun noon–5pm, ☎718/816-4506; suggested donation $3). Easily reachable by the S51 bus to Hylan Boulevard (walk down the hill), this Victorian cottage faces the waters of the Narrows, and from the front lawn it's easy to understand why Alice Austen's grandparents dubbed their house "Clear Comfort." But the attraction of this place is actually the story of Alice Austen herself, a pioneering photographer whose work comprises one of the finest records of turn-of-the-century American life. At a time when photography was both difficult and expensive, Alice Austen developed her talent and passion for the art expertly. Her tragedy is that she never considered the possibility of going professional, even when the stock market crash of 1929 lost her the family home and left her in the poorhouse, and her work was only rediscovered shortly before her death in 1952. The house exhibits a relatively small selection of photographs, but they're fascinating to look at, and as more of the rooms are restored and refurnished, the museum can only improve.

South Beach and the southeast shore

Stretching below the Verrazano Narrows, along the eastern part of the island, are a series of public beaches, starting with **South Beach**, a once-thriving resort for New York's wealthy, and stretching down to **Great Kills Park**, a place surfed by locals. Few visitors come to New York for its beaches, and those who do most likely head to the Rockaways in Queens – for good reason – but these aren't bad if you're looking for less crowded and more casual alternatives. At South Beach, reachable by the S51 bus, there is a two-and-a-half mile boardwalk – the fourth largest in the world and a great place to jog or rollerblade; otherwise, just hit its fairly quiet sands for sunning. If you're in need of nourishment, great pizza can be had nearby at *Goodfella's Brick Oven Pizza*, on 1718 Hylan Boulevard (☎718/987-2422).

Lighthouse Hill: The Jacques Marchais Museum of Tibetan Art

In the middle of Staten Island's residential heartland, the **Jacques Marchais Museum of Tibetan Art** at 338 Lighthouse Avenue (April–Nov Wed–Sun 1–5pm, other times by appointment; $3, $2.50 seniors, $1 kids; ☎718/987-3500) is an unlikely find; the bus drivers don't know it's there, so ask to be let off at Lighthouse Avenue, and then walk up the hill until you hit it on your right. Jacques Marchais was the alias of Jacqueline Klauber, a New York art dealer who reckoned she'd get on better with a French name. She did, and used her own comfortable income and that of her husband to indulge her passion for Tibetan art. Eventually she assembled the largest collection in the Western world, reproducing a *gompah*, or Buddhist temple, on the hillside in which to house it. Even if you know nothing about such things the exhibition is small enough to be accessible, with magnificent bronze Bodhisattvas, fearsome deities in union with each other, musical instruments, costumes, and decorations from the mysterious world of Tibet. Give it time – after a while the air of the temple and its gardens is heady. Best time to visit is on a Sunday, when lectures focus on different aspects of Asian culture around the world, and in the first or second week of October when the Tibetan festival takes place: Tibetan monks in maroon robes perform the traditional ceremonies, and Tibetan food and crafts are sold. Phone ahead for the exact date.

While you're up on the hill, there are two more items of note, neither of which is open to the public – but walking by won't hurt anyone. The **Staten Island Lighthouse** on Ediboro Road can be seen from Lighthouse Avenue, appropriately enough, and though it's a strange thing to see so far inland, it's been in pretty much constant use since it first starting guiding ships into New York Harbor in 1912. Around the corner, at **48 Manor Court**, the private home known as "Crimson Beech" was designed by Frank Lloyd Wright. Not one of his more inspiring efforts, but it bears some significance as the only residence designed by Wright within the New York City limits.

The Richmond Town Restoration

Back on the main Richmond Road, a short walk, or the S74 bus from the central terminal, brings you to the **Richmond Town Restoration** (July & August Wed–Fri 10am–5pm, Sat & Sun 1–5pm; Sept–June Wed–Sun 1–5pm; $4, $2.50 students, seniors and under-18s; ☎718/351-1611), a likable gathering of a dozen or so old houses and miscellaneous buildings transplanted from their original sites and grafted on to the eighteenth-century village of Richmond. Starting from the **Historical Museum**, half-hourly tours negotiate the best of these – including the **Voorlezer's House**, oldest elementary school in the country; a picture-book general store; and the lovely, atmospheric **Guyon-Lake-Tysen House** of 1740. What brings it to life are the craftspeople using old techniques to weave cloth and fire kilns, and knowledgeable, costumed workers who enthusiastically fill you in on the facts. It's all carried off to picturesque and ungimmicky effect, and by the end of your visit you're likely to be so won over that you'll want to work there yourself – or at least come back for one of their special events. The rustic setting makes it difficult to believe you're just twelve miles from downtown Manhattan.

Conference House

At the southern tip of the island is the **Conference House**, at 7455 Hylan Boulevard, a preserved seventeenth-century structure that, while pleasant enough, is only of interest to the most ardent of revolutionary history buffs. Its claim to fame is acting as host to failed peace talks, led by Ben Franklin and John Adams, during the American Revolution – and it feels like it hasn't seen much action since, other than perhaps the manicuring of its rolling lawns. Today, the house is open for tours (call ☎ 718/984-6046); step inside for a peek at the period furnishings and its original kitchen, now restored to working order.

Chapter 15

Museums and Galleries

As a city, New York does not lack visual stimulation, and you may find there's enough on the streets to look at without walking inside a **museum**. But you should be aware of what you're missing. For in the big two Manhattan museums – the **Metropolitan** and the **Museum of Modern Art** – there are few aspects of Western art left untapped. The Metropolitan, in particular, is exhaustive (mercilessly so, if you try to take in too much too quickly), with arguably the world's finest collection of European art as well as superlative displays of everything from African artifacts to medieval sculpture. The Museum of Modern Art (MoMA) takes over where the Met leaves off, emphasizing exactly why (and how) New York became the art capital of the world.

Among the other **major museums**, there are exciting collections of modern art and invariably excellent temporary shows at the **Whitney** and **Guggenheim**; a wide array of seventeenth- and eighteenth-century paintings at the **Frick**; and – amid unexpectedly pastoral scenes – a glorious display of medieval art at **The Cloisters**. All things, time permitting, are worth seeing. So also are some of the **minor museums**, often quirkily devoted to otherwise total obscurities.

Opening hours

Opening hours don't fall into any fixed patterns; many museums are closed on Mondays (and national holidays) and are open into the early

---

Free museums

The following museums are free at the stated times:

Tuesday Cooper-Hewitt (5–9pm), International Center of Photography Uptown and Midtown (6–8pm, pay what you wish), Jewish Museum (5–8pm).

Thursday Asia Society Gallery (6–8pm), Whitney (6–8pm).

Friday Guggenheim (6–8pm, pay what you wish), Museum of Modern Art (4.30–8.30pm, pay what you wish).

Saturday New Museum of Contemporary Art (6–8pm).

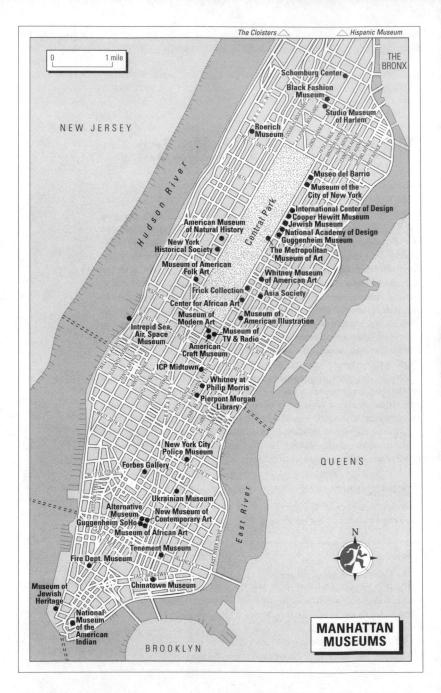

The Cloisters △   △ Hispanic Museum

THE BRONX

0 ___ 1 mile

NEW JERSEY

Schomburg Center

Black Fashion Museum

Studio Museum of Harlem

Roerich Museum

Museo del Barrio

Museum of the City of New York

International Center of Design

Cooper Hewitt Museum

Jewish Museum

National Academy of Design

Guggenheim Museum

American Museum of Natural History

New York Historical Society

The Metropolitan Museum of Art

Museum of American Folk Art

Whitney Museum of American Art

Frick Collection

Center for African Art

Asia Society

Museum of Modern Art

Museum of American Illustration

Intrepid Sea, Air, Space Museum

Museum of TV & Radio

American Craft Museum

ICP Midtown

Whitney at Philip Morris

Pierpont Morgan Library

New York City Police Museum

Forbes Gallery

QUEENS

Ukrainian Museum

Alternative Museum

New Museum of Contemporary Art

Guggenheim SoHo

Museum of African Art

Tenement Museum

Fire Dept. Museum

Chinatown Museum

Museum of Jewish Heritage

National Museum of the American Indian

BROOKLYN

Hudson River

Central Park

East River

N

MANHATTAN MUSEUMS

evening one or two nights a week. Admission charges are high, with a slight discount for those with student ID cards; to offset the prices, many major museums are free or offer a much-reduced entrance charge one evening a week. Many NY museums utilize the "voluntary donation" system. In theory, this means you're allowed to give as little or as much as you'd like for an entry fee (hence enabling museums to keep their charitable status); in practice, you'll need to be pretty brazen to give any less than the (not particularly low) recommended minimum.

The Metropolitan Museum of Art

5th Ave at 82nd St. Subway #4, #5 or #6 to 86th St–Lexington Ave Tues–Thurs & Sun 9.30am–5.15pm, Fri & Sat 9.30am–8.45pm, closed Mon. Recorded info ☎535-7710 or 879-5500. Admission by voluntary donation, suggested $8, students $4 (includes admission to The Cloisters on the same day; see p.258). Free conducted tours, "Highlights of the Met," daily; also highly detailed tours of specific galleries; recorded tours of the major collections, $4.

The Met, as it's usually called, is the foremost museum in America. Its galleries take in over three-and-a-half million works of art and span the arts and cultures not just of America and Europe (though these are the most famous collections), but also of China, Africa, the Far East, and the Classical and Islamic worlds. Any overview of the museum is out of the question: the Met demands many and specific visits or, at least, self-imposed limits.

Broadly, the Met breaks down into six **major collections**: European Painting, American Painting, Medieval Art, "Primitive" Art, Egyptian Antiquities and Asian Art, the latter with newly expanded galleries for Chinese works that have greatly increased its prominence. You'll find the highlights of these detailed below. Keep in mind, however, that there is much, much more for which space forbids anything other than a passing mention. Among the **less famous Met collections** are Greek and Roman Galleries (second only to those in Athens), Islamic Art (possibly the largest display anywhere in the world), Arms and Armor Galleries (the largest and most important in the Western hemisphere), a Musical Instrument Collection (containing the world's oldest piano) and what would, anywhere else, be seen as essential Twentieth-Century Art Galleries (with Picasso's *Portrait of Gertrude Stein* and Pollock's *Parsiphaë*, for a start).

Despite the museum's size, **initial orientation** is not too difficult. There is just one main entrance, and once you've passed through it you find yourself in the **Great Hall**, a deftly lit Neoclassical cavern where you can consult plans, check tours and pick up info on the Met's excellent lecture listings. Directly ahead is the Grand Staircase and what is, for many visitors, the single greatest attraction – the European Painting galleries.

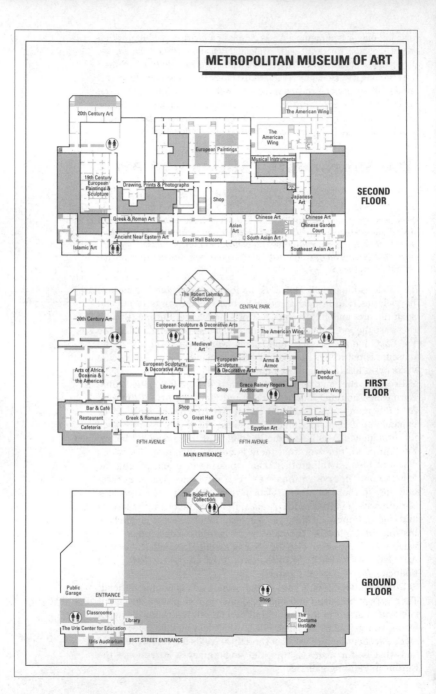

METROPOLITAN MUSEUM OF ART

SECOND FLOOR

20th Century Art

19th Century European Paintings & Sculpture

Drawing, Prints & Photographs

European Paintings

The American Wing

The American Wing

Musical Instruments

Shop

Japanese Art

Greek & Roman Art

Ancient Near Eastern Art

Asian Art

Great Hall Balcony

Chinese Art

South Asian Art

Chinese Art

Chinese Garden Court

Islamic Art

Southeast Asian Art

FIRST FLOOR

The Robert Lehman Collection

CENTRAL PARK

20th Century Art

European Sculpture & Decorative Arts

The American Wing

Medieval Art

Arts of Africa, Oceania & the Americas

European Sculpture & Decorative Arts

European Sculpture & Decorative Arts

Arms & Armor

Temple of Dendur

Library

Shop

Grace Rainey Rogers Auditorium

The Sackler Wing

Bar & Café

Restaurant

Cafeteria

Greek & Roman Art

Shop

Great Hall

Egyptian Art

Egyptian Art

FIFTH AVENUE

FIFTH AVENUE

MAIN ENTRANCE

GROUND FLOOR

The Robert Lehman Collection

Public Garage

ENTRANCE

Classrooms

Shop

Library

The Uris Center for Education

The Costume Institute

Uris Auditorium

81ST STREET ENTRANCE

Problems in visiting the Met

There are three main difficulties in visiting, other than the obvious frustrations of size and time:

Scheduling. Certain collections are open only on a rotating basis, so if you're intent on seeing anything less than obvious, phone ahead (☎535-7710). The rotating schedule affects galleries only on Tuesdays, Wednesdays and Thursdays.

Layout. The Met has developed in a piecemeal way, for its nineteenth-century multimillionaire benefactors were often as intent on advertising their own tastes as setting America on the cultural high road. Therefore, their bequests often stipulated that their donations be housed in distinct galleries. If you're interested in one particular period or movement of art, you won't necessarily find all of its examples in the same place.

Reorganization. The museum is constantly reorganizing its galleries: rotating the works, creating space for special exhibits, loaning out pieces for retrospectives and refurbishing rooms. This means that although the master works stay pretty much in the same locations, the order in which we've listed various standouts may not be that in which they appear.

European Painting galleries

The Met's European Painting galleries are divided in two parts: the European Painting section – which traces several centuries worth of work – and the nineteenth-century European Paintings and Sculpture section.

The former begins with a scattering of portraits then branches off into **two paths**: One path moves through the Italian Renaissance, chronicles the seventeenth-century Dutch masters, passes through a small but fine English collection and ends with a clutch of Spanish, French and Italian works painted in the Baroque style; the other path begins in the Gothic period, passes through the religious works of the Northern Renaissance, offers glances at Baroque and Italian Mannerism and finally culminates in Italian Baroque.

The nineteenth-century galleries, located to the west of this exhibit, are dominated by a tremendous core group of Impressionist painting. Ideally, take a break in the café between each of these halves: these are large collections.

Spanish and Italian Painting

After looking through a preliminary section that contains works by the Italian **Tiepolo** and Neoclassical/Romantic portraits by **David** and **Greuve**, you'll arrive at the beginning of the Italian secular painting.

The **Italian Renaissance** isn't spectacularly represented, but there's a worthy selection from the various Italian schools, including an early *Madonna and Child Enthroned with Saints* by Raphael, a late **Botticelli**, the crisply linear *Three Miracles of Saint Zenobius*,

The Metropolitan Museum of Art

and **Filippo Lippi**'s *Madonna and Child Enthroned with Two Angels*. Among the **Mannerists**, best of the Italian collections, is **Bronzino**'s *Portrait of a Young Man*. Make sure you backtrack into rooms 4A and 4B, where you will see a smaller series of religious paintings, including **Michele de Verona**'s handsome *Madonna and Child with the Infant John the Baptist*, rendered in the fifteenth-century Italian tradition with a marmoreal surface bathed in soft light. Also look out for the roaring dragon in **Crivelli**'s *St George* and **Mantegna**'s rigid and sculptural *Adoration of the Shepherds*.

Dutch Painting

Adjacent to room 4B is the **Benjamin Altman Collection**, here cleverly jigsawed into the main gallery. A small number of Dutch works, including **Memling**'s *Tommaso Portinari and his Wife* and a *Mystical Marriage of St Catherine*, prelude the main Dutch Painting section. This collection, dominated by the major works of **Rembrandt, Vermeer** and **Hals**, is the culmination of the main European galleries – and arguably the finest single group of paintings in the museum.

Vermeer, genius of the domestic interior, is represented by some of his best works. His *Young Woman with a Water Jug*, which hints at themes of purity and temperance, is a perfect example of his skill in composition and tonal gradation, combined with an uncannily naturalistic sense of lighting. *A Girl Asleep* is deeper in its composition – or at least appears to be, the rich fabric separating the foreground from the rooms beyond. Vermeer often used this trick, and you'll see it again in *Allegory of the Faith*, where the drawn curtain presents the tableau and separates the viewer from the lesson presented. Most haunting of all is the great *Portrait of a Young Woman*, displaying Vermeer at his most complex and the Met at its most fortunate.

As Vermeer's pictures depict the domestic harmony of seventeenth-century Holland, **Hals**'s early paintings reveal its exuberance. In *Merrymakers at Shrovetide*, the figures explode out from the canvas in an abundance of gesture and richness. *Young Man and a Woman at an Inn*, painted five years later, shows a more subdued use of color (yet not at the expense of vitality).

The best of **Rembrandt**'s works here are also portraits. There is a beautiful painting of his common-law wife, *Hendrike Stoffjels*, finished three years before her early death – a blow that marked a further decline in the artist's fortunes. In 1660, he went bankrupt, and the superb *Self-Portrait* of that year shows the self-examination he brought to later works. A comparison between the flamboyant 1632 *Portrait of a Lady* and the warmer, later *Lady with a Pink* reveals his maturing genius.

In addition to these three famous artists, the Dutch rooms also display a good scattering of works by their contemporaries. Most memorable is **Pieter de Hooch**'s *Two Men and a Woman in a*

Courtyard of a House – his acknowledged masterpiece, with its perfect arrangement of line, form and color. While de Hooch was painting peaceful courtyards and Vermeer lacemakers and lute players, **Adrian Brouwer** was turning his eye to the seamier side of Dutch life. When he wasn't drunk or in prison he came up with works like *The Smokers*, typical of his tavern scenes. Traditionally, *The Smokers* is a portrait of Brouwer and his drinking pals – he's the one in the foreground, in case you hadn't guessed.

English Painting

Though the Met's **English Gallery** is essentially a prelude to the other major collections here, it's an unusually brilliant and elegant clutch of paintings. At its heart are a group of portraits by **Sir Joshua Reynolds**, **William Gainsborough** and **Thomas Lawrence**, the trio of great, eighteenth-century English portraitists. **Gainsborough's** *Mrs Grace Dalrymple Elliott* is typical of his portrait style – an almost feathery lightness softening the monumental pose. Lawrence is best represented by *The Calmady Children*, a much-engraved portrait that was the artist's favorite among his works, and by his likable and virtuoso study of *Elizabeth Farren*, which he painted at the precocious age of 21. Upon seeing the picture, Sir Joshua Reynolds remarked, "This young man begins where I leave off," a rather modest comment considering the number of portraits by Reynolds that are included here.

Continue on, and as you loop back toward the initial two galleries, you'll pass through another smattering of works by **Spanish**, **French** and **Italian** painters, most notably **Goya** and **Velázquez**. The latter's piercing and somber *Portrait of Juan de Parej* shouldn't be missed; when it was first exhibited, a critic dramatically remarked, "All the rest are art, this alone is truth."

Early Flemish and Netherlandish Painting

Follow the left-hand fork from the preliminary rooms and you'll arrive at *Early Flemish and Netherlandish Painting*, precursors of both the Northern and Italian Renaissances. Inevitably, the first paintings are by **Jan van Eyck**, who is generally attributed with beginning the tradition of North European realism. His *The Crucifixion* and *The Last Judgement* – painted early in Van Eyck's career and much like the miniatures he painted for the Turin-Milan Hours – are bright, realistic and full of expressive (and horrific) detail. *The Annunciation* adjacent is probably by Van Eyck too; its perspective is tidily, if not totally accurately, drawn, the Romanesque right-hand side of the portal and the Gothic left symbolizing the transition from Old Testament to New.

There's more allusion to things Gothic in **Rogier van der Weyden's** *Christ Appearing to his Mother*, the apocryphal visit surrounded by tiny statuary depicting Christ's earlier and Mary's later life. It's one of the most beautiful of all van der Weyden's works, quite different in feel to Van Eyck, with a warmth of design and feeling replacing the former's hard draughtsman's clarity. This development is continued through the third great Northern Gothic painter, **Gerhard David**, as is the vogue for setting religious scenes in Low Countries settings. The background to David's exquisite *Virgin and Child with Four Angels* is medieval Bruges; in *The Rest on the Flight to Egypt* landscape features are added to by Low Country genre scenes. **Bruegel's** *Harvesters*, one of the Met's most reproduced pictures and part of the series of twelve paintings that included his (Christmas-card familiar) *Hunters in the Snow*, shows how these innovations were assimilated.

Cutting left at this point brings you to more **Mannerists** and **Italian Baroque**, which culminates in a room dedicated to the formidable works of **El Greco**. His extraordinary *View of Toledo* – all brooding intensity as the skies seem about to swallow up the ghost-like town – is perhaps the best of his works anywhere in the world, and a satisfying conclusion to the gallery.

The nineteenth-century galleries

A suite of twenty rooms recently designed in Beaux Arts style (the decorative detail was adapted from designs made for the museum by architects McKim, Mead and White early this century) displays a startling array of **Impressionist and Post-Impressionist** art and nineteenth-century European sculpture.

Impressionist Painting

The **Manet** gallery is the largest of the rooms and serves as a focal point, flanked by galleries devoted to **Courbet**, **Degas** and the **Barbizon School**. To the west are rooms of **Impressionist** and **Post-Impressionist paintings**, as well as works from the Annenberg Collection.

The display, fittingly, centers around **Édouard Manet**, the Impressionist movement's most influential precursor, and whose early style of contrasting light and shadow with modulated shades of black can be firmly linked to the tradition of Hals, Velázquez and Goya. The *Spanish Dancer*, an accomplished example of this heritage, was well received on Manet's debut at the Paris Salon in 1861. Within a few years, though, he was shocking the same establishment with *Olympia*, *Déjeuner sur l'Herbe* and the striking *Woman with a Parrot* – the same woman, incidentally, modeled for all three paintings. Later, Manet's style shifted again as he adopted the Impressionist lightness of handling and interest in perception. He worked for a time with Renoir and Monet, a period of which *Boating* is typical – a celebration of the middle classes at play.

Claude Monet, who was influenced by Manet's style before Impressionism, was one of the movement's most prolific painters.

He returned again and again to a single subject to produce a series of images capturing different nuances of light and atmosphere. Three superb examples – *Rouen Cathedral, The Houses of Parliament from the Thames* and *The Doge's Palace Seen from San Giorgio Maggiore* – show the beginnings of his final phase of near-abstract Impressionism.

Paul Cézanne's technique was very different. He labored long to achieve a painstaking analysis of form and color, something clear in the *Landscape of Marseilles*. Of his few portraits, the jarring, almost Cubist angles and spaces of *Mme Cézanne in a Red Dress* seem years ahead of their time. Take a look, too, at *The Card Players*, whose dynamic triangular structure thrusts out, yet retains the quiet concentration of the moment. **Claude Renoir** is perhaps the best represented among the remaining Impressionists, though his most important work here dates from 1878, when he began to move away from the mainstream techniques he'd learned while working with Monet. *Mme Charpentier and her Children* is a likable enough piece, one whose affectionate if unsearching tone manages to sidestep the sugariness of Renoir's later work. Better, or at least more real, is his *Waitress at Duval's Restaurant*.

Post-Impressionist Painting

The Post-Impressionists, logically enough, follow, with **Paul Gauguin**'s masterly *La Orana Maria*. The title, the archangel Gabriel's first words to Mary at the Annunciation, is the key to the work. The scene was a staple of the Renaissance, transferred here to a wholly different culture in an attempt to unfold the symbolic meaning, and perhaps voice the artist's feeling for the native South Sea islanders, whose cause he championed. *Two Tahitian Women* hangs adjacent, a portrait of his lover Pahura – skillful, studied simplicity.

Henri de Toulouse-Lautrec delighted in painting the world Gauguin went to Tahiti to escape. *The Sofa* is one of a series of sketches he made in Paris brothels. The artist's deformity distanced him from society, and he identified with the life of the prostitutes in his sketches. He also hated posed modeling, which made the bored women awaiting clients an ideal subject.

Gustave Courbet and **Degas**, too, are well represented – Courbet especially, with examples of every phase and period of his career, including *Young Ladies from the Village*, a virtual manifesto of his idea of realism, and *Woman with a Parrot*, a superbly erotic and exotic work that gave Manet the idea for his work of the same name. Degas constantly returned to the subject of dancers, and there are studies in just about every medium – from pastels to sculpture. Unlike the Impressionists, Degas subordinated what he saw to what he believed, and his *Dancers Practicing at the Bar* shows this – the painting is about structure, alluded to in the way the dancer on the right picks up the form of the watering can used to lay the dust in the studio. Also here is a vaguely macabre casting of his *Little Dancer*, complete with real tutu, bodice and slippers.

All of this scratches little more than the surface of the galleries. There's also work by **Van Gogh**, **Rousseau** and **Seurat**; paintings from the **Barbizon School**; portraits by **Ingres**; sculpture by **Rodin**; a quick overview of Romanticism and a peripheral gallery of paintings that express the official taste of the nineteenth century.

The Lehman Pavilion

The **Lehman Pavilion** was tacked on to the rear of the Met in 1975 to house the collection of Robert Lehman, millionaire banker and art collector. This section breaks from the Met's usual sober arrangement of rectangular floor plans: Rooms are laid out beside a brilliantly lit atrium, with some rooms re-created from Lehman's own home.

Most important, Lehman's enthusiasms fill the gaps in the Met's account of **Italian Renaissance** painting. This period was his passion, and his collection is shown on the first floor of the pavilion. The heart of the group centers around **Botticelli's** *Annunciation*, a small but exquisite celebration of the Florentine discovery of perspective. From the Venetian school comes a sculptural *Madonna and Child* by **Giovanni Bellini** and two unaffected portraits by **Jacometto Veneziano**. Then, following **Bartolomeo Vivarini's** exquisitely detailed altarpiece *Death of the Virgin*, there's a quartet of works by the Sienese **Giovanni di Paolo**; most notable are *The Creation of the World* and the *Expulsion from Paradise*, in which an angel gently ushers Adam and Eve from Eden, while a Byzantine God points to their place of banishment.

Continuing on, there is a small but strong group of sixteenth-century portraits by **El Greco**, **Ingres** (the luminescent *Princesse de Broglie*), **Ter Bosch** and **Velázquez**. One painting stands out from them all, though: **Rembrandt's** *Portrait of Gerard de Lairesse*. Although de Lairesse was supposedly disliked for his luxurious tastes and unpleasant character, his most apparent flaw was his disfigured face – ravaged by congenital syphilis.

In the gallery left of this collection are works from the **Northern Renaissance**, highlighted by a trio of paintings by Memling, Holbein and Petrus Christus. **Christus's** untypically large canvas of *St Elegius*, patron saint of goldsmiths, shows an Eyckian attention to detail in its depiction of the saint's jewels and precious stones – an insight into the work of the fifteenth-century goldsmith. Memling, working around thirty years later, used a lighter palette to achieve the delicate serenity of his *Annunciation*, in which cool colors and a gentle portrayal of Mary and her attendant angels illuminate the Flemish interior. **Hans Holbein the Younger's** *Portrait of Erasmus of Rotterdam* was one of three he painted in 1523 that established his reputation as a portraitist.

On the ground floor, where the time frame moves toward the **nineteenth and twentieth centuries**, the collection loses its authority. There are minor works by major artists here – Renoir, Van Gogh, Gauguin, Cézanne and Matisse. Have a look at **Suzanne Valadon**'s *Reclining Nude*: Valadon is largely ignored today, and is best known as a model for Toulouse-Lautrec, Renoir and Degas (who encouraged her to become a painter in her own right). But her boldly colored canvases show originality and also her influence on her son, **Maurice Utrillo**, whom she taught to paint as an attempt to wean him off the drink and drugs that were his downfall. Utrillo's *40, Rue Ravignon* stands here near his mother's painting.

Twentieth-century art

Housed over two floors in the Lila Acheson Wallace Wing, the Met's **twentieth-century collection** is a fascinating and compact group of paintings. The first floor begins with the collection's recent acquisitions, proceeds through a temporary exhibit of relevant works and concludes with a chronological installation of American and European art **from 1905 to 1940**. Such paintings as **Charles Demuth**'s *The Figure Five in Gold* and **Picasso**'s *Portrait of Gertrude Stein* are here, hung alongside works by Klee, Matisse, Braques, Freud and Klimt. There's also a small design collection, featuring changing pieces of furniture, ceramics and almost anything else from the museum's holdings.

The second floor contains European and American painting **from 1945 to the present**, opening with a room filled with the gigantic, emotional canvases of Abstract Expressionist **Clyfford Still**. Highlights on this floor include **Jackson Pollock**'s masterly *Autumn Rhythm (Number 30)*, **Thomas Hart Benton**'s rural idyll *July Hay*, **R.B. Kitaj**'s *John Ford on his Deathbed*, a dream-like painting of the director of western movies, and **Andy Warhol**'s final *Self-Portrait*; hung alongside are works by Max Beckmann, Roy Lichtenstein (*Painting Since 1945*), Mark Rothko, and Gilbert and George. In the summer months, you also can continue up to the **Cantor Roof Garden**, located on top of the Wallace Wing, which displays **contemporary sculpture** against the dramatic backdrop of the New York skyline.

Asian Art

Recently redesigned and greatly expanded, the second floor's **Asian Art galleries** – while lacking in the prestige and the named artists of the Western holdings – gather an impressive and vast array of Chinese, Japanese, Indian and southeast Asian sculpture, painting and the like, centered on an indoor replica of a Chinese garden. Approach from the Great Hall balcony: lining the corridor's back wall is an exhibit of fifth- to eighth-century Kuran pottery, which holds some fancifully glazed and decorated ceremonial pieces among the everyday jugs and bowls.

First up is **Chinese Sculpture**, a hodgepodge of stone works arranged around two twenty-foot-high buddhas. The focal point, however, is not any one sculpture but an enormous (and exquisite) fourteenth-century mural, *The Paradise of Bhaishajyaguru*. This piece, masterfully reconstructed after being severely damaged in an earthquake, is a study in calm reflection.

Take the right fork from this gallery to arrive at **South Asian Art**. Note the ancient pair of golden earrings from India as you enter – actually quite rare, for it was custom there to melt down and recast jewelry after the owner died to avoid inheriting that person's karma. **Statues** of Hindu and Buddhist deities form the bulk of work, alongside numerous pieces of **friezes**, many of which still possess exceptional detail despite years of exposure. *The Great Departure and the Temptation of the Buddha*, carved in the third century, is a particularly lively example: Siddhartha setting out on his spiritual journey being chased by a harem of dancing girls and grasping cherubs.

Past a set of stairs that leads to a small third-floor gallery (for temporary exhibits) is **Chinese art**. The works here tend to run into one another, though there are some worthwhile parchments painted in the fifteenth and sixteenth centuries by scholar-artists – an underclass of unemployed scholars that blurred the line between amateur painters and the more educated court artists. The highlight in this area, however, is the **Chinese Garden Court**, a serene, minimalist retreat enclosed by the galleries. The naturally lit garden is a reconstruction of ones found in Chinese homes, assembled by experts from the People's Republic: a pagoda and small waterfall and stocked goldfish pond landscaped by limestone rocks, trees and shrubs – all of which conjure an airy and peaceful feel. The surrounding windows add to the calm: each is filled with a different geometric shape, intended to give the illusion of continuous space.

After your meditation, forge right to the Sackler Wing, part of a cluster of rooms dedicated to **Japanese art**. Less structured than the other galleries, this section holds objects from the prehistoric era to the present, divided into thematic sections: "Gods and Ancestors," "Spirits and Teachers," "Characters in a Story" and "The Moral and Immoral." Complementing this core are rotating exhibits of textiles, paintings and prints. Earliest of Japanese **religious art** are the *dogu*, female figurines dating from 10,500 BC up to 400 BC, none of which remains a whole piece. Probably due to deliberate acts of superstition rather than general wear and tear, the figures are broken or missing a limb. The coming of Buddhism in the sixth century changed the strategy of Japanese art, and the results – greatly exaggerated depictions of physical perfection – can be well seen in the **Japanese Buddhist painting and sculpture** collection. All of which is a prelude to the exhibit's crown jewel – the several galleries of seventeenth- and eighteenth-century **hand-painted Kano screens**. The screens range from the elegantly mundane (books on a shelf) to elaborate scenes of historical allusion and divine fervor, such as *Gods of Good Fortune and Chinese Children*, a six-fold screen of delicate inkwork and vivid colors by **Kano Chikanobu** that resides in a place of honor in the *shoin* (study) room.

The American wing

The American wing comes nearest to being a museum in its own right, and it's a thorough introduction to the development of fine and decorative art in America.

Galleries – and almost immediately, a series of **furnished historical rooms** – take off from the **Charles Engelhard Court**, a shrub-filled sculpture garden enclosed at the lower end by the *Facade of the United States Bank*, lifted straight from Wall Street. Step through this facade and you'll be standing in the **Federal period rooms,** surrounded by the restrained Neoclassical elegance of the late eighteenth century. (If this is your first visit to this section of the Met, go up to the third floor and work your way down from there; that way you'll see the rooms in chronological order.) The **early Colonial period**, represented most evocatively in the Hart room of around 1674, begins the tour; **Frank Lloyd Wright's** *Room from the Little House, Minneapolis*, originally windowed on all four sides to demonstrate Wright's concept of minimizing interior–exterior division, ends it. On the second floor balcony, be sure not to miss the iridescent Favrile glass of **Louis Comfort Tiffany**: an elegant Art Nouveau accompaniment to the decor.

The collection of American paintings

The **collection of American paintings** begins on the second floor with **eighteenth-century** portraits, but really gets going with the works of **Benjamin West**, an artist who worked in London and taught or influenced many of the American painters of his day – *The Triumph of Love* is typical of his Neoclassical, allegorical works. More heroics come with **John Trumbull**, one of West's pupils, in *Sortie Made by the Garrison of Gibraltar* and the fully blown Romanticism of *Washington Crossing the Delaware* by **Emanuel Leutzes**. This last shows Washington escaping across the river in the winter of 1776; although historically and geographically inaccurate – the American flag, shown dramatically flowing in the background, hadn't yet been created – the picture is nonetheless a national icon.

Early in the nineteenth century, American painters gained the confidence to move away from European themes. **William Sidney Mount** depicted genre scenes on his native Long Island, often with a sly political angle – as with *Cider Makers* and *The Bet* – and the painters of the **Hudson Valley School** apotheosized that landscape in their vast lyrical canvases. **Thomas Cole**, the school's doyen, is represented by

The Oxbow, his pupil **Frederick Church** by an immense *Heart of the Andes* – combining the grand sweep of the mountains with minutely depicted flora. **Albert Bierstadt** and **S.R. Gifford** continued to concentrate on the American west – their respective works *The Rocky Mountains, Lander's Peak* and *Kauterskill Falls* have a near-visionary idealism, bound to a belief that the westward development of the country was a manifestation of divine will.

Winslow Homer is allowed a gallery to himself – fittingly for a painter who was to influence greatly the late nineteenth-century artistic scene in America. Homer began his career illustrating the day-to-day realities of the Civil War – there's a good selection here that shows the tedium and sadness of those years – and a sense of recording detail carried over into his late, quasi-Impressionistic studies of seascapes. *Northeaster* is one of the finest of these, close to Courbet in its strength of composition and color.

The mezzanine below brings the Met's account of American art into the **twentieth century**. Some of the initial portraiture here tends to the sugary, but **J.W. Alexander**'s *Repose* deftly hits the mark – a simple, striking use of line and light with a sumptuous feel and more than a hint of eroticism. By way of contrast, there's **Thomas Eakin**'s subdued, almost ghostly *Max Schmitt in a Single Scull*, and **William Merritt Chase**'s *For the Little One*, an Impressionist study of his wife sewing. Chase studied in Europe and it was there that he painted his *Portrait of Whistler*. Whistler returned the compliment but destroyed the work on seeing Chase's (quite truthful) depiction of himself as a dandified fop – and done in a teasing style that mimicked his own. Whatever Whistler's conceits, though, his portraits are adept: Witness the *Arrangement in Flesh Color and Black: Portrait of Theodore Duret* nearby.

The reputation of **John Singer Sargent** has suffered its ups and downs over the years, but now he seems to be coming back into fashion. There is certainly a virtuosity in his large portraits, like that of *Mr and Mrs I.N. Phelps Stokes*, the couple purposefully elongated as if to emphasize their aristocratic characters. *Padre Sebastiano* is a smaller, more personal response. The *Portrait of Madam X* (Mme Pierre Gautreau, a notorious Parisian beauty) was one of the most famous pictures of its day: Exhibited at the 1884 Paris salon, it was considered so improper that Sargent had to leave Paris for London. "I suppose it's the best thing I've done," he said wearily on selling it to the Met a few years later.

Medieval art

In theory, you could move straight on to the **medieval galleries** from the American wing. But this would be heavy-going; you'd miss out on the museum's carefully planned approach.

Instead, enter these galleries via the **corridor** leading in from the Great Hall; there you'll see displays of the sumptuous **Byzantine** metalwork and jewelry that J.P. Morgan donated to the museum in its early days. At the end of the corridor is the main **sculpture hall**, piled high with religious statuary and carvings (a tremendous *St Nicholas Saving Three Boys in the Brine Tub*) and split with a *reja* (altar screen) from Valladolid Cathedral.

Right from here the **medieval treasury** has an all-embracing – and magnificent – display of objects religious, liturgical and secular. And beyond are the **Jack and Belle Linski Galleries**: Flemish, Florentine and Venetian painting, porcelain and bronzes.

Dotted throughout the medieval galleries are later **period rooms**: paneled Tudor bedrooms and Robert Adam fineries from England, florid Rococo boudoirs and salons from France, and an entire Renaissance patio from Velez Blanco in Spain. It's all a bit much, leaving you with the feeling that Morgan and his robber baron colleagues would probably have shipped over Versailles if they could have laid their hands on it.

The Egyptian collection

"A chronological panorama of ancient Egypt's art, history and culture," boasts the blurb to the **Egyptian collection**, and the display is certainly lavish. Brightly efficient corridors steer you through the treasures of the digs of the 1920s and 1930s, art and artifacts from the prehistoric to Byzantine periods of Egyptian culture.

The **statuary** are the most immediately striking of the exhibits, though after a while it's the smaller **sculptural** pieces that hold the attention longest. Figures like *Merti and his Wife* were modeled as portraits, but often carvings were made in the belief that a person's *Ka*, or life force, would continue to exist in an idealized model after his or her death. There's a beautifully crafted example in the *Carving of Senebi* in gallery 8; what was probably Senebi's tomb is displayed nearby. Also in this room is the dazzling collection of *Princess Sithathorunet's jewelry*, a pinnacle in Egyptian decorative art from around 1830 BC; the *Models of Mekutra's House* (around 1198 BC); and the radiant *Fragmentary Head of a Queen*, sensuously carved in polished yellow jasper.

The Temple of Dendur

At the end of all this sits the **Temple of Dendur**, housed in a vast airy gallery designed to give hints and symbols of its original site on the banks of the Nile. Built by the Emperor Augustus in 15 BC as an attempt to placate a local chieftain, the temple was moved here as a gift of the Egyptian people during the construction of the Aswan High dam – otherwise it would have been drowned. Sadly, the gallery, rather than suggest the empty expanses of the Nile, dwarfs what is essentially an unremarkable building, one that might be more engaging if you could explore inside. The temple needs a helping hand, and gets it at night, illuminated on a corner of Central Park with at least some of the mystery that's missing during the day.

The Michael C. Rockefeller Wing

Son of Governor Nelson Rockefeller, Michael C. Rockefeller disappeared during a trip to West New Guinea in 1961. The Rockefeller Wing stands as a memorial to him, including many of his finds alongside the Met's comprehensive collection of art from Africa, the Pacific Islands and the Americas. It's a superb gallery, the muted, reassuring decoration throwing the **"Primitive" Art** exhibits into sharp and often frightening focus. You don't need much knowledge of early indigenous cultures to feel the intensity of the work here: the blackened reliquary heads from Gabon once contained the skulls of a family's ancestors and issued magical protection; the elegant spared lines of terracotta heads from Ghana put you in mind of Modigliani portraits; and the rich geometry of the South American jewelry and ornaments too often seems startlingly contemporary.

Other collections

The Met's **other collections** include the **Costume Institute**, which shows rotating exhibitions drawn from its collection of more than 60,000 costumes and accessories, dating from the fifteenth century to the present day. The expanding **Department of Photographs** has been busily acquiring work, and now commands a collection to rival that of the Museum of Modern Art.

MANHATTAN

The Museum of Modern Art

11 W 53rd St, Subway E or F to 5th Ave–53rd St. Sat–Tues 11am–6pm, Thurs & Fri noon–8.30pm, closed Wed; $8.50, students $5.50, Fri 4.30–8.30pm pay what you wish. Recorded audio tour $4. Free gallery talks held Mon & Tues 1pm & 3pm; Thurs & Fri 3pm, 6pm & 7pm; and Sat & Sun 1pm & 3pm. Call ☎ 708-9480 for exhibit information.

Instigated in 1929, moved to its present home ten years later, and extensively updated in the mid-1980s with a steel pipe and glass renovation that doubled its gallery space, **The Museum of Modern Art** (plain MoMA to the initiated) offers the finest and most complete account of late nineteenth- and twentieth-century art you're likely to find. Yet another extension is in the works, to be completed by 2000. The competition to design it has brought the current space under fire; indeed, maverick architect Rem Koolhaas, who submitted an ambitious proposal for the future addition, criticized the old space as "shabby" and the newer parts as "tacky." Such candor apparently didn't help his cause – his plans for a cohesive update were turned down.

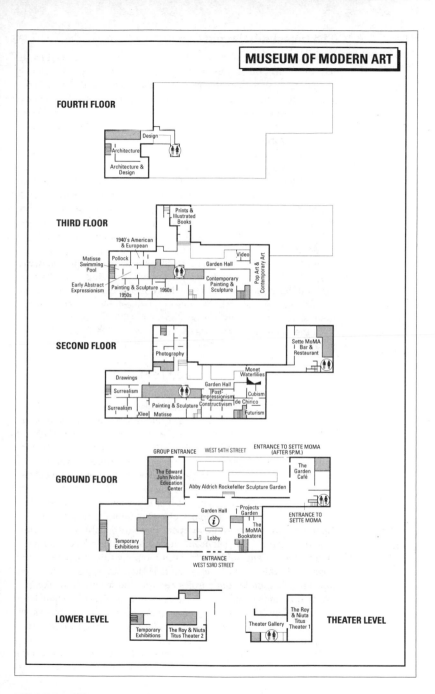

The museum's layout

The MoMA building is designed to guide you effortlessly and easily into the collections – and, with glass-enclosed landings and gliding escalators, it's an enjoyable place to walk inside. On the **first floor**, you'll find the usual pairing of restaurant and shop, as well as a video room and film theater (pick up a leaflet for a list of current showings); outside, a **sculpture garden,** designed by Philip Johnson, offers the works of Rodin and Matisse alongside such artifacts as an Art Nouveau Paris metro sign. The museum proper begins upstairs, with the second and third floors devoted to the **main painting and sculpture galleries,** the fourth to **architecture and design.** The roster of artists and major movements in the main rooms remains fairly constant; however, apart from a few key works, paintings are changed regularly, and some of the pieces we've commented on below may not be up when you visit – though there will usually be something by the same artist in its place.

In addition to the three main sections, the museum also has galleries devoted to **photographs**, **prints** and **drawings**, all of which give rotating displays of the museum's collections. The photographs, in particular, are marvellous – one of the finest, most eclectic collections around and a vivid evocation of twentieth-century America, from the dramatic landscapes of Ansel Adams to Stieglitz's dynamic views of New York to the revealing portraits of Man Ray.

Second floor: painting and sculpture

Once you reach the second floor, **Cézanne**'s *Bather* of 1885, hung alongside some of his other works, pulls you toward further **Post-Impressionist** oeuvres – principally paintings by **Gauguin**, **Seurat** and **Van Gogh**, the latter whose *Starry Night* is included here. In the third room, paintings by the Belgian James Ensor, by Redon and Bonnard, and by **Rousseau** (*The Dream*) lead to galleries devoted to works by the major Cubist painters, including a handful by **Picasso** and **Braque**. Most notable is Picasso's *Demoiselles d'Avignon* (1907), a jagged, sharp and, for its time, revolutionary clash of tones and planes which some hold to be the heralder (and initial arbiter) of Cubist principles – though **Derain**'s *Bathers* in the previous room may have equal claim to the title.

A room off to the left from this Cubist gallery holds **Monet**'s *Water Lilies*: enormous, stirring attempts to abstract color and form, and which cover well over half their gallery's space, their swirling jades, pinks and purples creating the feeling of sitting in a giant aquarium. To the right are more **Cubist** canvases, mainly later works like Picasso's *Three Women at the Spring* (1921) and *Three Musicians*, hung opposite Léger's jokier evocation of the same subject, painted in 1944.

Rooms encapsulating entire periods and movements follow, cursory glances that contain a staggering quality of material. There are paintings by **Chagall**; **Kirchner's** *Dresden* and *Berlin* street scenes are the focus of a gallery devoted to the glaring realities of the **German Expressionists**; while the whirring abstractions of **Boccioni** are the mainstay of a room devoted to the **Futurists'** paeans to the industrial age. A further room takes in the work of **De Stijl**, principally **Mondrian**, following the artist's development from early limp Cubist pieces to later works like *Broadway Boogie Woogie*. This, painted in 1940 after he had moved to New York, reflects his love of jazz music – its short, sharp stabs of color conveying an almost physical rhythm.

Beyond here (and past a staircase leading up to the next painting and sculpture floor), **Matisse** has a large room to himself. MoMA's collection centers on the *Dancers* of 1909, taking in other lesser-known works like his pudgy series of *Heads of Jeanette*, where straight Impressionism becomes, in the final head, no more than a series of disfiguring lines and lumps. Look out, also, for the *Red Studio*, a depiction of Matisse's studio in France in which all perspective is resolved in shades of rusty red, and, if it's hung (which it's often not), *Le Bateau*. When this painting was first exhibited, MoMA had it hanging upside down for 47 days before noticing the mistake.

The next gallery holds paintings by **Klee**, some swirling canvases by **Kandinsky**, the smooth shapes of **Brancusi's** sculpture, and leads through to late works by **Braque** and **Picasso**: *Night Fishing at Antibes*; the *Seated Bather*; and the *Charnel House*, which, like *Guernica*, is an angry protest against the horrors of war.

In contrast, a room on are the brooding skies of **de Chirico**; a room containing works by **Miró**, notably his hilarious *Dutch Interior*; and a handful of dreamlike paintings by **Dali**, **Magritte** (*The Menaced Assassin*), **Delvaux** (*Phases of the Moon*) and **Balthus**: illogical scenes but disturbing in their clarity and undercurrents of eroticism. In Balthus's *The Living Room*, the static poses of the adolescent girls and carefully positioned guitar hint at notions of sexual awakening; while his rather odd portrait of Derain shows the anxious artist in front of a half-dressed young girl.

Third floor: painting and sculpture

The second painting and sculpture gallery continues chronologically, and, perhaps inevitably, with a more American slant. **Andrew Wyeth's** *Christina's World*, one of the best known of all modern American paintings, is often hung here, usually along with a couple of typically gloomy canvases by **Edward Hopper** – *House by the Railroad* and *New York Movie*, potent and atmospheric pieces that give a bleak account of modern American life. Contrast these with **Sheeler's** *American Landscape*: "the industrial landscape pastoralized," a critic noted, and almost toytown in its neat vision of industrialization, in which nothing moves and all gleams.

More abstract pieces follow: early Jackson Pollocks, **Gorky's** Miró-like doodles, some neat satires by **Dubuffet** and, at the end of the room, the anguished scream of **Bacon's** *No. 7 from 8 Studies for a Portrait*. What many come here for, however, is to see the later paintings of the artists of the **New York School** – large-scale canvases meant to be viewed from a distance, perfect for MoMA's large airy rooms. The paintings of **Pollock** and **de Kooning** – wild, and in Pollock's case, textured patterns with no clear beginning or end – mingle with the more ordered efforts of the Color Field artists and the later works of artists like **Matisse** and **Miró**. Matisse's work here is mainly paper cutouts, most striking the bold blue shapes of his *Swimming Pool* which the aging artist made to decorate the walls of his apartment in Nice. The work of the so-called **Color Field artists** is more vivid but emphasizes the importance of color in a similar way. In **Barnett Newman's** words, their paintings, "drained of impediments of memory, association, nostalgia, legend, myth, and what have you," are nothing but pure color, as in Newman's own *Vir Heroicus Sublimus*, sheer red and huge against the wall; in the radiating, almost humming blocks of **Mark Rothko**; and, perhaps most palpable, in the black canvases of **Ad Reinhardt**. **Robert Motherwell's** *Elegy to the Spanish Republic*, one of a series of more than a hundred such paintings, is slightly different: color is less important, and the broad splashes of black are meant to hint at the rituals of the *corrida*, the shapes roughly reminiscent of the testicles displayed at the finale of a bullfight.

The last of the painting and sculpture rooms is in part made up of donations by Philip Johnson – **Pop Art** mainly, including **Jasper Johns's** *Flag*, a well-known piece in which the Stars and Stripes is painted onto newsprint, transforming America's most potent symbol into little more than an arrangement of shapes and hues. You might also see work by **Robert Rauschenberg** and **Claes Oldenburg**, though these galleries are also regularly given over to contemporary work from the museum's collection.

Fourth floor: architecture and design

Architecture and design are, after painting and sculpture, MoMA's most important concern. The galleries on the fourth floor take in models and original drawings by the architects of key modern buildings – **Frank Lloyd Wright's** *Falling Water*, and projects by **Le Corbusier** and **Mies van der Rohe**. Further aspects of modern design are traced through the swollen glasswork of **Tiffany**, **Guimard's** flowery Art Nouveau furniture and, in addition to a couple of **Rietveld** chairs, a Rietveld sideboard that looks as if it could do with a spot of Rietveld paint. There are also chairs and other **furniture** designed by Mies van der Rohe, Alvar Alto and Henri van den Velde, some of which have been more successful examples of applied design than others. Look out, too – indeed you can't miss them – for the oversized items at the top of the escalator, notably a green Bell helicopter from 1945, poised delicately in the open space of the landing.

The Guggenheim Museum

1071 5th Ave (E 88th St). Subway #4, #5 or #6 to 86th St. Sun–Wed 10am–6pm, Fri & Sat 10am–8pm; closed Thurs; $10, Fri 6–8pm pay what you wish. Exhibit information ☎ 423-3500.

Multistory parking lot or upturned beehive? Whatever you think of the **Guggenheim Museum**, it's the building that steals the show. Frank Lloyd Wright's purpose-built structure, sixteen years in the making, caused a storm of controversy when it was unveiled in 1959, bearing little relation to the statuesque apartment buildings of this most genteel part of Fifth Avenue. Reactions, though Wright didn't live long enough to hear many, ranged from disgusted disbelief to critical acclaim. Even now, though the years have given the building a certain respectability, the jury is still out – as the furor over the museum's extension proved. From 1990 to summer 1992 the museum was closed, undergoing a $60 million facelift of the original Lloyd Wright building that opened the whole space to the public for the first time. Dull offices, storage rooms and bits of chicken wire were all removed to expose the uplifting interior spaces so that the public could experience the spiral of the central rotunda from top to bottom. This, along with the clever extension, has added the sort of tall, straight-walled, flat-floored galleries that the Guggenheim needed to offset its distinct shape. The new consensus is that the building is both a better museum and a better work of architecture.

The Guggenheim SoHo has annually changing exhibits from the main gallery; see p.264.

Some history

Solomon R. Guggenheim was one of America's richest men, his mines extracting silver and copper – and a healthy profit – all over the USA. Like other nineteenth-century American capitalists, the only problem for Guggenheim was what to spend his vast wealth on, so he started collecting Old Masters – a hobby he continued half-heartedly until the 1920s, when various sorties to Europe brought him into contact with the most avant-garde and influential of European art circles. Abstraction in art was then considered little more than a fad, but Guggenheim, always a man with an eye for a sound investment, started to collect modern paintings with fervor, buying wholesale the work of Kandinsky, adding items by Chagall, Gleizes, Léger and others, and exhibiting them to a bemused American public in his suite of rooms in the *Plaza Hotel*. In 1976, the collector Justin K. Thannhauser bequeathed masterworks by Cézanne, Degas, Gauguin, Manet, Toulouse-Lautrec, Van Gogh and

Picasso, among others, to the museum. The Guggenheim's collection of American Minimalist art from the 1960s is also particularly rich.

The collection

It's these works, added to with special purchases and the odd donation, that form the nucleus of the permanent collection; between the extension and the rotunda, a significant part of the museum's collection will always be displayed. There are also regular exhibitions based on aspects of the collection, picking up themes from the various styles and periods – which means there's little you can say about the Guggenheim without predicting what's going to be on show.

Even so, it's the space itself which dominates – "one of the greatest rooms erected in the twentieth century," wrote Philip Johnson, quite rightly. Even if you hate the sight of the place from the outside, it's hard not to be impressed by the tiers of cream concrete that open up above like the ribs of some giant convector fan. Most of the temporary exhibits are shown in the circular galleries, which increase upward at a gentle slope. On the way to the top, two galleries offer a representative sample of the Guggenheim's **permanent collection**: The first, in the **new extension**, gives a quick glance at the Cubists, Chagall and, most completely, Kandinsky; the other, the **Thannhauser Galleries** in the restored small rotunda, offers a collection of Post-Impressionist and early Modern masterpieces. High points here are a handful of late nineteenth-century paintings, not least the exquisite Degas *Dancers* and other Post-Impressionists, Van Gogh's *Mountains at St Rémy* and some sensitive early Picassos.

The Frick Collection

1 E 70th St. Subway #6 to 68th St–Lexington Ave. Tues–Sat 10am–6pm, Sun 1–6pm, closed Mon; $5, students $3. Audio-visual installation tells Henry Clay Frick's story and details the mansion and its collection at a quarter past each hour between 11.15am and 4.15pm. Concerts of classical music are also held each month: pick up a leaflet or call ☎288-0700 for details.

Some history

Housed in the former mansion of Henry Clay Frick, the immensely enjoyable **Frick Collection** comprises the art treasures hoarded by Frick during his years as one of the most ruthless of New York's robber barons. Vicious, uncompromising and anti-union, Frick broke strikes with state troopers and was hated enough to survive narrowly a number of assassination attempts. However, the legacy of his self-aggrandizement – he spent millions on the best of Europe's art treasures – is a superb collection of works, and as good a glimpse of the sumptuous life enjoyed by New York's big industrialists as you'll find.

First opened in the mid-1930s, the museum has been largely kept as it would have looked when the Fricks were living there. It's in dubious taste for the most part, much of the furniture heavy eighteenth-century French, but the nice thing about it – and many people rank the Frick as their favorite New York gallery because of this – is that it strives hard to be as unlike a museum as possible. Ropes are kept to a minimum, and even in the most sumptuously decorated rooms there are plenty of chairs you can freely sink into. When weary, you can take refuge in the central closed courtyard, whose abundant greenery, fountains and marble are arranged with a classical attention to order, and whose serenity you'd be hard pushed to find anywhere else in the city.

The collection

The collection itself was acquired under the direction of Joseph Duveen, notorious – and not entirely trustworthy – adviser to the city's richest and most ignorant. For Frick, however, he seems to have picked out the cream of Europe's post-World War I private art hoards, even if the opening ensemble of the **Boucher Room** is not to twentieth-century tastes, decorated with succulent representations of the arts and sciences. Next along, the **Dining Room** is more reserved, its Reynoldses and Hogarths overshadowed by the one non-portrait in the room, **Gainsborough**'s *St James's Park*: a subtly moving promenade under an arch of luxuriant trees – "Watteau far outdone," wrote a critic at the time. Outside there's more lusty French painting (Boucher again) and, in the next room, **Fragonard**'s *Progress of Love* series, which was painted for Madame du Barry in 1771 – and rejected by her soon after.

Better paintings follow, not least of them **Bellini**'s *St Francis*, which suggests his vision of Christ by means of pervading light, a bent tree and an enraptured stare. **El Greco**'s *St Jerome*, above the fireplace, reproachfully surveys the riches all around. In the South Hall hangs one of Boucher's very intimate depictions of his naked wife – loaded with meaning – and an early **Vermeer**, *Officer and Laughing Girl*: similarly suggestive, and full of lewd allusions to forthcoming sex. In the opposite direction, the Library holds a number of British works, most notably one of **Constable**'s *Salisbury Cathedral* series, and in the North Hall hangs an engaging and sensitive portrait of the *Comtesse de Haussonville* by **Ingres**.

The West Gallery

The **West Gallery**, beyond here, is the Frick's major draw, holding some of its finest paintings. Two **Turners**, views of Cologne and Dieppe, hang opposite each other, both a blaze of orange and creamy tones; **Van Dyck** pitches in with a couple of uncharacteristically informal portraits of Frans Snyders and his wife – two paintings only reunited when Frick purchased them; and across the room **Frans Hals** reveals himself in a boozy and rare self-portrait. **Rembrandt**, too, is represented by a set of piercing self-portraits and (although serious doubt has recently been thrown on its authenticity) the enigmatic *Polish Rider* – more fantasy-piece than portrait.

At the far end of the West Gallery **Whistler** shares the Oval Room with **Houdon's** *Diana*, his portrait of fellow-artist *Rose Corder* posed to the point where she would have to faint before Whistler would stop painting. Past here, the East Gallery holds more paintings still, but more interesting is the tiny room on the other side of the West Gallery. This houses an exquisite set of Limoges enamels, mainly sixteenth century, as well as a collection of small-scale paintings that includes a *Virgin and Child* by **Jan van Eyck** – one of the artist's very last works, and among the rare few to have reached America.

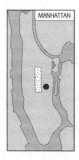

MANHATTAN

The Whitney Museum of American Art

945 Madison Ave (75th St). Subway #6 to 77th St–Lexington Ave. Wed, Fri–Sun 11am–6pm; Thurs 1–8pm, closed Mon & Tues; $8, students with ID $6; Thurs 6–8pm free for all. Excellent – and free – gallery talks take place Wed–Sun; call for times. Exhibit information ☎570-3652.

A gray-faced Brutalist arsenal designed by Marcel Breuer, the **Whitney's** oblique windows and cantilevered floors have an intimidating and suspiciously institutional air. Within, however, all such impressions are quickly dispelled. This is some of the best gallery space in the city and the perfect forum for the works that it owns one of the pre-eminent collections of twentieth-century American art. It is also a superb exhibition locale and, like the Guggenheim, devotes much of its time and rooms to this end, the majority of these given over to retrospectives and debuts of lesser-known themes. Every other year, though, there is an exhibition of a wholly different nature – the **Whitney Biennial** – designed to give a provocative overview of what's happening in contemporary American art. It is often panned by critics but always packed with visitors; catch it if you can between March and June in odd-numbered years.

In late 1997, the Whitney added on a fifth floor of galleries that increased the size of the exhibition area by about thirty percent. This space is being given over to a permanent display of core holdings, so some of the works mentioned below may well have been moved there.

The permanent collection

Gertrude Vanderbilt Whitney, a champion of American art, founded the collection in 1930 around works by Hopper, Thomas Hart

Benton, George Bellows and other living painters. Currently, the gallery owns over 12,000 pieces of painting, sculpture, photography and film by artists as diverse as Calder, Nevelson, O'Keefe, de Kooning, Rauschenberg, Le Witt and Nam June Paik. The **Highlights of the Permanent Collection**, a somewhat arbitrary pick of the Whitney's best, are arranged by both chronology and theme. The works form a superb introduction to twentieth-century American art, best evaluated with the help of the gallery talks, designed to explain and locate the paintings and sculptures in their various movements.

Gertrude Whitney's taste tended toward **Realism**, and the paintings often tie in with the expectations of the genre. **George Bellows's** *Dempsey and Firpo*, though, is a sort of Neo-Mannerist view of a boxing match, full of movement and flesh – "I don't know anything about boxing; I'm just painting two guys trying to kill each other," said Bellows.

The collection is particularly strong on **Edward Hopper** (his works were bequeathed to the museum), and several of his best paintings are here: *Early Sun Morning* is typical, a bleak urban landscape, uneasily tense in its lighting and rejection of topical detail. The street could be anywhere (in fact it's Seventh Avenue); for Hopper, it becomes universal.

As if to balance the figurative works that formed the nucleus of the collection, more recent purchases include much **abstraction**. **Marsden Hartley's** *Painting Number 5* is a strident, overwhelmed work, painted in the memory of a German officer friend killed in the early days of the Great War. **Georgia O'Keefe** called it "a brass band in a closet," and certainly her own work is gentler, though with its darknesses: *Abstraction* was suggested by the noises of cattle being driven to the local slaughterhouse. Have a look, too, at O'Keefe's flower paintings: verging on abstraction but hinting at deeper organic, erotic forms.

Featuring strongly are the **Abstract Expressionists**, with great works by high priests **Pollock** and **de Kooning**, leading on to **Rothko** and the **Color Field** painters – though you need a sharp eye to discern any color in **Ad Reinhardt's** *Black Painting*. In a different direction, **Warhol**, **Johns** and **Oldenburg** each subvert the meanings of their images. Warhol's silk-screened *Coke Bottles* fade into motif; Jasper Johns's celebrated *Three Flags* once again erases the emblem of

---

The Philip Morris Building collection

Situated in the atrium of the **Philip Morris Building** at 120 Park Avenue at 42nd Street (subway #4, #5 or #6 to Grand Central–42nd St), this Whitney satellite has two sections: a small **Picture Gallery** (Mon–Wed & Fri 11am–6pm, Thurs 11am–7.30pm; free) with changing exhibitions on just about any modern theme that you care to mention; and a **Sculpture Court** (Mon–Sat 7.30am–9.30pm, Sun 11am–7pm; free) festooned with works. A much better place to wait for a train than across the road in Grand Central.

patriotism and replaces it with ambiguity; and Claes Oldenburg's lighter-hearted *Soft Sculptures*, with squidgy toilets and melting motors, falls into line with his declaration, "I'm into art that doesn't sit on its ass in a museum." Finally, don't – you can't – miss **Ed Keinholz**'s *The Wait*, perhaps the best macabre joke in town.

MANHATTAN

The Cloisters

Fort Tryon Park. Subway A to 190th St–Washington Ave. Museum open Tues–Sun 9.30am–5.15pm (closes 4.45pm Nov–Feb), closed Mon. Suggested donation $8, students $4 (includes admission to Metropolitan Museum on same day); call ☎923-3700 for exhibition information.

High above the Hudson in Fort Tryon Park, **The Cloisters** stands like some misplaced Renaissance palazzo-cum-monastery, which was presumably the desired effect. For this was the folly of collectors George Barnard and John D. Rockefeller, Jr, who in turn spent the early years of this century shipping over the best of medieval Europe that was going: Romanesque chapels and Gothic halls, transplanted brick by brick and now housing the best part of the Metropolitan Museum's **medieval collection**. If you're familiar with the type of buildings that have been cannibalized, then the place can't help but feel like something of a Frankenstein's monster: an assemblage of parts to make a distorted whole. Nevertheless, it is all undeniably well carried off, not without atmosphere, and in detail superb.

The collection

The best approach – from the 190th Street subway – is directly across the park; Rockefeller Jr thoughtfully bought up the land on the other side of the river so as not to spoil the views. Starting from the entrance hall and working counterclockwise lays out the collection in a loosely chronological order. First off is the simple monumentality of the **Romanesque Hall**, consisting of French remnants and the frescoed Spanish **Fuentiduena Chapel**, both thirteenth century and immediately inducing a reverential hush. They corner on the prettiest of the four sets of cloisters here, those from **St Guilhelm**, strong and busily carved capitals from thirteenth-century France. More or less contemporary, and again from France, is the nearby **Langon Chapel**, attractive enough in itself and enhanced by a twelfth-century **ciborium** that manages to be formal and graceful in just the right proportions, and protects an emotive **Virgin and Child** beneath.

At the center of the museum is the **Cuxa cloister**, from the twelfth-century Benedictine monastery of Saint Michel de Cuxa near Prades in the French Pyrenees; its capitals are brilliant peasant art, many carved with weird, self-devouring grotesque creatures. Pastiche additions to the scene are the gardens, planted with fragrant, almost overpowering, herbs and flowers and (bizarrely) piped plainsong.

The museum's smaller **sculpture** is equally impressive. In the Early Gothic Hall are a number of carved figures, one a memorably tender and refined **Virgin and Child**, carved in England in the fourteenth century, probably for veneration at a private altar. The collection of **tapestries** is special, too, including a rare surviving Gothic work showing the **Nine Heroes**. The heroes, popular figures of the ballads of the Middle Ages, comprise three pagans (Hector, Alexander, Julius Caesar), three Hebrews (David, Joshua, Judas Macabeas) and three Christians (Arthur, Charlemagne, Godfrey of Bouillon). Five of the nine are here, clothed in the garb of the day (around 1385) against a rich backdrop. The **Unicorn Tapestries**, in the succeeding room, are even more spectacular – brilliantly alive with color, observation and Christian symbolism.

Most of the Met's medieval painting is to be found downtown, but one important exception here is **Campin**'s *Merode Altarpiece*. Housed in its own antechamber, this triptych depicts the Annunciation scene in a typical bourgeois Flemish interior of the day. On the left, the donors gaze timidly on through an open door; to the right, St Joseph works in his carpenter's shop. St Joseph was mocked in the literature of the day, which might account for his rather ridiculous appearance – making a mousetrap, a symbol of the way the Devil traps souls. Through the windows behind, life goes on in a fifteenth-century market square, perhaps Campin's native Tournai.

With the ground floor, you move into Gothic architecture – or at least into a pseudo-Gothic chapel, built around the monumental **sarcophagus of Ermengol VII**, with its whole phalanx of family and clerics carved around to send him off. Two further cloisters are here to explore, along with an amazing downstairs **Treasury**. This is crammed with items but two can easily be singled out: the *Belles Heures de Jean, Duc de Berry*, perhaps the greatest of all medieval Books of Hours, executed by the Limburg Brothers with dazzling genre miniatures of seasonal life; and the twelfth-century **altar cross** from Bury St Edmunds in England, a mass of tiny expressive characters from biblical stories. Finally, hunt out a minute **rosary bead** from sixteenth-century Flanders: with a representation of the Passion inside, it seems barely possible it could have been carved by hand.

The American Museum of Natural History

Central Park West (W 79th St). Subway B or C to 81st St–Central Park West. Sun–Thurs 10am–5.45pm; Fri & Sat 10am–8.45pm; suggested donation $7, students $5. Call ☎769-5100 for exhibit information.

According to the *Guinness Book of Records*, this is the largest museum in the world bar none, and once you've paced the length of its

The American Museum of Natural History

The Hayden Planetarium, home to the museum's astronomy department, is closed while a new center devoted to earth and space is constructed. This project, to include a new Hayden Planetarium, is scheduled to be completed by 2000.

exhibition hall and witnessed a fair number of its 34 million displays, you'll feel it in your feet. This is to say, be selective: anthropologists could have a field day here, but for anyone else a highly discriminating couple of hours should be ample.

The main entrance on Central Park West is the one to make for, leaving you well placed for a loop of the more interesting halls on the first floor: principally intelligently mounted artifacts from Asia and Africa, backed up with informal commentary and lent atmosphere with drums and ethnic music.

From there, run – don't dally – to the rehauled **dinosaur display** on the fourth floor. More than 120 specimens are here – it's one of the largest collections in the world – and they're imaginatively shown: you can watch two robotic dinosaur heads chew; walk on a transparent bridge erected over a fifty-foot long Barosaurus spine; and touch fossils. The exhibits benefit from the latest scientific knowledge, and not only do they correct past presentation foibles, but they're also supplemented by diagrams and claymation videos that, for some reason, make all the dinosaurs look like they're smiling. "Profiles in Palaeontology" are also included – glamorous blurbs about those who dug these treasures out of the dirt.

If you have time, also worth a look is the **Hall of Meteorites**: well laid out and including some strikingly beautiful crystals – not least the *Star of India*, the largest blue sapphire ever found. The *NatureMax* theater, with the biggest viewing screen in NYC, also presents some worthwhile IMAX films; check to see what's playing. One thing you can't see, at least for a while, is the adjacent **Hayden Planetarium**, closed for renovations until, supposedly, the year 2000.

Other museums

While you could fill weeks wandering through New York's great museums listed earlier in this chapter, the city is awash with smaller museums, and the collections are so varied as to have something to interest everyone. On a highly selective basis, highlights include the **International Center for Photography**, the **National Museum of the American Indian**, the **Lower East Side Tenement Museum**, a clutch of first-rate **ethnic museums** and, for anyone less than enamored of current New York television, the **Museum of Television & Radio** and the **American Museum of the Moving Image**.

Art, visuals and design

Alternative Museum

594 Broadway (between Houston and Prince sts). Subway N or R to Prince St. Tues–Sat 11am–6pm, closed mid-Aug to mid-Sept; suggested donation $3. ☎966-4444 for exhibition information.

Temporary exhibitions of contemporary art, emphasizing international developments. Well organized and adventurous, with displays supplemented by regular musical events and poetry readings.

American Craft Museum

40 W 53rd St. Subway E or F to 5th Ave–53rd St. Tues 10am–8pm, Wed–Sun 10am–5pm; $5, students $2.50, free Tues 5–8pm. ☎956-3585 for exhibition information.

A showcase of modern crafts as chosen by the American Craft Council. Bright, brash and good fun.

American Museum of the Moving Image

35th Ave at 36th St, Astoria, Queens. Subway R or G to Steinway St. Tues–Fri noon–5pm, Sat & Sun noon–6pm, closed Mon; $7, students $4; price includes all film and video programs. ☎718/784-0077 for exhibition information.

Housed in a part of Astoria Studios previously used by Woody Allen and the *Cosby Show*, among others, this museum chronicles the art, technology and cultural impact of film, TV and video. The second and third floors contain its core exhibition, "Behind the Screen," which has ten interactive displays and four hours' worth of audio and visual material. You can view demonstrations of nonlinear editing and computerized special effects; select a song from a soundtrack jukebox and learn more about its composer; and read a scene from *Dressed to Kill* and see how it was actually shot on film.

Aside from "Behind the Screen," the museum allots a substantial amount of space to temporary exhibits (a recent show was on computer games, where visitors could play their way through the history of video game technology); it also offers screenings designed to explain the technical development of an art form that, to millions around the world, defines America. You can listen in to directors explaining sequences from famous movies; watch short films made up of well-known clips; add your own sound effects to movies; and view original sets and costumes. A fascinating place, and well worth a visit. See also "Astoria" in Chapter 14, *The Outer Boroughs*.

American Numismatic Society

Broadway (155th St). Subway #1 to 157th St–Broadway, or B to 155th St–Amsterdam Ave. Tues–Sat 9am–4.30pm, Sun 1–4pm (exhibition hall only), closed Mon; free. ☎234-3130 for exhibition information.

For those who think that coin collecting is sheer dullsville, the Numismatic Society might change your mind: it's dedicated to the preservation and study of coins, medals and paper money, and offers changing exhibits on numismatic history, design and politics. The Society's library contains an enormous number of numismatic periodicals, books and illustrations – all there for the researcher or intrigued collector.

Asia Society Gallery

*725 Park Ave (70th St). Subway #6 to 68th St–Lexington Ave. Tues & Wed,
Fri & Sat 11am–6pm, Thurs 11am–8pm, Sun noon–5pm; $3, students $2;
free Thurs 6–8pm. ☎517-ASIA for exhibit information.*

Small permanent display of the Rockefeller collection of Asian art.
Worth the admission fee if the accompanying temporary exhibition
looks promising. Asia House also holds intriguing performances, lectures, films and free events.

Black Fashion Museum

*155 W 126th St. Subway #2 or #3 to 125th St–Lenox Ave. Mon–Fri
noon–8pm; suggested donation $1.50, students $1. Call in advance
☎666-1320 for an appointment.*

It's on the premise that black fashion designers have gone largely
unrecognized that the Black Fashion Museum organizes its exhibits,
which draw upon a wide variety of costumes designed and made by
blacks from the eighteenth century on. The second floor has a quirky
group of robes and gowns, including a slave dress of finely stitched
cotton and Mary Todd Lincoln's velvet inaugural gown designed by
Elizabeth Keckley, a freed slave. The museum's situation up on
Lenox Avenue, however, likely makes for specialist interest only.

Bronx Museum of the Arts

*1040 Grand Concourse, corner of 165th St, the Bronx. Subway #4 to 161st
St–Grand Concourse. Wed 3–9pm, Thurs & Fri 10am–5pm, Sat & Sun
1–6pm; suggested donation $3, students $2. ☎718/681-6000 for exhibition information.*

Contemporary American art, none of any great note, plus changing
exhibitions of Bronx-based artists.

The Brooklyn Museum

*200 Eastern Parkway, Brooklyn. Subway #2 or #3 to Eastern
Parkway–Brooklyn Museum. Wed–Sun 10am–5pm; $4, students $2.
☎718/638-5000 for exhibition information. The museum's gift shop sells
genuine ethnic items from around the world at reasonable prices.*

When Judy Chicago's *Dinner Party* was exhibited here back in the
early 1980s, the Brooklyn Museum had people lining up all the way
around the block. Since then, however, the museum has reverted to
its former status: good in its own right, but perpetually doomed to
stand in the shadow of the Met. Which is a pity, for it's a likable
place, and – together with a visit to the adjacent Botanical Garden –
is a good reason for forsaking Manhattan for an afternoon.

A trip through the museum does require considerable selectivity, for
on offer are over five floors stacked with exhibits. The highlights
include the arts and applied arts from **Oceania and the Americas** on
the ground floor; the **Classical and Egyptian** antiquities on the second
floor; and the evocative **American period rooms** on the fourth floor.

Be sure to also look in on the American and European **picture galleries** on the top story, which progress from eighteenth-century portraits – including one of George Washington by Gilbert Stuart – and bucolic paintings by members of the Hudson River School to works by Eastman Johnson and John Singer Sargent to pieces by Charles Sheeler and Georgia O'Keefe. A handful of paintings by European artists – Degas, Cézanne, Toulouse-Lautrec, Monet and Dufy, among others – are also displayed, although nothing approaching their best work.

Cooper-Hewitt Museum

2 E 91st St. Subway #4, #5 or #6 to 86th St–Lexington Ave. Tues 10am–9pm, Wed–Sat 10am–5pm, Sun noon–5pm; $3, students $1.50, free Tues 5–9pm. ☎860-6868 for exhibition information. The gift shop boasts an array of innovative and inexpensive items.

When he decided to build at what was then the unfashionable end of Fifth Avenue, millionaire industrialist Andrew Carnegie asked for "the most modest, plainest and most roomy house in New York." And that's nearly what he got – a series of wood-paneled boxes too decorative to be plain, too large to be modest. These beautiful and spacious boxes now constitute the gallery space for the Cooper-Hewitt's collection of designs. Three floors' of exhibits focus on the history of objects – both commercial and high art – and explain how and why innovations occurred. The skillful curating and insightful commentary make a trip to the Cooper-Hewitt highly entertaining. Themes vary, so check what's on first.

Dahesh Museum

601 5th Ave (at 48th St). Subway B, D, F or Q to 47th–50th St (Rockefeller Center)–6th Ave. Tues–Sat 11am–6pm; free. ☎759-0606 for exhibition information.

A small museum featuring a rotating group of nineteenth- and early twentieth-century paintings collected by Dr Dahesh, a Lebanese writer and philosopher passionate about European academic art.

Forbes Galleries

62 5th Ave (12th St). Subway #4, #5 or #6 to 14th St–Union Square, or F to 14th St & 6th Ave. Tues & Wed, Fri & Sat, 10am–4pm; free. ☎206-5549 for exhibition information.

The world's largest collection of Fabergé eggs, along with five hundred toy boats and twelve thousand toy soldiers.

Grey Art Gallery & Study Center, New York University

33 Washington Place. Subway A, B, C or D to W 4th St, or R to 8th St, or #6 to Astor Place. Tues, Thurs & Fri 11am–6.30pm, Wed 11am–8.30pm, Sat 11am–5pm; free. ☎988-6780 for exhibition information.

This, the gallery of New York University's Art Department, displays two outstanding collections: the **New York University art collection**

Other museums

– known for its American painting from the 1940s onwards, and for prints by Picasso, Miró and Matisse – and the **Abbey Weed Grey Collection of Contemporary Asian and Middle Eastern Art.**

Guggenheim Museum SoHo

575 Broadway at Prince St. Subway N or R to Prince Street–Broadway, or #6 to Spring St; Wed–Fri & Sun 11am–6pm; Sat 11am–8pm; $5, students $3; two-day pass for both uptown and SoHo Guggenheims $11, students $7. ☎ *423-3500 for exhibition information.*

By renting three floors of a loft building in the heart of SoHo, the Guggenheim is the first major museum to move downtown to where New York's contemporary art scene really happens. Showcasing the more established of the modern artists, the museum both provides an historical context for the area's new art and helps erode the barrier between stodgy uptown museums and irreverent downtown artists. It's certainly worth dropping by to see what's on. Make sure to stop into the museum's shop – it's an excellent source for art books, colorful jewelry and creative household objects.

International Center of Photography – Midtown

1133 Ave of the Americas (at 43rd St). Subway B, D, F or Q to 42nd St. Hours and admission prices same as ICP below; free Tues 6–8pm. ☎ *768-4682 for exhibition information.*

Smaller, changing exhibitions of photographs from the main collection – see below for more detail.

International Center of Photography – Uptown

1130 5th Ave at 94th St. Subway #6 to 96th St–Lexington Ave. Tues 11am–8pm, Wed–Sun 11am–6pm; $4, students $2.50, free Tues 6–8pm. ☎ *860-1777 for exhibition information.*

Founded and directed by Cornell Capa, brother of Robert, the ICP exhibits photography in all its aspects. The Center's permanent archived collection holds most of the greats – Cartier-Bresson, Adams, Kertesz, Eugene Smith – and there are often three temporary shows on at any given time. At least one of these is bound to be worthwhile, often featuring the city's most exciting avant-garde and experimental work. Overall, an excellent adjunct to MoMA's static collection.

Isamu Noguchi Garden Museum

32–37 Vernon Blvd, Long Island City, Queens. Subway N to Broadway station, Queens, or weekend shuttle bus from Asia Society (Park Ave and E 70th St) every hour on the half-hour 11.30am–3.30pm, with return trip every hour on the hour 1–5pm, $5 round trip; call ☎ *718/204-7088 for more info. Museum open April–Nov Wed–Fri 10am–5pm; Sat & Sun 11am–6pm; suggested donation $4, students $2. Tours available upon request.*

Although it seems ironic that a garden museum is located in an abandoned industrial area in Queens, it's fitting in this instance. **Isamu**

Noguchi (1904–88), an abstract Japanese sculptor, strove to integrate art with nature and the urban environment. More than three hundred of his stone, metal, wood and paper works are on show in this gutted warehouse and small garden; the pieces are elegant and Zen-like in their simplicity.

Museum of American Folk Art

2 Lincoln Sq., Columbus Ave (66th St). Subway #1 or #9 to 66th St. Tues–Sun 11.30am–7.30pm; free. ☎595-9533 for exhbition information.

Changing exhibitions of traditional handicrafts with the emphasis on the domestic; could be just the place if the splendors the Met offers aren't your cup of tea.

Museum of American Illustration

128 East 63rd St. Subway #4, #5 or #6 to 59th St–Lexington Ave. Tues 10am–8pm, Wed–Fri 10am–5pm, Sat noon–4pm, closed Sun and Mon; free. ☎838-2560 for exhbition information.

Rotating selections from the museum's permanent collection of illustrations – from wartime propaganda to contemporary ads, with all manner of cartoons and drawings in between. Exhibitions center on theme or illustrator – designed primarily for aficionados, but always accessible, well mounted and topical.

Museum of Television & Radio

25 W 52nd St (btwn 5th and 6th aves). Subway E or F to 5th Ave–53rd St. Tues & Wed noon–6pm, Thurs noon–8pm, Fri–Sun noon–6pm (theaters open until 9pm Friday). Suggested donation $6, students $4. ☎621-6600 for information on daily events.

An archive of 60,000 mostly American TV and radio broadcasts. The museum's excellent computerized reference system allows you to research news, public affairs, documentaries, sports, comedies, advertisements and other aural and visual oddities. You can select up to four programs at a time, and watch them on one of the eight dozen video consoles. Service is quick, and multiple copies exist of the more popular choices; perfect if you want to settle down to a day's worth of *I Love Lucy*.

To appease wary pop cult critics, the museum also conducts educational seminars and screenings in its four theaters; organizes thematic festivals; and broadcasts live from its in-house radio station. A warning, though: The museum becomes a noisy hothouse on weekends and holidays, so try to visit at other times.

National Academy of Design

1083 5th Ave (89th St). Subway #4, #5 or #6 to 86th St–Lexington Ave. Wed–Thurs, Sat–Sun noon–5pm, Fri noon–8pm; $3.50, students $2. ☎369-4880 for exhibit information.

Samuel Morse founded the National Academy of Design along the lines of London's Royal Academy, and though 1083 Fifth Avenue is not nearly as grand as Burlington House, similarities remain: a school of fine art, exclusive membership and regular exhibitions which, as you'd imagine, are usually American. There's a tradition that academicians and associates give a work of art on their election here: associates a self-portrait, academicians a "mature work." One hundred and fifty years' worth of these pictures are now held by the Academy and form the mainstay of the Selection from the Permanent Collection – varied throughout the year but always with a strong slant toward portraiture. The icing on the cake is the building itself: a faintly snooty Beaux Arts townhouse donated to the academy by the husband of sculptor Anna Hyatt Huntingdon; her *Diana* gets pride of place below the cheerful rotunda.

New Museum of Contemporary Art

583 Broadway (btwn Prince and Houston). Subway N or R to Prince St, or #6 to Spring St. Wed–Fri, Sun noon–6pm, Sat noon–8pm; $3.50, students and artists $2.50, free Sat 6–8pm. ☎219-1355 for exhibition information.

Regularly changing exhibitions by contemporary American and international artists. Offbeat and eclectic, the New Museum will mount risky works that other museums are unable – or unwilling – to show. Its SoHo-center library (Wed–Fri noon–6pm; free access, but appointments preferred) claims to be the only library in the world devoted entirely to contemporary art criticism and theory. Pick up the museum's calendar for details on current and forthcoming exhibits and lectures. A must.

The Pierpont Morgan Library

29 E 36th St. Subway #6 to 33rd St–Park Ave. Tues–Fri 10.30am–5pm, Sat 10.30am–6pm, Sun 12–6pm, closed Sun in July & Aug; $5, students $3. Tours at 2:30pm Tues–Fri. ☎ 685-0610 for more information.

Built by McKim, Mead and White for J. Pierpont Morgan in 1917, this gracious Italian-style nest, feathered with the fruits of the financier's magpie-ish trips to Europe, is one of New York's best small museums – though many of the exhibits are changed so regularly that it's difficult to say precisely what you'll see.

The focal points are two main rooms, access to which is along a corridor usually lined with a fine assortment of **Rembrandt prints**. The first room you come to, the **West Room**, served as Morgan's study and has been left much as it was when he worked here, with a carved sixteenth-century Italian ceiling, a couple of paintings by Memling and Perugino and, among the few items contemporary with the building, a desk custom-carved to a design by McKim. There's a portrait of J.P.'s father over the fifteenth-century Florentine fireplace, and a portrait of J.P. Junior on the far wall, swathed in the academic finery of an honorary Cambridge degree conferred in 1919. From here, through a

domed and pillared hallway, lies the **East Room** or library, a sumptuous three-tiered cocoon of rare books, autographed musical manuscripts and various trinkets culled from European households and
churches. In a changing exhibit, there are original manuscripts by
Mahler (the museum holds the world's largest collection of his work);
a Gutenberg Bible from 1455 (one of eleven surviving); the only complete copy of Thomas Malory's *Morte d'Arthur*; as well as literary manuscripts of everyone from the letters of Vasari and George Washington
to works by Keats and Dickens. All in all, a fascinating display.

Other
museums

Roerich Museum

*319 W 107th St. Subway #1 to 110th St–Broadway. Tues–Sun 2–5pm;
free. ☎864-7752.*

Nicolas Roerich was a Russian artist who lived in India, was influenced by Indian mysticism, and produced strikingly original paintings. A small, weird and virtually unknown collection.

Socrates Sculpture Park

*Broadway at Vernon Blvd, Long Island City, Queens. Subway N to
Broadway. Daily 10am–sunset; free. ☎718/956-1819.*

Disused park turned interactive sculpture gallery. Not well kept, but
worth peeking into after visiting the Isamu Noguchi Garden Museum
(p.264).

City history

Fraunces Tavern

*54 Pearl St (at Broad). Subway #4 or #5 to Bowling Green, or #1 or #9
to South Ferry, or #2 or #3 to Wall Street. Mon–Fri 10am–4.45pm, Sat
noon–4pm; $2.50, students $1. ☎425-1778 for exhibition information.*

Revolutionary-era rooms and objects, with rotating exhibitions; see
"The Financial District" in Chapter 3, *The Financial District and
the Civic Center.*

Museum of Bronx History

*3266 Bainbridge Ave, the Bronx. Subway D to 205th St–Bainbridge Ave,
or #4 to Kingsbridge Rd. Mon–Fri 9am–5pm by appointment, Sat
10am–4pm, Sun 1–5pm; $2. ☎718/881.8900 for exhibit information.*

Bronx-related artifacts from Indian times to the Depression.

Museum of the City of New York

*Fifth Ave (103rd St). Subway #6 to 103rd St–Lexington Ave. Wed–Sat
10am–5pm, Sun 1–5pm; suggested donation $5, students $4. ☎534-1672
for exhibit information.*

Spaciously housed in a purpose-built neo-Georgian mansion on the
fringes of Spanish Harlem, the museum gives a competent if unex-

citing rundown on the history of the city from Dutch times to the present. Paintings, furniture and a slide show – plus the museum runs Sunday walking tours of New York neighborhoods (see "Information, Maps and Tours" in *Basics*).

Museum of Immigration

Ellis Island: access by Circle Line Statue of Liberty Ferry from Battery Park. Ferry ($7) runs daily 9.30am–5.30pm in summer, 9.30am–5pm in winter, though you need to be on the 3pm ferry at the latest to be able to see the museum. Entry to museum is free.

Artifacts, photographs, maps and personal accounts tell the story of the immigrants who passed through Ellis Island on their way to a new life in America. For extensive details, see Chapter 2, *The Harbor Islands*.

New York City Police Museum

235 E 20th St. Subway #6 to 23rd St–Park Ave. Mon–Fri 9am–2pm, by appointment only (☎477-9753); free.

A collection of memorabilia of the New York Police Department, the largest and oldest in the country. It's used to inculcate reverence for the force in young cadets, and just about merits itself to anyone not wildly interested in law and order. It's not about crime or punishment so much as the personal effects of New York's Finest: night sticks, uniforms, photos and the like. There's a copper badge of 1845 as worn by the sergeants of the day, earning them the nickname of "coppers." If you're into firepower, search out the tommy gun in a violin case – original gangster issue.

The New York Historical Society

Central Park West (77th St). Subway B or C to 81st St–Central Park West. Wed–Sun noon–5pm; $3, students $1. Library and Prints, Photographs, and Architecture Room opened Wed–Fri noon–5pm; appointments preferred – call ☎873-3400 ext 228.

More a museum of American than New York history, this is a venue well worth keeping an eye on: Its temporary exhibitions are more daring than you'd expect, mixing high and low culture with intelligence and flair. The permanent collection of paintings on the second floor repays a visit in its own right: **James Audubon**, the Harlem artist and naturalist who specialized in lovingly detailed watercolors of birds, is the focus of one room; other galleries hold a broad sweep of **nineteenth-century American painting**, principally portraiture (the "missing" White House portrait of Jacqueline Kennedy Onassis, a slobbish Aaron Burr, and the picture of Alexander Hamilton that found its way on to the $10 bill) and Hudson River School landscapes (among them Thomas Cole's famed and pompous *Course of Empire* series).

On a more historical note, and for a small additional fee, you can look around the museum **library**, which boasts such diverse items as the original Louisiana Purchase document and the correspondence between Aaron Burr and Alexander Hamilton that led up to their duel (see p.187). An interesting museum, and often overlooked.

New York Transit Museum

Old subway entrance at Schermerhorn St and Boerum Place, Brooklyn. Subway #2, #3, #4, #5 and F to Borough Hall. Tues, Thurs, Fri 10am–4pm; Wed 10am–6pm; Sat & Sun noon–5pm; $3. ☎718/243-5839 for exhibition information.

Subway cars from the turn of the century, artifacts and ephemera connected with the world's largest underground railway. Cheap and engaging, even for non-enthusiasts, and made all the better by being housed in a disused subway station.

Queens Museum of Art

Flushing Meadows–Corona Park. Subway #7 to Willets Point–Shea Stadium. Wed–Fri, Sat 10am–5pm, Sun noon–5pm, closed Mon & Tues; $3, students $1.50. ☎718/592-9700 for exhibit information.

Primarily worth the trip for its one and only permanent item: an 18,000-square-foot model of the five boroughs of New York City, spectacularly lit, constantly remodeled and originally conceived for the 1964 World's Fair by Robert Moses. Great fun if you know the city, and useful orientation if you don't. The zoo here has an aviary in one of Buckminster Fuller's geodesic domes.

Community and ethnic

Chinatown Museum

8 Mott St. Subway N or R to Canal St. Mon–Sat 10am–6pm, closed Sun.

A hoard of Chinese costumes, Buddhas and religious accoutrements located at the end of a sleazy amusement arcade (which itself includes an incredibly cruel contraption caging a "live, dancing chicken"). A great stopoff on any tour of Chinatown, but bring several friends – the museum is open only to groups of eight or more.

The Hall of Chinese History

246 Bowery, between Prince and Houston sts. Open for groups only, by appointment; call ☎962-3634.

Lifesize terracotta warriors and horses of the Qin dynasty are the high spot of this collection of Chinese art across the ages.

Hispanic Society of America

Audubon Terrace, 3753 Broadway (155th St). Subway #1 to 157th St–Broadway. Tues–Sat 10am–4.30pm, Sun 1–4pm; free. ☎690-0743 for exhibit information.

A chocolate-colored, terracotta interior, a scattering of Spanish masters, and, best of all, the joyful Murals of Spain by Joaquin Sorolla y

Bastida. The **library** of 200,000 books is a major center for research on Portuguese and Spanish art, history and literature (Tues–Fri 1–4.30pm, Sat 10am–4.30pm, closed Aug).

Jewish Museum

1109 5th Ave (92nd St). Subway #4, #5 or #6 to 92nd St. Sun–Thurs 11am–5.45pm, Tues 11am–8pm; $7, students $5, free Tues 5–8pm. Closed on major federal and Jewish holidays. ☎ 423-3200 for exhibit information.

The largest museum of Judaica outside Israel. Its centerpiece is the permanent exhibition on the Jewish experience – the basic ideas, values and culture developed over four thousand years. More vibrant and exciting, however, are the changing exhibitions of works by major international artists on the ground floor, as well as the children's "hands-on" area on the fourth floor.

Kurdish Library and Museum

Park Place at Underhill Ave, Brooklyn. Subway D to 7th Ave, or #2 or #3 to Grand Army Plaza. Mon–Thurs 1–4pm; Library opened same hours or by appointment (☎ 718-783-7930); free.

A collection of Kurdish photos, scholarly books, traditional costumes and crafts that seek to place in context the fourth largest group of people in the Middle East. The museum, American founded and sponsored, also publishes two journals about Kurds.

Lower East Side Tenement Museum

97 Orchard St. Subway F to Delancey St–Essex St. Tues–Sun 11am–5pm; $7, students $6, free on Tues. The museum also organizes tours of a renovated tenement building: Tues–Fri, the tours commence at 1pm, 2pm & 3pm; on Sun, the tours run every 45min, with the first at 11am and the last at 4.15pm. In addition, walking tours of different ethnic areas are conducted every Sat & Sun at 12.30pm and 2pm. Call ☎ 431-0233 for prices and details.

Housed in a former tenement building, the Tenement Museum aims to present a complete picture of lower Manhattan's immigrant history via a variety of temporary exhibitions. The two galleries show photos and community-based displays, which concentrate on the multiple ethnic heritages in the area. If you elect to take the tour (which is well worth your time), you'll be taken across the street to New York's first tenement building, which has been preserved more or less as it was when it was occupied by immigrant families earlier this century. Two of the rooms – vacant since the 1930s – serve as "living history" displays; they're decorated in styles circa the late 1800s and 1930. In all, an earnest and sympathetic attempt to document the immigrant experience.

Museo del Barrio

1230 5th Ave (104th St). Subway #6 to 103rd St. Wed–Sun 11am–5pm; suggested donation $4, students $2. ☎ 831-7272 for exhibition information.

"The neighborhood museum," the Museo was founded in the 1960s by a group of Puerto Ricans from Spanish Harlem who wanted to teach their children about their roots. Now, although the emphasis remains largely Puerto Rican, the museum embraces the whole of Latin America, with five major loan exhibits of painting, photographs and crafts each year. Make sure to see the *santos de palo* – an exquisite collection of carved votive figures.

Museum of African Art

593 Broadway. Subway N, R or Q to Prince St. Tues–Fri 10.30am–5.30pm, Sat & Sun noon–6pm; $4, students $2. ☎966-1313 for exhibition information.

Changing exhibitions of the best of traditional African art. An eye-opener compared to the token ethnic collections that are usually found.

Museum of Jewish Heritage

18 1st Place, Battery Park City, Subway #1, 9 to South Ferry, #4, 5 to Bowling Green; N, R to Whitehall, Sun–Wed 9am–5pm, Thurs 9am–8pm, Fri 9am–2pm, closed Sat and Jewish holidays (☎968-1800); $7, tickets available at museum and Ticketmaster.

Its doors just opened in late 1997, the Museum of Jewish Heritage attempts to contextualize the Holocaust, with modest displays varying from the prison garb suvivors wore in Nazi concentration camps to the practical accoutrements of everyday Eastern European Jewish life. Multimedia montages and achival film catalog the Jewish experience this century: Europe's pre-WWII ghettos, the establishment of Israel, even the successes of entertainers and artists like Samuel Goldwyn and Allen Ginsberg. The hexagonal granite structure is itself symbolically part of the exhibit – referencing the six million jews who perished and the six points of the star of David.

The National Museum of the American Indian

Alexander Hamilton US Customs House, One Bowling Green. Subway #1 or #9 to South Ferry, or #4 or #5 to Bowling Green, or N or R to Whitehall Street. Open daily, 10am–5pm; free. ☎825-6992 for exhibition information.

An excellent and innovative assemblage of artifacts from almost every tribe native to the Americas, revamped and relocated to the Customs House on Bowling Green in Lower Manhattan (see Chapter 3). This collection might seem a little overpowering, but the curators have made it lively: they've incorporated multiple media, experimented with presentation and used stories to convey information. Aside from the garments and masks, highlights include the seven-foot house posts shaped like animals; elegant featherwork from Amazonia; and a tribe's worth of elaborately beaded moccasins. Best by far is the instalment that recreates a living room of the federally subsidized **HUD house**, the type of house that the government built on Native American reservations. You're invited to sit on the living room couch, glance around at the mixture of Indian and European furnishings, flip through the photo album and watch a biting satire of Native American culture conflict: aerobics to tribal drums and an advertisement for a telephone helpline that connects you to your tribal Clan Mother when you're "having doubts about being an Indian."

Schomburg Center for Research in Black Culture

515 Malcolm X Blvd (135th St). Subway #2 or #3 to 125th St–Lenox Ave. Mon–Wed noon–8pm, Thurs–Sat 10am–6pm, Sun 1–5pm; free. ☎491-2200 for exhibit information.

Thought-provoking exhibitions of documents, art, photos and sculpture that detail the history of blacks in the US. The five million items in its collections make the Center the world's pre-eminent research facility for the study of black history and culture.

Studio Museum in Harlem

144 W 125th St. Subway #2 or #3 to 125th St–Lenox Ave. Wed–Fri 10am–5pm, Sat–Sun 1–6pm; $5, students $3. ☎864-4500 for exhibition information.

Exhibitions of contemporary (and often local) painting, photography and sculpture.

Ukrainian Museum

203 2nd Ave. Subway #4, #5 or #6 to Astor Place. Wed–Sun 1–5pm; $1, students 50¢. ☎228-0110 for exhibition information.

Situated in the heart of the Ukrainian East Village, this small collection offers little to entice outsiders. Crammed into two tiny floors, the museum divides itself between recounting the history of Ukrainian immigration to the US and showing (more interestingly) some ethnic items and constumes from the country. Look out for the hand-painted Easter eggs or *pysanky* – a craft that's still practiced today because, according to Ukrainian folklore, when production ceases the world will end.

Commercial galleries

Art, and especially contemporary art, is big in New York: there are roughly 500 art galleries in NYC, the majority in SoHo, and as many as 90,000 artists living in and around the city. Even if you have no intention of buying, many of these galleries are well worth seeing, as are some of the alternative spaces, run on a nonprofit basis and less commercial than mainstream galleries.

Broadly, galleries fall into five main areas: along **Madison Avenue** in the 60s and 70s for antique works and the occasional (minor) Old Master; **57th Street** between Sixth and Park avenues for contemporary big names; **SoHo** for whatever is fashionable; and **TriBeCa** and the western edge of **Chelsea** for more experimental displays. A few of the more exclusive galleries are invitation only, though one of the best ways to see the galleries is with *Art Tours of Manhattan* (see "Information, Maps and Tours" in *Basics*), which runs informed (if pricey) conducted tours. Also, pick up a copy of the *Gallery Guide* – available upon request in the larger galleries – for listings of current shows and each gallery's specialty. The weekly *Time Out New York* offers broad listings of the major commercial galleries, although its coverage is spotty.

Listed below are some of the more interesting options in the main Manhattan locations. **Opening times** are roughly Tuesday to Saturday 11am–6pm, but note that many galleries have truncated summer hours and are closed during August. The best time to gallery-hop is on weekday afternoons; the absolute worst time is on Saturday, when out-of-towners flood into the city's trendy areas. Openings – usually free and identifiable by crowds of people drinking wine from clear plastic cups – are excellent times to view work and eavesdrop on art gossip.

SoHo and TriBeCa galleries

123 Watts, 123 Watts St ☎219-1482. Trendy gallery known for its photography; often shows work by Robert Mapplethorpe.

14 Sculptors Gallery, 164 Mercer St ☎966-5790. Just as the name implies, a gallery formed by fourteen sculptors to exhibit figurative and abstract contemporary art.

A.C.E. Gallery New York, 275 Hudson St ☎255-5599. Hosting several shows at a time, Ace is the place to see the work of young, emerging artists.

The Drawing Center, 35 Wooster St ☎219-2166. Specializes in oversized painting, sculpture and construction.

Edward Thorp, 103 Prince St ☎431-6880. Mainstream figurative painting.

Gemini GEL at Joni Weyl, 375 Broadway, 2nd Floor ☎219-1446. New and vintage prints, including works by Roy Lichtenstein and Robert Rauschenberg.

Holly Soloman, 172 Mercer St (at Houston) ☎941-5777. Emphasis on installations and narrative art, including multimedia works by Laurie Anderson, who happens to show her pieces here.

Jay Gorney Modern Art, 100 Greene St ☎966-4480. Hosts group shows and installations.

John Gibson, 2nd floor, 568 Broadway (at Prince) ☎925-1192. Avant-garde and old school conceptualist, with emphases upon land art, constructions and abstract works.

Commercial galleries

John Weber, 3rd floor, 142 Greene St ☎966-6115. Conceptual, minimalist and highly unusual works, including those by Sol LeWitt and younger, similarly inspired, artists.

Leo Castelli, 2nd floor, 420 West Broadway ☎431-5160. One of the original dealer-collectors and a cult unto himself, Castelli was instrumental in aiding the careers of Rauschenberg and Warhol, and offers big names at big prices. His other gallery is at 578 Broadway (between Houston and Prince sts; ☎431-6279).

Louis Meisel, 141 Prince St (at West Broadway) ☎677-1340. The place to find out what Abstract Illusionism looks like. Meisel claims to have invented the term, along with Photorealism – also well in evidence here.

Mary Boone, 417 West Broadway ☎431-1818. Leo Castelli's protégée who specializes in installations and up-and-coming European and American artists.

Nahan Galleries, 380 West Broadway ☎966-9313. Contemporary abstract painting, sculpture and graphic art.

O K Harris, 383 West Broadway ☎431-3600. Named after a mythical traveling gambler, O K is the gallery of Ivan Karp, a cigar-munching champion of Super-Realism. One of the first SoHo galleries and, although not as influential as it once was, worth a look.

Paula Cooper, 155 Wooster St ☎674-0766. Minimalist and abstract works, and much more.

Sonnabend, 3rd floor, 420 West Broadway ☎966-6160. Across-the-board painting, photography and video from American and European artists, including Robert Morris and Gilbert and George.

Sperone Westwater, 2nd floor, 142 Greene St ☎431-3685. Flashy European and American painting.

Vorpal, 459 West Broadway ☎777-3939. Contemporary and Old Masters.

Galleries elsewhere

Annina Nosei Gallery, 530 W 22nd St (2nd floor) ☎741-8965. Global works, especially contemporary pieces by Latin American artists.

Knoedler & Co., 19 E 70th St ☎794-0550. Very highly renowned gallery specializing in European Old Masters and some of the best-known twentieth-century American artists.

Marlborough/Marlborough Graphics, 40 W 57th St ☎541-4900. Internationally renowned galleries that show the cream of British and American artists and graphic designers.

Matthew Marks Gallery, 522 W 22nd St ☎243-1650. A very hot gallery that carries the work of such well-known Minimalist and abstract artists as Cy Twombly and Lucien Freud.

Morris-Healy, 530 W 22nd St ☎243-3753. Installations, drawings and sculpture at a former SoHo gallery.

PaceWildenstein, 32 E 57th St ☎421-3292. Well-known gallery that holds a large stock of modern American art works and shows a bit of everything. Downtown satellite located at 142 Greene St.

Pat Hearn, 530 W 22nd St ☎727-7366. Thematic works that create very specific environments. Does host risky exhibits.

Robert Miller, 41 E 57th St ☎980-5454. Twentieth-century American art of all media.

Alternative spaces

The galleries listed above are part of a system designed to channel artists' work through the gallery spaces and, eventually, into the hands of the collector. While initial acceptance by a major gallery is an important rite of passage for an up-and-coming artist, it shouldn't be forgotten that the gallery system's philosophy is centered on making money for the owners, who normally receive a third to a half of a piece's sale price. For an artist's work to be uncommercial is perhaps even more damning than to be socially or politically unacceptable. The galleries below, often referred to as **alternative spaces**, provide a forum for the kind of risky and noncommercially viable art (such as installations) that many galleries may not be able to afford to show. The recession of the 1990s has given the alternative space a new lease of life, and those mentioned here are at the cutting edge of new art in the city.

Art in General, 79 Walker St ☎219-0473. An experimental arts factory with multimedia exhibits and performances.

Artists' Space, 38 Greene St (3rd floor) ☎226-3970. One of the most respected alternative spaces, with frequently changing theme-based exhibits, film screenings, video art and installations, and events. Their Artists' File is a computerized slide registry of more than 2500 New York State artists, and can be scanned free of charge.

The Broken Kilometer, 393 West Broadway ☎431-3789. Adventurous new work – painting, graphics, sculpture and installations – in a remarkable gallery space filled with five hundred solid, highly polished brass rods.

Clocktower, 108 Leonard St ☎233-1096. Temporary exhibitions and an annual studio program in which artists work in the studio space within the clock tower. When this is happening, you're allowed to wander around and talk to the artists about their work. Go just to see the incredible views of Downtown.

DIA Art Foundation, administrative offices 107 Franklin St ☎431-3789. Nonprofit organization that commissions and exhibits work by new artists in three galleries: the New York Earth Room, the Broken Kilometer and the DIA Center for the Arts. New York's major alternative art organization.

DIA Center for the Arts, 548 W 22nd St ☎431-3789. The foundation's largest gallery space shows year-long exhibitions of work by artists such as Joseph Beuys, Dan Graham, Robert Ryman and Kids of Survival. The exhibition space on the roof has a café and usable chairs designed by artists.

Exit Art, 548 Broadway ☎966-7745. A young, hip and (often) gay crowd frequents this huge gallery that favors big constructions made from common objects and art about the body. Make sure to have some espresso and ginger cookies from the café.

New York Earth Room, 141 Wooster St (between Prince and Houston sts) ☎431-3789. An incredible gallery, filled, as the name suggests, with masses of dirt. Changing exhibitions, installations and performances by contemporary artists.

PS 1, 46-01 21st St in Long Island City, Queens ☎718/784-2084. $2 suggested donation. Part of the same organization (the Institute for Art and Urban Resources) as Clocktower, and based in an old schoolhouse, and the source from which several Downtown galleries cull new talent.

PS 122, 150 First Ave ☎228-4249. Nonprofit gallery space open from September to June, which highlights emerging artists.

Storefront for Art and Architecture, 97 Kenmare ☎431-5795. Innovative design shows exploring the use of urban space, be it in the form of architects' drawings, sculpture or painting. Housed in an incredible building that literally folds out.

Thread Waxing Space, 476 Broadway ☎966-9520. A trendy downtown space that recreates the 1960s "loft scene" – multimedia events, performance artists and even live bands play in this gallery decorated with avant-garde paintings, computer art and the like. Admission charges vary.

White Columns, 154 Christopher St (2nd floor) ☎924-4212. Curator Bill Arning has a finger on the pulse of what's happening in the NYC art world. The gallery has a more responsible attitude than many, and is very influential for emerging artists. Check out the changing group shows, open Wed–Sun noon–6pm.

Part 3

Listings

Chapter 16

Accommodation

Accommodation in New York is a major cost. The majority of **hotels** in the city charge well over $100 a night, not to mention the **taxes** tacked on to that. Obviously the best way to cut this expense is to utilize contacts in the New York area – friends, or friends of friends – and perhaps sleep on a few floors along the way. However, there are a number of exceptions to the hotel rule – places that offer decent double rooms for as little as $65 a night – and some other less grand, but more practical, options for finding a bed for the night.

For the young and sociable there are plenty of **hostels** with dormitory accommodation offering a bed for as little as $15 a night. Other budget options include private rooms in a **YMCA/YWCA** (a Y as they're known), which run to around $50 for a double, or a **bed and breakfast**, which basically means staying in somebody's spare room, but with all the amenities of a private apartment. These rooms go for $65 and up for a double and can be booked through any of the agencies listed under "Bed and breakfast" on p.282

Whichever option you decide to go for, **booking ahead** is very strongly advised. At certain times of the year – Christmas and summer particularly – you're likely to find everything (and we mean this) chock full. You can book a room in a hotel or hostel yourself, by phoning direct to the hotel (☎001/212 before the listed number if you're dialing from Britain, or if there's an 800 number

listed you can use it to call toll-free from within the States, but only outside the city), or by going through a specialist **travel agent** – which can sometimes work out cheaper (see "Getting there" in *Basics* for addresses). Bear in mind, too, the possibilities of all-in flight and hotel package vacations, again detailed under "Getting there." For hotels, there are also booking services – listed under "Hotels" – that reserve rooms at discount prices and usually for no extra charge.

Hostels and YMCAs

Hostels and **YMCAs** are just about the only option for cash-strapped backpackers in New York, with dorm beds for as little as $15 a night. Most hostels are fine as long as you don't mind sleeping in a bunk bed and sharing a room with strangers (if you're traveling in a group of four or six you could get a room to yourselves), though they do vary in quality. YMCAs are better if you want privacy because they have private single and double rooms, though they tend to have a more institutional feel than the more relaxed hostels. Note that hostels are especially busy and fairly rowdy in August and September when the legions of camp counselors descend on the city. For a comprehensive listing of hostels in New York and across North America you should obtain *The Hostel Handbook* for $3 by phoning ☎926-7030, faxing ☎238-0108 or emailing *InfoHostel@aol.com*. Or, if you are

For the precise locations of most of the hotels and hostels we've listed, see the Accommodation map at the back of the book.

Accommodation

online, you can visit the *Internet Guide to Hosteling Web Site* at *http://www. hostels.com/us.ny.ny.html*. The following is a small selection of the best hostels and Ys.

Banana Bungalow, 250 W 77th St, NY 10024 ☎769-2441; fax ☎877-5733; email: *NYres@bananabungalow.com*. Popular new dorm hostel at the corner of 77th St and Amsterdam Ave, on the Upper West Side. Rates are $12–18 per person per night. Sun deck on the roof and a shared kitchen and lounge.

Blue Rabbit International House, 730 St Nicholas Ave, NY 10031 ☎491-3892; fax ☎283-0108; email: *infohostel@aol.com*. Recently opened by the owners of *International House – Sugar Hill*, four doors away, and charging the same price for dorms. However, it also has double rooms for $18 per person per night, which may be the cheapest doubles in the city. Check-in between 9am and 10pm. Has kitchens, and bed linen is included in the price.

Chelsea Center Hostel, 313 W 29th St near 8th Ave, NY 10001 ☎643-0214; fax ☎473-3945. Office hours: 8.30am to 11pm. No curfew. Small, clean, safe and friendly Chelsea hostel has beds for $20 with breakfast and clean sheets included. The privately run hostel has no sign outside, which adds to its security, and it's well situated for Midtown, Chelsea and the West Village. It's good to book one and a half to two weeks in advance in high season. Two mixed dorms sleep twenty each, and facilities include a safe for valuables and summer barbecues in the garden courtyard.

Chelsea International Hostel, 251 W 20th St, NY 10011 ☎647-0010; fax ☎727-7289. Very well located in the heart of Chelsea, between 7th & 8th aves, this is the closest hostel to Downtown. Beds (130 in all) are $18 a night, including tax, and the rooms, which sleep four or six, are small, clean and rudimentary, with bathrooms in the hall (though there are larger rooms for six at the back of the hostel which have

For details of **long-stay residences**, particularly ones geared specifically to women, see "Staying On" in *Basics*.

their own bathrooms). They also have private rooms for two at $40 a night. There are communal areas, a backyard, and free beer and pizza parties once a week, but it's the location – which can't be beaten for a night on the town – which is the hostel's main attraction. 24-hour check-in, though it's worth calling ahead.

De Hirsch Residence at the 92nd St Y, 1395 Lexington Ave between 91st and 92nd sts, NY 10128 ☎415-5650; fax ☎415-5578. Not for tourists, but a good option for a long-term stay in the city, especially for students, the *De Hirsch Residence* has single or shared bright study-bedrooms for $685 (or $550 each if shared) per month, or smaller shared doubles for $465 each per month, a little more for rooms with air conditioning. Cooking and laundry facilities are available on each floor, along with shared bathroom facilities. Applications for residence must be made months in advance and in the fall they only take applications for stays of two months or more. An added bonus: the *92nd St Y* is renowned for its poetry and music events (to which residents get a discount), along with a host of other social activities.

Gershwin Hotel, 7 E 27th St, NY 10016 ☎545-8000; fax ☎684-5546. A fun new hostel/hotel superbly located in the Flatiron district, just off 5th Ave, and handy for just about any part of town. Beds in dorms (which sleep four to twelve) are $22 a night including tax, the only catch being they cannot be reserved – it's a first-come, first-served basis (there are 230 beds). Imaginatively decorated with a Pop Art theme, and geared toward young travelers, there's an astroturfed rooftop terrace (where parties are held on summer weekends), a small bar, a well-priced restaurant, and friendly staff. Highly recommended. See also "Hotels" for details of the *Gershwin's* private rooms.

Hosteling International – New York, 891 Amsterdam Ave at W 103rd St, NY 10025 ☎932-2300; fax ☎932-2574. High up on the Upper West Side, this historic building has 480 dormitory-style beds for $22–24 for *IYHA* members (on-the-spot membership is $27) and $27 for nonmembers per night. Two-month stays for students can be arranged during the school year. A double room costs $400 each per month, a single $550. Facilities include a library, kitchen, lounge, coffee bar and a large outdoor patio. Though large there's a good chance it'll be heavily booked, so book at least 24 hours in advance (48 hrs in the summer). Open 24 hours.

International House of New York, 500 Riverside Drive at 122nd St, NY 10027 ☎316-8400. This graduate student residence hall up at Columbia University also functions as a hostel for travelers, though the cheapest rooms, with shared bathrooms, are only available to nonstudents during Christmas and summer, and cost $40 a night, or $35 if you stay fifteen days or more. Singles with private bathroom are available year-round for $95, doubles for $105 and triples for $120. Write or phone for reservations.

International House – Sugar Hill, 722 St Nicholas Ave at 145th St, NY 10031 ☎926-7030; fax ☎283-0108; email: *infohostel@aol.com*. Friendly, well-run dorm hostel in a reputedly safe, middle-class neighborhood on the border of Harlem and Washington Heights. $18 per night, tax included, no curfew, no chores and no lockout during the day. Hostel sleeps about 35 with 6 people per dorm. Check-in between 9am and 10pm. You will need to book in advance for Aug and Sept. Take the A or D train to 145th St – the hostel is just across the road.

International Student Center, 38 W 88th St ☎787-7706. One of the oldest hostels in the country and it's beginning to show. However, though this is bottom-

line accommodation, with little more than a few grubby, roach-ridden dorms sleeping eight to ten, it's cheap and in a good location on the Upper West Side, near the park. Rates are around $15 a bed, and there are kitchen facilities and a lounge with TV. Phoning ahead is advised as reservations are not accepted, and keeping an eye on your belongings is essential (the dorms don't go in for the luxury of lockers for your gear, but you can leave valuables at the front desk).

McBerny YMCA, 24th St and 7th Ave ☎741-9226; fax ☎741-8724. Usefully situated in Chelsea, just behind busy 23rd St. Single rooms are between $40 and $47, doubles are $56, triples $70 and quads $88. Bathrooms are shared. Staying in the Y gives you free access to the pool, gym and sauna. You should reserve at least 48 hours in advance if possible, four to five days in summer.

Newark YMWCA, 600 Broad St, Newark, NJ 07102 ☎201/624-8900. Worth considering as a major cost-cutting option if you want a private room and don't mind not being based in Manhattan. The *Newark YMWCA* is basic, but has a gym and swimming pool, and single rooms at $30 per person per night, $90 per week after you've stayed for 14 days. Doubles are $40 a night. The building is ten minutes' walk from Newark's Penn Station, where frequent PATH and NJ Transit trains run into Manhattan for $1. It's also reasonably close to the airport.

Uptown Hostel, 239 Lenox Avenue at 122nd St ☎666-0559. Small hostel just north of Central Park, and well situated for the clubs, restaurants and shopping in Harlem. Room for 25–30 people a night at $14 per person.

Vanderbilt YMCA, 224 E 47th St ☎756-9600. Smaller and quieter than the hostels mentioned above, and neatly placed in midtown Manhattan, just five minutes' walk from Grand Central Station. Inexpensive restaurant, swimming pool, gym and laundromat. Singles $53, doubles $66.

Accommodation

Accommodation

Webster Apartments, 419 W 34th St, NY 10001 ☎967-9000, outside city ☎800/242-7909; fax ☎268-8569. One of the nicer women-only residences, founded in 1923, the *Webster* has 390 rooms and is mainly for single women working short-term in the city, rather than for tourists. Though the rooms – all singles, with shared bathrooms on each floor – are small and rudimentary, the communal areas are the building's greatest asset. There are several lounges with piano or stereo, a large dining room and a library, and, best of all, the plant-filled rooftop terrace which has amazing views, and the lovely, leafy private garden, which is an invaluable haven in New York. The immediate location outside is unexciting, but it is well placed for access to all parts of the city. Contact the *Webster* on a weekday to set up a personal interview. The weekly rate is $142–187 depending on salary, $168 for those with an internship, and $190 for students. This includes two meals a day and daily maid service; all prices before taxes. Visitors can stay for $50 a night including full breakfast.

Westside YMCA, 5 W 63rd St ☎787-4400; fax ☎875-1334. A wonderfully located *Y* right next to Central Park and Lincoln Center with single rooms for $53 a night, doubles for $65, and free use of the pool and gym. Book two weeks in advance.

Camping

You won't save a great deal on any of the above options by **camping**. All of the campsites that could conceivably serve New York City are situated so far out as to make travel in and out a major cost. For the dedicated, though, these are the most accessible.

Battle Row Campground, Claremont Rd, Old Bethpage, Long Island ☎516/572-8690. The nearest site to the city – a short way up Long Island. You'll need either your own vehicle or a taxi to reach Manhattan since public transport is virtually nonexistent. Site is open April to

November; cost is $7 and up for a tent-site, first come, first served.

Hecksher State Park Campground, East Islip, Long Island ☎516/581-2100. Beautiful situation and easier to reach than *Battle Row* – from Penn Station take the Long Island Railroad to Great River Station. Open mid-May to mid-September; prices around $12 for a tent and up to six people. Campers must be over 21.

Bed and breakfast

Bed and breakfast has taken off in a big way in America of late, particularly in New York where Manhattanites need all the cash possible to pay their astronomical rents. For the visitor, it can be a good way of staying bang in the center of Manhattan at a reasonably affordable price. Don't expect to socialize with your temporary landlord/lady – chances are you'll have a self-contained room and hardly see them – and don't go looking for B&Bs on the streets; all rooms – except for a few which we've found off the beaten track (listed below) – are let out via the following official agencies and they all recommend making your reservations as far in advance as possible – especially for the cheapest rooms.

B&B agencies

Bed and Breakfast in Manhattan, PO Box 533 New York, NY 10150-0533 ☎472-2528; fax ☎988-9818. The ex-casting director head of this agency really knows her hosts and will match you up with the place and people where you'll be most comfortable. Rooms in a hosted apartment cost between $80 and $100 a night; unhosted places go for between $100 and $250 a night; an unusual option are the semi-hosted places (a private floor in a townhouse, for example) where you have plenty of space and privacy but there are hosts on hand for advice if you need it.

Bed and Breakfast Network of New York, Suite 602, 134 W 32nd St, NY 10001 ☎645-8134, Mon–Fri 8am–6pm.

Growing network with hosted singles for $60–80, doubles $90–100; prices for unhosted accommodation run from $100 to luxury multibedded apartments for $300. Weekly and monthly rates also available. For an assured booking write at least a month in advance, though short-notice reservations should be made by phone.

City Lights Bed & Breakfast, PO Box 20355, Cherokee Station, New York, NY 10021 ☎737-7049. More than 400 carefully screened B&Bs on its books, with many of the hosts involved in the-ater and the arts. Hosted singles run from $70–75, doubles $75–95. Unhosted accommodation costs $95 to $300 per night depending on whether it's a studio or four-bedroom apartment. Minimum stay two nights, with some exceptions. Reserve well in advance.

Colby International, 139 Round Hey, Liverpool L28 1RG England ☎0151/220-5848. If you want guaranteed B&B accommodation, *Colby International* is without doubt your best bet – and they can fix up accommodation from the UK. Excellent-value double rooms start at $70 a night, studios from a mere $90: book at least a fortnight ahead to be sure of a room in high season, though it's worth trying for last-minute reservations.

Gamut Realty Group, 301 E 78th St, ground floor, New York, NY 10021 ☎879-4229, outside city ☎800/437-8353; fax ☎517-5356; email: *gamuthq@aol.com*. Fully automated agency that can fax or email you sample listings of available rooms and apart-ments for nightly or longer-term stays. Hosted singles and doubles for $95; unhosted studio apartments for $115–130, and one-bedroom apart-ments for $145 and up. Has accommo-dation all over Manhattan, some in luxu-ry buildings or artists' lofts.

New World Bed & Breakfast, Suite 711, 150 5th Ave, New York, NY 10011 ☎675-5600; outside city ☎800/443-3800; fax ☎675-6366. Budget hosted singles $60–70, doubles $80–90; budget

unhosted studios $85–110. Private apart-ments are available; call for a brochure.

Urban Ventures, PO Box 426, New York, NY 10024. Personal visitors welcome at Suite 1412, 38 W 32nd St ☎594-5650. The first and largest registry in the city. Their budget double rooms go for $75 upwards, "comfort range" rooms (with private bath) from about $85. If you wish, you can rent a studio apartment minus hosts from $105 a night. Two nights minimum stay for hosted B&B, three nights for unhosted. You can book up until the last minute.

B&B properties

Bed & Breakfast on the Park ☎718/499-6115. In Brooklyn. A hand-some 1892 limestone town house with views over Prospect Park, with seven double rooms ranging $110–$250 a night.

Chelsea Brownstone ☎206-9237. Conveniently located on a safe, quiet street in Chelsea, this well-maintained, family-run brownstone contains a num-ber of private, self-contained apartments costing between $110 and $140 per night, each with their own TV, phone, bathroom and fully equipped kitchen. One has its own patio, and one has access to a back garden. Best to book well in advance by phone, though last-minute bookings are possible.

Foy House ☎718/636-1492. Beautiful 1894 brownstone in Park Slope, with rooms for $79, $89, $119, and a garden suite for $150. Close to subways. Smoking not permitted.

New York Bed and Breakfast, 134 W 119th St at Lenox Ave ☎666-0559; fax ☎663-5000. A lovely old brownstone in the heart of Harlem, just north of Central Park with nice double rooms for $45 a night for two people. The owner also runs a small dorm hostel a few blocks up the road with beds for $14 a night.

Hotels

Most of New York's **hotels** tend to be in midtown Manhattan, which is fine if you

Accommodation

Accommodation

want to be close to theaters and the main tourist sights, and fairly near the Park, but is hardly the loveliest part of the city. Unfortunately there aren't many other options, but if you're going to be spending a lot of time in the East or West Village or SoHo, you might want to try one of the handful of downtown hotels. Or if museums, the park and Lincoln Center are more your kind of thing, you should try the Upper West Side. The selections below cover the range from the cheapest to New York's most luxurious, the latter a small and select grouping of really special places for which it's worth paying over the odds. Within each area group below, the hotels are listed alphabetically. For an overview of where to find a listed hotel, see the map at the back of the book.

Taxes and other hidden costs

The bad news is that there are **additional taxes** added to your hotel bill, and that hotels will nearly always quote you the price of a room *before* tax. The good news is that New York City and State hotel taxes have dropped quite considerably in the past few years. Taxes will add 13.25% to your bill (State taxes are 8.25%, city taxes 5%), and there is also an additional $2 per night "occupancy tax." This will add $15 to a $100 room. (But a few years ago you would have added $27!) The **price codes** at the end of each of the following listings represent the price of the hotel's cheapest double room inclusive of all taxes.

Most hotels do not offer free **breakfast**, though continental breakfasts, for what they're worth, are becoming increasingly popular. If you have to pay for breakfast you can probably get better value at a nearby diner. At the more upmarket hotels, **tipping** will absorb at least some of your cash: unless you firmly refuse, a bell hop will grab your bags when you check in and expect $5 for carrying them to your room. It's appreciated if you tip the cleaning staff when you leave. Watch out for the luxuriously stocked **minibars**, with booze and chocolate goodies at astronomical

Hotel booking services

Accommodations Express
☎ 609/391-2100; ☎ 1-800/444-7666;
fax ☎ 609/525-0111.
CRS ☎ 407/339-4116; ☎ 1-800/950-0232; fax ☎ 407/339-4736.
Express Reservations ☎ 1-800/356-1123. Weekdays only.
Meegan's Services ☎ 718/995-9292;
from outside the city ☎ 1-800/441-1115.
The Room Exchange 450 7th Ave, NY 10123 ☎ 760-1000. Weekdays only.

prices, and hotel shops that sell basic necessities at three times the street price. Also, it's worth checking on the hotel's **phone charge** policy. Some hotels will charge you even if you call toll-free numbers or use your own calling card, so beware.

Discounts and special deals

With almost any hotel room it's possible to **cut costs** slightly if you can fill a double with three or even four people. This is normal practice in the US and managements rarely mind, providing an extra bed or two for an extra $20 or so. If you're staying long enough, you may also be able to pay a special **weekly rate**, maybe getting one night in seven for free. Some hotels, particularly those that see tourists as a major part of their revenue, also lay on special **weekend discounts** if you stay two nights or more, though these seem not to be available during the busiest season from September through December. One good thing: almost all US hotels, even the most basic, have TVs in their rooms as a matter of course – so if you've spent all your money on a bed for the night you can always curl up in front of David Letterman...

For full hotel listings and prices, consult the New York Convention and Visitors Bureau **leaflet**, *Hotels in New York City*, available from one of their offices.

Hotel price codes

The code in the following listings refers to the price of a hotel's cheapest double room and includes all taxes (State tax at 8.25%, city tax at 5% and occupancy tax of $2). Where prices are based on a per-person rate, however, they are given in dollars. Hotels in each geographical section are listed alphabetically.

① under $80
② $81–100
③ $101–130
④ $131–160
⑤ $161–200
⑥ $201–250
⑦ over $250

Downtown: Below 14th Street

Holiday Inn Downtown, 138 Lafayette St, NY 10013 at corner of Howard St ☎966-8898. An idiosyncratic member of the well-known chain, in the heart of Chinatown. This is a possible base for exploring the area, though the rooms themselves are small for the highish price. Has a new fitness center. ⑤.

Larchmont, 27 W 11th St, NY 10011 ☎989-9333; fax ☎989-9496. Brand-new budget hotel in the heart of Greenwich Village, on a beautiful tree-lined street, just off Fifth Ave. Hotels are a rarity in this lovely residential area, so this is a real find. Rooms are small but nicely decorated and clean, and all have TV, air conditioners, phones and wash-basins. Small kitchens and bathrooms with showers are on each corridor. Prices include continental breakfast. Very small singles as low as $60 a night plus tax, with doubles at ②.

Marriott Financial Center, 85 West St, NY 10006 ☎385-4900. On the weekend, doubles at ⑤ make this civilized business hotel with superb views of the World Trade Center, the Hudson and New York Harbor fairly affordable. Weekdays are a different story, but the high rates (⑦) are well worth it. Service is excellent.

Millennium Hilton, 55 Church St, NY 10007 ☎693-2001; ☎800/752-0014. The *Millennium* is designed for style-conscious businesspeople on expense accounts – but lower weekend rates with full breakfast and use of the hotel pool and fitness center make it well worth consideration. Relax in the sky-lit swimming pool overlooking St Paul's Chapel, enjoy your cocktail at the bar overlooking the World Trade Center Plaza, or eat in two, not overly expensive, restaurants, or the café. Rooms are fairly luxurious: ask for one with a view (unforgettable) of the Brooklyn Bridge. ⑦, but sometimes as low as ⑤ on weekends.

Off SoHo Suites, 11 Rivington St, NY 10002 ☎979-9808; ☎800/OFF-SOHO; fax ☎979-9801. These small, apartment-style suites are well located for Little Italy and Chinatown, but are in a rather depressed Lower East Side neighborhood. Very good value for two or four, the suites include fully equipped kitchen, VCR, and use of laundry and fitness room. This part of town can be a little tense – you may want to make use of the hotel's discount cab service at night. Suite for two with a shared bathroom ②; suites for four with private bath ④.

Soho Grand Hotel, 310 West Broadway at Grand St ☎965-3000. Great location at the edge of Soho, and many guests exude the attitude that comes with the territory: models, actors and the like who might not be so friendly. Still, the staff is surprisingly helpful, the rooms are stylishly appointed (if a bit small), and you can get free espresso at a machine on every floor. The hotel also has a bar, restaurant and fitness center. ⑥.

Washington Square, 103 Waverly Place, NY 10011 ☎777-9515; ☎800/222-0418; fax ☎979-8373. An ideal location: bang in the heart of Greenwich Village, just off Washington Square Park, and a stone's throw from the NYU campus. Don't be deceived by the grand-looking lobby – the rooms are what you'd expect for the price, and the staff can be surly.

Accommodation

Continental breakfast and use of the exercise room are included in the price. ③.

Chelsea and the West Side: 14th to 36th streets

Arlington Hotel, 18 W 25th St, NY 10010 ☎645-3990; fax ☎633-8952. Chinese-run hotel with very good prices for clean and recently redone accommodation near Madison Square Park and equidistant between Downtown and Midtown. ①; with two-room suites for four at ③.

Best Western Manhattan, 17 W 32nd St, NY 10001 ☎736-1600. Recently refurbished, reasonably priced hotel (previously called the *Aberdeen*) in a good location just off 5th Ave. ③.

Chelsea, 222 W 23rd St, NY 10011 ☎243-3700. One of New York's most noted landmarks, both for its aging neo-Gothic building and, more importantly, its long list of alumni, from Dylan Thomas to Bob Dylan and Leonard Cohen, to Sid Vicious, doomed punk icon, and his girlfriend Nancy (see p.113 for the full cast). It's still something of a haunt of musicians and art-school types, though these days it's as much an apartment building as a hotel with its majority of guests being semi-permanent. If you check into the *Chelsea* you may find yourself staying in somebody's apartment, surrounded by their belongings. Ask instead for a renovated room with polished wood floors, log-burning fireplaces, and plenty of space to cram a few extra friends into. ④ for a studio room, ⑦ for a suite.

Chelsea Inn, 46 W 17th St, NY 10011 ☎645-8989. Well-situated rooming house in the heart of Chelsea, not too far from the Village, a bit low on services but with a choice of guest rooms, studios and suites, most equipped with kitchenettes. Two with bath shared with one other guest room; studio with bathroom ③.

Comfort Inn Manhattan, 42 W 35th St, NY 10001 ☎947-0200. The best thing about the *Comfort Inn* is the free hot coffee, Danish pastries and newspapers

they give you in the elegant lobby each morning. It's a solid, good-value place to stay but the management can be unhelpful – you won't be able to see a room before you hand over your cash, for example. ⑤.

Herald Square, 19 W 31st St, NY 10001 ☎279-4017. Home of the original *Life* magazine, and with Philip Martiny's sculptured cherub known as *Winged Life* still presiding over the doorway of this Beaux Arts building. That's where the ornamentation stops – inside, the hotel has few frills, but rooms are fine for the price. ①; triples and quads ③. Very small single rooms go for as low as $50 a night with shared bathroom.

Hotel Pennsylvania, 401 7th Ave, NY 10001 ☎736-5000. Boasting the same telephone number since 1917 (the "Pennsylvania six five thousand" of the Glenn Miller song), this is now the world's largest *Ramada Hotel*. It's located across from Madison Square Garden, and offers every possible convenience, though you can't help thinking it looked better when it was a good old-fashioned hotel. ④.

Howard Johnson's 34th Street, 215 W 34th St, NY 10001 ☎947-5050. A fairly cheap, recently renovated hotel opposite Penn Station; used to be called the *Penn Plaza*. The rooms are decent enough and there's a private second-floor lobby lounge to get away from the 7th Ave madness. ③.

Southgate Tower, 371 7th Ave, NY 10001 ☎563-1800. A member of the excellent Manhattan East Suites chain, *Southgate Tower* is opposite Penn Station and Madison Square Garden. All rooms are suites with kitchens. ⑤.

Stanford, 43 W 32nd St, NY 10001 ☎563-1480. Clean, inexpensive hotel on the block known as "Little Korea." As well as the basic hotel facilities the *Stanford* offers room service and valet laundry, an American café in the lobby and good Korean cuisine in the very relaxing surroundings of the *Gam Mee Ok* restaurant. ②.

Wolcott, 4 W 31st St, NY 10001 ☎268-2900. A surprisingly relaxing budget hotel, with a gilded, ornamented lobby and more than adequate rooms, all with bathrooms. A very good deal. ②.

Midtown Manhattan East: 14th to 45th streets

Carlton, 22 E 29th St, NY 10016 ☎532-4100. A very well-priced, nicely modernized hotel in a Beaux Arts building. There are two pluses: you're in the safe residential area of Murray Hill, and you also get room and valet service, not often associated with hotels in this price bracket. ④.

Carlton Arms, 160 E 25th St, NY 10010 ☎684-8337. A strong contender for the city's latest bohemian hangout, with eclectic interior decor by would-be artists, very few comforts, and a clientele made up of Europeans, down-at-heel artists and longstay guests. People either love it or hate it − so check it out before you commit yourself to staying. Discount rates available for students and foreign travelers, with an extra 10% discount if you stay more than 7 nights. Singles can be as low as $49 plus tax. Reserve well in advance for summer. ①.

Doral Park, 70 Park Ave at 38th St, NY 10016 ☎687-7050. A multimillion-dollar restoration has turned the *Doral Park* into one of the snazziest deluxe hotels, with re-creations of classical friezes and frescoes and original designs for lighting and furnishings. Service is excellent. ⑤.

Gershwin Hotel, 7 E 27th St, NY 10016 ☎545-8000; fax ☎684-5546. A great new young persons' hotel just off 5th Ave in the Flatiron district which also functions as a hostel (see "Hostels"). There are 70 private double rooms with bathrooms which cost between $75 and $120 a night including tax − a great bargain. The cheapest have no phone or TV but are bright and clean. Imaginatively decorated with a Pop Art theme, the *Gershwin* has an astroturfed rooftop terrace in the summer (where parties are held on the weekend), a small bar, a

well-priced restaurant, friendly staff, and is highly recommended. Try to book well in advance. ①.

Gramercy Park, 2 Lexington Ave, NY 10010 ☎475-4320. Pleasant enough hotel located next to the only private park in the city (residents get a key to the gate) and popular with Europeans. There are smoking and non-smoking rooms (you really know when you're in one of the former) and a mixture of newly renovated and tatty rooms. ④.

Jolly Madison Towers, Madison Ave at 38th St, NY 10016 ☎685-3700. The lobby and Whaler Bar are looking very dated these days, but the rooms are restful, clean and fairly spacious. Among the facilities is an Oriental health spa with whirlpool bath and sauna. ⑤; weekends ④, not always available.

Martha Washington, 30 E 30th St, NY 10016 ☎689-1900; fax ☎689-0023. A women-only hotel with very low room rates, but a character that's a little on the depressing side, although some rooms are renovated. There's a choice of single or twin-bedded rooms, with or without bathrooms. Singles without bathroom cost $52, singles with bath $69, doubles without bathroom $76, doubles with bath $98. Weekly rates work out to between $27 and $41 a night (all prices include tax). ①.

Morgans, 237 Madison Ave, NY 10016 ☎686-0300. Created by the instigators of *Studio 54* and the *Palladium* nightclub, this is self-consciously − and quite successfully − one of the chicest flophouses in town. Discreet furnishings are by André Putnam, good-looking young staff clothed in Klein and Armani. These days the stars stay at the *Royalton*, but those wanting to keep a low profile still frequent the place, able as they are to slip in and out unnoticed. The black-white-gray decor is starting to look too self-consciously 1980s and hence a little passé, but you do get a jacuzzi, a great stereo system and cable TV in your room. ⑦; weekends ⑤.

Accommodation

Accommodation

Murray Hill Inn, 143 E 30th St, NY 10016 ☎683-6900. It's easy to see why young travelers and backpackers line the *Inn's* narrow halls. Though the rooms are smallish and fairly undecorated, the amenities are surprising for the price: air-con, telephone, cable TV, and sink; toilets and showers are shared but clean. With a friendly staff and a residential locale that offers a breather from the bustle. Singles for $65; doubles start at $85, additional costs if more than two in a room. Ask for weekly rates. ②.

Quality Hotel 5th Avenue, 3 E 40th St, NY 10016 ☎447-1500. This is a motel-style hotel, owned by a Canadian chain. If you're here on business, the PC/fax dataports, desks and same-day valet service will come in handy. Rooms are bright and well-furnished, and there's a very comfortable lounge and restaurant on the premises. ⑤ with low weekend rates, ③ for up to four in a room.

Roger Williams, 28 E 31st St, NY 10016 ☎684-7500. A good choice for families or friends traveling together on a budget. Rooms in this Murray Hill ex-apartment building have kitchenettes (two-burner gas stove, sink, refrigerator and cabinet), simple furnishings, and color cable TV. There's a 24-hour deli-salad bar on the same block, and the friendly staff will provide a "Kitchen Kit" of kettle, pots and pans, plastic crockery and tea, coffee, sugar and salt as well as a copy of their twelve-page guide to the area called *Herald Square/Murray Hill Tips*. Doubles and triples ②, quads ③.

Seventeen, 225 E 17th St, NY 10003 ☎475-2845; fax ☎677-8178. Budget accommodation as you'd expect it to look: rudimentary bedrooms, and bathrooms on the corridors that have seen better days. But *Seventeen* is clean and friendly, and it can't be beaten either for location – it's on a nice, tree-lined street between 2nd and 3rd aves; *the* hotel if you want to spend your time in the East Village, only a few blocks away – or for price: if you stay for a week the prices come to $41 a night for a single, $59 for a double. For single nights doubles are

$77 and single rooms are $65. Not to be sneezed at. ①.

Shelburne Murray Hill, 303 Lexington Ave, NY 10016 ☎689-5200. Another reliable Manhattan East Suite hotel, in the most elegant part of Murray Hill. The outstanding features are the *Secret Harbor Bistro* with dishes of the day chalked up above the bar, and the stunning open-air penthouse roof garden. ⑥, with lower promotional rates; weekends as low as ④ if available.

UN Crowne Plaza, 304 E 42nd St, NY 10017 ☎986-8800. One of the more stylish hotels close to Grand Central Station, in the unique residential area built in the 1920s known as "Tudor City." Rooms are deluxe, with minibar, cable and in-room movies, hair dryer and opulent marble bathrooms. There's a fitness room and sauna too. Service is excellent. ⑤; weekends less.

Midtown Manhattan West: 36th to 60th streets

Algonquin, 59 W 44th St, NY 10036 ☎840-6800. New York's classic literary hangout, as created by Dorothy Parker and her associates and perpetuated by Noel Coward, Bernard Shaw, Irving Berlin and most names subsequent. Decor remains little changed except in the bedrooms which have all been refurbished to good effect. Ask about summer and weekend specials. ⑦; weekends ⑤.

Ameritania, 230 W 54th St, NY 10019 ☎247-5000. One of the best values of the city's inexpensive hotels: you get a well-furnished room with marble bathroom, cable TV, individual climate control and a cocktail bar, restaurant and pizza parlor off the high-tech, neon-lit lobby. $5 off if you mention *Rough Guides*. ⑤.

Amsterdam Court Hotel, 226 W 50th St, NY 10019 ☎459-1000; fax ☎265-5070. Well positioned and eminently affordable, the *Amsterdam Court* sports a coffee shop, bar and exercise room – and some of the best prices in town. Rooms with private bathrooms, and quad rooms without, fall into category ②: all others (including triples) are ①.

Best Western President, 234 W 48th St, NY 10036 ☎246-8800. This solid, reasonably priced hotel between 8th Ave and Broadway offers small, recently renovated rooms. ⑤.

Best Western Woodward, 219 W 55th St, NY 10019 ☎247-2000. Recently renovated and handy for the Museum of Modern Art; includes continental breakfast. For a single ③, for a double ⑤.

Broadway Bed & Breakfast Inn, 264 W 46th St, NY 10036 ☎997-9200; ☎800-826-6300; fax ☎768-2807. Brand-new, small, well-priced hotel in the heart of the theater district, on the corner of charmless 8th Ave, but a skip away from Times Square and Restaurant Row. All rooms are pleasant, have private bathrooms with tub or shower, and a couple have jacuzzis. Continental breakfast is included in the price and all guests get a 20% discount at the restaurant downstairs. ②.

Casablanca, 147 W 43rd St, NY 10036 ☎869-1212. Inexpensive hotel on a theater-lined street. Fairly recently revamped rooms, each has color TV and telephone. There's a general Moroccantheme, plus a second-floor sitting area and helpful staff. Doubles, triples and quads for ③.

Days Inn, 790 8th Ave, between W 48th and W 49th sts, NY 10019 ☎581-7000. A rooftop pool open during the summer months is the main attraction of this slightly characterless chain hotel (formerly a Ramada Inn). Still, rooms are in good condition, and the rates are reasonable. ④.

Edison, 228 W 47th St, NY 10036 ☎840-5000. The most striking thing about the 1000-room *Edison* is its beautifully restored Art Deco lobby, re-creating the original from 1931. All rooms have been recently renovated. ③.

Essex House, 160 Central Park South, NY 10019 ☎247-0300. A beautiful hotel for a special occasion, *Essex House* has been restored by new Japanese owners

to its original Art Deco splendor. The best rooms have spectacular Central Park views. Despite the excellent service the atmosphere is not at all formal or hushed. ⑦, dropping to ⑥ at weekends.

Gorham, 136 W 55th St, NY 10019 ☎245-1800; ☎800-735-0710. Good-value, newly renovated midtown hotel between 6th and 7th aves, handy for Central Park. Suites have whirlpool baths and self-service kitchen. Doubles ⑤; suites ⑥.

Helmsley Windsor, 100 W 58th St, NY 10019 ☎265-2100. Enjoy coffee on the house each morning in the richly decorated, wood-paneled lobby. Like the other *Helmsley* hotels, the *Windsor* has a pleasantly old-fashioned air, with plenty of useful extras in the rooms, and all with private bathrooms. Central Park is a short walk away. ⑤.

Howard Johnson Plaza, 8th Ave at 52nd St, NY 10019 ☎581-4100. Not the usual bland, chain hotel you might have expected, the 300-room hotel offers very well-decorated rooms, space to spread out, and a piano bar and restaurant. ⑤.

Iroquois, 49 W 44th St, NY 10036 ☎840-3080. The rooms are better than the lobby suggests – they're well furnished with plush carpets. This is a family-run hotel (some of the family are more helpful than others), and its low rates are unusual for this part of town. ③.

Mansfield, 12 W 44th St, NY 10036 ☎944-6050. The real-value alternative to both the nearby *Algonquin* and the *Royalton*, with better-than-average rooms for the price. The deli off the lobby will make up snacks for you, or continental breakfast is included. ⑤.

Marriott Marquis, 1535 Broadway at 45th St, NY 10036 ☎398-1900. The enormous *Marquis* is perfect for conference and convention guests; it's worth dropping by to gawp at the split-level atrium and to ride the glass elevators to NY's only revolving restaurant, but the rooms themselves are modest for the high price. ⑥.

Accommodation

Accommodation

Michelangelo, 152 W 51st St, NY 10019 ☎765-1900. An Italian chain took over recently and created a palazzo on Broadway, with acres of marble, and no expenses spared in the luxurious and super-large rooms. In terms of decor you have a choice: rooms are in Art Deco, Empire or Country French styles. On weekends and special holidays (New Year's Eve and Valentine's Day, for example), prices are lowest. ⑦; weekends ⑥.

Milford Plaza, 270 W 45th St, NY 10036 ☎869-3600. Rooms are tiny and the atmosphere is impersonal, but hoardes of theater-goers still flock here for the "Lullabuy [sic] of Broadway" deals. ⑤.

Millennium Broadway, 145 W 44th St, NY 10036 ☎768-4400. Black marble and wall-to-ceiling art works dominate the *Millennium Broadway's* lobby; the sleek lines continue in the beautiful off-white bedrooms. A good place to come for an intimate after-theater supper, even if you decide against the (justifiably) high room rates. ⑥; weekends ⑤.

Novotel, 226 W 52nd St, 10019 ☎315-0100. Chain hotel large enough to offer a decent range of facilities, while small enough to avoid anonymity. The decor is sophisticated, the food good, as you would expect from a French-owned establishment, and the hotel offers special rooms for the disabled. ⑤.

Paramount, 235 W 46th St, NY 10036 ☎764-5500. For the past few years now, this has been one of the hippest places in town to stay, popular with a pop and media crowd, who come to enjoy an interior designed by Philippe Starck and be waited on by sleek young things. Doubles aren't as pricey as you'd think, and they sport prints of Vermeer's *Lacemaker* as headboards along with VCRs and designer bathrooms. The branch of *Dean and DeLuca* off the lobby, the *Whiskey Bar* and the newly opened *Coco Pazzo Teatro* restaurant are all busy and fun. ⑤.

Plaza, 768 5th Ave, NY 10019 ☎759-3000. The last word in New York luxury, at least by reputation, and worth the money for the fine old pseudo-French chateau building if nothing else. Doubles start at $235 and run to $15,000 (no kidding!) for a specialty suite, and that's before taxes. A place to stay if someone else is paying. ⑦.

Portland Square, 132 W 47th St, NY 10036 ☎382-0600. A theater hotel since 1904, and former home to Jimmy Cagney and other members of Broadway casts. The *Portland* has a few more comforts than its sister hotel *Herald Square*, but is still a budget operation, good for a few nights' sleep but not for hanging out in. The cheapest rooms go as low as $50 plus tax for a small single with a shared bathroom. Doubles ②; triples and quads ③.

Quality, 59 W 46th St, NY 10036 ☎719-2300. Near Diamond Row and a stone's throw from Rockefeller Center, this budget hotel has recently undergone a spruce-up. All rooms come with private bath, cable TV and telephone; there's a garden, too. Singles ②; standard doubles ④.

Remington, 129 W 46th St, NY 10036 ☎221-2600. A very tacky, but spotless, hotel right in the heart of things. Service is brusque and efficient; all rooms have private bathrooms, air conditioning, cable TV and a telephone. ③.

Roosevelt, 45 W 45th St, NY 10017 ☎661-9600, reservations ☎1-800/223-0888. The *Roosevelt's* heyday was in the Railway Age, when its proximity to Grand Central Station meant that thousands of travelers came to stay. It has recently undergone extensive renovations, with new suites and the prices to match. Has nice, if traditional, bar and restaurant. ⑦.

Royalton, 44 W 44th St, NY 10036 ☎869-4400. Owned by the same management as the *Paramount*, the *Royalton* attempts to capture the market for the discerning style-person, with more interiors designed by Philippe Starck. It has tried to become the *Algonquin* of the 1990s, and is as much a power-lunch venue for NYC's media and publishing set as a place to stay. ⑦.

St Moritz on the Park, 50 Central Park South, NY 10019 ☎755-5800. If you'd like a view of Central Park but you don't want to pay the $300–400 a night room rates of the other hotels around here, then this is the place for you. The catch is that the rooms are tiny, so enjoy the views and then spend time in the *Sidewalk Café*, piano bar or *Rumpelmayer's Ice Cream Parlor* on the premises. ④.

Salisbury, 123 W 57th St, NY 10019 ☎246-1300. Good service, large rooms and proximity to Central Park are the main attraction of this recently renovated hotel. The famous *Russian Tea Room* is across the street. ⑤.

Travelodge Midtown, 132 W 45th St, NY 10036 ☎921-7600. Located on the edge of the theater district, this recently renovated hotel (previously called the *Chatwal Inn*) nevertheless manages to be an oasis of calm. Suites are very spacious and can easily accommodate four people; decor is in restful Queen Anne and Federal styles. Continental breakfast is included in the price. ④.

Warwick, 65 W 54th St, NY 10019 ☎247-2700. Stars of the 1950s and 1960s – including Cary Grant, Rock Hudson, the Beatles, Elvis Presley and JFK – stayed at the *Warwick* as a matter of course. Although the hotel's lost its showbusiness cachet now, it's an exceptionally spacious, pleasant place to stay, from the elegant lobby and Italian restaurant to the apartment-sized renovated rooms with views of 6th Ave. ⑥.

Wellington, 7th Ave at 55th St, NY 10019 ☎247-3900. The *Wellington's* gleaming, mirror-clad lobby is the result of recent renovations, and similar attention has been paid to the rooms. Some have kitchenettes, and family rooms offer two bathrooms. Close to Carnegie Hall and handy for Lincoln Center, the hotel's a fair price for this stretch of town. ④.

Westpark, 308 W 58th St, NY 10019 ☎246-6440. The best rooms look out over Columbus Circle and the southwest-ern corner of Central Park. The rooms were more recently decorated than the public areas, which have a slightly seedy air, but it's great value for the area, especially handy for Lincoln Center and the Park. ②.

Wyndham, 42 W 58th St, NY 10019 ☎753-3500. The *Wyndham's* large rooms and suites vary enormously in terms of decor and it's the kind of place where the hotel's devotees – many of whom are Broadway actors and actress-es – request their favorite each time they stay. All the rooms are homely, though, and the place feels more like an apart-ment building than a hotel. ③.

The Mid and Upper East Side: East 45th to 92nd streets

Allerton House, 130 E 57th St, NY 10022 ☎753-8841. Well located in a busy East Side shopping district, the women-only *Allerton House* has tiny rooms (with or without private bath). There's also a roof-top terrace, bar and laundry, and gym facilities nearby. They could do with some less creepy male staff. ①, with singles as low as $42 plus tax.

Barbizon, 140 E 63rd St, NY 10021 ☎838-5700. Pleasant, recently renovat-ed hotel with bar and gym, and good views from the terrace suites. Located three blocks from *Bloomingdale's*. ⑤.

Beekman Tower, 3 Mitchell Place (49th St and 1st Ave), NY 10017 ☎355-7300. One of the more expensive of the Manhattan East Suite Hotel chain. Suites are of a similar size and high standard, however, and the Art Deco top floor *Top of the Towers* restaurant offers superb East Side views. ⑥; weekend rates occa-sionally available at ④.

Beverly, 125 E 50th St at Lexington Ave, NY 10022 ☎753-2700. Nicely furnished, comfortable rooms in an otherwise slightly rundown-looking building. Laundry and valet service, safe-deposit boxes, free continental breakfast, room service, a steakhouse restaurant, concierge and 24-hour pharmacy are some of the many extras. ⑤.

Accommodation

Accommodation

Box Tree, 250 E 49th St, NY 10017 ☎758-8320. Thirteen elegant rooms and suites fill two adjoining brownstones and make one of New York's more eccentric lodgings. The Egyptian-, Chinese- and Japanese-style rooms have fur throws on the beds, great lighting and ornaments and decoration everywhere. A $100 dining credit toward a meal in the excellent *Box Tree Restaurant* is included in the weekend room rate. Worth it for a splurge. ⑤; weekends unusually very much more expensive ⑦.

Drake, 440 Park Ave at 56th St, NY 10022 ☎421-0900. A first-class hotel, and member of the Swissotel chain, with bustling cocktail bar and superb French restaurant, a spa and gym. This used to be an apartment building, so the rooms are large. ⑥.

Elysee, 60 E 54th St, NY 10022 ☎753-1066. The *Elysee* was until recently famed for its eccentric, theatrical style, but sadly enthusiastic new management have refurbished the whole place in the best possible taste. A fine place to stay if you can afford it, and close to 5th Ave. ⑥.

Fitzpatrick Manhattan, 687 Lexington Ave between 56th and 57th sts, NY 10022 ☎355-0100; outside city ☎800/367-7701; fax ☎355-1371. Opened in 1991, this handsome Irish-owned and Irish-themed hotel is perfectly located for Midtown shopping, Upper East Side museums and Central Park. A hearty Irish breakfast is served all day long. Doubles and suites for ⑦, with weekend deals available.

Lexington, 511 Lexington Ave at E 48th St, NY 10017 ☎755-6963. This large, elegantly renovated old hotel successfully gathers a very good Chinese restaurant, Western-style nightclub ("A shot of country with a splash of rock 'n' roll"), American-style coffee shop and refined north-Italian restaurant under one roof. The rooms are small and unexciting but the prices are reasonable for this high-quality accommodation. ⑤.

Loews, 569 Lexington Ave at E 51st St, NY 10022 ☎752-7000. There's a Deco-esque theme throughout the *Loews* New York, from the beautiful circular *Lobby Bar* and *Lexington Avenue Grill* to the very well-decorated guest rooms. ⑥; weekends ⑤.

Lowell, 28 E 63rd St, NY 10021 ☎838-1400. Madonna loved to work out so much when she stayed here (so it's said) that the *Lowell* built a suite, with its own fitness machines. Then Roseanne and Tom Arnold stayed in it and now you can too, for just $815, plus taxes. Along with the room you get great views of New York, a woodburning fireplace and tons of posh seclusion. ⑦.

Lyden House, 320 E 53rd St, NY 10022 ☎888-6070. One of the friendliest of the Manhattan East Suite chain, where even the smallest suites are apartment-sized by New York standards and could sleep four (second two adults at $20 plus tax per person per night). All suites have eat-in kitchens and have the luxury of a maid to do the dishes. ④; weekend specials if available.

Mark, Madison Ave at E 77th St, NY 10021 ☎744-4300. One of a handful of NYC's hotels which really does live up to its claims of sophistication and elegance. A recent renovation has kitted the lobby out with Biedermeier furniture and sleek Italian torchieres. In the guest rooms, restaurant, and invitingly dark *Mark's Bar* there's a similar emphasis on the best of everything. ⑦.

Pickwick Arms, 230 E 51st St, NY 10022 ☎355-0300. A thoroughly pleasant budget hotel, and for the price, one of the best deals you'll get on the East Side. All 400 rooms are air-conditioned, with cable TV, direct-dial phones and room service. The *Pickwick's* open-air roof deck with stunning views and cafe are added attractions. A single room with a shared bathroom is $50. ②.

Pierre, 795 5th Ave at 61st St, NY 10021 ☎838-8000. The *Pierre* has consistently retained its reputation as one of New York's top hotels and is certainly luxurious. It was Salvador Dali's favorite place to stay in the city, but the only surreal aspects today are the prices. If these prohibit a stay, have afternoon tea in the gloriously frescoed *Rotunda*, or experience a power-breakfast in the *Café Pierre*. ⑦.

Plaza 50, 155 E 50th St, NY 10022 ☎751-5710. A Manhattan East Suite hotel with guest rooms as well as one-bedroom suites, particularly good for business travelers. The *Plaza 50* also offers concierge, valet and room service. ⑤; weekends are good value at ④.

Roger Smith, 501 Lexington Ave at 47th St, NY 10017 ☎755-1400. One of the best midtown hotels with very helpful service, individually decorated rooms, a great restaurant which doubles as a jazz bar, and art works and sculpture on display in the public areas. Breakfast is included in the price, along with a refrigerator and coffee-maker in most rooms and VCRs with 2000 videos available from the hotel's library. Popular with bands, and guests who like the arty ambience. ⑥; weekends drop to ④.

San Carlos, 150 E 50th St, NY 10022 ☎755-1800. The *San Carlos* is well-located in the East 50s near plenty of bars and restaurants, and the large rooms all have fully equipped kitchenettes. This is a useful standby when everything else is booked solid. ④.

Sherry Netherland, 781 5th Ave, NY 10022 ☎355-2800. The place to rent a whole floor and live in permanently, if a large sum of money ever comes your way. Many of the *Sherry Netherland*'s guests already do this, and the service is geared to satisfying their every whim. Room service is by renowned restaurateur Harry Cipriani. ⑦.

Surrey, 20 E 76th St, NY 10021 ☎288-3700. A genteel Manhattan East Suite hotel, in the heart of the "Museum Mile." Recently renovated, with a new fitness center. ⑥.

Waldorf-Astoria, 301 Park Ave at E 50th St, NY 10022 ☎355-3000. One of the great names among New York hotels,

and restored to its 1930s glory, making it a wonderful place to stay if you can afford it or someone else is paying. ⑦.

Wales, 1295 Madison Ave on 92nd St, NY 10128 ☎876-6000. Almost in Spanish Harlem, though very definitely Upper East Side in feel. Excellent prices for the high standard of accommodation: the original oak moldings and mantles have been lovingly restored, and tea, cookies and classical music are served up every afternoon in the parlor. ⑤.

The Upper West Side: Above 60th Street

Beacon, 2130 Broadway at 75th St, NY 10023 ☎787-1100. A pleasantly buzzing hotel with generously sized rooms, high ceilings, deep closets, color cable TV and fully equipped kitchenettes. They have suites for four for $150. *Zabar's*, NYC's famous gourmet deli, is conveniently situated across the road. ③.

Broadway American, 2178 Broadway at 77th St, NY 10024 ☎362-1100. Newly renovated budget hotel decorated in minimalist Art Deco style with shared kitchen and laundry facilities on each floor. Singles as low as $55; cheapest doubles are those with shared bathrooms ②; with private bathrooms ③.

Excelsior, 45 W 81st St ☎362-9200. Old-fashioned hotel situated across from the Natural History Museum in the heart of the liveliest stretch of the Columbus Ave scene. All the rooms are a decent size, and they have larger suites that would be good for four sharing. ③.

Malibu Studios, 2688 Broadway at W 103rd St, NY 10025 ☎222-2954; outside the city ☎800/647-2227; fax ☎678-6842. Probably the best-value budget accommodation in the city. A fair step from the heart of things up at the Morningside Heights end of the Upper West Side, but adjacent to the 103rd St stop on the #1 subway line, and within walking distance of plenty of restaurants and nightlife due to the nearby presence of Columbia University. Prices, all before taxes, are $45 for a single room ($69

Accommodation

Accommodation

with private bath), $59 for a double ($79 with private bath). The hotel has just added 50 'deluxe' rooms, that start at $79 for a single. Mention the *Rough Guides* and pay for 3 nights or more upfront and get a 10 percent discount on any room. Friendly management too, who will help get you discount tickets for the city's best clubs if you ask. ①.

Mayflower, 15 Central Park West at 61st St, NY 10023 ☎265-0060. A slightly down-at-heel but very comfortable hotel a few steps from Central Park and Lincoln Center. It's so close to the latter, in fact, that performers and musicians are often to be seen in the hotel's very good *Conservatory Café*. ⑤; ⑥ for views over the park.

Milburn, 242 W 76th St ☎362-1006; ☎800/833-9622; fax ☎721-5476. Welcoming and well-situated suite hotel, great for families, which has recently been renovated in very gracious style. There are studios and one- and two-room suites with fully equipped kitch-

enettes, bathrooms and TV. Practical extras are in-room safes, laundry and maid service. ④.

Radisson Empire, 44 W 63rd St, NY 10023 ☎265-7400. A lavishly renovated member of the Radisson chain, the *Empire* will suit music lovers – not only is it opposite the Metropolitan Opera House and Lincoln Center, but also each (box-sized) room comes equipped with excellent CD player/tape deck and VCR. ⑤.

Riverside Tower, 80 Riverside Drive at W 80th St, NY 10024 ☎877-5200. The area's alternative budget accommodation, this time in a quiet, residential part of the Upper West Side. Restaurants and bars are just a few blocks away, which is just as well as the rooms are not designed to make you want to spend much time in them. They are decent and clean though, with telephone and TV, and views of the Hudson River. It's worth noting that the triples and quads work out at around $25 per person, per night. ①.

Chapter 17

Eating

There are plenty of good reasons why New Yorkers like to **eat** out so much. Many of them work long hours and don't have time to cook dinner; still more live in very small apartments, and restaurants serve as their dining rooms. Of course, there are other reasons – New York is a rich port city that can get the best foodstuffs from anywhere in the world, and, as a major immigration gateway, it attracts chefs who know how to cook the world's cuisines properly, sometimes exceptionally. So not only can you get Senegalese, French provincial, or any other kind of food you can think of, you can also get outstanding versions of it. As you stroll through the heavenly odors that emanate from the city's delis, bagel shops, Chinese restaurants and upscale eateries, it's hard not to work up an appetite.

Budget food

In the early morning you'll see frazzled New Yorkers lining up in front of street **vendors** for a breakfast on the run of bagels, doughnuts and coffee. Summer's chilly treats include ice-cream bars, soft ice cream and *helados* – shaved ice with syrup poured on top – while street staples like hot dogs, gyros and honey-roasted nuts are available all year round. Street food makes for a cheap, greasy and sometimes sublimely satisfying meal, or for around $1.50 you can always get a slice of **pizza**. Of course,

there are the predictable *Burger King* and *McDonald's* **burger chains**, but with the abundance of good, cheap food available, you shouldn't have to resort to them.

For **quick snacks**, many delis also do ready-cooked hot meals. Though most are truly less than appetizing, delis are a sure-bet, and often all-night, place to get a salad or quick precooked meal in a pinch. **Diners** are a little more expensive, but you get the advantage of a table, seat, bathroom and possibly a quiet pay telephone. They serve filling breakfasts, burgers, sandwiches and basic American fare from a usually enormous menu, which often includes good-value lunchtime specials, either at formica-topped tables or at stools set around a counter. Prices are around $6 for a heavily garnished burger and fries, $8 or so for anything more elaborate, making diners a good value for a filling lunch on a budget, and they have a distinctly overdone style with an ambience all their own.

Breakfast

Although many hotels serve a breakfast of some kind, it is usually much cheaper (not to mention more interesting) to go out to a coffee shop for the first meal of the day. Most diners offer **breakfast specials** until 11am, allowing you to eat and drink until you're full for under $5. Figuring prominently on **breakfast menus** are sausages and bacon (streaky, cut very thin and fried to a

Eating

crisp), along with eggs, toast, waffles and pancakes – the latter thick and heavy, and usually served with a smothering of maple syrup. Be prepared to be interrogated as to how you want your eggs, and be ready to snap back with an answer – breakfast may be taken seriously, but it is never taken slowly. Basically, "sunny side up" means fried unturned and "over easy" turned for a few seconds only. A typical breakfast special usually includes some combination of eggs (fried or scrambled), home fries (chunky potatoes fried with onions) or French fries, toast, juice and coffee for a fixed price.

Lunch

Aside from coffee shops, most **restaurants** in New York open at lunchtime. Some of the best lunchtime deals can be had in **Chinatown**, where you can get a massive plate of meat with noodles or rice for around $5, or, if you're feeling a little more adventurous, feast at a dim sum restaurant for $7–8. Dim sum (literally "your heart's delight") consists of small dishes that you choose from a moving trolley and pay for at the end, according to the empty dishes in front of you. For the inexperienced (and dim sum is not recommended to vegetarians) there's an element of chance, since Chinatown waiters tend not to speak English and the dishes themselves are often unrecognizable until the first bite. But duckwebs aside, it's mostly pretty accessible fare.

Another option for lunch – and one that's not just limited to Manhattan – is to get a **sandwich "to go"** from a **deli**. Once again, be prepared for a quick-fire question-and-answer session with the counter person, who will not only ask which kind of bread you want – white, whole wheat, rye or French – but also whether you want mayonnaise, lettuce or anything else. Deli sandwiches are custom-built and constrained only by your imagination, so bear in mind the size of the thing you're creating; if you hear them say "full house" it means you've ordered

everything. You can expect to pay around $5 for a sandwich, but it is easily a meal in itself.

Brunch

Brunch can also be a good-value deal, and is something of a New York institution, usually served on weekends between noon and 4pm. Lox and cream cheese on a bagel, omelettes, French toast, and pancakes are favorite brunch items. Many restaurants compete for customers by laying on a special well-priced brunch menu – sometimes including a free cocktail. This can be because the food isn't so good, or because the place specializes in dinner fare and wants to fill some seats in the afternoon. (A quick look at the food on other people's tables should tell you which is the case.) There's a list of recommended brunch venues on p.327.

Bar food and bargains

Bars are often the cheapest places to eat in New York, but they're by no means the only budget option. In the **ritzier bars** there are almost invariably hot **hors d'oeuvres**, laid out during happy hour between 5pm and 7pm Monday to Friday, one of the city's best scams if you're on a tight budget. For the price of a single drink (it won't be cheap) you can stuff yourself silly on pasta, seafood, chili or whatever. Remember, though, that the more you look like an office-person (it's for them, after all, that the hors d'oeuvres are put out) the easier you'll blend in with the free-loading crowds.

Most **bars** serve food of one kind or another, and you'll find a substantial – and inevitable – crossover between our *Eating* and *Drinking* chapters. Even in the lowliest bar there's a good chance they'll cook you at least a burger or a plate of potato skins, and many places offer a full menu, particularly the more upscale Irish and American hangouts. Though bars stay open late, their kitchens are usually closed by midnight. Bars that serve serious food are detailed along

Eating

Service, tipping . . . and home deliveries

Whatever you eat, **service** is likely to be decent, since not only is the notion of customer service deeply ingrained into the American psyche, but the system of tipping, whereby (in New York) you double the figure on the bill for tax (just over 8 percent) to work out the minimum tip, can make the staff almost irritatingly attentive. There's no way round this: if you either refuse or forget to tip there's little point in going back to that restaurant. As far as actual **payment** is concerned, many – although by no means all – restaurants take credit/charge cards

(if you use one you'll find a space left for you to write in the appropriate tip); travelers' checks are also widely accepted (see *Basics*, "Money and Banks").

If you're not in the mood to get dressed up or fight the crowds, you might consider having food delivered to your hotel or host's home. These days almost every kind of New York neighborhood restaurant offers this service for free if the order exceeds a given minimum and you're within a reasonable distance – though you should, of course, tip the bearer.

---

with restaurant **listings** later in this chapter.

For further cheap eating options, be sure to look also at the places detailed in the following "Restaurants" section. Although Chinese and east European food, and of course pizza, are perhaps the only cuisines that are reliably cheap pretty much everywhere, there are bargains to be had in every category.

Coffee, tea and soft drinks

Served black or "regular" (with cream or milk, though in other parts of the States "regular" coffee is black coffee), **coffee** is usually freshly brewed (high-maintenance New Yorkers consume coffee in large quantities), though it frequently tastes stale. You can get coffee "to go" in most delis, and many restaurants serve a "bottomless cup," i.e. you can keep asking for refills at no extra charge. *Sanka* is the most popular type of decaffeinated, but more and more restaurants (and even some delis) provide brewed water-decaffeinated coffee (if you see two glass-globe pots of coffee in the bus-station or behind the counter, and one has an orange or green band around the neck instead of a black or brown one, that's usually brewed decaf). **Tea** is becoming more popular and will normally be served

straight or with lemon; if you want milk request it, and specify if you want it hot or it will come ice cold. **Soft drinks** (sodas) come in caffeine-free versions as well. These are drunk in three sizes: small (large), regular (bigger) and large (practically a bucket); stick to cans and bottles so you'll know what you're in for.

New York has a number of **cafés** and **tea rooms**, which don't always serve alcohol but concentrate instead on providing fresh coffee and tea, fruit juices and pastries and light snacks, and sometimes full meals. Many of the more long-established cafés are downtown, congenial places with a European emphasis; indeed they're often determinedly Left Bank in feel (like the grouping at the junction of Bleecker and MacDougal streets) and perfect for lingering or just resting up between sights. The more upscale midtown **hotels** are good places to stop for tea too, if you can afford the prices they charge for the English country-house atmosphere they often try to contrive.

American food and ethnic cuisines

American cooking, as served by New York restaurants, tends to be served in huge portions. Salads are frequently eaten with meals, not as a main course

Eating

but as an appetizer, and ordering one entails fielding more rapid questions as to the kind of dressing you want. Italian (more like European "French"), French (nothing like European "French"), Thousand Island, and blue cheese are the usual alternatives. When in doubt, go with the tried and true oil-and-vinegar option. Main dishes include steaks and burgers (which are near ubiquitous) and often a choice of fish and seafood. Vegetables will almost certainly include a choice of French fries and baked potato. Ordering a burger may be more complicated than you're used to: they're treated like regular steaks and you'll be asked how you want them cooked – rare, medium or well-done. (Only have them rare if you're sure of the quality of the meat.)

In New York City, at least, so-called American food inevitably fades into the background when you're confronted with the startling variety of **regional** variations and different **ethnic cuisines**. Among them, none has had so dominant an effect as Jewish food, to the extent that many **Jewish** specialities – bagels, pastrami, lox and cream cheese – are now considered archetypal New York. Others retain more specific identities. **Chinese** food, available not just in Chinatown but all over Manhattan, is most frequently (and familiarly) Cantonese, though many restaurants serve the spicier Szechuan and Hunan dishes. Chinese prices are usually among the city's lowest, especially in the numerous Fukinese take-out places, which are usually not very good. **Japanese** food is generally expensive – sushi (raw fish), in particular, is served as much for the aesthetic arrangement as for the taste, which you'll either love or hate. Other Asian cuisines include **Indian**, becoming more widespread though still nothing like as ubiquitous – or as good – as their British counterparts, and a broad and increasing sprinkling of **Thai**, **Korean** and **Indonesian** restaurants, all of which tend to be pricier than Chinese but not prohibitively so.

Irish food dominates the city's pubs, with corned beef (more like salt beef than the tinned British bully), cabbage and Irish stew. **Italian** cooking is also widespread and not terribly expensive, especially if you stick to pizza; as is **Spanish**, whose huge seafood paella dishes can make an economical night out for those in a group. **French** restaurants tend to be wildly overpriced, mediocre or both, although there are an increasing number of bistros and brasseries turning out authentic and reliable French nosh for attractive prices.

More realistically, a whole range of **eastern European** restaurants – Russian, Ukrainian, Polish and Hungarian – serve well-priced filling fare. Other sundry places include **Cuban-Chinese** and **Kosher-Chinese** hybrids, and any number of vegetarian and wholefood eateries to cater for any taste or fad. The key is to keep your eyes peeled and not be afraid to be adventurous. Eating is the great joy of being in New York, and it would be a shame to waste it on the familiar.

Restaurant prices

New York's ethnic make-up is at its most obvious and accessible in the city's restaurants. Don't, however, make the mistake of assuming ethnic food is necessarily inexpensive. Often it's not. You pay Manhattan's highest prices for the better Italian, French and Japanese eateries; Greek and Spanish food, too, often work out to be expensive, and really only Chinese, Jewish and east European (and sometimes Mexican) are dependably low-budget. (One other thing to bear in mind is that these days many of New York's better and more affordable ethnic restaurants are in the Outer Boroughs.) Selections given here shouldn't break the bank, and at lunchtime you'll often find special deals or set menus – though we have tried to include the best of Manhattan's restaurants as well as the cheapest. The listings that follow are by neighborhood and then country of origin, with closing sections on seafood and vegetarian options.

More on ethnic food – our divisions and where to find it

AMERICAN, LATIN AND SOUTH AMERICAN

Dishes from these cuisines often overlap, so the restaurants are grouped together here for simplicity. Regional American restaurants can be fairly sedate, and portions are consistently generous. Some serve interesting regional variations, like **Southern**, **Southwestern**, and **Cajun Creole**. In the past few years there has been an eruption of **Contemporary American** restaurants, which serve French-tinged traditional American fare with a light and creative twist. **Tex-Mex** cuisine is a common hybrid all over America (though not at its best in New York City); it's honest grub by any standards, and as variable as you might expect, although you always get plenty and there are no extras to push up the bill.

ASIAN

Chinese cuisine provides one of the city's best bargains, particularly if you pick up dim sum and other lunchtime specials. As far as areas go, Chinatown not surprisingly has the highest restaurant concentration, but there's another good contingent in the Upper West Side 90s. More expensively, **Thai** food has become more prevalent of late, and you'll find Thai restaurants springing up all over Manhattan, as well as an increasing number of **Vietnamese** restaurants – many of which are, like Chinese spots, quite inexpensive.

FRENCH

French restaurants tend to trade on their names in New York: those that are good know it and make you pay accordingly, although a handful have slipped through with value-for-money intact. Beware the wine list: prices for French vintages can be considerably more than Californian wines of comparable quality.

GREEK AND MIDDLE EASTERN

While **Greek** restaurants are plentiful, few make it on to anyone's list of top ten places to eat: vegetarians in particular may be faced with few options, and for the best Greek cooking you should head for Astoria in Queens, home turf of most of the city's Greek population. Greek tends to be pricey for what you get, as do the city's **Turkish** restaurants. Other than a handful of places serving pita-related snacks, **Middle Eastern** food was rather thin on the ground in Manhattan till recently; some splendid restaurants of Saharan origin have now begun to crop up.

INDIAN, PAKISTANI, AFRICAN

Two good places to look for **Indian** food in New York are in midtown Manhattan, along Lexington Avenue between 28th and 30th streets, and (much cheaper) in the East Village, on the block-long stretch of 6th Street between First and Second avenues – the latter one of the city's best budget eating options. Budget **African** restaurants are becoming increasingly common, their pulse-based meals almost always including vegetarian options.

ITALIAN

Little Italy is the most obvious location for **Italian** food, though much of the area is geared toward tourists these days and consequently can be pricey: pick with care. For the real thing it's again best to head out to the Outer Boroughs – Belmont in the Bronx or Carroll Gardens in Brooklyn – or content yourself with pizza, either from *Ray's* (or a similar snack joint), or a regular sit-down restaurant.

JAPANESE

When sushi arrived on the scene in the 1980s, **Japanese** food took off in a big way, and it's still one of the city's most popular cuisines. It tends to be expensive, however, with many of the restaurants in the pricier reaches of midtown Manhattan. But if you know where to go

Eating

Eating

Glossary of American food terms for foreign visitors

Term	Definition	Term	Definition
A la mode	With ice cream	*Hero*	Sandwich made with French bread
Au jus	Meat served with a gravy made from its own juices	*Home fries*	Thick-cut fried potatoes, often cooked with onions and spiced with pepper
BLT	Bacon, lettuce and tomato toasted sandwich		
		Jello	Jelly
Broiled	Grilled	*Jelly*	Jam
Brownie	A gooey biscuit of chocolate and fudge	*Maitre d'*	Head waiter
		Muffin	Leavened cake made with bran, blueberry, etc.
Brunch	Originally a meal between breakfast and lunch; now a midday meal at weekends		
		Pecan pie	Dessert dish made of pastry, pecan nuts and caramel syrup
Caesar salad	Lettuce in egg dressing with anchovy paste, olives and lemon served with garlic croutons and Parmesan cheese	*Popsicle*	Ice lolly
		Potato chips	Crisps
		Pretzels	Savory circles of glazed pastry
Check	Bill	*Scrod*	Young Atlantic cod
Clam chowder	A thick soup made with clams and other seafood. Very tasty and, with bread, almost a meal in itself	*Seltzer*	Fizzy/soda water
		Sherbet	Sorbet
		Shrimp	Prawns
		Soda	Generic term for any soft drink
Club sandwich	Traditionally, a triple-decker sandwich with various combinations of meats, cheese, lettuce and tomato	*Soft-shell crab*	A kind of crab with a soft edible shell. Eating an entire crab shell and all may be a bit hard to get used to, but persevere – it's rightly considered a delicacy on the East Coast
Doggy bag	Not a bag but a stylish wrapping-up of your leftovers for reheating later at home		
		Squash	Marrow
		Tab	Bill
Egg cream	Neither eggs nor cream but a drink containing milk, chocolate or vanilla syrup and seltzer	*Teriyaki*	Chicken or beef, marinated in soy sauce and grilled
Eggplant	Aubergine	*Waffles*	Like pancakes but thicker and crispier; egg batter cooked in an iron and served with maple syrup or honey and butter
English muffin	Toasted bread roll, similar to a crumpet		
Fillet	The same as in England but pronounced "fillay"		
Frank	Frankfurter (hot dog)		
(French) fries	Chips	*Waldorf salad*	Celery, chopped apple and walnuts served on lettuce leaves with a mayonnaise dressing
Half-and-half	Half cream, half milk		
Hash browns	Mashed potato shaped into cubes and fried in fat		
		Zucchini	Courgettes

Glossary of ethnic food terms

Eating

Jewish

The Jewish faith allows two types of restaurant: those in which meat can be eaten and those where dairy products can be consumed. The two types of cooking can't be mixed. This section includes some Russian and Ukrainian dishes, which, though occasionally spelled differently on menus, are often much the same.

Bagel	Hard bread roll, in the shape of a ring, often toasted
Blintz	Crêpe filled with cheese or fruit and eaten with sour cream
Borscht	Beetroot soup
Challah	Egg-bread, eaten traditionally as part of the Friday evening Sabbath meal
Falafel	(Middle Eastern) Deep-fried spiced chick pea balls
Glatt kosher	Type of cuisine and restaurant catering to the diet of ultra-orthodox Jews
Kasha	Cracked buckwheat cooked until tender and served with soup or as a side dish
Knaidel	Flour dumpling. Also known as matzo balls
Knish	Pastry filled with cheese, meat, potato, fruit or anything else that comes to hand
Kreplach	Noodle-dough shells filled with kasha, meat, potato, etc.
Kugel	Potato or noodle pudding
Lox	Smoked salmon
Matzo	Flat unleavened bread eaten all year round but particularly at Passover
Pareve	Term for "neutral," i.e. something that can be eaten with meat or dairy food
Pirogen	Baked envelopes of dough filled with potato, meat or cheese
Schmaltz	Chicken fat
Tzimmes	Literally "a mixture." Casserole of meat, vegetables and fruit

Italian

Al forno	Cooked in the oven
Alfredo	Tossed with cream, butter and cheese
Alla carbonara	Sauce made with bacon and egg
Alla Veneziana	Cooked with onions and white wine
Cacciatore	"Hunter's style" – cooked with tomatoes, mushrooms, herbs and wine
Calzone	Pizza folded in half so the topping is inside
Posillipo	Tomato cooked with garlic, Neapolitan style
Puttanesca	Literally "whore style," cooked with tomato, garlic, olives, capers and anchovies
Zabaglione	Dessert of whipped egg yolks, sugar and Marsala

Pasta

Cannelloni	Large pasta tubes, stuffed with minced meat and tomato and baked
Cappelleti	"Little hats" stuffed with chicken, cheese and egg
Cappelli d'angeli	"Angel's hair," very fine pasta strands
Fettuccine	Flat ribbons of pasta
Fusilli	Pasta spiral
Gnocchi	Pasta and cheese dumplings
Linguine	Flat pasta noodles, like fettuccine

Eating

Manicotti	Squares stuffed with cheese; ravioli are the same, only with meat
Tortellini	Rings of pasta stuffed with either spiced meat or cheese
Vermicelli	Very thin spaghetti
Ziti	Small tubes of pasta, often baked with tomato sauce

Japanese

California roll	Mild-tasting sushi with a slice of avocado
Gyoza	Meat and vegetable dumplings
Karagei	Fried chicken
Larmen	Noodles in spicy broth
Negimayaki	Sliced beef with scallions
Okonomi	Literally "as you like it," used with regard to sushi when choosing the topping
Sake	Strong rice wine, drunk hot
Sashimi	Thinly sliced raw fish eaten with soy sauce or wasabi
Soba	Thin rice noodles, best cold
Sushi	Raw fish wrapped up in rice in seaweed. See also below
Tempura	Seafood and vegetables deep-fried in batter
Tonkatsu	Deep-fried pork with rice
Udon	Thick buckwheat noodles in broth
Wasabi	Hot green horseradish sauce

Sushi/Sashimi

Anago	Sea eel
Chirashi	Mixed fish on rice
Ebi	Shrimp
Ikura	Salmon roe
Kappa (*maki*)	Cucumber with rice and seaweed
Maguro	Tuna
Nigiri	Rice topped with fish
Tai	Red snapper
Tekka (*maki*)	Tuna with rice rolled in seaweed (*nori*)
Toro	Extra meaty part of the tuna

Chinese

Cantonese	Szechuan/Hunan	
Chow	Chao	Stir-fried
Daofu	Doufu	Bean curd
Fun, fon	Fun	Rice
Gai, gee	Ji	Chicken
Har, ha	Xia	Shrimp (prawns)
Siu	Shao	Roasted
Jyu yuk	Zhu rou	Pork
Ngow yuk	Niu rou	Beef
Opp, opp	Ya	Duck
Ow	Zha	Deep-fried
Yu	Yu	Fish

Dim Sum (Cantonese)

Bao, bau	Bun (generally steamed)
Cha siu bao	Steamed bun filled with sweet cubes of roast pork
Chow fun	Fried flat rice noodles
Chow mai fun	Fried rice vermicelli
Har gow	Steamed shrimp dumplings
Jook	Congee, or rice gruel
Kow, gow	Dumplings
Lo mein	Stir-fried noodles
Mai fun	Rice noodles
Tong mein	Soup noodles
Wonton, won ton	Thin-skinned dumplings filled with fish, usually served in broth

Greek

Baklava	Very sweet, flaky pastry with nuts and honey
Dolmades	Vine leaves stuffed with rice and meat
Feta	Crumbly white cheese made with goat's milk
Gyro	Minced lamb
Horta	Greens, often dandelion leaves
Kasseri	Rubbery cheese made with sheep's milk
Kokeretsi	Grilled lamb innards

Moussaka	Baked aubergine pie, topped with cheese sauce		and chili, and used as a topping
Pastitsio	Lamb pie topped with macaroni	Margarita	The cocktail to drink in a Mexican restaurant, made with tequila, triple sec, lime juice and limes, and blended with ice to make slush. Served with or without salt
Souvlaki	Shish kebab		
Spanakopita	Spinach pie		
Stifado	Lamb stew		
Taramasalata	Paste made of cod's roe, olive oil and lemon juice		
Tiropita	Cheese pie	Mariscos	Seafood
Tzatziki	Yoghurt with garlic and cucumber	Menudo	Soup made from a cow's stomach, said to be a cure for hangovers
		Nachos	Tortilla chips topped with melted cheese
Mexican			
Arroz	Rice, usually prepared in tomato sauce	Quesadilla	Folded soft tortilla containing melted cheese
Burritos	Folded tortillas stuffed with refried beans or beef, and grated cheese	Salsa	Chilies, tomato, onion and *cilantro*, served in varying degrees of spiciness
Chiles rellenos	Green chilies stuffed with cheese and fried in egg batter	Tacos	Folded, fried tortillas, stuffed with chicken, beef, pork or (occasionally) tongue
Enchiladas	Soft tortillas filled with meat and cheese or chilli and baked	Tamales	Corn mill dough with meat and chili, wrapped in a corn husk and baked
Fajitas	Soft flour tortillas served with a prawn, chicken or beef dish to wrap inside	Tortillas	Corn or flour dough pancakes used in most dishes
Frijoles	Refried beans, i.e. mashed fried beans	Tostada	Fried, flat tortillas, smothered with meat and vegetables
Guacamole	Thick sauce made from avocado, garlic, onion,		

Eating

it is possible to experiment reasonably cheaply.

JEWISH AND EASTERN EUROPEAN

The city's large **Jewish** community, most of whom originated in eastern Europe, means that kosher restaurants (serving dairy and non-dairy menus) are found all over town, with Manhattan's highest concentration in the East Village and Lower East Side. They cover all price ranges, but usually represent good, and very filling, value – as do the various and consistently delicious **Polish**, **Hungarian** and Ukrainian restaurants.

SPANISH

Downtown, in Greenwich Village especially, are a number of enjoyable **Spanish** restaurants, mostly not too pricey, and certainly nowhere near as expensive as their French counterparts. Paellas, often intended to be eaten by two, will cut costs, and house wines are affordable.

FISH AND SEAFOOD

Budget **fish restaurants** are a rarity in the city, especially since the area around the downtown fish market was dolled up into the South Street Seaport. However, fish and particularly seafood

Eating

remain something New York does extremely well, and a couple of the places listed here are among its most unmissable culinary treats – though they rarely come cheap.

VEGETARIAN

Surprisingly, exclusively **vegetarian** restaurants are a rarity in New York, although most places serve fish and poultry along with meatless dishes, and unless you're in a real carnivore's haven it's unusual to find a menu that doesn't have something completely meat-free.

New York's restaurants

The **listings** below follow (though not slavishly) the chapter divisions of our guide. For a quick refresher on the whereabouts of the following neighborhoods, turn to the map on p.54. For an overview of specialty restaurants see below.

Financial District and Civic Center

The culinary focal point of lower Manhattan is the *Fulton Fish Market*, so not surprisingly many of the restaurants in the **Financial District** and **Civic Center** serve seafood. Unfortunately, with few exceptions, most overcharge the power-broking lunch regulars for relatively unimpressive fare. And remember, the place revolves around trading hours, so many restaurants close early.

AMERICAN

Bridge Café, 279 Water St (at Dover St) ☎227-3344. They say there's been a bar here since 1794, but this place looks very up to the minute. The good crab cakes come from the local fish market, and there are plenty of upscale beers with which to wash them down.

Fraunces Tavern, 54 Pearl St (at Broad St) ☎269-0144. Where George Washington ate back when; they try to keep it as much like that as modern hygiene allows. The food's so-so, but atmosphere is the reason to come.

Hamburger Harry's, 157 Chambers St (between W Broadway and Greenwich St) ☎267-4446. Handy diner serving gourmet burgers with exotic toppings; a bit less elegant than its Theater District cousin. Some claim its burgers are the best in town.

Harry's at Hanover Square, 1 Hanover Square (between Pearl and Stone sts) ☎425-3412. Bar that gets into its stride when the floor traders come in after work. Great burgers, but only open during the work-week.

FISH AND SEAFOOD

Jeremy's Alehouse, 254 Front St (at Dover St) ☎964-3537. Once a waterside sleaze bar in the shadow of the Brooklyn Bridge, *Jeremy's* fortunes changed with the aggrandizement of the nearby South Street Seaport. However, it still serves well-priced pint mugs of beer and excellent fish fresh from the adja-

---

Specialty eating

In this chapter we've gathered together **particular types and styles of restaurant**, and places to eat that can't easily be listed elsewhere, and listed them on the following pages.

---

cent *Fulton Fish Market*, as well as burgers. Expect to spend $10, all told.

Johnny's Fish Grill, 4 World Financial Center ☎385-0333. Cozy New England-style seafood house featuring very fresh clams on the half-shell and superior grilled swordfish at moderate prices. Open Mon–Fri, serving dinner until 10pm.

Sloppy Louie's, 92 South St (at Fulton St) ☎509-9694. If you take in the South Street Seaport, you'll have a lot of fresh fish options. You could do worse than this clean, well-lit joint, where you can get in large combination platters just about anything that comes out of the nearby waters.

Chinatown, Little Italy and the Lower East Side

Three of New York's most prominent cuisines huddle together in these adjoining neighborhoods. If authentic Chinese, Thai and Vietnamese food is what you're after, best head for the busy streets of **Chinatown**, where you'll find *the* best budget eats in the city. Little Italy and the Lower East Side are less of a bargain but as much of an institution. Mulberry Street is **Little Italy**'s main drag, and though often crowded with Bridge and Tunnel weekend tourists, the southern Italian food and carnival atmosphere make dinner and coffee a worthwhile excursion. A turn down one street may leave you standing in front of an overpriced and quintessentially touristy restaurant. The next turn down a side street, and the **Lower East Side** at times seems like a throwback to early immigrant sweatshop days and others an overpriced and tourist experience. Either way, it's still the best place to get a pickle.

BAKERIES AND CAFÉS

Café Gitane, 242 Mott St (between Prince and Houston sts) ☎334-9552. Sunny little café serving coffee and creative light lunch fare.

Caffè Biondo, 141 Mulberry St (between Grand and Hester sts) ☎226-9285. A little brick-walled cappuccino shop with excellent Italian desserts.

Caffè Roma, 385 Broome St (between Mulberry and Mott sts) ☎226-8413. Old Little Italy pasticceria, ideal for a drawn-out coffee and pastry. Try the home-made Italian cookies, exceptionally good cannoli (plain or dipped), or gelato at the counter out back.

Ceci-Cela, 55 Spring St (between Mulberry and Lafayette sts) ☎274-9179. Tiny French patisserie with a stand-up counter and bench out front for immediate consumption of coffee and delectable baked goods. Croissants and palmiers are divine.

Ferrara's, 195 Grand St (between Mott and Mulberry sts) ☎226-6150. The best-known and most traditional of the Little Italy coffee houses, this neighborhood landmark has been around since 1892. Try the cheesecake, cannoli or granite (Italian ices) in summer. Outside seating.

AMERICAN, LATIN AND SOUTH AMERICAN

El Cibao, corner of Clinton and Rivington sts, no phone. The best of a slew of Dominican and Puerto Rican restaurants in the Lower East Side. Hearty and inexpensive fare, with great sandwiches, particularly the *pernil* (pork), toasted crisp in a sandwich press.

El Sombrero, corner of Stanton and Ludlow sts, no phone. Known to the local demimonde as "The Hat," this unprepossessing Mexican restaurant serves generous portions of wholesome food and wonderful frozen margaritas.

ASIAN

Bo Ky, 80 Bayard St (between Mott and Mulberry sts) ☎406-2292. Cramped Chinese-Vietnamese serving very inexpensive noodle soups and seafood dishes. The house specialty is a big bowl of rice noodles with shrimp, fish or duck.

Canton, 45 Division St at the Manhattan Bridge (between Bowery and Market sts) ☎226-4441. Fairly upscale compared to other Chinatown restaurants in terms of style and service, but only marginally

Eating

Eating

more expensive. Seafood is the specialty here; bring your own booze. Closed Mon and Tues.

Chinatown Ice Cream Factory, 65 Bayard St (between Mott and Elizabeth sts) ☎608-4170. A must after you've stuffed yourself in one of the restaurants nearby, but the wondrously unusual flavors make it good anytime. Specialties include green tea, ginger, almond cookie and lychee.

Excellent Dumpling House, 111 Lafayette St (between Canal and Walker sts) ☎219-0212. The thing to order is obviously the most highly excellent dumplings, any way you like them.

Joe's Shanghai, 9 Pell St (between Bowery and Doyers sts) ☎233-8888. New Chinatown entry of famed Queen's restaurant, this place is most always packed, with good reason. Start with the soup dumplings and work through some seafood dishes for the main course.

Nice Restaurant, 35 E Broadway (between Catherine and Market sts) ☎406-9510. Vast Cantonese restaurant especially good for dim sum (and barbecued duck). Usually crowded, particularly on Sundays.

Nom Wah, 13 Doyers St (between Bowery and Pell sts) ☎962-6047. A fairly mellow, even downbeat place to enjoy tea and Chinese snacks.

Oriental Pearl, 103 Mott St (between Hester and Canal sts) ☎219-8388. Great dim sum served in a huge and hectic Chinatown restaurant.

Pho Pasteur, 85 Baxter St (between Canal and Bayard sts) ☎608-3656. Quick, hot, and filling Vietnamese noodles. Very cheap.

Say Eng Look, 5 E Broadway (at Chatham Square) ☎732-0796. Good-value Shanghai restaurant that'll tailor your meal to fit your budget. Just tell them how much you can afford and they'll do the rest. They rarely miss.

Silver Palace, 50 Bowery (between Bayard and Canal sts) ☎964-1204. A predominantly dim sum restaurant. Take the escalator up to the enormous dining room with dragon pillars and peacock murals. Not recommended for vegetarians.

Thailand Restaurant, 106 Bayard St (at Baxter St) ☎349-3132. This Chinatown restaurant is a bit pricier than its neighbors, with entrées at about $15, but it's well worth the extra few dollars. The deep sea bass, crispy and spicy, is a standout.

Wo Hop, 17 Mott Street (between Canal St and Park Row) ☎267-2536. Heaping plates of food, many for less than $5. Anything with duck and noodles is recommended. Best of all, *Wo Hop* is open all night.

Wong Kee, 113 Mott St (between Canal and Hester sts) ☎226-9018/966-1160. Good, cheap, reliable Cantonese.

FISH AND SEAFOOD

20 Mott, 20 Mott St (at Canal St) ☎964-0380. The place for shark's-fin soup and other Hong Kong-style maritime delicacies.

Vincent's Clam Bar, 119 Mott St (at Hester St) ☎226-8133. Little Italy restaurant serving cheap, spicy seafood dishes – clams, mussels and squid.

ITALIAN

Benito I, 174 Mulberry St (between Grand and Broome sts) ☎226-9171; **Benito II**, 163 Mulberry St (between Grand and Broome sts) ☎226-9012. The smell of garlic lures you in to these two homey little Italian spots that serve simple Sicilian fare. Closed Sunday.

Grotta Azzurra, 387 Broome St (at Mulberry St) ☎925-8775. Bustling Little Italy institution that serves garlicky home-cooked Sicilian food. Closed Monday.

Il Fornaio, 132a Mulberry St (between Hester and Grand sts) ☎226-8306. Stylish, bright, tiled Italian restaurant with good lunch deals – fine calzone and pizza for $4. Affordable and decent southern Italian cooking, too – Italian stews and the like. Recommended.

La Luna, 112 Mulberry St (between Canal and Hester sts) ☎ 226-8657. Surrounded by the valet-parked limos and eating palaces of Little Italy, this must be one of the city's cheapest Italian restaurants: honest and unassuming in every way, from the vast peasant portions of pasta they serve to the gruff Brooklyn manner of the waiters and the fact that you have to walk through the kitchen to sit down.

La Mela, 167 Mulberry St (between Grand and Broome sts) ☎ 431-9493. Established Little Italy restaurant serving food in huge portions. A huge selection of pastas.

Pellegrino, 138 Mulberry St (between Hester and Grand sts) ☎ 226-3177. Laid-back Little Italy restaurant serving good food for good prices.

Puglia, 189 Hester St (between Mulberry and Mott sts) ☎ 226-8912. One of Little Italy's more affordable (and tacky) restaurants, where they cut costs and sharpen the atmosphere by sitting everyone at communal trestle tables. Consistently good southern Italian food, consumed loudly and raucously. Closed Monday.

JEWISH/EASTERN EUROPEAN

Katz's Deli, 205 E Houston St (between Essex and Ludlow sts) ☎ 254-2246. Cafeteria-style or sit down and be served. The pastrami or corned beef sandwiches, doused with mustard and with a side pile of pickles, should keep you going for about a week. If you've seen the movie *When Harry Met Sally*, you may recognize this as the site of the famous "orgasm" scene.

Ratner's, 138 Delancey St (between Norfolk and Suffolk sts) ☎ 677-5588. Massive dairy restaurant, crowded at all times of the day. High on atmosphere, though on the pricey side. Some of the best prune danishes in the city. Closed Sat.

Sammy's Roumanian Restaurant, 157 Chrystie St (between Delancey and Rivington sts) ☎ 673-0330. Surrounded by the boarded-up shopfronts of Chrystie

Street, *Sammy's* is some indication of just how far the Upper East Side is swayed by a restaurant's reputation. The food, if you've got $25 or so to burn for a full meal, is undeniably good, but most people come for the raucous live music. Remember: no *spritzing* your date with the seltzer bottles!

Yonah Schimmel's, 137 E Houston St (between Forsyth and Eldridge sts) ☎ 477-2858. Knishes, baked fresh on the premises, and wonderful bagels. Unpretentious and patronized by a mixture of wrinkled old men wisecracking in Yiddish and – on Sundays especially – young uptowners slumming it while they wade through the *New York Times*. Closed Saturday.

SoHo and TriBeCa

Still New York's two trendiest neighborhoods, in **SoHo** and **TriBeCa** you most often pay for the vista than the victuals. Even so, there are appropriately divine meals, and on occasion even deals, to be had. And the view's not bad either.

BAKERIES AND CAFÉS

Yaffa Tea Room, 353 Greenwich St (at Harrison St); 19 Harrison St (at Greenwich St) ☎ 274-9403. Hidden in an unassuming corner of TriBeCa these side-by-side restaurants serve Mediterranean-style dinners, good brunch and a cozy high tea (reservations required). Eclectic decor composed of flea market bric a brac finds.

AMERICAN, LATIN AND SOUTH AMERICAN

Bodega, 136 W Broadway (between Thomas and Duane sts) ☎ 285-1155. Across the street from its pricier sister, *Odeon* (see p.310), this family-style restaurant serves great burritos, burgers and home-cooked specials all for under $10 per entree.

Brisa del Caribe, 489 Broadway (at Broome St) ☎ 226-9768. Very good and very cheap rice and beans in an unlikely SoHo no-frills eatery.

Eating

Eating

Bubby's, 120 Hudson St (between Franklin and N Moore sts) ☎219-0666. A relaxed TriBeCa restaurant serving homey health-aware American food. Great scones, mashed potatoes, rosemary chicken, and soups.

Cupping Room Café, 359 W Broadway (between Broome and Grand sts) ☎925-2898. Absurdly quaint American restaurant that serves good wholesome food to live jazz on Friday and Saturday nights. Brunches are excellent, with huge portions of freshly baked breads and muffins, though you'll probably need to wait. Recommended.

Ear Inn, 326 Spring St (between Washington and Greenwich sts) ☎226-9060. Once an activist hangout, this bar/restaurant has cheap, basic pub fare (all under $10), a good jukebox, and a long-standing tradition of hosting poetry readings. Live folk and country music on Tuesday nights. Good draught *Guinness*, and tables with paper tablecloths with crayons for doodlers.

Elephant and Castle, 68 Greenwich Ave (between 6th and 7th aves) ☎243-1400. Old Village favorite serving up well-priced food and drink. Known for its burgers, excellent omelettes, and Caesar salad.

El Teddy's, 219 W Broadway (between Franklin and White sts) ☎941-7070. Eccentrically decorated restaurant that serves creative Mexican food, like goat cheese quesadillas, and the best margaritas in town. Try the fried tortillas wrapped around spicy chicken for starters. Entrées, around $15–19, are a little pricey.

Jerry's Restaurant, 101 Prince St (between Greene and Mercer sts) ☎966-9464. Casual American-French restaurant with a funky, upscale diner atmosphere. Good lox for brunch. Moderate prices. Closed Sun night.

La Cigalle, 231 Mott St (between Spring and Prince sts) ☎334-4331. A comfortable, quiet, garden-equipped eatery where you can have plain (pork chops, steak) or fancy (ceviche, farfalle), all good, relatively inexpensive, and served with a refreshing lack of pretension.

Layla, 211 W Broadway (at Franklin St) ☎431-0700. Middle Eastern theme restaurant from the *TriBeCa Grill* boys, where you can get a very nice $24 kebab, as well as calamari stuffed with merguez sausage. Belly-dancers add a great deal to the experience.

Moondance Diner, 80 6th Ave (between Grand and Canal sts) ☎226-1191. This authentic old diner car turns out cheap and filling meals of great burgers, omelettes and apple pancakes. Draught beers for $1 (Mon–Fri 4–7pm). Open 24 hours on weekends.

Nick and Eddie, 203 Spring St (at Sullivan St) ☎219-9090. Great home-cooked American food at modest prices. Has a pleasant outdoor garden.

Prince Street Bar, 125 Prince St (at Wooster St) ☎228-8130. SoHo bar and restaurant used by the local art-house clique. Broad array of different foods, and, for the area, not terribly expensive.

Silver Spurs, 490 LaGuardia (at Houston St) ☎228-2333. Brighter and better sister to the lower Broadway original. Burgers are the specialty, cooked on an open grill under metal pots to lock in the juices.

SoHo Kitchen and Bar, 103 Greene St (between Prince and Spring sts) ☎925-1866. Stylish burger-pizza-pasta place frequented by local gallery-goers. Average food, moderately priced, and supplemented, if you so wish, by a fine list of wines and beers. More than 100 wines offered by the glass and regular wine, beer and champagne tasting.

Spring Street Market, 111 Spring St (between Mercer and Greene sts) ☎226-4410. Wonderful deli. The best sandwiches downtown.

Tennessee Mountain, 143 Spring St (at Wooster St) ☎431-3993. Though situated in the heart of SoHo, this is a very un-SoHo-like restaurant, serving huge portions of barbecued meat and fish. A good value if you're hungry.

Eating

Breakfast: coffee shops and diners

You rarely have to walk more than a block or two in Manhattan to find somewhere that serves breakfast. Coffee shops and diners all over town serve up much the same array of discounted specials before 11am. But when you're desperate for a shot of early morning coffee, the following checklist should help you avoid traipsing too far from wherever you happen to be staying. You'll find full reviews elsewhere in this chapter; otherwise just expect standard American burgers, sandwiches and breakfasts.

Lower Manhattan

Around the Clock, 8 Stuyvesant St (between 2nd and 3rd aves) ☎598-0402

Bendix Diner, 219 8th Ave (at W 21st St) ☎366-0560

Jones Diner, 371 Lafayette (at Great Jones St) ☎673-3577

Kiev, 117 2nd Ave (at E 7th St) ☎674-4040

KK Restaurant, 192–194 1st Ave (between E 11th and 12th sts) ☎777-4430

Odessa, 117–119 Ave A (between E 7th St and St Mark's Place) ☎473-8916

Triumph Restaurant, 148 Bleecker St (between LaGuardia and Thompson sts) ☎228-3070

Veselka, 144 2nd Ave (between E 9th St and St. Mark's Place) ☎228-9682

Waverly Restaurant, 385 6th Ave (between W 8th St and Waverly Place) ☎675-3181

Midtown Manhattan

Broadway Diner, 590 Lexington Ave (at E 52nd St) ☎486-8838; 1726 Broadway (at W 55th St) ☎765-0909

Chez Laurence, 245 Madison Ave (between E 37th and 38th sts) ☎683-0284

Ellen's Stardust Diner, 1377 6th Ave (at W 56th St) ☎307-7575; 1650 Broadway (at W 51st St) ☎956-5151

Jerry's Metro Delicatessen, 790 8th Ave (at W 48th St) ☎581-9100

Market Diner, 572 11th Ave (at W 43rd St) ☎695-0415

Olympic Restaurant, 809 Eighth Ave (between W 48th and 49th sts) ☎956-3230

Upper Manhattan

EJ's Luncheonette, 433 Amsterdam Ave (between W 81st and 82nd sts) ☎873-3444

Googie's Diner, 1491 2nd Ave (at E 78th St) ☎717-1122

Gracie Mews Diner, 1550 First Ave (at E 81st St) ☎861-2290

Tom's Restaurant, 2880 Broadway (at W 112th St) ☎864-6137

Tramway Coffee Shop, 1143 2nd Ave (at E 60th St) ☎758-7017

Viand, 673 Madison Ave (between E 61st and 62nd sts) ☎751-6622

Westway Diner, 614 Ninth Ave (between 43rd and 44th St) ☎582-7661

TriBeCa Grill, 375 Greenwich St (at Franklin St) ☎941-3900. Part-owned by Robert de Niro, so some people come for a glimpse of the actor when they should really be concentrating on the food – fine American cooking with Asian and Italian accents at around $30 a main course. The setting is nice too; an airy, brick-walled eating area around a central Tiffany bar (rescued from the legendary Upper East Side singles' hangout, *Maxwell's Plum*). Well worth the money.

Zoë, 90 Prince St (between Broadway and Mercer St) ☎966-6722. One of SoHo's trendier places to eat, with a California-style setting and menu packed full of the intriguing and often delicious combinations. Not cheap; entrées are around $16–25, but chic and highly popular.

ASIAN

E&O, 100 W Houston St (at Thompson St), ☎254-7000. "Wok-seared filet

Eating

mignon" says it all: a mix of Southeast Asian cookery and rich American tastes. It's good, though, and the room is comfortable and attractive.

Kelley and Ping, 127 Greene St (between Prince and W Houston sts) ☎228-1212. Sleek pan-Asian restaurant that serves a tasty bowl of noodle soup. Dark wooden cases filled with Thai herbs and cooking ingredients add to the casually elegant setting.

Nobu, 105 Hudson St (at Franklin St) ☎219-0500. Robert De Niro's best-known New York restaurant. A lavish woodland decor complements already superlative Japanese cuisine.

Rice, 227 Mott St (between Prince and Spring sts) ☎ 226-5775. Small, inexpensive pan-Asian spot, where you mix-and-match various rices (black, sticky, etc) with interesting meat choices (lemongrass chicken, beef salad and the like).

Thai House Café, 151 Hudson St (at Hubert St) ☎334-1085. Small, friendly TriBeCa Thai restaurant, popular for its well-priced authentic food. Pad Thai and red curries are excellent. Closed Sun.

FRENCH

Capsouto Frères, 451 Washington St (at Watts St) ☎966-4900. Tucked away in a discreet corner of TriBeCa is this wonderful, if pricey, French bistro with a lofty feel. Dinner entrées are expensive, about $14–24. Try the duck with ginger and cassis and don't miss the dessert soufflés the *Frères* is best known for.

Chanterelle, 2 Harrison St (at Hudson St), ☎966-6960. One school of thought says, while in New York you should live on stale bread all week, and spend all your money on one of Chef David Waltuck's meals here. Haute cuisine of the finest order, with wines so rare you are advised to reserve your bottle ahead of time so they can properly decant it, all served impeccably in a small, stately room.

L'Ecole, 462 Broadway (at Grand St) ☎219-3300. Students of the French Culinary Institute serve up affordable French delights. They rarely miss. Closed Sun.

Manhattan Bistro, 129 Spring St (between Greene and Wooster sts) ☎966-3459. Your basic bistro – familiar French dishes, plus pastas and foccacia sandwiches – that has lasted in a fad-obsessed neighborhood because the food is well-prepared and not overpriced, and the room is classy and quiet.

Montrachet, 239 W Broadway (between Walker and White sts) ☎219-2777. Nouvelle cuisine food with a relaxed bistro ambience. The salmon and seared tuna are exceptional.

Odeon, 145 W Broadway (at Thomas St) ☎233-0507. Very long-established restaurant serving French Mediterranean food to a still largely chic clientele. Entrées go for around $15–20 and, on the whole, are worth it. Steak frites and crab fritters are recommended.

Provence, 38 MacDougal St (between Prince and Houston sts) ☎475-7500. Very popular SoHo bistro that serves excellent food but – at around $15–19 up for a main course – ain't that cheap. A nice place for a special occasion, though, with a lovely airy eating area and a garden for the summer.

Raoul's, 180 Prince St (between Sullivan and Thompson sts) ☎966-3518. French bistro seemingly lifted from Paris. The food, especially the *steak au poivre*, and service are wonderful, as you'd expect at these prices. Closed Aug.

GREEK AND MIDDLE EASTERN

Delphi, 109 W Broadway (at Reade St) ☎227-6322. Accommodating Greek restaurant with good menu, great portions and unbeatable prices. The antipasti and fish are excellent value at $8–10.75 or there's kebabs and the like from $7–10 and sandwiches as low as $3.75. Best Manhattan choice for bargain Greek eating.

INDIAN, PAKISTANI, AFRICAN

Abyssinia, 35 Grand St (between 6th Ave and W Broadway) ☎226-5959. A comfy

Ethiopian restaurant popular with a youthful crowd. A good array of vegetarian dishes.

ITALIAN

Arturo's, 106 W Houston St (at Thompson St) ☎677-3820. Coal oven pizza comparing favorably to *John's* in the West Village, and a lot less crowded. Sidewalk dining in warm weather.

JEWISH/EASTERN EUROPEAN

Triplet's Roumanian, 11–17 Grand St (at 6th Ave) ☎925-9303. Noisy neighborhood restaurant that is like crashing a loud Jewish wedding. Egg creams made at your table are a real highlight. A guaranteed blast. Closed Mon and Tues.

VEGETARIAN

Bell Caffè, 310 Spring St (between Greenwich and Hudson sts) ☎334-2355. Cheap crunchy granola-style fare in an unhurried atmosphere.

Spring Street Natural Restaurant, 62 Spring St (at Lafayette St) ☎966-0290. Pricier, and not wholly vegetarian, but very good. From $9.

Greenwich Village

The bohemian edge that once characterized the **West Village** became the most seductive of marketing ploys, attracting visitors from near and far. Now restaurants are overcrowded and overpriced, particularly in and around the New York University area. Move a little west to Hudson or north toward the meat packing district and you'll find some cosier Continental nooks. In spite of tourist traffic, the hub of Italian cafés around Bleecker and MacDougal remains a good place to recuperate with a healthy infusion of sugar and caffeine.

BAKERIES AND CAFÉS

Anglers & Writers, 420 Hudson St (at St Luke's Place) ☎675-0810. Village café serving high tea from 4pm to 7pm, as well as decent Continental fare – soups and desserts are a specialty. A good place to just have a coffee, a snack or a full meal.

Café Le Figaro, 184 Bleecker St (at MacDougal St) ☎677-1100. Former Beat hangout during the 1950s and the ersatz Left Bank at its finest. If you want to watch weekend tourists flooding West Village streets, this is a good place to do it.

Caffè Dante, 79 MacDougal St (between Bleecker and Houston sts) ☎982-5275. A morning stopoff for many locals since 1915. Good cappuccino, double espresso and caffè alfredo with ice cream. Often jammed with NYU students and teachers.

Caffè Reggio, 119 MacDougal St (between Bleecker and W 3rd sts) ☎475-9557. One of the first Village coffee houses, dating back to the 1920s, usually crowded and with tables outside for people- or tourist-watching.

Caffè Vivaldi, 32 Jones St (between Bleecker and W 4th sts) ☎929-9384. An old-fashioned Viennese-style coffee house with fireside coziness.

Peacock Caffè, 24 Greenwich Ave (between W 10th and Charles sts) ☎242-9395. Puccini arias as background music accompany rich desserts, hot chocolate, and Café Royale – coffee with whipped cream.

Rumbul's Pastry Shop, 20 Christopher St (between Gay St and Waverly Place) ☎924-8900; 559 Hudson St (between Perry and W 11th sts) ☎929-8783. Dark wood café with huge slices of rich cakes and other baked goods.

Tea and Sympathy, 108 Greenwich Ave (between W 12th and 13th sts) ☎807-8329. Self-consciously British tearoom, serving an afternoon high tea full of traditional British staples like jam roly-poly and treacle pud, along with shepherd's pie and scones. Perfect for British tourists feeling homesick.

AMERICAN, LATIN AND SOUTH AMERICAN

Aggie's, 146 W Houston St (at MacDougal St) ☎673-8994. Funky

Eating

Eating

upscale diner serving fresh and generous, if a bit overpriced, salads and sandwiches. *Aggie's* friendly cats roam their turf while you eat.

Bagel Buffet, 406 6th Ave (between W 8th and 9th sts) ☎477-0448. Wide selection of fillings and good-value bagel salad platters for around $5. Open 24 hours.

Benny's Burritos, 113 Greenwich Ave (at Jane St) ☎633-9210; 93 Avenue A (at E 6th St) 254-2054. Huge burritos with all kinds of fillings and speedy service. Cheap too. First-rate margaritas.

Brother's Bar-B-Q, 275 Varick St (between Clarkson and W Houston sts) ☎727-2775. They've moved to a large room with kitschy Dixie-ana displays, but still serve some of the best barbecue food north of the Mason-Dixon line. The mashed potatoes and collard greens are not to be missed. Cheap too – two people can eat handsomely for around $20.

Caliente Cab Co, 61 7th Ave (at Bleecker St) ☎243-8517. Average Tex-Mex food but with some good bargains: Mon–Fri happy hour (4–8pm) has free bar food; weekend brunch buffet (Sat & Sun noon–3pm) comes with as many margaritas, mimosas or screwdrivers as you can drink.

Caribe, 117 Perry St (between Hudson and Greenwich sts) ☎255-9191. A funky Caribbean restaurant filled with a leafy jungle decor and blasted with reggae music. Jerk chicken, washed down with wild tropical cocktails, makes it the place for a fun night out. Entrées in the range of $7–10.

Carmella's Village Garden, 49 Charles St (at W 4th St) ☎242-2155. Cheap café serving omelettes, pasta and the like for $5 up.

Corner Bistro, 331 W 4th St (at the corner of 8th Ave and W 12th St) ☎242-9502. Somewhat dark and dingy pub with cavernous cubicles and healthy servings of burgers, fries, beer, and desserts for reasonable prices. Long-standing haunt of West Village literary and arty types.

Cowgirl Hall of Fame, 519 Hudson St (at W 10th St) ☎633-1133. Down-home Texan-style barbecue amidst cowboy kitsch and memorabilia. Huge selection of tequilas served in a glass cowboy boot. Try the meaty ribs or chicken-fried chicken.

Dave's Pot Belly, 94 Christopher St (at Bleecker St) ☎242-8036. Friendly all-night restaurant with inexpensive American food in very large helpings – burgers for around $9. The desserts are easily enough for two.

Day-O, 103 Greenwich Ave (at W 12th St) ☎924-3161. A young crowd enjoys the grub at this downtown Caribbean/Southern joint. Deadly tropical drinks too.

Drover's Tap Room, 9 Jones St (between Bleecker and West 4th sts) ☎627-1233. Owned by the same people who made *Home* a local institution, this microbrew-centric boîte serves solid American-style food and bar chow.

Flying Fish, 395 West St (between Christopher and W 10th sts) ☎924-5050. Crowded Caribbean place that sells cheap Jamaican food.

Fuddrucker's, 87 7th Ave South (between Barrow and Grove sts) ☎255-9349. Burger restaurant imported from Texas, and serving suitably giant-size burgers and other down-home American food. Outdoor seating when it's warm enough.

Home, 20 Cornelia St (between Bleecker and W 4th sts) ☎243-9579. There's no place like it, as the saying goes. *Home* is one of those rare restaurants that manages to pull off quaint and cozy with flair. Creative American food is always fresh and wonderful, perhaps a better deal at lunch than dinner. Try the cheese fondue or cumin-crusted pork chops.

Lupe's East LA Diner, 110 6th Ave (at Watts St) ☎966-1326. Very laid-back, hole-in-the-wall restaurant serving excellent burritos and enchiladas. Good fun, and cheap.

Mi Cucina, 57 Jane St (at Hudson St) ☎627-8273. Authentic Mexican food (but without the grease) in a simple setting. Good prices – entrées in the range of $9–14.

The Pink Teacup, 42 Grove St (between Bleecker and Bedford sts) ☎807-6755. Long-standing soul-food institution in the heart of the Village. Relatively inexpensive, homey, and filling.

Riviera Café, 225 W 4th St (at 7th Ave) ☎242-8732. Central Village restaurant serving acceptable food at low prices. In the 1960s this was very much the place to be seen.

Shopsin's General Store, 63 Bedford St (at Morton St) ☎924-5160. Leave your attitude at the door when you come to *Shopsin's*. This tiny family-run restaurant serves a Bible-length menu of soups and sandwiches. Closed weekends . . . because they feel like it.

Tortilla Flats, 767 Washington St (at W 12th St) ☎243-1053. Cheap West Village Mexican dive with great margaritas, a loud jukebox, and plenty of kitsch.

Violet Café, 80 Washington Square Park East (at W 4th St) ☎529-5428. Coffee shop-cum-restaurant popular with NYU students. Best for inexpensive sandwiches and breakfasts. Closed Sunday.

ASIAN

Omen, 113 Thompson St (between Prince and Spring sts) ☎925-8923. Zen-inspired SoHo spot featuring authentic Kyoto flavors and flair.

Toons, 417 Bleecker St (at Bank St) ☎924-6420. Relatively high prices, but a low-lit place with an intimate atmosphere. A Thai community favorite.

FISH AND SEAFOOD

Jane Street Seafood Café, 31 8th Ave (at Jane St) ☎242-0003. A cozy New England-style seafood restaurant with moderate prices and friendly service. Something of a neighborhood favorite.

Le Pescadou, 18 King St (off 6th Ave, south of W Houston St) ☎924-3434. A trendy seafood bistro in a charming French setting. Moderate prices.

FRENCH

Au Troquet, 328 W 12th St (at Greenwich St) ☎924-3413. Romantic Village haunt that has an authentic Parisian feel. Decent food, moderately priced.

Café de Bruxelles, 118 Greenwich Ave (at W 13th St) ☎206-1830. Not French, but a very authentic – and popular – Belgian restaurant in Greenwich Village. Moderately priced, interesting food – try the *Waterzooi*, a rich and creamy chicken stew. Excellent frites and mussels for the less adventurous.

Chez Brigitte, 77 Greenwich Ave (between Bank St and 7th Ave) ☎929-6736. Only a dozen people fit in this tiny restaurant that serves homey soups, all-day roast meat dinner for under $10, and other bargains from a simple menu.

Chez Ma Tante, 189 W 10th St (between W 4th and Bleecker sts) ☎620-0223. A tiny French bistro that's most fun in summer, when the doors open out on to the street. NYC rustic, but charming nevertheless.

Chez Michallet, 90 Bedford St (at Grove St) ☎242-8309. A cozy Village version of a French country inn. Moderate to expensive but, at $19.95 for a three-course meal, the nightly prix fixe menu is great value.

Florent, 69 Gansevoort St (between Washington and Greenwich aves) ☎989-5779. Ultra-fashionable bistro on the edge of the meat-packing district that serves good French food, either à la carte or from a prix fixe menu ($18.50, or $16.50 before 7.30pm). Coffee shop decor, always busy. The mussels are so good it almost doesn't matter how obnoxious the waiters are. They also serve weekend brunch. Open late.

French Roast Café, 456 6th Ave (at W 11th St) ☎533-2233. A stylish café where you can while away hours reading the newspapers and magazines while drinking café au lait. Decent food and snacks; open 24 hours.

Eating

Eating

Smoker-friendly restaurants

At 12:00:01am on April 10, 1995 a hitherto inconceivable thing happened in New York: restaurants, or at least the majority of them, went **smokeless**. A complicated new law prohibits smoking in the dining area of all New York restaurants with a capacity of more than 35 people. In these restaurants, smoking is restricted to the bar area or designated enclosed lounges. Smoking is still permitted in bars and establishments that seat fewer than 35 persons. When in doubt, call ahead, or ask before you light up. What follows is a listing of some restaurants that, at the time of writing, continue to permit smoking.

Lower Manhattan

Admiral's Gallery, 160 South (at Dover St) ☎608-6455

Au Troquet, 328 W 12th St (at Greenwich St) ☎924-3413

Baby Jake's, 14 1st Ave (between E 1st and 2nd sts) ☎254-2229

Bayamo, 704 Broadway (between E 4th St and Washington Place) ☎475-5151

Bell Caffè, 310 Spring St (between Greenwich and Hudson sts) ☎334-2355

Benito I, 174 Mulberry St (between Grand and Broome sts) ☎226-9171

Café Tabac, 232 E 9th St (between 2nd and 3rd aves) ☎674-7072

Corner Bistro, 331 W 4th St (between W 12th and Jane sts) ☎242-9502

Cucina Della Fontana, 368 Bleecker St (at Charles St) ☎242-0636

Ear Inn, 326 Spring St (between Washington and Greenwich sts) ☎226-9060

El Teddy's, 219 W Broadway (between Franklin and White sts) ☎941-7070

Fanelli, 94 Prince St (at Mercer St) ☎226-9412

Florent, 69 Gansevoort St (between Washington and Greenwich aves) ☎989-5779

Gotham Bar & Grill, 12 E 12th St (between 5th Ave and University Place) ☎620-4020

Home, 20 Cornelia St (between Bleecker and W 4th sts) ☎243-9579

John's of 12th Street, 302 E 12th St (between 1st and 2nd aves) ☎475-9531

La Cigalle, 231 Mott St (between Spring and Prince sts) ☎334-4331

Le Pescadou, 18 King St (off Sixth Ave, south of West Houston St) ☎924-3434

La Bohème, 24 Minetta Lane (between W 3rd and Bleecker sts) ☎473-6447. Bright and amiable, if cramped, restaurant in the heart of the Village with pasta, brick-oven pizza, and meat and fish dishes for $12–15. Good food, and nice in the summer when they open the French doors to the street. Closed Sun and Mon during Aug.

La Metairie, 189 W 10th St (at W 4th St) ☎989-0343. Charming West Village bistro serving excellent French country fare. Entrées in the range of $14–24.

Paris Commune, 411 Bleecker St (between W 11th and Bank sts) ☎929-0509. Romantic West Village bistro with reliable French home cooking.

Memorable French toast and wild mushroom ravioli at moderate prices. Long lines for brunch.

ITALIAN

Arturo's Pizza, 106 W Houston St (at Thompson St) ☎475-9828. Moderate to expensive entrées and coal-oven pizzas big enough to share for even less. While-you-eat entertainment includes live music. Convivial, if not the cheapest feed in town.

Cent' Anni, 50 Carmine St (between Bleecker and Bedford sts) ☎989-9494. Small Village restaurant serving consistently delicious, and not overpriced, Florentine food.

Lucky Strike, 59 Grand St (between W Broadway and Wooster St) ☎941-0479

Raoul's, 180 Prince St (between Sullivan and Thompson sts) ☎966-3518

Rio Mar, 7 9th Ave (at W 12th St) ☎243-9015

TriBeCa Grill, 375 Greenwich St (at Franklin St) ☎941-3900

Midtown Manhattan

Aquavit, 13 W 54th St (between 5th and 6th aves) ☎307-7311

Blue Moon Café, 150 8th Ave (between W 17th and 18th sts) ☎463-0560

P.J. Clarke's, 915 3rd Ave (between E 55th and 56th sts) ☎759-1650

The Coffee Shop, 29 Union Square West (between E 16th and 17th sts) ☎243-7969

Dawat, 210 E 58th St (between 2nd and 3rd aves) ☎355-7555

El Rio Grande, 160 E 38th St (between Lexington and 3rd aves) ☎867-0922

La Bonne Soupe, 48 W 55th St (between 5th and 6th aves) ☎586-7650

Landmark Tavern, 626 11th Ave (between W 45th and 46th sts) ☎757-8595

Live Bait, 14 E 23rd St (between Broadway and Madison Ave) ☎353-2400

Mickey Mantle's, 42 Central Park South (W 59th St between 5th and 6th aves) ☎688-7777

Mike's American Bar & Grill, 650 10th Ave (between W 45th and 46th sts) ☎246-4155

Orson's, 175 Second Ave (between 11th and 12th sts) ☎475-1530

Oyster Bar, Lower level, Grand Central Terminal (at 42nd St and Park Ave) ☎490-6650

Symphony Café, 950 8th Ave (at W 56th St) ☎397-9595

Trattoria dell'Arte, 900 7th Ave (between W 56th and 57th sts) ☎245-9800

Zarela, 953 2nd Ave (between E 50th and 51st sts) ☎644-6740

Upper Manhattan

Asia, 1155 3rd Ave (between E 67th and 68th sts) ☎879-5846

Bangkok House, 1485 1st Ave (between E 77th and 78th sts) ☎249-5700

Bella Donna, 307 E 77th St (between 1st and 2nd aves) ☎535-2866

Madame Romaine de Lyon, 29 E 69th St (between Park and Madison aves) ☎759-5200

Rathbones, 1702 2nd Ave (between E 88th and 89th sts) ☎369-7361

Eating

Cucina Della Fontana, 368 Bleecker St (at Charles St) ☎242-0636. From the outside this place looks like a normal bar, but out the back there's a plant-filled atrium where you can eat fine Italian food. Mussels, fish, pasta all very good.

Cucina Stagionale, 275 Bleecker St (between 6th and 7th aves) ☎924-2707. Enormously popular restaurant in the West Village, with most dishes at around $6. Expect to wait in line, and bring your own wine – there's no license. Try the calamari or *pasta puttanesca.*

Ennio and Michael, 539 LaGuardia Place (between Bleecker and W 3rd sts)

☎677-8577. Old-fashioned Italian bistro favorite, intimate and homey.

John's Pizzeria, 278 Bleecker St (between 6th and 7th aves) ☎243-1680. No slices, no takeaways. One of the city's best and most popular pizzas. The crust is thin and coal-charred. Be prepared to wait in line. Uptown branches at 408 E 64th St (between 1st and York aves) ☎935-2895; and 48 W 65th St (between Columbus Ave and Central Park West) ☎721-7001.

Mezzogiorno, 195 Spring St (between Sullivan and Thompson sts) ☎334-2112. Bright SoHo restaurant that's as much a place to people-watch as eat. A little overpriced, but a good and inventive

Eating

menu, including excellent wood-burning-oven pizzas, great salads and carpaccio – thinly sliced raw beef served in various ways. Sister restaurant is *Mezzaluna* – see p.341.

Minetta Tavern, 113 MacDougal St (at Minetta Lane) ☎475-3850. One of the oldest bars in New York, decorated with murals showing Greenwich Village as it was in the 1930s. A restaurant out back turns out dependable Italian food.

MIDDLE EASTERN

Moustache, 90 Bedford St (between Grove and Barrow sts) ☎229-2220. There are scores of felafel joints in the West Village, but *Moustache* is a real step up: clean, delicious and clever as well. The gimmick is "pitza," fresh pitas with pizza-like toppings; better still is the lamb sandwich. It does take a while though.

SPANISH

Café Español, 63 Carmine St (at 7th Ave South) ☎675-3312; 172 Bleecker St (between MacDougal and Sullivan sts) ☎353-2317. Hole-in-the-wall restaurant serving garlicky Spanish fare for $10–15 a plate. Try the paella or *mariscada* – a filling seafood dish that can easily feed two.

El Faro, 823 Greenwich St (at Horatio St) ☎929-8210. A dark, lively restaurant, where garlic smells from the kitchen and the look of the food at the next table (it's that cramped!) are guaranteed to stir any appetite. You can't go wrong with the paella or seafood in green sauce. Moderate prices too, and you can share most main dishes.

Panchito's, 105 McDougal (between West 3rd and Bleecker sts) ☎473-5239. No, it's not "authentic," but so what? A big, lively and attractive room, with cheap and filling food (beans, rice, burritos). And the bar is excellent, with some very rare brandies.

Rio Mar, 7 9th Ave (at W 12th St) ☎243-9015. A welcoming Spanish restaurant that serves low-priced and authentic food, albeit in a fairly downbeat setting. Recommended.

Spain, 113 W 13th St (between 7th and 8th aves) ☎929-9580. Budget prices and large portions are the prime attractions of this cozy Spanish restaurant. Order the paella and split it with a friend.

VEGETARIAN

Eva's, 11 W 8th St (between 5th and 6th aves) ☎677-3496. Healthy food in a coffee-shop setting. Nice grub, speedily served, and very cheap. Try the vegetarian falafel combo.

Souen, 210 6th Ave (at Prince St) ☎807-7421; 28 E 13th St (between 5th Ave and University Place) ☎627-7150. Politically correct vegetarian seafood.

Vegetarians' Paradise, 144 W 4th St (between MacDougal St and 6th Ave) ☎260-7130; 33–35 Mott St (between Bayard and Worth sts) ☎460-6988; 48 Bowery ☎571-1535. East Village vegetarian Chinese – pricier than ordinary downtown Chinese restaurants but still pretty reasonable.

East Village

Less precious than its western counterpart, the **East Village** is a mixed bag of radicals, runaways, immigrants (mostly Puerto Ricans and older eastern Europeans), and an increasingly large number of young professionals. It seems a new upscale Italian restaurant, sushi bar, or trendy café opens every day on Avenue A. By contrast the homey and cheap restaurants of **Little India**, E 6th St between 1st and 2nd aves, and **Little Ukraine**, around E 7th to E 9th St between 1st and 3rd aves, remain consistently good and satisfying.

BAKERIES AND CAFÉS

Caffè Della Pace, 48 E 7th St (between 1st and 2nd aves) ☎529-8024. Dark and cozy East Village café with decent food and a great selection of coffees and desserts, especially the tiramisu.

Eating

Coffee and tea

Lately, New York has been invaded by cookie-cutter **coffee chains**, large and small, each professing to offer the final word in the java experience. Chains like *Starbuck's*, *New World Coffee*, *Pasqua*, *Dalton's*, *Timothy's*, *Seattle Coffee Roasters* are consistently good and serve just about any caffeinated concoction you can dream up. But when you're looking to get your caffeine high, you might just want a little more ambience. For that kind of mood, we suggest the following:

Lower Manhattan

@ Cafe, 12 St Mark's Place (between 2nd and 3rd aves) ☎979-5439

alt.coffee, 137 Ave A (between 9th and 10th sts) ☎529-2233

Anglers & Writers, 420 Hudson St (at St Luke's Place) ☎675-0810

Café Gitane, 242 Mott St (between Prince and Houston sts) ☎334-9552

Caffè Della Pace, 48 E 7th St (between 1st and 2nd aves) ☎529-8024

Caffè Vivaldi, 32 Jones St (between Bleecker and W 4th sts) ☎929-9384

Cyber Cafe, 273 Lafayette (at Prince St) ☎334-5140

Danal, 90 E 10th St (between 3rd and 4th aves) ☎982-6930

Dean and DeLuca Café, 121 Prince St (between Wooster and Greene sts) ☎254-8776; 75 University Place (at E 11th St) ☎473-1908

De Robertis, 176 1st Ave (between E 10th and 11th sts) ☎674-7137

Limbo, 47 Ave A (between E 3rd and 4th sts) ☎477-5271

Peacock Caffè, 24 Greenwich Ave (between W 10th and Charles sts) ☎242-9395

Rumbul's Pastry Shop, 20 Christopher St (between Gay St and Waverly Place) ☎924-8900; 559 Hudson St (between Perry and W 11th sts) ☎929-8783

Sticky Fingers, 131 Ave A (between St Mark's Place and E 9th St) ☎614-0560

T, 142 Mercer St (at Prince St) ☎925-3700

Tea and Sympathy, 108 Greenwich Ave (between W 12th and 13th sts) ☎807-8329

Thé Adoré, 17 E 13th St (between 5th Ave and University Place) ☎243-8742

Veniero's, 342 E 11th St (between 1st and 2nd aves) ☎674-4415

Yaffa Tea Room, 353 Greenwich St (at Harrison St) ☎274-9403

Midtown Manhattan

Algonquin Oak Room, 59 W 44th St (between 5th and 6th aves) ☎840-6800

Big Cup, 228 8th Ave (between W 21st and 22nd sts) ☎206-0059

City Bakery, 22 E 17th St (between Broadway and 5th Ave) ☎366-1414

Kaffeehaus, 131 8th Ave (between W 16th and 17th sts) ☎229-9702

News Bar, 2 W 19th St (between 5th and 6th aves) ☎255-3996; 366 W Broadway (at Broome St) ☎343-0053

Upper Manhattan

The Bread Shop, 3139 Broadway (at W 123rd St) ☎666-4343

Café Lalo, 201 W 83rd St (between Broadway and Amsterdam Ave) ☎496-6031

Café Mozart, 154 W 70th St (between Central Park West and Columbus Ave) ☎595-9797

Caffè la Fortuna, 69 W 71st St (between Central Park West and Columbus Ave) ☎724-5846

Food Attitude, 127 E 60th St (between Lexington and Park aves) ☎980-1818

Les Friandises, 922 Lexington Ave (between E 70th and 71st sts) ☎988-1616; 655 Amsterdam Ave (between W 92nd and 93rd sts) ☎316-1515

Eating

Cloister Café, 238 East 9th St (between 2nd and 3rd aves) ☎777-9128. Don't come here for the food, which hovers somewhere between bad and *really* bad. Come for the garden and a big bowl of coffee.

De Robertis, 176 1st Ave (between E 10th and 11th sts) ☎674-7137. Good, strong coffee in a small, cafeteria-style café, but desserts are better at *Veniero's* across the street.

Limbo, 47 Ave A (between E 3rd and 4th sts) ☎477-5271. Sweets are decent (the blackout cake is more than that) and the coffee is good. You end up sharing tables with would-be screenwriters and novelists. A good selection of magazines to read. Avoid the infrequent poetry readings.

Moishe's, 115 Second Ave (between E 7th St and St Mark's Place) ☎505-8555. The best prune danish in the city, excellent humentashen, seeded rye and other heavy kosher treats.

Sticky Fingers, 131 Ave A (between St Mark's Place and E 9th St) ☎614-0560. Friendly East Village refuge with kids' artwork on the wall. If you ask for your coffee extra-strong, you get it that way. Try smoothies, made with your choice of frozen fruits and milk, yoghurt or soy milk, in summer.

Taylor's, 175 2nd Ave (between E 11th and 12th sts) ☎674-9501; 523 Hudson St (between W 10th and Charles sts) ☎645-8200; 228 W 18th St (between 7th and 8th aves) ☎366-9081. They have soups and salads, but come for the oversized muffins and astonishing pastries. Try the monkey bread, a kind of sugary baked doughnut, or the zebra brownies. Flourless chocolate soufflé cake and blueberry muffins.

Thé Adoré, 17 E 13th St (between 5th Ave and University Place) ☎243-8742. Charming little tearoom with excellent pastries, scones, croissants and coffee. Sit upstairs and have a sandwich and a tasty bowl of soup. Closed weekends in the summer.

Veniero's, 342 E 11th St (between 1st and 2nd aves) ☎674-4415. East Village bakery and almost century-old institution that sells wonderful pastries and has a recently expanded seating area in the back. Desserts and decor are fabulously over-the-top. Try the ricotta cheesecake and homemade gelati in the summer.

AMERICAN, LATIN AND SOUTH AMERICAN

Around the Clock, 8 Stuyvesant St (between 2nd and 3rd aves) ☎598-0402. Centrally situated East Village restaurant serving crepes, omelettes, burgers and pasta at reasonable prices. Open 24 hours.

Baby Jake's, 14 1st Ave (between E 1st and 2nd sts) ☎254-2229. Funky East Village restaurant serving Cajun crab cakes, fried catfish, salmon fajitas, and po' boy delights.

Bayamo, 704 Broadway (between E 4th St and Washington Place) ☎475-5151. Chinese-Cuban food, served in vast portions at moderate prices – around $10–16 for entreés. Try the stir-fried duck with rice and Cuban chicken cutlets.

Boca Chica, 13 1st Ave (at 1st St) ☎473-0108. This is real Brazilian stuff, piled high and washed down with black beer and fancy, fruity drinks. It gets crowded, especially late and on weekends, and the music is loud, so come in a party mood.

Bowery Bar & Grill, 358 Bowery (at E 4th St) ☎475-2220. A former gas station turned restaurant serving overpriced and rather ordinary fare, but the place to be for the terminally hip.

First, 87 1st Ave (between E 5th and 6th sts) ☎674-3823. Sophisticated East Village newcomer serving innovative combinations of New American fare, like tuna *steak au poivre* and double-thick pork chops. Moderately priced – entrées average about $14.

Great Jones Café, 54 Great Jones St (between Bowery and Lafayette St) ☎674-9304. Blackened catfish, Cajun popcorn, molasses cornbread, beer and

Cajun martinis in an intentionally hip and divy neighborhood restaurant. Southern weekend brunch highlight: andouille-peppered Crescent City eggs with grits and biscuits 'n' gravy.

Life Café, 343 E 10th St (between Ave A and B) ☎477-8791. Peaceful and long-established East Village haunt right on Tompkins Square that hosts sporadic classical and other music concerts. Food is sandwiches, California/Mexican, and vegetarian – plates all around $8–10.

Marion's Continental Restaurant and Lounge, 354 Bowery (between Great Jones and E 4th sts) ☎475-7621. Superb *steak au poivre* and martinis in a casually elegant atmosphere. Turf is consistently better than surf.

Miracle Grill, 112 First Ave (between E 6th and 7th sts) ☎254-2353. Moderately priced Southwestern specialties with interesting taste combinations and an attractive garden out back. Save room for the vanilla bean flan.

Old Devil Moon, 511 E 12th St (between Ave A and B) ☎475-4375. Filled with thrift store *tchotchkes*, this restaurant and East Village hangout serves enormous brunch portions, most notably the Road Side breakfast (sloppy, greasy and perhaps better described as "road kill"). Try the catfish sandwich or corn meal pancakes with fresh fruit of the day.

Pedro Paramo, 430 E 14th St (between 1st Ave and Ave A) ☎475-4851. Authentic Mexican in a quiet, homey restaurant. Have a mole and an excellent margarita. Entrées are about $8–12.

Stingy Lulu's, 129 St Mark's Place (between 1st Ave and Ave A) ☎674-3545. This retro diner serves decent simple fare and is a good place to people-watch.

Time Café, 380 Lafayette St (between Great Jones and E 4th sts) ☎533-7000. Happening restaurant with an eclectic California-Southwestern menu and a downstairs lounge, *Fez*, that offers poetry readings, regular live jazz (usually on Wednesdays) or just a cozy place to drink.

ASIAN

Dok Suni, 119 1st Ave (between E 7th St and St Mark's Place) ☎447-9506. This dimly lit chic East Village restaurant has fast become a favorite for Korean home cooking. Try the spicy squid and black bean rice.

Indochine, 430 Lafayette St (between E 4th and Astor Place) ☎505-5111. Not the kind of place you go to save money; more to lap up the elegant surroundings and French-Vietnamese food. Good people-watching, too.

Japonica, 100 University Place (at E 12th St) ☎243-7752. Some of the freshest sushi in the city, at some of the most reasonable prices. Sat and Sun brunch deals are excellent – big plates of sushi or sashimi (teriyaki too), with salad and beer or plum wine for around $12 a head. Be prepared to wait in line after 7pm.

Lucky Cheng's, 24 1st Ave (between 1st and 2nd sts) ☎473-0516. Creative combinations of California and Asian cuisines, with many vegetarian options, served by fabulous waiters in drag. $6–16 for entrées.

Mee Noodle Shop, 219 1st Ave (between E 13th and 14th sts) ☎995-0333; 922 2nd Ave (at E 49th St) ☎888-0027. You can create endless combinations of noodles, broths and toppings at *Mee*. The food is so well-priced that you won't notice the lack of decor. Try Mee Fun Soup with chicken or Dan Dan noodles, served with black mushrooms in a spicy meat sauce.

Sapporo Village Japanese Restaurant, 245 E 10th St (at 1st Ave) ☎260-1330. You're better off with noodles since the sushi isn't always up to par. The remarkably low prices keep this restaurant crowded and lively.

Shabu Tatsu, 216 E 10th St (between 1st and 2nd aves) ☎477-2972. Great Japanese barbecue. Choose a combination of foods, and cook them at your table.

Siam Square, 92 2nd Ave (between E 5th and 6th sts) ☎505-1240. Small restau-

Eating

Eating

Bagels

Theories abound as to the origin of the modern **bagel**. Most likely, it is a derivative of the pretzel, with the word *bagel* coming from the German *beigen*, "to bend." Modern-day bagels are probably softer and have a smaller hole than their ancestors – the famous hole made them easy to carry on a long stick to hawk on street corners. Whatever their birthplace, it is certain that bagels have become a **New York institution**. Since they are boiled before being baked, bagels have a characteristically chewy texture. They can be served with white fish, red onions, tomatoes or, most famously, with cream cheese and lox (smoked salmon).

Until the 1950s bagels were still hand-crafted by eastern European Jewish immigrants in two- or three-man cellars scattered around New York's Lower East Side. Today they can be found **almost everywhere**, but here is a list of some of the better bagelsmiths.

Bagel Buffet, 406 6th Ave (between W 8th and 9th sts) ☎477-0448

Bagel Palace, 36 Union Square (between 16th St and Park Ave South) ☎673-0452

Bagelry, 1324 Lexington Ave (between E 88th and 89th sts) ☎996-0567

Bagels on the Square, 7 Carmine Street (between Bleecker St and 6th Ave) ☎691-3041

Columbia Hot Bagels, 2836 Broadway (between W 110th and 111th sts) ☎222-3200

Ess-A-Bagel, 359 1st Ave (at E 21st St) ☎260-2252

H & H Bagels, 2239 Broadway (at W 80th St) ☎595-8000

Yonah Schimmel's, 137 E Houston St (between Forsyth and Eldridge sts) ☎477-2858

---

rant serving decent Thai food for reasonable prices. Fine service, tacky decor.

Takahachi, 85 Ave A (between E 5th and 6th sts) ☎505-6524. Superior sushi, the best in the neighborhood, at affordable prices. For dinner you'll probably have to wait.

FISH AND SEAFOOD

Pisces, 95 Ave A (between E 6th and 7th sts) ☎260-6660. Innovative and fresh fish combinations and sinful desserts. A great seafood value.

FRENCH

Bel Air, 110 St Mark's Place (between Ave A and 1st Ave). ☎677-6563 Casual, open-air restaurant, with limited but winning menu. Try the skate, served over greens.

Danal, 90 E 10th St (between 3rd and 4th aves) ☎982-6930. Charming and cozy French café in what used to be an antiques store. French toast made with croissants and topped with cinnamon

apples. Great for dinner, brunch and high tea. Closed Mon and Tues.

Jules, 65 St Mark's Place (between 1st and 2nd aves) ☎477-5560. Comfortable and authentic French restaurant, a rarity in the East Village, serving up adequate bistro fare.

Opaline, 85 Ave A (between E 5th and 6th sts) ☎475-5050. It's hip, it's loud, it has roast ostrich – but you can also get crepes and confit, and you don't have to dress up (but bring a full wallet).

GREEK AND MIDDLE EASTERN

Khyber Pass, 34 St Mark's Place (between 2nd and 3rd aves) ☎473-0989. Afghan food, which, if you're unfamiliar, is filling and has plenty to offer vegetarians (pulses, rice, eggplants are frequent ingredients). Excellent value for under $10.

INDIAN, PAKISTANI, AFRICAN

Gandhi, 345 E 6th St (between 1st and 2nd aves) ☎614-9718. One of the best and least expensive of the E 6th Street Indian restaurants.

Mingala Burmese, 21 E 7th St (between 2nd and 3rd aves) ☎529-3656; 325 Amsterdam Ave (between W 75th and 76th sts) ☎873-0787. Indian and Chinese cuisines combine in these bargain Burmese kitchens. Try the Thousand Layer Pancakes.

Mitali East, 334 E 6th St (between 1st and 2nd aves) ☎533-2508. Though more expensive than the other 6th Street Indians, this one is well worth it, and still at half the price of spots further uptown. Another branch across town, *Mitali West,* at 296 Bleecker St (at 7th Ave) ☎989-1367.

Passage to India, 308 E 6th St (between 1st and 2nd aves) ☎529-5770. North Indian tandoori dishes and breads at very cheap prices.

Raj Mahal, 322 E 6th St (between 1st and 2nd aves). Better-than-average portions and live Indian music, at low prices.

Rose of India, 306 E 6th St (between 1st and 2nd aves) ☎533-5011. Good workmanlike curries, and if you tell them it's your birthday they'll turn on the "disco lights" and bring you a free dessert.

Sonali, 324 E 6th St (between 1st and 2nd aves) ☎505-7517. Good, cheap, substantial Indian food.

ITALIAN

Cucina di Pesce, 87 E 4th St (between 2nd and 3rd aves) ☎260-6800. There are better Italian restaurants around, but not at these prices. The room is attractive and underlit, and the help is friendly. Squid-ink linguine and various seafood specials are the standouts. There's a big local crowd at dinnertime; get a drink at the bar and nibble on the free stewed mussels while you wait.

John's of 12th Street, 302 E 12th St (between 1st and 2nd aves) ☎475-9531. Heaped portions of southern Italian food – including good brick-oven pizza – in a dark, candlelit room.

La Foccaceria, 128 1st Ave (at 11th St) ☎254-4946. Cheap, filling meals of the steam-table variety, with wine served in water glasses.

Lanza Restaurant, 168 1st Ave (between E 10th and 11th sts) ☎674-7014. A prix-fixe lunch for $8.50 or a late-night prix-fixe at 9–11pm for $11.95 makes this basic Italian-fare, like linguine with white clam sauce, seem extra-special.

Orologio, 162 Ave A (between E 10th and 11th sts) ☎228-6900. Clocks are the theme in this rustic Italian eatery that offers reasonably priced food in a happening, though usually very crowded, environment.

Stromboli Pizzeria, 112 University Place (between E 12th and 13th sts) ☎255-0812. Excellent thin-crust pizzas – a good place for a quick slice.

Two Boots, 37 Ave A (between E 2nd and 3rd sts). Unique East Village restaurant serving thin crust pizzas with a Cajun flavor – crawfish and jalapeño peppers are common toppings. Main dishes, too, follow the same bias – spicy pasta and seafood options mainly. Excellent value.

Two Boots To Go, 42 Ave A (at 3rd St) ☎505-5450; 74 Bleecker St (at Broadway) ☎777-1033; 514 2nd St (between 7th and 8th aves); Park Slope, Brooklyn ☎718-499-3253. An even cheaper way to sample the thin-crust Cajun-Italian pizza combinations available at the restaurant.

JEWISH/EASTERN EUROPEAN

B & H Dairy, 127 2nd Ave (between E 7th St and St Mark's Place) ☎505-8065. Tiny luncheonette serving homemade soup, challah and latkes. You can also create your own juice combination to stay or go.

Christine's, 208 1st Ave (between E 12th and 13th sts) ☎505-0376. Long-standing Polish coffee shop, one of several such places in the area – great soups, blintzes and *pierogies.*

Kiev, 117 2nd Ave (at E 7th St) ☎674-4040. Eastern European dishes and

Eating

Eating

burgers. Great and affordable food at any time of the day or night. Open 24 hours.

KK Restaurant, 192–194 1st Ave (between E 11th and 12th sts) ☎777-4430. Polish home cooking with cheap breakfast specials. Try to sit in the tranquil garden out back.

Odessa, 117–119 Ave A (between E 7th St and St Mark's Place) ☎473-8916. The scramble for a seat may put you off, but the food here – a filling array of dishes from the Caucasus – and prices (around $5 for a meal) are impressive. Coffee-shop decor, loud, plastic and brightly lit – not the sort of place to chew the fat.

Second Avenue Deli, 156 2nd Ave (between E 9th and 10th sts) ☎677-0606. An East Village institution, serving up marvellous burgers, hearty pastrami sandwiches, and other deli goodies in ebullient, snap-happy style. The star plaques in the sidewalk out front commemorate this area's Yiddish theatre days.

Veselka, 144 2nd Ave (between E 9th St and St Mark's Place) ☎228-9682. East Village institution, though given a recent sprucing up, that offers fine homemade hot borscht (and cold in summer), latkes, *pierogies*, and great burgers and fries. Open 24 hours.

VEGETARIAN

Anjelica Kitchen, 300 E 12th St (between 1st and 2nd aves) ☎228-2909. Seasonal vegetarian macrobiotic restaurant with various daily specials for a decent price. Patronized by a colorful downtown crowd.

Dojo, 24–26 St Mark's Place (between 2nd and 3rd aves) ☎674-9821; also at 14 W 4th St (between Broadway and Mercer Sts) ☎505-8934. Popular East Village hangout, with reasonably priced vegetarian and Japanese food in a brash, fun environment. One of the best-value restaurants in the city, and certainly one of the cheapest Japanese menus you'll find.

Chelsea

Retro diners, Cuban-Chinese greasy spoons along 8th Ave, and cute brunch spots characterize **Chelsea** – a neighborhood of mixed and multiple charms. Perhaps the best and most reasonably priced offerings are to be had in the area's Central American establishments, though there is also a mosaic of international cuisines – Thai, Austrian, Mexican, Italian, and traditional American – to choose from.

BAKERIES AND CAFÉS

Kaffeehaus, 131 8th Ave (between W 16th and 17th sts) ☎229-9702. Amazing desserts and Viennese coffee. Austrian food – Wiener schnitzel, warm cheese strudel – with a creative twist.

News Bar, 2 W 19th St (between 5th and 6th aves) ☎255-3996; 366 W Broadway (at Broome St) ☎343-0053; 969 3rd Ave (at E 57th St) ☎319-0830. Tiny minimalist café with equally great selections of pastries and periodicals. The 19th St location draws photographer and model types, but all three are good for people-watching.

AMERICAN, LATIN AND SOUTH AMERICAN

Blue Moon Café, 150 8th Ave (between W 17th and 18th sts) ☎463-0560. Standard Mexican food at moderate prices. Hockey fans may be interested to know the restaurant is owned by the NY Rangers.

Eighteenth and Eighth, 159 8th Ave (between W 17th and 18th sts) ☎242-5000. Ever so tiny upscale Chelsea coffee shop popular with a hip, gay crowd. Great for homey brunch fare, especially the brioche French toast.

Empire Diner, 210 10th Ave (between W 22nd and 23rd sts) ☎243-2736. With its gleaming chrome-ribbed Art Deco interior, this is one of Manhattan's original diners, still open 24 hours and still serving up plates of simple American food. The food is very average, but the place is a beauty. Free postcards, too.

Eating

Food Bar, 149 8th Ave (between W 17th and 18th sts) ☎243-2020. The food at this very gay Chelsea restaurant is not quite as good as the view. Even so, well-priced salads and sandwiches.

Kitchen, 218 8th Ave (between W 21st and 22nd sts) ☎243-4433. Mexican cuisine to go with a slew of daily burrito specials to choose from.

Mary Ann's, 116 8th Ave (at W 16th St) ☎633-0877. Cheap and filling Mexican food, most for under $10, also available from a branch in the East Village at 300 E 5th St ☎475-5939. Potent margaritas.

Mesa Grill, 102 5th Ave (between W 15th and 16th sts) ☎807-7400. One of lower Manhattan's more fashionable eateries, serving unique and eclectic Southwestern grill fare at highish prices. Full of publishing and advertising types doing lunch.

Moran's, 146 10th Ave (at 19th St) ☎924-6659. Listed in the phone book as "Moran's Chelsea Sea Food," but while you can get good swordfish, lobster and sole here, it's the steaks and chops that impress – as well as the plush stained-wood decor. Try and get the cozy back room, especially in winter, when the fireplace is roaring.

The Old Homestead, 56 9th Ave (between 14th and 15th sts) ☎249-9040. Steak. Period. But really gorgeous steak, served in an almost comically old-fashioned walnut dining room by waiters in black vests.

O'Reilly's, 56 W 31st St (between Broadway and 6th Ave) ☎684-4244. Posh Irish pub/restaurant with standard American dishes at $6–12. Good value.

Sam Chinita, 176 8th Ave (between W 19th and 20th sts) ☎741-0240. Old-fashioned boxcar diner serving cheap Cuban-Chinese combos.

ASIAN

Bendix Diner, 219 8th Ave (at W 21st St) ☎366-0560. For breakfast, your all-American greasy-spoon diner, but with an unusually large lunch and dinner menu that includes a lot of Thai-inspired dishes.

Meri Ken, 189 7th Ave (at W 21st St) ☎620-9684. Stylish Art Deco sushi place.

Royal Siam, 240 8th Ave (between 22nd and 23rd sts) ☎741-1732. Reasonably priced Thai restaurant, with surprisingly flavorful renditions of the old standards.

FRENCH

La Luncheonette, 130 10th Ave (between W 18th and 19th sts) ☎675-0342. Creative Parisian-style bistro serving good-quality French food, though in an unfortunately downbeat and out-of-the-way location.

Man Ray, 169 8th Ave (between W 18th and 19th sts) ☎627-4220. French food in a sleek Art Deco setting conveniently located next to the Joyce Theater. Try the calamari appetizer and seared rare tuna with garlic cream sauce for dinner. Very reasonable – entrées in the range of $8–14.

GREEK AND MIDDLE EASTERN

Periyali, 35 W 20th St (between 5th and 6th aves) ☎463-7890. Gourmet Greek food that's a cut above the rest, both in quality and price, in a cheerful Mediterranean setting. Closed Sun.

ITALIAN

Caffè Bondí, 7 W 20th St (between 5th and 6th aves) ☎691-8136. This Flatiron district restaurant serves up Sicilian specialties and divine desserts. Try to sit in the garden.

Chelsea Trattoria, 108 8th Ave (between W 15th and 16th sts) ☎924-7786. A brick-walled northern Italian restaurant that's cozy and enjoyable for the ambience as much as the moderately priced food.

Frank's, 85 10th Ave (at W 15th St) ☎243-1349. Long-established Italian-American restaurant with pasta dishes from $5 up. A taste of old New York.

Le Madri, 168 W 18th St (at 7th Ave) ☎727-8022. Named after the Italian

Eating

"mothers" who work in the kitchen, this elegant Tuscan eatery's marvellous food and wine is only slightly marred by the snooty service and clientele. On the pricey side, but worth it. Try and get a table in the patio out back – if you can get one at all.

JEWISH/EASTERN EUROPEAN
Eisenberg's Sandwich Shop, 174 5th Ave (between W 22nd and 23rd sts) ☎675-5096. This narrow little restaurant is a Flatiron institution. A tuna sandwich and some matzoh ball soup will cure what ails you.

SPANISH
El Quijote, 226 West 23rd St (between 7th and 8th aves) ☎929-1855. Has changed very little over the years; it was recently used as setting for a dinner scene in *I Shot Andy Warhol* (which takes place in 1968) with minimal makeover. Still serves lovely *mariscos* and fried meats as rich as the deep burgundy lighting and dark-stained wood.

Union Square, Gramercy Park, Murray Hill
Due at least in part to the success of the Union Square Greenmarket, the area around **Union Square** and **Gramercy Park** has become the site of many a culinary excursion of late. Save some of the more expensive restaurants for lunch, but by all means come to sample the fresh and largely Californian cuisine-influenced restaurants the Flatiron district has to offer. Like Little India in the East Village, the area **around Lexington Ave in the upper 20s** is a good place to sample cheap and filling Indian fare.

BAKERIES AND CAFÉS
Chez Laurence, 245 Madison Ave (between E 37th and 38th sts) ☎683-0284. Well-placed, friendly little patisserie that makes cheap breakfasts and decent, inexpensive lunches – and good coffee at any time of the day. Closed Sun.

City Bakery, 22 E 17th St (between Broadway and 5th Ave) ☎366-1414;

550 Madison Ave (between E 55th and 56th sts) ☎833-8020. Minimalist bakery that uses fresh Greenmarket ingredients from around the corner. Serves reasonable soups and light lunch fare, but above all masterfully delicate tartlets, creamy hot chocolate, and crème brûlée. Closed Sunday.

La Boulangère, 49 E 21st St (between Broadway and Park Avenue South) ☎475-8772; also 495 Broadway (at Broome St) ☎475-8582. French bakery-café with a menu of breads, pastries, soups and salads. Good for a midday pick-me-up.

AMERICAN, LATIN AND SOUTH AMERICAN
Alva, 36 E 22nd St (between Broadway and Park Ave South) ☎228-4399. Mirrors and photos of Thomas Alva Edison cover the walls in this eclectic American restaurant. Specialties include grilled duck, double garlic roast chicken, and soft-shell crabs. It's expensive, but the prix-fixe dinner on Monday is good value. If you have the cash, it's certainly an excellent place to explore American cooking.

Bagel Palace, 36 Union Square (between 16th St and Park Ave South) ☎673-0452. Bagels topped with just about anything, plus a hundred different omelettes.

Café Beulah, 39 E 19th St (between Broadway and Park Ave South) ☎777-9700. A little pricey but still the best southern food in Midtown. Try the free-range duck in a tangy barbecue wine sauce.

El Rio Grande, 160 E 38th St (between Lexington and 3rd aves) ☎867-0922. Long-established Murray Hill Tex-Mex place with a gimmick: you can eat Mexican, or if you prefer, Texan, by simply crossing the "border" and walking through the kitchen. Personable and fun – and the margaritas are earth-shattering. Try the swordfish or grilled shrimp.

Friend of a Farmer, 77 Irving Place (between E 18th and 19th sts) ☎477-

2188. Rustic Gramercy café known for its old-fashioned chicken pot pie and homey "comfort meals."

Jackson Hole Wyoming, 521 3rd Ave (between E 35th and 36th sts) ☎679-3264; 1611 2nd Ave (between E 83rd and 84th sts). Midtown burger chain with a reputation for obscenely large burgers. Good value for dyed-in-the-wool carnivores.

Mayrose, 920 Broadway (at E 21st St) ☎533-3663. High-ceilinged upscale diner serving solid American food in the Flatiron district. Crowded at lunch.

Reuben's, 244 Madison Ave (at E 38th St) ☎867-7800. Busy midtown diner that makes a fine and filling haven in between the sights and shops of 5th Ave.

Sarge's, 548 3rd Ave (between E 36th and 37th sts) ☎679-0442. Large coffee shop serving enormous portions of deli grub. Open 24 hours a day.

Scotty's Diner, 336 Lexington Ave (at E 39th St) ☎986-1520. Conveniently placed midtown diner, close to Grand Central and the Empire State. Solid diner food, good breakfasts until 11am and a friendly Spanish owner.

Union Square Café, 21 E 16th St (between 5th Ave and Union Square West) ☎243-4020. Choice California dining with a classy but comfortable downtown atmosphere. No one does salmon like they do. Not at all cheap – prices average $100 for two – but the creative menu, not to mention the stylish, bustling environment, is a real treat. Don't miss it if you have the bucks.

Verbena, 54 Irving Place (at E 17th St) ☎260-5454. This simple and elegant restaurant serves a seasonal menu of creative American food. Don't miss the crème brûlée with lemon verbena, the herb for which the restaurant was named.

Whaler Bar, Madison Towers Hotel, 22 E 38th St (at Madison Ave) ☎802-0600. Casual atmosphere and choice of cheese and veggie dishes.

ASIAN

Choshi, 77 Irving Place (at E 19th St) ☎420-1419. Modestly priced Gramercy Japanese serving first-rate fresh sushi. The prix-fixe menu is a good deal.

Jaiya Thai, 396 3rd Ave (between E 28th and 29th sts) ☎889-1330. Spicy, delicious and affordable. Pad Thai for $8.

Tina, 249 Park Ave South (at E 20th St) ☎477-1761. Good Chinese in an area not usually known for its Chinese restaurants.

FRENCH

La Maison Japonaise, 125 E 39th St (between Park and Lexington aves) ☎682-7375. Creative combinations of French and Japanese cuisines in a peaceful townhouse. Closed Sun.

Les Halles, 411 Park Ave South (between E 28th and 29th sts) ☎679-4111. Noisy, bustling bistro with the carcasses dangling in a butcher's shop in the front. Very pseudo *rive gauche*. A little pricey; dinners in the range of $13–22. Not recommended for veggies.

L'Express, 249 Park Ave South (at 20th St) ☎254-5858. A good, airy bistro with the usual food (galatine, smoked salmon a la Lyonnaise) at the usual prices, but with two important points of distinction: the waiters are actually friendly, and it's open 24 hours – by far the classiest all-night place south of the *Brasserie*.

Park Bistro, 414 Park Ave South (between E 28th and 29th sts) ☎689-1360. Sister to *Les Halles* (see above) and similar in prices and style, though a little less hectic. Friendly bistro à la Paris in the 1950s.

Steak Frites, 9 E 16th St (between Union Square West and 5th Ave) ☎463-7101. As the name suggests, great steak and frites, for about $19. Main courses $12–20.

GERMAN

Rolf's, 281 3rd Ave (at 22nd St) 473-8718. A nice, dark, chintz-decorated Old World feeling dominates this East Side

Eating

Eating

institution. Schnitzel and sauerbraten are always good but somehow taste better at the generous bar buffet, commencing around 5pm all through the week.

INDIAN, PAKISTANI, AFRICAN

Annapurna, 108 Lexington Ave (between E 27th and 28th sts) ☎679-1284. Good value Indian restaurant.

Curry in a Hurry, 119 Lexington Ave (between E 27th and 28th sts) ☎683-0900. One of the first fast-food joints in "Little India." Quick, inexpensive and good – eat for around $5.

Madras Mahal, 104 Lexington Ave (between E 27th and 28th sts) ☎684-4010. A kosher vegetarian's dream . . . and really good for everyone else, too. Around $10.

FISH

City Crab, 235 Park Ave S (at E 19th St) ☎529-3800. A large and very popular joint that prides itself on a large selection of fresh East Coast oysters and clams, which can be had in mixed sampler plates. Overall, a hearty place to consume lots of bivalves and wash 'em down with pints of ale. Sometimes with jazz at weekend brunch.

VEGETARIAN

Zen Palate, 34 Union Square East (at E 16th St); 663 9th Ave (at W 46th St) ☎582-1669. Stylish and modern, with what it calls a "Zen atmosphere," this serves up health-conscious vegetarian Chinese food prepared to look, and sometimes even taste, like meat. Sit at the counter and pick an appetizer from the extensive list of "Tasty Morsels" for quick snacks alone.

Midtown (west)

Manifold good meals await you on the **western side of Midtown**, a neighborhood whose restaurants encompass Greek, South American, Japanese, African, French, and everything in between. **Restaurant Row**, W 46th St between 8th and 9th aves, is a frequent stopover for

theater-goers seeking a late-night meal, though **9th Ave** often offers better and cheaper alternatives. Further east is the infamous galaxy of **Planets** – Hollywood, Harley Davidson, Hard Rock, and Fashion – that are not worth a visit as much as a laugh.

BAKERIES AND CAFÉS

Algonquin Oak Room, 59 W 44th St (between 5th and 6th aves) ☎840-6800. The archetypal American interpretation of the English drawing room. Good for afternoon teas.

Au Café, 1700 Broadway (at W 53rd St) ☎757-2233. A rare midtown place where you can linger over coffee. The menu offers a range of soups, salads and sandwiches. Outdoor seating.

Cupcake Café, 522 9th Ave (at W 39th St) ☎465-1530. A delightful little joint, offering decent soup and sandwiches at bargain prices, and great cakes, cupcakes and pies. Anything with fruit is a must.

Poseidon Bakery, 629 9th Ave (between W 44th and 45th sts) ☎757-6173. Decadent baklava and other sweet Greek pastries and cookies, as well as spinach pies. Known most of all for its hand-rolled phyllo dough that supplies many restaurants. Closed Mon.

AMERICAN, LATIN AND SOUTH AMERICAN

American Festival Café, 20 W 50th St (at Rockefeller Plaza) ☎246-6699. For the views, at least, there's no better place to sample regional American cooking – everything from Louisiana catfish to Mississippi mud pie. A nice place to warm up after a spin on the Rockefeller rink, though it doesn't come cheap – count on $15 and up for a dinner entrée.

Arriba Arriba, 762 9th Ave (at W 51st St) ☎489-0810. Boozy Tex-Mex place, popular with the after-work crowd for the great margaritas as much as the meals.

Bryant Park Grill, 25 W 40th St (between 5th and 6th aves) 840-6500.

Brunch

Weekend brunch is a competitive business in New York, and the number of restaurants offering it is constantly expanding. Selections below (most of which are covered in more detail elsewhere in the listings) all offer a good weekend menu, sometimes for an all-in price that includes a free cocktail or two – though offers of freebies are to be treated with suspicion by those more interested in the food than getting blitzed. Above all, don't regard this as a definitive list. You'll find other possibilities all over Manhattan.

Eating

Lower Manhattan

Aggie's, 146 W Houston St (at MacDougal St) ☎673-8994

Anglers & Writers, 420 Hudson St (at St Luke's Place) ☎675-0810

Caliente Cab Co, 61 7th Ave (at Bleecker St) ☎243-8517

Cupping Room Café, 359 W Broadway (between Broome and Grand sts) ☎925-2898

Danal, 90 E 10th St (between 3rd and 4th aves) ☎982-6930

Elephant and Castle, 68 Greenwich Ave (between 6th and 7th aves) ☎243-1400

Home, 20 Cornelia St (between Bleecker and W 4th sts) ☎243-9579

Japonica, 100 University Place (at E 12th St) ☎243-7752

Jerry's Restaurant, 101 Prince St (between Greene and Mercer sts) ☎966-9464

Old Devil Moon, 511 E 12th St (between aves A and B) ☎475-4375

Paris Commune, 411 Bleecker St (between W 11th and Bank sts) ☎929-0509

7A, 109 Ave A (between E 6th and 7th sts) ☎673-6853

Yaffa Tea Room, 353 Greenwich St (at Harrison St); 19 Harrison St (at Greenwich St) ☎274-9403

Midtown Manhattan

Eighteenth and Eighth, 159 8th Ave (between W 17th and 18th sts) ☎242-5000

Food Bar, 149 8th Ave (between W 17th and 18th sts) ☎243-2020

Friend of a Farmer, 77 Irving Place (between E 18th and 19th sts) ☎477-2188

Royal Canadian Pancake Restaurant, 1004 2nd Ave (between E 53rd and 54th sts) ☎980-4131; 2286 Broadway (between W 82nd and 83rd sts) ☎873-6052; 180 3rd Ave (between E 16th and 17th sts) ☎777-9288

Upper Manhattan

Barking Dog Luncheonette, 1678 3rd Ave (at E 94th St) ☎831-1800

Copeland's, 547 W 145th St (between Broadway and Amsterdam Ave) ☎234-2357

E.A.T., 1064 Madison Ave (between E 80th and 81st sts) ☎772-0022

EJ's Luncheonette, 433 Amsterdam Ave (between W 81st and 82nd sts) ☎873-3444

Good Enough to Eat, 483 Amsterdam Ave (between W 83rd and 84th sts) ☎496-0163

Popover Café, 551 Amsterdam Ave (between W 86th and 87th sts) ☎595-8555

Sarabeth's Kitchen, 423 Amsterdam Ave (between W 80th and 81st St) ☎496-6280; 1295 Madison Ave (between E 92nd and 93rd sts) ☎410-7335

Shark Bar, 307 Amsterdam Ave (between W 74th and 75th sts) ☎874-8500

Outer Boroughs

Montague Street Saloon, 122 Montague St (between Henry and Hicks sts), Brooklyn Heights ☎718/522-6770.

Oznot's Dish, 79 Berry (at N 9th St) ☎718/599-6596.

Eating

The food is standard-upscale (Caesar salad, grilled chicken), but the real reason to come is atmosphere, provided by the Park, whether viewed from within the spacious dining room or enjoyed al fresco.

Cabana Carioca, 123 W 45th St (between 6th Ave and Broadway) ☎581-8088. Animated restaurant decorated with colorful murals. A great place to try out Brazilian-Portuguese specialties, like *feijoada* (black bean and pork stew), washed down with fiery *caipirinhas*. Portions large enough for two make it reasonably inexpensive.

Ellen's Stardust Diner, 1377 6th Ave (at W 56th St) ☎307-7575; 1650 Broadway (at W 51st St) ☎956-5151. Another 1950s-style diner serving traditional American food and built around the "missed my subway home" theme.

Fashion Café, 51 Rockefeller Plaza (at W 51st St) ☎765-3131. The latest and greatest in the line of theme restaurants of the Hard Rock variety, this one founded by supermodels Elle Macpherson, Claudia Schiffer and Naomi Campbell, and including their personal favorite recipes – as if they ever cook.

Hamburger Harry's, 145 W 45th St (between Broadway and 6th Ave) ☎840-0566. Handy diner just off Times Square; cousin to its downtown location but more refined. Some claim its burgers are the best in town.

Hard Rock Café, 221 W 57th St (between Broadway and 7th Ave) ☎489-6565. Burger restaurant that for some reason continues to pull in celebrity New York, or at least the odd rock star. Full to bursting most nights, especially on weekends. The food isn't bad, but only really worth it if you've a teenager in tow.

Jerry's Metro Delicatessen, 790 8th Ave (at W 48th St) ☎581-9100. Large deli restaurant with a huge choice of sandwiches, omelettes and burgers, etc. Good breakfasts, too.

Joe Allen's, 326 W 46th St (between 8th and 9th aves) ☎581-6464. Tried and true formula of checkered tablecloths, old-fashioned bar-room feel, and reliable American food at moderate prices. The calf's liver with spinach and potatoes hasn't been off the menu in 20 years. Have a Bloody Mary.

Landmark Tavern, 626 11th Ave (between W 45th and 46th sts) ☎757-8595. Long-established Irish tavern popular with the Midtown yuppie crowd. The Irish soda bread is baked fresh every hour. Good food and huge portions.

Market Diner, 572 11th Ave (at W 43rd St) ☎695-0415. The ultimate 24-hour diner, chrome-furnished and usually full of weary clubbers filling up on breakfast. A good place to refuel early evening, too.

Mike's American Bar & Grill, 650 10th Ave (between W 45th and 46th sts) ☎246-4155. Funky "downtown" bar in Midtown west (aka "Hell's Kitchen"). The decor changes each season, but the menu stays basic: burgers, nachos and the like for under $25.

Motown Café, 104 W 57th St (between 6th and 7th aves) ☎581-6030. The chow is decent, tending toward mild soul food and burgers. Guess what kind of music they play? Still, clean and lively, and fast becoming a favorite among African-American couples out on a date.

Planet Hollywood, 140 W 57th St (between 6th and 7th aves) ☎333-7827. A tourist trap in the *Hard Rock Café* vein, but with movie rather than music memorabilia. Co-owned by Bruce Willis, Sylvester Stallone and Arnold Schwarzenegger.

Stage Deli, 834 7th Ave (between W 53rd and 54th sts) ☎245-7850. Another reliable all-night standby, and long-time rival to the *Carnegie Deli*, p.331. More genuine New York attitude.

Symphony Café, 950 8th Ave (at W 56th St) ☎397-9595. Situated between Carnegie Hall and Lincoln Center, it's not surprising to find a restaurant with a "symphony" theme. The food is nouvelle American, the surroundings pleasant, and in summer you can sit outside; moderately priced.

Via Brasil, 34 W 46th St (between 5th and 6th aves) ☎997-1158. Excellent place to taste *feijoada*, Brazil's national dish, a meaty black bean stew. A bit pricey – entrées in the range of $13–22. Live music Wed–Sat nights.

Victor's Café 52, 236 W 52nd St (between Broadway and 8th Ave) ☎586-7714. Cuban food at moderate prices. Great black bean soup and sangria.

Virgil's Real BBQ, 152 W 44th St (between Broadway and 6th Ave) ☎921-9494. Hard-core ribs and biscuits for barbecue enthusiasts though the ambience leaves something to be desired. A bit pricey, so order light. Chances are you'll still end up with too much.

Wine and Apples, 117 W 57th St (between 6th and 7th aves) ☎246-9009. A kind of hybrid Greek-Hungarian diner with meals priced from $5–8 and inexpensive booze. A life-saver in this part of Midtown.

Zuni, 598 9th Ave (at W 43rd St) ☎765-7626. Pricey haute Mexican cuisine in an informal setting. They make the guacamole fresh at your table.

ASIAN

Dish of Salt, 133 W 47th St (between 6th and 7th aves) ☎921-4242. Tired of the linoleum-table Cantonese fare in Chinatown? For approximately five times as much money, you can dig into roast plum duckling and spinach with crabmeat, served impeccably at huge polished-wood tables at this midtown institution.

Oishi Noodle, 1117 6th Ave (at W 43rd St) ☎764-3075. One of the best Japanese noodle restaurants in the city.

Pongsri Thai Restaurant, 244 W 48th St (between Broadway and 8th Ave) ☎582-3392; 106 Bayard St (between Baxter and Canal sts) ☎349-3132; 331 2nd Ave (between E 18th and 19th sts) ☎477-4100. Restaurant popular at lunchtime with local business people for its extensive and good-value lunch menu – rice and noodle combos a specialty. A massive menu in the evenings.

Siam Inn, 916 8th Ave (between W 54th and 55th sts) ☎489-5237; **Siam Inn Too**, 854 8th Ave (between W 51st and 52nd sts) ☎757-3520. Unpretentious restaurant serving average-priced spicy Thai fare. Try the *masaman* curry or the chili and garlic fried sea bass. Seafood is always fresh and good, and the prix-fixe dinner is great value.

FRENCH

Café Un, Deux, Trois, 123 W 44th St (between Broadway and 6th Ave) ☎354-4148. French brasserie-style restaurant close to Times Square serving fair-to-middling food. Crayons for table-top doodling while you wait for your order. $12–25 for a main course.

Chantal Café, 257 W 55th St (between Broadway and 8th Ave) ☎246-7076. Quiet little bistro serving a savory chicken with rosemary and other Continental specialties.

Chez Napoleon, 365 W 50th St (between 8th and 9th aves) ☎265-6980. The West Side's proximity to the docks, where landed French soldiers, made it the spot for several highly authentic Gallic eateries in the 1940s and 1950s. They live on as old-fashioned places like this. Bring a wad to enjoy the tradition, though.

Hourglass Tavern, 373 W 46th St (between 8th and 9th aves) ☎265-2060. Tiny midtown French restaurant – around eight tables in all – which serves an excellent-value, two-course prix-fixe menu for just $12.75. Choose between two appetizers and half a dozen or so main courses – a small range that guarantees good cooking. The gimmick is the hourglass above each table, the emptying of which means you're supposed to leave and make way for someone else. In reality they seem to last more than an hour, and they only enforce it if there's a line. Cash only.

La Bonne Soupe, 48 W 55th St (between 5th and 6th aves) ☎586-

Eating

Eating

7650. Traditional French food at reasonable prices. Steaks, omelettes, snails and fondues from $14.

La Cité, 120 W 51st St (between 6th and 7th aves) ☎956-7100. A handsome midtown French steakhouse. Expensive – entrées are $20–30.

La Fondue, 43 W 55th St (between 5th and 6th aves) ☎581-0820. Swiss chocolate and fondues for about $10.

Le Madeleine, 403 W 43rd St (between 9th and 10th aves) ☎246-2993. Pretty midtown French bistro with modest prices. Try and get a seat in the outdoor garden.

René Pujol, 321 W 51st St (between 8th and 9th aves) ☎246-3023. See *Chez Napoleon* above. This room is a little brighter and the food less traditional, *tant pis.*

West Bank Café, 407 W 42nd St (at 9th Ave) ☎695-6909. Some French, some American, all delicious and not as expensive as you'd think – from $9–16.

GERMAN

Hallo Berlin, 402 W 51st (between 9th and 10th aves) ☎541-6248. On the West Side, the best for wursts. The owner used to sell this stuff from a pushcart, and made enough to open a restaurant. Pleasant bench-and-table beer-garden setting.

GREEK AND MIDDLE EASTERN

Ariana Afghan Kebab, 787 9th Ave (between W 52nd and 53rd sts) ☎262-2323. A casual neighborhood restaurant serving inexpensive kebab (chicken, lamb and beef) and vegetarian meals. Also at 1345 2nd Ave (between E 70th and 71st sts) ☎517-2776 and 155 W 46th St (between 6th and 7th aves) ☎768-3875.

Lotfi's Couscous, 358 W 46th St (between 8th and 9th aves) ☎582-5850. Moderately priced Moroccan hidden away on the second floor. Lots of spicy dishes, vegetarian options and inexpensive salads. Closed in Aug.

Uncle Nick's, 747 Ninth Ave (between W 50th and 51st sts) ☎315-1726. A clean, sunny little restaurant with unimpassioned but wholesome Greek standards.

INDIAN, PAKISTANI, AFRICAN

Darbar, 44 W 56th St (between 5th and 6th aves) ☎432-7227. Some of the best Indian food in an enchanting setting. Try the vegetable pakoras and chicken tikka masala. Moderate to expensive.

Ngone International Gourmet, 823 6th Ave (between W 28th and 29th sts) ☎967-7899. Senegalese food at bargain prices. Lunch specials are a particularly good deal. "Chef Ousmane welcomes you." Try their yassa fish or *lamb mafe* – chunks of lamb in a thick peanut sauce.

ITALIAN

Becco, 355 W 46th St (between 8th and 9th aves) ☎397-7597. A welcome addition to "Restaurant Row" – and as such is busy with the pre-theater crowd – where you get generous amounts of antipasto and pasta for around $20.

Corrado, 1373 6th Ave (between W 55th and 56th sts) ☎333-3133. Northern Italian eatery with a breezy decor and great pasta. Moderately priced. Next door is *Corrado Kitchen*, the takeout version of the restaurant.

Julian's, 802 9th Ave (between 53rd and 54th sts) ☎262-4800. Light and inventive Mediterranean fare in a bright, pleasing room and clever dining garden tucked in an alley. Whether you want sandwiches or scalloppine, a safe bet in Hell's Kitchen.

Manganero's, 492 9th Ave (between 37th and 38th sts) ☎947-7325. This is as close as you're going to get to good, solid, working-class Italian north of *Puglio's* – emphasis on "solid." Linoleum tables, steam-table cutlets, rice balls with sauce ($1.75!) like mama used to make. Their giant "hero-boy" sandwiches come up to six-feet long and are popular at local offices.

Prego, 1365 6th Ave (between W 55th and 56 sts) ☎307-5775. Good pasta joint with a wide choice of generously spooned dishes for about $7 but an off-puttingly bathroom-like interior. Not for the hungover. Fill up and move on.

Supreme Macaroni Co., 511 9th Ave (between W 38th and 39th sts) ☎502-4842. A macaroni shop with a small, divy but lovable restaurant attached.

Trattoria dell'Arte, 900 7th Ave (between W 56th and 57th sts) ☎245-9800. Unusually nice restaurant for this rather tame stretch of Midtown, with a lovely airy interior, excellent service and good food. Great, wafer-thin crispy pizzas, decent and imaginative pasta dishes for around $15 and a mouth-watering antipasto bar – all eagerly patronized by an elegant out-to-be-seen crowd. Best to reserve.

JEWISH/EASTERN EUROPEAN

Carnegie Deli, 854 7th Ave (between W 54th and 55th sts) ☎757-2245. This place is known for the size of its sandwiches – by popular consent the most generously stuffed in the city, and a full meal in themselves. The chicken noodle soup is good, too. Not cheap, however, and the waiters are among New York's rudest. The consummate New York experience.

Uncle Vanya Café, 315 W 54th St (between 8th and 9th aves) ☎262-0542. White Russian delicacies, including more than just the obligatory borscht and caviar. Moderately priced; closed Sunday.

Midtown (east)

Catering mostly to lunchtime office-going crowds that swarm the sidewalks on weekdays, the **eastern side of Midtown** overflows with restaurants, most of them on the pricey side. You probably won't want to make it the focal point of too many culinary excursions but, that said, there are a few time-worn favorites in the neighborhood.

AMERICAN, LATIN AND SOUTH AMERICAN

Broadway Diner, 590 Lexington Ave (at E 52nd St) ☎486-8838; 1726 Broadway (at W 55th St) ☎765-0909. An upscale coffee shop with 1950s-style ambience.

The Champion, Marriott Hotel, 525 Lexington Ave (between E 48th and 49th sts) ☎755-4000. One of the most popular happy hours, with excellent hors d'oeuvres disappearing rather quickly. Don't arrive much after 6pm.

Lipstick Café, 885 3rd Ave (at E 54th St) ☎486-8664. Unlike most restaurants in the neighborhood, this one serves up delectable lunchtime food at affordable prices. Tasty homemade soups, salads and delicious baked goods. Closed weekends.

Rosen's Delicatessen, 23 E 51st St (between 5th and Madison aves) ☎541-8320. Enormous Art-Deco restaurant, renowned for its pastrami and corned beef, and handily situated for those suffering from midtown shopping fatigue. Good breakfasts too.

Royal Canadian Pancake Restaurant, 1004 2nd Ave (between E 53rd and 54th sts) ☎980-4131; 2286 Broadway (between W 82nd and 83rd sts) ☎873-6052; 180 3rd Ave (between E 16th and 17th sts) ☎777-9288. A memorable restaurant serving numerous kinds of vast – and delicious – pancakes, with fillings ranging from lager to white chocolate and almond to berries and bananas. Come hungry, and try sharing.

Ryan McFadden's, 800 2nd Ave (between E 42nd and 43rd sts) ☎599-2226. A long-established hangout of *Daily News* reporters (or it was, till the *News* moved west) and expats. Always crowded and fun.

Top of the Sixes, 666 5th Ave, 39th floor (between 52nd and 53rd sts) ☎757-6662. No better place to freeload really. Hot hors d'oeuvres every evening, Mon to Fri, and some great views over Manhattan.

Eating

Eating

Smith and Wollensky, 201 E 49th St (at 3rd Ave) ☎753-1530. Clubby atmosphere in a grand setting, where waiters – many of whom have worked here for twenty years or more – serve you the primest cuts of beef imaginable. Quite pricey – you'll pay at least $30 a steak but worth the splurge. Go basic with the sides and wines.

Zarela, 953 2nd Ave (between E 50th and 51st sts) ☎644-6740. A reaction against the "nachos with everything, washed down with tequila," the food here is fresh and authentic: if you've ever wondered what regional home-cooked Mexican food really tastes like, this festive restaurant is the place to go. It's noticeably more expensive than most regular places, but worth every bit. Don't miss *Zarela's* red snapper hash.

ASIAN

Hatsuhana, 17 E 48th St (between 5th and Madison aves) ☎355-3345; 237 Park Ave (at E 46th St) ☎661-3400. Every sushi lover's favorite sushi restaurant, now with two branches. Not at all cheap, so try to get there for the prix-fixe lunch.

Vong, 200 E 54th St (between 2nd and 3rd aves) ☎486-9592. This is the eccentrically decorated (call it Temple Glitz) restaurant everyone was talking about last month – or was it last year? In any case it's still hot enough to make your wallet smoke. The chefs take a French colonial approach to Thai cooking, doing things like putting mango in *foie gras*, and sesame and tamarind on Moscovy Duck. Somehow it works. You can get a "tasting menu" of samples for the bargain price of $65 per person.

FISH AND SEAFOOD

Goldwater's, 988 2nd Ave (between E 52nd and 53rd sts) ☎888-2122. Fish dishes in huge portions for $10–15 a head.

Oyster Bar, Lower level, Grand Central Terminal (at 42nd St and Park Ave) ☎490-6650. Wonderfully atmospheric turn-of-the-century place, down in the vaulted dungeons of Grand Central, where midtown office workers break for lunch. Fish, seafood, and of course oysters, though none of it exactly budget-rated – reckon on $20 upwards. If you're hard up, settle for the clam chowder with bread – delicious, quite ample and around $3 – or great creamy bowls of pan-roast oysters or clams for around $10.

FRENCH

Brasserie, 100 E 53rd St (between Park and Lexington aves) ☎751-4840. At this writing, closed for renovations and vague about when they'll be finished. Better call ahead. Always more highly regarded for its 24-hour opening policy than its food, and perhaps rightly so.

SPANISH

Solera, 216 E 53rd St (between 2nd and 3rd aves) ☎644-1166. Tapas and other Spanish specialties in a stylish town-house setting. As you'd expect from the surroundings and the ambience, it can be expensive.

VEGETARIAN

Great American Health Bar, 821 3rd Ave (between E 50th and 51st sts) ☎758-0883; 35 W 57th St (between 5th and 6th aves) ☎355-5177. This Manhattan chain comes well praised, but in reality the food can be rather bland and uninviting. Committed veggies only.

Hangawi, 12 E 32nd St (between 5th and Madison aves) ☎213-0077. If *Great American* sounds a little grim for you, here's a more exciting option: a genuine Korean restaurant. Pumpkin porridge, shredded mountain root and bamboo rice are among the standouts. A little pricey.

Upper West Side and Morningside Heights

Most of the restaurants in **Upper West Side** are not particularly cheap, but as you move north you'll find more and better-priced cafeteria-style Central American eateries. There are lots of generous burger joints, amiable coffee houses, and delectable, if a bit pricey, brunch spots, so you'll never be at a loss for decent, or better, meals.

BAKERIES AND CAFÉS

Boathouse Café, Central Park Boating Lake (72nd St entrance) ☎517-2233. Peaceful retreat from a hard day's trudg-ing around the 5th Ave museums. You get great views of the famous Central Park skyline for steep prices. Closed from Oct to March.

The Bread Shop, 3139 Broadway (at W 123rd St) ☎666-4343. Rich homemade breads and buttermilk biscuits in the bakery section and soup and pizza in the cozy little restaurant section. A good place to rest up if you're in the neighborhood.

Café Lalo, 201 W 83rd St (between Broadway and Amsterdam Ave) ☎496-6031. A West Side coffee house with scrumptious chocolate and berry desserts.

Café Mozart, 154 W 70th St (between Central Park West and Columbus Ave) ☎595-9797. Faded old Viennese coffee house that serves rich tortes and apple strudel.

Caffè la Fortuna, 69 W 71st St (between Central Park West and Columbus Ave) ☎724-5846. The walls are covered with records and black and white photos of stage personalities. Dark and comfy. You can sip a coffee all day long in the shade of their peaceful garden. Recommended.

AMERICAN, LATIN AND SOUTH AMERICAN

All State Café, 250 W 72nd St (between Broadway and West End Ave) ☎874-1883. Hamburgers, steaks and American food from $10–14 make this a popular Upper West Side hangout. Seating is limited, and it closes at 11.30pm; get here early to be sure of a place.

Amsterdam's, 428 Amsterdam Ave (between W 80th and 81st sts) ☎874-1377. Bar-restaurant serving burgers, great fries, chicken, pasta and the like for $12–15. Downtown branch at 454 Broadway (at Grand St) ☎925-6166.

Big Nick's, 2175 Broadway (between 76th and 77th sts) ☎362-9238. If you want a hamburger or pizza on the Upper West Side, this is the place. In his crowded, chaotic little wooden-

Eating

Eating

table restaurant, Big Nick has been serving them up all night long to locals for 20-plus years. Wash the stuff down with 12-ounce draft beers at $1 a pop.

La Caridad, 2199 Broadway (at W 78th St) ☎ 874-2780. Something of an Upper West Side institution, a tacky little dump doling out plentiful and cheap Cuban-Chinese food to hungry diners. Bring your own beer, and expect to wait in line.

Dallas BBQ, 27 W 72nd St (between Columbus Ave and Central Park West)

☎ 873-2004; 1265 3rd Ave (at E 73rd St) ☎ 772-9393; 21 University Place (at E 8th St) ☎ 674-4450; 132 2nd Ave (at St Mark's Place) ☎ 777-5574. A real-value budget option for this part of town, just off Central Park, though the Upper East Side branch has a better reputation. Barbecue chicken and burgers for $5–8, chili for less. Whichever branch you try it'll be crowded, however, and the service can be poor, to say the least.

Diane's Uptown, 249 Columbus Ave (between W 71st and 72nd sts) ☎ 799-

6750. Fast, quick hearty burgers, and handy for Ben & Jerry's ice cream next door.

EJ's Luncheonette, 433 Amsterdam Ave (between W 81st and 82nd sts) ☎873-3444. Diner that does its best to look old, with mirrors, booths upholstered in turquoise vinyl, and walls adorned with 1950s photographs. Unpretentious, affordable American food that includes pancakes in many guises and banana splits to die for. Expect long lines for brunch on Sun.

Flor de Mayo, 2651 Broadway (at W 101st St) ☎663-5520. Very cheap, very popular Cuban-Chinese restaurant with coffee-shop decor and lots of food, though not much for vegetarians – spicy chicken, Cuban-style steaks, etc. You can eat well for around $12.

Good Enough to Eat, 483 Amsterdam Ave (between W 83rd and 84th sts) ☎496-0163. Cutesy Upper West Side restaurant known for its cinnamon-swirl French toast, award-winning meatloaf, and excellent brunch value.

Gray's Papaya, 2090 Broadway (at W 72nd St) ☎799-0243. Order two all-beef franks and a papaya juice for a true New York experience. No ambience, no seats, just good cheap grub.

Hi-Life Bar and Grill, 477 Amsterdam Ave (at W 83rd St) ☎787-7199; also 1340 1st Ave (at E 72nd St) ☎249-3600. An in spot for Upper West and East Siders for basic American fare, Olympic-sized tables, and good people-watching.

Josephina, 1900 Broadway (between W 63rd and 64th sts, across from Lincoln Center) ☎799-1000. Large airy restaurant painted with colonial murals (albeit cut in half by their new banquette seating). Good salads, soups and the like; moderate prices.

Main Street, 446 Columbus Ave (between W 81st and 82nd sts) ☎873-5025. Homey American restaurant lauded for its meatloaf, mashed potatoes and sweet potato fries in particular. In a city where even the most average por-

tions tend to be large, Main Street has a reputation for serving vast plates – usually enough to feed two at least.

Popover Café, 551 Amsterdam Ave (between W 86th and 87th sts) ☎595-8555. Excellent, if overly cutesy (the place is filled with teddy bears!) uptown eatery whose dishes come served with a pop-over – a sort of dyspeptic brioche from the Midwest. Expect a long wait on weekends.

Positively 104th St, 2725 Broadway (between W 104th and 105th sts) ☎316-0372. Basic but good American food, with excellent steaks and a friendly atmosphere, make this a good choice for this part of town. Reasonably priced too.

Sarabeth's Kitchen, 423 Amsterdam Ave (between W 80th and 81st St) ☎496-6280; 1295 Madison Ave (between E 92nd and 93rd sts) ☎410-7335. Best for brunch, this country restaurant serves delectable baked goods and impressive omelettes. Dinner is pricey, so you're better off at brunch. But expect to wait in line.

Tom's Restaurant, 2880 Broadway (at W 112th St) ☎864-6137. Cheap, greasy-spoon fare. This is the *Tom's* of *Seinfeld* and Suzanne Vega fame.

Vince & Eddie's, 70 W 68th St (between Columbus Ave and Central Park West) ☎721-0068. Slightly pseudo country-style American restaurant serving grub like American grannies supposedly used to make – hearty, wholesome and delicious. Moderately priced.

ASIAN

Fujiyama Mama, 467 Columbus Ave (between W 82nd and 83rd sts) ☎769-1144. The West Side's best – and most boisterous – sushi bar, with hi-tech decor and loud music.

Hunan Balcony, 2596 Broadway (at W 98th St) ☎865-0400; 1417 2nd Ave (at E 74th St) ☎517-2088. Cheap and reliable Hunan-style food from $6–11. Soft-shell crab for $12.95.

Eating

Eating

Lemongrass Grill, 2534 Broadway (between W 94th and 95th sts) ☎666-0888. Very reasonable Upper West Side Thai restaurant serving delicious chicken soup with lime juice and red pepper, spicy curries, basil chicken, and Pad Thai from $8–15.

Lenge, 200 Columbus Ave (at W 69th St) ☎799-9188; 1465 3rd Ave (between E 82nd and 83rd sts). Decent Japanese restaurant, averagely priced.

Monsoon, 435 Amsterdam Ave (at W 81st St) ☎580-8686. It's best to come here for lunch when the crowds are smaller and the food is apt to be more dependable. Otherwise be prepared to wait. Try the grilled chicken on skewers or coconut curry shrimp noodle soup.

Ollie's Noodle Shop, 2315 Broadway (at W 84th St) ☎362-3111; 2957 Broadway (at W 116th St) ☎932-3300; and 190 W 44th St (between Broadway and 8th Ave) ☎921-5988. Downscale Chinese fast-food noodle shop that serves marvellous noodles and spare ribs. Not, however, a place to linger. Very cheap, very crowded and very noisy.

Rikyu, 210 Columbus Ave (between W 69th and 70th sts) ☎799-7847. A wide selection of Japanese food, including sushi made to order. Inexpensive lunches and early-bird specials make this place a bargain.

FISH AND SEAFOOD

Dock's Oyster Bar, 2427 Broadway (between W 89th and 90th sts) ☎724-5588; 633 3rd Ave (at E 40th St) ☎986-8080. Some of the freshest seafood in town at these popular uptown restaurants. The Upper West Side is the original and tends to have the homier atmosphere – though both can be noisy.

Fish, 2799 Broadway (at 108th St) ☎864-5000. A nice compromise between *nouvelle* and old-fashioned; the dishes here are unfussy, but still incredibly tasty. Fried calamari with anchovy butter is a good example; prawns roasted with bacon, cognac and scallions is

another. Or just content yourself with impeccably fresh raw oysters.

Fishin' Eddie, 73 W 71st St (between Central Park West and Columbus Ave) ☎874-3474. Fresh fish in a homey New England-style setting.

FRENCH

Café Luxembourg, 200 W 70th St (between Amsterdam and West End aves) ☎873-7411. Trendy Lincoln Center area bistro that packs in (literally, some say) a self-consciously hip crowd to enjoy its first-rate contemporary French food. Not too pricey – two people can eat for $50 or so.

La Boite en Bois, 75 W 68th St (between Central Park West and Columbus Ave) ☎874-2705. Rustic, moderately priced Lincoln Center bistro that has good country French food.

GREEK AND MIDDLE EASTERN

Symposium, 544 W 113rd St (between Broadway and Amsterdam aves) ☎865-1011. Neighborhood restaurant near Columbia University, serving favorite Greek dishes in a relaxed, studenty atmosphere.

INDIAN, PAKISTANI, AFRICAN

Blue Nile, 103 W 77th St (between Amsterdam and Columbus aves) ☎580-3232. Ethiopian restaurant, where the food is served on a communal tray at low tables. Eat with your fingers using soft, flat *injera* bread. The food consists of rich meat stews and lentil and vegetable concoctions washed down with sharp African beer. Main dishes priced around $10.

Mughlai, 320 Columbus Ave (at W 75th St) ☎724-6363. Uptown, upscale Indian with prices about the going rate for this strip: $10–15.

ITALIAN

Carmine's, 2450 Broadway (between W 90th and 91st sts) ☎362-2200; also in Midtown at 200 W 44th St (between Broadway and 8th Ave) ☎221-3800. The original large Upper West Side restaurant justifiably made a name for itself for its combination of decent (and decently priced) home-style southern Italian food, in mountainous portions (careful not to over-order), and the noisy, convivial atmosphere in which it's served. If you're in a group of six or more you can book; otherwise be prepared to wait in line.

Ernie's, 2150 Broadway (at W 75th St) ☎496-1588. Casual, extra-large Upper West Side Italian, serving staple, affordable food.

Perretti, 270 Columbus Ave (between W 72nd and 73rd sts) ☎362-3939. Basic neighborhood Italian with below-average prices.

Presto, 2770 Broadway (between W 106th and 107th sts) ☎222-1760. An inexpensive Italian that's not bad for its pasta dishes – huge platefuls for around $9.

Sambuco, 20 W 72nd St (between Columbus Ave and Central Park West) ☎787-5656. Best described as *Carmine's* without the superior attitude, noise and long lines, this serves up great portions of good food at excellent prices.

Sfuzzi, 58 W 65th St (between Central Park West and Broadway) ☎385-8080. Swinging bar scene and lots of Italian hors d'oeuvres – easily enough to make yourself a mini dinner. Try the frozen *sfuzzi* – fresh peach nectar, champagne, and peach schnapps.

V&T Pizzeria, 1024 Amsterdam Ave (between W 110th and 111th sts) ☎663-1708. Checkered tableclothed pizzeria near Columbia that draws a predictably college-aged crowd. Good, though, and very inexpensive.

Vinnie's Pizza, 285 Amsterdam Ave (between W 73rd and 74th sts) ☎874-4332. Some say the best, cheesiest pizzas on the Upper West Side. Cheap too.

JEWISH/EASTERN EUROPEAN
Barney Greengrass (The Sturgeon King), 541 Amsterdam Ave (between W 86th and 87th sts) ☎724-4707. A West Side deli that's been around since time

began. The smoked salmon section is a particular treat.

Fine & Schapiro, 138 W 72nd St (between Broadway and Columbus Ave) ☎877-2721. Long-standing Jewish deli that's open for lunch and dinner and serves delicious old-fashioned kosher fare – an experience that's getting harder to find in New York. See Chapter 24, *Shops and Markets*.

Upper East Side

Upper East Side restaurants cater mostly to a discriminating and well-heeled clientele; many of our French and Italian "Expense-account restaurants" (see overleaf) call this neighborhood home. Otherwise, the cuisine here is much like that of the Upper West Side: a mixture of Asian, standard American, and more reasonable Italian cafés. For a change of pace, try a wurst and some strudel at one of **Yorkville's** old-world luncheonettes.

BAKERIES AND CAFÉS
Food Attitude, 127 E 60th St (between Lexington and Park aves) ☎980-1818. Sweet fruit tarts and chocolate truffle cakes make this tiny café a good place to rest up between sights. A display of crusty bread creatures graces the front window. Closed Sun.

Les Friandises, 922 Lexington Ave (between E 70th and 71st sts) ☎988-1616; 655 Amsterdam Ave (between W 92nd and 93rd sts) ☎316-1515. A paradise of French pastries on the Upper East and West sides. Wonderful croissants and brioches and a sublime *tarte tatin*.

Patisserie & Bistro, 1032 Lexington Ave (between 72nd and 73rd sts) ☎717-5252. This is real Parisian pastry, buttery, creamy, over the top. Cookies, cakes, and crème brûlée made to the exacting standards of the local millionaires' kitchen staffs.

AMERICAN, LATIN AND SOUTH AMERICAN
Arizona 206, 206 E 60th St (between 2nd and 3rd aves) ☎838-0440.

Eating

Eating

Expense-account restaurants

Should you win the lottery or have rich relatives, New York has some superb restaurants to choose from, most of them serving French or French-tinged American food, or in some cases variations on California-style cuisine. Go expecting to pay upwards of $100 a head, dress up, and phone first. If, however, you want to try one of these more expensive eateries but have neither the will nor the way to pay for it, go for lunch instead. You'll get a much better deal, often for a fixed price.

Ambassador Grill, E 44th St at 1st Ave ☎ 702-5014. In the *United Nations Hotel*, so you know what kind of clientele it serves: one that appreciates quiet and demands excellent food and service. Food tends toward the old-fashioned coq au vin and medallions of whatever, but you aren't going to see it done much better elsewhere, and the sleek dining room is truly ambassadorial.

Aquavit, 13 W 54th St (bet 5th and 6th aves) ☎ 307-7311. Superb Scandinavian food – pickled herrings, salmon, even reindeer – in a lovely atrium restaurant. A real treat.

Arcadia, 21 E 62nd St (between 5th and Madison aves) ☎ 223-2900. This small, beautifully decorated restaurant in a charming townhouse serves French-accented American food cooked up by one of America's leading young chefs.

Aureole, 34 E 61st St (between Madison and Park aves) ☎ 319-1660. Magical French-accented American food in a gorgeous old brownstone setting. The prix-fixe options should bring the cost down to $70 per head.

Le Bernadin, 155 W 51st St (between 6th and 7th aves) ☎ 489-1515. Renowned as perhaps the best place in New York to eat fish, for which the chef has received rave reviews. However, to enjoy both that and the clubby teak decor of this place you have to book months in advance. And

it's one of the city's most expensive restaurants, of any kind. Not for the dilettante eater.

Bouley, 165 Duane St (between Greenwich and Hudson sts) ☎ 608-3852. One of New York's best French restaurants, serving modern French food made from the freshest ingredients under the eye of chef David Bouley. Popular with city celebrities, but costs for the magnificent meals can be softened by opting for the prix-fixe lunch and dinner options.

Le Cirque, 58 E 65th St (between Madison and Park aves) ☎ 794-9292. This place is widely thought of as the city's top-rated restaurant. Very orchestrated, very expensive, and honored by such names as Liza Minnelli, Richard Nixon and Ronald Reagan. Not for the likes of us.

Elaine's, 1703 2nd Ave (between E 88th and 89th sts) ☎ 534-8103. Remember the opening shots of Woody Allen's *Manhattan*? That was *Elaine's*, and today her restaurant is still something of a favorite with New York celebrities – though it's hard to see why. If you want to star-gaze there's no better place to come; if you're hungry or watching the pennies, best go somewhere else.

Four Seasons, 99 E 52nd St (between Park and Lexington aves) ☎ 754-9494. Housed in Mies van der Rohe's Seagram

Intriguing southwestern decor and inventive food, though it doesn't come cheap, and the service is variable. The next-door café section is more casual and cheaper, serving essentially the same food in smaller portions.

Barking Dog Luncheonette, 1678 3rd Ave (at E 94th St) ☎ 831-1800. Puppy motif at this uptown diner with extra-special mashed potatoes and grilled cheese sandwiches. Expect lines for brunch.

Eating

Building, this is one of the city's most noted restaurants, not least for the decor, which includes murals by Picasso, sculptures by Richard Lippold and interior design by Philip Johnson. The food isn't at all bad either, and there's a relatively inexpensive pre-theater menu – around $40 – If you want to try it.

Gotham Bar & Grill, 12 E 12th St (between 5th Ave and University Place) ☎ 620-4020. This restaurant serves marvellous American fare in an airy, trendy setting. Generally reckoned to be one of the city's truly best restaurants; and it's at least worth a drink in the bar to see the city's beautiful people drift in.

Hudson River Club, 4 World Financial Center, Upper Level (between Liberty and Vesey sts) ☎ 786-1500. Worth the $70 or so per head for the view over the harbor to the Statue of Liberty. Food is American, with special emphasis on cooking from New York State's Hudson River Valley. Try the pumpkin-apple soup or the roast free-range chicken with beet risotto, but save room for one of the scrumptious chocolate desserts.

Lutece, 249 E 50th Street (between 2nd and 3rd aves) ☎ 752-2225. Once rated as the best restaurant in the country, and still well up there with the best of the places that New Yorkers (those who can afford it) will kill to get a table at. Again, big bucks and best dress.

The Rainbow Room, 30 Rockefeller Plaza, 65th floor (between W 49th and 50th sts) ☎ 632-5100. The city's best views, most overpriced food, and tacki-est entertainment in the form of the Rainbow Room Orchestra. Early evening, though, you might find it worth the price of a cocktail to take in the city skyline in comfort. Once again, Sunday best only.

River Café, 1 Water St (at the East River), Brooklyn ☎ 718/522-5200. You probably won't be able to afford the food, but for the price of a drink you can enjoy the best view of the Lower Manhattan skyline there is. Try brunch – it's the best bargain.

Russian Tea Room, 150 W 57th St (between 6th and 7th aves) ☎ 265-0947. Has been closed for a while, but scheduled to reopen in the late 1998. Rates are perhaps not as high as in the city's top French dining spots; plus it's easier to get a table. The wonderfully garish interior makes eating here a real occasion, too, though choose care-fully on the rather overrated menu, and stick to the old favorites – the blinis are among the city's best, as is the chicken kiev.

21 Club, 21 W 52nd St (between 5th and 6th aves) ☎ 582-7200. Though its days when the likes of Dorothy Parker regularly dined here are over, this remains a stylish, power-broking restau-rant, enormously popular despite its high (some might say through-the-roof) prices. (You can, however, get a prix-fixe luncheon for $24.)

Windows on the World, World Trade Center, 107th floor (at West St) ☎ 938-1111. Recent renovations have cleaned it up a bit; the views remain unchanged and are the main attraction. But if you've money to burn the food's good too, and the wine cellar is said to be among the best in New York. A nice venue for Sunday brunch; weekday lunch, previously only served to lunch club members, is now open to anyone with the money.

Brother Jimmy's BBQ, 1461 1st Ave (at E 76th St) ☎ 288-0999. Casual, fun bar-becue restaurant whose motto is "Pig Out!".

Canyon Road, 1470 1st Ave (between E 76th and 77th sts) ☎ 734-1600.

Yuppie Upper East Side place effecting a Santa Fe atmosphere. Moderate prices.

E.A.T., 1064 Madison Ave (between E 80th and 81st sts) ☎ 772-0022. Expensive and crowded but excellent

Eating

food – especially the soups and breads, and particularly the ficelles and Parmesan toast. Unlike most in the city, the mozzarella, basil and tomato sandwiches are fresh and heavenly.

El Pollo, 1746 1st Ave (between E 90th and 91st sts) ☎996-7810. Fast-food Peruvian-style chicken restaurant, serving rotisserie chicken flavored with a variety of spices to eat in or take out. Delicious – and very cheap.

Googie's Diner, 1491 2nd Ave (at E 78th St) ☎717-1122. Arty diner with funky decor and Italian-influenced American food.

Madhatter, 1485 2nd Ave (between E 77th and 78th sts) ☎628-4917. Casual pub serving decent burgers and other simple food.

Rathbones, 1702 2nd Ave (between E 88th and 89th sts) ☎369-7361. Opposite *Elaine's* (see "Expense-account restaurants", pp.338–339) and an excellent alternative for ordinary humans. Take a window seat and watch the stars arrive, and eat for a fraction of the price. Burgers, steak, fish for under $10 – and a wide choice of beers.

Serendipity 3, 225 E 60th St (between 2nd and 3rd aves) ☎838-3531. Long-established daytime eatery and ice-cream parlor adorned with Tiffany lamps. The frozen hot chocolate, a trademarked and copyrighted recipe, is out of this world.

The Velvet Room, 209 E 76th St (between 1st and 2nd aves) ☎628-6633. Upper East Siders used to have to go downtown to sit on plush, mismatched couches and eat *tapas* and light continental food. Now they don't, thanks to this eccentric but cozy room. Food is served till 3am.

Viand, 673 Madison Ave (between E 61st and 62nd sts) ☎751-6622. A bit pricier than most diner fare but worth it for the enormous turkey sandwiches, remarkable burgers, and tasty vanilla Cokes.

ASIAN

Asia, 1155 3rd Ave (between E 67th and 68th sts) ☎879-5846. Pan-Asian cuisine in a handsome wood-paneled setting.

Bangkok House, 1485 1st Ave (between E 77th and 78th sts) ☎249-5700. Terrific Thai food, fairly priced. Try the deep-fried fish with chili sauce, Pad Thai for $8.75, or masaman curry with shrimp, chicken or beef for $10.75–11.50.

Pig Heaven, 1540 2nd Ave (between E 80th and 81st sts) ☎744-4333. Good-value Chinese restaurant decorated with images of pigs. Lean and meaty spare ribs. In case you hadn't guessed, the accent is on pork.

Sala Thai, 1718 2nd Ave (between E 89th and 90th sts) ☎410-5557. Restaurant serving creative combinations of hot and spicy Thai food for under $15 a head.

FRENCH

Bistro du Nord, 1312 Madison Ave (at E 93rd St) ☎289-0997. A cozy bistro with excellent Parisian fare. Very stylish atmosphere with moderate to expensive prices – entrées run from $18–20. Try the duck confit.

Le Refuge, 166 E 82nd St (between Lexington and 3rd aves) ☎861-4505. Quiet, intimate and deliberately romantic old-style French restaurant situated in an old city brownstone. Bouillabaisse and other seafood dishes are delectable. Expensive but worth it; save for special occasions. Closed Sun during the summer.

Mme Romaine de Lyon, 29 E 61st St (between Madison and Park aves) ☎758-2422. The best place for omelettes: they've got 550 on the lunch menu, and dinner features an expanded non-omelette menu.

Voulez Vous, 1462 1st Ave (at E 76th St) ☎249-1776. Decently priced Upper East Side French bistro serving superlative deserts. Entrées are about $14–20. Known for their steak tartare and crème brûlée.

Eating

FISH AND SEAFOOD

Katch, 339 E 75th St (between 1st and 2nd aves) ☎396-4434. Not only is the fish fresh and well prepared, it's available till 3am all week long. And most of the entrées are under $10.

GREEK AND MIDDLE EASTERN

Uskudar, 1405 2nd Ave (between E 73rd and 74th sts) ☎988-2641. Authentic Turkish cuisine at a rather spartan Upper East Side venue. Great prices – plan on $25 or so for two.

INDIAN, PAKISTANI, AFRICAN

Dawat, 210 E 58th St (between 2nd and 3rd aves) ☎355-7555. The best elegant gourmet Indian dining in the city. Try the Cornish game hen with green chili or a leg of lamb. A bit pricey – entrées average about $16. For an extra charge, Beverly will give you a tarot card reading.

ITALIAN

Bella Donna, 307 E 77th St (between 1st and 2nd aves) ☎535-2866. Quaint Italian storefront restaurant with home-made pastas, low prices and long waits for a table.

Caffè Buon Gusto, 243 E 77th St (between 2nd and 3rd aves) ☎535-6884. This stretch of the Upper East Side has plenty of cool, Italian joints: what *Buon Gusto* lacks in style it makes up for in taste and prices.

Carino, 1710 2nd Ave (between E 88th and 89th sts) ☎860-0566. Family-run Upper East Side Italian, with low prices, friendly service and good food. Two can eat for under $25.

Contrapunto, 200 E 60th St (at 3rd Ave) ☎751-8616. More than twenty fresh pastas daily at this friendly, shopping neighborhood Italian restaurant. Reasonably priced as well.

Ecco-Là, 1660 3rd Ave (between E 92nd and 93rd sts) ☎860-5609. Unique pasta combinations at very moderate prices make this place one of the Upper East Side's most popular Italians. A real find if you don't mind waiting.

Il Vagabondo, 351 E 62nd St (between 1st and 2nd aves) ☎832-9221. Hearty southern Italian food in a casual setting that includes the restaurant's own bocci court.

Mezzaluna, 1295 3rd Ave (between E 74th and 75th sts) ☎535-9600. Sister restaurant to the SoHo eatery *Mezzogiorno*, this claims to be the place that introduced carpaccio to Manhattan. Whatever the truth of that, the food here is fine (great pizzas, inventive pastas), though the environment doesn't really justify the moderate-to-high prices.

JEWISH/EASTERN EUROPEAN

Café Geiger, 208 E 86th St (between 2nd and 3rd aves) ☎734-4428. Famed Yorkville eatery known for its elaborate German cakes and pastries. There is also an extensive and reasonably priced dinner menu, including sauerbraten.

Heidelburg, 1648 2nd Ave (between E 85th and 86th sts) ☎628-2332. The atmosphere here *mittel*-European kitsch, with gingerbread trim and waitresses in Alpine goatherd costumes. But the food is the real deal, with excellent liver dumpling soup, Bauernfruestuck omelettes, and pancakes (both sweet and potato). And they serve Weissbeer the right way, too – in giant, boot-shaped glasses.

Ideal Restaurant, 238 E 86th St (between 2nd and 3rd aves) ☎535-0950. Before renovations a few years back, this was the place. Now, we're not so sure. But you can still get wursts and sauerkraut in huge portions for paltry prices.

Mocca Hungarian, 1588 2nd Ave (between E 82nd and 83rd sts) ☎734-6470. Yorkville restaurant serving hearty portions of Hungarian comfort food – schnitzel, cherry soup, goulash and chicken paprikash, among others. Moderately priced, but be sure to come hungry.

SPANISH

Malaga, 406 E 73rd St (between 1st and York aves) ☎737-7659. Intimate Spanish

Eating

restaurant frequented by locals. Good, wholesome food at decent prices.

Harlem, Washington Heights, Inwood

Cheap Cuban, African, Caribbean, and the best soul-food restaurants in the city abound in and around **Harlem**; even institutions like *Sylvia's*, touristy and crowded as it may be, remain reasonably priced. Too many visitors to New York forego excursions, culinary and otherwise, to Harlem, but it's well worth the trip.

BAKERIES AND CAFÉS

Wilson's Bakery and Restaurant, 1980 Amsterdam Ave (at W 158th St) ☎923-9821. Luscious Southern specialties, like sweet potato pie and peach cobbler, but much more than desserts – try the chicken and waffle combination.

AFRICAN

Koryoe Restaurant and Café, 3151 Broadway (between Tiemann Place and LaSalle St) ☎316-2950. Huge portions of West African specialties served with your choice of meat and sauce. Try the *wacheay*, rice with black-eyed peas, plantains, and your choice of meat for $9. Also a vegetarian section.

Zula, 1260 Amsterdam Ave (at W 122nd St) ☎663-1670. High-quality and inexpensive ($7 up) Ethiopian food that's popular with the folk from Columbia. Spicy chicken, beef and lamb dishes mainly, though a few veggie plates too.

AMERICAN, LATIN AND SOUTH AMERICAN

Caridad Restaurant, 4311 Broadway (at W 184th St) ☎781-0431. Not to be confused with the Upper West Side restaurant of (almost) the same name, this place serves mountains of Dominican food at cheap prices. Try the *mariscos* or seafood, specialty of the house and eaten with lots of *pan y ajo*, thick slices of French bread, grilled with olive oil and plenty of garlic. Be sure to go feeling hungry.

Copeland's, 547 W 145th St (between Broadway and Amsterdam Ave) ☎234-2357. Soul food at good prices for dinner or Sunday brunch, with a more reasonably priced cafeteria next door. Try the Louisiana gumbo. Live jazz on Fri and Sat nights.

Emily's, 1325 5th Ave (at E 111th St) ☎996-1212. Barbecued chicken and some of the best ribs in New York in a convivial atmosphere.

Londel's, 2620 8th Ave (between 139th and 140th sts) ☎234-6114. A little soul food, a little Cajun, a little Southern-fried chicken. This is an attractive down-home place where you can eat upscale items like steak diane or more common treats like fried chicken; either way, follow it up with some sweet potato pie.

Sylvia's Restaurant, 328 Lenox Ave (between 126th and 127th sts) ☎996-0660. Legendary Southern soul-food restaurant in Harlem with exceptional greens and Southern fried chicken. Go early on a Wednesday night and get free tickets for amateur night at the *Apollo*. A New York must.

The Outer Boroughs

If you decide to explore the **Outer Boroughs**, food could be as good a motivation as any. The ethnic communities here have for the most part retained their closed character – and their restaurants are similarly authentic, generally run by and for the locals. All of New York's ethnic groups are well represented, and you can eat more or less anything: **Brooklyn** has some of New York's best West Indian and Italian food, not to mention its most authentic Russian restaurants; **Queens** holds the city's biggest Greek and South American communities; while Belmont in the **Bronx** is one of the best places in the city to eat authentic Italian cuisine.

BROOKLYN: BROOKLYN HEIGHTS AND ATLANTIC AVENUE

Gage & Tollner, 372 Fulton St (between Jay and Boerum sts), downtown

Eating

24-hour food

This is simply a checklist for **late-night** – and mainly budget-constrained – hunger. For details, either check the listings in the above sections, or assume they serve a straight coffee-shop menu. If you're nowhere near any of the addresses below, don't despair. There are numerous additional all-night delis (for takeout food), and in most neighborhoods of the city you'll also find at least one 24-hour Korean greengrocer – good for most food supplies.

Lower Manhattan

Around the Clock, 8 Stuyvesant St (between 2nd and 3rd aves) ☎598-0402

Bagel Buffet, 406 6th Ave (between W 8th and 9th sts) ☎477-0448

Dave's Pot Belly, 94 Christopher St (at Bleecker St) ☎242-8036

French Roast Café, 456 6th Ave (at W 11th St) ☎533-2233

Greenwich Cafe, 75 Greenwich Ave (between 7th Ave S and Bank St) ☎255-5450

Kiev, 117 2nd Ave (at E 7th St) ☎674-4040

L'Express, 249 Park Ave South (at 20th St) ☎254-5858

7A, 109 Ave A (between E 6th and 7th sts) ☎673-6853

Triumph Restaurant, 148 Bleecker St (between LaGuardia and Thompson sts) ☎228-3070

Veselka, 144 2nd Ave (between E 9th St and St Mark's Place) ☎228-9682

Waverly Restaurant, 385 6th Ave (between W 8th St and Waverly Place) ☎675-3181

Yaffa Café, 97 St Mark's Place (between Ave A and 1st Ave) ☎677-9001

Midtown Manhattan

Brasserie, 100 E 53rd St (between Park and Lexington aves) ☎751-4840

Empire Diner, 210 10th Ave (between W 22nd and 23rd sts) ☎243-2736

Gemini Diner, 641 2nd Ave (at E 35th St) ☎532-2143

Lox Around the Clock, 676 6th Ave (at W 21st St) ☎691-3535

Market Diner, 572 11th Ave (at W 43rd St) ☎695-0415

Sarge's, 548 3rd Ave (between E 36th and 37th sts) ☎679-0442

Stage Deli, 834 7th Ave (between W 53rd and 54th sts) ☎245-7850

West Side Diner, 360 9th Ave (at W 31st St) ☎560-8407

Upper Manhattan

Big Nick's, 2175 Broadway (between 76th and 77th sts) ☎362-9238.

Gray's Papaya, 2090 Broadway (at W 72nd St) ☎799-0243

Green Kitchen, 1477 1st Ave (at E 77th St) ☎988-4163

H & H Bagels, 2239 Broadway (at W 80th St) ☎595-8000

Tramway Coffee Shop, 1143 2nd Ave (at E 60th St) ☎758-7017

Brooklyn ☎718/875-5181. Old-fashioned seafood restaurant with an extensive menu that's long been part of the downtown Brooklyn eating scene. Not as expensive as it looks. Serves great crab cakes, Charleston she-crab soup and clam bellies.

Henry's End, 44 Henry St (at Cranberry St), Brooklyn Heights ☎718/834-1776. Neighborhood bistro with a wide selection of seasonal dishes, appetizers and desserts. Normally crowded, and don't expect it to be all that cheap. Known for its wild-game festival in fall and winter.

Montague Street Saloon, 122 Montague St (between Henry and Hicks sts), Brooklyn Heights ☎718/522-6770. Burgers and salads for under $10; good fried calamari and Cajun catfish.

Eating

Moroccan Star, 205 Atlantic Ave (between Court and Clinton sts), Brooklyn Heights ☎718/643-0800. Perhaps New York's best Moroccan restaurant, with wonderful *tajines* and couscous with lamb. The chef once worked at the *Four Seasons*, and the quality of his cooking remains undiminished.

Moustache Pitza, 405 Atlantic Ave (at Bond St) ☎718/852-5555. Original and best branch of small Middle-Eastern chain that has since migrated to Mahattan (see p.316).

Oznot's Dish, 79 Berry (at N 9th St) ☎718/599-6596. Technically Middle Eastern, but in decor and spirit more Middle-East-Village. Plop down on one of the antique chairs and try grilled shrimp with jalapeño vinagrette served on a grilled mango, or lamb chunks over basmati rice with melted leeks and tomatillos.

Patsy's Pizza, 19 Old Fulton St (between Water and Front sts) ☎718/858-4300. Delicious, thin and crispy pies that bring even Manhattanites across the water.

Peter Luger's Steak House, 178 Broadway (at Driggs Ave), Williamsburg ☎718/387-7400. Pricey (around $40 a head) place, but reckoned by aficionados to have the best steaks in the city – which is quite a claim. Good service and pleasant ambience make it a great place to eat a charred porterhouse steak.

Petite Crevette, 127 Atlantic Ave (between Henry and Clinton sts) ☎718/858-6660. Reasonable, comfortable French bistro with many simple fish dishes.

PlanEat Thailand, 184 Bedford Ave (between N 6th and 7th sts), Williamsburg ☎718/599-5758. A welcome addition to Bedford Ave that serves reasonably priced spicy Thai food. Worth a trip on the L train if you're in Manhattan.

Stacy's, 85 Broadway (at Berry St) ☎718/486-8004. Cheap neighborhood restaurant serving an eclectic mix of Moroccan, Middle Eastern and American fare. Works by local artists, a majority of the clientele, are displayed on the walls.

Teresa's, 80 Montague St (between Hicks St and Montague Terrace) ☎718/797-3996. Large portions of Polish home-cooking – blintzes, *pierogies* and the like – make this a good lunchtime stopoff for those on tours of Brooklyn Heights.

Tripoli, 156 Atlantic Ave (at Clinton St), Brooklyn Heights ☎718/596-5800. Lebanese restaurant serving fish, lamb and vegetarian dishes for a low $8 or so. Miniature lamb pies in yoghurt sauce is a standout.

BROOKLYN: CENTRAL BROOKLYN

Aunt Sonia's, 1123 8th Ave (at 12th St), Park Slope ☎718/965-9526. Seasonal eclectic menu featuring everything from Caribbean to Thai to Italian to traditional American. Main courses for around $10.

Aunt Suzie's, 247 5th Ave (between Garfield Place and Carroll St), Park Slope ☎718/788-3377. Neighborhood Italian serving decent food for as little as $10 a person. Not a restaurant to drive from Manhattan for, but if you happen to be in the area, it's one of the best-value places around.

Cucina, 256 5th Ave (between Garfield Place and Carroll St), Park Slope ☎718/230-0711. Warm and inviting Italian restaurant serving exemplary food for affordable prices.

Fatoosh Babecue, 311 Henry St (at Atlantic Ave) ☎718/596-0030. Call it "hippie Middle Eastern," fresh, hearty felafel and babaganoush in a funky boîte on a shady Cobble Hill street.

Ferdinando's, 151 Union St (between Hicks and Columbia sts) ☎718/855-1545. Authentic Italian, cooked and served by the family that owns this tiny dining room. Nothing fancy, just your basic sauces, meats, and pastas made the same way they've been making them out here for decades.

Leaf 'n' Bean, 83 7th Ave (between Union and Berkeley sts), Park Slope ☎718/638-5791. Exotic coffees and teas plus excellent homemade soups and gourmet truffle candies. Brunch for about $10 on weekends. Outdoor seating when it's fine.

Once Upon a Sundae, 7702 3rd Ave (at 77th St), Bayridge ☎718/748-3412. Turn-of-the-century ice cream parlor.

Sam's, 238 Court St (between Baltic and Kenneth sts), Cobble Hill ☎718/596-3458. Long-established restaurant serving standard Italian fare at reasonable prices.

BROOKLYN: CONEY ISLAND AND BRIGHTON BEACH

Carolina, 1409 Mermaid Ave (at W 15th St), Coney Island ☎718/714-1294. Inexpensive, family-run Italian restaurant that's been around forever. Great food, great prices.

Gargiulo's, 2911 W 15th St (between Surf and Mermaid aves) ☎718/266-4891. A gigantic, noisy family-run Coney Island restaurant famed for its large portions of cheap and hearty Neapolitan grub.

Mrs Stahl's, 1001 Brighton Beach Ave (at Coney Island Ave), Brighton Beach ☎718/648-0210. Long-standing knishery with over 20 different varieties.

Nathan's Famous, Surf and Stillwell Ave, Coney Island ☎718/266-3161. New York's most famous hot dogs and crinkle-cut French fries. Not the ultimate in gastronomy but a legend nonetheless.

Odessa, 1113 Brighton Beach Ave (between 13th and 14th sts), Brighton Beach ☎718/332-3223. Excellent and varied Russian menu at unbeatable prices. Dancing and music nightly.

Primorski, 282 Brighton Beach Ave (between 2nd and 3rd sts), Brighton Beach ☎718/891-3111. Perhaps the best of Brighton Beach's Russian hangouts, serving up a huge menu of authentic Russian dishes, including blintzes and stuffed cabbage, at absurdly cheap prices. Live music in the evening.

THE BRONX

Dominick's, 2335 Arthur Ave (between 187th St and Crescent Ave), Fordham ☎718/733-2807. All you could hope for in a Belmont Italian: great, rowdy atmosphere, wonderful food and low(ish) prices.

Marlo's, 2342 Arthur Ave (between 187th St and Crescent Ave), Fordham ☎718/584-1188. Pricey but impressive cooking, enticing even die-hard Manhattanites to the Bronx.

QUEENS: ASTORIA

Omonia Café, 32–20 Broadway (at 33rd St), Astoria ☎718/274-6650. Affordable Greek neighborhood restaurant.

Uncle George's, 33–19 Broadway (at 34th St), Astoria ☎718/626-0593. This 24-hour joint serves excellent and ultra-cheap authentic Greek food.

QUEENS: JACKSON HEIGHTS

Inti-Raymi, 86–14 37th Ave (between 86 and 87th sts), Jackson Heights ☎718/424-1938. Unpretentious restaurant serving substantial low-priced Peruvian food in a jovial atmosphere. Try the *ceviche de mariscos* (raw fish in lime juice) or the Peruvian version of *lo mein*.

Jackson Diner, 37–03 74th St (between 37th and Roosevelt Ave), Jackson Heights ☎718/672-1232. Come here hungry and stuff yourself silly with amazingly light and cheap Indian fare. Samosas and mango lassis are not to be missed.

La Pequeña Colombia, 83–27 Roosevelt Ave (at 90th St), Jackson Heights ☎718/478-6528. Literally "Little Colombia," this place doles out heaped portions of seafood casserole, pork and tortillas. Try the fruit drinks too, *maracuay* (passion fruit) or *guanabana* (sour soup).

Las Americas, 93–09 37th Ave (at 90th St), Jackson Heights ☎718/458-1638. Colombian cakes, pastries and full meals. Good for inexpensive lunches.

Eating

Eating

Tabaq 74, 73-21 37th Ave (between 74th and 75th sts) ☎718/898-2837. Pakistani barbecue of the highest order. If you don't like beef brains (the house specialty), you can have chicken, lamb, or quail, generously spiced and prepared with skill and care.

QUEENS: FOREST HILLS, JAMAICA, BAYSIDE, KEW GARDENS

Pastrami King, 124-24 Queens Blvd (at 82nd Ave), Kew Gardens ☎718/263-1717. The home-smoked pastrami and corned beef are better than any you'll find in Manhattan. Closed Sat.

STATEN ISLAND

Aesop's Tables, 1233 Bay St (at Hylan Blvd), Rosebank ☎718/720-2005. Cozy and rustic restaurant serving interesting American variations. Try the catfish over greens or jerk chicken.

Goodfella's Pizza, 17-18 Hylan Blvd ☎718/987-2422. Not worth a special trip, but if you've ferried across, you'll find the pizza here more than up to the snuff.

Chapter 18

Drinking

Despite the image many Europeans have of puritanical, abstemious Americans living on bottled water, New York is a drinking town. You can't walk a block along most Manhattan avenues (and many of the sidestreets) without passing one or two **bars**. You can swig $1 dollar drafts at your local dive or sip martinis in the city's most plush hotel bars. Specific **savings** on drinking can often be made in the larger bars by ordering quart or half-gallon pitchers of beer, which represent a considerable discount on the price per glass. Look out, too, for "happy hour" bargains (see below) and two-for-the-price-of-one deals. Also, avoid bars or clubs that offer "free drinks for ladies" – they tend to be cattle markets or worse. Remember too that many serve some form of food,

from basic chicken wings and ribs to full-blown meals.

Bars generally **open** from mid-morning (around 10am) to the early hours – 4am at the latest, when they have to close by law. As for prices, in a basic bar you'll be paying $2–2.50 for a glass of draft beer (a little over a half-pint), $3–4 a bottle, although in a swankier and/or more fashionable environment, or in a singles joint, this may go up considerably. Detailed listings and recommendations begin on p.350.

What to drink

When you've made your choice of bar, the problem is deciding **what to drink**.

Beer

Despite its successful incursion into overseas markets in recent years, American

---

Happy hours and free food

At the turn of the last century, Bowery barkeeps offered a "free lunch" of pickles and boiled eggs to attract workingmen during their mid-day break. This has evolved into **happy hour**, now designed to pull in the after-work crowds. It's generally a two-hour period, often 5–7pm, Monday to Friday only. Discounts are offered, either in two-for-one deals, or sometimes with special prices on specific drinks. Bars often put out thirst-inducing **snacks** like popcorn or pretzels during happy hour, but some

offer free hors d'oeuvres, particularly the swell midtown joints. Since the idea in these cases is to draw in well-heeled clientele, you'll do well to **dress** appropriately, though most of these places will accommodate you as long as you perform with confidence and don't too obviously clear the tables. The **cost** of a regular drink or cocktail should work out around $3. For happy hour devotees, there are possibilities in addition to those listed: just check out the more upscale midtown bars and hotels.

Drinking

The age rage

The drinking age in New York, as in the rest of the US, is 21 and, unlike some states, that's not just for hard liquor. Order *any* kind of alcohol and you're likely to be "carded" or "proofed" – carry ID just in case. If you're underage, you won't get in trouble for trying to buy alcohol; just prepare yourself for embarrassment if you're turned down. It's also not uncommon for staff to ask for proof of your age even when you're *obviously* well over 21: this either seems to be a ploy to irritate you – or to pick you up. In the Giuliani era, neighborhoods with a high youth population (ie, near colleges) have been subject to "sweeps" by local police, so if you aren't carded at a place one day, don't count on avoiding it the next.

beer has long enjoyed something of a reputation for being fizzy, tasteless and with a relatively low alcoholic content. On the bright side, it's normally served so chilled that the taste barely matters anyway. The major brands available everywhere are *Budweiser, Miller* and *Rolling Rock*, of which the last is the most palatable, but increasingly you'll see more interesting American beers in bottles or on tap – *Anchor Steam, Pete's Wicked* and *Samuel Adams* are some of the better brands you'll often encounter in New York. Also imported beers like Canadian *Molson*, Mexican *Dos Equis* and the familiar European varieties are widely available. At least a few "boutique beers" can be found in most bars above the "dive" category – they usually cost around $4 a pint. If price is a problem, then bear in mind you can walk into any supermarket or corner store and buy beer at around $1 a can.

Wines

By all means sample Californian **wines**. They are not only very good but also fairly inexpensive at around $8–10 for a bottle in a liquor store, less than this if you buy a so-called "jug wine" – basically the nastiest, lowest-quality wine there is. If you're keen to sample something decent, try the varieties from the Napa or Sonoma valleys, just north of San Francisco, which between them produce some of the best-quality wines in the country. New York State also produces wine, though of a lesser quality than California. French and Italian wines come more expensive, but they're still by no means costly. In all cases, however, wine does demand a better-filled wallet when in a restaurant or bar: expect 100 percent mark-up on the bottle.

Spirits and liquor

As for the **hard stuff**, there are a number of points of potential confusion for overseas visitors. First bear in mind that whether you ask for a drink "on the rocks" or not, you'll most likely get it poured into a glass full to the brim with ice; if you don't want it like this ask for it "straight up." Don't forget either that if you ask for whiskey you will get one of the American kinds, most likely rye, of which the most common brand is *Seagram's 7*. If you want bourbon, Scotch or Irish whiskey you should ask for them by name. Pick a brand if you want something better than "speed rack" liquor (the cheap stuff a bartender serves if a brand choice is not indicated); it will cost more, but it will also be infinitely more drinkable. *Jim Beam, Wild Turkey*, and *Maker's Mark* are among the better readily available bourbons. For Irish, *Paddy, Bushmill's* and *Murphy's* are the safe bets, and unless you want to get into the thicket of single-malts available in the better bars, *Johnny Walker* (*Black* or *Red*) is the most popular Scotch. And neither should you ask for *Martini* if you want the herby drink drunk by beautiful people. To Americans a martini is a mixture of gin and vermouth, usually with an olive or two, served in an elegant stemmed glass (and still drunk by beautiful people) – vermouth (pronounced "vermooth") to an American being what the British would call *Martini*.

Cocktails

Cocktails are popular all over the States, especially during happy hours and weekend brunch. The standards are listed overleaf, but really varieties are innumerable, sometimes specific to a single bar. With any names you come across, experiment – that's half the fun. Look out for something called **jello-shots**, an intoxicating sort of gelatinous matter: they're served in some of the livelier bars and restaurants, only made with vodka instead of water. For novice drinkers, a word of advice: go slow with any drink containing more than three ingredients.

Non-alcoholic drinks

By law, all NYC bars must serve selections of **non-alcoholic drinks**. Even if you plump for (say) the dubious delights of the alcohol-free beers that have become popular in recent years, quaffing a *Kaliber* in an Irish bar is a bit like having a bath with your raincoat on. See "Coffee and tea," p.317, in the previous chapter for details of places specializing in genteel refreshment – and those that will provide you with a serious caffeine hit.

Buying your own booze

When buying your own alcohol, you'll need to find a **liquor store** – supermarkets only have beer, just one of New York State's complex **licensing laws**. Other regulations worth keeping in mind are that you have to be over 21 to buy or consume alcohol in a bar or restaurant (and you'll be asked to provide evidence if there's any dispute); that it's against the law to drink alcohol on the street (which is why you see so many people furtively swigging from brown paper bags, though this still doesn't make it legal); and that you can't buy your own booze, other than beer, anywhere on a Sunday.

Where to drink

It's in Manhattan – and more specifically below about 23rd Street – that you're likely to spend most time **drinking** (as well as eating). Many of the city's better bars are situated in this part of town, as well the majority of the cheaper (and ethnic) restaurants. For drinking only, you'll find some of the bars listed here (music and gay-oriented places, most obviously) cross over into the *Nightlife* chapter that follows, both in terms of feel and often escalating prices.

The bar scene

The **bar scene** in New York City is a varied one, with a broader range of places to drink than in most American cities, and prices to suit most pockets. At the bottom end of the scale, the cheapest watering holes you'll find, all over the city, are roughish places – convivial enough, though difficult ground for women on their own, and sometimes for men. In addition to these, there are more mixed hangouts, varying from some of the long-established haunts in Greenwich Village to newer, louder and more deliberately stylish places that spring up – and die out – all the time in the downtown neighborhoods. Bars with some kind of theme are particularly big right now. Finally there are also bars, known as **"singles bars,"** many of which concentrate in Midtown on the east side, which New Yorkers tend to use to pick up a member of the opposite (or same) sex. Expect prices to be hiked up greatly anywhere like this.

Selections that follow are personal favorites. The potential choice, obviously, is a lot wider – below 14th Street it's hard to walk more than a block without finding a bar – and takes in the whole range of taste, budget and purpose. (Bear in mind that many places double as bar and restaurant, and you may therefore find them listed not here but in the previous chapter, *Eating*.) The best hunting grounds are in the East Village, SoHo, and TriBeCa; there's a good choice

Drinking

Drinking

of midtown bars – though here bars tend to be geared to an after-hours office crowd and (with a few notable exceptions) can consequently be pricey and rather dull; uptown, the Upper West Side, between 60th and 85th streets along Amsterdam and Columbus, has a good array of bars though these tend to cater to more of a clean-cut and dully collegiate crowd.

Hours of opening are generally mid-morning through to 1am or 2am; some stay open later but by law all must close by 4am. Bar kitchens usually stop operating around midnight or a little before. Wherever you go, even if you just have a drink you'll be expected to **tip**: the going rate is roughly ten percent of the bill or 50¢ for a single drink.

Groupings follow, approximately, the chapter divisions outlined in the *Guide*. For ease of reference, however, all specifically gay and lesbian bars are gathered together in a single section on p.357.

Financial District and Civic Center

Greatest Bar on Earth, 1 World Trade Center, 107th Floor, Liberty St ☎524-7000. Posh, expensive bar with obviously excellent views; holds a popular lounge party on Wed.

Jeremy's Alehouse, 254 Front St (at Dover St) ☎964-3537. Earthy bar near the South Street Seaport, and one of the best in an otherwise bland area. Fried calamari for $5.95 and fried clams for $4.95.

SoHo and TriBeCa

Broome Street Bar, 363 W Broadway (between Broome and Grand sts) ☎925-2086. A popular and long-established local haunt, these days more restaurant than bar, serving reasonably priced burgers and salads in a dimly lit setting. A nice place just to nurse a beer too, especially when footsore from SoHo's shops and galleries.

Buddha Bar, 150 Varick St ☎255-4433. This red-lit bar opens at 10pm; quite cozy early but gets raunchy quickly as the clubbers arrive.

Café Noir, 32 Grand St (at Thompson St) ☎ 431-7910. Faux-Moroccan decor (think Sidney Greenstreet's place in *Casablanca*, without the flies) and lush cocktails. A place to be seen.

Fanelli, 94 Prince St (at Mercer St) ☎226-9412. Established in 1872, *Fanelli* is one of SoHo's oldest bars, relaxed and informal. Food is simple Italian-American fare: burgers, Maryland crab cakes and homemade soups.

Knitting Factory, Leonard St (between Church St and Broadway) ☎219-3055. Cozy downstairs taproom with 18 draft micros. $1 draughts from 5pm to 6pm weekdays.

La Jumelle, 55 Grand St (between Wooster St and W Broadway) ☎941-9651. Just down from the *Lucky Strike* in SoHo (see opposite), and similar in many

ways, though more popular with young Europeans.

Lucky Strike, 59 Grand St (between W Broadway and Wooster St) ☎941-0479. Convivial bar/bistro patronized by a mixed bunch of young and middle-aged SoHo-ites. Food served out back (nothing special and not cheap), and DJs on Fri, Sat and Sun nights, when the scene can be buzzing – though it's really best at lunchtime, when it's less frenetic.

McGovern's, 305 Spring St (between Hudson and Washington) ☎243-8804. Looks a bit down-at-the-heels, but a cozy neighborhood joint with excellent "guest" beers that change monthly and live bands on weekends.

Ñ, 33 Crosby St (between Broome and Grand sts) ☎219-8856. Laid-back in summer and packed on frosty winter nights, this long and narrow bar serves *paté de aceitunas* and other tasty tapas. $15 pitchers of not-too-sweet sangria are a great value. A favorite on the SoHo scene.

Puffy's Tavern, 81 Hudson St (at Harrison St) ☎766-9159. Small, funky TriBeCa bar with lunchtime food and bar pizza, cheap booze, and a great jukebox.

Drinking

Hotel bars

There's no better place to go for a martini in New York when you're feeling fabulous. Hotel bars are posh watering holes for the well bred and well maintained and, lest you forget, their sole purpose is comfort. Sure the drinks are expensive, but you're paying for atmosphere, too. Sink back into a comfy banquette, sip your precious booze slowly and with dignity, and watch the parade of foreign dignitaries, royalty, well-groomed businesspeople, and mysterious strangers conducting important affairs.

Bemelman's, The Carlyle, 35 E 76th St (at Madison Ave) ☎744-1600

The Blue Bar, The Algonquin Hotel, 59 W 44th St (between 5th and 6th aves ☎840-6800

5757, The Four Seasons, 57 E 57th St (between Madison and Park Ave) ☎758-5700

44, The Royalton, 44 W 44th St (between 5th and 6th aves) ☎944-8844

King Cole Bar, St Regis Hotel, 2 E 55th St (between 5th and Madison aves) ☎339-6721

The Lounge, The Inn at Irving Place, 54 Irving Place (between E 17th and 18th sts) ☎533-4600

The Oak Bar, The Plaza Hotel, 768 Fifth Ave (at 59th St) ☎546-5320

The View, The Marriott Marquis, 1535 Broadway (at W 45th St) ☎398-1900

Drinking

Sporting Club, 99 Hudson St (between Leonard and Franklin sts) ☎219-0900. Sports bar with a large electronic screen to keep up with the action. Up to nine different events can be screened at once, with college and pro scores posted on an electronic scoreboard. Closed on weekends during the summer.

Spring Lounge, 48 Spring St (at Mulberry St) ☎965-1774. The former *Shark Bar*, peopled by trendy youths, though even with expanded space it's still a downbeat hole-in-the-wall.

Greenwich Village

Chumley's, 86 Bedford St (between Grove and Barrow sts) ☎675-4449. Not easy to find, and with good reason – this place used to be a speakeasy and is obviously so well known now it doesn't need to advertise its presence. High on atmosphere and with a good choice of beers and food from around $8. Best arrive before 8pm if you want to eat at one of the battered tables – at which, supposedly, James Joyce put the finishing touches to *Ulysses*.

Corner Bistro, 331 W 4th St (between W 12th and Jane sts) ☎242-9502. Get here early for a booth in this dark and smoky tavern. Excellent BLTs, grilled chicken sandwiches, burgers and fries and a great jazz jukebox.

Fannie's Oyster Bar, 765 Washington St ☎255-5101. Tiny oyster bar with live blues music, good gumbo, and other Cajun specialties. Closed Mon.

Fifty Five, 55 Christopher St (between 6th and 7th aves) ☎929-9883. Near the site of the late, lamented *Lion's Head*, this bar has a great jazz jukebox and live jazz performances seven nights a week.

Hogs & Heifers, 859 Washington St (at W 13th St) ☎229-0930. Hogs as in the burly motorcycles parked outside; heifers as in, well, ladies. Though there's no more bar dancing (Julia Roberts was famously photographed doing so here) due to a recent bust, you can still drink to excess in this rough-and-tumble meat-packing district joint, which plenty do.

Jekyll and Hyde, 91 7th Ave South (between Barrow and Grove sts) ☎989-7701; 1409 6th Ave (between W 57th and 58th sts). Novelty pub with a haunted house theme that appeals to a mainly under-25 crowd.

Orbit Café & Bar, 46 Bedford St (between Leroy St and 7th Ave) ☎463-8717. Cocktails, oysters and a Spanish-American menu. Pan-seared trout and a good selection of pizzas.

Peculier Pub, 145 Bleecker St (between La Guardia and Thompson sts) ☎353-1327. Popular local bar whose main claim to fame is the number of beers it sells – more than 300 in all and examples from any country you care to mention.

Scrap Bar, 130 W 3rd St (no phone). Built on the site of the folk club where Bob Dylan had his first residency, a small punky bar with loud music.

The Universal, 44 Bedford St (between Leroy St and 6th Ave) ☎989-5621. A gay club that welcomes straights who can get with the cheerful cross-gender vibe. There's decent food, and if you tell them it's your birthday (don't be afraid to lie), disco lights come on and the busboys run to your table in outrageous headdresses to shimmy to some cheesy song or other (such as the "I Dream of Jeannie" theme).

Village Idiot, 355 W 14th St (at 9th Ave) ☎989-7334. Like *Hogs & Heifers* minus the crowds and celebs. Tommy, the owner, eats beer cans and (when he's feeling really perky) shot glasses. For a dollar, you can feed a goldfish to the bar's snapping turtle.

White Horse Tavern, 567 Hudson St (at W 11th St) ☎243-9260. Village bar where Dylan Thomas supped his last before being carted off to hospital with alcoholic poisoning, and where today you can buy burgers, chili and the like for around $5. Little changed, apart from the excellent jukebox, since Dylan fell off his bar stool.

Lower East Side, East Village

Ace, 531 E 5th St (between Ave A and Ave B) ☎979-8476. Behind the architectural glass brick is a noisy and strangely cavernous bar, with pool table, darts and a good jukebox.

bOb, 235 Eldridge St (between Stanton and Houston sts) ☎777-0588. A hip lounge with occasional DJs who do little to disturb the languid atmosphere. Nice garden in the back, too.

Cedar Tavern, 82 University Place (between E 11th and 12th sts) ☎929-9089. Legendary beat and artists' meeting point in the 1950s and now a cozy bar with food and well-priced drinks. Have some pork chops or a burger. In the summer you can eat in their covered roof garden upstairs.

d.b.a., 41 1st Ave (between E 2nd and 3rd sts) ☎475-5097. A beer lover's paradise, *d.b.a.* has 60 bottled beers, 12 beers on tap, and an authentic hand pump.

Doc Holliday's, 141 Avenue A (between 10th and 11th sts) ☎979-0312. A very rowdy bar with a cowboy theme; barmaids will, with the slightest provocation, hoot, holler and pour liquor straight from the bottle into your mouth.

Grassroots Tavern, 20 St Mark's Place (between 2nd and 3rd aves) ☎475-9443. Basement bar at the center of the East Village hum: not expensive, and with a good oldies jukebox and two darts boards.

Holiday Cocktail Lounge, 75 St Mark's Place (between 2nd and 3rd aves) ☎777-9637. East Village dive bar that attracts a mixed bag of customers, from old-world grandfathers to the young and trendy. Good place for an afternoon beer. Closes early.

Hotel Galvez, 103 Ave B (between 6th and 7th sts) ☎358-9683. Newcomer with good, live music, above-average Southwestern food and a lot of youthful drinkers.

International Bar, 120 1/2 1st Ave (between E 7th St and St Mark's Place)

☎777-9214. Christmas lights year-round make this neighborhood bar a cozy choice for the East Village. Bring crisp bills and choose from two moody juke-boxes.

Joe's, E 6th St (between aves A and B), no phone. Cowboy music, cheap beer and pool table in a tatty East Village setting.

KGB, 85 E 4th St (between 2nd and 3rd aves) ☎505-3360. Soviet motif bar on the second floor. Popular with off-off Broadway theater crowds.

Lakeside Lounge, 162 Avenue B (between 10th and 11th sts) ☎529-8463. Opened by a local DJ and a record producer who have stocked the jukebox with old rock, country and R&B to keep annoying college students out. A down-home hangout, with occassional live music.

Lansky Lounge, 38 Delancey St (between Norfolk and Suffolk sts) ☎677-5588. The venerable dairy restaurant *Ratner's* has spun its back room into a retro cocktail lounge, to which jaded urban sophisticates flock.

Luna Lounge, 171 Ludlow (between Houston and Stanton sts) ☎260-2323. Across the street from *Max Fish* (see below), it gets the substantial spillover. Noisy rock bands or stand-up comedians perform in the back.

Max Fish, 178 Ludlow St (between Houston and Stanton sts) ☎529-3959. Pretentious, but prototypical, tragically hip Downtown music and art crowd. Holds regular art exhibitions.

McSorley's, 15 E 7th St (between 2nd and 3rd aves) ☎473-9148. New York City's longest-established watering hole, so it claims, and a male-only bar until just over a decade ago. These days it retains a saloon look, with a youthful gang indulging themselves on the cheap strong ale. There's no trouble deciding what to drink – you can have beer, and you can have it dark or light.

Mona's, Ave B (between E 13th and 14th sts) ☎353-3780. A favorite East

Drinking

Drinking

Village dive bar that's been discovered by the younger set.

Nation, 50 Ave A (between E 3rd and 4th sts) ☎473-6239. Coffeehouse by day, bar by night. An abundance of tall mirrors makes for good people-watching. A different live DJ every night of the week.

Noho Star, 330 Lafayette St (between Bleecker and Houston sts) ☎925-0070. Laid-back NoHo ("North of Houston") bar decorated by its artist clientele and serving a mix of American and Thai-influenced Asian food.

Sapphire Lounge, 249 Eldridge St (between Houston and Stanton) ☎777-5153. Very small, very dark, and very popular with the cocktail-dress-and-martini-glass tribe.

Sophie's, 507 E 5th St (between aves A and B) ☎228-5680. $1 draft beer and oh-so-cheap mixed drinks make this bar the consummate East Village hang-out. Pool table and jukebox.

Temple Bar, 332 Lafayette St (between Bleecker and Houston sts) ☎925-4242. Small, dark, elegant bar serving champagne and, some claim, Manhattan's best martinis to a self-consciously Beautiful Bunch. Exceptionally good people-watching.

Tenth Street Lounge, 212 E 10th St (between 2nd and 3rd aves) ☎473-5252. Dim red lighting and cushy couches make this an elegant atmosphere for watching model-wannabes, despite the overpriced cocktails.

2A, corner of 2nd St and Ave A, no phone. A long, thin and wildly popular bar catering to longtime East Village residents. Bar sometimes manned by "Handsome Dick" Manitoba of the legendary punk rock group The Dictators.

Vazac's, 108 Ave B (between E 6th and 7th sts) ☎473-8840. Known as "7 B" for its location on the corner of Tompkins Square, this is a popular East Village hangout, with an extremely mixed crowd, that's often used as a sleazy set in films and commercials – perhaps most

famously in the film *Crocodile Dundee*.

Union Square, Gramercy Park, Murray Hill and Midtown East

The Coffee Shop, 29 Union Square West (between E 16th and 17th sts) ☎243-7969. A former coffee shop turned trendy bar and restaurant that is still a place to be seen. Still with the curvy counter and bar stools of the old coffee shop, the bar is a nice place to hang out at any time. The noisy adjacent restaurant, complete with booths, serves vaguely Brazilian-style food – a little overpriced at around $16 a main course but not half bad, and there's cheaper stuff as well, making it a decent alternative for lunch.

Green Derby, 994 2nd Ave ☎688-1250. Just opposite *Murphy's*, this tries hard to be Irish through and through. Basically, though, a singles hangout, convivial if not especially cheap.

Harglo's, 974 2nd Ave (between E 51st and 52nd sts) ☎759-9820. Kitschy, Cajun bar and restaurant that serves a mean *étouffé*. An exceptionally lively happy hour full of midtown professionals.

Live Bait, 14 E 23rd St (between Broadway and Madison Ave) ☎353-2400. Cajun bar/restaurant run by the same people as *The Coffee Shop* (see above) and popular with the after-office crowd. Not the place for a quiet drink or a good meal but a hopping atmosphere nonetheless.

Molly Malone's, 287 3rd Ave (between E 22nd and 23rd sts) ☎725-8375. Comfortable Irish bar with solid, if unexciting, food.

Murphy's, 977 2nd Ave (between E 51st and 52nd sts) ☎751-5400. Irish bar attracting midtown singles. Drinks are costly but food less so – a rare and useful standby in this part of town.

Old Town Bar and Restaurant, 45 E 18th St (between Broadway and Park Ave South) ☎473-8874. One of the oldest bars in the city, and a favorite with publishing types, artists, models and photographers from the surrounding

Flatiron district. High on atmosphere, and with an excellent, if standard, menu of chili, burgers and the like. Was often featured in the old NBC version *David Letterman Show.*

Paddy O'Reilly's 519 2nd Ave (between 29th and 30th sts) ☎686-1210. A good place to enjoy a few Guinness drafts while pretending you're Irish.

Pete's Tavern, 129 E 18th St (at Irving Place) ☎473-7676. Convivial watering hole and former speakeasy that claims to be the oldest bar in New York, opened in 1864 – though these days it inevitably trades somewhat on its history. The restaurant serves enormous burgers, rib-eye steak, prime ribs, and standard Italian-American fare.

P.J. Clarke's, 915 3rd Ave (between E 55th and 56th sts) ☎759-1650. One of the city's most famous watering holes, this is a spit-and-sawdust alehouse with a not-so-cheap restaurant out the back. You may recognize it as the location of the film *The Lost Weekend.*

Chelsea, Garment District and Midtown West

Chelsea Commons, 242 10th Ave (at W 24th St) ☎929-9424. Not only a personable bar but a great place to eat – outside meals for $7–10. Choice burgers. Very much a local hangout. Summer garden and winter fireplace.

Full Moon Saloon, 735 8th Avenue (between W 43rd and W44th sts) ☎664-9829. If you really want to *drink*, here's the place: a dark, airless box with loud country music, $2 drafts and nearly inedible microwaved White Castle burgers to soak them up.

Mickey Mantle's, 42 Central Park South (W 59th St between 5th and 6th aves) ☎688-7777. As you'd imagine, a bar that's entirely given over to sports, with numerous TV screens showing different events, and even a video library of sports tapes. Decent food – burgers, squid and good desserts.

Rudy's Bar and Grill, 627 9th Ave (between W 44th and 45th sts) ☎974-

9169. One of New York's cheapest, friendliest, and liveliest dive bars, a favorite with local actors and musicians. Great jukebox, free hot dogs, and a backyard in the summer.

Russian Vodka Room, 265 W 52nd St (between Broadway and 7th Ave) ☎307-5835 They have several different kinds of vodka, as you might expect, and a lot of Russian and eastern European expatriates.

Siberia, 250 W 50th St (in the IRT subway station) ☎333-4141. One of New York's oddest exemplars of the "location, location, location" school: this small bar is in the 1/9 subway station at 50th street. It looks and feels like your parents' rec room; a good place for a shot of vodka or a late-night beer.

Ye Olde Tripple Inn, 263 W 54th St (between Broadway and 8th Ave) ☎245-9849. Basic Irish bar that serves inexpensive food at lunchtime and early evening. A useful place to know about if you're after affordable food in this part of town.

Upper West Side and Morningside Heights

Augie's Pub, 2751 Broadway (at W 105th St) ☎864-9834. One of the more interesting places on this stretch of Broadway, downbeat and unpretentious, and favored by local jazz fans for its live music from 10.30pm onwards. Also has inexpensive snacks and food.

Café Luxembourg, 200 W 70th St (between Amsterdam and West End aves) ☎873-7411. Sleek, sophisticated Upper West Side retro bar and restaurant. Serves great steak frites and herb-roasted chicken.

Cannon's Pub, W 108th St at Broadway, no phone. Longtime favorite haunt of Columbia students. Four TVs, usually playing sporting events; $5 *Rolling Rock* pitchers, darts, and draft Guinness.

Donohue's, 174 W 72nd St (at Broadway) ☎874-9304. Surprisingly, it's very much a local place – fairly atmospheric and good for an early drink or two.

Drinking

Drinking

Dublin House, 225 W 79th St (between Broadway and Amsterdam Ave) ☎874-9528. Brash Irish bar with a young crowd, good jukebox and inexpensive drinks. Recommended if you're up this way.

Lucy's Retired Surfers, 503 Columbus Ave (between W 84th and 85th sts) ☎787-3009. Day-Glo painted, surfboard-decorated bar with killer cocktails with names like "Shark Attack." Inevitably popular with upwardly mobile Upper West Siders. Same people run *Pop's Pizza* next door.

Night Café, 938 Amsterdam Ave (between 106th and 107th). A sports bar with cheap beer and a large screen TV playing local games. Very downscale, not for the faint of heart.

Raccoon Lodge, 480 Amsterdam Ave (at W 83rd St) ☎874-9984. Simple bar with cheap drinks, jukebox, pinball and pool table. Also on the East Side at 1439 York Ave ☎650-1775 and downtown at Warren St ☎766-9656.

The Saloon, 1920 Broadway (at W 64th St) ☎874-1500. Large bar/restaurant with a vast menu. Good for brunch.

Shark Bar, 307 Amsterdam Ave (between W 74th and 75th sts) ☎874-8500. High-class, well-dressed crowd. Delectable $15.95 soul-food brunch on weekends.

Upper East Side

Australia, 1733 1st Ave (at 90th St) ☎876-0203. The reigning Aussie-theme bar. "No wombats allowed."

Bear Bar, 1770 2nd Ave (between 92nd and 93rd sts) ☎987-3633. Happy hour starts at 4pm; drafts and buffalo wings are each 25 cents apiece, and go up 25 cents every half-hour thereafter until they hit full price around 7pm or so. Also have tons of microbrews.

Border Café, 244 E 79th St (between 2nd and 3rd aves) ☎535-4347. Friendly neighborhood hangout good for satisfying cravings for fajitas, frozen margaritas and the like. It remains a down-to-earth place despite its upscale location.

The Clubhouse, 1586 York Ave (between E 83rd and 84th sts) ☎288-3218. Upper East Side sports bar next door to *Casey's Dance Hall.*

Jim McMullen, 1341 3rd Ave (between E 76th and 77th sts) ☎861-4700. Upper East Side bar usually crammed with the local professionals. Restaurant serves steak and pot pies.

Ruby's River Road Café & Bar, 1754 2nd Ave ☎348-2328. Home of the famous jello-shots (shots of liquor made with different colored jellies), and a fun bar with a Cajun café in the back.

Rusty's, 1271 3rd Ave ☎861-4518. Small bar, good for burgers and brew, that's run by an ex-Mets baseball player and has the sporting paraphernalia to match – including a big-screen TV to watch the action. Another branch – known as *Rusty Staub's* – is at 575 5th Ave in a shopping mall (☎682-1000), where the food is probably better.

Subway Inn, 143 E 60th St (at Lexington Ave) ☎223-8929. Downscale neighborhood dive bar surprisingly located across the street from *Bloomingdale's*. Definitely ungentrified, and great for a late after-noon beer.

Gay and lesbian bars

New York's gay men's bars cover the spectrum: from relaxed, mainstream cafés to some hard-hitting clubs full of glamour and attitude. Most of the more established places are in Greenwich Village, with the East Village and Murray Hill–Gramercy Park areas (the east 20s and 30s) up-and-coming. Things tend to get raunchier further west as you reach the bars and cruisers of the wild West Side Highway and meat-packing districts, both of which are hard-line and occasionally dangerous. Lesbian bars are fast growing in popularity, especially in the East Village. Perhaps even more popular are the roving "nights" that operate certain days of the week in bars throughout Downtown, like the **Clit Club** (☎529-3300). See *Nightlife*, chapter 19, for full listings. Check local weeklies, like the

Village Voice and MetroSource, and club-land's free 'zines like *H/X, H/X for Her, Female FYI* for up-to-the minute listings.

Mainly for men

The Bar, 68 2nd Ave (at E 4th St) ☎674-9714. A long-standing neighborhood hideaway in the East Village. Relaxed, and with a pool table.

The Boiler Room, 86 E 4th St (between 1st and 2nd aves). Recent addition popular with NYU students and locals.

Crowbar, 339 E 10th St (between Ave A and B) ☎420-0670. The nature of the crowd changes with the night of the week but consistently filled with lots of happy, shiny boys having fun.

The Duplex, 61 Christopher St (at 7th Ave South) ☎255-5438. Big, welcoming piano bar with two levels. Very mainstream.

Hell, 59 Gansevoort St ☎727-1666. A relatively new, upscale lounge on the outer fringes of the West Village.

Keller's, 384 West St (at Christopher St) ☎243-1907. This friendly West Village bar at historic Christopher Street draws a largely African-American crowd.

Marie's Crisis, 59 Grove St ☎243-9323. Well-known cabaret/piano bar popular with tourists and locals alike. Features old-time singing sessions on Fri and Sat nights. Often packed, always fun.

The Monster, 80 Grove St ☎924-3558. Large, campy bar with a drag cabaret, piano and video. Very popular with a strong "neighborhood" feel. Downstairs is a cozier lounge.

Oscar Wilde, 221 E 58th St (at 2nd Ave). As you might guess from the name, not particularly rambunctious, but pleasant nonetheless.

Rawhide, 212 8th Ave (at 21st St) ☎242-9332. Hell-bent for leather, Chelsea's Rough Rider Room opens at 8am for those who are not yet ready for breakfast (and closes fairly late too).

Spike, 120 11th Ave (at W 20th St) ☎243-9688. Chelsea institution with a mostly middle-aged jeans and leather crowd.

Stonewall, 53 Christopher St (between Waverly Pl and 7th Ave South) ☎463-0950. Yes, *that* Stonewall, mostly refurbished and flying the pride flag like they own it – which, one supposes, they do.

Uncle Charlie's, 56 Greenwich St (between 6th and 7th aves) ☎255-8787. As long as you're in town you may as well visit your dear Uncle Charlie. This large, long-lived bar isn't the hottest spot around, but it's friendly, familiar and unpretentious.

Wonder Bar, 505 E 6th St (between Ave A and Ave B) ☎777-9105. Cramped, festive and lesbian-friendly, though still boy-dominated.

The Works, 428 Columbus Ave (at W 81st St) ☎799-7365. Laid-back tropical theme bar. Cool, pleasant and one of the few options for this part of town. $1 margaritas on Thurs.

Mainly for women

Café Tabac, 232 E 9th St (between 2nd and 3rd aves) ☎674-7072. New York's exquisite, ultra-chic femmes assemble here upstairs Sun nights.

Crazy Nanny's, 21 7th Ave South (at Leroy St) ☎366-6312. Comfortable neighborhood bar with DJs Wed–Sat. Cowgirls on Thurs and free pizza on Mon.

Cubby Hole, 281 W 12th St (at W 4th St) ☎243-9041. Still happening.

Henrietta Hudson, 438 Hudson St (between Morton and Barrow sts) ☎924-3347. Laid-back in the afternoon but brimming by night, especially on weekends.

Julie's, 204 E 58th St (at Madison Ave) ☎688-1294. Not exactly sedate, but not a riot-grrl joint either. One of your few choices around Midtown or Uptown, too.

Meow Mix, 269 E Houston St (at Suffolk St) ☎254-1434. The girl club of the moment, way east downtown. Bands or performances most nights, for which men are welcome if they behave themselves.

Sanctuary, 44 7th Ave (at 15th St), Brooklyn ☎718-832-9800. Park Slope has the biggest Outer Borough lesbian scene, and this is its prime women's bar. Bands or performances most nights.

Drinking

Chapter 19

Nightlife

New York's **music scene** reflects the city's diversity. Traditional and contemporary **jazz** are still in abundance, with the annual *JVC* and *Knitting Factory's* "What Is Jazz?" festivals bringing top international talent to the city every year. The downtown **avant-garde** scene – best personified by John Zorn, Arto Lindsay and Laurie Anderson – has petered out since the 1980s but still exists; its attendant art noise bands – the most famous being Sonic Youth – continue to influence the area's musicians both directly (the band runs the Sonic Youth Recordings label, and Thurston Moore does informal talent scouting) and indirectly (Kim Gordon's *X-Girl* fashion line). **Spoken word performers**, along with the current crop of singer/songwriters, are reviving the Beats' poetry scene. And, if you travel to the Outer Boroughs, you'll find pockets of **Brazilian music, West Indian music,** reggae and hip-hop.

But if you stay within Manhattan (and chances are that you will), **indie rock** will fill your ears. The city's guitar bands have gotten sexier recently, with the punk revival giving way to acts that incorporate ethnic and electronica elements into their tunes.

Despite what the designers on any avenue would like you to believe, New York is not uptight about appearance. In the trendiest **clubs**, however, appearances do matter: acolytes must adhere to the current look, with bouncers guarding the doors against the gauche.

But if you just want to dance, there are plenty of more casual places, especially the city's **gay clubs**, which often offer more creative music and less hassle.

The sections that follow provide accounts of the cream of current venues. Remember, though, that the music – and especially the club scenes – change continually. To ensure that techno night isn't now a drag-queen party, consult weekly **listings** magazine *Time Out New York* or monthly mag *Paper*. Also worth checking are *The Village Voice* and *Homo Xtra*, both of which are free in Manhattan and contain detailed club, theater and venue listings for the gay and straight scenes. Remember to take your **ID** (driver's license or passport) with you when you go out: Venues and bars do enforce the legal drinking age of 21, especially so since Giuliani has taken over as mayor.

Rock music

New York's **rock music** scene is still built on white-boy guitar bands, with three-chord rock the default setting. That said, many foreign acts – especially British bands – travel to New York's shores first when trying to break into America. Frequently you'll have the opportunity to see these groups play in small venues at low admission prices.

Rising rents have forced many musicians out of Manhattan and into the Outer Boroughs and New Jersey; although the scene is still in Manhattan, the center has become more diffused. There is a thriving off-Manhattan hub in Hoboken, New Jersey, centering on *Maxwell's* (see p.360); hip-hop, techno, house, ambient, and drum'n'bass are big in the clubs; and in Brooklyn and Queens, large Latin, South American, Indian, and reggae contingents exist – although the venues themselves are way off the average tourist circuit.

In Manhattan, most of the energy is provided by bars and venues located in the East Village and TriBeCa. The listings below should point you to the major spots; more obscure locales can be found in the publications suggested above.

The big performance venues

Madison Square Garden, 7th and 8th aves, W 31st–33rd sts ☎465-6741. New York's principal large stage, the *Garden* hosts not only hockey and basketball but also a good proportion of the stadium rock acts that visit the city. Seating 20,000-plus, the arena is not the most soulful place to see a band, but it may be the only chance that you get.

Meadowlands Stadium, East Rutherford, New Jersey ☎201/935-3900. The city's other really large venue, again with room for 20,000 of your closest friends.

Radio City Music Hall, 6th Ave and 50th St ☎247-4777. Not the prime venue it once was; most of the acts that play here now are firmly in the mainstream. The building itself has as great a sense of occasion, though, and Rockette dolls are still sold in the gift shop.

Smaller venues

Apollo Theatre, 253 W 125th St (between 8th Ave and Powell Blvd) ☎749-5838 (show info) ☎864-0372 (tkts). Stars are born and legends are still made at the *Apollo*, which features a cast of black music acts, as well as weekly amateur nights (Wed) and the odd dog show. $10–30.

Arlene Grocery, 95 Stanton St (between Ludlow and Orchard sts) ☎358-1633.

An intimate, erstwhile *bodega* that hosts nightly free gigs by local indie bands. Frequented by musicians, some talent scouts and open-minded rock fans.

Beacon Theater, 2124 Broadway (74th St) ☎307-7171. A restored theater hosting big, off-the-mainstream names, at $20–40.

The Bitter End, 147 Bleecker St ☎673-7030. Young MOR bands in an intimate club setting. The famous people who've played the club are listed by the door: don't expect to see them there nowadays. Cover $5–10, with a two-drink minimum.

The Bottom Line, 15 W 4th St (corner of Mercer St) ☎228-7880. Not New York's most adventurous venue but one of the better known – and where you're most likely to see singer-songwriters. Cabaret setup, with tables crowding out any suggestion of a dance floor. Entrance $15–20, with shows at 7.30pm & 10.30pm. Cash only.

Brownies, 169 Ave A (between 10th and 11th sts) ☎420-8392. The place to see major-label one-offs, bands on the cusp of making it big and impressive local talent. Around $8. Bring ID.

CBGB (and OMFUG), 315 Bowery (Bleecker St) ☎982-4052. Living off its history, this legendary punk bastion (host to Richard Hell, Patti Smith and Talking Heads) is hardly as cutting-edge as it once was. Noisy rock bands are the order now, often four or five a night. Weekdays shows begin at 8pm, weekend shows at 9.30pm, and Sun hardcore matinees at 3pm. Prices about $3–9.

CB's 313 Gallery, 313 Bowery (at Bleecker St) ☎677-0445. Seven nights a week, *CB's* clean little counterpart features folk, acoustic, and experimental music. $5.

Coney Island High, 15 St Mark's Place (between 2nd and 3rd aves) ☎674-7959. Punk lives on, with the venue's pierced patrons waiting for the next Sex Pistols reunion. Club nights attract distinctly different audiences (see *Konkrete Jungle* p.364). Around $7.

Nightlife

Nightlife

Continental Club, 25 3rd Ave (between St Mark's and E 9th St) ☎529-6924. Home to frat boys and loud alternative rock, with $2 shots at all times. Free entrance during the week, $5 on weekends.

The Cooler, 416 W 14th St (between 9th and 10th aves) ☎645-5189. Maybe it's the indigo lighting that lends a *Blue Velvet* feel to this underground bunker – or perhaps it's because the club is a former meat refrigerator. Adventurous indie rock and avant-garde attract a youthful, hip crowd. Mon–Thurs shows begin at 9pm; Fri & Sat shows start at 10pm. Free on Mon, otherwise $5–10.

Fez (Under Time Café), 380 Lafayette St (Great Jones St) ☎533-2680. Although the mirrored bar and sparkling gold stage curtain suggest a crap disco fantasy, *Fez's* poetry readings and acoustic performances are of a high caliber. Around $10.

Irving Plaza, 17 Irving Place (between E 15th and E 16th sts) ☎249-8870. Once home to an off-Broadway musical (hence the dangling chandeliers and blood-red interior), now host to an impressive array of rock, electronic and techno acts. Room has wildly divergent acoustics; stand toward the back on the ground floor for truest mix of sound. $10–25.

Koyote Kate's, 307 W 47th (8th Ave) ☎956-1091. A baying coyote decorates the outside, while blues, jazz, and rock musics are performed live inside. No cover; bands daily except for Sun and Mon, with sets beginning at 9.30pm.

Manhattan Center, 311 W 34 St (between 8th and 9th aves) ☎564-4882. Recently refurbished ballroom that hosts a few shows a month, mostly indie rock and electronic music, in a 4,000-seat venue. Uptight bouncers limit movement between seating levels and prohibit smoking on the balconies. $16–40.

Manny's Car Wash, 1558 3rd Ave (87th St) ☎369-2583. Smoky, Chicago-style blues bar with a small dance floor, reasonable prices and Upper East Side clientele. Shows from 9.15pm. No cover Sun for blues jams; Mon women are admitted free and enjoy *gratis* tap beer and house wine. Otherwise, $4–15.

Maxwell's, Washington and 11th sts, Hoboken, New Jersey ☎201/798-4064. Neighborhood rock club hosting up to a dozen bands a week: some big names and one of the best places to check out the tri-state scene. Admission $6–10.

Mercury Lounge, 217 E Houston St (Essex St) ☎260-7400. Just as the name implies, an intimate lounge favoring finely crafted pop and art rock. Books lots of Downtown and UK acts. Around $10.

Roseland, 239 W 52nd St (between Broadway and 8th Ave) ☎249-8870. A ballroom dancing school that, six times a month, turns into a venue for pop and rave-type electronic bands. Take a gander at the shoes and photographs displayed in the entry hall. $10–30.

SOB's (Sounds of Brazil), 204 Varick St (corner of Houston St) ☎243-4940. Premier place to hear Brazilian, West Indian, Caribbean, and World Music acts within the confines of Manhattan. Vibrant, with a high quality of music. Two shows nightly, times vary. Admission $12–20.

Supper Club, 240 W 47th St (between Broadway and 8th Ave) ☎921-1940. White linen tablecloths, a large dance floor, and upscale lounge jazz/hip-hop groups. Around $20.

Tramps, 51 W 21st St (between 5th and 6th aves) ☎727-7788. Blues, funk, and rock bands almost nightly. Excessively air-conditioned, so bring a sweater. Entrance $5–20. Cash only for tickets.

Under Acme, 9 Great Jones St (Lafayette St) ☎420-1934. Seamy but laidback basement club specializing in up-and-coming indie bands. Around $7.

Wetlands Preserve, 161 Hudson St (Laight St) ☎966-4225. A self-proclaimed "ecosaloon" that books reggae, hip-hop, and psychedelic blues bands. Admission $7–15.

Jazz

The late 1980s and early 1990s were tough times for New York **jazz**. The city's clubs went through a rough patch, from which many a joint – including the landmark *Village Tavern* – did not survive. A clutch of new clubs has revived the scene, however, and there still are more than forty locations in Manhattan that present jazz regularly. Look mostly to **Greenwich Village** for a good place; midtown jazz clubs tend to be slick dinner-dance joints – expensive and overrun by business people looking for culture.

To find out who's playing, check the usual sources, notably the *Voice*, *Hothouse*, a free monthly magazine that sometimes is available at the venues; or the jazz monthly *downbeat*. The city's jazz-oriented **radio stations** are also sources of information: two of the best are **WBGO** (88.5 FM), a 24-hr jazz station, and **WKCR** (98.7 FM), Columbia University's radio station. As a final resort, the **Jazz Line** (☎479-7888) provides recorded information about the week's events.

Price policies vary from club to club, but at most there's a hefty cover ($10–15) and always a minimum charge for food and drinks. An evening out at a major club will cost at least $15 per person, and more along the lines of $25–30 per person if you'd like to eat. Piano bars – smaller and often more atmospheric – come cheaper; some have neither an admission fee nor a minimum, but expect to pay inflated drink prices.

Jazz venues

Arthur's Tavern, 57 Grove St ☎675-6879. Small, amiable piano bar with some inspired performers and no cover or minimum. Drinks are pricey.

Birdland, 315 W 44th (8th and 9th aves) ☎581-3080. Not the original place where Charlie Parker played, but an established supper club that's recently moved to Midtown. Hosts some big names. Sets nightly at 9pm and 11pm, with an additional 12.30am show on Fri

& Sat. Music charge of $5–15 at the bar, $10–30 at the tables, with a one-drink minimum.

The Blue Note, 131 W 3rd St (6th Ave) ☎475-8592. Famous names with the attendant high prices. Cover charges vary wildly, from $7 to $65, plus a $5 minimum per person at the tables or a one-drink minimum at the bar. Depending on who's playing, there is also a surcharge of $5–15 per table. Sets are at 9pm & 11.30pm. On Fri & Sat, the 1am set is free if you've seen the previous set, $5 if you haven't. Also offers a decent Sunday brunch for $14.50 that includes live music.

Detour, 349 E 13th St (1st Ave) ☎533-6212. Coffee and cocktail bar that fancies itself a bit of Paris in the East Village. Modern jazz and avant-garde experimentation nightly, no cover.

Downstairs at the Metropolis, 31 Union Sq West (16th St) ☎675-2300. Walk through the *Metropolis'* imposing white marble facade and take the stairs to the left: at the bottom you'll find trad jazz and big band swing performed in a club that oozes cool elegance. Around $15.

Fifty Five, 55 Christopher St (between 6th and 7th aves) ☎929-9883. See Chapter 18, *Drinking*.

Iridium Room, 44 W 63rd St (Columbus Ave) ☎582-2121; for current listings, ☎956-HORN. Contemporary jazz performed 7 nights a week in a surrealist decor described as "Dolly meets Disney." Cover $12–20, with one-drink/$5 minimum.

Knickerbocker's, 9th St and University Place ☎228-8490. A piano bar/restaurant decorated with Hirschfelds and featuring high-caliber bass/piano duos. Cover ($3–4) and minimum one-entree ($12–17) at the tables; cover ($3–4) and one-drink/$5 minimum at the lounge; and no cover but one-drink/$5 minimum at the bar (which offers the best view of the performers). Music begins at 9.45pm and continues until 1–3am.

Knitting Factory, 71 Leonard St (between Broadway and Church sts) ☎219-3006.

Nightlife

Nightlife

When it moved from its grubby East Village digs to a chichi space in TriBeCa, the *Knit* lost its street cred but gained an affluent clientele. The refurbished club – two performance spaces, two bars and a microbrewery with eighteen beers on draft – may be a baby boomer's dream, but for the rest of us, it's a place to see avant-garde jazz, experimental acts, and big-name rock bands in an intimate setting. $8–15, with shows beginning around 8pm & 10pm on weekdays, 9pm & 11pm on weekends.

Smalls, 183 W 10th St (7th Ave South) ☎929-7565. Cozy West Village club has the best jazz bargain in NY: ten hours of music for $10. The program comprises two sets and a late-night jam, by well-knowns and unknowns. Free juice and non-alcoholic beverages, or BYOB. Daily performances run 10pm–8am.

Sweet Basil, 88 7th Ave (between Grove and Bleecker sts) ☎242-1785. One of New York's major – and most crowded – jazz spots, particularly at weekends, when there's brunch and free jazz 2–6pm. The walls are covered with photographs of former clients – just mere mortals like Dizzy Gillespie. Weekday evenings are the best times to go, and shows usually start at 9pm and 11pm. $17.50 cover and a $10 minimum per set at the tables; $18 cover and one-drink minimum at the bar, with one free drink from the house. Fri and Sat offer an additional set at 12.30am.

Village Vanguard, 178 7th Ave (W 11th St) ☎255-4037. A NYC jazz landmark that celebrated its fiftieth anniversary a few years back, the *Vanguard* supplies a regular diet of big names. Mon admission is $12, with a $10 minimum; Tues–Sun entry is $15, with a $10 minimum.

Visiones, 125 MacDougal St (W 3rd St) ☎673-5576. A Spanish restaurant four doors down from *The Blue Note* that hosts an eclectic range of acts. The atmosphere is looser and the clientele younger than many of NY's jazz venues. Shows nightly at 9pm and 11pm, with an additional 1am show/after-hours jam

on Fri–Sat. Cover charge ranges $10–12, with $10 minimum at the tables and $12–15 (plus a free drink) at the bar.

Folk, country and spoken word venues

Maybe it's the legacy of New York's Beatnik writers, so verbal and prolific in the 1950s and 1960s, or maybe it's backlash against punk and grunge trends. Whatever the reason, there's been a resurgence of interest in poetry in New York's music scene. **Singer-song-writers** have returned, as have **readings**. Spoken word acts have evolved too: words are no longer just read off scraps of paper in a shaky voice – now they're also shouted and accompanied by music.

Centerfold Coffee House, Church of St Paul and St Andrew, 263 W 86th St (at Broadway). A 75-seat space with incredible acoustics that hosts occasional folk, jazz and bluegrass performances as well as small theater productions. Around $10.

Louisiana Community Bar and Grill, 622 Broadway (at Houston) ☎460-9633. Zydeco music and Cajun cooking in dowdy Greenwich Village. No cover, but the bands merit one. Open 5–11pm (midnight on the weekends).

Nuyorican Poet's Café, 236 E 3rd St (between aves B & C) ☎505-8183. Beat poetry for the 1990s, performed both a cappella and accompanied by jazz and hip-hop. Café opens at 5pm; two shows nightly Tues–Sun. $5–7.

O'Lunney's, 12 W 44th St ☎840-6688. Restaurant serving steaks, hamburgers and the like to traditional folk sounds.

Rodeo Bar, 375 3rd Ave (27th St) ☎683-6500. Dust off your spurs, grab your partner and head down to the *Rodeo* for live country tunes seven days a week.

The Speakeasy, 107 MacDougal St ☎598-9670. The only folk club in NYC with music seven nights a week. Something of a hangout for musicians and folkies alike. $5–10 cover; bland health-food menu.

Nightclubs

New York's – especially Manhattan's – **club life** is a rapidly evolving creature. While many of the name DJs remain the same, venues shift around, opening and closing according to finances and fashion. Musically, techno and house hold sway at the moment, with the emphasis on the deep, vocal style that's always been popular in the city; but reggae, hip-hop, funk, ambient and drum'n'bass all retain interest.

Recently, though, the club scene has endured tough times, with Mayor Rudolph Guiliani introducing a conservative strain into the city's nightlife. Under the guise of "quality of life" improvements, Guiliani has enacted laws requiring each nightspot to have a cabaret license in addition to an alcohol license if it intends to allow dancing. So while many bars might have a DJ playing in the corner, only the ones with the costly extra paperwork will permit their patrons to shake their hips.

Another problem that has dampened the scene has come from within. Peter Gatien, the owner of New York's three largest nightclubs – *Limelight*, *Tunnel* and *Palladium* – was indicted in May 1996 on drug distribution and conspiracy charges, and his biggest party promoter, Michael Alig, is currently in jail, charged with the murder of club kid Angel Melendez. *Limelight* was closed after the debacle (it may have re-opened by now), and drug sweeps at other clubs have caused some temporarily to shutter their doors. Though drugs are regarded by many as a natural accompaniment to clubbing, a word of warning: if you feel you must indulge, be very discreet.

Despite all this, **clubs** in New York can offer a good night out. The scene constantly changes, so to ensure that the party is still there, check such listings mags as *Time Out New York*, *Paper Magazine* or *Homo Xtra*.

Clubbing can be costly. In order to get the most for the least amount of money, here are some guidelines:

• The best time to club is during the week. Crowds are smaller, prices are cheaper, service is better, and clubbers are more savvy than during the weekend, which is when out-of-towners flood the floor.

• The fliers placed in record and clothing stores in the East Village and SoHo are the best way to find out about the latest clubs and one-off nights. Many fliers also offer substantial discounts.

• Style can be important, so make an effort and you'll probably get beyond the velvet rope (if there even is one).

• Nothing much gets going before midnight, so many places offer reduced admission before then.

• Expect to be thoroughly frisked by security before entering the larger dance clubs. Drugs, weapons and hip flasks will be confiscated; any sharp objects that could be used as weapons (Swiss Army knives, metal combs) will be held at the door, as will pepper sprays and bottles of water. Basically, if you'd like to keep it, don't take it to the club.

• When you eventually stagger out into the morning light, keep your wits about you. If you're taking a cab, specify the most direct route home, or you might find yourself taking a tour of the city.

999999's, held Sun at *Flamingo East*, 219 2nd Ave (between E 13th and E 14th sts) ☎533-2860. Part Dadaist cabaret and part pure pretension, the *9's* attempts to recreate Berlin in the 1920s. A decent effort, but thwarted by the crowd it attracts. $5, $3 if outfitted in suit jacket or dress, free before 11pm.

Bar d'O, 29 Bedford St (Downing St) ☎627-1580. Drag-queens-about-town Joey Arias and Raven-O belt out show tunes that would bring a tear to any Streisand fan's eye. Tues, Sat & Sun. $3.

b0b, 255 Eldridge St (E Houston St) ☎777-0558. A friendly, 20-something art-school crowd lounges on the sofas

Nightlife

Nightlife

while DJs spin hip-hop and soul grooves. Nightly, free.

Body and Soul, held Sun 2–10pm at *Vinyl*, 157 Hudson St (King St) ☎343-1379. DJs John Davis and François Kevorkian dish up old-school garage at this afternoon party. Popular with a mid-20s crowd that prefers dancing to body piercing. $10.

Cafe Con Leche, held Sun at *Expo*, 124 W 43rd St (between 6th and 7th aves) ☎819-0377. Banjee boys and sexy sisters pack into this Latin-house hotspot. $15–20.

Crow Bar, 339 E 10th St (between aves A and B). ☎420-0670. Cheap (around $5) and lively, this East Village hole-in-the-wall serves up tunes to a predominantly gay male crowd who like to move.

Delia's, 197 E 3rd St (between aves A and B) ☎254-9184. A supper club whose sleazy location appeals to Upper East Siders. *Delia's* is anything but squalid, however: inside, the formidable mistress presides over a plush environment that caters to the needs of diners and dancers alike. Open Fri and Sat, with prix-fixe dinner/dancing $35; dancing alone $10.

Den of Thieves, 145 E Houston St (Eldridge St) ☎477-5005. The cleanest club in the East Village – no small feat – and offering a democratic mix of hip-hop, soul, funk, and electronica. A varied crowd, too. $5–10.

Don Hill's, 511 Greenwich St (corner of Spring) ☎334-1390. Drag queens, creative types, and slumming stars congregate at this dive on the outskirts of SoHo. Less trendy than it used to be, but still the place where your rubber gear won't get a second glance. Fri is Squeezebox, a cauldron of glam, punk and disco; on Sat, genders bend with Fraggle Rock. $10.

Giant Step, venues vary, call ☎414-8001 for time and place. After single-handedly flooding NY with acid jazz, *Giant Step* has mercifully reinvented itself as a proponent of drum'n'bass and trip-

hop. Hosts low-key shows that aren't well publicized, offering the chance to see name acts for cheap prices in small venues. $10–15.

Konkrete Jungle, held Mon at *Coney Island High*, 15 St Marks Place (between 2nd and 3rd aves) ☎604-4224. NY's most reliable place to hear quality drum'n'bass. Brings in big names from the UK on a monthly basis; look for fliers on upcoming events and discounted admission. $7–15.

Les Poulets, 16 W 22nd St (between 5th and 6th Aves) ☎229-2000. Big names in Latin music and sensuously performed salsa – the only place in central Manhattan where the twain do meet. Frequented by a serious dance clientele, and extremely crowded on weekends. Open for dinner and dancing Thurs–Sat, with prices around $5–20. Call for details on discount admissions; free all night Thurs.

Life, 158 Bleecker St (at Thompson) ☎420-1999. Mirrored pillars, a huge dance floor, and "hidden" seating behind the bar make this trendy nightspot antiseptic and anachronistic, executed without a trace of humor. JFK Jr has been spotted here, as has Mariah Carey. Need we say more? Wed is Latin night, with women free before 10pm; Thurs is Get a Life, a favorite of the fashion crowd. Tues–Sun, with prices $10–20.

Meow Mix, 269 Houston St (Suffolk St) ☎254-1434. Lipstick lesbians, leather ladies, and all types in between drink and dance at this temple devoted to les femmes. DJs play tunes that range from 1980s hits to sinewy soul. Free–$5.

Mother, 432 W 14th St (Washington St) ☎366-5680. Located among the warehouses and loading docks of the meatpacking district, this recently redesigned funhouse is so happening that it was immortalized in an Absolut vodka ad. Probably one of the few NY clubs left where anything goes. Fri is the Clit Club, a techno, tribal extravaganza for women only; Sat is Click + Drag, where leather and pleather fetishes reach cyberspace;

Tues is the long-running Jackie 60, a dress-to-excess party that sets no bounds. $10.

Nation, 50 Ave A (between 3rd and 4th sts) ☎473-6239. Here they serve coffee by day and spin electronica by night. Laidback atmosphere with comfy couches in the back room. Free–$15.

Nell's, 246 W 14th St (between 7th and 8th aves) ☎675-1567. First of the so-called "supper clubs," it's still a place to be seen pouting. Tues is open mike, with the occasional celebrity guest ascending the stage. $10–15.

Palladium, 126 E 14th St (at Irving Place) ☎473-7171. Biggest and for some still among the best of New York clubs, although its popularity peaked in the 1980s, when Madonna used to hang out there. Housed in an enormous old theater, the dance floor, 3-D laser light and sound systems take some beating, especially midweek. Sat is Arena, the new hard house party by the Sound Factory's old resident DJ, Junior Vasquez. Admission $10–20.

Plush, 431 W 14th St (between 9th Ave and Washington St) ☎367-7035. House, hip-hop and drum'n'bass in the meat-packing district's spot of the moment. Thurs is Jungle Nation, a notable purveyor of breakbeats and deep bass. $10.

Robots, 25 Ave B (between 2nd and 3rd sts) ☎995-0968. The after-hours East Village club that starts up when the other nightspots are winding down. A dubious clientele, many of whom are more wired than welcoming. Mon–Sat 11pm–noon, entrance $8–15.

Sapphire Lounge, 249 Eldridge St (at Houston) ☎777-5153. Cheesy'n'sleazy, with a black-lit interior and "arty" films in the back room. Mon is Tang, where hip Lower East Siders soak in Latin, soul and funk. Free–$5.

Sound Factory, 618 W 46th St (between 11th and 12th aves) ☎643-0728. Relocated yet again, the Sound Factory has been reborn as a mainstream house and techno club with security so tight that they'll frisk your socks. The crowd lacks the flavor of the Factory's old days, and the spirit, though willing, is weak. Open Fri ($20) & Sat ($10–15).

Tunnel, 220 12th Ave (W 27th St) ☎695-7292. Although its psychotropic lights will stun you, its maze-like floor-plan will confuse you, and its chronically overflowing toilets will disgust you, the *Tunnel* is still a premier techno and house hall. The hip-hop lounge down-stairs offers sanctuary. Open Fri–Sun; $15–20.

Twilo, 530 W 27th St (between 10th and 11th aves) ☎268-1600. Gay boys galore, moving till dawn to house and trance. Features name European DJs each Fri. Open Thurs–Sat; $15–20.

Vinyl, 157 Hudson St (King St) ☎343-1379. This big, dark, low-ceilinged ware-house is a techno sweatshop: packed full of rave kids and other slaves to the beat. Li'l Louis Vega spins here each Sat; expect to wait in line for a long time. Fri–Sun. $12–20.

Nightlife

Chapter 20

The Performing Arts and Film

From Broadway glitter to NoHo grunge, from the high-culture polish of Lincoln Center to the rawest experimentalism of the Lower East Side, the range and variety of the performing arts in New York is exactly what you might expect. And prices, of course, vary accordingly, from $100 nights at the opera to free bring-your-own chair performances of Shakespeare in downtown parking lots. Broadway, and even Off-Broadway **theater** is notoriously expensive, but if you know where to look, there are a variety of ways to get tickets cheaper, and on the Off-Off-Broadway fringe you can see a play for little more than the price of a movie ticket. **Dance**, **music** and **opera** are superbly catered for: again the big mainstream events are extremely expensive; but smaller ones are often equally as interesting as well as far cheaper. As for **cinema**, New York gets the first run of most American films and many foreign ones long before they reach Europe, and has a very healthy art-house and revival scene.

"What's on" listings for the arts can be found in a number of places. The most useful sources are the clear and comprehensive listings in *Time Out New York*, the free *Village Voice* (especially the pull-out *Voice Choices* section), or the *New York Press*, all especially useful for things Downtown and vaguely "alternative." For tonier events try the "Cue"

section in the weekly *New York Magazine*, the "Goings On About Town" section of *The New Yorker*, or Friday's "Weekend" or Sunday's "Arts and Leisure" sections of *The New York Times*. Specific Broadway listings can be found in the free *Official Broadway Theater Guide*, available from theater and hotel lobbies or the *New York Convention and Visitors' Bureau* (see "Information, Maps and Tours" in *Basics*). A new alternative to listings magazines is Microsoft's Sidewalk Web site at *http://www.sidewalk.com*, which has up-to-the-minute information on arts and events in New York.

Theater

Theater venues in the city are referred to as **Broadway**, **Off-Broadway**, or **Off-Off-Broadway**, groupings that represent a descending order of ticket price, production polish, elegance and comfort (but don't necessarily have much to do with the address) and an ascending order of innovation, experimentation, and theater for the sake of art rather than cash. Though **Broadway**'s 1996–97 season was especially successful, with record receipts and the second-highest attendance in Broadway history (behind the 1980–81 season) – perhaps stemming from the attention lavished on vital new shows like *Rent* and *Bring in 'da Noise*,

Bring in 'da Funk (both Off-Broadway transplants) – the Great White Way remains dominated by grandiose musicals and revivals. As William Grimes wrote not long ago in *The New York Times*, "The shows making the most money today are, for the most part, the same ones that were making big money five years ago: *Cats, The Phantom of the Opera, Miss Saigon* and *Les Miserables*." There still remains next to no new serious drama in Times Square – perhaps an Ibsen revival or two, but not much else. Fortunately a new private coalition called the Broadway Initiative has begun moves to establish a $10 million annual fund to reverse this trend and to improve the quality and range of Broadway theater. At a time when the Disneyfication of Times Square is proceeding apace, this move is heartening.

But for now, for quality drama and name playwrights from Shakespeare to Shepard, **Off-Broadway** is still the place to go. Off-Broadway theaters provide polished production qualities, but combine them with a greater willingness to experiment. It's Off-Broadway where you'll find social and political drama, satire, ethnic plays and repertory: in short, anything that Broadway wouldn't consider a surefire money-spinner. Lower operating costs also mean that Off-Broadway often serves as a forum to try out what sometimes ends up as a big Broadway production.

Off-Off-Broadway is New York's fringe. Unlike Off-Broadway, Off-Off doesn't have to use professional actors, and shows range from shoestring productions of the classics to outrageous and experimental performance art. Prices Off-Off range from cheap to free, and quality can vary from execrable to electrifying. Use weekly reviews as your guide; the listings here should give you an idea of which venues and companies are worth a look.

For the record, it's the size of the theater that technically determines the category it falls into: under 100 seats and a theater is Off-Off; 100 to 500 and it's Off. Most Broadway theaters are located in the blocks just east or west of Broadway between 41st and 53rd sts; Off- and Off-Off-Broadway theaters are sprinkled throughout Manhattan, with a concentration in the East and West Villages, Chelsea, and several in the 40s and 50s west of the Broadway theater district.

Tickets

Tickets for Broadway shows can cost as much as $75 for orchestra seats and as little as $15 for same-day standing-room tickets for some of the longer-running shows. Off-Broadway's best seats are cheaper than those on Broadway, averaging between $35–45, but often there is only one price for every seat in the house. Off-Off Broadway, however, tickets should rarely set you back more than $15 at most. There are also a couple of methods for obtaining cheap seats on and Off-Broadway.

• Line up at one of two Manhattan **TKTS booths** run by the Theater Development Fund (☎768-1818), where you can obtain cut-rate tickets on the day of performance (up to half-off plus a $2.50 service charge) for many Broadway and Off-Broadway shows (though not always for the more recently opened popular shows). The booth in Times Square, at Broadway and 47th St, has the longest lines and opens Mon–Sat 3–8pm, 10am–2pm for Wed and Sat matinees, and 11am–7pm for all Sun performances. There's a less busy downtown *TKTS* booth on the mezzanine of 2 World Trade Center (preferable if it's raining) open Mon–Fri 11am–5.30pm, Sat 11am–3.30pm, and on Fri and Sat tickets are sold for the *following day's* matinee shows. Both booths take cash or traveler's checks only; best days for availability and short lines are Tues, Wed and Thurs.

• Look for **twofer discount coupons** in the *New York Convention* and *Visitors' Bureau* and many shops, banks, restaurants and hotel lobbies. These entitle two people to a hefty discount (though the days when they really offered two-for-the-price-of-one are long gone) and

The
Performing
Arts and
Film

The Performing Arts and Film

unlike *TKTS* it's possible to book ahead, though don't expect to find coupons for the latest shows. The *Hit Show Club* (630 9th Ave at 44th St ☎581-4211) also provides discount vouchers up to fifty percent off which you present at the box office.

• If you're prepared to pay full price you can, of course, go directly to the theater, or call one of the following ticket sales agencies. **Telecharge** (☎239-6200), **Ticketmaster** (☎307-7171), and **Ticketron** (☎1-800/SOLD OUT Mon to Fri) sell tickets over the phone to Broadway shows, while **Tickets Central** (☎279-4200) sells tickets to many Off- and Off-Off-Broadway theaters 1–8pm daily. All these services charge a service fee of a couple of dollars or more. You can also buy theater tickets over the internet at Ticketmaster's Web site (*http://www.ticketmaster.com*) or through Playbill-On-Line (*http://www.playbill.com*).

Though you will want to check out the aforementioned listings magazines to see what's playing, the following theaters are worth attention for their specialized repertoire or for their long-running shows.

Off-Broadway

Actor's Playhouse, 100 7th Ave South ☎463-0060. West Village venue specializing in gay-themed theater.

American Jewish Theater, 307 W 26th St ☎633-9797. Produces four classical and contemporary plays a year on Jewish themes.

Astor Place Theater, 434 Lafayette St ☎254-4370. Showcase for much exciting work since the 1960s, when Sam Shepard's *The Unseen Hand* and *Forensic and the Navigators* had the playwright on drums in the lobby. Since 1992 the theater has been running the absurdist performance show *Tubes* by the very eccentric Blue Man Group.

Brooklyn Academy of Music, 30 Lafayette St, Brooklyn ☎718/636-4100. Despite its name, *BAM* regularly stages theater on its three stages. They have

imported a number of stunning productions directed by Ingmar Bergman in recent years, and every autumn the annual Next Wave festival is the city's most exciting showcase for large-scale performance art by the likes of Robert Wilson, Robert LePage, Laurie Anderson and Pina Bausch. Not so much Off-Broadway as Off-Manhattan, but well worth the trip.

Irish Repertory Theater, 132 W 22nd St ☎727-2737. Specializes in Irish or Irish-themed theater.

The Joseph Papp Public Theater, 425 Lafayette St ☎260-2400. This major downtown Off-Broadway venue produces serious and challenging theater from new, mostly American playwrights all year round, as well as being the major producer of Shakespeare productions in the city. In the summer the *Public* runs the free Shakespeare Festival at the open-air *Delacorte Theater* in Central Park (☎539-8750). Tickets are available on the day both at the *Public* downtown and the *Delacorte* uptown, but be prepared for long lines.

Manhattan Theater Club, 131 W 55th St ☎581-1212. Major Midtown venue for serious new theater, many of whose productions eventually transfer to Broadway. See them here first.

Orpheum Theater, 126 2nd Ave (at St Mark's Place) ☎477-2477. One of the biggest theaters in the East Village, known for showing David Mamet and other new American theater, and home for the last few years to the British percussion performance troupe Stomp.

The SoHo Playhouse, 15 Vandam St ☎691-1555. Home of the participation comedy *Grandma Sylvia's Funeral*, which stages a mock Jewish funeral in the *Tony'n'Tina* mold (see below). Ticket price (around $50) includes the funeral meal.

St John's Church, 81 Christopher St ☎279-4200. This West Village church has for the past ten years been host to the audience participation comedy *Tony'n'Tina's Wedding*. The audience attends a boisterous Italian-American wedding and then joins the party for dinner at a nearby restaurant (a pricey night out at $70 a ticket).

Sullivan St Playhouse, 181 Sullivan St ☎674-3838. Greenwich Village theater which has been home to *The Fantasticks*, the longest running show in American history, since 1960.

Vivian Beaumont Theater and Mitzi E. Newhouse Theater, 150 W 65th St at Lincoln Center. Technically Broadway theaters, though far enough away from Times Square in distance and, usually, quality, to qualify as Off. The place to see new work by Stoppard, Guare and the like.

Westside Theater, 407 W 43rd St ☎315-2244. Small basement theater known for productions of Shaw, Wilde, Pirandello and the like.

Off-Off-Broadway and performance art spaces

Samuel Beckett Theater, 410 W 42nd St ☎332-0894. A repertory program of classic and new plays.

Jean Cocteau Repertory, Bouwerie Lane Theater, 330 Bowery (at Bond St) ☎677-0060. Genet, Sophocles, Shaw, Strindberg, Sartre, Wilde, Williams, etc, along with unknowns.

Dixon Place, 258 Bowery (between Prince and Houston sts) ☎219-3088. Very popular small venue upstairs in a Bowery loft dedicated to experimental theater.

Expanded Arts, 85 Ludlow St (below Delancey) ☎253-1813. Produces free outdoor Shakespeare performances all summer long on a Lower East Side Parking Lot.

Franklin Furnace, 112 Franklin St ☎925-4671. An archive dedicated to installation work and performance art, the *Franklin Furnace* has launched the careers of performers as celebrated and notorious as Karen Finley and Eric Borgosian. Performances do not take place at the TriBeCa *Furnace* but at related venues downtown.

Hudson Guild Theater, 441 W 26th St (between 9th and 10th aves) ☎760-9800. Introduces new American and European playwrights.

The Kitchen, 512 W 19th St (between 10th and 11th aves) ☎255-5793; Web site: *http://www.panix.com/~kitchen*. Well-established Chelsea venue for avant-garde performance art, theater, music and dance.

Knitting Factory, 74 Leonard St (between Broadway and Church) ☎219-3006; Web site: *http://www.knittingfactory.com*. In its new, improved TriBeCa space this much-loved alternative music venue now hosts theater and performance art in its *Alterknit Theater*.

La Mama E.T.C. (Experimental Theater Club), 74A E 4th St (between the Bowery and 2nd Ave) ☎475-7710. The mother of all Off-Off-theaters and venue for some of the most exciting theater, performance and dance seen in the city in the past 30 years.

Nuyorican Poets Cafe, 236 E 3rd St (between aves B and C) ☎505-8183. For a number of years now the *Nuyorican* in Alphabet City has been one of the most talked-about performance spaces in town. Its "poetry slams" made it famous, but they also host theater and film script readings, occasionally with well-known downtown stars.

Ontological Theater at St. Mark's Church, 131 E 10th St ☎533-4650. Produces some of the best radical theater in the city; especially famous for the work of downtown theater legend Richard Foreman.

Performing Garage, 33 Wooster St ☎966-3651. The well-respected experimental Wooster Group (whose most famous alumnus is Willem Dafoe) perform regularly in this SoHo space.

P.S. 122, 150 1st Ave (at 9th St) ☎477-5829. A converted school house in the East Village that is a perennially popular venue for a jam-packed schedule of radical performance art, dance, and one-person shows.

Surf Reality, 172 Allen St (between Stanton and Rivington sts) ☎673-4182.

The Performing Arts and Film

The Performing Arts and Film

Eclectic performance art and comedy space on the Lower East Side.

Theater for the New City, 155 1st Ave (at 10th St) ☎254-1109. Known for following the development of new playwrights and integrating dance, music, and poetry with drama. TNC also performs outdoors for free at a variety of venues throughout the summer.

Thread Waxing Space, 476 Broadway ☎966-9774. Beautifully named performance space in SoHo, inside an old factory, mostly used for music, but often hosts performance-based art too.

WPA Theater, 519 W 23rd St ☎206-0523. The *Workshop of the Players Art* performs neglected American classics and American Realist plays, many from the South, acted in a style described as "derived from Stanislavski."

Dance

With the astounding success of recent shows like *Riverdance*, *Tap Dogs*, *Bring in 'Da Noise* and *Forever Tango*, **dance** is experiencing an unparalleled surge in popularity in New York. And, as with theater, the range of dance on offer in the city is vast. New York has five major ballet companies, dozens of modern troupes and untold thousands of soloists and you would have to be very particular indeed in your tastes not to find something of interest. Events are listed in broadly the same places as for music and theater – though you might also want to pick up *Dance Magazine*. The official dance season runs from September to January and April to June. The following is a list of some of the major dance venues in the city though a lot of the smaller, more esoteric companies also perform at many of the spaces like the *Kitchen* and *P.S.122*, which are listed above under "Off-Off Broadway and Performance Art."

Brooklyn Academy of Music, 30 Lafayette St (between Flatbush Ave and Fulton St), Brooklyn ☎718/636-4100. Universally known as *BAM*, this is America's oldest performing arts academy and one of the busiest and most daring producers in New York. In the autumn, *BAM*'s Next Wave Festival showcases the hottest international attractions in avant-garde dance and music; in winter visiting artists appear, and each spring *BAM* hosts the annual *DanceAfrica Festival*, America's largest showcase for African and African-American dance and culture, now in its twentieth year. A great venue and one definitely worth crossing the river for.

City Center, 131 W 55th St (between 6th and 7th aves) ☎581-1212 and ☎581-7907. This large midtown venue hosts some of the most important troupes in modern dance, such as the Merce Cunningham Dance Company, the Paul Taylor Dance Company, the Alvin Ailey American Dance Theater, the Joffrey Ballet, and the Dance Theater of Harlem.

Dance Theater Workshop's Bessie Schönberg Theater, 219 W 19th St (between 7th and 8th aves) ☎691-6500; Web site: http://www.dtw.org. Founded in 1965 as a choreographers' collective for the support of emerging artists in alternative dance, *DTW* boasts more than 175 performances from nearly 70 artists and companies each season. Located on the second floor of a former warehouse, the theater has an unintimidating, relaxed atmosphere and ticket prices are very reasonable.

Danspace Project, St Mark's-Church-in-the-Bowery, 131 E 10th St (at 2nd Ave) ☎674-8194. Experimental contemporary dance, with a season running from September to June in one of the more beautiful performance spaces.

Emanu-El Midtown YM/YWHA, 344 E 14th St ☎674-7200. Has been presenting dance for decades. The facility is actually a gymnasium and can be stifling on warm days. Still, the range of talents seen here (and the budget-priced admission) make it a space to know about.

The Joyce Theater, 175 8th Ave (at 19th St) ☎242-0800. Situated in Chelsea, the *Joyce* is perhaps the best-known downtown dance venue. Hosts short seasons by a wide variety of acclaimed dance troupes such as Pilobolus, the Parsons Dance Company and Donald Byrd/The Group. The *Joyce* also recently opened a new space in SoHo at 155 Mercer St between Prince and Houston ☎431-9233.

The Judson Church, 55 Washington Square South (at Thompson St) ☎477-6854. Greenwich Village's historic venue for experimental dance.

Julliard Dance Workshop, Julliard Theater, 155 W 65th St (at Broadway) ☎799-5000. The dance division of the Julliard School often gives free workshop performances.

Merce Cunningham Studio, 55 Bethune St at Washington St ☎780-3463. The new home of the Merce Cunningham Dance Company stages performances by emerging modern choreographers.

Metropolitan Opera House, Columbus Ave at 64th St, Lincoln Center ☎362-6000. Home of the renowned American Ballet Theater, which performs at the Opera House from early May into July. Prices for ballet at the *Met* range from more than $100 for the best seats to $15 for standing-room tickets, which go on sale the morning of the performance.

New York State Theater, Columbus Ave at 64th St, Lincoln Center ☎870-5585. Lincoln Center's other major ballet venue is home to the revered New York City Ballet, which performs for a nine-week season each spring.

92nd Street Y, 1395 Lexington Ave at 92nd St ☎415-5552. Hosts performances and discussions, often for free, at the Y's Harkness Dance Center.

Classical music and opera

New Yorkers take **serious music** seriously. Long lines form for anything popular, many concerts sell out, and summer

---

Free summer concerts

In the light of high concert ticket prices, it's welcoming that so many events in the city, especially in summer, are free. **The Summerstage Festival** (☎360-2777) in **Central Park** puts on an impressive range of free concerts throughout the summer. Performances take place at the Rumsey Playfield (near the 72nd St and 5th Ave entrance). Pick up a calendar of events around town or look in *Time Out New York* or *The Village Voice* for details. Every Wednesday night the **New York Grand Opera** performs a different Verdi opera at Summerstage. Central Park is also one of the many open-air venues for the **New York Philharmonic's Concerts in the Park** series (☎875-5709), which turns up all over the city and the Outer Boroughs in July, and the similar **Met in the Parks** series (☎362-6000) in June.

All summer **Lincoln Center Out-of-Doors** (☎875-5108) hosts a varied selection of free performances of music and dance on the plaza, while the beautifully made-over **Bryant Park** has free concerts on the grass. And at MoMA the **Summergarden** series (☎708-9480) presents free music concerts in the sculpture garden on Friday and Saturday evenings in July and August.

Downtown, **CenterStage at the World Trade Center** (☎435-4170) hosts free lunchtime and evening performances of jazz and R&B throughout July and August. And there is free classical music in the Village at the **Washington Square Music Festival** (☎431-1088) on Tuesdays at 8pm from mid-June to mid-July.

On July and August weekends the **Prospect Park Bandshell** serves as venue for the Celebrate Brooklyn Festival (☎718/768-0699); recent attractions have included artists as diverse as the Piccolo Teatro dell' Opera performing *Othello*, and the Brooklyn Gospel Festival.

The Performing Arts and Film

evenings can see a quarter of a million people turning up in Central Park for free performances by the New York Philharmonic. The range of what's on offer is wide, but it's big names at big venues that pull the crowds, leaving you with a good number of easily attended selections.

Opera venues

Amato Opera Theater, 319 Bowery ☎228-8200. This downtown venue presents an ambitious and varied repertory of classics performed by up-and-coming young singers and conductors. Performances at weekends only, closed in the summer.

Julliard School, 155 W 65th St (at Broadway) ☎799-5000. Right next door to the Met, Julliard students often perform under the control of a famous conductor, usually for low ticket prices.

Metropolitan Opera House, Columbus Ave at 64th St, Lincoln Center ☎362-6000. Known as *the Met*, New York's premiere opera venue is home to the Metropolitan Opera Company from September to late April. Tickets are expensive and can be quite difficult to get hold of, though 175 standing-room tickets for $11–15 go on sale every Saturday morning at 10am (though the line has been known to form at 5am).

The New York State Theater also in Lincoln Center (☎870-5570) is where Beverley Sills' New York City Opera plays David to the *Met's* Goliath. Its wide and adventurous program varies wildly in quality – sometimes startlingly innovative, occasionally mediocre, but seats go for less than half the *Met's* prices.

Concert halls

The Avery Fisher Hall, in Lincoln Center ☎875-5030; Web site: *http://www. newyorkphilharmonic.org*. Permanent home of the New York Philharmonic, and temporary one to visiting orchestras and soloists. Ticket prices for the Philharmonic are in the range of $12–50. An often fascinating bargain are the NYP open rehearsals at 9.45am on concert

days. Tickets for these, nonreservable, cost just $6. Avery Fisher also hosts the very popular annual *Mostly Mozart* Festival (☎875-5103) in August.

The Alice Tully Hall ☎875-5050, also in Lincoln Center, is a smaller venue for chamber orchestras, string quartets and instrumentalists. Prices similar to those in *Avery Fisher*.

Brooklyn Academy of Music, 30 Lafayette St, Brooklyn ☎718/636-4100. See "Dance."

Bargemusic, Fulton Ferry Landing, Brooklyn ☎718/624-4061. Chamber music in a wonderful river setting below the Brooklyn Bridge on Thursdays and Fridays at 7.30pm, and Sundays at 4pm.

Carnegie Hall, 154 W 57th St (at 7th Ave) ☎247-7800. The greatest names from all schools of music performed here in the past, from Tchaikovsky and Toscanini to Gershwin and Billie Holiday. The acoustics remain superb. Expect music of just about any sort, and moderate prices.

Kaufman Concert Hall, in the 92nd St Y at 1395 Lexington Ave ☎996-1100.

Lehman Center for the Performing Arts, Bedford Park Boulevard, the Bronx ☎718/960-8232. First-class concert hall drawing the world's top performers.

Merkin Concert Hall, Abraham Goodman House, 129 W 67th St ☎362-8719.

Symphony Space, 2536 Broadway (at 95th St) ☎864-5400.

Town Hall, 123 W 43rd St (between 6th and 7th aves) ☎840-2824.

Cabaret and comedy

Comedy clubs and cabaret spots are rife in New York, with shows varying from stand-up and improvised comedy (amazing if you've never seen it before – quick-fire wit being part of the city psyche) to singing waiters and waitresses, many of whom are professional performers waiting for their big break. Most clubs have shows every night, with two at weekends, and charge a cover and usually a two-drink minimum. The list below represents the best-known venues in town, but check *Time Out New York* and *New York Magazine* for the fullest and most up-to-date listings.

Asti, 13 E 12th St ☎741-9105. Celebrating 70 years in business, *Asti* is an East Village restaurant with daily live entertainment from professional opera stars and singing waiters. A rowdy, fun night out. No cover. Closed in the summer.

Boston Comedy Club, 82 W 3rd St (between Thompson and Sullivan sts) ☎477-1000. This long-running club in the heart of the Village has what *New York Magazine* calls "an *Animal House* ambience" so be warned. $5 cover Tues–Thurs, $10 Fri–Sat. Two-drink minimum.

Brandy's Piano Bar, 235 E 84th St ☎650-1944. Small, Upper East Side piano bar featuring bar staff and waitresses who sing popular Broadway show hits and old TV theme tunes. Opens at 9.30pm; there's a two-drink minimum charge at the tables but no cover.

Caroline's Comedy Club, 1626 Broadway at 49th St ☎757-4100. Moved to Times Square from its old location at the Seaport, *Caroline's* still books some of the best stand-up acts in town. $12–15 cover Sun–Thurs, $15–17 Fri and Sat. Two-drink minimum. Also has a restaurant, *Comedy Nation*, upstairs.

Catch a Rising Star, 253 W 28th St (between 7th and 8th aves) ☎244-3005. One of New York's classiest comedy clubs, which comes complete with its own restaurant, the *Catch Bar & Grill*. Hosts a mixture of stand-up and revue comedy. $8 cover Tues–Thurs; $12.50–15 Fri and Sat. Two-drink minimum.

Chicago City Limits Theater, 1105 1st Ave (at 61st St) ☎888-5233. Improvisation theater playing one show nightly, two on weekends. Closed Tues and Sun. Ticket prices $10–17.50. New York's oldest improv club.

Comedy Cellar, 117 MacDougal St (between W 3rd and Bleecker sts) ☎254-3480. Popular Greenwich Village comedy club now in its 17th year of

existence. A good late-night hangout (open til 2.30am). $5 cover Sun–Thurs, $12 Fri–Sat. Two-drink minimum.

Comic Strip, 1568 2nd Ave (between 81st and 82nd sts) ☎861-9386. Famed showcase for stand-up comics and young singers going for the big time. Cover $8 Sun–Wed, $12 Fri and Sat. Two-drink minimum.

Dangerfield's, 1118 1st Ave (between 61st and 62nd sts) ☎593-1650. Vegas-style new talent showcase founded 20 years ago by Rodney Dangerfield. Cover $12.50–15, with, unusually, no minimum drinks charge.

Don't Tell Mama, 343 W 46th St (between 8th and 9th aves) ☎757-0788. Lively and convivial West Midtown piano bar and cabaret featuring rising stars and singing waitresses. Shows at 8pm & 10pm. Cover $10–20, two-drink minimum.

Duplex, 61 Christopher St and 7th Ave ☎255-5438. West Village cabaret popular with a boisterous gay crowd; it was here that Joan Rivers was discovered. Has a rowdy piano bar downstairs and a cabaret room upstairs. Hosts a "Star Search" show on Fri nights. Open 4pm–4am. Cover $3–12, two-drink minimum.

Eighty Eight's, 228 W 10th St ☎924-0088. West Village cabaret, owned by entertainers who have been playing the circuit for years. Cabaret upstairs, piano bar downstairs; cover $8–15. Two-drink minimum.

Gotham Comedy Club, 34 W 22nd St (between 5th and 6th aves) ☎367-9000. A swanky and spacious comedy venue in the Flatiron district. Cover $8 Sun–Thurs, $12 Fri and Sat. Two-drink minimum.

The Original Improv, 433 W 34th St (between 9th and 10th aves) ☎279-3446. New comic and singing talent – most, as the name suggests, improvised. Cover $10. $9 drinks minimum. Shows at 9pm on Thurs; 8.30pm and 10.30pm on Fri & Sat nights.

Stand Up New York, 236 W 78th St at Broadway ☎595-0850. Upper West Side

The Performing Arts and Film

The Performing Arts and Film

forum for established comics, many of whom have appeared on Leno, Letterman and the like. Nightly shows, three on weekends. Weekdays $7 cover, Fri & Sat $12. Two-drink minimum.

Film

For **movie** fans, an added bonus of any trip to New York is a chance to see new American films long before they reach Europe, and there are plenty of great theaters to catch them in, as well as a fair share of dives. In general, Times Square cinemas are small, noisy and to be avoided, except for the enormous **Astor Plaza** (44th St and Broadway ☎869-8340), which is one of the city's largest screens, and the new four-screen **State Theater** within the Virgin Megastore (1540 Broadway ☎391-2900). Around town the largest multiplexes (the *Cineplex Odeons* and *Sonys*) are your best bet for large screens, comfortable seats and good sightlines, and, let's face it, if you're going to see the latest blockbuster you don't really want to watch it in a room the size of a small car. The jewel in the crown is the venerable **Ziegfeld** (54th St at 6th Ave ☎765-7600), an old-style midtown movie palace that makes almost any film seen in it look good. Also worth a trip, if only to sit in an old-time movie balcony, is the recently reopened **Paris Fine Arts** (58th St and 5th Ave ☎980-5656). Best of the multiplexes is the new **Sony Lincoln Square** (Broadway at 68th St ☎336-5000), near Lincoln Center, which has a lobby like a crowded airport but comfortable seats and large screens throughout, as well as a giant **3-D Imax** theater. For new foreign films the six-screen **Lincoln Plaza** (Broadway at 62nd St ☎757-2280), also on the Upper West Side, is the place to go. For cultier, more American-indie fare make your way to Downtown's ever popular six-screen **Angelika Film Center** (corner of Houston and Mercer ☎995-2000), whose spacious café lobby is a great place to meet, or to the smaller four-screen **Quad** (13th St at 6th Ave ☎255-8800), the

single-screen **Cinema Village** (22 E 12th St ☎924-3363), or the brand-new TriBeCa **Screening Room** (54 Varick at Canal ☎334-2100) with its very own cocktail bar and restaurant. The **Film Forum** (see *Revivals*) also screens a very outré selection of new low-budget films and documentaries. If you're a fan of Hong Kong cinema you should definitely check out the last remaining Chinatown theater, the **Music Palace**, on the Bowery just above Canal Street, which, though it's rarely listed in newspapers, does have a regular turnover of new films, all with English subtitles. For listings your best bets are the weekly *Village Voice*, or the *New York Press* (both free), *Time Out New York*, or the daily papers on a Friday when reviews come out. The weekly magazines (*New York*, *The New Yorker*) publish listings but without showtimes. You should also look out for the new handy *Pocket Flicks* movie guides, distributed throughout the city. Beware that listings in papers are not *always* entirely accurate, but you can phone 777-FILM for accurate showtimes and computerized film selections. Ticket prices have recently risen to as high as $9, and there are no reduced matinee prices in Manhattan, nor cheap evenings, but if you're strapped for cash the six-screen **Worldwide** (50th St between 8th & 9th aves ☎504-0960) is a godsend, showing new films only just past their prime for $3. Note that theaters are very busy on Friday and Saturday nights, and tickets for hot new releases can sell out early in the day on opening weekend.

Festivals

There always seems to be some film festival or other running in New York. The granddaddy of them all, **The New York Film Festival**, starts at the end of September, runs for two weeks at the Alice Tully Hall at Lincoln Center, and is well worth catching if you're in town. Unfortunately, tickets sell out quickly in mid-September for the most popular films, but it's often possible to purchase tickets on the night from people selling unwanted tickets at face value outside the theater (especially if the film has been panned that morning in *The New York Times*). Other New York film festivals include the **New York Jewish Film Festival** in January; **New Directors/New Films Festival** – which speaks for itself – at the Museum of Modern Art, and the rival downtown **Underground Film Festival**, both in March; the **GenArt Film Festival** of American independents and the **Avignon/New York Festival** of French and American films in April; the **Human Rights Watch Film Festival**, the **Lesbian and Gay Film Festival**, the **Women's Film Festival**, and the **Sierra Club Film & Video Festival** of environmental activist films in June; the **Asian American International Film Festival** and the **New York Video Festival** in July; the **Harlem Week Black Film Festival** in August; the **Hong Kong Film Series** at the *Cinema Village* in August and September; and the **Margaret Meade Festival** of anthropological films at the Museum of Natural History in October.

Revivals

Outside of Paris, New York may well be the best city in the world to see a wide selection of old movies, but the cinema landscape has changed considerably in the past decade. The old repertory houses showing a regular turnover of scratchy prints of old chestnuts and recent favorites have all gone (the last five closed in the 1990s, including the much-loved **Theater 80 St Mark's**). But what remains, or has sprung up in its place, is an impressive selection of museums and revival houses showing imaginatively programmed series of films – whether retrospectives of particular directors or actors, series from particular countries, or programs of particular genres. The theaters showing these films range from the dryly academic to the purely pleasurable, but what most of them have in common is an emphasis on good-quality prints (there are exceptions of course) and comprehensiveness. Of course, as a visitor, what you get to see is a matter of chance. If you're lucky your trip may coincide with retrospectives of your favorite director, your movie heartthrob, and that series of Lithuanian silents you'd been waiting all your life to see.

Schedules can be found in the publications listed above, and all the following revival houses and museums publish calendars that can be picked up at the box office.

The American Museum of the Moving Image, 35th Ave (at 36th St), Queens ☎718/784-0077. Showing films only on weekends during the day, *AMMI* is well worth a trip out to Queens (it's not as far as it sounds – call ☎718/784-4777 for directions) either for the films – serious director retrospectives, silent films, and a good emphasis on cinematographers – or for the cinema museum itself.

Anthology Film Archives, 32 2nd Ave (at 2nd St) ☎505-5181; Web site: *http://www.arthouseinc.com/anthology*. The bastion of experimental filmmaking has recently been given a new lease of life by the addition of Fabiano Canosa, formerly of *Film at the Public*, to its staff. Now the programs of mind-bending abstraction, East Village grunge-flicks, and the year-round *Essential Cinema* series rub shoulders with some of the best of recent international art cinema. Now if they'd only do something about the seats.. Around the corner, on E 4th St between 2nd and 3rd aves, **Millennium Film Workshop** keeps the experimental candle burning with occasional screenings of new abstract and avant-garde work in film and classes in low-budget filmmaking.

Film Forum, 209 W Houston (between 6th and 7th aves) ☎727-8110; Web site: *http://www.filmforum.com*. The cozy three-screen *Film Forum* has an eccentric but famously popular program of new independent movies, documentaries and foreign films on two of its screens, and a repertory program in *Film Forum 2* specializing in silent comedy, camp classics and cult directors. With its cappuccinos and popcorn and lively crowds, *Film Forum* is always worth a visit.

The Museum of Modern Art, 11 W 53rd St ☎708-9480; Web site: *http://www.*

The
Performing
Arts and
Film

The Performing Arts and Film

moma.org. Famous among local cinephiles for its vast collection of films, its exquisite programming and its regular audience of cantankerous senior citizens. Films range from Hollywood screwball comedies to hand-painted Super 8, and entry to either of *MoMA*'s large movie theaters is free with museum admission.

Walter Reade Theater, 65th St between Broadway and Amsterdam ☎875-5600; Web site: *http://www.filmlinc.com*. Programmed by the Film Society of Lincoln Center, the *Walter Reade* is simply the best place in town to see great films. Opened in 1991, this beautiful modern theater with perfect sightlines, a huge screen and impeccable sound elevates the art of cinema to the position it deserves within Lincoln Center. The emphasis is on foreign cinema and the great auteurs.

Also of note

On Mondays, at sunset throughout the summer, **Bryant Park** (6th Ave and 42nd St ☎512-5700) hosts free, outdoor screenings of old Hollywood favorites, while **River Flicks** at the new Chelsea Piers (Pier 62 at W 23rd St) has free summer screenings of water-themed crowd-pleasers (like *Jaws* and *The Poseidon Adventure*) on Wednesday nights. Though primarily music venues, **Symphony Space** (2537 Broadway at 95th St ☎864-5400) hosts a repertory program of old favorites one night a week, and the **Knitting Factory** (74 Leonard St ☎219-3055) occasionally shows silent films with live modern accompaniment. There are also regular screenings, often of experimental cinema, at the **Whitney Museum** (see Chapter 15, *Museums and Galleries*) in conjunction with its exhibitions. German, Asian, Japanese and French cinema can often be found at, respectively, the **Goethe House** (1014 5th Ave ☎439-8706), the **Asia Society** (725 Park Ave at 70th St ☎517-2742), the **Japan Society** (333 E 47th St ☎832-1155) and the **French Institute** (55 E 59th St ☎355-6160). And for night-owls, there are special midnight screenings on Friday and Saturday nights at the **Angelika Film Center** and the **Screening Room** (see above); not to forget that New York institution, *The Rocky Horror Picture Show*, which has returned to the city with midnight shows at the **Village East** (189 2nd Ave at 12th St ☎529-6799).

Chapter 21

Sports and Outdoor Activities

Sports in America are big business, which is to say that for all spectator sports financial considerations come first. The Brooklyn Dodgers, New York's official baseball team, upped and left (for LA) as long ago as 1957, and every other professional team intermittently threatens to do the same. Yet New Yorkers are themselves highly sports-conscious: the city's newspapers devote a great many pages to the subject, as do the TV stations, which cover most of the regular season games and all of the post-season games in the big four American team sports – **football**, **baseball**, **basketball** and **ice hockey** (known simply as hockey). If you want to watch a game, bear in mind that some tickets can be hard to come by and don't come that cheap. Remember, also, that bars – often known as **sports bars** – are a good alternative to actually being there, especially those with king-size screens (see box on p.382 for listings).

Many **participation sports** are affordable. You can **swim** (either at the local pools or the borough beaches) or **jog**, still one of the city's main obsessions. If you're into soccer there are generally lots of pick-up games on the Great Lawn – recently refurbished – in Central Park on summer Sundays. However, it is hard to find facilities for some sports, such as **tennis**, if you are not either a club member or a city resident. Many New Yorkers

spend around $100 a month to be members of private health clubs. For anyone interested, these places fill sizable sections of the city's *Yellow Pages*.

Spectator sports

In this section we've included details of each of the main **spectator sports** in New York – including a run-through of the rules, where necessary – followed by a section detailing the venues.

American football

If you're a foreign visitor and haven't seen an **American football** game before you arrive in New York you won't have long to wait. All big games are featured on TV and they're a major slot in most neighborhood bars. For the uninitiated, the spectacle of all-American razzmatazz is probably novelty enough, though the game does get more interesting if you can pick up at least some of the rules (see box overleaf).

The **season** stretches from September to the end of December, when the playoffs take place to decide who goes to the Super Bowl – America's version of the FA Cup Final, played on the third Sunday of January. New York's teams are the **NY Jets** and the **NY Giants**, neither of whom actually play in New York: both play at Giants Stadium in the Meadowlands Sports Complex in New

Sports and Outdoor Activities

Jersey. The two teams have been in a bit of a nosedive through the 1990s, but the Jets – hoping to revive themselves and steal some of the Giants' (the more successful franchise) thunder – recently hired Bill Parcells, ex-coach of the Giants and winner of two Super Bowls with them. The cheapest tickets can be tough to get. If you don't manage to get any, don't worry too much: at least two games are shown on TV every Sunday afternoon, with another on Monday night during the regular season.

Baseball

Baseball is America's game. No other sport generates as much interest in the US over the whole season, and nothing else compares with the tradition and mystique that surround this still essentially parochial and small-town game. Baseball has a complex set of rules that only a true aficionado completely understands, but it is easy to get the general idea. Games are played (162 each season) all over the US close to every day from April through September, with the season culminating in the modestly titled World Series in October – the final best-of-seven playoff between the champions of the two leagues, the National and the American. The bitter feelings caused by the players' strike that cut short the 1994 season, canceling the World Series and delaying the start of the 1995 season, have generally blown over. And New York fans are still heady from the ticker tape parade celebrating the Yankees' 1996 World Series championship. Watching a game, even if you don't understand what's going on, can at least be a pleasant day out, drinking beer and eating hot dogs outdoors: tickets are

---

The rules of baseball and football: an explanation for foreign visitors

Baseball

The basic set-up looks like the English game of rounders, with four **bases** set at the corners of a 90-foot-square **diamond**; at the bottom corner the base is called **home plate** and serves much the same purpose as do the stumps in cricket. Play begins when the **pitcher**, standing on a low pitcher's mound in the middle of the diamond, throws a **ball** at upwards of 100 mph, making it curve and bend as it travels toward the **catcher**, who crouches behind home plate; seven other defensive players take up **positions**, one at each base and the others spread out around the field of play. A **batter** from the opposing team stands beside home plate and tries to hit the ball with a tapered, cylindrical wooden **bat**. If the batter swings and misses, or if the pitched ball crosses the plate above the batter's knees and below his chest, it counts as a **strike**; if he doesn't swing and the ball passes outside of this strike zone, it counts as a **ball**. If the batter gets **three strikes**

against him he is out; **four balls** and he gets a free **walk**, and takes his place as a runner on first base.

If he succeeds in hitting the pitched ball into **fair territory**, the wedge between the first and third bases, the batter runs toward first base; if the opposing players catch the ball before it hits the ground, the batter is out. Otherwise they field the ball and attempt to relay it to first base before the batter gets there; if they do he is **out**, if they don't the batter is **safe** – and stays there, being moved along by subsequent batters until he makes a complete circuit of the bases and scores a **run**. The most exciting moment is the **home run**, when a batter hits the ball over the outfield fences, a boundary often times 400 feet away from home plate; he and any runners on base when he hits the ball each scores a run. If there are runners on all three bases it's a **grand slam** and earns four runs.

Games take up to three hours to play and each side – made up of nine play-

---

not too expensive and the crowds usually friendly and sociable.

New York has two baseball teams, the **Yankees** and the **Mets**. The Yankees, who play at Yankee Stadium in the Bronx, are the oldest team (alumni include Joe di Maggio and Babe Ruth). They have won more World Series (26) than any team in history, are the most recognized sports franchise in the world, and are among the top five wealthiest. The Mets are a relatively young team, launched in 1962 to compensate for the loss of the Brooklyn Dodgers. They play at Shea Stadium in Flushing, Queens, and last won the World Series back in 1986. Now, interest in the Yankees and the Mets is running pretty even. Tickets for the Yankees are $21, $18 and $12 ($6 for bleacher seats); for the Mets they are $18, $14, $13, and $7. (For rules, see box below)

Basketball

Basketball is perhaps the most popular American game to be played outside the US; it's also by far the most athletic of American team sports, and the most graceful to watch. Played over 48 minutes, the game is nonstop action conducted at a blistering pace. Since the clock only runs when the ball is in play, a game generally lasts about two hours. Its most popular player, **Michael "Air" Jordan**, is America's most recognizable sports icon; he's paid like it, too, receiving nearly $40 million from his championship team, the Chicago Bulls.

The men's basketball season begins in November and runs until the third week of June, when the NBA Finals take place. The two professional teams in the New York area are the **NY Knickerbockers** (Knicks), who play at Madison Square

Sports and Outdoor Activities

ers – bats through nine innings; each side gets **three outs** per **inning**. Games are normally held at night. There are no tied games; the teams play **extra innings** until either side pulls ahead and wins.

American football

Basically, American football is like rugby. The aim is to reach the **end zone** with the ball and score a **touchdown** earning the team six points (though players don't actually have to place the ball on the ground). The action is organized into a series of **plays** and each time the player with the ball is **tackled** to the ground or the ball goes off the pitch, that play is concluded. On each play the quarterback will either **hand-off** to a runner or fire off a **pass** to a teammate. Meanwhile, blockers try to prevent the defensive team from tackling the player with the ball.

The measurement of advancement is a **down**; with every **ten yards** counting as a **first down**. The offensive team has four attempts to move forward the ten yards. (Thus the enigmatic phrases uttered by commentators – Third

(down) and 6 (yards are needed). If it seems unlikely that the offensive team will make their first down (i.e. Fourth and 9), a **kicker** may attempt a **field goal** (worth three points) by sending the ball through the goalposts. If the ball is too far to attempt a field goal and they have not achieved the first down, the ball is turned over to the opposition by having a **punter** drop-kick it as far downfield as possible. If a team makes a touchdown, they usually attempt to kick the ball between the goalposts for an **extra point**; although they may try to garner two points by running a player back into the end zone. Once either of these has been attempted, the ball is then kicked off a tee to the opposing team.

The game lasts for one hour of play, divided into four **quarters** with a break after the second quarter. However, the clock only runs when the game is in progress, which means that it can run for three hours or more – more than enough time to master the complexities if you're prepared to sit back and listen, since on TV every moment is analyzed and reanalyzed ad nauseam.

Sports and Outdoor Activities

Garden, and the New Jersey **Nets**, whose venue is the Continental Airlines Arena at the Meadowlands Sports Complex in New Jersey. The Knicks are by far the more beloved of the two teams. In 1994, they were in the finals, but lost by one excruciating game to the Houston Rockets. While they made it to the playoffs in 1995, 1996 and 1997, they were knocked out in the second round of games each time. They should, however, remain playoff contenders in the years ahead, whereas the Nets seem to be constantly rebuilding – in other words, losing.

Tickets to Knicks games are scarce and as a result expensive: for a popular game you might have to pay upwards of $100 to an agency. "Courtside tickets" in the first row of Madison Square Garden for the Knicks (where the celebrities appear) cost $1000 per seat, per game. New York team games during the regular season are usually shown on TV and all playoff and finals games are, so catch a game at one of the sports bars if you can't get tickets.

The women's basketball season (**WNBA**) opens in June and runs through the summer to its playoffs in September. The league kicked off in 1997; the area team is the **NY Liberty**, runners-up for the title their first year. They play at Madison Square Garden too, and the games are a bargain compared to the Knicks. Seats start at $10 and go to $45, and while many games have near sellout crowds, you can usually get a ticket – unlike at Knicks games.

College basketball is also hugely popular, and worth watching if you can catch it on TV. Some games are also played at Madison Square Garden; call for schedule information. The college season culminates in a 64-team playoff – aptly titled "March Madness" – with the top four teams participating in the "Final Four" the first week in April, which crowns the college basketball champion.

Horse racing

There are four **race tracks** in the New York area: the **Aqueduct Race Track**, the **Belmont Race Track**, the **Meadowlands**

Race Track and **Yonkers Raceway**. Both the Aqueduct ("The Big A") and Belmont have thoroughbred racing. Meadowlands has both thoroughbred and standardbred racing and Yonkers has only standardbred.

The **Aqueduct** in Rockaway, Queens, has racing from October through May, and hosts smaller races. To get there take Subway A to the Aqueduct station. The **Belmont Race Track** is in Elmont, Long Island, and is home to the Belmont Stakes, which, along with the Kentucky Derby and Preakness, is one of the big three American races of the year (the "Triple Crown"). The racing takes place May–July and September–October, with the Belmont Stakes held in June. You have two options to get there by public transportation: take Subway E or F to 169th St and then the #16 bus will get you to the track, or take the Long Island Railroad to the Belmont Race Track, stop which is directly across from the track. For both Belmont and the Aqueduct, call ☎718/641-4700. Admission at both tracks is $2 general parking, $4 preferred parking, $2 to sit in the Grandstand, and $4 to view from the Clubhouse.

The **Meadowlands Race Track**, in the Meadowlands Sports Complex in New Jersey, holds harness racing eight months of the year (December–August) and thoroughbred racing September–December (☎201/935-8500). From Manhattan, the easiest way to get there is on NJ Transit, bus #164 from Port Authority. Parking is free, admission is $1, and entry to the Clubhouse is $3. **Yonkers Raceway** holds harness racing only, but operates all year round (☎914/968-4200). Take Subway #4 to Woodlawn and transfer to the #20 bus. If you drive, parking is $1.50; admission is $3.25.

To **place a bet** anywhere other than the race track itself you'll need to find an **OTB** – Off Track Betting – office. There are plenty around the city; call ☎221-5200 for locations (opening hours are Monday to Saturday 11.30am–7pm, Sunday 11.30am–6.30pm). You need an established account to place a phone bet: to set one up, call ☎800 OTB 8118. To watch a race or two in comfort, try *The Inside Track* (run by *OTB*) at 991 2nd Ave at 53rd St (☎752-1940). They are open from 11.30am until the last race ends and offer food, drink and wagering on the premises.

Ice hockey

To someone who isn't familiar with the game, **hockey**, as it is called in the US, might seem a very odd excuse for getting a bunch of guys to beat the hell out of each other for the benefit of the paying public. However, this would be a serious misrepresentation of one of the country's best-loved – and patronized – games. It is a violent sport, certainly, and some players are without doubt chosen mainly for their punching ability. But there's a huge amount of skill involved, too. It takes some watching to work out where the puck is – the speed the action takes place at is, without question, phenomenal. The two New York teams are the **Rangers**, who play at Madison Square Garden, and the less purely New York **Islanders**, whose venue is out at the Nassau Coliseum on Long Island. There's also a local New Jersey side, the **Devils**, who play at Meadowlands. The season culminates in the Stanley Cup Finals. New York teams have been on top in recent times, with the Rangers taking the Cup in 1994 for the first time in 40 years. The Devils won the Cup in 1995.

Soccer

There is a new professional soccer league in the US; the **New York/New Jersey MetroStars** are the area's representatives, and the team plays at the Meadowlands. The season runs from April to September, and tickets are $22, $16, and $11. New York was one of the venues for 1994 World Cup matches, and this greatly heightened the mainstream's awareness of the game (and helped secure the franchise). In the South and Latin American communities

of Queens, and the Italian areas of the Outer Boroughs and New Jersey, soccer is enormously popular. However, apart from the occasional British game shown on the sports cable channels, most of the soccer shown on TV is confined to the Spanish-language stations – usually every Sunday on channels 31 and 41. You can also catch soccer matches at Irish pubs throughout the city, like *McCormick's* on 3rd Ave between 26th and 27th sts. There are some decent-quality college matches played out at Rutgers University in New Jersey.

Tennis

The **US Open Championships**, held in Queens each September at the National Tennis Center, Flushing Meadows, is the top **tennis** event of the year. In 1997, the Flushing complex opened a new center court, the Arthur Ashe Stadium. When David Dinkins, an avowed sports fan, was mayor, he ordered the nearby La Guardia Airport planes to be rerouted during the championships, which greatly improves the volume level. For tickets, call the Tennis Center's box office ☎718/760-6200 ext 3, Mon–Fri, 9am–5pm. *Telecharge* (☎888/673-6849) handles tickets for the promenade level of the stadium: prices are $22–66. If they are sold out, keep trying up to the day of the event because often corporate tickets are returned. Tickets for the big matches are incredibly difficult to get – you can either take a chance with scalpers or try your luck at the *Will Call* window for people who don't show up. Madison Square Garden also boasts annual international tennis matches in the form of the WTA Tour Championships, held each year in the middle of November.

Track and field

The **Chase Bank Melrose Games**, played at Madison Square Garden in February each year, feature world-class athletes. The games include almost every **track and field** event such as the one-mile race, sprints, pole-vault, the high jump,

Sports and
Outdoor
Activities

Sports and Outdoor Activities

Sports bars

Boomer's Sports Club, 349 Amsterdam between 76th and 77th sts ☎362-5400. Named after quarterback Boomer Esiason, the club is filled with memorabilia.

Brother Jimmy's Bar-B-Que, 1461 1st Ave at 76th St ☎288-0999. Great place to watch college football. If one of the ACC (Atlantic Conference Championships) schools wins the season, their name is painted in big letters on the wall like a giant trophy. Also a good place for basketball.

Jimmy's Corner, 140 W 44th St ☎221-9510. Bar loaded with boxing paraphernalia, including pictures of Jimmy with any number of the champs. A few TVs and a lot of smoke in the air.

Kinsdale Tavern, 1672 3rd Ave, at 93rd St ☎348-4370. Comfortable Irish bar with 15 TVs.

Mickey Mantle's, 42 Central Park South between 5th and 6th aves ☎688-7777. Started by one of America's baseball heroes. Restaurant serving American food, with a lot of TVs and sports memorabilia.

Mustang Sally's, 324 7th Ave, between 28th and 29th sts ☎695-3806. Pre-Madison Square Garden crowd as well as ticketless fans watching on big screens. Same owner as *Mustang Harry's*, 354 7th Ave ☎2688930, just down the block, which is bigger but has only TV-size screens.

The Polo Grounds Bar & Grill, 147 3rd Ave at 83rd St ☎570-5590. Named after the old Polo Grounds in New York.

Sporting Club, 99 Hudson St between Franklin and Leonard sts ☎219-0900. Rated the number 1 sports bar in Manhattan by *New York* magazine. Has 7 giant screens, a dozen smaller TVs, plus a pool table and other games.

Turtle Bay, 987 2nd Ave, between 53rd and 52nd sts, ☎223-4224. Irish bar-restaurant with 7 TVs downstairs.

the long jump and much more. The event is well attended, but tickets are easier to come by than other city sporting events. Call Madison Square Garden (☎465-6741) for more information.

Ultimate frisbee

From 1989 to 1993, New York's **ultimate frisbee** team beat more than twenty nations to win five consecutive World Ultimate Frisbee Championships. Since they disbanded, several of the team's members have regrouped to form new teams, variously called the *Cojones, Randall's Island,* and *Kill Van Kull.* To find out about game times and places (and their current name), call ☎914/698-6218.

Each team has seven members, and the object is to pass a disk to a teammate in the end zone. Watching the antics and sometimes extraordinary lengths players go to is great fun, plus it is a laidback sport with no referees – the players call their own fouls! A good place to catch pick-up games is at the North Meadow in Central Park between 96th and 100th St (West), on Sunday afternoons.

Wrestling

Wrestling, held regularly at Madison Square Garden, is perhaps the least "sporting" of all the sports you can watch in New York, more of a theatrical event really, with a patriotically charged, almost salivating crowd cheering on all-American superheroes against evil and distinctly un-American foes. Bouts start with a rendition of *The Star-Spangled Banner,* after which the action – a stagey affair between wrestlers with names like Hulk Hogan and the Red Devil – takes place to a background of jingoistic roars, the true-blue US spirit invariably winning the day. Recently, some of the more flamboyant professional athletes from other sports – basketball's Dennis Rodman, football's Kevin Greene – have even tried their hands in the ring. For details of bouts, call Madison Square Garden direct (☎465-6747).

Tickets and venues

Tickets for most events can be booked ahead with a credit card through *Ticketmaster* ☎307-7171 and collected at the gate, though it's cheaper ─ and of course riskier for popular events ─ to pick up tickets on the night. You can also call or go to the stadium's box office and buy advance tickets. When the box office has sold out, you can call a **ticketing agency** such as **1-800 SOLD OUT** (☎800 765-3688), which buys quantities of tickets for resale. Expect to pay a little bit more to substantially more, depending on the importance of the game and the seats – look in the *Yellow Pages* under tickets for others. **Scalping** (buying a ticket from an individual, usually the day of the event outside the arena at an inflated price) is illegal. If all else fails, simply catch the action on the big screen in a sports bar.

Madison Square Garden Center, W 33rd St and 7th Ave ☎465-6741. Subway #1, #2, #3 to 34th Street Penn Station. Box office Mon–Sat noon–6pm.

Meadowlands Sports Complex, containing both Giants Stadium and the Continental Airlines Arena, off routes 3, 17, and Turnpike exit 16, East Rutherford, New Jersey ☎201/935-3900. Regular buses from Port Authority Bus Terminal on 42nd St and 8th Ave. Box office open for all arenas Mon–Fri 9am–6pm, Sat 10am–6pm, Sun noon–5pm.

Nassau Coliseum, Hempstead Turnpike, Uniondale, New York ☎516/794-9300. Long Island Railroad to Hempstead, then bus N70, N71 or N72 from Hempstead bus terminal, one block away. Box office daily 10.30am–5.45pm.

Shea Stadium, 126th St at Roosevelt Ave, Queens ☎718/507-8499. Subway #7, direct to Willets Point/Shea Stadium Station. Box office Mon–Fri 9am–6pm,

Sat & Sun 9am–5pm. Dress warmly in autumn and winter as Shea is a windy icebox.

Yankee Stadium, 161st St and River Ave, the Bronx ☎718/293-6000. Subway C, D or #4 direct to 161st St Station. Although the surrounding neighborhood has a bad reputation, the stadium and walkway to the subway are well guarded, brightly lit and quite safe. Box office Mon–Sat 9.30am–5pm, Sun 10am–5pm and during evening games.

Participatory sports

Central Park is the focus for all sports: from croquet to chess, ultimate frisbee to hacky-sack, sunning to swimming. Joggers, in-line skaters, walkers and cyclists have the roads to themselves on weekdays 10am–3pm & 7–10pm; on weekends 7pm Fri to 6am Mon; and 7pm the night before a holiday until 6am the day after. To find out what, where and when, go to the *Arsenal*, at 64th St and 5th Ave in Central Park, and pick up the following, or call and ask for them to be mailed to you:

• **Green Pages**, which tell you about every activity, from archery to wild-food walks, ☎360-8111 ext 310.

• **Special Events Calendar**, a day-by-day listing of events in the parks in all the boroughs April–Dec. There are races, dances, track meets, rodeos, as well as a lot of concerts and events for children, ☎360-1492.

• **The Central Park Calendar**, a quarterly publication giving information about recreation centers, croquet lawns, athletic fields, handball and boccie courts, historic houses and model airplane fields, ☎360-8236.

Chelsea Piers Sports and Entertainment Complex

Chelsea Piers is located at 23rd St and the Hudson River, between 17th and 23rd sts; ☎336-6666 for general info. To get there, take the A, C, or E trains to 23rd St and walk west, or the 23rd St bus, which will drop you off at the front door.

Sports and
Outdoor
Activities

Sports and Outdoor Activities

The complex is the complete renovation of four piers originally designed in 1912 by Warren & Wetmore, the architects of Grand Central Station. Jutting out into the Hudson River, the location couldn't be more scenic. Non-sports-minded people can enjoy Chelsea Piers by strolling along the Esplanade (free) or eating at one of its three restaurants – such as the microbrewery *Chelsea Brewing Company* or the family-priced *Crab House*.

There are five different **facilities** at Chelsea Piers:

The **Golf Club** at Pier 59 features Manhattan's only outdoor driving range. The hours are basically daily 7am–11pm, and to midnight in the summer. You buy tee time at $15 for 108 balls. ☎336-6400.

The **Field House** connects the four piers. This facility houses the largest gymnastics facility in the state, and is where soccer, lacrosse and field hockey leagues play. You can also rock climb or play basketball without being in a league. ☎336-6500.

Sports Center at Pier 60 features a quarter-mile running track, the largest rock climbing wall in the Northeast, two basketball courts, a boxing ring, a 24-yard swimming pool and whirlpool, indoor sand volleyball courts, exercise studios scheduling over 100 classes weekly, cardiovascular weight-training room, a sundeck right on the Hudson River, and spa services.

You must be 16 or older to use the Sports Center. Day passes are available for $31 on weekdays and $50 on weekends. Mon–Fri 6am–11pm & weekends 7am–10pm. ☎336-6000.

The **Roller Rinks** are on Pier 62. They are outdoors and open April–Nov, weather permitting. Daily session starts at noon, exact times vary. $4; $3 for children under 12. Rentals available. ☎336-6200.

The **Sky Rink** is on Pier 61. Ice-skate year-round on this indoor rink. Daily sessions start at noon, exact times vary. $9; $7 for children under 12; $6 seniors. Rentals are $4. ☎336-6100.

Jogging

Jogging is still very much the number one fitness pursuit: the number of yearly coronaries in Central Park, the most popular venue, probably runs well into double figures. A favorite circuit in the park is 1.58 miles around the Receiving Reservoir; just make sure you jog in the right direction – counterclockwise. The East River Promenade and almost any other stretch of open space long enough to get up speed are also well jogged. One of the more beautiful and longer routes is through the Bronx's Botanical Garden (☎718/817-8705): it's a two-mile loop with eight miles of adjoining trails. For company, contact the **New York Runners Club** and find out their schedule: E 89th St ☎860-2280. They do several races/runs such as the Frostbite 10 Miler and the Valentine Run each year.

If, rather than bust your own guts, you'd prefer to see thousands of others do so, the **New York Marathon** takes place on the first Sunday of November. Two million people turn out each year to watch the 16,000 runners complete the 26-mile course, which starts in Staten Island, crosses the Verrazano Narrows Bridge and passes through all the other boroughs before ending up at the *Tavern on the Green* in Central Park. To take part you need to apply for an entry form from the New York Road Runners' Club (see above).

Roller- and ice-skating . . . and tobogganing

In winter, the freezing weather makes for good **ice-skating**, while in summer **rollerskating** is a popular activity, on the paths in Central Park and specifically the northwest corner of the Sheep Meadow; also at Riverside Park and even the smaller open spaces. **Tobogganing** is another popular winter activity, up on the slopes of Van Cortlandt Park in the Bronx; phone ☎718/549-6494 to see if the snow's deep enough.

Lasker Rink, 110th St, Central Park ☎534-7639. The lesser-known ice rink in Central Park, at the north end of the park. Much cheaper than the Wollman Rink, though less accessible, and the neighborhood isn't great at night. Open Mon–Thurs 10am–9.30pm, Fri & Sat 10am–11pm. Admission $2.50 plus $2 for skate rentals.

Rockefeller Center Ice Rink, between 49th and 50th St off 5th Ave ☎332-7654. Without doubt the slickest place to skate, though you may have to wait in line and it's pricier than anywhere else. Open Mon–Thurs 9am–10pm, Fri & Sat 9am–midnight, Sun 9am–10pm. Admission $8 plus $4 for skate rentals.

Wollman Rink, 62nd St, Central Park ☎396-1010. Lovely rink, where you can skate to the marvelous, inspiring back-drop of the lower Central Park skyline – incredibly impressive at night. Open Mon 10am–5pm, Tues–Thurs 10am–9.30pm, Fri–Sun 10am–11pm. Admission $6 plus $3.50 for skate rentals.

In-line skating

You'll see commuters to freestylists on in-line skates – also known as **rollerblades** – in New York. For the best place to watch freestylists, go to the skate circle near Naumberg Bandshell in Central Park at 72nd St. World-class bladers maneuver between cones with all kinds of fancy footwork just inside Central Park's *Tavern on the Green* entrance, by 68th St. Other than Central Park, the best places to skate are Battery Park, and Flushing Meadow Park in Corona, Queens, which is forty minutes from Midtown on the #7 train.

Wollman Rink, 62nd St Central Park, ☎396-1010. See above description, dur-ing the summer. Admission $6 plus $6.50 for in-line skate rental.

Blades. Their many locations make it a convenient shop to rent in-line skates:

120 W 72nd St between Columbus and Broadway ☎787-3911.

160 E 86th St between Lexington and 3rd Ave ☎996-1644.

1414 2nd Ave at 73rd St ☎249-3178.

659 Broadway between Bleecker and 3rd Ave ☎477-7350.

$16 for two hours on weekends, $27 a day on weekends, $16 for 24 hours Sun–Thurs starting at 4pm. No overnight rentals on Fri or Sat.

Stephen Baum's In-Line Skating Clinics & Tours ☎800-24-SKATE. Sightseeing skating tours of NYC landmarks uptown, downtown and Central Park. $20 per person for three hours, and $30 for five hours. Clinics are available for groups and individuals, prices vary.

Bicycling

There are 100 miles of **cyclepaths** in New York; other than Central Park, Riverside Park and the East River Promenade are some of the nicest. If you want to go further, the deal of the century is a *MetroNorth Railroads* lifetime bike pass for $5, available at the ticket windows of Grand Central Station. These trains will bring you to the scenic small towns of lower Hudson Valley and coastal Connecticut. When riding on the street, remember that by law you must wear a helmet. It's not enforced, but it's the safe thing to do. Most bike stores rent bicycles by the day or hour. What follows is a list of clubs and other good cycling info:

Bicycle Habitat, 244 Lafayette St ☎431-3315. Known for an excellent repair ser-vice and prices, as well as rentals $25 a day, plus a deposit equal to the value of the bike, and $7.50 an hour with a two-hr minimum. You can also call ahead and have your bike shipped here and assembled and tuned-up for about $60 if you think you'll be riding a lot. The very knowledgeable staff here will be able to help you no matter what level of cyclist you are. They also offer group rides.

Five Borough Bike Club. If you happen to be in New York during early May, the club sponsors *Bike NY: The Great Five Borough Tour* with the *International Hostel Association*. Meet at Battery Park at 8am, and 42 miles later there's a party in Staten Island. Call ☎932-2300 ext 115 for registration information.

Sports and Outdoor Activities

Sports and Outdoor Activities

They do other rides throughout the year as well.

Loeb Boathouse in Central Park at 74th St and the East Drive ☎861-4137. Bike rentals $8–14 an hour or $32 per day. Avoid if possible; the bikes here are junky. Go to a local bike shop and rent a nicer bike for the whole day. Most bike shops have rental bikes.

Metropolitan Cycling Club ☎302-5857. If you are interested in racing give them a call.

New York Cycle Club ☎886-4545. A large club that offers many rides. Call for registration information.

Times Up ☎802-8222. They do a variety of rides such as New York Historical Rides, Moonlight Rides, Cyclone Rides (to Coney Island). Call for a schedule.

Transportation Alternatives, 92 St Marks Place ☎629-8080. They have many interesting programs and many knowledgeable staffers. Stop by or call to find out more information.

Pool and snooker

Aside from bars and nightclubs, the new thing to do of an evening in Manhattan is play **pool**, not in dingy halls but in gleaming bars where well-heeled yuppies mix with the regulars. A number of sports bars and dive bars have pool tables as well, though these are often much smaller than regulation size.

Snooker fans will also find a few tables throughout the city.

Amsterdam Billiards, 344 Amsterdam Ave at 77th St ☎496-8180. Very popular uptown billiards club with 31 tables. They have a full sandwich bar and serve beer.

The Billiard Club, 220 W 19th St between 7th and 8th aves ☎206-7665. A pool club with a nice, vaguely European atmosphere and a small bar serving soft drinks and cappuccinos.

Chelsea Billiards, 54 W 21st St between 5th and 6th aves ☎989-0096. A casual place with both snooker and pool tables. Refreshments from machines or you can bring your own if you don't cause a stir.

Hiking

For hikes, nature walks and other special activities around the city, you can try either of the following organizations:

Urban Park Rangers ☎360-2774 or ☎800-201-PARK.

Shorewalkers ☎330-7686.

Horse riding and carriage rides

Carriage Rides, Central Park South, between 5th and 6th aves. For some, the ideal way to see Central Park, and some carriages are willing – with a little persuasion – to take you further afield. Not cheap, though – around $34 per carriage for twenty minutes – and bear in mind the warning on p.152. Every day, all day, until the late evening. ☎246-0520.

Appalachian Mountain Club

To go off the beaten track and mix with locals, participate in the New York/New Jersey chapter of the worldwide **Appalachian Mountain Club**.

With friendly people of all ages, you can cycle through the partying streets of the East Village at four in the morning, raft the Hudson River, learn yoga on Fire Island, canoe on the East River, tour the historic neighborhoods of Park Slope in a singles' gathering, hike the scenic Shawangunks and watch world-class rock climbers scale the cliffs.

Because of the many requests by nonmembers to attend these trips, this chapter has developed a special four-month membership. You'll receive a temporary membership card and complete seasonal schedule packed with more outings than you'll have time for. Send $15, with your name and mailing address, to: *AMC*, 5 Tudor City Place, NY, NY 10017.

Claremont Riding Academy, 175 W 89th St ☎724-5100. For riding in Central Park, this place hires out ponies by the hour for $33. Saddles are English-style; lessons $38 per half-hour. You must be an experienced rider.

Jamaica Bay Riding Academy, 7000 Shore Parkway, Brooklyn ☎718/531-8949. Trail riding, with western-style saddles, around the eerie landscape of Jamaica Bay. Very much the more atmospheric riding alternative, and a little less expensive than *Claremont* at $23 for a 45-min ride; lessons $45 an hour.

Riverdale's Equestrian Center in Bronx's Van Cortlandt Park ☎718/548-4848. Lessons only: $35 for 30min, $65 for full hour. Brand-new, beautiful country trails.

Tenpin bowling

Bowlmor Lanes, 110 University Place between 11th and 12th sts ☎255-8188. Long-established and large bowling alley with a bar and shop. Open Sun–Thurs 10–1am, Fri & Sat 10–4am; $3.25 per game per person, plus $1 shoe-hire.

Leisure Time Bowling, on 2nd floor of Port Authority, 625 8th Ave, near 40th St ☎268-6909. Five years old, the nicest place in the city to bowl. Price $3.75 per game per person, plus $2 shoe-hire.

Tennis

Court space is at a premium in Manhattan so finding a court and being able to afford it could be tough, but you can call the following:

New York City Courts ☎360-8133 for information on all city courts.

Sutton East Tennis Club (Oct–April) 488 E 60th St ☎751-3452.

Health and fitness: pools, gyms and baths

There are several newly renovated city recreation centers that you can become a member of for $25 per year. All have gym facilities and most have an indoor and/or outdoor pool. Call ☎447-2020 or look in the Manhattan *Blue Pages* (with-

in *White Pages*) under NY City Parks; there is a listing of centers under *Recreation* and under *Swimming Pools*.

East 54th St Pool, 342 E 54th St ☎397-3154. Good-sized indoor pool; annual membership just $25. Bring check or money order, no cash. Exercise classes too. Open afternoons and evenings only Mon–Fri, all day until 5pm Sat & Sun.

John Jay Pool, 77th and Cherokee Place ☎794-6566. Above the FDR Drive, this six-lane, fifty-yd pool is surrounded by playgrounds and park benches. While it opened in 1940, it is in remarkably great condition. Free to anyone; bring a padlock.

Riverbank State Park, W 145th St and Riverside Drive ☎694-3600. Beautiful new facility built on top of a waste refinery in Harlem. Sounds strange, and it is, but there are great tennis courts, an outdoor track, an ice skating rink and indoor facilities. Admission is free.

Sutton Gymnastics and Fitness Center, 20 Cooper Union ☎533-9390. One of the few gyms in New York where you don't have to be a member to use the facilities. Gymnastic and exercise classes for around $20. Open Mon–Fri all day, for adults noon, and at weekends for kids.

Tenth Street Turkish Baths, 268 E 10th St ☎473-8806. An ancient place, something of a neighborhood landmark and still going, with steam baths, sauna and pool, as well as exercise rooms, whirlpool, massage, etc. A restaurant too. Admission $19, access to the various facilities extra. Open daily 9am–10pm; men only Sun & Thurs; women only Wed; co-ed Mon, Tues, Fri & Sat.

West 59th St Pool, 533 W 59th St and West End Ave ☎397-3159. Two pools, one indoor and another outdoor, gym and climbing wall. $25 annual membership, paid by check or money order. The pool is open 11am–7pm, and the gym is open 11am–10.30pm. Closed Sun.

Sports and Outdoor Activities

Sports and Outdoor Activities

Boating

Downtown Boathouse, Hudson River, Pier 26 ☎966-1852. Free kayaking on the weekends.

Loeb Boathouse, Central Park ☎517-2233. Rowing boats for hire between April and Oct, daily 9am–6pm. Rates are $10 an hour plus $30 deposit. Also gondola rides for $35 a half-hour.

Beaches

Few visitors come to New York for the **beaches**, and those New Yorkers with money tend to turn their noses up at the city strands, preferring to move further afield to Long Island, just a couple of hours away and much better. But the city's beaches, though often crowded, are a cool summer escape from Manhattan and most are also just a subway token away.

BROOKLYN

Coney Island Beach, at the end of half a dozen subway lines: fastest is the D train to Stillwell Ave. After Rockaway (see opposite), NYC's most popular bathing spot, jam-packed on summer weekends. The Atlantic here is only moderately dirty and there's a good, reliable onshore breeze.

Brighton Beach, D train to Brighton Beach. Technically the same stretch as Coney, but less crowded and given color by the local Russian community (pick up ethnic snacks from the boardwalk vendors).

Manhattan Beach, D train to Sheepshead Bay Rd, walk to Ocean Ave and cross the bridge. Small beach much used by locals.

QUEENS

Rockaway Beach, A and C trains to any stop along the beach. Forget California: this seven-mile strip is where New Yorkers – up to three-quarters of a million daily in summer – come to get the best surf around. So good that the Ramones wrote a song about it. Best beaches are at 9th St, 23rd St, and 80–118th sts.

Jacob Riis Park, IRT #2 train to Flatbush Ave, then Q35 bus. Good sandy stretches, the western ones used almost exclusively by a gay male crowd.

THE BRONX

Orchard Beach, subway train #6 local to Pelham Bay Park, then Bx12 bus. Lovingly known as "Horseshit Beach" – and in any case less easy to get to than the rest.

STATEN ISLAND

Great Kills Park, bus #103 from Staten Island Ferry Terminal. Quiet and used by locals.

South Beach, bus S52. New ballfields, rollerblading areas and low-key beaches.

Wolfe's Pond Park, bus #103 to Main St Tottenville, at Hylan and Cornelia. Regularly packs in the crowds from New Jersey.

Chapter 22

Parades and Festivals

The other big daytime activities in New York, and often worth timing your visit around, are its **parades** and **street festivals**. The city takes these, especially the parades, very seriously. Almost every large ethnic group in the city holds an annual get-together, often using 5th Ave as the main drag; the events are often political or religious in origin, though now are just as much an excuse for music, food and dance. Chances are your stay will coincide with at least one: the list that follows is roughly chronological.

Also prominent in New York are **summer-long arts festivals**, or performance series, often held outdoors – Central Park, Prospect Park and South Street Seaport are all prime locations – and usually free. For more details and exact dates of parades, festivals and the like, phone ☎800 NYC-VISIT, or visit their Web site: http://www.nycvisit.com. Also, look at listings in *New York* magazine's CUE section, *The New Yorker* magazine's "Goings on About Town" section, the Friday *New*

York Times's "Weekend" section, and the *Village Voice*'s "Cheap Thrills" section.

January
Chinese New Year (first full moon after January 21): a noisy, colorful occasion celebrated around Mott St. Dragons dance in the street, firecrackers chase away evil spirits and the chances of getting a meal anywhere in Chinatown are slim; phone ☎431-9740 for further details.

February
Winter Festival (usually the second weekend of the month): an outdoor family festival at Chelsea Piers. Don't worry if there is no snow on the ground – they make it, ☎336-6666.

Empire State Building Run Up Foot Race (mid-month): where contenders race up 1575 steps, ☎736-3100.

Manhattan Antiques and Collectibles (last two weekends of the month): Triple Pier Expo at the Passenger Ship Terminal, ☎691-7297.

Block fairs

Look out, too, for neighborhood block fairs. These are like urban village fêtes, and more than 5000 crop up annually, most frequently in midsummer. They're advertized locally, on noticeboards and in newspapers, and depending on the neighborhood it can be well worth going. More significant-

ly, block fairs are a good way of getting a taste of real, neighborhood New York, beyond the sirens and skyscrapers. For a free, very comprehensive list of street events, go to 51 Chambers St, room 608, Mon–Fri, 10am–4pm. Updated monthly. They will not mail or fax.

Parades and Festivals

Presidents Day Parade (third Mon): for Abe and George. It's on 5th Ave, from 35th to 50th sts.

March

New York Flower Show (ten days at the beginning of March): at the New York Coliseum at Columbus Circle, ☎914/421-3293.

Spring Crafts Market (second and third weekend of the month): at Columbia University, ☎866-2239.

St Patrick's Day Parade (weekend nearest March 17): Celebrating an impromptu march through the streets by Irish militiamen on St Patrick's Day 1762, it has become a draw for every Irish band and organization in the US and Ireland, which in recent years has meant increasing political overtones, with Noraid and Sinn Fein out in full force. Much of the city lines the route up 5th Ave from 44th to 86th sts, and general dementia runs especially high in Irish bars – should you find yourself in one, steer clear of politics. A good vantage point is St Patrick's Cathedral, where the bishop of New York greets the marching pipes and bands.

Greek Independence Day Parade (March 25): not as long or as boozy as St Pat's, more a patriotic nod to the old country from floats of pseudo-classically dressed Hellenes. When Independence Day falls in the Orthodox Lent, the parade is shifted to April or May. It kicks off from 5th Ave at 49th St.

Easter Parade (Easter Fri): from Central Park down to Rockefeller Center on 50th St, an opportunity for New Yorkers to dress up in outrageous Easter bonnets. There's also an **Eggstravaganza**, a children's festival including an egg-rolling contest in Central Park on the Great Lawn (ages 5–13).

New York Coliseum Antiques Show (toward the end of the month; call for exact date): at the Coliseum at Columbus Circle, ☎691-7297.

The Circus Animal Walk (call for exact date): where animals from Ringling Brothers' Barnum & Bailey Circus march from their point of arrival to Madison Square Garden. Call the Garden for details at ☎465-MSGI.

New York Underground Film Festival (third week of the month): a bit out of the mainstream, often held at the Anthology Film Archives, but location can vary, ☎925-3440.

April

First Run Film Festival, (beginning of the month): NYU's annual showcase of student shorts, at Cinema Village (☎924-3363) and Town Hall (☎840-2824).

New Directors, New Films (beginning of the month): Lincoln Center and MOMA have presented this popular film festival for more than 25 years (☎708-0480).

Vintage Poster Fair (first weekend): a tradition for more than 15 years at the Metropolitan Pavilion at 110 W 19th St ☎206-0499; $10 admission.

Annual Antiquarian Book Fair at the Park Ave Armory, Park Ave and 67th St ☎777-5218. Admission $10.

Macy's Annual Flower Show (mid-April): Landscapers from all over the NY area bring you wonderful garden paths to walk through, ☎494-4495.

Rockefeller Center Flower and Garden Show (mid-April): more garden paths, ☎632-3975.

Fine Art and Craft Show (third and fourth weekends): located on 59th St between 5th and 7th aves; call ☎463-0200 ext 225 for info.

Earth Day (April 22): In the weeks surrounding it, there are dozens of activities at parks and schools around the five boroughs, ranging from compost demonstrations to shad festivals. Call ☎922-0048 for a schedule.

May

Bike NY: The Great Five Borough Bike Tour (first weekend): More than 30,000 bicyclists show up for this big cycling event. (See Sports section for details.)

Happy Birthday Brooklyn Bridge

If you can plan it right, walk across the **Brooklyn Bridge** on **May 24**, in the early evening. As you approach the midway overlook point, people in party hats will pull you into a birthday party for the bridge, complete with champagne, party food and friendly spirit. This yearly celebration is an informal reunion from previous bridge parties. One regular is Christopher, a boy who shares his birthday with the bridge – 100 years apart. Many years, a New York City fireboat salutes the bridge above with majestic plumes of water. Playwright Joe Caldwell started this celebration in the late 1950s as a toast among friends. His love affair with the Gothic structure, which led to his writing the play *On the Bridge*, stems from being able to climb out of the bathroom window of his Hague St apartment directly onto the bridge. The city has long since razed the block of tenements under the bridge, but Joe's party lives on.

Parades and Festivals

Ukrainian Festival (two weeks after Easter): This fills a weekend on E 7th St between 2nd and 3rd aves with marvellous Ukrainian costume, folk music and dance plus authentic foods. At the *Ukrainian Museum* (12th Ave and 2nd St) there's a special exhibition of *pysanky* – traditional hand-painted eggs; ☎228-0110 for festival details.

Brooklyn Bridge Day Parade (mid-month): Marchers and bands come over the bridge. When the weather is good, it is magnificent. (See box above.)

Fine Art & Craft Show (third weekend): on 59th St between 5th and 7th aves, call ☎463-0200 ext 225 for info.

Martin Luther King Jr Memorial Day (May 17): a procession along 5th Ave from 44th to 86th sts to celebrate his work for equal rights for African Americans.

Ninth Ave International Food Festival (weekend in mid-May; call for exact dates): It closes down the avenue between 37th and 57th sts for the weekend, 10am–7pm, giving you the chance to snack your way along the strip of delis and restaurants that come out on to the street with their wares. Street performers, balloons, and of course, food. Plus, many restaurants charge only the year – $19.98 and so on – for lunches. ☎581-7217.

Lower East Side's Loisada Street Fair (traditionally held on the last weekend in May).

Crafts on Columbus (call for dates): Columbus Ave between 77th and 81st sts, ☎866-2239.

Salute to Israel Parade (call for date): on 5th Ave, between 58th and 79th sts, ☎339-6918.

Fleet Week (end of May): the annual welcome of sailors from the US, Canada, Mexico, and the UK to New York, held at the Intrepid Sea-Air-Space Museum, ☎245-0072. Ships are open for free, there are jet and helicopter demonstrations, and the US Marine Corps does formations in Central Park.

Irish American Festival (last weekend): at Gateway National Recreation Area in Brooklyn, ☎718/338-3687.

Washington Square Outdoor Art Exhibit (end May/beginning June): It's free, held for over 65 years, and features over 200 artists, ☎982-6255.

International Children's Festival (end May/beginning June): The parking lot at the *Brooklyn Academy of Music (BAM)* is transformed for this kidfest. A day pass is $15, ☎718/636-4129 for details.

June

Museum Mile Festival (first Tues evening in June): on 5th Ave from 82nd St to 105th St. Ten museums are open free 6–9pm.

Puerto Rican Day Parade (first Sun of June): the largest of several Puerto Rican celebrations in the city, three hours of

Parades and Festivals

bands and baton-twirling from 44th to 86th sts on 5th Ave, then across to 3rd.

Avenue of the America's Springfest (around the second week of June): held on 6th Ave from 42nd to 57th sts, ☎809-4900.

Lower East Side Jewish Spring Festival (the second Sun): on E Broadway between Rutgers and Montgomery sts, featuring glatt kosher foods, Yiddish and Hebrew folk singing and guided tours of the Jewish Lower East Side.

Mermaid Parade (first Saturday after June 21): hilarious event where the participants are dressed up like mermaids and King Neptunes, and they saunter down the boardwalk of Brooklyn's Coney Island, after which everyone throws fruit into the sea.

The Festival of St Anthony (starts first Thurs of month): a two-week long, fun Italian celebration on Sullivan St from Spring to West Houston sts, culminating in a procession of Italian bands, led by a life-size statue of the saint carried on the shoulders of four men, ☎777-2755.

Welcome Back to Brooklyn Homecoming Festival (second week of June): one of Brooklyn's largest festivals, held at Grand Army Plaza in Prospect Park, ☎718/855-7882.

Gay Pride March (last Sun in June): the culmination of Lesbian and Gay Pride Week, commemorating the Stonewall riots of 1969 (see Chapter 6, *Greenwich Village and the East Village*) – a well-attended celebration of gay rights running south from Columbus Circle, ☎807-7430.

July

Independence Day (July 4th): *Macy's* fireworks display – visible all over lower Manhattan but best seen from Battery Park from around 9.00pm.

The Great July 4th Festival: at Battery Park ☎809-4900, a fantastic fair and more fireworks. For oratory, go to City Hall.

Bastille Day (Sun following July 14th): In Greenwich Village, celebrate the French

way with food by *Florent*, a tea dance, a fashion show and Marie Antoinette impersonators. All proceeds benefit Housing Works, an AIDS social service. Call ☎989-5779. Uptown, you can celebrate with the Alliance Francaise on 60th St between Park and 5th Ave, ☎355-6100.

American Crafts Festival (first two weekends): at Lincoln Center. More than crafts, you'll also see demonstrations, puppets, clowns and singing.

Fiestas de Loiza Aldea (second weekend of July): miniature versions of the great Fiestas de Santiago Apostol (Festival of St James the Apostle) in the town of Loiza Aldea, Puerto Rico. Following mass at the Church of San Pueblo at Lexington and 117th St, separate processions of women, men and children each carry a statue of the apostle to the footbridge at 102nd St and East River Drive to Ward's Island. After the procession there's a festival of Latin music, dance and salsa on Ward's Island, with plenty of Puerto Rican food.

Japanese Obon Festival (Sat nearest July 15th): early evening in Riverside Park Mall at W 103rd St. Slow, simple dancing in the lantern-hung park makes this well worth catching, ☎678-0305. Also that same weekend are usually the **NYC Unfolds** street fair, on W 3rd St from Broadway to La Guardia, and the **Magic on Madison Ave Fair**, from 37th to 57th sts.

Lollapalooza Festival (call for date): at Downing Stadium on Randall's Island is supposedly the best of the new bands, a one-day 1990s version of Woodstock, although it has already become pretty establishment, ☎249-8870.

August

Tudor City Festival (usually the first weekend): on 2nd Ave from 38th to 47th sts.

Harlem Week (second week): call ☎862-7200 for info.

Crafts at the South Street Seaport Marketplace (call for dates): For sunshine, salt air and handcrafted gifts, this is the place. Call ☎866-2239.

Macy's Tap A Mania (mid-Aug): It starts at noon, and there is a rain date. There have often been more than 3500 dancers, and *Guinness* lists this as the "record for the largest line of dancers ever to tap in unison." 34th St and 7th Ave, near Broadway, ☎494-5247.

Festival of Families (weekend before Labor Day): down in Battery Park, ☎809-4900.

Fiesta Folklorica (Sun before Labor Day): an all-singing, all-dancing spectacle that fills Central Park.

September

Labor Day Parade and Street Fair (Labor Day): go march down 5th Ave and then you head to the street fair on 42nd St between 9th and 10th aves. Labor Day weekend also hosts the **Big Apple Balloon Festival** on Central Park's Great Lawn at 81st St.

Tugboat Challenge (Labor Day): Labor Day Weekend also hosts this kid-pleasing annual, the race between NY's working tugs. The finish line is the Pier 86. It is the culmination of **Seafest** – ship visits and pier events at the *Intrepid Sea-Air-Space Museum*, ☎245-0072.

Broadway on Broadway (first Sunday of the month): Free performances feature songs performed by casts of virtually every Broadway musical, culminating in a shower of confetti. At Times Square, ☎768-1560.

Fine Art & Craft Show (the third and fourth weekends): more from Central Park South, on 59th St between 5th and 7th aves; call ☎463-0200 ext 225 for info.

Julliard's Focus! (mid-month): from *Julliard School of Music*, the renowned high school, an annual festival with six concerts, ☎769-7406.

Festival San Gennaro (ten days in mid-Sept): celebrating the patron saint of Naples, held along Mulberry St in Little

Italy. This feast has been held here for over 70 years: wonderful food, great people watching, and fun things to buy. A high spot is a procession of the saint's statue through the streets, with donations of dollar bills pinned to his cloak.

New York is Book Country (usually third Sun): events and fair, 11am–5pm on 5th Ave between 48th and 57th sts, and from Madison to 6th Ave on 52nd and 53rd sts. Every bookstore, publisher and even bookbinders have stalls, carts or stands, ☎207-7242.

African American Day Parade (call for exact date): runs from 111 St and Adam Clayton Powell Blvd to 142 St then right to 5th Ave, Harlem, ☎374-5176.

Korean American Parade (call for exact date): from 41st St and Broadway to 23rd St, ☎255-6969.

Steuben Day Parade (third weekend): the biggest German-American event. Baron von Steuben was a Prussian general who fought with Washington at the battle of Valley Forge, which is as good an excuse as any for a costumed parade in his honor from 61st to 86th sts and 5th Ave, ☎239-0741.

West Indian Day Parade and Carnival (Labor Day weekend): in Crown Heights (see description in *Brooklyn* section).

New York Armory Antiques Show (call for dates): colossal event at the 7th Regiment Armory at Park Ave at 67th St, ☎677-5040. $10 buys access to hundreds of dealers from style centers across the globe.

Washington Square Outdoors Art Exhibit (call for dates): along the sidewalks of the village centered around Waverly Place from 6th Ave to Broadway, ☎982-6255.

Gracie Square Art Show (call for date): 11am–dusk, at Carl Shultz Park, on East End Ave from 84th to 87th sts, ☎535-9132.

Annual Broadway Flea Market and Grand Auction (end of Sept): on Shubert Alley between 44th and 45th sts.

Parades and Festivals

Parades and
Festivals

October

Promenade Art Show (usually the first weekend): on Brooklyn's historic walkway overlooking downtown Manhattan ☎718/625-0080.

Lexington Ave Octoberfest (usually the first weekend): on Lexington from 42nd to 57th sts, ☎808-4900.

Pulaski Day Parade (call for exact date): on 5th Ave for the city's Polish immigrants, ☎254-1180.

Hispanic Day Parade (on or around Oct 8): running on 5th Ave between 44th and 72nd sts.

Columbus Day Parade (on or around Oct 12): one of the city's largest binges, commemorating the day America was put on the map. Runs on 5th Ave from 44th to 86th sts, ☎249-9923.

Village Halloween Parade (Oct 31): a procession on 6th Ave from Spring to 23rd sts. You'll see spectacular costumes, wigs and make-up. The music is great, the spirit is wild. There's a tamer children's parade earlier that day, around Washington Square Park.

Antique and craft fairs include **Crafts on Columbus**, which runs for several weekends behind the Museum of Natural History, ☎866-2239; the **Fall Antiques Show at the Pier**, on Passenger Pier 92, at W 52nd and Hudson River, ☎977-7120; the **New York Coliseum Antiques Fair**, at Columbus Circle, 300 dealers for $10 admission; and **St Ignatius Loyola**

Macy's Thanksgiving Day Parade

See Mickey Mouse and the other floats being inflated the night before the parade. It's not as crowded, and you can experience something not televised to every home in America. They're blown up right on W 81st St, in front of the Museum of Natural History. Wander around these huge objects and watch their shapes appear. It starts at dusk and can go past midnight.

Antiques Show at Park Ave and 84th St, an annual show of mainly affordable home stuff.

November

New York City Marathon (second week): Runners from all over the world assemble for this 26.2-mile run on city pavement through the five boroughs. One of the best places to watch is Central Park South, almost at the finish line, ☎860-4455.

Veteran's Day Parade (Nov 11): The United War Veterans sponsor this annual event, which runs down 5th Ave from 39th St to 24th sts, ☎693-1475.

Triple Pier Expo (two weekends, midmonth): The largest metropolitan antiques fair, on piers 88, 90, and 92, ☎255-0020.

Macy's Thanksgiving Parade (last Thurs in Nov): New York's most televised parade, with floats, dozens of marching bands from around the country, the Rockettes, and Santa Claus's first appearance of the season. More than two million spectators watch it from 77th St down Central Park W to Columbus Circle, afterwards down Broadway to Herald Square, 9am–noon, ☎494-5432.

Thanksgiving Weekend Annual Uptown/Downtown Thanksgiving Crafts Fair: For a more sedate scene, start your holiday shopping here. Uptown: Landmark on the Park/Downtown: Loeb Student Center, at *NYU*, ☎866-2239.

December

'Miracle on Madison Avenue' Children's Festival (first Sun): covers 15 blocks, between 57th and 72nd sts, with a variety of things for children to do and buy, ☎988-4001.

Rockefeller Center (beginning of month): The center lights up its Christmas tree with more than 25,000 bulbs early in the month at dusk and decorates Channel Gardens, so beginning the festivities, ☎632-3975.

Chanukah Celebrations (first night of Chanukah; check calendar): Everyone is invited to the 92nd St YMCA, at Lexington and 92nd St, ☎427-6000. For the eight nights of this holiday, a *menorah* lighting ceremony takes place at 59th St and 5th Ave.

Holiday Windows (the two Sun before Christmas): The windows on 5th Ave are fun to look at, although you might have to wait on line especially for *Lord & Taylor* and *Saks*. 5th Ave is closed to traffic, with entertainment on the streets. Santa Claus holds court in *Macy's* for a photo opportunity.

New Year's Eve (Dec 31): traditionally marked by 200,000 people gathering on Times Square where the last seconds of the year signal drunken but good-natured revelry in the snow, ☎768-1560. There are also fireworks at South St Seaport, and Brooklyn's Prospect Park. A more family-oriented, alcohol-free festival has started, called **First Night**, with dancing, music and food throughout the city, ☎818-1777.

Summer arts' festivals

There are a number of **performance series** or ongoing **arts festivals**, mostly music-oriented, that take place throughout the summer in New York; best of all, most of these are free.

Anchorage Music and performance art inside the Brooklyn Bridge. Call for info, ☎260-6674.

Bryant Park Summer Film Festival Mon nights at sunset (Tues rain date), mid-June to Labor Day, behind the 42nd St NY Public Library, between 5th and 6th. Much better sound than you'd expect. Bring a blanket and a picnic. Also comedy on Thurs, 1–2pm, and readings, concerts and dance selected evenings and noons. Call ☎512-5700 for info. Free.

Buskers' Fair and Ball Traditional street performers June 3–18 on the World Trade Center Plaza, and on the streets of lower Manhattan. Call ☎435-4170 for info. Free.

Celebrate Brooklyn Mid-June through mid-August. Concerts, plays and readings

free in Prospect Park. Call ☎718/855-7882 ext 52. See *Brooklyn* section of *Outer Boroughs*.

JVC Jazz Festival City-wide during June, hear mythic names and new groups, indoors and out, in clubs and halls; some are even free. Call *Jazz Line* at ☎479-7888 for info or *JVC Jazz* at ☎501-1390.

Lincoln Center Out-of-Doors Aug evenings and weekends at Lincoln Center's outdoor plazas and Damrosch Park. Annual highlights include Roots of American Music, which celebrates the best in blues, gospel and folk with the likes of Odetta and Nancy Griffith. Call ☎875-5108 for info. Free.

Midsummer Night Swing Every Wed through Sat from mid-June to mid-July, 8.15–11.00 at Lincoln Center's outdoor plaza. Dance to live swing, mambo, merengue, samba, country, zydeco and other bands, plus a special day for kids. Dance lessons included Wed–Fri 6.30–7.30pm. Call ☎875-5766 for info. $9, but you can dance and listen to the music from the areas surrounding the stage for free.

Mostly Mozart July–Aug, at Lincoln Center's *Avery Fisher Hall* and *Alice Tully Hall*, at 8pm. Distinguished guests join the orchestra. Call ☎875-5103 for info. $15–40.

Music at Castle Clinton Free music performances by top named performers in Battery Park. Call ☎835-2789 for details.

Opera in the Park Mid-June through mid-July the Metropolitan Opera performs opera for free in New York parks. Check *Village Voice* for listings.

South Street Seaport Free concerts June to Aug at the South Street Seaport. Includes the Seaport Arts and Crafts Fair at Pier 17 the second two weekends in Aug, *Dancin' on the Docks*, *Thursday Night Concert Series* and the *Outdoor Cinema*. Call ☎SEA-PORT for info.

New York Philharmonic Free concerts in all five boroughs with fireworks. Call ☎875-5709 for schedule.

Parades and Festivals

Parades and Festivals

The Panasonic Village Jazz Festival Usually around Aug 15–25, includes films, free concerts, special club events, walking tour, exhibition, Jazz Fair. Call ☎929-5149 for info.

River Flicks Summer Film Series at Pier 62 (23rd St). All films are free and have a water theme – *Jaws, On the Waterfront,* etc. Call ☎353-0366 during business hours for info.

Shakespeare in the Park *Delacorte Theater* in Central Park, Tues–Sun July–Aug. ☎260-2400 for info. Free tickets given out at 6.15pm for 8pm performances, but line forms early in the morning.

Sounds at Sunset at the Battery Park Esplanade June, July and Aug, at 6.30pm Call ☎416-5300 for info. Free.

Summergarden Concerts Museum of Modern Art concerts in the sculpture garden, 54th St between 5th and 6th aves. Fri and Sat, June–Aug at 8.30pm. First come, first served, but it will be canceled if raining. Call ☎708-9491 for info. Free.

Summerstage at Central Park June–Aug at Rumsey Playfield in Central Park, mid-park at 72nd St. Concerts, performances and readings, plus the New York Grand Opera. Call ☎360-CPSS for info. Free.

Washington Square Music Festival Classical and contemporary, near the statue of Garibaldi, Tues at 8pm, July & Aug. Call ☎431-1088 for info.

The World Financial Center Arts & Events June–Aug. Dance on the waterfront to various types of music from Hungarian to swing. Call ☎945-0505 for info. Free.

Chapter 23

Kids' New York

Despite what you may hear on the evening news, New York can be a wonderful city to visit with **children** of all ages. There are the obvious attractions such as skyscrapers and ferries, simple pleasures of just walking the streets, seeing the buskers and taking in the hopping scene. Your main problem won't be finding stuff to do with your kids, but perhaps how to transport the younger ones around: though some natives navigate the streets and subways with a stroller, many prefer to keep infants and toddlers safely contained in a **backpack** or **front carrier**; indeed, most of the attractions listed below do not allow strollers. The majority of restaurants, art galleries and stores, however, are tolerant of children, if not actually child-friendly, and many of the city's museums and theaters have specific children's programs. Below we have detailed some of the attractions that are especially appealing to kids. For a further listing of what is available when you're in town, see "Activities for Children" in *New York* magazine as well as *The Village Voice*. An excellent automated directory of family-oriented current events all around the city is available through the *New York Convention and Visitors Bureau*, 2 Columbus Circle, NY, NY 10019, 1-800/692-8474 (Web site: *http://www.nycvisit.com*). They also have a free seasonal booklet, *The Big Apple Visitor's Guide*, with a good map, directions and coupons. Always be sure to phone ahead for specific times, programs and availability to avoid any disappointment.

Museums

One could spend an entire holiday just checking out the city's many museums, which almost always contain something of interest for the kids; the following should evoke more than just the usual enthusiasm.

American Museum of Natural History

Central Park West at 79th St ☎769-5100. Sun–Thurs 10am–5.45pm, Fri & Sat 10am–8.45pm; Discovery Room noon–4pm; Hayden Planetarium closed until the year 2000 due to massive new renovations; IMAX shows 10.30am–4.30pm, every hour on the half-hour. Suggested donation $8, children $4.50, students/seniors $6. Special exhibits and IMAX additional charge, combination packages available.

One of the best museums of its kind, an enormous building full of fossils, meteorites and many more natural artifacts. Several large dinosaur halls are sure to please all ages and are a good first stop. Extensive dioramas of animals from around the world allow children an up-close look at wildlife.

American Museum of the Moving Image

35th Ave at 36th St, Astoria, Queens ☎718/784-0077. Tues–Fri noon–5pm, Sat & Sun 11am–6pm; $8, students/seniors $5, children 5–18 $4;

Remember that children under 44 inches (112cm) tall ride free on the subway and buses when accompanied by an adult.

Kids'
New York

under five free. (Museum admission includes film screenings.)

Free film screenings in a lovely old movie palace, filled with historic costumes, cameras and props.

Brooklyn Children's Museum

145 Brooklyn Ave, on the corner of St Mark's Ave ☎718/735-4400. Wed–Mon 2–5pm, Sat & Sun noon–5pm; suggested contribution $3.

Founded in 1899, this is the world's first museum for children. A participatory and hands-on museum stacked full of authentic ethnological natural history and technological artifacts with which to play. Fun for children of all ages as well as adults.

Children's Museum of the Arts

72 Spring St between Broadway and Lafayette St ☎274-0986. Thurs 5–7pm, Sat & Sun 11am–5pm; $5, 18 months and under free.

Art gallery of works by and/or for children. Children are encouraged to look at different types of art and then create their own, with paints, clay, plaster of Paris and any other simple medium. There are even projects for small toddlers.

Children's Museum of Manhattan

212 W 83rd St between Broadway and Amsterdam in the Tisch building ☎721-1234. Tues–Sun 10am–5pm; children and adults $5, under age 1 free.

Another participatory museum concentrating on the world around us. Also a Media Center where children can produce their own television shows. Primarily directed at ages up to 12 years. Art workshops, special holiday workshops, guest performers and storytellers.

Fire Museum

278 Spring St between Hudson and Varick ☎691-1303. Tues–Sun 10am–4pm; $4, students $2, children 12 and under $1.

A sure hit with the preschool crowd, it's an unspectacular but pleasing homage to New York City's firefighters, and indeed firepeople everywhere. On display are fire engines from the last century (hand-drawn, horse-drawn and steam-powered), helmets, dog-eared photos and a host of motley objects on three floors of a disused fire station. A neat and endearing display.

Intrepid Sea-Air-Space Museum

Far western end of 46th St at Pier 86. ☎245-0072. May–Sept Mon–Sat 10am–5pm, Sun 10am–6pm; Oct–April Wed–Sun 10am–5pm, last admission 1 hour prior to closing; $10, children 12–17 $7.50, children 6–11 $5, ages five and under first child free, each additional child $1.

This old aircraft carrier has a distinguished history, including hauling Neil Armstrong and co out of the ocean following the Apollo 11 moonshot. Today it holds a dubious celebration of military might, such as the A-12 Blackbird – the world's fastest spy plane, and the *SS Growler* – a guided missile submarine. With other modern and vintage air and seacraft; interactive CD-rom exhibits; and a restaraunt on the premises.

Museum of the City of New York

5th Ave at 103rd St ☎534-1672. Wed–Sat 10am–5pm, Sun 1–5pm; suggested donation $5, children and students $4, families $10.

A museum, obviously, about the history of New York City. Antique toy and photograph exhibits on specific themes change regularly. Excellent archaeological exhibits.

National Museum of the American Indian (Smithsonian Institution)

1 Bowling Green ☎668-6624. Daily 10am–5pm, Thurs until 8pm; free.

A beautiful museum housing the largest collection in the world devoted to North, Central and South American Indian cultures. Though much of the exhibit is behind glass, the layout makes it very accessible and the background sound and music set the mood. Kids will enjoy looking at the ancient dolls, moccasins and the replicas of a reservation home and school room. They often have programs that include theater troupes, performance artists, dancers and films.

New York Hall of Science

47–01 111th St, Flushing Meadows, Corona, Queens ☎718/699-0005. Wed–Sun 10am–5pm; $4.50, children $3. (Open Mon and Tues during the summer.)

Built for the 1964–65 World's Fair, this museum contines to add the latest in technological displays, with hands-on exhibits that make it more fun for kids. Not worth a special trip in itself, but certainly merits a visit on the way out to nearby Shea Stadium, the Queens Zoo, Queens Art Museum or the World's Fair grounds in Flushing Meadow Park.

New York Transit Museum

130 Livingston St. Old subway entrance at Schermerhorn St and Boerum Place, Brooklyn ☎718/243-3060. Tues–Fri 10am–4pm, Sat & Sun noon–5pm; $3, children $1.50.

Housed in an abandoned subway station, there's more than 100 years worth of transportation memorabilia, including old subway cars and buses. Frequent activities for children, and best for schoolkids.

South Street Seaport Center and Museum

12 Bowling Green ☎748-8600. April–Sept daily 10am–6pm, Thurs until 8pm; Oct–March 10am 5pm, closed Tues; $6, students $4, children $3.

Eighteenth- and nineteenth-century buildings house three galleries, a children's center, a large fleet of historic ships, a maritime craft center and a library. **New York Unearthed** is a site the museum has devoted to archaeological work currently being done in the city. Children can watch archaeologists work, see how artifacts discovered tell the story of New York's history and ride an elevator into a simulated 'dig' site. During July and August there are also free concerts on Saturday evenings.

Babysitting

The Babysitters' Guild, 60 E 42nd St ☎ 682-0227, offers babysitting services, with approved sitters, 16 foreign languages spoken. Fees are $12 an hour, depending on the age and how many children there are, plus a flat fee of $4.50 to cover transportation. (After midnight the fee for transportation is $7.) All sitters have teaching and nursing backgrounds, and are fully licensed and bonded. As always, call for the full picture. Be sure to book as far in advance as you can – at the latest the day before you need the sitter, if possible.

Staten Island Children's Museum

Snug Harbor Cultural Center, 1000 Richmond Terrace, Staten Island ☎718/273-2060. Tues–Sun noon–5pm, closed Mon; $4, children under 2 free.

This is a good way to round off a trip on the Staten Island ferry; it's reachable on a trolley bus from the ferry terminal. There are many hands-on exhibits, covering subjects like the environment and technology, puppets and toys. In the summer months the downstairs gallery hosts many special exhibits which are free with admission, but the space is often full. Call for reservations.

Sights and entertainment

New York Aquarium

W 8th St and Surf Ave, Coney Island, Brooklyn ☎718/265-3474. Daily 10am–6pm; $7.75, children 2–12 $3.50, under 2 free.

First opened in 1896, the aquarium is a division of the Wildlife Conservation Society. Mostly it's a series of darkened halls containing creatures from the deep, but open-air shows of marine mammals are held several times daily, as are the shark, sea otter and walrus feedings. This is also the sight of the famous

Kids'
New York

See also Bronx Zoo, detailed on p.223, and Central Park Zoo, p.153.

Kids'
New York

Times Square

Just north of 42nd St, where Broadway and 7th Ave converge in midtown Manhattan, is the new **Times Square**, which has been transformed from an infamous den of iniquity into a family-oriented entertainment zone. Much of this has to do with Disney's new and very obvious presence in the area. For more on the neighborhood, see p.145. Below are some of the more kid-oriented options in the district.

The Disney Store, Broadway and 42nd St ☎ 221-0430. This retail outlet is found in many American malls, though this one is considerably larger than the standard. There is a giant movie screen running advertisements for DisneyWorld in Orlando, Florida, and of course segments of the many Disney movies.

New Victory Theater, 209 W 42nd St ☎ 382-4000. The city's first year-round theater for families. There is always a rich mix of theater, music, dance, story-telling, film and puppetry, in addition to pre-performance workshops and post-performance participation. The interior has been beautifully restored, the seats are plush but small. Everything about

this theater is child-oriented from the affordable cost (most shows $10–20) to the duration of performances (60–90 minutes).

XS Virtual Game Arena, 1457 Broadway between 41st and 42nd sts ☎ 1-888/972-7529, Web site: *http://www.xsnewyork.com*. Sun–Thurs 10am–midnight, Fri & Sat 10–2am. This is a must stop for the age 10 and above crowd. Upon entering this very dark and very loud futuristic world all senses go into overdrive, which is exactly the idea. There are tons of virtual reality games to try, from hand-gliding to a Western shoot-out, plus an underground lasertag arena and a number of computers with Internet access.

Coney Island boardwalk and amusement park – older children and teens will find it a good spot to people watch.

New York Botanical Garden

200th St & Southern Blvd (Kazimiroff Blvd) Bronx, NY ☎ 718/817-8777; Web site: *http://www.nybg.org*. Tues–Sun 10am–6pm; $3, children $1, free admission on Wednesday.

One of America's foremost public gardens. The Enid A. Haupt Conservatory has been magnificently restored and is currently housing a rainforest containing several thousand medicinal herbs, which are illustrative of the thousands used around the world.

Skyride

350 5th Ave at 34th St in the Empire State Building ☎ 279-9777. Daily 10am–10pm; $11.50, children 5–11 $9.50. Combination ticket to skyride and observatory $14 and $9.

The New York Skyride is a big-screen thrill ride through the most well-known sights in the city, complete with tilting seats and surround sound. Bring a strong stomach; it may be too much for small children. The observatory is at the top of the Empire State Building, offering spectacular day and nighttime views 1050 feet above Manhattan.

Sony Imax Theater

1998 Broadway & 68th St ☎ 336-5000, Web site: *http://www.sony.com*. Adults $9.50, 12 and under $6.

See the city past and present in 3D. Also housed in the Lincoln Square Entertainment Complex is a Sony twelve-screen movie theater and the *Real Java Café*. Show times vary daily.

Sony Wonder Technology Lab

550 Madison Ave at 56th St ☎ 833-8100. Tues–Sat 10am–6pm, Thurs 8pm closing, Sun noon– 6pm; free.

A hands-on experience with communication technology, including everything from rock videos to editing or producing TV programs. Very futuristic; every person receives a card-key that imprints your photo image, name, and a voice sample and a completion certificate at the end.

Shops: toys, books and clothes

Barnes & Noble, Jr, 120 E 86th St between Lexington and Park aves ☎427-0686. One of the largest children's bookstores in Manhattan. Storytelling sessions on Tues at 10.30am, 11:30am and Thurs at 5.30pm.

Big City Kites, 1210 Lexington Ave at 82nd St ☎472-2623. Manhattan's largest and best kite store, with a huge range to choose from.

Books of Wonder, 132 7th Ave at 18th St ☎989-3270, also 16 W 18th St,

between 5th and 6th aves. Excellent kids' bookstore, with a great story-hour on Sun at 11.45am.

Chocolate Soup, 946 Madison Ave between 74th and 75th sts ☎861-2210. Upscale clothing store specializing in hand-made sweaters and hand-painted clothes.

Cozy's Cuts for Kids, 1125 Madison Ave at 84th St ☎744-1716. Second location 448 Amsterdam Ave, between 81st and 82nd ☎579-2600. For the first haircut through 12 years old, kids can get their hair cut while sitting in a play jeep and watching videos. Little ones receive an honorary diploma for their first haircut.

Enchanted Forest, 85 Mercer St between Spring and Broome sts ☎925-6677. A marvellous shop that hides its merchandise – stuffed animals, puppets, masks and the like – partly in the branches of its mock forest.

Kids'
New York

Central Park

Central Park in the summer is equipped to provide sure-fire entertainment for children of all ages. From storytelling to rollerblading, here are the places to go:

Alice in Wonderland Statue, 72nd St on the East Side. An enchanting homage to the storybook character, but an even better climbing spot.

Belvedere Castle, 79th St on the West Side. A fairytale castle resting atop Central Park's highest point. It's home to the Children's Discovery Chamber.

The Carousel, 64th St mid-park. For just 90 cents, children can take a spin on the country's largest hand-carved horses.

Conservatory Water, 72nd St on the East Side. Adult enthusiasts race remote-controlled model boats here every Saturday in the summer.

Hans Christian Andersen statue, 72nd St on the East Side. Forty-or-so-year tradition of storytelling sessions. Sat 11am–noon, June to Sept.

Loeb Boathouse, 72nd St mid-park. Rent a rowboat and enjoy the views or take a gondola ride in the evening. Bike rentals available too.

Swedish Marionette Theater, 81st St on the West Side ☎988-9093. $5; children $4. A puppet theater, housed in a former Swedish school building that was brought to New York in the nineteenth century. Shows during the day, call for times. Reservations required.

Wild Life Center, 5th Ave at 64th St. Adults $2.50, 3–12 50 cents, under 3 free. Daily Mon–Fri 10am–5pm, Sat & Sun 10:30am–5:30pm A very do-able zoo, with an indoor rain forest, polar bears and penguins.

Wollman Rink, 62nd St mid-park ☎396-1010. $6; children $3. Roller/in-line skating during the summer and ice-skating during the winter. Skate rental and instruction available.

Kids' New York

New York for teens

Manhattan itself should be enough to excite and enrapture **teenagers**, but if you're searching for additional entertainment, there are any number of options. For high-tech thrills, check the **Sony Wonder Technology Lab** (p.400) or **XS Virtual Game Arena** (p.400). Or you could hit one of the city's many music stores. **Manny's Music**, 156 W 48th St, has walls covered with hundreds of autographed photographs of music's biggest stars, past and present, in addition to musical instruments and recording gear. The **Virgin Megastore**, 1540 Broadway at 46th St, is true to its name and has every kind of merchandise for the music enthusiast. There is a café on the basement level, and its late hours (open until 1am on Thurs, 2am Fri and Sat) make it a favorite haunt of older teens who want to be out on the town but aren't ready for the club scene. For a backstage look at real television production, take the **NBC Studio Tour** (30 Rockefeller Plaza–50th St between 5th and 6th aves Mon–Sat 9.30am–4.30pm, approximately every 15min; $8.25 per person; children under 6 not admitted). The tour is about one hour long and

shows the stages of *NFL Live* and *Saturday Night Live*, as well as general production facilities. The **Kramer Reality Tour** (P.O. Box 391, NY, NY 10036 ☎268-5525; Sat & Sun tours at noon, $37.50) is a tour of New York spots highlighted in the popular *Seinfeld* sitcom, led by the person who inspired the character of Cosmo Kramer. For the sports enthusiast the **Madison Square Garden Tour** (7th Ave between 33rd & 31st ☎465-5800) offers a behind-the-scenes look at the arena, theater, and Knick and Ranger locker rooms. For a rockin' eating experience, there are the established favorites: **Hard Rock Café** (221 W 57th St ☎489-6565); **Planet Hollywood** (140 W 57th St ☎333-7827); **Harley Davidson Café** (1370 6th Ave ☎245-6000), which also has a cool retail shop; **Fashion Café** (51 Rockefeller Plaza ☎ 765-3131); and **The All Star Cafe** (corner of 45th & 7th ☎840-8326), a sports-fan's paradise, owned by Andre Agassi, Wayne Gretzky and Joe Montana. For that clothes-shopping spree, head to the East Village and SoHo for all the funky stores and "in" fashions.

The Exclusive Oilily Store, 870 Madison between 70th and 71st sts ☎628-0100. Fun, bright and busy clothing from Holland.

F.A.O. Schwarz, 767 5th Ave at 58th St ☎644-9400. Showpiece of a nationwide chain sporting three floors of everything a child could want. Fans of Barbie will want to check out the Barbie store, in the back of *F.A.O. Schwarz* on Madison Ave.

Little Eric, 1331 3rd Ave between 76th and 77th sts ☎288-8987 and 1118 Madison between 83rd and 84th sts ☎769-1610. Large selection of shoes, mostly imported from Italy, for children of all ages. Kids won't mind shopping here since they play videos and cartoons all day.

Monkeys and Bears, 506 Amsterdam Ave between 84th and 85th sts ☎873-2673. Upscale, funky clothes for kids. Can be pricey, but good value.

Noodle Kidoodle, 112 E 86th St between Lexington and Park aves ☎427-6611. Well-stocked educational toy shop.

Penny Whistle Toys, 1283 Madison Ave at 91st St ☎369-3868; 448 Columbus Ave at 81st St ☎873-9090. Shop selling a fun, imaginative range of toys that deliberately eschews guns and war accessories.

Red Caboose, 23 W 45th St between 5th and 6th aves; lower level-flashing railroad sign in back of lobby ☎575-0155. Another shop specializing in models, but concentrating on trains and train sets.

Second Childhood, 283 Bleecker St between 6th and 7th aves ☎989-6140. Toys dating back to 1850, with a wide assortment of miniatures, soldiers and lead animals.

Space Kiddets, 46 E 21st St off Park Ave ☎420-9878. Eclectic mix of unusual, funky clothes from newborn to size 12. They also have shoes and toys.

Warner Brothers Studios Store, 1 E 57th St off 5th Ave ☎754-0300. A dizzying array of merchandise featuring the Warner Bros cartoon characters. As if the merchandise isn't enough for children, video screens show cartoons around the clock.

Theater, puppet shows, circuses and others

The following is a highly selective round-up of other activities, particularly cultural ones, that might be of interest to young children. Bear in mind that you can – as always – find out more by checking the pages of Friday's *Daily News* or *New York Times*; or take a look at *New York* magazine or the *Village Voice*, which also sometimes lists kid-oriented events. Note too that stores like *Macy's* and *F.A.O. Schwarz* often have events for children – puppet shows, story-hours and the like – as do the better children's bookstores, most of which regularly have storytelling sessions (see above).

Barnum & Bailey Circus, Madison Square Garden ☎465-6741. This large touring circus is usually in New York between the end of March and the beginning of May.

Big Apple Circus, Lincoln Center ☎875-5400. Small circus that performs in a tent behind Lincoln Center, from late Oct to early Jan. Tickets $10–45.

Bronx Zoo, Bronx River Pkwy at Fordham Rd, Bronx ☎718/367-1010. The largest urban zoo in America hosts a number of interesting activities and exhibits including a special children's area where the small ones can climb inside a tortoise shell, pretend to be a prairie dog inside Plexiglas tunnels and ride on a camel.

Miss Majesty's Lollipop Playhouse, performances at the *Grove St Playhouse*, 39 Grove St ☎741-6436. Sat and Sun at 1.30pm & 3pm; $7 adults and children. Children's theater company closed in the summer.

Puppet Playhouse, 555 E 90th St ☎369-8890. Puppet theater that puts on shows on weekends. Adults $6, kids $5; performances at 10.30am and noon. Seasons run Oct to May – call for a schedule; reservations only.

Thirteenth Street Repertory Company, 50 W 13th St between 5th and 6th aves ☎675-6677. Sat & Sun 1pm; $7 adults and children. Original musicals specifically for "little humans" year round. Reservations needed, as these are very popular shows.

Kids'
New York

Baby-changing facilities

All the above establishments have restrooms, many with **baby-changing facilities**. Fast-food restaurants, too, will usually allow you to use their facilities without purchase; there are also facilities in hotel lobbies and larger department stores.

Chapter 24

Shops and Markets

New York is the consumer capital of the world. Its **shops** cater to every possible taste, preference, creed and perversity, in any combination and in many cases at any time of day or night – and, as such, they're as good a reason as any for visiting the city. The best, the biggest, the oddest and the oldest stores still exist, yet the face of New York shopping, particularly in Chelsea, the East Village and Times Square, is changing. With the invasion of superstores and chains, *Barnes & Noble*, *Filenes Basement*, *T.J. Maxx*, *Bradleys* and even the world's largest *K-Mart* now have retail space in Manhattan. And there seems to be a *Gap* on every corner (25 at last count, and 11 *Baby Gap*). While their vast inventory and lower prices are appealing, nothing beats discovering a quirky, independent store that may only specialize in vintage cufflinks or rubber rats.

When to shop, how to pay

Most parts of the city are at their least oppressive for shopping early weekday mornings, and at their worst around lunchtimes and on Saturday. There are few days of the year when everything closes (really only Thanksgiving, Christmas and New Year's Day) and many shops, including the big midtown department stores, regularly open on Sunday. Remember, however, that certain (usually ethnic) communities close their shops in accordance with religious and other holidays: don't bother to shop on the Lower East Side on Friday after-

noon or on Saturday, for example, though places there are open on Sunday. By contrast, Chinatown is open all day every day, while the stores of the Financial District follow the area's nine-to-five routine and for the most part are shut all weekend.

Opening hours in midtown Manhattan are roughly Monday–Saturday 9am–6pm, with late closing on – usually – Thursday; downtown shops tend to stay open later, at least until 8pm and sometimes until about midnight; bookstores especially are often open late.

As far as **payment** goes, credit and charge cards are as widely accepted as you'd expect: even the smallest of shops will take *Visa*, *American Express*, *MasterCard* (*Access*) and *Diners Club*; many department stores also run their own credit schemes. Travelers' checks are a valid currency too, though they must be in US dollars and you may have to provide ID. Remember that an 8.25 percent **city sales tax** will be added to your bill; this is bypassed sometimes when paying cash in a market or discount store. Finally, wherever you're shopping, be careful. Manhattan's crowded, frenzied stores are ripe territory for pickpockets and bag-snatchers.

Shopping neighborhoods of Manhattan

As in most large cities, New York stores are concentrated in specific **neighborhoods**, so if you want something par-

Shops and Markets

ticular you invariably know exactly where to head.

SOUTH STREET SEAPORT/FINANCIAL DISTRICT

This area is mostly composed of three malls – one at **South Street Seaport** and the other two in the **World Trade Center** and the **World Financial Center**. All contain stores that you can pretty much find elsewhere. South Street especially is very touristy but can be nice in the summer with the open-air concerts and a great view of the Brooklyn Bridge. There aren't too many other places to shop downtown, with the notable exception of two discount department stores: *Century 21* (12 Cortlandt St) and *Syms* (42 Trinity Place).

LOWER EAST SIDE

Bordered by Canal St on the south and Houston St on the north, Orchard St is the main artery of the Jewish **Lower East Side**. It's worth a trip for its cheap clothes stores, especially on Sunday when its 200 shops are open only to pedestrians. With merchandise out on the street, it is something of an open-air bazaar. Some merchants, like *Ben Freedman* (137 Orchard), have been there since its pushcart heyday around the turn of the century.

Shops and Markets

CHINATOWN

Bustling with energy and activity all the time, a trip to **Chinatown** is worthwhile just for the sights. While the two main streets are Canal and Mott, which bisect each other, Chinatown continues to grow. It has now completely encircled Little Italy, making it a sort of island in a Chinese sea. If you're interested in shopping, there are a few things that are worth checking out. Some of the cheapest electronics in the city can be found on Canal St toward the Lower East Side. Chinatown is also known for its abundance of fresh (and cheap) food. Buy from the street carts; for the cheapest selections venture south of Canal on Mott St. You can also get prepared food (noodles, fried rice, etc) for a few dollars from carts on the south side of Canal St. There is a wonderful grocery store, *Kam-Man* (200 Canal off Mulberry), that sells all sorts of paraphernalia downstairs, including dishware; *Pearl River Mart* (277 Canal St) is a popular Chinese department store in the neighborhood.

SOHO

The area **So**uth of **Ho**uston, north of Broome and between Lafayette and 6th Ave, is one of the most lively and fashionable areas in the city. Along Broadway is an odd conglomeration of shoe stores and chains such as *Eddie Bauer* and *Pottery Barn*; it's west of here, down Prince and Spring sts, that you encounter high fashion, trendy shoes, beautiful antiques and home furnishings along with all of the accompanying attitude – this is the place to go for up-to-the-minute fashion.

Just east of SoHo and north of Little Italy is a fairly new shopping neighborhood (with a number of nicknames, none of which have quite stuck yet) around Mott, Mulberry and Elizabeth sts. Many local artists, jewelry-makers and designers have set up shop here, such as at *Push* (240 Mulberry St), *Kelly Christy* (235 Elizabeth St) and *Micheal Anchin Glass Co.* (250 Elizabeth St). It's also a good place to get away from central SoHo's more madding crowds.

GREENWICH VILLAGE

The **Village** plays host to a wide variety of more offbeat stores: small boutiques, secondhand bookshops and almost pedantically specialized stores, selling nothing but candles or a hundred different types of caviar. On Christopher St to the west of 7th Ave are several stores catering specifically to gays, with all sorts of merchandise options. Most shops are small and charming and can be found on the streets that fit the same description; the atmosphere itself makes this a fun shopping neighborhood.

THE EAST VILLAGE

For some shopping on the funkier side of life, hit the **East Village** – at its best along 9th St and also down Ave A. This neighborhood is crammed with one-of-a-kind shops and boutiques like *Gabbriel Ichak Studio* (430 E 9th St between 1st Ave and Ave A), where they specialize in accessories made of recycled materials, and the self-explanatory *Kimono House* (93 E 7th St at 1st Ave). There are many other hip stores, mostly of local designers and elegant home furnishings, on 9th St between 2nd Ave and Ave A. If you are on the prowl for vintage clothes, head to the area to the south and west of Tompkins Square Park, mostly along side streets such as 7th St. The most famous consumer strip in the neighborhood, **St Mark's Place**, is now somewhat of a charmless sidewalk sale; unless you're looking for cheap CDs, T-shirts or jewelry, you may want to miss it altogether.

CHELSEA

Sixth Ave in **Chelsea** is lined with places to shop, mostly giant superstores; there's *Barnes & Noble* and *Bed, Bath & Beyond*, and cheap clothiers like *Filene's Basement*, *Old Navy*, and *Today's Man*. However, as you move west toward 7th and 8th aves you encounter some smaller, more unusual shops like *Eclectic Home* (224 8th Ave at 21st St) and *Roger & Dave* (123 7th Ave between 17th and 18th sts), the latter good for kitschy T-shirts. Chelsea is also the home of the city's largest lesbian and gay bookstore (*A Different Light* at 151 W 19th St between 6th and 7th aves) as well as several other gay-friendly stores. For odds and ends, there's the Chelsea Antiques Fair and Flea Market at 26th St and 6th Ave on weekends. The **Flower District** is nearby on 6th Ave between 26th and 30th sts and has the city's largest concentration of plants and flowers. If you can't find what you want here, be it houseplant, tree, dried, cut or artificial flower, then it's a fair bet it's not available anywhere else in New York.

LOWER FIFTH AVENUE/FLATIRON

Between the Flatiron Building at 23rd St and Union Square at 14th St, **5th Ave and Broadway**, and their side streets, have become a great shopping neighborhood. You'll find street fashion standards like *Banana Republic* (17th St and 5th) and *J. Crew* (5th at 17th St) as well as new and established designers such as *Lola's* hat shop (east of 5th on 17th St), *Eileen Fisher* (5th between 17th and 18th sts) and *Matsuda* (5th and 20th St). Home furnishings are reigned over by *ABC Carpet and Home* (19th St and Broadway) and *Domain* (Broadway at 22nd St); and off-beat merchandise such as vintage gravy boats can be procured at *Fishs Eddy* (19th St and Broadway).

HERALD SQUARE

The small triangular park where 6th Ave and Broadway intersect, at 34th St, is named **Herald Square**, an unlikely center of New York's busiest shopping district. Locals and tourists alike come here for clothes, shoes and accessories; during holidays, the crowds are almost unfathomable. The main reason, of course, is *Macy's* department store, where 35,000 shoppers visit daily. Located one block east on 34th St are *Limited Express, NY Lerner*, Manhattan's flagship *Gap*, an *HMV* music store, and *Athlete's Foot*. On the bargain end, there are several *Conways* for inexpensive clothes and housewares. There's also *Daffy's, Toys R Us* and

Manhattan Mall along 6th Ave. **The Garment District** – basically the blocks between 6th and 7th aves in the 30s – can be a good place for picking up designer clothes, fabric and trimmings (beads, buttons and ribbon) at a discount. There's an office here for every women's garment retailer and manufacturer in the country, and though some are wary of selling to nonwholesale customers, you can pick up some enviable bargains at sample sales. The best fabric shops are on 40th and 41st sts, between 7th and 8th aves. For a wonderful array of tassels and buttons, start at *M & J Trimming* (1008 6th Ave at 38th St).

FIFTH AVENUE

Just south of Central Park, **5th Ave** in the 50s is a neighborhood filled with the best-known international designer stores: department stores like *Henri Bendel* (at 56th St), *Saks* (at 50th St, across the street from Rockefeller Center), and *Takashimaya* (between 54th and 55th sts); jewelry stores such as *Bulgari* (at 57th St) and *Cartier* (at 52nd St); and designer boutiques including *Christian Dior* (at 55th St) and *Gucci* (at 54th St). A lot of the little shops have been replaced by big business, like the *Warner Brothers Studio Store* (at 57th St) and the *Coca-Cola Store* (at 55th St). As you travel downtown toward 34th St, the prices and merchandise continually get more middle class. West of 5th Ave in the 40s is the **Diamond District**, where you can browse the jewelry marts and select your own gems and settings. South of 42nd St are *Lord & Taylors* (at 39th St), many electronics and camera stores and inexpensive "going-out-of-business" shops selling fakes.

57TH STREET

This is one of the most exclusive shopping streets in the world, bound by Lexington on the east, and capped by 7th Ave and Carnegie Hall on the west. Almost all top international designers have a boutique on **57th St**, some otherwise only found in Paris, Milan and LA.

Shops and Markets

Shops and Markets

Its classiness is firmly anchored by *Bergdorf Goodman, Tiffany, Chanel, Escada,* and *Tourneau.* However, the type of shopping is changing, evidenced by *Daffy's* discount department store taking over 125 Madison, formerly the home of *Place des Antiquares.* The *Original Levi's Store* (3 E 57th St) customizes women's jeans. You will also find the chains like *Pottery Barn, Victoria's Secret, Limited Express, Bolton's,* and a *Borders* superstore. On Lexington, the shopping experience extends to 59th St for *Bloomingdales, Banana Republic, Urban Outfitters* and *Levi's 501* store.

UPPER WEST SIDE

Most of the shopping done between 66th and 86th sts, west of Central Park and north of Lincoln Center, happens on Broadway, Columbus Ave, and Amsterdam Ave. The **Upper West Side** has perhaps the city's greatest concentration of intellectuals, especially if judged by the number of bookstores and cafés. The giant *Barnes & Noble* (at Broadway at 66th St) hosts readings almost every night, and the *Tower Records/Video* (across the street) lets you sample before you buy. There is an array of off-the-wall stores to challenge any funky area in the city. On upper Broadway and Columbus Ave you'll find shopping staples of the 1990s: *Ann Taylor, Gap, Body Shop, Banana Republic, Limited Express, Pottery Barn* and *Talbots,* as well as unusual clothes and home shops like *April Cornell* (487 Columbus Ave). Amsterdam Ave in the 70s and 80s is a little more interesting, with antique shops, secondhand clothing, craft and design shops, including *Allan & Suzi* (416 Amsterdam at 80th St), which claims to have restarted the platform shoe craze.

UPPER EAST SIDE

Madison Ave in the 60s, 70s and 80s – the core of the **Upper East Side** shopping neighborhood – is filled with exclusive clothiers and antique and art dealers. *Bloomingdale's* department store marks the southern end of this neighborhood, at 59th St and Lexington Ave. Between 62nd and 72nd sts there are no less than twenty designer shoe stores, as well as dozens of European fashion boutiques including *Armani, Gianni Versace, Krizia, Valentino* and *Prada.* *Polo-Ralph Lauren* (at 71st St) is one of the few American designers here; also unusual is the designer discount store *Bis* (24 E 81st). Because it is also a residential neighborhood, there is a smattering of children's stores, coffee shops, restaurants and bars. The waning German community influence is most visible at the intersection of 82nd St and 2nd Ave, with *Kramer's Pastries* and *Schaller & Webber* butcher. Most of the museums on Museum Mile have shops, most notable the Metropolitan Museum.

HARLEM

The main shopping district of **Harlem**, New York's most famous African-American community, is 125th St. The shopping district extends from Park Ave, where the MetroNorth commuter trains stop, to Frederick Douglas Blvd, where the *Apollo Theater* is located. The stores are mostly mundane; among the most appealing are chain stores such as *The Body Shop.* Though many vendors have been moved from the street due to political wrangling, *Mart 123* (125th St between Frederick Douglas and Adam Clayton Powell Blvds) holds nearly forty, selling everything from fresh produce and T-shirts to incense and kitchen appliances. Don't miss the *Malcolm Shabazz Harlem Market* (Lenox at 116th St) for beautiful African imports, and the museum store at The Studio Museum in Harlem (144 W 125th St). The best shop in the city for African crafts is **African Paradise** (27 W 125th St), with its herbal medicines, black soaps, baskets, musical instruments and much more.

Department stores and malls

In *Saks, Bloomingdale's* and *Macy's,* New York has some of the great **depart-**

ment stores of the world. However, the last few years have seen a number of the better established ones close down, while others have gone upmarket, making them less places to stock up on essentials and more outlets for designer clothes and chi-chi accessories, full of concessions on the top-line names. If you want to buy something in a hurry without turning it into a major New York shopping experience, you'd often do better to use a more specialized shop; if, on the other hand, you are on the look-out for a specific item, especially clothes, a department store might be a good first stop. With the exchange rate reasonable for most European visitors, prices are not too prohibitive, and during sale-times you may well find some excellent bargains; visit on and around holiday periods and watch the newspapers for timings.

Most department stores offer restaurants and complimentary personal shopping, alterations, and concierge service: they'll make your dinner reservations, secure tickets to the theater, call a taxi and more. Ask for details at each store's information desk.

Manhattan also has a number of **shopping malls**: shopping precincts basically, housed in purpose-built locations or in conversions of older premises, whose anodyne locations are on occasion reasonable places to browse – though they're not at all what New York does best. The larger and more important ones are listed below.

Department stores

Barney's, Madison and 61st St ☎826-8900. Mon–Fri 10am–8pm, Sat 10am–7pm, Sun noon–6pm. Though a proper department store, *Barney's* actually concentrates on clothes, particularly men's, with the emphasis on high-flying, up-to-the-minute designer garments, alongside a relatively new women's wear department. If you've the money, there's no better place in the city to look for clothes. There's a smaller branch at 225 Liberty St in the World Financial Center mall ☎945-1600.

Bergdorf Goodman, 754 5th Ave at 57th St ☎753-7300. Mon–Fri 10am–7pm, Thurs 10am–8pm, Sat 10am–6pm. The name, the location, the thick pile carpets and discreetly hidden escalators – everything about *Bergdorf's* speaks of its attempt to be New York City's most gracious department store. Lucky that most of the folk who shop here have purses stacked with charge cards – the rustle of money would utterly ruin the feel. The men's store is across 5th Ave at 58th St.

Bloomingdale's, 1000 3rd Ave at 59th St ☎355-5900. Mon–Fri 10am–8.30pm, Sat 10am–7pm, Sun 11am–7pm. New Yorkers are proud of *Bloomingdale's*: somehow it's an affirmation of their status, their sense of style, and not surprisingly, they flock here in droves. You may not be so impressed. *Bloomingdale's* has the atmosphere of a large, bustling bazaar, packed full with concessions to perfumiers and designer clothes. It's certain, though, that whatever you want, *Bloomies* – as the store is popularly known – is likely to stock it.

Henri Bendel, 712 5th Ave at 56th St ☎247-1100. Mon–Sat 10am–7pm, Sun 11am–6pm. *Bendel's* is and always has been deliberately more gentle in its approach than the biggies, with a name for exclusivity and top-line modern designers. One of Manhattan's most refined shopping experiences.

Lord & Taylor, 424 5th Ave at 38th St ☎391-3344. Mon, Tues & Sat 10am–7pm, Wed–Fri 10am–8.30pm, Sun 11am–6pm. The most established of the New York stores, and to some extent its most pleasant, with a more traditional feel than *Macy's* or *Bloomingdale's*. Though no longer at the forefront of New York fashion, it's still good for classic designer fashions, petites, household goods and accessories, and the more basic items.

Macy's, Broadway at 34th St ☎695-4400. Mon–Sat 10am–8.30pm, Sun 11am–7pm. Quite simply, the largest department store in the world, with two buildings, two million square feet of floor space, ten floors (four for women's garments alone). These days it's also a seri-

Shops and Markets

Shops and Markets

ous designer fashion rival to *Saks* and *Bloomingdale's*. To compete with the burgeoning bargain stores in the midtown area, Macy's has started a $100 million renovation both in physical space and in attitude. Eventually the narrow escalators will be gone, the perfume sprayers already are. Wander around even if you don't want to buy: if you see only one of the city's large department stores, it should really be this.

Saks Fifth Avenue, 611 5th Ave at 49th St ☎753-4000. Mon–Fri 10am–7pm, Thurs 10am–8pm, Sat 10am–6.30pm, Sun noon–6pm. The name is virtually synonymous with style, and, although *Saks* has retained its name for quality, it has also updated itself to carry the merchandise of all the big designers. In any case, with the glittering array of celebrities that use the place regularly, *Saks* can't fail.

Sterns, 899 6th Ave at 33rd St ☎244-6060. Mon, Thurs & Fri 10am–8pm, Tues, Wed & Sat 10am–11pm. Located in the Manhattan Mall, this store is similar in look and merchandise to ones found in suburbs across the nation. Go to shop, not to soak in atmosphere.

Takashimaya, 693 Fifth Ave between 54th and 55th aves ☎800/753-2038. Mon–Fri 10am–6pm, Thurs 10am–7pm. A relative newcomer to New York, with other locations in Tokyo and Paris. Beautiful Japanese department store with a scaled-down assortment of expensive merchandise, simply displayed, and exquisitely wrapped purchases. Stop by the cafe, *The Tea Box*, on the lower level where there is also an assortment of teapots and loose tea.

Shopping malls

Manhattan Mall, Sixth Ave and 33rd St. Perhaps because of its location a block away from *Macy's*, this large, mirror-fronted and rather glitzy shopping center has never really been a success, a humdrum string of mainstream stores in what resembles nothing so much as a suburban shopping mall. Unless there's a specific shop you want, or you want to pig out at the various ethnic nosh

counters in the food hall, you'd be better off in *Macy's*.

Pier 17, South Street Seaport. Again, not quite the shopping experience it has been cracked up to be, although it has a more interesting selection of shops than the chain stores of Manhattan Mall, in a more sensitively converted location.

Trump Tower, 5th Ave and 56th St. The gaudiest and most expensively meretricious of the Manhattan malls, with a range of exclusive boutiques set around a deep, marbled atrium that mark it out as a tourist attraction in itself.

World Financial Center, Battery Park City. Centered around the huge, greenhouse-like Winter Garden, this is worth a visit just for a look at the development as a whole, and it has a handful of intriguing stores. On the other hand, it's rather out of the way just for a spot of shopping.

Clothes and fashion

Dressing right is important to many in Manhattan, and fashion is a key reference point, though you may find that **clothes** are more about status here than setting trail-blazing trends. Although New York may be streets in front of the rest of the country fashion-wise, compared to Europe it can sometimes seem pretty staid unless you are in an international designer's boutique. If you are prepared to search the city with sufficient dedication you can find just about anything, but it's **designer clothes** and the snob values that go with them that predominate. **Secondhand clothes**, of the "vintage" or "antique" variety, have caught on of late and you can therefore find some very upscale vintage stores that specialize in designer vintage. Unfortunately this popularity has driven the prices up a bit, but it is still possible to find bargains here and there.

Chain stores

Ann Taylor, 575 5th Ave at 47th St (flagship store) ☎922-3621. Medium-priced business and elegant casual clothing for women. More than ten branches throughout the city; check the phone book for exact locations.

Banana Republic, 655 5th Ave at 52nd St (flagship store) ☎644-6678. Owned by the same company that owns *Gap*, these stores originally stocked expensive wear for the chic traveler: boots, bags, designer safari suits, etc. Now they offer an upscale version of *Gap* clothing. Ten branches throughout the city; check the phone book for exact locations.

Benetton, 597 5th Ave at 48th St ☎317-2501. Youthful, contemporary, casual, bright-colored clothing for women, men and children. The flagship shop is located in the landmark Scribners building, an insult to many serious book buyers. Their store at 666 5th Ave (☎399-9860) carries only the Cicely line, the upper end of Benetton.

Burberry's, 9 E 57th St between 5th and Madison aves ☎371-5010. If you're still not sure how to identify a yuppie, take a look at the clothes they sell here.

Diesel, 770 Lexington at 60th St ☎308-0055. One of five stores in the States that sell this Italian-designed label. Funky, some vintage-inspired club wear, lots of denim. Two floors including a café.

Eileen Fisher, 103 5th Ave between 17th and 18th sts ☎924-4777. This is the largest of their four NY shops full of loose and elegantly casual clothes for women. Their outlet is on 9th St between 1st and 2nd aves ☎529-5715.

Gap, 60 W 34th St and Herald Square (flagship store) ☎643-8960. Dressing most of the people in the States. You can get the essentials here; lots of denim, and some stores now carry shoes. Branches on every other corner of the city (25 in Manhattan); check the phone book for exact locations.

J Crew, 99 Prince St at Mercer (flagship store) ☎966-2739. Better known as a mail-order company, but its retail stores are popping up all across the country. Serving both men and women, the casual clothing is a safe bet although they do offer some dressier pieces. Another

at 91 5th Ave and 16th St, and 203 Front St (South Street Seaport area).

Laura Ashley, 398 Columbus Ave at 79th St ☎496-5110. Expanded beyond the floral prints this store is known for. Contemporary cotton, linen and silk clothing for women and children as well as country-style home furnishings.

The Limited, 691 Madison Ave at 62nd St ☎838-8787; another branch at the World Financial Center. Moderately priced casual clothing for women.

Limited Express, 7 W 34th St between 5th and 6th aves ☎629-6838; twelve branches including South Street Seaport and 46th St at 3rd Ave. An offshoot of *The Limited* stores, they carry similar, albeit trendier, versions of the same type of clothing.

Urban Outfitters, 628 Broadway between Houston and Bleecker sts ☎475-0009, at 360 6th Ave and Waverly Place and 127 E 59th St at Lexington Ave. A good range of stylish clothing at reasonable prices.

Designer stores

As you might expect, New York has an unrivaled selection of **designer clothing stores**, and if you have any interest in clothes at all these should not be missed, even for only an afternoon of people-watching. Internationally known **design houses** are concentrated uptown on 5th Ave in the 50s; on 57th St; and on Madison Ave in the 60s and 70s. Downtown the newer, younger designers are found in either SoHo or lower 5th Ave. In either neighborhood they are close enough to enjoy walking from one to another. Dress well, and you'll be welcomed whether browsing or buying. Most are open Monday to Saturday 10am to 6pm, but call to check.

Agnes B, 116 (men's) and 118 (women's) Prince St between Greene and Wooster sts ☎925-4649; 79 Greene St 431-4339; 13 East 16th St ☎741-2585; 1063 Madison Ave between 80th and 81st sts ☎570-9333.

Shops and
Markets

Shops and Markets

Anna Sui, 113 Greene St between Prince and Spring sts ☎941-8406.

Beau Brummel, 421 West Broadway between Prince and Spring sts ☎219-2666.

Betsey Johnson, 130 Thompson St between Prince St and Houston ☎420-0169.

Chanel, 5 E 57th St at 5th Ave ☎355-5050.

Christian Dior, 712 5th Ave at 55th St ☎582-0500.

Comme des Garçons, 116 Wooster St between Prince and Spring sts ☎219-0660.

Cynthia Rowley, 108 Wooster between Prince and Spring sts ☎334-1144.

Emanuel Ungaro, 792 Madison Ave at 67th St ☎249-4090.

Gianni Versace, 817 Madison Ave ☎744-6868 and 816 Madison Ave ☎744-5572 between 68th and 69th sts.

Giorgio Armani, 815 Madison Ave at 68th St ☎988-9191. This is the couture line only, but you can find the lower priced, more mass-produced line at **Emporio Armani**, 110 5th Ave at 18th St. And for his most relaxed, inexpensive look, head for **Armani A/X**, 568 Broadway at Prince St.

Gucci, 685 5th Ave at 54th St ☎826-2600.

Hermes, 11 East 57th St ☎751-3181.

Krizia, 769 Madison Ave between 65th and 66th sts ☎879-1211

Paul Smith, 108 5th Ave at 16th St ☎627-9770.

Polo, 867 Madison Ave ☎606-2100 and **Polo Sport**, 888 Madison Ave ☎434-8000.

Todd Oldham, 123 Wooster St between Prince and Spring sts ☎226-4668.

Valentino Boutique, 825 Madison Ave at 63rd St ☎772-6969.

Vivienne Tam, 99 Greene St between Prince and Spring sts ☎966-2398

Yohji Yamamoto, 103 Grand St at Mercer St ☎966-9066

Yves Saint Laurent Boutique, 855 Madison Ave between 70th and 71st sts ☎988-3821.

Designer boutiques

Here's one-stop designer fashion. New York's department stores also all have **designer boutiques** clustered together on one or more floors.

Bagutta, 402 W Broadway ☎925-5216. A confluence of top designers including Helmut Lang, Prada, Gaultier, Plein Sud, Dolce & Gabbana.

Brooks Brothers, 346 Madison Ave ☎682-8800. Something of an institution in New York, priding itself on its non-observance of fashion and still selling the same tweeds, gabardines and quiet-ly striped shirts and ties it did fifty years ago. It's a formula that seems to work.

Charivari, 18 W 57th St ☎333-4040, a good selection of ready to wear New York street fashion.

Paul Stuart, Madison Ave at 45th St ☎682-0320. Classic men's garb, not unlike *Brooks Brothers* but more stylish.

Vintage/secondhand

The East Village is the neighborhood for this brand of shopping. Wander up and down the side streets east of 3rd Ave and west of Ave A, where the stores are too numerous to mention. But there are good options throughout the city.

Alice Underground, 481 Broadway between Broome and Grand sts ☎431-9067. A large assortment contained in bins you have to dig through. A good selection of vintage linens, dresses, lin-gerie and shoes.

Canal Jean Co, 504 Broadway between Spring and Broome sts ☎226-1130.

Enormous warehousey store sporting a prodigious array of jeans, jackets, T-shirts, hats and more, new and second-hand. Young, fun and reasonably cheap.

Cheap Jack's, 841 Broadway between 13th and 14th sts ☎777-9564. Large vintage clothing store that's not so cheap, but you can find good bargains if you look hard enough. Lots of jeans and loads of leather jackets. A helpful staff that will give you an honest opinion.

Darrow, 7 W 19th St between 5th and 6th aves ☎255-1550. Designer and never-worn vintage, with a friendly and helpful staff. Popular with top models.

Designer Resale, 324 E 81st St between 1st and 2nd aves ☎734-3639. A resale store for slightly used designer clothes.

Fan Club, 22 W 19th St between 5th and 6th aves ☎929-3349. An amazing selection of vintage clothes, many from movies, TV and theater, with a good supply of Marilyn Monroe frocks usually on display in the front window. The store benefits three AIDS charities.

Housing Works Thrift Shop, 143 W 17th St between 6th and 7th aves ☎366-0820. Upscale thrift store where you can find secondhand designer wear in very good condition. All proceeds benefit *Housing Works*, an AIDS social service organization.

Love Saves the Day, 119 2nd Ave at 7th St ☎228-3802. Fairly cheap vintage as well as classic lunch boxes and a few other kitschy items.

Memorial Sloan Kettering Thrift Shop, 1440 3rd Ave at 82nd St ☎535-1250. Good thrift store with a fairly contempo-rary selection of clothes and tons of other bits and pieces.

Michael's: The Consignment Shop, 1041 Madison at 79th and 80th sts ☎737-7273. For bridal wear as well as slightly used designer women's clothing from names like Ungaro, Armani and Chanel.

Out of Our Closet Consignment, 136 W 18th St between 6th and 7th aves ☎633-6965. Specializing in top-end

Shops and Markets

Shops and Markets

designers like Gucci, Prada and Helmut Lang. You can also find new clothes direct from the showroom.

Reminiscence, 74 5th Ave between 13th and 14th sts ☎243-2292. Funky secondhand and new clothes for men and women. Quite inexpensive. Great off-the-wall gifts too.

Resurrection, 123 East 7th St between 1st Ave and Ave A ☎228-0063. Specializing in designer vintage (Pucci, Christian Dior) in excellent condition at a reasonable price.

The Ritz Thrift Shop, 107 W 57th St between 6th and 7th aves ☎265-4559. Calls itself "The Miracle on 57th Street" and sells only used furs. Imagine, get a $15,000 mink for only $2000!

Screaming Mimi's, 382 Lafayette St between 4th St and Great Jones ☎677-6464. Good selection of vintage clothes (including lingerie) at reasonable prices.

Stella Dallas, 218 Thompson St between Bleecker and 3rd sts ☎674-0447. A relatively small selection, but very nice quality vintage clothing with a beautiful selection of scarves (most $1–3). Also hand-embroidered vintage linens.

Tokio 7, 64 E 7th St between 1st and 2nd aves ☎353-8443. Unique, expensive consignment items.

The Village Scandal, 19 E 7th St between 2nd and 3rd aves ☎460-9358. Small and friendly, with fashionable clothing at decent prices.

Funky

Look on 7th St and 9th St between 3rd Ave and Ave A for a prodigious amount of stores carrying **funky clothing**. You may also want to check out Ludlow St south of Houston.

Big Drop, 174 Spring St between Thompson and W Broadway ☎966-4299. Clothes for forward-thinking women.

Liquid Sky, 241 Lafayette between Spring and Prince sts ☎343-0532. Lots of club clothes and transferred T-shirts. Very trendy. For men and women.

Patricia Fields, 10 E 8th St between 5th Ave and University Place ☎254-1699. Touted as Manhattan's most inventive clothes store, *Pat Fields* was one of the first NYC vendors of "punk chic" and has since blossomed into one of the few downtown emporia that yuppie uptowners will actually visit.

Pierre Garroudi, 139 Thompson St between Houston and Prince sts ☎475-2333. A limited design line with unusual fabrics, colors and styles. All of the clothes are made on the premises and they can make any item for you overnight. Reasonable prices.

Smylonylon, 222 Lafayette between Spring and Broome sts ☎431-0342. Psychedelic store with lots of stock. Funky secondhand clothing including go-go boots, halter tops, tube-tops, slinky mylar shirts and more. Most items around $20. For men and women.

TG-170, 170 Ludlow St between Houston and Stanton sts ☎995-8660. Small, unique store featuring many local designers. A favorite with the East Village crowd.

Trash 'n' Vaudeville, 4 St Mark's Place between 2nd and 3rd aves ☎982-3590. Famous to the extent that it advertises its wares in British magazines like *ID*. Great clothes, new and "antique," in the true East Village spirit.

X-Girl, 248 Lafayette between Prince and Spring sts ☎226-0151. Very girlie clothes for the club kid. All of the fastest, newest trends are here.

Discount clothing

Aaron's, 627 5th Ave, between 17th and 18th sts, Brooklyn ☎718/768-5400. This 10,000-square-foot store carries discounted designer fashions ranging from Jones New York to Adrienne Vittadini at the beginning of each season, not the end. Prices are marked down about 25 percent. It's 30 minutes from Manhattan – take the R train to Brooklyn, get off at the Prospect Ave Station/4th Ave and 17th St in Brooklyn. Walk one block east to 5th Ave.

Sample sales

At the beginning of each season, designers and manufacturers' showrooms are full of **leftover merchandise** that is removed via these informal sales. You'll always save at least fifty percent off the retail price, though you may not be able to try on the clothes and you can never return them. While some take credit cards, be prepared with cash. The best times for sample sales are in April, May, June, and October, November and December. Short of waiting for advertisement fliers to be stuffed into your hands while walking through the garment district, the following two small magazines are helpful. While they are also filled with advertisements for discount stores you could find for yourself, you will learn exactly where and when the Anne Klein, Armani, Escada, Nina Ricci, Donna Karan, and Calvin Klein, among other hot sales, take place.

Fashion Update (Web site: *http://www.fashionupdate.com*). Quarterly magazine that outlines a self-guided tour of sample sales. A yearly subscription is $70 and includes *Sample Sale Supplements* – send check to *Fashion Update*, 1274 49th St, Suite 207, Brooklyn, NY 11219. **Fashion Update Tours** are available, too: bargain expert Sarah Gardner (who writes the "Deals to Die For" column in the *NY Post*) will take you individually, or with a group, on a three-hour sample sale tour geared to your needs, from bridal to sportswear, inside the designer showrooms of NY's garment district. They are held Monday to Friday, 10am–noon, and are fun but no bargain

– prices start at $75 per person. Call ☎ 718/ 377-8873 for details.

S&B Report. Find out about designer showroom sales, as well as the best retail sales, and consignment and thrift shops in the *Sales and Bargains* magazine. It is published monthly by NYC's other bargain expert, Elysa Lazar, who *Redbook* magazine called "the world's smartest shopper." Send $9.95 for the month's issue that coincides with your trip to NY: each is available by the 24th of the preceding month and will be sent out to you immediately. Or you can subscribe for $49 a year. Address: *The S&B Report*, 108 East 38th St, Suite 2000 NY, NY 10016 ☎ 683-7612.

Bolton's. Eleven locations include: 225 E 57th St between 2nd and 3rd aves ☎ 755-2527; 27 W 57th St between 5th and 6th aves ☎ 935-4431; and 111 51st St at 6th and 7th aves ☎ 245-5227. Designer clothes at vast reductions.

Century 21, 12 Cortlandt St ☎ 227-9092. A department store with designer brands for half the cost, a favorite among budget yet label-conscious New Yorkers. Only snag – no dressing rooms. If you can make the trip, better prices and more selection in the Brooklyn store at 472 86th St ☎ 718/748-3266.

Conway. Nine stores in NYC; the biggest one is 1333 Broadway at 35th St ☎ 967-3460. For general info, call ☎ 967-5300. This no-frills store sells chil-

dren's and adult clothing and in some stores toiletries, linens and jewelry very inexpensively. Can be crowded, and no dressing rooms.

Dave's A & N Jeans, 779 6th Ave at 26th St ☎ 989-6444. Comes recommended as the best place to buy jeans in Manhattan. Helpful assistants, no blaring music, and brands other than just Levi's.

Daffy's. Four locations in Manhattan; the biggest one is at Herald Square, 6th Ave and 34th St ☎ 736-4477. Name-brand clothes at discount prices for men, women and children. Specializes in Italian designers such as Les Copian.

Filene's Basement, a newcomer to NY's discount shopping, a favorite in the sub-

Shops and Markets

urbs. 620 6th Ave, at 18th St is the bigger one ☎620-3100: there is also one at Broadway and 79th St.

Gabay's Outlet, 225 1st Ave, between 13th and 14th sts ☎254-3180. Overordered, flawed or returned goods from the upmarket midtown department stores. Well worth a rummage.

Labels for Less, biggest branch is at 1345 6th Ave at 54th St ☎956-2450. The name says it all – a national chain with 13 stores in Manhattan selling discount designer labels for women.

Loehmann's, biggest branch is at 101 7th Ave between 16th and 17th sts, ☎352-0856. New York's best-known store for designer clothes at knockdown prices. No refunds and no exchanges, but this one does offer free personal shopping, as well as individual dressing rooms. Other locations are 2103-2127 Emmons Ave, Brooklyn ☎718/368-1428; 60-06 99th St, Rego Park, Queens ☎718/271-4000; and the original store at 5740 Broadway, the Bronx ☎718/543-6420.

Orva, 155 E 86th St, between Lexington and 3rd ave ☎369-3448. Discount fashion clothing and shoes for women. Great bargains.

Syms, 42 Trinity Place ☎797-1199, and 54th St and Park Ave ☎317-8200. "Where the educated consumer is our best customer." Combine the downtown *Syms* and *Century 21* in the same trip.

T.J. Maxx, 620 6th Ave, at 18th St ☎229-0875. Another suburban discount chain, a lot like *Filene's,* and in the same shopping center.

Shoes

Most department stores carry two or more **shoe** salons – one for less expensive brands and one for finer shoes. Both *Bloomingdale's* and *Lord & Taylor* are known for their shoe departments, and *Loehmann's* has a vast selection of designer shoes at discount prices. You'll find shoe stores in all clothes-shopping areas, such as 34th St, Columbus Ave, Broadway from Astor Place to Spring St,

and Bleecker going south to 6th Ave. The greatest concentration of bargain shoe shops in hip fashions is on West 8th St between University Place and 6th Ave in the Village and on Broadway below West 8th St. **Shoes on Sale** is the largest shoe sale open to the public, with more than 50,000 pairs of shoes. It is held each year around the second week in October, in a tent in Central Park at 5th Ave and 60th St. Check the newspaper for details.

Anbar Shoes, 60 Reade St, between Church St and Broadway ☎227-0253. All different name brands, savings up to 50 percent – and in a pleasant setting.

Fluevog, 104 Prince St ☎431-4484. Innovative designs for a walk about town. Mostly casual, always hip shoes.

Kenneth Cole, 353 Columbus Ave at 77th St ☎873-2061; call for more locations.

Lady Continental, 932 Madison Ave at 73rd St ☎744-2626. If you have $300 to spend, you can't go wrong with these stylish Italian shoes that last 10 years and more.

Manolo Blahnik, 15 West 55th St between 5th and 6th aves ☎582-3007. Feminine, fashion-forward shoes that have been featured in *Vogue, Harper's* and *Cosmopolitan.*

Otto Tootsi Plohound, 137 5th Ave ☎460-8650; 413 W Broadway ☎925-8931; 1116 3rd Ave ☎249-0671. If you want to run with a trendy crowd these shoes will help. Very current designs.

Patrick Cox, 702 Madison Ave between 62nd and 63rd sts ☎759-3910. *Patrick Cox* runs the gamut from fun sneakers to elegant evening shoes. Innovative styles and textures.

Salvatore Ferragamo, 661 5th Ave at 52nd St ☎759-3822 (women's) and 725 5th Ave at 56th St, in the Trump Tower ☎759-7990 (men's). Wonderful Italian shoes, as well as accessories and clothing.

Sigerson Morrison, 242 Mott St at Prince St ☎219-3893. Kari Sigerson and Miranda Morrison make rather timeless, simple and elegant shoes for women.

Steve Madden, 150 E 86th St at Lexington ☎426-0538; 540 Broadway at Prince ☎343-1800. Very popular downtown chic shoes.

Unisa, 701 Madison Ave ☎753-7474. The only retail shop for these comfortable affordable shoes imported from Spain and Brazil.

Finishing touches: hair, make-up, glasses

As a rule of thumb you will find these **accessories** in major department stores and in areas where there is a high concentration of shopping such as SoHo and the Upper East Side. You can spend very little or a fortune – whatever suits you. What follows is sampling of the best.

GLASSES

Alain Mikli, 880 Madison Ave between 71st and 72nd sts ☎472-6085. A wide selection of European and vintage frames for men and women.

Cohen's Optical, 117 Orchard St ☎674-1986. Nicaragua's Daniel Ortega supposedly spent $3000 here on a pair of bullet-proof ones. You can probably get away with something less.

Lens Crafters, Manhattan Mall at 34th St and 6th Ave ☎967-4166; call for more locations. Chain store for glasses in an hour or a repair.

Morgenthal-Frederics, 944 Madison Ave near 75th St ☎744-9444. Nice custom-made spectacles.

HAIR

Astor Place Haircutters, 2 Astor Place ☎475-9854. People line up six deep here. They'll do any kind of style, and, most important, don't cost the earth – around $10 (plus tip) for a straight cut.

Shops and Markets

The Diamond District

The strio of 47th St between 5th and 6th aves is known as the **Diamond District** of New York. The industry is traditionally run by Hasidic Jews from Poland, but now the business people are from all over the world. Crammed into this one block are more than 100 shops: combined they sell more jewelry than any other block in the world.

At the street level are dozens of retail shops and over twenty "exchanges" – marts containing booths where many different dealers sell very specific merchandise. For example, 55 W 47th St is home to 115 independent jewelers and repair specialists. Lesser known is the *Swiss Center* at 608 5th Ave at 49th St, specializing in antique and estate jewelry and housed in an historic Art Deco building.

There are different dealers for all the different gems, for gold and silver – even someone who will string your beads for you. Some jewelers trade only among themselves; some sell retail; and

others do business by appointment only. Most shops are open Monday through Saturday 10am–5.30pm, though a few close on Saturday for religious reasons, and the standard vacation time is from the end of June to the second week in July.

It is very important that you go to the exchanges **educated**. Research what you are looking for and be as specific as possible. It's always better to go to someone that has been recommended to you if possible. Some good starting points are *Andrew Cohen, Inc* (579 5th Ave, 15th floor), for diamonds; *Myron Toback* (25 W 47th St), a trusted dealer of silver findings; and *Bracie Company Inc* (608 5th Ave, suite 806), a friendly business specializing in antique and estate jewelry. Once you buy, there's *A&A Pearl Co* (10 W 47th St), the industry's choice for pearl and gem stringing; and, if you want to get your gems graded, the *Gemological Institute of America* (580 5th Ave, 2nd floor).

Shops and Markets

Jean Louis David, 1385 Broadway at 37th St ☎869-6921; call for more locations. They're everywhere if you need a cheap respectable cut. You don't need an appointment but it helps.

Peter Coppola, 746 Madison Ave between 64th and 65th sts ☎988-9404. Extremely fashionable place to get your hair coiffed – also extremely expensive.

The Spot, 521 Madison Ave between 53rd and 54th sts ☎688-4450. Get a great cut by some of the best apprentices in the city at a reduced rate. Starts at $50.

MAKE-UP

If you are looking for make-up lines such as Clinique, Elizabeth Arden, and the like, start by going to any of the department stores, since they all have large cosmetics departments. If you are looking for something a little different check out the following:

Aveda, 233 Spring between 6th Ave and Varick St (7th Ave) ☎807-1492. Call for more locations.

Face Stockholm, 110 Prince St ☎334-3900 and 224 Columbus Ave between 70th and 71st sts ☎769-1420.

MAC, 14 Christopher St between 6th and 7th Ave ☎243-4150 and 113 Spring St ☎334-4641.

Sporting goods

The **sporting goods** scene is dominated by chains such as **Foot Locker, Athlete's Foot, Sports Authority**, and **Modell's**, though there are a few other options: "theme park" sports clothes stores, as well as stores tightly focused on one sport. Use them for merchandise as well as a wealth of information about that sport in NY.

Superstores

Niketown, 6 E 57th St between 5th and Madison ☎891-6453. You can enter this temple through the Trump Tower, literally hearing crowds cheer as you pass through the door. Every 30 minutes, a screen descends the full five stories of the store and shows Nike commercials. There's tons of memorabilia, most notably of Michael Jordan. Oh, and you can also purchase Nike clothing and accessories.

Reebok Concept Store, 160 Columbus Ave ☎595-1480. This is the flagship Reebok store; their other big shop is at Chelsea Piers. Not as dazzling as *Niketown*, but it does show ads on two big screens and it houses the Reebok Sports Club. Reebok merchandise, Greg Norman golf apparel, as well as European Reebok lines not found anywhere else in the States are all here.

Specialty stores

Bicycle Habitat, 244 Lafayette ☎431-3315. This unassuming store is frequented by bike messengers. Buy a bike here, and they'll service your brakes forever.

Blades, Board & Skate, 120 W 72nd St between Broadway and Columbus Ave ☎787-3911. Rent or buy rollerblades, snowboards and the like.

Mason's Tennis Mart, 911 7th Ave ☎757-5374. NY's finest tennis shop that lets you demo all racquets.

Paragon, 867 Broadway at 18th St ☎255-8036. Family owned, with three levels of general merchandise.

Super Runners Shop, 1337 Lexington Ave at 89th St ☎369-6010; 360 Amsterdam Ave at 77th St ☎787-7665, and 416 3rd Ave at 29th St ☎213-4560. Experienced runners work at all four locations.

Tent & Trail, 21 Park Place ☎227-1760. Bizarrely located in the Wall Street neighborhood, this small shop is a hiker's dream.

The World of Golf, 147 E 47th St between Lexington and 3rd aves ☎755-9398. Known for their large selection and discount policy.

Food and drink

Food – the buying as much as consuming of it – is a New York obsession. Nowhere do people take eating more seriously than Manhattan, and there's no better place to shop for food. Where to buy the best bagels, who stocks the widest – and weirdest – range of cheeses, are questions that occupy New Yorkers a disproportionate amount of time. The shops themselves are mouth-watering, and even the simplest street-corner deli should be enough to get your tastebuds jumping; more sophisticated places, gourmet or specialty shops for example, will be enough to make you swoon.

The listings below, while comprehensive, are by no means exhaustive. Wander the streets and you'll no doubt uncover plenty more besides. If you're after **drink**, remember that you can only buy liquor – i.e. wines, spirits or anything else stronger than beer – at a liquor store, and that you need to be 21 or over to do so.

Supermarkets, delis and greengrocers

For the most **general food requirements**, there are a number of **supermarket** chains that pop up all over the city. *Big Apple*, *Sloan's*, and *Food Emporium* you'll find pretty much everywhere; *D'Agostino* and *Gristedes* tend to appear in the fancier neighborhoods. In addition, many of the department stores listed above – principally *Macy's* and *Bloomingdale's* – have food halls. At night, there's *Food Emporium*; their 15 locations are open 24hrs on weekdays, and on Saturday and Sunday they close at midnight (see the phone book for locations).

On a smaller scale, there are **delis and greengrocers** that sell basic food and drink items, as well as sandwiches and coffee to take away, and sometimes hot ready meals and the chance to dip into a copiously provided salad bar. You should never have to walk more than a couple of blocks to find one, and most are open late or all night.

Gourmet shops

Gourmet shops are essentially a step up from delis and are gloriously stocked places, selling all manner of edible items

in a super-abundant environment that will make your taste buds jump. In general – though not exclusively – they supply the more gentrified neighborhoods with their most obscure (and more mainstream) objects of desire.

Balducci's, 424 6th Ave between 9th and 10th sts ☎673-2600. This is the long-term, non-Jewish, downtown rival of *Zabar's* (see overleaf), a family-run store that's no less appetizing – though some say it's slightly pricier.

Citarella, 2135 Broadway at 75th St ☎874-0383. Famous fish store gone full-service gourmet market (see also "Fish and seafood").

Dean & Deluca, 560 Broadway between Prince and Spring sts ☎431-1691. One of the original big neighborhood food emporia. Very chic, very SoHo and not at all cheap. There is also a café on Prince St.

EAT Gourmet Foods, 1064 Madison Ave at 80th St ☎772-0022. A brother to *Zabar's*, primarily based in the East Side and packed with gourmet delights. Try the wonderful Eli's bread.

Faicco's, 260 Bleecker St between 6th and 7th aves ☎243-1974. Very authentic Italian deli.

Fairway, 2127 Broadway between 74th and 75th sts ☎595-1888. Long-established Upper West Side grocery store that for many locals is the better-value alternative to *Zabar's*. They have their own farm on Long Island, so the produce is always fresh, and their range in some items is enormous.

Fine & Schapiro, 138 W 72nd St between Broadway and Columbus Ave ☎877-2874. Excellent, principally kosher, meals to go and renowned sandwiches and cold meats. Also a restaurant – see Chapter 17, *Eating*.

Food Works, 10 W 19th St between 5th and 6th aves ☎352-9333. Full-service gourmet market with eat-in café. Good selection of cheeses and better prices than most gourmet shops.

Gourmet Garage, 453 Broome St at Mercer ☎941-5850. Excellent values on

Shops and Markets

Shops and Markets

cheeses, olives, produce and ready-made sandwiches.

Grace's Marketplace, 1237 3rd Ave at 71st St ☎737-0600. Gourmet deli off-spring of *Balducci's* that is a welcome addition to the Upper East Side food scene. An excellent selection of just about everything.

Russ & Daughters, 179 E Houston St between Allen and Orchard sts ☎475-4880. Technically, this store is known as an "appetizing" – the original Manhattan gourmet shop, set up at the turn of the century to sate the appetites of home-sick immigrant Jews, selling smoked fish, caviar, pickled vegetables, cheese and bagels. This is one of the oldest.

Schaller & Weber, 1654 2nd Ave between 85th and 86th sts ☎879-3047. Culinary heart of the Upper East Side's now sadly diminished German-Hungarian district of Yorkville, this shop is a riot of cold cuts, salami and smoked meats. Not for vegetarians.

Todaro Brothers, 555 2nd Ave between 30th and 31st sts ☎532-0633. An excellent selection of imported and domestic gourmet foods, plus a bakery.

Zabar's, 2245 Broadway at 80th St ☎787-2000. The apotheosis of New York food-fever, *Zabar's* is still the city's most eminent foodstore. Choose from an astonishing variety of cheeses, cooked meats and salads, fresh baked bread and croissants, excellent bagels, and cooked dishes to go. Upstairs stocks implements to help you put it all togeth-er at home. Not to be missed.

Bakeries and patisseries

Cupcake Cafe, 522 9th Ave at 39th St ☎465-1530. Special-occasion cakes and cupcakes, all with buttercream frosting. Also serves light meals. Cozy place to sit.

Damascus Bakery, 56 Gold St, Brooklyn ☎718/855-1456. Syrian bakery, long established, with the city's best supply of different pita breads, as well as a dazzling array of pastries.

Ferrara, 195 Grand St between Mulberry and Mott sts ☎226-6150. Little Italy

café-patisserie with four branches throughout New York City. Specializes in gelati, cakes, and coffees. Sit-down café.

Fung Wong, 30 Mott St ☎267-4037. Chinese pastries.

H&H Bagels, 639 W 46th at 12th Ave ☎595-8000 and 2239 Broadway at 80 St. Open 24hr, seven days a week, this is the reputed home of New York's finest bagel.

Hungarian Pastry Shop, 1030 Amsterdam Ave between 110th and 111th sts ☎866-4230. *Rigojanci,* bitter-sweet chocolate mouse cake, linzer tarts and other authentic Hungarian desserts as well as a bottomless cup of coffee. Good either for an afternoon snack or to round off a meal nearby. Popular with Columbia students.

Kossar's, 367 Grand St at Essex St ☎473-4810. Jewish baker specializing in bialys.

Krispy Kreme, 265 W 23rd St between 7th and 8th aves ☎620-0111. The donuts come out of the fryer and bathe in hot glaze right before your eyes. A Southern newcomer, delighting NY. Also on 125th St and in Penn Station.

Little Pie Company, 424 W 43rd St between 9th and 10th aves ☎736-4780. Specializes in traditional American pies and cakes.

Moishe's, 181 E Houston St between Allen and Orchard sts ☎475-9624; 115 2nd Ave between E 6th and E 7th aves ☎505-8555. New York's most authentic Jewish bakery.

Orwasher's, 308 E 78th St between 1st and 2nd aves ☎288-6569. Handmade breads and rolls, all certified kosher and parve.

Sticky Fingers, 121 1st Ave at 7th Ave and St Marks Place ☎529-2554. Fresh breads daily, and homemade desserts.

Taylor's, 156 Chambers St ☎962-0519. Baked goods, entrees and desserts to go, all baked on premises. Also at 523 Hudson, 228 W 18th St and 175 2nd Ave.

Veniero's, 342 E 11th St between 1st and 2nd aves ☎674-7264. Century-old Italian-style patisserie.

Vesuvio, 160 Prince St between Thompson St and W Broadway ☎925-8248. SoHo's most famous Italian bakery.

Yonah Schimmel's, 137 E Houston St between 1st and 2nd aves ☎477-2858. Specialists in home-made knishes, with a variety of fillings (kasha, potato, cheese, etc), which you can take away or consume on the premises; their knishes taste nothing like the mass-produced kind.

Zaro's, Grand Central Station; Penn Station and several other locations in Manhattan; check the phone book for addresses. Croissants, bagels, and all good things. A good place to stop off for a breakfast on your feet.

Zito's, 259 Bleecker St between 6th and 7th aves ☎929-6139. Long-established downtown Italian baker, renowned for its fine round *pane di casa*.

Cheese and dairy

Alleva Latticini, 188 Grand St at Mulberry St ☎226-7990. Italian cheesery and grocer makes own smoked mozzarella and ricotta.

Cheese Unlimited, 240 9th Ave between 24th and 25th sts ☎691-1512. The name says it all . . . more than 40 varieties of cheese.

Di Paolo, 206 Grand St at Mott St ☎226-1033. A wide array of different cheeses, including fresh Italian dairy varieties made on the premises.

Ideal Cheese Shop, 1205 2nd Ave between 63rd and 64th sts ☎688-7579. A fine cheese emporium.

Joe's Dairy, 156 Sullivan St at Houston St ☎677-8780. Family store that's the best bet for fresh mozzarella.

Murray's Cheese Shop, 257 Bleecker St between 6th and 7th aves ☎243-3289. A variety of more than 300 fresh cheeses.

Third Avenue Cheese Shop 141 3rd Ave between 9th and 10th sts ☎477-1221. Very inexpensive, with a nice selection; good breads, to boot.

Fish and seafood

Caviarteria, 502 Park Ave; enter on 59th St between Park and Madison aves ☎759-7410. Mainly caviar – more than a dozen varieties – and a stock of smoked fish and patés.

Citarella, 2135 Broadway at 75th St ☎874-0383. The largest and most varied fish and seafood source in the city, now with gourmet baked goods, cheese, coffee, meat, prepared food. Still, the specialty is seafood; there's a wonderful bar serving prepared oysters, clams and the like to take away. Great, artistic window displays, too. Also at 1313 E 75th at 3rd Ave.

Fulton Fish Market. For New York's freshest fish if you're up early enough (5am – see "Information, Maps and Tours" in *Basics*). The market itself is a lively affair to visit.

Murray's Sturgeon Shop, 2429 Broadway between 89th and 90th sts ☎724-2650. Another popular Upper West Side haunt, this place specializes in smoked fish and caviar.

Petrossian, 182 W 58th St and 7th Ave ☎245-2214. This well-known shop imports only the finest Russian caviar, alongside a range of other gourmet products – smoked salmon and other fish mainly – as well as pricey implements to eat it all with. Quite the most exclusive place to shop for food in town, and with a restaurant attached to complete the experience.

Health food, vegetarian and spice shops

Angelica's Herbs, 147 1st Ave at 9th St ☎677-1549. An excellent selection of herbs, tinctures, spices and books.

Aphrodisia, 264 Bleecker St between 6th and 7th aves ☎989-6440. For herbs and spices only, this place is hard to beat.

Commodities, 165 1st Ave at 10th St ☎260-2600; 117 Hudson St between N Moore and Franklin sts ☎334-8330. Huge health food store.

General Nutrition Center (GNC). The city's largest health food chain (check the phone book for addresses), though

Shops and Markets

Shops and Markets

often the one-off downtown health shops are better.

Good Earth Foods, 1330 1st Ave between 71st and 72nd sts ☎472-9055; 167 Amsterdam Ave at 68th St ☎496-1616. Not cheap but one of the best-equipped health food outlets in the city. Has a worthy juice and food café.

Good Food Co-op, 58 E 4th St. Cooperatively run but open to the public. Full market with a good amount of organic food.

Gramercy Natural Food Center, 427 2nd Ave between 24th and 25th sts ☎725-1651. Best known for its fish, poultry and organic dairy products.

The Health Nut, 2611 Broadway at 99th St ☎678-0054 and other Manhattan locations. Good general health food and macrobiotic chain.

Kalustyan's, 123 Lexington Ave between 28th and 29th sts ☎685-3451. The best of the fooderies that make up the tiny Little India district of Manhattan. Good spice selection.

Nature Food Center, 348 W 57th between 8th and 9th aves ☎757-4180 and locations across Manhattan. The "department store" of natural foods – an excellent selection.

Prana, 125 1st Ave between St Mark's and 7th St ☎982-7306. Wholefood shop where you can make your own peanut butter.

Whole Foods in SoHo, 117 Prince St between Greene and Wooster ☎982-1000; 2421 Broadway and 89th St ☎874-4000. Health food supermarket, open daily with a very wide selection.

Ice cream

Two chains have largely carved up the city's appetite for ice cream between them: *Baskin-Robbins*, who have about half a dozen outlets spread between Wall St and Harlem, and the considerably better *Haagen-Dazs*, who trade from about fifteen locations across Manhattan; again, the phone book has details.

While their ice cream is excellent and comes in myriad different flavors,

there are a few smaller operators which die-hard New York ice cream freaks swear by. Of these *Steve's* (2294 Broadway between 82nd and 83rd sts) and *Ben & Jerry's* (680 8th Ave at 43rd St; 41 3rd Ave between 9th and 10th sts; World Financial Center) both have their vehement defenders; and the *Chinatown Ice Cream Factory* (65 Bayard St, south of Canal between Mott and Elizabeth sts) incurs the most bemused reactions, since it's the only place that serves up mango, green tea and lychee flavors.

Sweets, nuts and chocolates

Bazzini, 339 Greenwich St at Jay St ☎334-1280. Fabulous selection of nuts in all shapes and sizes. A wide selection of sweets, too.

David's Cookies. A chain with branches around the city (see the phone book for exact locations) selling excellent cookies.

Economy Candy, 108 Rivington St between Essex and Ludlow sts ☎254-1531. Best of a bunch of unpretentious Lower East Side stores, selling tubs of sweets, nuts and dried fruit.

Elk, 240 E 86th St between 2nd and 3rd aves ☎650-1177. A Yorkville candy store selling Yorkville-style candies – rich and marzipaned.

Godiva, 701 5th Ave between 54th and 55th sts ☎593-2845. This renowned Belgian chocolatier has branches all over Manhattan – unbeatable for satisfying anyone's chocolate craving.

Li-Lac, 120 Christopher St between Hudson and Bleecker sts ☎242-7374. Delicious chocolates that are hand-made on the premises since 1923. One of the city's best treats for those with a sweet tooth.

Teuscher, 620 5th Ave between 49th and 50th sts ☎246-4416; 251 E 61st St ☎751-8482. The truffles of this Upper East Side store are renowned.

Treat Boutique, 200 E 86th St at 3rd Ave ☎737-6619. Six different kinds of home-made fudge and a broad selection of dried fruit and nuts.

Tea and coffee

McNulty's, 109 Christopher St between Bleecker and Hudson sts ☎242-5351. Coffee, and a wide selection of teas.

Oren's, 31 Waverly Place (Greenwich Village) ☎420-5958, call for other locations along the East Side. Among the best beans in the city.

Porto Rico, 201 Bleecker St between 6th Ave and McDougal St ☎477-5421, also 40 1/2 St Mark's off 2nd Ave and 107 Thompson St between Prince and Spring. Best for coffee, and with a bar for tasting.

The Sensuous Bean, 66 W 70th St just off Columbus Ave ☎724-7725. Mostly coffee, with some tea.

Liquor stores

Prices for all kinds of **liquor** are controlled in New York State and vary little from one shop to another. There are, however, a number of places that either have a particularly good selection or where things tend to be a touch less expensive. It's those that are listed here. Bear in mind there's a state law forbidding the sale of strong drink on Sundays, a day on which all liquor stores are closed. Many places will take orders over the phone if you would like your drink to come to you.

Acker Merrall & Condit, 160 W 72nd St between Broadway and Columbus Ave ☎787-1700. Holds a very wide selection of wine from the US, especially California. Open until 11.30pm.

Astor Wines and Spirits, 10 Astor Place at Lafayette St ☎674-7500. Manhattan's best selection and most competitive prices.

Beekman Liquor Store, 500 Lexington Ave between 47th and 48th sts ☎759-5857. Good, well-priced Midtown alternative to *Astor*.

Columbus Circle Liquor Store, 1780 Broadway at 57th St ☎247-0764. Ditto for uptown.

Cork & Bottle, 1158 1st Ave between 63rd and 64th sts ☎838-5300. Excellent selection; deliveries too.

Garnett Wine & Liquor, 929 Lexington Ave at 68th St ☎772-3211. Another good-value liquor store.

Maxwell Wine & Spirits, 1657 1st Ave between 86th and 87th sts ☎289-9595. Upper East Side liquor store that opens until midnight on weekends.

Morrell & Co, 535 Madison Ave ☎688-9370. One of the best selections of good-value wine in town.

Schapiro's, 126 Rivington St between Essex and Norfolk sts ☎674-4404. Kosher wines made on the premises. Free tours of the cellars, with wine tasting, Sun 11am–4pm on the hour.

Schumer's, 59 E 54th St between Park and Madison aves ☎355-0940. Stays open until midnight Fri & Sat, and will also deliver.

Sherry-Lehman, 679 Madison Ave ☎838-7500. New York's foremost wine merchant.

Spring Street Wines, 187 Spring St between Thompson and Sullivan sts ☎219-0521. Well-stocked SoHo liquor store.

Warehouse Wines and Spirits, 735 Broadway between 8th and Waverly, ☎982-7770. The top place to get bang for your buck, with a wide selection.

Books

Book lovers bemoan the steady stream of independent bookstores that are closing in New York and directly attribute this to the 15 (at last count) *Barnes & Noble* stores. But there's still a fantastic selection of **books** in New York. Stores servicing a niche, such as mystery, are flourishing as a place to purchase books as well as meet like-minded people. More than 90 percent of the nation's publishers are located here, with their wares sold in more than 500 bookstores. New or secondhand, US or foreign, there's little that isn't available somewhere. If there's a particular book you want to look at, but not buy, don't forget the New York Public Library at 42nd St and 5th Ave.

Shops and Markets

Shops and Markets

Superstores and chains

Barnes & Nobles are among the nicest places in the city to buy books – and their enormous stock makes it likely you'll be able to find what you're looking for. Their superstores are designed like a library with comfy chairs and a café; author readings take place about five evenings a week, and hours are 9am to midnight, every day. **Barnes & Noble Jr** at 120 E 86th St at Lexington ☎427-0686 has only children's books and readings; 105 5th Ave at E 18th St ☎807-0099 concentrates on **college text books**, and their **sales annex** is located at 128 5th Ave at W 18th St ☎691-3770.

There are eight **superstores** in Manhattan:

4 Astor Place at Broadway and Lafayette ☎420-1322; 675 6th Ave at W 22nd St ☎727-1227; 600 Fifth Ave at W 48th St ☎765-0590; Citicorp building at E 54th St and 3rd Ave ☎750-8033; 2289 Broadway at W 82nd St ☎362-8835; 1280 Lexington at E 86th St ☎423-9900; Lincoln Center at 1960 Broadway ☎595-6859; Union Square at 33 E 17th St ☎253-0810.

Borders Books and Music, 5 World Trade Center at Church and Vesey sts ☎839-8037. This Ann Arbor-based chain rivals *Barnes & Noble*. Should be a 42,000 square foot superstore at Park Ave and 57th St open by the time you read this.

B. Dalton, 396 6th Ave at 8th St ☎674-8780. A nationwide chain, but this is the only branch left in Manhattan.

General interest and new books

Coliseum Books, 1771 Broadway at 57th St ☎757-8381. Very large store, good on paperbacks and academic books.

Dover Books, 180 Varick St ☎255-6399. Go upstairs to the small bookstore, filled to the brim with hard-to-find Dover reproductions.

Gotham Book Mart, 41 W 47th St ☎719-4448. Located in the heart of the Diamond District. For more than 75 years this jewel has focused on the creative arts, stocking both new publications as well as out-of-print books. The art department and gallery are on the second floor. Huge film and theater section, and excellent for the more obscure literary stuff. A noticeboard downstairs advertises readings and literary functions, and a gallery has sporadic exhibitions.

Labyrinth Books, 536 W 112th St ☎865-1588. Largest scholarly bookstore east of the Mississippi.

McGraw Hill, 1221 6th Ave at 49th St ☎512-4100. Specializes in business, technical and scientific books.

Papyrus, 2915 Broadway at 114th St ☎222-3350. New and used titles, especially good on literature.

Posman Books, 2955 Broadway and 116th St ☎961-1524. General college bookstore, affiliated with Barnard College. Also a downtown location, at 1 University Place ☎533-2665.

Shakespeare & Co., 939 Lexington at 68th and 69th sts ☎570-0201, and 716 Broadway and Washington Place ☎529-1330. Both have new and used books, paper and hardcover, great for fiction and psychology.

Spring Street Books, 169 Spring St between W Broadway and Thompson ☎219-3033. SoHo's most wide-ranging and pleasant bookshop, good for paperbacks and magazines from home and abroad.

St Mark's Bookshop, 31 3rd Ave, between 8th and 9th sts ☎260-7853. Nice selection of new titles from mainstream to way alternative; see p.427, under "Radical," for more.

Three Lives, 154 W 10th St and Waverly Place ☎741-2069. Excellent literary bookstore that has an especially good selection of books for and by women, as well as general titles.

Tower Books, 383 Lafayette St at 4th St ☎228-5100. The literary arm of *Tower Records*, next door, focusing on pop culture, music, travel and film.

Secondhand books

A neighborhood to browse through for book bargains is centered around 5th Ave and 18th St. There you'll find used bookstores **Academy Books**, **Skyline Books**, **Books of Wonder** (for children) as well as the **Barnes & Noble Sales Annex**. The Strand is four blocks away at 12th St and Broadway. The **Metropolitan Book Auction** sells fine and rare used books – they're on the 4th floor of 123 W 18th St; call ☎929-4488 for schedule.

Academy Books, 10 W 18th St between 5th and 6th aves ☎242-4848. Small shop of used, rare and out-of-print books.

Argosy Bookstore, 116 E 59th St between Lexington and Park aves ☎753-4455. Unbeatable for rare books, and also sells clearance books and titles of all kinds, though the shop's reputation means you may well find mainstream works cheaper elsewhere.

Gryphon Bookshop, 2246 Broadway between 80th and 81st sts ☎362-0706. Used and out-of-print books, records, CDs and laser discs. Art books, illustrated books and antique children's books.

Housing Works Used Books Cafe, 126 Crosby St between Houston and Prince sts ☎334-3324. Very cheap books, comfy and spacious. Proceeds benefit AIDS charity.

Ninth Street Books, 436 East 9th St between 1st Ave and Ave A ☎254-4603. General used books.

Pageant Book & Print Shop, 114 W Houston between Thompson and Sullivan sts ☎674-5296. Large selection of secondhand books, prints, engravings and maps.

Ruby's Book Sale, 119 Chambers St ☎732-8676. Civic Center's used bookstore, dealing especially in paperbacks and ancient dog-eared magazines. Excellent value.

Skyline Books, 13 W 18th St between 5th and 6th aves ☎675-4773. Concentration of beat literature, first editions and uncommon art and photography books. Cheerfully does book searches.

Strand Bookstore, 828 Broadway at 12th St ☎473-1452. With around eight miles of books and a stock of over two million, this is the largest book operation in the city – and one of the few survivors in an area once rife with secondhand book stores. As far as recent titles go, you can pick up review copies for half price; more ancient books go for anything from 50¢ up.

Special interest bookstores

Like most large cities, New York has a good number of stores specializing in books on one particular area, from travel and art to more arcane subjects. The following is a fairly selective list.

TRAVEL

The Civilized Traveler, 2003 Broadway between 68th and 69th sts ☎875-0306; 864 Lexington at 65th St ☎288-9190; Two World Trade Center ☎786-0687. Similar to *The Complete Traveler*, with luggage, magazines and other travel accessories..

The Complete Traveler, 199 Madison Ave at 35th St ☎685-9007. Manhattan's premier travel bookshop, excellently stocked, secondhand and new.

Rand McNally Map and Travel Store, 150 E 52nd St between Lexington and 3rd aves ☎758-7488. As much a map shop as a place for guide books, with maps of all the world and specialist ones of New York State and city.

Travelers Choice Bookstore, 11 Greene between Prince and Spring sts ☎941-1535. Affiliated with a travel agency and has a large, well-stocked store.

ART AND ARCHITECTURE

Hacker Art Books, 45 W 57th St ☎688-7600. On the fifth floor.

Printed Matter, 77 Wooster St between Spring and Broome sts ☎925-0325. Retail arm of historic Municipal Art Society. Great space, exhibitions.

Urban Center Books, 457 Madison Ave between 50 and 51st sts ☎935-3592. Architectural book specialists.

Shops and Markets

Shops and Markets

PHOTOGRAPHY, CINEMA AND THEATER

Applause Theater Books, 211 W 71st St at Broadway ☎496-7511. Theater, film, television, screenplays of films – new and used.

Drama Bookshop, 723 7th Ave between 48th and 49th sts on second floor ☎944-0595. Theater books, scripts and publications on all manner of drama-related subjects.

A Photographer's Place, 133 Mercer St just below Prince St ☎431-9358. Lovingly run bookshop specializing in all aspects of photography and out-of-print titles.

Richard Stoddard Performing Arts Books, 18 E 16th St, room 605 ☎645-9576. Purchase a playbill from Broadway's yesteryear hits, plus good out-of-print theater book selection.

Theater Circle, 268 W 44th St ☎391-7075. Theater books, posters, sheet music and souvenirs.

CRIME

Black Orchid, 303 E 81st St ☎734-5980. Secondhand and new novels.

Murder Ink, 2486 Broadway between 92nd and 93rd sts ☎362-8905, and 1465 2nd Ave ☎517-3222. The first bookstore to specialize in mystery and detective fiction in the city, it's still the best, billed as stocking every murder, mystery or suspense title in print, and plenty out.

Mysterious Bookshop, 129 W 56th St between 6th and 7th aves ☎765-0900. The founder started Mysterious Press (now owned by Warner Books). Signed first editions of new and used titles.

Partners in Crime, 44 Greenwich Ave ☎243-0440. Crime novels. Also home to the Cranston and Spade Theater Co. who perform classic radio scripts from the 1940s on Saturday nights. Call ☎462-3027 for info.

SCI-FI AND COMICS

Forbidden Planet, 840 Broadway and 13th St ☎473-1576. Science fiction, fantasy and horror fiction, graphic novels and comics. T-shirts and the latest toys.

Science Fiction Mysteries and More, 140 Chambers St ☎385-8798. Basic sci-fi bookstore.

Science Fiction Shop, 168 Thompson between Bleecker and Houston sts ☎473-3010. New and used science fiction records and books.

St Mark's Comics, 11 St Mark's Place ☎598-9439. Tons of comic books, including underground comics; well known for their large stock. Action figures, trading cards, and a whole room of back issues.

LANGUAGE AND FOREIGN

Irish Book Shop, 580 Broadway, room 1103 ☎274-1923. Irish books and gifts.

Kinokuniya Bookstore, 10 W 49th St at 5th Ave ☎765-1461. The largest Japanese bookstore in NY, with English books on Japan, too.

Lectorum, 137 W 14th St ☎929-2833. Spanish books: fiction, reference, children's and business.

Liberation Bookstore, 421 Lenox Ave and 131st St ☎281-4615. Works from Africa and the Caribbean.

Librairie de France/Libreria Hispanica/The Dictionary Store, 610 5th Ave in the Rockefeller Center Promenade ☎581-8810. Small space housing a wealth of French and Spanish books, a dictionary store with over 8000 dictionaries of more than 100 languages, and a department of teach-yourself language books, records and tapes.

Rizzoli, 31 W 57th St between 5th and 6th aves ☎759-2424. Manhattan branches of the prestigious Italian bookstore chain and publisher, specializing in European publications, with a selection of foreign newspapers and magazines.

SPIRITUALITY

C.G. Jung Center Bookstore, 28 E 39th St ☎697-6433. Jungian thought.

Christian Publications Bookstore, 315 W 43rd St between 8th and 9th aves ☎582-4311. New Christian titles, as well as classics, greeting cards, Christian merchandise; Spanish books as well.

East West Books, 78 5th Ave between 13th and 14th sts ☎243-5994. Bookshop with a mind, body and spirit slant.

J. Levine Jewish Books and Gifts, 5 W 30th St, between 5th and 6th aves ☎695-6888. The ultimate Jewish bookstore.

Logos Bookstore, 1575 York between 83rd and 84th sts ☎517-7292. Christian books and gifts.

Paraclete Book Center, 146 E 74th St at Lexington ☎535-4050. Catholic scholarly books.

Quest, 240 E 53rd St ☎758-5521. New Age books.

St. Paul Book and Media Center, 150 E 52nd St between 3rd and Lexington aves ☎754-1110. Catholic books and tape store operated by the Daughters of St Paul.

Synod Bookstore, 75 E 93rd St ☎369-0288. Specializes in Eastern Orthodox Christian books.

GAY AND LESBIAN

A Different Light, 151 W 19th St between 6th and 7th aves ☎989-4850. Excellent gay/lesbian bookstore, as well as a center for contacts and further information. Has café, and it is open to midnight.

Oscar Wilde Memorial Bookshop, 15 Christopher St ☎255-8097. Gay and lesbian bookstore, with extensive rare book collection, signed and first editions, and framed signed letters from authors including Edward Albee, Gertrude Stein, and Tennessee Williams.

RADICAL

Blackout, 50 Ave B between 3rd and 4th sts ☎777-1967. Anarchist books, magazines and pamphlets as well as a meeting place for the activist community.

Revolution Books, 9 W 19th St ☎691-3345. New York's major left-wing bookshop and contact point. A wide range of

political and cultural books, pamphlets, periodicals and information on current action and events.

St Mark's Bookshop, 31 3rd Ave, between 8th and 9th sts ☎260-7853. Largest and best-known "alternative" bookstore in the city, with a good array of titles on politics, feminism and the environment, literary criticism and journals, as well as more obscure subjects. Good postcards too, and one of the best places to buy radical and art New York magazines. Open late.

MISCELLANEOUS

Audiobook Store, 125 Maiden Lane ☎248-7800, specializing in fiction, and 30 Rockefeller Plaza ☎399-9300, with more business titles. The biggest books-on-tape selection in New York.

Biography Bookshop, 400 Bleecker at 11th St ☎807-8655. Letters, diaries, memoirs.

Kitchen Arts & Letters, 1435 Lexington Ave at 94th St ☎876-5550. Cookbooks and books about food, run by a former cookbook editor.

Military Bookman, 29 E 93rd St between Madison and 5th Ave ☎348-1280. Historical aspects of war, as well as fiction and strategy.

See Hear, 33 St Mark's Place between 2nd and 3rd aves ☎505-9781. Great zines and small press books, mostly about music and radical culture.

Music

Before you arrive, make a list of all those favorite LPs now too scratched to play: CDs in the US are considerably cheaper than in most European countries, usually retailing at around $12–17 – though as low as $10 for new CDs in certain Village shops. Some savings too can be made on musical instruments, electric guitars in particular.

CDs, tapes and records

At the **Virgin Megastore** (1540 Broadway at 45th St) in Times Square you can

Shops and Markets

Shops and Markets

browse endless rows of CDs, get a cappuccino, book a flight on Virgin Atlantic and watch a movie all under one roof if you ever have occasion to do such a thing. This store is vast.

Other general stores to try are:

Tower Records at 692 Broadway at 4th St, 1961 Broadway at 66th St and 725 5th Ave between 56th and 57th sts. Extensive rock, world, jazz and classical sections and a little of everything else. Best of all they're open till midnight daily. This was the largest store in town until the *Virgin Megastore* moved in.

HMV, 2081 Broadway ☎721-5900. Similar to *Tower*. Also at 86th St and Lexington Ave and 34th and 6th Ave (Herald Square).

J&R Music World, 34 Park Row between Beekman and Anne sts ☎238-9000. A large downtown store with a decent selection and good prices.

Record Explosion, 142 W 34th St between 6th and 7th aves ☎714-0450. A smaller chain. Check phone book for more locations.

Sam Goody, 50 W 34th St in the Manhattan Mall ☎594-4330. A chain store with a selection limited to mainstream, popular music. Many more locations; check the phone book for addresses.

Special interest and used

Adult Crash, 66 Ave A between 4th and 5th sts ☎387-0558. Specializing in modern independent and hard to find CDs and vinyl.

Bleecker Bob's, 118 W 3rd St at McDougal St ☎475-9677. Long-established record store specializing in punk and new wave that has sadly of late become something of a tourist rip-off. Best avoid.

Dance Tracks, 91 E 3rd St at 1st Ave, ☎260-8729. Large collection of underground house music.

Finyl Vinyl, 204 E 6th St between 2nd Ave and Cooper Square ☎533-8007. Specializes in records from the 1930s to the 1970s.

Footlight Records, 113 E 12th St between 3rd and 4th aves ☎533-1572. The place for show music – everything from Broadway to Big Band, Sinatra to Merman. A must for record collectors.

The Golden Disc, 239 Bleecker St between Carmine and Cornelia St (just west of 6th Ave) ☎255-7899. Jazz, rock oldies, blues and gospel. This store is in the process of changing names but not locations.

Gryphon Record Shop, 251 W 72nd St between Broadway and West End on second floor ☎874-1588. Specializes in rare LPs.

House of Oldies, 35 Carmine St between Bleecker and 6th Ave ☎243-0500. Just what the name says – oldies but goldies of all kinds. Vinyl only.

Kim's Underground, 144 Bleecker at La Guardia St ☎260-1010. Downstairs. Walk through the video section to the back of the store for the CDs. Specializing in alternative and indie rock (independent labels), *Kim's* has a great sales staff that will play stuff for you and turn you on to new artists.

Other Music, 15 E 4th St between Broadway and Lafayette ☎477-8150. Around the corner from *Tower*, this is an excellent spot for "alternative" CDs, both old and new, that can be hard to find.

Rebel Rebel, 319 Bleecker St between Grove and Christopher sts ☎989-0770. Good supply of old and new vinyl and CDs.

Record Mart in the Subway, near the N train in the Times Square subway station, 1470 Broadway ☎840-0580. One of the best places in the city to find Caribbean – not to mention Central and South American – music. A knowledgeable staff too; good browsing for the enthusiast.

Second Coming, 231 Sullivan St between Bleecker and 3rd Ave ☎228-1313. The place to come for heavy metal and hard-core punk.

Smash, 33 St Mark's Place between 2nd and 3rd aves ☎473-2200. New, discounted and used. Good selection, but the new stock is a bit overpriced.

Sounds, 20 St Mark's Place between 2nd and 3rd aves ☎677-3444. New and used records; good prices and selection.

Strange, 445 E 9th St just off Ave A ☎505-3025. Specializes in techno/ambient/rave music, with lots of British imports. (You'll pay top dollar for the imports, but if you live in the States it's worth it.) The sales staff are very helpful and will play the music for you. There are two other shops specializing in this style of music on E 9th St, **Breakbeat Science** (no. 335) and **Etherea** (no. 441). **Vinylmania**, 60 Carmine St between Bleecker and 6th Ave ☎924-7223. This is where DJs come for the newest, rarest releases, especially of dance music. Hard-to-find imports too, as well as home-made dance tapes.

Musical instruments and accessories

New York's heaviest concentration of **musical instrument stores** is located on one block of W 48th St between 6th and 7th aves: **Manny's**, at 156 ☎819-0576, **Rudy's** at 169 ☎391-1699, and **Alex** at 164 ☎765-7738, are the best known in a row of many. A treat for guitar lovers, though harder to get to, is **Mandolin Brothers** at 629 Forest Ave on Staten Island ☎718/981-8585, which has one of the world's best collections of vintage guitars.

Sheet music

Carl Fischer, 56-62 Cooper Square ☎777-0900. A vast resource for sheet music for all different instruments and vocal arrangements.

Colony Record & Tape Center, 1619 Broadway at 49th St ☎265-2050. Printed sheet music and hard-to-find records.

Sam Ash, 155–160 W 48th St between 6th and 7th aves ☎719-2299. Five adjacent buildings, carrying all instruments, recording equipment, music-driven software and sheet music. One of the world's largest music stores, famous for discounts.

Pharmacies and drugstores

There's a **pharmacy** or **drugstore** on every corner in New York, and during the day it shouldn't be too difficult to find one. If you can't, the *Yellow Pages* have complete listings of places selling medicines and toiletries, listed under "pharmacies." Most pharmacies are open roughly Monday to Saturday 9am–6pm, though many also open on Sunday in busy shopping or residential neighborhoods. Corner **delis** carry some basic necessities; although you'll pay more they are great for late-night needs. Some of the better or more specialized pharmacies are listed below, along with a selection of those that stay open longer hours in case of need.

Everywhere

Duane Reade. A chain of drugstores that has cornered the market on discount medicines, toiletries, cigarettes and basic stationery over much of Manhattan, especially Midtown. Five locations are opened 24 hours a day, 7 days a week: 224 W 57th St and Broadway ☎541-9708; 2465 Broadway at 91st St ☎799-3172; 1279 3rd Ave at 74th St ☎744-2668; 378 6th Ave at Waverly Place ☎674-5257; 485 Lexington at 47th St ☎682-5338.

Other drugstore chains are **McKay, CVS, Genovese, Rite-Aid** and **Valu-Rite**. Check exact locations in the phone book.

Lower Manhattan

Bigelow Pharmacy, 414 6th Ave between 8th and 9th sts ☎533-2700. Established in 1882, this is one of the oldest chemists in the city – and that's exactly how it looks, with the original Victorian shopfittings still in place. Specializes in homeopathic remedies. Open seven days a week.

Kawa Trading Co, 80 Mulberry St ☎964-2017. Herbal Chinese remedies: snakeskin, shark's teeth and the like.

Shops and Markets

Shops and Markets

Midtown Manhattan

Caswell-Massey Ltd, 518 Lexington Ave at 48th St ☎755-2254. The oldest pharmacy in America, and a national chain, selling a shaving cream created for George Washington and a cologne blended for his wife, as well as more mainstream items. Other locations at South Street Seaport, World Trade Center and Trump Tower.

Edward's Drug Store, 225 E 57th St between 2nd and 3rd aves ☎753-2830. General pharmacy, closed on Sunday.

Freeda Vitamins and Pharmacy, 36 E 41st St between 5th and Madison aves ☎685-4980.

Kaufmans, 557 Lexington Ave at 50th St ☎755-2266. Open till midnight. Will deliver for the cost of a two-way cab ride.

Westerly Pharmacy, 911 8th Ave at 55th St ☎247-1096. Closed on Sun.

Upper Manhattan

Alexander Pharmacy, 1751 2nd Ave at 91st St ☎410-0060. Open seven days.

Plaza Pharmacy, 251 E 86th St between 2nd and 3rd aves ☎427-6940. Open daily until 10pm.

Star Pharmacy, 1540 1st Ave at 80th St ☎737-4324. Open seven days.

Windsor Pharmacy, 1419 6th Ave at 58th St ☎247-1538. Open until midnight seven days a week.

Antiques

You'd have to be pretty crazy – or very rich – to come to New York to buy **antiques**: prices are outrageous by European (and most American) standards. New York is, however, the premier antique source in the country, excellent for browsing, with museum-quality pieces available as well as lots of interesting, fairly priced stuff at the junkier end of the market. Sections of the city with a concentration of antique shops are the East Village and West Village, SoHo, Chelsea, lower Broadway, and the Upper East Side. Recently Lafayette St, from SoHo to just above Houston St, has become a prime spot for finding early twentieth-century American design. A handful of shops on E Houston (between Lafayette and Bowery) have decent furniture, with the most interesting pieces at a sidewalk market on the north side of the street where Houston meets Elizabeth.

The Village and around

American Folk Art Gallery, 374 Bleecker between Hudson and Perry sts ☎366-6566. American country painted furniture and hooked rugs, from 1790 to the 1920s.

Carl Victor, 55 E 13th St ☎673-8740. This breathtaking shop carries antique lighting, marble fireplaces and more.

Kitschen, 380 Bleecker between Perry and Charles sts ☎727-0430. Fun vintage housewares.

Susan Parrish, 390 Bleecker between Perry and W 11th sts ☎645-5020. Americana and Indian art.

SoHo

Chameleon, 231 Lafayette St, ☎343-9197. Interesting collection of antique lighting fixtures dating from the nineteenth century up to the 1960's. Many from New York residences.

Cobweb, 116 W Houston St ☎505-1558. Mon–Fri noon–7pm, Sat noon–5pm. Tiled tables, iron beds and cabinets from southern Europe, Egypt, Morocco, Indonesia and Argentina.

Elan, 345 Lafayette Street ☎529-2724. Twentieth-century furniture, mostly mid-century, from top designers.

Historical Materialism, 125 Crosby St ☎431-3424. Eclectic decorative antiques and unique objects from the 1870s to 1920s.

280 Modern, 280 Lafayette St ☎941-5825. Tribal art pre-1920s and American design from 1920s to 1970s.

Urban Archeology, 285 Lafayette St ☎431-6969. Large-scale accessories and furniture, mainly American turn-of-the-century, often rented out for film sets. Great place for browsing.

Chelsea

Annex Antiques Fair and Flea Market, on 6th Ave between 26th and 27th sts. The biggest antiques fair in the city – with 600 dealers of furniture, rugs, collectibles, photos and more – is the hub of a burgeoning antiques neighborhood. Admission $1. Open every Saturday and Sunday, year round. Look one block north, between 26th and 27th sts, for another weekend flea market, and on Sundays you'll find more spillover on 26th St and on 24th St between 6th Ave and Broadway. And in a parking lot on 7th Ave between 25th and 26th aves, the Chelsea Flea Market is starting up.

Chelsea Antiques Building, 110 W 25th St between 6th and 7th aves ☎929-0909. Better quality, better condition, and higher prices than above listings. 150 dealers on 12 floors of exceptional estate treasures. Open daily 10am–6pm. *Café Mozart* on 8th floor.

The Garage, 112 W 25th St between 6th and 7th aves. Just a block away from the Annex Antiques Fair is this market located in a parking garage. In the basement level and first floor are 150 dealers - check out the great vintage eyeglass frames.

Metropolitan Arts and Antiques Pavilion, 110 W 19th St between 6th and 7th aves ☎463-0200. Open a few times a month for special-interest auctions and fairs ranging from vintage fashion to antique toys.

The Showplace, 40 W 25th St between 6th Ave and Broadway ☎633-6063. Indoor market of over 100 dealers of antiques and collectibles plus an espresso bar every Sat & Sun 9am–6pm.

The Upper East Side

American Hurrah, 766 Madison Ave ☎535-1930. Aged Americana mainly. A wonderful selection of quilts, rugs and samplers.

Christie's, 502 Park Ave at 59th St. The premier British auction house. You are welcome here, even if you don't bid. Busy times are autumn and spring. For

schedule of auctions or catalogue, call ☎800/395-6300. Catalogues $10–75. Seating is first come, first served; for evening auctions make reservations. Also *Christie's East* at 219 E 67th St.

56th Street Art & Antiques Center, 160 East 56th St ☎755-4252. Three levels of antique furniture, paintings, objects d'art and more.

Manhattan Art and Antiques Center, 1050 2nd Ave at 55th St ☎355-4400. Around 70 dealers, spread over three floors, stocking a vast assortment of goodies – everything from American quilts to Oriental ceramics, with an emphasis on small items.

Newel Galleries, 425 E 53rd St, east of 1st Ave ☎758-1970. Dazzle your eyes in this six-floor collection of one-of-a-kind big pieces – many for rent.

Sotheby's, York Ave and 72nd St. Mon–Fri 9am–5pm ☎606-7000. The big US auction house: open to the public. Come in for a newsletter, which gives auction schedule for 2–3 months. To have one sent you must subscribe for $25 annually. Previews are 3–4 days beforehand; bring two types of ID to bid. Watch for more affordable Arcade Auctions.

Electronic equipment and cameras: bargains for overseas visitors

Given even a reasonable exchange rate, **electronic goods** of almost any description are extremely cheap in America when compared to prices in Europe. The best place for discount shopping is 7th Ave a little north of Times Square in the 50s, where there are any number of stores selling cameras, stereo equipment, radios and the like; for **cameras**, anywhere in midtown from 30th and 50th sts between Park and 7th aves is the patch. (See overleaf for more listings.) You'll be offered different prices depending on whether you buy the equipment with or without a guarantee (ask for the price with guarantee to prevent any misunderstanding), and it's no use going

Shops and
Markets

Shops and Markets

into a shop without an *exact* idea of the model you want. Be on your guard for fake equipment (usually easily spotted) or inferior products that have had the labels of better makes carefully and illegally applied. Yes, it's a jungle out there.

Don't be tempted by American **TVs or videos** – they won't work on British or most European systems – and make sure that anything you buy is **dual voltage** if you want it to work in a country with 240 volts, like Britain.

Provided the voltage matches and the machine is pulse/tone dial switchable (and you change the plug for a BT one), most **phones and answering machines** will work in the UK – though neither we nor the shops will guarantee that.

Computers, computer peripherals and software are also particularly cheap, but again you may be faced with the voltage compatibility problem, though most quality equipment has switchable voltage. Peripherals (like CD-rom players, laptop computers and modems), usually have an external power supply which you can replace with a domestic model when you return home. One problem that's impossible to overcome is that a bulky machine is hard for customs officials to miss – legally, you are obliged to pay both import duty and VAT when bringing most of the items mentioned above into European Union countries (see opposite). And, though cameras and laptop computers are easily concealed, their serial numbers indicate their place of origin. Don't say we didn't warn you.

Tactics and places

The best advice initially is to get a ballpark figure on the item you desire by checking the newspapers: look in the "Science" section in Tuesday's *NY Times*, and ads in the *Village Voice*. Then shop around as widely as possible, as prices vary hugely – extremely hard-nosed bargaining is the order of the day, and you should be prepared for rudeness followed by a rapid drop in price when you walk out on someone's "best offer." Remember too that you'll get a better price for cash than if you use a credit or charge card.

If all this sounds too daunting, head for one of the chains. One of the largest (though never the cheapest) is **Nobody Beats The Wiz** ☎677-4111, 726 Broadway at Waverly Place and eight other locations. It's a convenient place to shop, and a good place to benchmark prices.

For real bargains, though, head for Canal St, between Essex and Ludlow. Take the F train to the E Broadway stop. On this small block there are three main electronics shops: compare the prices. Bring cash. You cannot return merchandise, but they will exchange it. Save your receipt for showing the manufacturer if repairing defective merchandise. Don't be dismayed by the small space each has – the local warehouse will (usually) ship your request to the store within minutes.

ABC Trading Corporation, 31 Canal St ☎228-5080. Sun–Thurs 10am–6pm, Fri 10am–1pm.

Best Hi Fi, 37 Canal St ☎529-7777. Seven days a week, 10am–7pm. Specializes in cameras, stereo equipment, phones, TVs, selling all major brands like SONY and Panasonic.

Prism Electronics, 28 Canal St ☎227-4088. Seven days a week, 10am–6pm. Specializes in multi-systems, VCRs and TVs, Nintendo and Sega games.

Traditional retailers

Bang & Olufsen, 952 Madison Ave at 75th St ☎879-6161. Incredibly good, high-quality audio and some video, in sleek modern Danish design.

B&H Photo and Video, 119 W 17th St ☎807-7474. For specialty equipment; knowledgeable sales help will take the time to guide you through a buying decision. Closed Saturday.

Cello Music & Film Systems, 41 E 62nd St ☎207-4016. Call for an appointment at this boutique company that sells and installs state-of-the-art A/V equipment. If you are setting up a record label in your basement, come here. Prices are high, but it's worth it.

CompUSA, 420 5th Ave ☎764-6224. This superstore runs a computer camp for kids, training for adults, and carries the largest inventory in the city.

DataVision, 445 5th Ave ☎689-1111. Superstore filled with computer and video equipment.

Grand Central Camera and Computer, 420 Lexington Ave at 44th St ☎986-2270. Huge selection, and the staff speak several languages.

Harvey Electronics, 2 W 45th St at 5th Ave ☎575-5000. Top-of-the-line equipment, sold by experts.

J&R Music and Computer World, 23 Park Row between Beekman and Anne sts ☎238-9000. In this shop down by City Hall, you'll find a good selection and good prices for stereo and computer equipment.

Miscellaneous

The things listed below fit easily into none of the previous categories. They're either shops that might be interesting to visit simply for themselves; or they sell items that are cheaper in New York than in most other countries; or they're places that deserve a mention just because they're offbeat.

ABC Carpet and Home, 888 Broadway at 19th St ☎473-3000. Six floors of antiques and country furniture, knick-knacks, linens and carpets, of course. The set-up is half the fun. Wander to garner decorating ideas.

Arthur Brown Inc, 2 W 46th St between 5th and 6th aves ☎575-5555. America's

largest art suppliers, with a pen department that claims to stock every pen in the known universe.

Body Worship, 102 East 7th between 1st Ave and Ave A ☎614-0124. Fetish fashion and erotica. Get your latex and corsets here.

Condomania, 351 Bleecker St at W 10th St ☎691-9442. A store for the AIDS-conscious 1990s. Condoms of all shapes, sizes, colors and flavors. Some for jokes but most to use.

Gregory's Chateau Hip, 110 Greene St between Prince and Spring sts ☎941-8080. Small, funky but elegant home furnishings.

Hammacher Schlemmer, 147 E 57th St between Lexington and 3rd aves ☎421-9000. Established in 1848, and probably New York's longest-running trivia store. Unique items, both practical and whimsical. Claims to be the first store to sell the pop-up toaster.

J&R Tobacco Corp, 11 E 45th St between 5th and Madison aves ☎983-4160. Self-proclaimed largest cigar store in the world, with an enormous – and affordably priced – range including all the best-known (and some not so known) brands.

Kate's Paperie, 561 Broadway between Prince and Spring sts ☎941-9816. Any kind of paper you could imagine or want. 22,000 square feet of paper in stock from 30 different countries, including great handmade and exotic paper. If you can't find something – ask. They'll even custom-make paper for you. A smaller shop is located at 8 W 13th St, between 5th and 6th aves.

Kiehl Pharmacy, 109 3rd Ave between 13th and 14th sts ☎475-3400. Another ancient pharmacy but with a stock more in keeping with its age, including herbs, roots, dried flowers, oils and spices. Check out the great motorcycle collection in the adjoining room.

Little Rickie, 49 1/2 1st Ave at 3rd St ☎505-6467. A selection of kitsch: "Church of Elvis" fridge magnets, plastic nativity scenes for the dashboard, etc.

Shops and Markets

For toy shops, both new and antique, see Chapter 23, "Kids' New York".

Shops and Markets

Maxilla & Mandible, 451 Columbus Ave between 81st and 82nd sts ☎724-6173. Animal and human bones for collectors, scientists or the curious. Worth a visit even if you're not in the market for a perfectly preserved male skeleton.

Merrimack Publishing Corp, 85 5th Ave at 16th St ☎989-5162. Victorian repro toys, decorations, greetings cards, etc, as well as all manner of useless and trivial items – wind-up toys, yo-yos and the like.

New York Yankees Clubhouse Shop, 393 5th Ave between 36th and 37th sts ☎685-4693. In case you want that "NY" logo on all your clothing. Another location at 110 E 59th St between Park and Lexington aves ☎758-7844.

Our Name is Mud, 1566 2nd Ave between 81st and 82nd sts ☎570-6868. You can buy beautiful handmade pottery here, even an unfinished vessel and paint it with your own personal design. Call for West Side and downtown locations.

Pearl Paint Company, 308 Canal St between Church St and Broadway ☎431-7932. Five floors of artists' supplies including one for house painting. Another contender for title of the country's largest art shop.

Pink Pussycat Boutique, 167 W 4th St between 6th and 7th aves ☎243-0077. All manner of sex toys and paraphernalia.

The Sharper Image, 4 W 57th St between 5th and 6th aves ☎265-2550. Novelty items for yuppies – talking alarm clocks, massage devices and the sort of stuff you find in little catalogues that drop out of Sunday newspaper supplements.

Star Magic, 745 Broadway at E 8th St ☎228-7770. Out-of-this-world space-age gifts – crystals, celestial maps, books, cards and records.

Village Chess Shop, 230 Thompson St between W 3rd and Bleecker St ☎475-9580. Every kind of chess set for every kind of pocket. Usually packed with people playing. Open until midnight.

Markets

New York doesn't really go in for **markets** in a big way: those that exist are mostly highly organized, wholesale-only affairs with retail stores attached, or simply neighborhoods devoted to specific items. Street markets, on the other hand, can't compare with those in Europe.

Greenmarkets

Several days each week, long before sunrise, hundreds of farmers from Long Island and the Hudson Valley set out in their trucks transporting fresh-picked bounty to New York City, where they are joined by bakers, cheesemakers and others at greenmarkets. These are run by the city authorities, roughly between June and November. Usually you'll find apple cider, jams and preserves, flowers and plants, maple syrup, fresh meat and fish, pretzels, popcorn, flour, herbs, honey – just about any and everything that's produced in the rural regions around the city – not to mention occasional live worm composts and baby dairy goats.

Most greenmarkets are open 8am–5pm. To find the one nearest to you, call ☎477-3220, or see the list opposite.

Flea markets and craft fairs

Flea markets have yet to catch on in the States, though New York has more outlets than most American cities for old clothes, antiques and suchlike, as well as any number of odd places – parking lots, playgrounds, or maybe just an extra-wide bit of sidewalk – where people set up to sell their wares.

LOWER MANHATTAN

Essex St Covered Market, on Essex St between Rivington and Delancy. Mon–Fri 9am–6pm. In an old municipal building you'll find a kosher fish market along with Latino groceries and a Chinese green market, reflecting the diverse neighborhood. Also jewelry and clothes.

WHERE TO FIND GREENMARKETS

Manhattan

Bowling Green at Broadway & Battery Place Thurs, year round.

World Trade Center at Church & Fulton sts Tues, June–Nov, and Thurs, year round.

City Hall at Chambers & Centre sts Tues and Fri, year round.

Washington Market Park at Greenwich and Reade sts Sat, year round.

Federal Plaza at Broadway and Thomas sts Fri, year round.

Harrison Street at Greenwich and Harrison sts Wed, year round.

Lt. Petrosino Park at Lafayette & Spring sts Thurs, July–Nov.

Tompkins Square at 7th St & Avenue A Sun, June–Dec.

St. Mark's Church at E 10th St & 2nd Ave Tues, June–Nov.

Abingdon Square at W 12th St and 8th Ave Sat, May–Dec (8am–3pm).

Union Square at E 17th St & Broadway Mon, Wed, Fri and Sat, year round.

Sheffield Plaza at W 57th & 9th Ave Wed and Sat, year round.

W 70th St, between Amsterdam & West End aves, Sat, June–Nov.

Verdi Square at 72nd St and Broadway Sat, June–Nov.

I.S. 44 at W 77th St and Columbus Ave Sun, year round (10am–5pm)

W 97th St between Amsterdam & Columbus aves Fri, June–Dec.

Minisink Townhouse at W 143 St and Lenox Ave Tues, mid-July–Oct.

W 175th St at Broadway Thurs, June–Dec.

Bronx

Lincoln Hospital at E 149th St & Park Ave Tues and Fri, mid-July–Oct.

Poe Park, E 192nd St & Grand Concourse Tues, mid-July–Nov.

Brooklyn

Williamsburg at Havemeyer & Broadway Thurs, July–Oct.

Borough Hall at Court & Remsen sts Tues and Sat, year round.

Albee Square at Fulton St & DeKalb Ave Wed, mid-July–Oct.

Grand Army Plaza at entrance to Prospect Park Wed, May–Nov, and Sat, year round.

Staten Island

St George at St Markís & Hyatt sts Sat, July–Nov.

Shops and Markets

Tower Market, Broadway between W 4th and W 3rd sts, Sat & Sun 10am–7pm. House music, jewelry, clothes, woven goods from South America, New Age paraphernalia and the like.

SoHo Flea Market, 503 Broadway, between Spring and Broome sts, Sat, Sun & holidays, 10am–6pm. Not as established version of above; in fact, can be very slow.

SoHo Antiques and Collectibles Fair, Broadway and Grand Street, Sat & Sun 9am–5pm. Collectibles and crafts.

MIDTOWN MANHATTAN

Annex Weekend Antiques Fair and Flea Market, 6th Ave at 26th St, Sat & Sun 10am–6pm. Surrounded by antique shops, this is the fastest growing fair in New York with 600 vendors. Four other locations in the surrounding two blocks. Admission $1. (See Antiques section for more detailed information.)

Fifth Avenue Pavilion, 5th Ave and 42nd St, Mon–Fri 11am–7pm, Sat & Sun noon–6pm. Was under a tent, now has a small, crowded building to house 25

Shops and Markets

vendors – a mix of world crafts and NY souvenirs.

Grand Central Crafts Market, main waiting room, off 42nd St and Park Ave entrance. Christmas and spring seasons, with the best of New York shops displaying their wares. At other times, check out this beautifully renovated space, often used for off-beat art exhibits.

UPPER MANHATTAN

Antique Flea and Farmers Market, PS 183, E 67th St between 1st and York Ave, Sat 10am–6pm. Usually about 150 indoor and outdoor stalls of fresh food, odd antiques and needlework.

Columbus Circle Market, 58th St and 8th Ave, in front of the Coliseum. 7 days a week, 11am–7pm. Over 20 stalls in a convenient location, but only go if you're in the neighborhood.

Green Flea I.S. 44 Flea Market, Columbus Ave at 77th St. Every Sun (but the 3rd one in Sept) 10am–5.30pm. One of the best and largest markets in the city; antiques and collectibles, new merchandise and a farmer's market.

Malcolm Shabazz Harlem Market, Lenox Ave between 116th and 117th sts. Daily 8am–9pm. A dazzling array of West African cloth, clothes, jewelry, masks, Ashanti dolls and beads. Also sells leather bags, music and black pride T-shirts.

Chapter 25

Directory

AIRLINES Toll-free phone numbers of foreign airlines include: *Air India* ☎1-800/223-7776; *Air New Zealand* ☎1-800/262-1234; *British Airways* ☎1-800/247-9297; *El Al* ☎1-800/223-6700; *Japan Air Lines* ☎1-800/525-3663; *Korean Airlines* ☎1-800/438-5000; *Kuwait Airways* ☎1-800/458-9248; *Qantas Airways* ☎1-800/227- 4500; *Virgin Atlantic Airways* ☎1-800/862-8621. For the toll-free numbers of the major US and Canadian airlines, see p.9.

BRING . . . Film, toiletries, cosmetics, razor blades, all of which can work out more expensive (if just) in the States. And don't forget your credit card – you'll be considered barely human without it.

BUY . . . Good things to take home, especially with a decent exchange rate, include all American-style gear, such as baseball caps, basketball shoes, American Levis, and any kind of trainers. CDs are significantly cheaper, as is almost any photographic or electronic equipment; for the latter, however, make sure the voltages match or can be converted (see overleaf, and read our warnings on p.432).

CONSULATES Australia, 630 5th Ave (☎408-8400); Canada, 1251 6th Ave (☎596-1600); Denmark, 1 Dag Hammerskjöld Plaza (☎223-4545); Ireland, 345 Park Ave (☎319-2555); Netherlands, 1 Rockefeller Plaza (☎246-1429); Sweden, 1 Dag Hammerskjöld Plaza (☎583-2550); United Kingdom, 845 3rd Ave (☎745-0200).

CONTRACEPTION Condoms are available in all pharmacies and delis. If you're on the pill it's obviously best to bring a supply with you; should you run out, or need advice on other aspects of contraception, abortion or related matters, contact Planned Parenthood, 380 2nd Ave (☎677-6474), or the Women's Healthline (☎230-1111).

DATES Written the other way around to Europe. For example, 4.1.99 is not the 4th of January but the 1st of April.

DOGS Dog shit on the sidewalk is much less of a problem than it was, thanks to "pooper scooper" laws that make it illegal not to clear up after your mutt. This is firmly enforced, and wherever you go in the city you'll see conscientious dog owners scraping up after their pets with makeshift cardboard shovels and newspaper, then dumping the evidence in the nearest litter bin. So you might want to think twice before doing your New York friend a favor and walking the dog.

DRUGS While drug use of all kinds is pretty prevalent throughout New York, possession of any "controlled substance" is completely illegal. Should you be found in possession of a small amount of marijuana, you probably won't go to jail – but expect a hefty fine and, as with most run-ins with the law, the possibility of deportation. Street dealers proliferate in Washington Square Park and many other parts of the city; they'll approach you with urgent whispers of "smoke, smoke" or "sens, sens" (short for

Directory

sensamilia, a particular type of marijuana). If anyone offers you a "nickel bag" in the street they're not selling sweeties (probably not even selling real drugs) but touting a $5 deal of a hard drug - possibly crack, a refined form of cocaine which is highly addictive and can make the user extremely violent and aggressive. Periodic crackdowns make buying anything from street dealers an iffy business, and there's no telling that you won't end up with a bag full of oregano either. Best avoided.

ELECTRIC CURRENT 110V AC with two-pronged plugs. Unless they're dual voltage, all British appliances will need a voltage converter as well as a plug adapter. Be warned, some converters may not be able to handle certain high-wattage items, especially those with heated elements.

EMERGENCIES For Police, Fire or Ambulance dial ☎911.

FLOORS In the United States, the ground floor is known as the first floor, the first floor the second . . . so if someone you know lives on the third floor you only have to walk up two flights of stairs. Many older buildings (and some newer ones) count floors 11, 12, 14 . . . skipping the 13th floor out of superstition.

HOMELESSNESS Partly due simply to the lack of affordable accommodation, partly to a policy a few years back of releasing long-term mental patients into the community without any real provision of community care, you will be struck by the number of people living on the streets in New York − a population that is ever-growing.

ID Carry some at all times, as there are any number of occasions on which you may be asked to show it. Two pieces of ID are preferable and one should have a photo − passport and credit card are the best bets.

JAYWALKING This is how New Yorkers cross the streets − ie when they can, regardless of what the light might say, or if there's a light there at all. Hey, you're a grown-up . . . if you want to get run

over, that's your problem. David Dinkins suggested a crackdown after a British consular official complained. There was an outcry, and he is no longer mayor.

LAUNDRY Hotels do it but charge the earth. You're much better off going to an ordinary launderette (here called a laundromat) or dry cleaners, both of which you'll find plenty of in the *Yellow Pages* under "Laundries." Some budget hotels, YMCAs, and hostels also have coin-operated washers and dryers.

LEFT LUGGAGE The most likely place to dump your stuff is Grand Central Station (42nd St and Park Ave; ☎340-2555), where the luggage/lost and found department is open Mon–Fri 7am–8pm, Sat and Sun 10am–6pm, and charges $2 per item per day.

LIBRARIES The real heavyweight is the central reference section of the New York Public Library on 5th Ave at 42nd St (see p.132). However, as the name suggests, while this is a great place to work and its stock of books is one of the best in America and indeed the world, you can't actually take books home at the end of the day. To do this you need to go to a branch of the NYC Public Library (for a full list ask in the reference library) and produce proof of residence in the city. Across the board, library hours have been reduced drastically due to budget cuts. Not a problem for the visitor, but for the city's 9-to-5ers it's a definite bone of contention.

LOST PROPERTY Things lost on buses or on the subway: NYC Transit Authority, at the 34th St/8th Ave Station on the #A, #C and #E line (Mon–Wed & Fri 8am–noon, Thurs 11am–6.45pm; (☎718/625-6200). Things lost on Amtrak: Penn Station (Mon–Fri 7.30am–4pm; ☎630-7389). Things lost in a cab: Taxi & Limousine Commission Lost Property Information Dept, 221 W 41st St (☎302-8294) if you have a receipt or information on the driver or cab; otherwise the police precinct nearest your drop-off point (call ☎374-5000 to find it), or after 48 hours the Police Property Clerk (☎374-5084).

NOTICEBOARDS For contacts, casual work, articles for sale, etc, it's hard to beat the noticeboard just inside the doorway of the *Village Voice* office at 36 Cooper Square (just south of the Astor Place subway stop). Otherwise there are numerous noticeboards up at Columbia University, in the Loeb Student Center of NYU on Washington Square, and in the groovier coffee shops and restaurants in the East Village.

MEASUREMENTS AND SIZES The US has yet to go metric and measurements of length are for the moment in inches, feet, yards and miles, with weight measured in ounces, pounds and tons. Liquid measures are slightly more confusing in that an imperial pint is roughly equivalent to 1.25 American pints, and an American gallon thus only equal to about four-fifths of an imperial one. Add to this the fact that milk and orange juice are sold in quarts, while Coke and its equivalents are sold in litres. Clothing and shoe sizes are easier: women's garment sizes are always two figures less than they would be in Britain. Thus, a British size 12 will be a size 10 in the States, a size 14 a size 12. To calculate shoe sizes in America, simply add 1 to your British size – thus, if you're normally size 8 you'll need a size 9 shoe in New York. See the "Shops and Markets" chapter for more.

PUBLIC HOLIDAYS You'll find most offices, some stores and certain museums closed on the following days: January 1; Martin Luther King's Birthday (third Monday in January); Presidents' Day (third Monday in February); Memorial Day (last Monday in May); Independence Day (July 4); Labor Day (first Monday in September); Columbus Day (second Monday in October); Veterans Day (November 11); Thanksgiving (third Thursday in November); Christmas Day (December 25). Also, New York's numerous parades mean that on certain days – Washington's Birthday, St Patrick's Day, Gay Pride Day, Easter Sunday, and Columbus Day – much of 5th Ave is closed to traffic altogether.

RATS AND ROACHES You'll find both types of pest all around the city, in bigger versions than most anywhere else. Don't worry, though – they may be more afraid of you than you are of them.

SWIMMING POOLS See Chapter 21, *Sports and Outdoor Activities.*

TAX Within New York City you'll pay an 8.25 percent sales tax on top of marked prices on just about everything but the very barest of essentials, a measure brought in to help alleviate the city's 1975 economic crisis, and one which stuck. There is always talk of lifting the tax on clothing, and in 1997, there were even two "No Tax Weeks," when you could buy certain items up to, say, $1000, without any tax.

TIME Five hours behind Britain and Ireland, fourteen to sixteen hours behind East Coast Australia (variations for Daylight Savings Time), sixteen to eighteen hours behind New Zealand (variations for Daylight Savings Time), three hours ahead of West Coast North America.

TERMINALS AND TRANSIT INFORMATION Grand Central Terminal, 42nd St and Park Ave (Metro-North commuter trains ☎532-4900). Pennsylvania Station, 31st–33rd streets and 7th–8th aves (Amtrak ☎1-800/USA-RAIL and ☎582-6875; New Jersey Transit ☎201/762-5100; Long Island Railroad ☎718/217-5477). Port Authority Bus Terminal, 41st St and 8th Ave; George Washington Bridge Bus Terminal, W 179th St and Broadway (both ☎564-8484). Greyhound (☎1-800/231-2222); Trailways (☎1-800/343-9999); Bonanza (☎1-800/556-3815).

TIPPING It won't take long before you realize that tipping, in a restaurant, bar, taxi cab, hotel lobby or toilet, is a part of life in the States – in restaurants in particular, it's unthinkable not to leave something, even if you hated the service. There's not really any way around this, and in most cases you'll find that it's easier to simply cough up the minimum (15 percent of the bill or double the tax,

Directory

Directory

if your math isn't so good) than brave the withering glare of the staff, or worse, the horror-struck looks of your American friends. The secret is to save as much cash as possible by refusing all offers of help in public places – ie carry your own bags up to your room, open all doors yourself, and most importantly, never accept handouts of aftershave or perfume in posh washrooms.

TOILETS Several years ago, the city temporarily waived its ruling against paying public toilets to test a run of self-cleaning 25¢ sidewalk stalls. These proved immensely popular, so naturally they were removed, although if the city ever gets around to repealing the offending law, they'll be back. For now, the only one that remains is in City Hall park across from the Municipal Building, and it's such an unusual sight that you'll see people taking each other's picture going in and out. If you're anywhere else in the city, however, you have to resort to bravely flouting signs like "Restrooms for patrons only." Otherwise check out the lobbies of any of the swanky hotels in Midtown; the Trump Tower, where there are public loos on the Garden level; the New York Public Library at 42nd St and 5th Ave; and the Lincoln Center's Avery Fisher Hall and Library, both of which have several bathrooms. *Barnes & Noble Superstores*, and *Macy's* and *Bloomingdale's* department stores also have accessible and clean restrooms.

TRAVEL AGENTS *Council Travel*, America's principal student/youth travel organization, has an office at 205 E 42nd St (☎822-2700) and deals in airline and other tickets, inclusive tours, car rental, international student cards, guidebooks and work camps. Other agents worth trying are *STA Travel*, 10 Downing St (☎627-3111), and *Nouvelles Frontièrs*, 12 E 33rd St (☎779-0600). Bear in mind that Greyhound passes, etc, are better value if you purchase them before you leave home.

TURKISH BATHS Tenth Street Turkish Baths, 268 E 10th St (☎674-9250). Manhattan's longest-established bath, where you can use the steam rooms and pool for $20; a half-hour massage is $30 extra ($45 for a full hour).

WORSHIP There are regular services and masses at the following churches and synagogues. Anglican (Episcopal): Cathedral of St John the Divine, Amsterdam Ave at 112th St (☎316-7400); St Bartholomew's, 109 E 50th St (☎751-1616); Trinity Church, Broadway and Wall St (☎602-0800). Catholic: St Patrick's Cathedral, 5th Ave at 50th St (☎753-2261). Jewish (Reform): Temple Emanu-el, 5th Ave at 65th St (☎744-1400); Central Synagogue, Lexington Ave at 55th St (☎838-5122). Jewish (Conservative): Park Avenue Synagogue, 87th St at Madison Ave (☎369-2600). Unitarian: Church of All Souls, Lexington Ave at 80th St (☎535-5530).

Contexts

The historical framework

To Europe she was America, to America she was the gateway of the earth. But to tell the story of New York would be to write a social history of the world.

H.G. Wells

Early days and colonial rule

In the earliest times the area that is today New York City was populated by Native Americans. Each tribe had its own territory and lived a settled existence in villages of bark huts, gaining a livelihood from crop planting, hunting, trapping and fishing. In the New York area the Algonquin tribe was the most populous. Survivors of this and other tribes can still be seen at Long Island's **Shinnecook reservation** – as well as remnants of native culture at the upstate Turtle Center for the Native American Indian.

The native lifestyle represented a continuum of several thousand years, one that was to end with the arrival of European explorers. In 1524 **Giovanni da Verrazano**, an Italian in the service of the French King Francis I, arrived, following in the footsteps of Christopher Columbus 32 years earlier. On his ship, the *Dauphane*, Verrazano had set out to find the legendary Northwest Passage to the Pacific; instead he discovered **Manhattan**. "We found a very agreeable situation located within two small prominent hills, in the midst of which flowed to the sea a very great river, which was deep within the mouth; and from the sea to

the hills, with the rising of the tide, which we found at eight feet, any laden ship might have passed." Verrazano returned, "leaving the said land with much regret because of its commodiousness and beauty, thinking it was not without some properties of value," to woo the court with tales of fertile lands and friendly natives, but oddly enough it was nearly a century before the powers of Europe were tempted to follow him.

In 1609 **Hendrik Hudson**, employed by the **Dutch East India Company**, landed at Manhattan and sailed his ship, the *Half-Moone*, as far as Albany. Hudson found that the river did not lead to the Northwest Passage he had been commissioned to discover – but in charting its course for the first time gave his name to the mighty river. "This is a very good land to fall with," noted the ship's mate, "and a pleasant land to see." In a series of skirmishes Hudson's men gave the native people a foretaste of what to expect from future adventurers. Hudson sailed home to England, where he was promptly ticked off for working for the Dutch and sent on another expedition under the British flag: arriving in Hudson Bay, the temperature falling and the mutinous crew doubting his ability as a navigator, Hudson, his son and several others were set adrift in a small boat on the icy waters where, presumably, they froze to death.

The British fear that the Dutch had gained the upper hand in the newly discovered land proved well justified, for they had the commercial advantage and wasted no time in making the most of it. In the next few years the Dutch established a trading post at the most northerly point Hudson had reached, **Fort Nassau**. In 1624, four years after the Pilgrim Fathers had sailed to Massachusetts, thirty families left Holland to become New York's first European settlers, most sailing up to Fort Nassau but a handful – eight families in all – staying behind on a small island they called Nut Island because of the many walnut trees there: today's Governor's Island. Slowly the community grew as more settlers arrived, and the little island became crowded; the decision was made to move to the limitless spaces across the water, and **the settlement of**

Manhattan, an Indian word whose meaning is uncertain, began.

The Dutch gave their new outpost the name **New Amsterdam** and in 1626 **Peter Minuit** was sent out to govern the small community of just over three hundred. Among his first, and certainly more politically adroit, moves was to buy the whole of Manhattan Island from the Indians for trinkets worth 60 guilders (about $25 today); though the other side of the anecdote is even better – for the Indians Minuit dealt with didn't even come from Manhattan, let alone own it. As the colony slowly grew, a string of governors succeeded Minuit, the most famous of them **Peter Stuyvesant** – "Peg Leg Pete," a seasoned colonialist from the Dutch West Indies who'd lost his leg in a scrap with the Portuguese. Under his leadership New Amsterdam doubled in size and population, protected from British settlers to the north by an encircling wall (**Wall Street** today follows its course) and defended by a rough-hewn fort on what is now the site of the Customs House. Stuyvesant also built himself a farm (a *bowerie* in Dutch) a little to the north, that gave its name to the **Bowery**.

Meanwhile the **British** were steadily and stealthily building up their presence to the north. Though initially preoccupied by Civil War at home, they maintained their claim that all of America's East Coast, from New England to Virginia, was theirs, and in 1664 sent Colonel Richard Nicholls to claim the lands around the Hudson that King Charles II had granted to his brother, the Duke of York. To reinforce his sovereignty Charles sent along four warships and landed troops on Nut Island and Long Island. The Dutch settlers had by then had enough of Stuyvesant's increasingly dictatorial rule, especially the high taxation demanded by the nominal owners of the colony, the Dutch West India Company, and so refused to defend Dutch rule against the British. Captain Nicholls's men took New Amsterdam, renamed it **New York** in honor of the duke and settled down to a hundred-odd years of British rule, interrupted but briefly in 1673 when the dutch once more managed to gain the upper hand.

During this period not all was plain sailing. When King James II was forced to abdicate and flee Britain in 1689, a German merchant called **James Leisler** led a revolt against British rule. Unfortunately for Leisler it mustered little sympathy, and he was hanged for treason. Also, by now

black slaves constituted a major part of New York's population, and though laws denied them weapons and the right of assembly, in 1712 a number of slaves set fire to a building near Maiden Lane and killed nine people who attempted to stop the blaze. When soldiers arrived, six of the incendiaries committed suicide and twenty-one others were captured and executed. In other areas primitive civil rights were slowly being established: in 1734 **John Peter Zenger**, publisher of the *New York Weekly Journal*, was tried and acquitted of libeling the British government, establishing freedom for the press that would later bring about the First Amendment to the Constitution.

Revolution

By the 1750s the city had reached a population of 16,000, spread roughly as far north as Chambers Street. As the new community became more confident, so it realized that it could exist independently of the government in Britain. But in 1763 the **Treaty of Paris** concluded the Seven Years' War with France, and sovereignty over most of explored North America was conceded to England. British rule was thus consolidated and the government decided to try throwing its weight about. Within a year, discontent over British rule escalated with the passage of the punitive **Sugar, Stamp and Colonial Currency Acts**. Further resentment erupted over the **Quartering Act**, which permitted British troops to requisition private dwellings and inns, their rent to be paid by the colonies themselves. Ill feeling steadily mounted and skirmishes between soldiers and the insurrectionist **Sons of Liberty** culminated in January 1770 with the killing of a colonist and the wounding of several others. **The Boston Massacre**, in which British troops fired upon taunting protestors, occurred a few weeks later and helped formulate the embryonic feelings of the Revolution.

In a way, New York's role during the **War of Independence** was not crucial, for all the battles fought in and around the city were generally won by the side that lost the war. But they were the first military engagements between the British and American forces after the **Declaration of Independence**, proclaimed to the cheering crowds outside the site of today's **City Hall Park**, who then went off to tear down the statue of George III that stood on the Bowling Green. The British, driven from Boston the previous winter, resolved that New York should be the place where they would reassert their authority over the rebels, and in June and July of 1776 some two hundred ships under the command of **Lord Howe** arrived in New York Harbor. The troops made camp on Staten Island while the commander of the American forces, **George Washington**, consolidated his men, in the hope that the mouth of the harbor was sufficiently well defended to stop British ships from entering it and encircling his troops. But Howe managed to slip two frigates past Washington to moor north of the city and decided to make his assault on the city by land. On August 22 he landed 15,000 men, mainly Hessian mercenaries, on the southwest corner of Brooklyn. His plan was to occupy Brooklyn and launch an attack on Manhattan from there. In the **Battle of Long Island**, Howe's men penetrated the American forward lines at a number of points, the most important engagement taking place at what is today Prospect Park.

The Americans fell back to their positions and as the British made preparations to attack the fortifications, Washington could see that his garrison would be easily defeated. On the night of August 29, under cover of rain and fog, he evacuated his men safely to Manhattan from the ferry slip beneath where the Brooklyn Bridge now stands, preserving the bulk of his forces. A few days later Howe's army set out in boats from Green Point and Newtown Creek in Brooklyn to land at what is now the 34th Street heliport site. The defenders of the city retreated north to make a stand at Harlem Heights, but were pushed back again to eventual defeat at the **Battle of White Plains** in Westchester County (the Bronx), where Washington lost 1400 of his 4000 men. More tragic still was the defense of **Fort Washington**, perched on a rocky cliff 230 feet above the Hudson, near today's George Washington Bridge. Here, rather than evacuate the troops, the local commander made a decision to stand and fight. It was a fatal mistake: they were trapped by the Hudson to the West, and upwards of 3000 men were killed or taken prisoner. Gathering more forces, Washington retreated, and for the next seven years New York was occupied by the British as a garrison town. During this period many of the remaining inhabitants and most of the prisoners taken by the British slowly starved to death.

Lord Cornwallis's **surrender** to the Americans in October 1783 marked the end of the War of Independence, and a month later New York was finally relieved. Washington, the man who had held the American army together by sheer willpower, was there to celebrate, riding in triumphal procession down Canal Street and saying farewell to his officers at **Fraunces Tavern**, a building that still stands at the end of Pearl Street. It was a tearful occasion for men who had fought through the worst of the war years together: "I am not only retiring from all public employments," he declared, "but am retiring within myself."

But that was not to be. New York was now the fledgling nation's **capital** and, as Thomas Jefferson et al framed the Constitution and the role of president of the United States, it became increasingly clear that there was only one candidate for the position. On April 30, 1789, Washington took the oath of president at the site of the **Federal Hall National Memorial** on Wall Street. The federal government was transferred to Philadelphia a year later.

Immigration and civil war

In 1790 the first official census of Manhattan put the population at around 33,000: business and trade were on the increase, with the market under a buttonwood tree on Wall Street being a forerunner to the New York Stock Exchange. A few years later, in 1807, **Robert Fulton** launched the *Clermont*, a steamboat that managed to splutter its way up the Hudson River from New York to Albany, pioneering trade with upstate areas. A year before his death in 1814 Fulton also started a ferry service between Manhattan and Brooklyn, and the dock at which it moored became a focus of trade and eventually a maritime center, taking its name from the inventor.

But it was the opening of the **Erie Canal** in 1825 that really allowed New York to develop as a port. The Great Lakes were suddenly opened to New York, and with them the rest of the country; goods manufactured in the city could be taken easily and cheaply to the American heartlands. It was on this prosperity, and the mass of **cheap labor** that flooded in throughout the nineteenth and early twentieth centuries, that New York – and to an extent the nation – became wealthy. The first waves of **immigrants**, mainly **German** and **Irish**, began to arrive in the midnineteenth century, the latter forced out by the Potato Famine of 1846, the former by the failed Revolution of 1848–49, which had left many

German liberals, laborers, intellectuals and businessmen dispossessed by political machinations. The city could not handle people arriving in such great numbers and epidemics of yellow fever and cholera were common, exacerbated by poor water supplies, insanitary conditions and the poverty of most of the newcomers. But in the 1880s large-scale **Italian** immigration began, mainly of laborers and peasants from southern Italy and Sicily, while at the same time refugees from **eastern Europe** started to arrive – many of them Jewish. The two communities shared a home on the **Lower East Side**, which became one of the worst slum areas of its day. On the eve of the Civil War the majority of New York's 750,000 population were immigrants; in 1890 one in four alone of the city's inhabitants was Irish.

During this period life for the well-off was fairly pleasant and development in the city proceeded apace. Despite a great fire in 1835 that destroyed most of the business district downtown, trade boomed and was celebrated in the opening of the **World's Fair** of 1835 at the Crystal Palace on the site of Bryant Park – an iron and glass building that fared no better than its London namesake, burning down in 1858. In the same year work began on clearing the shantytowns in the center of the island to make way for a newly landscaped open space – a marvellous design by Frederick Law Olmsted and Calvert Vaux that became **Central Park.**

Two years later the **Civil War** broke out, caused by growing differences between the northern and southern states, notably on the issue of slavery. New York sided with the Union (north) against the Confederates (south), but had little experience of the hand-to-hand fighting that ravaged the rest of the country. It did, however, form a focus for much of the radical thinking behind the war, particularly with **Abraham Lincoln**'s influential "Might makes Right" speech from the **Cooper Union Building** in 1860. In 1863 a **conscription law** was passed that allowed the rich to buy themselves out of military service. Not surprisingly this was deeply unpopular, and New Yorkers rioted, burning buildings and looting shops: more than a thousand people were killed in these **Draft Riots**. A sad addendum to the war was the assassination of Lincoln in 1865: when his body lay in state in New York's City Hall, 120,000 people filed past to pay last respects.

The late nineteenth century

The end of the Civil War saw much of the country devastated but New York intact, and it was fairly predictable that the city would soon become the wealthiest and most influential in the nation. Broadway developed into the main thoroughfare, with grand hotels, restaurants and shops catering to the rich; newspaper editors **William Cullen Bryant** and **Horace Greeley** respectively founded the *Evening Post* and the *Tribune*; and the city became a magnet for writers and intellectuals, with **Washington Irving** and **James Fenimore Cooper** among notable residents. By dint of its skilled immigrant workers, its facilities for marketing goods, and the wealth to build factories, New York was also the greatest business, commercial and manufacturing center in the country. **Cornelius Vanderbilt** controlled a vast shipping and railroad empire, and **J.P. Morgan**, the banking and investment wizard, was instrumental in organizing financial mergers that led to the formation of a prototype corporate business. But even bigger in a way was a character who was not a businessman but a politician: **William Marcy Tweed**. From lowly origins Tweed worked his way up the Democratic Party ladder to the position of alderman at the age of 21, eventually becoming chairman of the party's State Central Committee. Surrounded by his own men – the **Tweed Ring** – and aided by a paid-off mayor, "Boss" Tweed took total control of the city's government and finances. Anyone in a position to endanger his money-making schemes was bought off by cash extorted from the huge bribes given by contractors eager to carry out municipal services. In this way $160 million found its way into Tweed's and his friends' pockets. Tweed stayed in power by organizing the speedy naturalization of aliens, who, in repayment, were expected to vote in Tweed and his sidekicks every so often. For his part, Tweed gave generously to the poor, who knew he was swindling the rich but saw him as a Robin Hood figure. As a contemporary observer remarked, "The government of the rich by the manipulation of the poor is a new phenomenon in the world." Tweed's swindles grew in audacity and greed until a determined campaign by **George Jones**, editor of the *New York Times*, and **Thomas Nast**, whose vicious portrayals of Tweed and his henchmen appeared in *Harper's Weekly*, brought him down. The people who kept Tweed in power may not have been able to read or write, but they could understand a cartoon – and Tweed's heyday was over. A committee was established to investigate corruption in City Hall and Tweed found himself in court. Despite a temporary escape to Spain he was returned to the US, and died in Ludlow Street jail – by pleasing irony a building he had commissioned as Chief of Works.

The latter part of the nineteenth century, however, was for some the city's golden age: elevated railways (the **Els**) sprung up to ferry people quickly and cheaply across the city, **Thomas Edison** lit the streets with his new electric light bulb, powered from the first electricity plant on Pearl Street, and in 1883, to the wonderment of New Yorkers, the **Brooklyn Bridge** was opened. Brooklyn itself, along with Staten Island, Queens and the part of Westchester that became the Bronx, became part of the city in 1898. All this commercial expansion stimulated the city's cultural growth; **Walt Whitman** eulogized the city in his poems, and **Henry James** recorded its manners and mores in novels like *Washington Square*. **Richard Morris Hunt** built palaces for the wealthy robber barons along Fifth Avenue, who plundered Europe to assemble art collections to furnish them – collections that would eventually find their way into the newly opened Metropolitan Museum. For the "Four Hundred," the wealthy élite that reveled in and owned the city, New York in the "gay nineties" was a constant string of lavish balls and dinners that vied with each other until opulence became obscenity. At one banquet the millionaire guests arrived on horseback and ate their meals in the saddle; afterwards the horses were fed gourmet-prepared fodder.

Further immigration and building

At the same time, emigration of Europe's impoverished peoples continued unabated, and in 1884 new immigrants from the Orient settled in what became known as **Chinatown**; the following year saw a huge influx of southern Italians to the city. As the Vanderbilts, Astors and Rockefellers lorded it over the mansions uptown, overcrowded tenements led to terrible living standards for the poor. Working conditions were little better, and were compassionately described by police reporter and photographer **Jacob Riis**, whose book *How the Other Half Lives* detailed

the long working hours, exploitation and child labor that kept the city's coffers full.

More Jewish immigrants arrived to cram the Lower East Side, and in 1898 the population of New York amounted to more than three million – the largest city in the world. Twelve years earlier Augustus Bartholdi's **Statue of Liberty** had been finished, holding a symbolic torch to guide the huddled masses; now pressure grew to limit immigration, but still people flooded in. **Ellis Island**, the depot that processed arrivals, was handling two thousand people a day, leading to a total of ten million by 1929, when laws were passed to curtail immigration. By the turn of the century, around half of the city's peoples were foreign-born, and a quarter of the population was made up of German and Irish migrants, most of them people living in slums. The section of Manhattan bounded by the East River, East 14th Street and Third Avenue, the Bowery and Catherine Street was probably the most densely populated area on earth, inhabited by "an underclass" who lived under worse conditions and paid more rent than the inhabitants of any other big city in the world. Yet, in 1900, J.P. Morgan's United States Steel Company became the first billion-dollar corporation.

The early 1900s saw some of this wealth going into adventurous new architecture. SoHo had already utilized the **cast-iron building** to mass-produce classical facades, and the **Flatiron Building** of 1902 announced the arrival of what was to become the city's trademark – the skyscraper. On the arts front **Stephen Crane**, **Theodore Dreiser** and Edith Wharton used New York as the subject for their writing, **George M. Cohan** was the Bright Young Man of Broadway, and in 1913 the **Armory exhibition** of Modernist painting by Picasso, Duchamp and others caused a sensation. Meantime the skyscrapers were pushing higher and higher, and in the same year a building that many consider the *ne plus ultra* of the genre, the **Woolworth Building**, was opened. Also that year **Grand Central Terminal** celebrated New York as the gateway to the continent.

The first two decades of the century saw a further wave of immigration, made up chiefly of Jews. In that period one-third of all the Jews in eastern Europe arrived in New York and upwards of 1.5 million of them settled in New York City, primarily in the Lower East Side. Despite advances in public building, caused by the outcry that followed Jacob Riis's reports, the area could not cope with a population density of 640,000 per square mile, and the poverty and inhuman conditions reached their worst as people strove to better themselves by working in the sweatshops of Hester Street. Workers, especially those in trades dominated by Jewish immigrants from socialist backgrounds, began to strike to demand better wages and working conditions. Most of the garment manufacturers, for example, charged women workers for their needles and the hire of lockers, and handed out swingeing fines for spoilage of fabrics. Strikes of 1910–11 achieved only limited success, and it took disaster to rouse public and civic conscience. On March 25, 1911, just before the **Triangle Shirtwaist Factory** at Washington Place was about to finish work for the day, a fire broke out. The workers were trapped on the tenth floor and 146 of them died (125 were women), mostly by leaping from the blazing building. Within months the state had passed 56 factory reform measures, and unionization spread through the city.

The war years: 1914–45

With America's entry into World War I in 1917 New York benefited from wartime trade and commerce. At home, perhaps surprisingly, there was little conflict between the various European communities crammed into the city. Although Germans comprised roughly one-fifth of the city's population, there were few of the attacks on their lives or property that occurred elsewhere in the country.

The postwar years saw one law and one character dominating the New York scene: the law was **Prohibition**, passed in 1920 in an attempt to sober up the nation; the character was **Jimmy Walker**, elected mayor in 1925 and who led a far from sober lifestyle. "No civilized man," said Walker, "goes to bed the same day he wakes up," and during his flamboyant career the Jazz Age came to the city. In speakeasies all over town the bootleg liquor flowed and writers as diverse as **Damon Runyon**, **F. Scott Fitzgerald** and **Ernest Hemingway** portrayed the excitement of the times. With the **Wall Street** crash of 1929 (see Chapter 2, *The Financial District and Civic Center*), however, the party came to an abrupt end. The Depression began and Mayor Walker was flushed away with the torrent of civic corruption and malpractice that the changing times had uncovered and unleashed.

By 1932 approximately one in four New Yorkers was unemployed, and shantytowns, blackly known as "Hoovervilles" after the then president, had sprung up in Central Park to house the workless and homeless. Yet during this period three of New York's most opulent – and most beautiful – skyscrapers were topped out: the **Chrysler Building** in 1930, the **Empire State** in 1931 (though it was to stand near-empty for years) and in 1932 the **Rockefeller Center** – all very impressive, but of little immediate help to those in Hooverville, Harlem or other depressed parts of the city. It fell to **Fiorello LaGuardia**, Jimmy Walker's successor as mayor, to take over the running of the crisis-strewn city. He did so with ruthless tax and rationalization programs that, surprisingly, won him the approval of the people in the street: Walker's good living had got the city into trouble, reasoned voters; hard-headed, straight-talking LaGuardia would get it out. Moreover President Roosevelt's **New Deal** supplied funds for roads, housing and parks, the latter undertaken by the controversial Parks Commissioner **Robert Moses**. Under LaGuardia and Moses, the most extensive public housing program in the country was undertaken; the Triborough, Whitestone and Henry Hudson bridges were completed; fifty miles of new expressway and five thousand acres of new parks were opened; and, in 1939, Mayor LaGuardia opened the airport that carries his name.

LaGuardia ran three terms as mayor, taking the city into the **war years**. The country's entry into World War II in 1941 had few direct effects on New York City: lights were dimmed, two hundred Japanese were interned on Ellis Island and guards placed on bridges and tunnels. But, more importantly, behind the scenes experiments taking place at Columbia University split the uranium atom, giving a name to the **Manhattan Project** – the creation of the first atomic weapon.

The postwar years

Though the beleaguered black community of Harlem erupted into looting and violence in 1943, the city maintained its pre-eminent position in the fields of finance, art and communications, both in America and the world, its intellectual and creative community swollen by refugees escaping the Nazi threat to Europe. When the **United Nations Organization** was seeking a permanent home, New York was the obvious choice: lured by Rockefeller-donated land, the UN began the building of the Secretariat in 1947.

The building of the UN complex, along with the boost in the economy that followed the war, brought about the development of midtown Manhattan. First off in the race to fill the once-residential Park Avenue with offices was the **Lever House** of 1952, quickly followed by skyscrapers like the **Seagram Building** that give the area its distinctive look. Downtown, the **Stuyvesant Town** and **Peter Cooper Village** housing projects went ahead, along with many others all over the city. As ever, there were plentiful scandals over the financing of the building, most famously concerning the **Manhattan Urban Renewal Project** on the Upper East Side.

A further scandal, this time concerning organized crime, ousted Mayor **William O'Dwyer** in 1950: he was replaced by a series of uneventful characters who did little to stop the gradual decline that had begun in the early 1950s as a general stagnation set in among the country's urban centers. New York fared worst: immigration from Puerto Rico had once more crammed East Harlem and the Lower East Side, and the nationwide trend of black migration from poorer rural areas was also magnified here. Both groups were forced into the ghetto area of Harlem, unable to get a slice of the city's wealth. Racial disturbances and riots occurred in what had for two hundred years been one of the more liberal of American cities. One response to the problem was a general exodus of the white middle classes – the **Great White Flight** as the media gleefully labeled it – out of New York. Between 1950 and 1970 more than a million families left the city. Things went from bad to worse during the 1960s with **race riots** in Harlem, Bedford-Stuyvesant and East Harlem.

The **World's Fair** of 1964 was a white elephant to boost the city's credit in the financial world, but on the streets the call for civil liberties for blacks and protest against US involvement in Vietnam were, if anything, stronger than in the rest of the country. What little new building went up during this period seemed wilfully to destroy much of the best of earlier traditions: a new **Madison Square Garden** was built on the site of the grandly Neoclassical **Pennsylvania Station**, and the **Singer Building** in the Financial District was demolished for an ugly skyscraper. In Harlem municipal investment stopped altogether and the community stagnated.

The 1970s and 1980s

Manhattan reached **crisis point** in 1975. By now the city was spending more than it received in taxes – billions of dollars more. In part, this could be attributed to the effects of the White Flight: companies closed their headquarters in the city when offered lucrative relocation deals elsewhere, and their white-collar employees were usually glad to go with them, thus doubly eroding the city's tax base. Even after municipal securities were sold, New York ran up a debt of $13,000 million. Essential services, long shaky through underfunding, were ready to collapse. The mayor who oversaw this farrago, **Abraham Beame**, was an accountant.

Three things saved the city: the **Municipal Assistance Corporation** (aka the **Big Mac**), which was formed to borrow the money the city could no longer get its hands on; the election of **Edward I. Koch** as mayor in 1978; and, in a roundabout way, the plummeting of the dollar on the world currency market following the oil price rises of the 1970s. This last effect, combined with cheap transatlantic airfares, brought European tourists into the city en masse for the first time, and with them came money for the city's hotels and service industries. Mayor Koch, cheerfully saying "Isn't it terrible?" to whatever he could not immediately put right, and asking "How am I doing?" each time he scored a success, gained the appreciation of New Yorkers, ever eager to look to their civic leaders for help or blame.

The slow reversal of fortunes coincided with the completion of two face-saving building projects: though, like the Empire State Building, it long remained half empty, the **World Trade Center** was a gesture of confidence by the Port Authority of New York and New Jersey, which financed it; and in 1977 the **Citicorp Center** added modernity and prestige to its environs on Third Avenue.

From the mid-1970s slump the city in some respects went from strength to strength. Ed Koch managed simultaneously to offend liberal groups and win the electoral support of ethnic groups, and despite the death of his friend and supporter Queens borough president **Donald Manes** (who committed suicide when an investigation into the city's various debt-collecting agencies was announced) he was probably the most popular mayor since LaGuardia – some measure of his adroitness as a politician.

Into the 1990s

A spate of building gave the city yet more fabulous architecture, notably **Battery City Park** downtown, while master builder Donald Trump provided housing for the super-wealthy. But the popularity of Ed Koch waned. Many middle-class constituents considered Koch to have only rich property-barons' interests at heart; he also alienated a number of minorities – particularly blacks – with off-the-cuff statements that he was unable to bluff away. And although he was not directly implicated, the scandals in his administration, beginning with the suicide of Donald Manes and continuing with the indictment (though she was acquitted) for bribery of another prominent friend, former Arts Commissioner Bess Myerson, took their political toll.

In 1989, Koch lost the Democratic nomination for the mayoral elections to **David Dinkins**, a 61-year-old, black ex-marine and borough president of Manhattan. In a toughly fought election the same year, Dinkins beat Republican Rudolph Giuliani, a hard-nosed US attorney (whose role as leader of the prosecution in a police corruption case was made into the film *Prince of the City*). But even before the votes were counted, pundits were forecasting that the condition of the city was beyond any mayoral healing.

By the end of the 1980s New York was slipping hard and fast into a **massive recession**: in 1989 the city's budget deficit ran at $500 million; of the 92 companies that had made the city their base in 1980, only 53 were left, the others having moved to cheaper pastures; and one in four New Yorkers was officially classed as poor – a figure unequaled since the Depression. The first black to hold the office, David Dinkins oversaw his first year as mayor reasonably well: the city's **Board of Estimate** had been declared unconstitutional by the Supreme Court (it violated the one person, one vote principle), and was abolished and replaced by a beefier City Council. Dinkins used his powers to quell racial unrest that had seemed about to explode in the spring, and skillfully passed a complex budget through the Council.

The date from which Dinkins's – and to some extent the city's – slide commenced was during the first week of the US Open tennis tournament in summer 1990. On his way to the match, Brian Watkins, a tennis fan from Utah, was stabbed to death in a subway station by a group of muggers while trying to protect his mother. Instead of holding a Koch-style "What is this city coming to?" press conference, Dinkins issued a statement saying that the media were exaggerating the importance of the murder – and then boarded a police helicopter to fly to the tennis event. As was predictable, the press latched onto this immediately, and Dinkins fell swiftly, and seemingly irrevocably, from popular favor, becoming known as the man "to whom everything sticks but praise."

From the summer on, the city's fortunes went into free fall. The unions went on the offensive when it was learned the city intended to lay off 15,000 workers; crime – especially related to the sale of crack (a cheap, cocaine-derived stimulant) – escalated; business failed. By the end of the year the city's budget deficit had reached $1.5 billion and city creditors were threatening to remove support for municipal borrowing unless the figure was reduced drastically.

Throughout 1991 the previous year's financial disasters started to have a knock-on effect on the city's **ordinary people**: homelessness increased as city aid was cut back, schools became no-go zones with armed police and metal detectors at the gates (fewer than half of high school kids in the city graduate, a far smaller proportion than elsewhere in the United States), and a garbage workers' strike in May left piles of rubbish rotting on the streets. Once again, New York seemed to have hit rock bottom, and this time there was no obvious solution. Unlike in 1976, the state government refused to bail the city out with aid loans; and, as far as the federal government was concerned, the coffers ran out for New York long ago. Neither did the new Clinton administration promise much for the city, other than the indirect hope that Hillary Clinton's much-vaunted reform of the health system would help the city's socially disadvantaged. In the 1993 mayoral elections, David Dinkins narrowly lost to the brash Republican lawyer **Rudolph Giuliani**. New York, traditionally a firmly Democrat city, had wanted a change, and with Giuliani – the city's first Republican mayor in 28 years – they got it.

Recent years

Though it might have been coincidental, Giuliani's first term helped usher in a dramatic upswing in New York's prosperity. A *New York Times* article described 1995 as "the best year in recent memory for New York City." Even the pope

Architectural chronology

1625	First permanent **Dutch settlement** on Manhattan.	No buildings remain of the period. **Wall Street** marks the settlement's defensive northern boundary in 1653.
Late 18th c.	New York under **British colonial rule**.	**St Paul's Chapel** (1766) built in Georgian style.
1812	British blockade of Manhattan.	**City Hall** built.
1825	Opening of **Erie Canal** increases New York's wealth.	**Fulton Street** dock and market area built. Greek Revival row houses popular – eg **Schermerhorn Row, Colonnade Row, St Mark's Place, Chelsea.** Of much Federal-style building, few examples remain: The **Abigail Adams Smith House**, the **Morris-Jumel Mansion** and **Gracie Mansion** the most notable.
1830–50	First wave of **immigration**, principally German and Irish.	The **Lower East Side** developed. **Trinity Church** built (1846) in English Gothic style, **Federal Hall** (1842) in Greek Revival.
1850–1900	**More immigrants** (more Irish and Germans, later Italians and east European Jews) settle in Manhattan. **Industrial development** brings extreme wealth to individuals. The **Civil War** (1861–65) has little effect on the city.	Cast-iron architecture enables buildings to mimic grand Classical designs cheaply. Highly popular in SoHo, eg the **Haughwout Building** (1859). Large, elaborate mansions built along Fifth Avenue for America's new millionaires. **Central Park** opened (1876). The **Brooklyn Bridge** (1883) links Gothic with industrial strength; **St Patrick's Cathedral** (1879) and **Grace Church** (1846) show it at its most delicate. **Statue of Liberty** unveiled (1886).
Early 20th c.		The **Flatiron Building** (1902) is the first skyscraper. Much civic architecture in the Beaux Arts Neoclassical style: **Grand Central Terminal** (1919), **New York Public Library** (1911), **US Customs House** (1907), **General Post Office** (1913) and the **Municipal Building** (1914) are the finest examples. The **Woolworth Building** (1913) becomes Manhattan's "Cathedral of Commerce."
1915		The **Equitable Building** fills every square inch of its site on Broadway, causing the first zoning ordinances to ensure a degree of setback and allow light to reach the streets.
1920	**Prohibition** law passed. Economic confidence of the 1920s brings the **Jazz Age**.	Art Deco influences show in the **American Standard Building** (1927) and the **Fuller Building** (1929).
1929	**Wall Street Crash**. America enters the **Great Depression**.	Many of the lavish buildings commissioned and begun in the 1920s reach completion. Skyscrapers combine the monumental with the decorative: **Chrysler Building** (1930), **Empire State Building** (1930), **Waldorf Astoria Hotel** (1931) and the **General Electric Building** (1931). The **Rockefeller Center**, the first exponent of the idea of a city-within-a-city, is built through the decade. The **McGraw-Hill Building** (1931) is self-consciously modern.
1930s	The **New Deal** and **WPA** schemes attempt to reduce unemployment.	Little new building other than housing projects. WPA murals decorate buildings around town, notably in the **New York Public Library** and **County Courthouse**.

Architectural chronology continued

1941	America enters **World War II**.	New zoning regulations encourage the development of the setback skyscraper: but little is built during the war years.
1950	**United Nations Organization** established.	The **UN Secretariat** (1950) introduces the glass curtain wall to Manhattan. Similar Corbusier-influenced buildings include the **Lever House** (1952) and, most impressively, the **Seagram Building** (1958), whose plaza causes the zoning regulations to be changed in an attempt to encourage similar public spaces. The **Guggenheim Museum** (1959) opens.
1960s	**Protest movement** stages demonstrations against US involvement in Vietnam.	Much early-1960s building pallidly imitates the glass box skyscraper. The **Pan Am** (1963) building attempts something different, but more successful is the **Ford Foundation** (1967). In the hands of lesser architects, the plaza becomes a liability. New **Madison Square Garden** (1968) is built on the site of the old Penn Station. The minimalist **Verrazano-Narrows Bridge** (1964) links Brooklyn to Staten Island.
1970s	Mayor Abraham Beame presides over **New York's decline**. City financing reaches **crisis point** as businesses leave Manhattan.	The **World Trade Center Towers** (1970) add a soaring landmark to the lower Manhattan skyline. The **Rockefeller Center Extensions** (1973–74) clone the glass-box skyscraper. Virtually no new corporate development until the **Citicorp Center** (1977) adds new textures and profile to the city's skyline. Its popular atrium is adopted by later buildings.
1975	Investment in the city increases.	**One UN Plaza** adapts the glass curtain wall to skilled ends.
1978	**Corporate wealth returns** to Manhattan. **Ed Koch elected mayor**.	The **IBM Building** (1982) shows the conservative side of modern architecture; postmodernist designs like the **AT&T Building** (1983) and **Federal Reserve Plaza** (1985) mix historical styles in the same building.
1980s	**Ed Koch returned as mayor**.	**Statue of Liberty** restoration completed. The mixed-use **Battery Park City** opens to wide acclaim.
1986	Wall Street **crashes**; Dow Jones index plunges 500 points in a day.	Property market takes a dive. **Equitable Building** on 7th Ave opens.
1989	**Ed Koch** loses Democratic nomination to **David Dinkins**, who goes on to become NYC's first black mayor.	**Rockefeller Center** sold to Japanese. **RCA Building** renamed **General Electric Building**.
1990	Major **recession** hits New York.	**Ellis Island** museum of immigration opens to public.
1991	NYC's **budget deficit** reaches record proportions.	**Guggenheim Museum** reopens with new extension.
1993	Republican **Rudolph Giuliani** bests Dinkins in mayoral race.	Famed **Ed Sullivan Theater** given complete overhaul.
1996	**NY Yankees** in first World series in almost 20 years	**SoHo Grand** opens – the first downtown hotel to be built for decades.
1997	**Murder rates** drop for fourth consecutive year.	Redevelopment of **Times Square**; opening of Battery Park City's **Museum of Jewish Heritage**.

came to town and called New York "the capital of the world." The city's reputation flourished, with remarkable decreases in crime statistics and a revitalized economy that helped spur the tourism industry to some of its best years ever.

Giuliani emerged as a very proactive mayor, riding the coattails of the movement to downsize government that has swept America in the last few years. Though the long-term effects of city agency reorganization and cutbacks and so-called work-fare reforms still aren't known, thus far the mayor has reduced crime and has happily taken on the scandal-ridden Board of Education. However popular Giuliani seems to be, he does tend to make political friends and enemies in equal measure – and with equal energy. His most famous *faux pas* came when he actively supported long-time Democratic New York State governor Mario Cuomo over his own party's eventual winner **George Pataki** in the 1994 elections. A red-faced Giuliani had to kowtow to Republicans so that New York City did not get its snout pushed out of the trough by State authorities. In the spring of 1996, Giuliani's constant battles with Police Commissioner Bratton, whose policies were widely considered responsible for the lower crime figures, forced the popular "Top Cop" into resigning. Many said that Giuliani simply didn't like Bratton sharing the spotlight. And in this showy town, that's what it's all about.

The spotlight and the high times have continued to grow for Giuliani and New York. More "improvements" in the city – the cleaning up of previously crime-ridden neighborhoods like Times Square, the influx of chain stores into Harlem – have only boosted the city's coffers, and the mayor's popularity. There were some hard knocks for the city in 1997, worst of all when a gunman went wild on top of the Empire State Building, killing one tourist and injuring seven others. A bitter fight over rent control (it was salvaged) in the spring, and shocking allegations of police brutality in the summer, followed, along with continued concern about overcrowding in the pinched school system. Still, Giuliani had an easy time of it come November's election, with barely a challenge mounted by his Democratic opponent, Ruth Messinger, and for the moment New York remains on cruise control, riding the feel-good wave toward the new millennium.

Twentieth-century American art

This is no more than a brief introduction to a handful of American painters; for more detailed appraisals, both of the century's major movements and specific painters, see "Books."

Twentieth-century American art begins with **The Eight**, otherwise known as the **Ashcan School**, a group of artists who were painting in New York in the first decade of this century. Led by Robert Henri, many of them worked as illustrators for city newspapers, and they tried to depict modern American urban life – principally in New York City – as honestly and realistically as possible, in much the same way as earlier painters had depicted nature. Their exhibitions, in 1908 and 1910, were, however, badly received, and most of their work was scorned for representing subjects not seen as fit for painting. Paralleling the work of the Ashcan School was that of the group that met at the **Photo-Secession Gallery** of the photographer Alfred Stieglitz on Fifth Avenue. They were more individual, less concerned with social themes than expressing their own individual styles, but were equally unappreciated. Art, for Americans, even for American critics, was something that came from Europe, and in the early years of the twentieth century attempts to Americanize it were regarded with suspicion.

Change came with the **Armory Show** of 1913: an exhibition, set up by the remaining Ashcan

artists (members of the new Association of American Painters and Sculptors), to bring more than 1800 European works together and show them to the American public for the first time. The whole of the French nineteenth century was represented at the show, together with Cubist and Expressionist painters, and, from New York, the work of the Ashcan painters and the Stieglitz circle. It was visited by over 85,000 people in its month-long run in New York, and plenty more caught it as it toured America. The immediate effect was uproar. Americans panned the European paintings, partly because they resented their influence but also since they weren't quite sure how to react; the indigenous American artists were criticized for being afraid to adopt a native style; and the press fanned the flames by playing up to public anxieties about the subversive nature of modern art. But there was a positive effect: the modern art of both Europe and America became known all over the continent, particularly abstract painting. From now on American artists were free to develop their own approach.

The paintings that followed were, however, far from abstract in style. The Great Crash of 1929 and subsequent Depression led to the school of **Social Realism** and paintings like **Thomas Hart Benton**'s *America Today* sequence (now in the Equitable Center at 757 Seventh Ave): a vast mural that covered, in realistic style, every aspect of contemporary American life. The New Deal and the resultant **Federal Art Project** of the WPA supported many artists through the lean years of the 1930s by commissioning them to decorate public buildings, and it became widely acknowledged that not only were work, workers and public life fit subjects for art, but also that artists had some responsibility to push for social change. Artists like **Edward Hopper** and **Charles Burchfield** sought to re-create, in as precise a way as possible, American contemporary life, making the particular (in Hopper's case empty streets, lone buildings, solitary figures in diners) "epic and universal." Yet while Hopper and Burchfield can be called great artists in their own right, much of the work of the time, particularly that commissioned as public works, was inevitably dull and conformist, and it wasn't long before movements were afoot to inject new life into American painting. It was the beginning of abstraction.

With these ideas so, the center of the visual art world gradually began to shift. The founding of the **Museum of Modern Art**, and also of the **Guggenheim Museum** some years later, combined with the arrival of many European artists throughout the 1930s (Gropius, Hans Hofmann, the Surrealists) to make New York a serious rival to Paris in terms of influence. **Hans Hofmann** in particular was to have considerable influence on New York painters, both through his art school and his own boldly Expressionistic works. Also, the many American artists who had lived abroad came back armed with a set of European experiences which they could couple with their native spirit to produce a new, indigenous and wholly original style. First and most prominent of these was **Arshile Gorky**, a European-born painter who had imbibed the influences of Cézanne and Picasso – and, more so, the Surrealists. His technique, however, was different: not cold and dispassionate like the Europeans but expressive, his paintings textured and more vital. **Stuart Davis**, too, once a prominent member of the Ashcan School, was an important figure, his paintings using everyday objects as subject matter but jumbling them into abstract form – as in works like *Lucky Strike*, which hangs in the Museum of Modern Art. Another artist experimenting with abstract forms was **Georgia O'Keefe**, best known for her depictions of flowers, toned in pastelly pinks and powder blues. These she magnified so they became no more than unidentified shapes, in their curves and ovular forms curiously erotic and suggestive of fertility and growth. The Whitney Museum holds a good stock of her work.

The **Abstract Expressionists** – or **The New York School** as they came to be known – were a fairly loose movement, and one that splits broadly into two groups: the first created abstractions with increasing gusto and seemingly endless supplies of paint, while the rest employed a more ordered approach to their work. Best known among the first group is **Jackson Pollock**, a farmer's son from Wyoming who had studied under Thomas Hart Benton in New York and in the 1930s was painting Cubist works reminiscent of Picasso. Pollock considered the American art scene to be still under the thumb of Europe, and he deliberately set about creating canvases that bore little relation to anything

that had gone before. For a start his paintings were huge, and it was difficult to tell where they ended; in fact Pollock would simply determine the edge of a composition by cutting the canvas wherever he happened to feel was appropriate at the time – a large-scale approach that was much imitated and in part determined by the large factory spaces and lofts where American artists worked. Also, it was a reaction against bourgeois (and therefore essentially European) notions of what a painting should be: the average Abstract Expressionist painting simply couldn't be contained in the normal collector's home, and as such was at the time impossible to classify. Often Pollock would paint on the floor, adding layers of paint apparently at random, building up a dense composition that said more about the action of painting than any specific subject matter: hence the term "action painting," which is invariably used to describe this technique. As a contemporary critic said: with Pollock the canvas became "an arena in which to act – rather than as a space in which to reproduce...."

Similar to Pollock in technique, but less abstract in subject matter, was the Dutch-born artist **Willem de Kooning**, whose *Women* series clearly attempts to be figurative – as do a number of his other paintings, especially the earlier ones, many of which are in the Museum of Modern Art. Where he and Pollock are alike is in their exuberant use of paint and color, painted, splashed, dripped or scraped on to the canvas with a palette knife. **Franz Kline** was also of this "gestural" school, though he cut down on color and instead covered his canvas with giant black shapes against a stark white background: bold images reminiscent of Chinese ideograms and Oriental calligraphy. **Robert Motherwell**, who some have called the leading light of the Abstract Expressionist movement (in so far as it had one), created a similar effect in his *Elegies to the Spanish Republic*, only here his symbols are drawn from Europe and not the East – and unlike Abstract Expressionist paintings they gain their inspiration from actual events. Again, for his work the Whitney and MoMA are good sources.

Foremost among the second group of Abstract Expressionists was **Mark Rothko**, a Russian-born artist whose work is easy to recognize by its broad rectangles of color against a single-hued background. Rothko's paintings are more controlled than Pollock's, less concerned with exuding their own painterliness than with expressing, as Rothko put it, "a single tragic idea." Some have called his work mystic, religious even, and his paintings are imbued with a deep melancholy, their fuzzy-edged blocks of color radiating light and, in spite of an increasingly lightened palette, a potent sense of despair. Rothko, a deeply unhappy man, committed suicide in 1970, and it was left to one of his closest friends, **Adolf Gottlieb**, to carry on where he left off. With his "pictographs" Gottlieb spontaneously explored deep psychological states, covering his canvases with "Native" American signs. He also used a unique set of symbols of cosmos and chaos – disks of color above a blotchy earth – as in his *Frozen Sounds* series of the early 1950s, currently in the Whitney collection.

The Abstract Expressionists gave native American art stature worldwide and helped consolidate New York's position as center of the art world. But other painters weren't content to follow the emotional painting of Pollock and Rothko et al, and toned down the technique of excessive and frenzied brushwork into impersonal representations of shapes within clearly defined borders – **Kenneth Noland**'s *Target* and the geometric (and later three-dimensional) shapes of **Frank Stella** being good examples. **Ad Reinhardt**, too, honed down his style until he was using only different shades of the same color, taking this to its logical extreme by ultimately covering canvases with differing densities of black.

Barnett Newman is harder to classify, though he is usually associated with the Abstract Expressionists, not least because of the similarities to Rothko of his bold "fields" of color. But his controlled use of one striking tone, painted with only tiny variations in shade, and cut (horizontally or vertically) by only a single contrasting strip, give him more in common with the trends in art that followed. **Helen Frankenthaler** (and later **Morris Louis**) took this one stage further with pictures like *Mountains and Sea*, which by staining the canvas rather than painting it lends blank areas the same importance as colored ones, making the painting seem as if it were created by a single stroke. With these two artists, color was the most important aspect of painting, and the canvas and the color were absorbed as one. In his mature period Louis began – in the words of a contemporary critic – "to think, feel and conceive almost exclusively in terms of open color." And as if in rejection of any other method, he destroyed most of his work of the previous two decades.

With the 1960s came **Pop Art**, which turned to America's popular media for subject – its films, TV,

advertisements and magazines – and depicted it in heightened tones and colors. **Jasper Johns**'s *Flag* bridges the gap, cunningly transforming the Stars and Stripes into little more than a collection of painted shapes, but most Pop Art was more concerned with monumentalizing the tackier side of American culture: **Andy Warhol** did it with Marilyn Monroe and Campbell's Soup; **Claes Oldenburg** by re-creating everyday objects (notably food) in soft fabrics and blowing them up to giant size; **Robert Rauschenberg** by making collages or "assemblages" of ordinary objects; **Roy Lichtenstein** by imitating the screen process of newspapers and cartoon strips; and **Ed Kienholz** through realistic tableaux of the sad, shabby or just plain weird aspects of modern life. But what Pop Art really did was to make art accessible and fun. With it the commonplace became acceptable material for the twentieth-century artist, and as such paved the way for what was to follow. **Graffiti** has since been elevated to the status of art form, and New York painters like **Keith Haring** (who died in 1990) and **Kenny Scharf** were celebrities in their own right, regularly called in to decorate Manhattan nightclubs. Haring's last finished work was an altar – complete with his trademark figures – installed in the Cathedral of St John the Divine.

On the whole New York's artistic star has waned over recent years. There has been a return to straight figurative depictions, either supra-realistically as in the poignant acetate figures of **Duane Hanson**, or in the more conventional nude studies of **Philip Pearlstein**. Perhaps the best-known artist of the last decade or so has been **Jean-Michel Basquiat**, if only for his well-publicized affair with Madonna, who owns several of his paintings. Basquiat began his career in the mid-Eighties as part of a two-man graffiti team called SAMO ("Same Old Shit"), and was marketed by the city's art dealers as a wild street kid – even though his family background was in fact comfortably middle-class. Sadly, their prophecy turned out to be a self-fulfilling one: Basquiat was a confirmed heroin user and died in 1989. The 1990s have yet to throw up a New York artist as famous internationally as Basquiat, whose life was recently made into a 1996 movie directed by fellow artist **Julian Schnabel**. One fairly big name on the scene has been **Jeff Koons**, who picked up the Pop Art mantle where Warhol and others left off, and who is perhaps an even greater self-promoter, but for the moment the city's artistic scene is still quieter than it has been for some time.

Books

Since the number of **books** on or set in New York is so vast, what follows is necessarily selective. Use it as a launchpad for further sleuthing. Publishers are given in the order British/American if they are different for each country; where a book is published only in one country, it is designated UK or US; o/p indicates a book out of print.

Essays and impressions

Djuna Barnes *New York* (Sun & Moon Press, US). This collection of newspaper stories – from 1913 to 1919 – looks mostly at out-of-the-way characters and places. Highly evocative of the times – a period in New York, and the world over, of great flux. See especially the piece on the "floating hotel for girls."

Anatole Broyard *Kafka Was the Rage* (Vintage, US). This new and highly readable account of "bohemian" 1940s Greenwich Village is occasionally misogynistic and somewhat self-congratulatory in parts. But Broyard's style and his descriptions of City College's radical/intellectual scene are gripping.

Jerome Charyn *Metropolis* (Abacus/Avon). A native of the Bronx, Charyn dives into the New York of the 1980s from every angle and comes up with a book that's still sharp, sensitive and refreshingly real. See also "New York in Fiction," p.460.

Josh Alan Friedman *Tales of Times Square* (Feral House). Chronicles activities on and around the square between 1978 and 1984, pornography's golden age. Its no-nonsense style of narration documents a culture under seige of impresarios, pimps and 25-cent thrills.

Frederico Garcia Lorca *Poet in New York* (Penguin/Grove Weidenfeld, o/p). The Andalusian poet and dramatist spent nine months in the city around the time of the Wall Street Crash. This collection of over thirty poems reveals his feelings on the brutality, loneliness, greed, corruption, racism and mistreatment of the poor.

Joseph Mitchell *Up in the Old Hotel* (Random House US). Mitchell's collected essays (he calls them stories), all of which appeared in the *New Yorker*, are works of a sober if manipulative genius. Mitchell depicts characters and situations with a reporter's precision and near-perfect style – he is the definitive chronicler of NYC street life.

Jan Morris *Manhattan '45* (Penguin/OUP). Morris's best piece of writing on Manhattan, reconstructing New York as it greeted returning GIs in 1945. Effortlessly written, fascinatingly anecdotal, marvellously warm about the city. See also *The Great Port* (OUP).

Georges Perec, Robert Bober *Ellis Island* (New Press, US). A brilliant, moving, original account of the "island of tears": parts history, meditation and interview-collection. Some of the stories are heartbreaking (between 1892 and 1924 there were 3000 suicides on the island), and the pictures are even more so.

Guy Trebay *In the Place to Be: Guy Trebay's New York* (Temple University Press, US). Collected columns by one of the more notable *Village Voice* writers. They celebrate populations on the margins, which, as the warm columns show, are the very fabric and spirit of the city – and hence not "marginal" at all.

History, politics and society

Herbert Asbury *The Gangs of New York* (Paragon House, US). First published in 1928, this fascinating account of the seamier side of New York is essential reading. Full of historical detail, anecdotes and character sketches of crooks, the book describes New York mischief in all its incarnations and locales.

Robert A Caro *The Power Broker: Robert Morris and the Fall of New York* (Vintage, US). Despite its foreboding size, this brilliant and searing critique of New York City's most powerful twentieth-century figure is one of the most important books ever written about the city and its environs. Caro's book brings to light the megalomania and manipulations responsible for the creation of the nation's largest urban infrastructure.

George Chauncey *Gay New York: The Making of the Gay Male World 1890–1940* (HarperCollins/Flamingo). Definitive, revealing account of the city's gay subculture, superbly researched. Though academic in approach, it's a highly readable chronicle of a much-neglected facet of New York's character.

Anne Douglas *Terrible Honesty: Mongrel Manhattan in the 1920s* (Picador/Farrar, Straus, Giroux). The media and artistic culture of the Roaring Twenties, a never-repeated fluke that was a casualty of the Depression.

Edward Robb Ellis *The Epic of New York City* (Marboro books, o/p). Popularized history of the city in which its major historical figures – Peter Stuyvesant, William Tweed and the rest – become a cast of characters as colorful as any historical novel. Interesting, but you sometimes wonder where Ellis gets his facts from.

Timothy J. Gilfoyle *New York City, Prostitution and the Commercialization of Sex 1790–1920* (W.W. Norton & Co, US). This dense read, chock-full of quotes, is worth plowing through for its vivid description of the sex trade. The development of New York City is linked inextricably with the (often fascinating) machinations of the brothel/dance hall world.

Kenneth T. Jackson (ed) *The Enyclopedia of New York* (Yale UP). Massive, engrossing and utterly comprehensive guide to just about everything in the city. Much dry detail, but packed with incidental wonders: did you know, for example, that there are more (dead) people in Calvary Cemetery, Queens, than there are (living) people in the whole borough? Or that Truman Capote's real name was Streckford Persons?

John A. Kouwenhoven *Columbia Historical Portrait of New York* (Doubleday US). Interpreting the evolution of the city in visual terms (with illuminating captions accompanying the illustrations), this opus is monumental, fascinating and definitive.

David Levering Lewis *When Harlem was in Vogue* (Penguin US). Much-needed account of the Harlem Renaissance, a brief flowering of the arts in the 1920s and 1930s. Just reissued, with a new introduction, this detailed but readable history traces the movement to its untimely end, a suffocation by the dual forces of depression and racism. Lewis also edited the *Portable Harlem Renaissance Reader* (Penguin), an anthology of the writing of the time.

Legs McNeil and Gillian McCain *Please Kill Me* (Abacus/Penguin). An oral history of punk music in New York, artfully constructed by juxtaposing snippets of interviews as if the various protagonists (artists, financiers, impresarios) were in a conversation. Sometimes hilarious, often quite bleak.

Michael Pye *Maximum City: The Biography of New York* (Picador, UK). Newish overview by a transplanted Brit; more synoptic, less impressionistic than Charyn's *Metropolis.*

Luc Sante *Low Life: Lures and Snares of Old New York* (Vintage US). This chronicle of the seamy side between 1840 and 1919 is a pioneering work. Full of outrageous details usually left out of conventional history, it reconstructs the day-to-day life of the urban poor with a shocking clarity. Sante's prose is poetic and nuanced, his evocations of the seedier neighborhoods, their dives and pleasure-palaces, quite vivid.

Art, architecture and photography

Lorraine Diehl *The Late Great Pennsylvania Station* (Four Walls Eight Windows, US). The anatomy of a travesty. How could a railroad palace, modeled after the Baths of Caracalla in Rome, stand for only fifty years before being destroyed? The pictures alone warrant the price.

H. Klotz (ed.) *New York Architecture 1970–1990* (Prestel/Rizzoli). Extremely well-illustrated account of the shift from Modernism to postmodernism and beyond.

Jacob Riis *How the Other Half Lives* (Dover/Hill & Wang). Republished photo-journalism reporting life in the Lower East Side at the end of the nineteenth century. The original awakened many to the plight of New York's poor.

Stern, Gilmartin, Mellins/Stern, Gilmartin, Massengale/Stern, Mellins, Fishman *New York 1900/1930/1960* (Rizzoli, US). These three exhaustive tomes, subtitled "Metropolitan Architecture and Urbanism," contain all you'd ever want or need to know about architecture and the organization of the city. The facts are dazzling and numbing, the photos nostalgia-inducing.

N. White and E. Willensky (eds.) *AIA Guide to New York* (Macmillan/Harcourt Brace). Perhaps even more than the above, the definitive contemporary guide to the city's architecture, far more interesting than it sounds.

Gerard R. Wolfe *New York: A Guide to the Metropolis* (McGraw-Hill, US). Only available in the States, this is more academic – and less opinionated – than Goldberger's book, but it does include some good stuff on the Outer Boroughs. Also informed historical background.

Specific guides

Richard Alleman *The Movie Lover's Guide to New York* (Harper & Row, US). More than two hundred listings of corners of the city with cinematic associations. Interestingly written, painstakingly researched and indispensable to anyone with even a remote interest in either New York or film history.

Joann Biondi & James Kaskins *Hippocrene USA Guide to Black New York* (Hippocrene, US). Borough-by-borough gazetteer of historic sites and contemporary shops of special Afro-American interest.

Judi Culbertson and Tom Randall *Permanent New Yorkers* (Chelsea Green, US). This unique guide to the cemeteries of New York includes the final resting-places of such notables as Herman Melville, Duke Ellington, Billie Holliday, Horace Greeley, Mae West, Judy Garland and 350 others.

Federal Writer's Project *The New York City Guide* (New Press). An indispensable artifact from 1940, the fruit of a project designed by the WPA to employ out-of-work writers. Recently reissued, this highly detailed guide still makes for fascinating reading.

Daniel Hurewitz *Stepping Out: 9 Walks through New York City's Gay and Lesbian Past* (Henry Holt & Co). An inspiring book, full of fascinating tidbits of gay-lore, and avowedly trashy. The book takes you on walking tours through every corner of the city, pointing out the signs and traces of gay life and gay culture in a conversational, anecdotal style.

Mark Leeds *Ethnic New York* (Passport Books, US, o/p). A guide to the city that details its major ethnic neighborhoods, with descriptions of restaurants, shops and festivals. Though its maps are

terrible, it's an excellent introduction to the city's ethnic locales, especially outside Manhattan.

Andrew Roth *Infamous Manhattan* (Carol Publishing Group, US). A vivid and engrossing history of New York crime, revealing the sites of Mafia hits, celebrity murders, nineteenth-century brothels, and other wicked spots, including a particularly fascinating guide to restaurants with dubious, infamous or gory pasts. As a walking tour guide it can't be beaten, but the stories and anecdotes of 350 years of Manhattan misdeeds are just as absorbing from an armchair. The most accurate and entertaining book on the subject yet published.

New York in fiction

Martin Amis *Money* (Penguin/Viking Penguin). Following the wayward movements of degenerate film director John Self between London and New York, a weirdly scatological novel that's a striking evocation of 1980s excess.

Paul Auster *The New York Trilogy: City of Glass, Ghosts* and *The Locked Room* (Faber/Viking Penguin). Three Borgesian investigations into the mystery, madness and murders of contemporary NYC. Using the conventions of the crime thriller, Auster unfolds a disturbed and disturbing picture of the city.

James Baldwin *Another Country* (Penguin/ Vintage). Baldwin's best-known novel, tracking the feverish search for meaningful relationships among a group of 1960s New York bohemians. The so-called liberated era in the city has never been more vividly documented – nor its knee-jerk racism.

John Franklin Bardin *The Deadly Percheron; The Last of Philip Banter; Devil Take the Blue-Tail Fly* (Penguin/Viking Penguin, all o/p). These three unique tales are the only work by Bardin, who disappeared from literary life in 1948; paranoid, almost surreal mysteries that use 1940s New York as a vivid backdrop for intricate storylines.

Jennifer Belle *Going Down* (Virago/Berkley). A brilliant first novel that chronicles the "descent" of an NYU student into working as a call girl. Full of surprising turns of phrase and some deadpan black humor.

Thomas Beller *Seduction Theory* (Abacus/Warner Books). Tales of youthful angst and yearning all set in New York City. Intelligent, penetrating and vaguely melancholic.

Lawrence Block *When the Sacred Ginmill Closes* (Phoenix/Avon). Tough to choose between this and *Dance at the Slaughterhouse*, or any of his other Matthew Scudder suspense novels. However, Block may be at his best here, with expert details of Hell's Kitchen, downtown Manhattan and far-flung parts of Brooklyn woven into this dark mystery.

William Boyd *Stars and Bars* (Penguin/Viking Penguin). Set partly in New York, part in the deep South, a well-observed novel that tells despairingly and hilariously of the unbridgeable gap between the British and Americans. Full of ringing home truths for the first-time visitor to the States.

Claude Brown *Manchild in the Promised Land* (Signet, US). Gripping autobiographical fiction set on the hard streets of Harlem and published in the mid-1960s; not as famous as *Invisible Man* (see Ralph Ellison opposite), but still worth the trip.

Truman Capote *Breakfast at Tiffany's* (Penguin/Random House). Far sadder and racier than the movie, this novel is a rhapsody to New York in the early 1940s, tracking the dissolute youthful residents of an uptown apartment building and their movements about town.

Caleb Carr *The Alienist* (Warner/Bantam). This thriller, set in 1896, evokes Old New York to perfection. The heavy-handed psycho-babble grates at times, but the story line (the pursuit of one of the first serial killers) is good enough. Best for its descriptions of New York's "in places" (and down-and-out locales), as well as saliva-inducing details of meals at long-gone restaurants.

Jerome Charyn *War Cries over Avenue C* (Abacus/Viking Penguin, o/p). Alphabet City is the derelict backdrop for this novel of gang warfare among the Vietnam-crazed coke barons of New York City. An offbeat tale of conspiracy and suspense. A later work, *Paradise Man* (Abacus), is the violent story of a New York hit man.

E.L. Doctorow *Ragtime* (Picador/Bantam). America, and particularly New York, before World War I: Doctorow cleverly weaves together fact and fiction, historical figures and invented characters, to create what ranks as biting indictment of the country and its racism. See also the earlier and equally skillful *Book of Daniel*; *World's Fair*, a beautiful evocation of a Bronx boyhood in the 1930s; *Loon Lake*, much of which is set in the Adirondacks; and the subsequent *Billy Bathgate*. All are published by Picador.

Ralph Ellison *Invisible Man* (Penguin/Random House). The definitive if sometimes long-winded novel of what it's like to be black and American, using Harlem and the 1950s race riots as a background.

Oscar Hijuelos *Our House in the Last World* (Serpent's Tail/Pocket Books). A warmly evocative novel of immigrant Cuban life in New York from before the war to the present day.

Chester Himes *The Crazy Kill* (Alison & Busby/Random House). Himes writes violent, fast-moving and funny thrillers set in Harlem, of which this is just one.

Andrew Holleran *Dancer from the Dance* (Penguin/NAL-Dutton). Enjoyable account of the embryonic gay disco scene of the early 1970s. Interesting locational detail of Manhattan haunts and Fire Island, but suffers from over-exaltation of the central character.

Henry James *Washington Square* (Penguin/Viking Penguin). Skillful examination of the codes and dilemmas of New York genteel society in the nineteenth century.

Joyce Johnson *Minor Characters* (Picador/Pocket Books). Women were never a prominent feature of the Beat generation; its literature examined a male world through strictly male eyes. This book, written by the woman who lived for a short time with Jack Kerouac, redresses the balance superbly well. And there's no better novel available on the Beats in New York. See also her *In the Night Café* (Flamingo), a novel that charts – again in part autobiographically – the relationship between a young woman and a struggling New York artist in the 1960s.

Joseph Koenig *Little Odessa* (Penguin/Ballantine). An ingenious, twisting thriller set in Manhattan and Brooklyn's Russian community in Brighton Beach. A readable, exciting novel, and a good contemporary view of New York City.

Mary McCarthy *The Group* (Penguin/Avon). Eight Vassar graduates making their way in the New York of the Thirties. Sad, funny and satirical.

Jay McInerney *Bright Lights, Big City* (Flamingo/Vintage). A cult book, and one that made first-time novelist McInerney a mint, following a struggling New York yuppie from one cocaine-sozzled nightclub to another.

David Levering Lewis (**ed.**) *The Portable Harlem Renaissance Reader* (Penguin). Though clunky and chunky as some anthologies tend to be, this offers a good introduction to a pivotal epoch of African-American arts and letters. Contains (selections from) essays, memoirs, poetry and fiction.

Henry Miller *Crazy Cock* (HarperCollins/Grove Weidenfeld, o/p). Semi-autobiographical work of love, sex and angst in Greenwich Village in the 1920s. The more easily available trilogy of *Sexus*, *Plexus* and *Nexus* (HC/Grove) and the famous *Tropics* duo (*...of Cancer*, *...of Capricorn*) contain generous slices of 1920s Manhattan as sandwich meat to bohemian life in 1930s Paris.

Dorothy Parker *Complete Stories* (Penguin). Parker's stories are, at times, surprisingly moving. She depicts New York in all its glories, excesses and pretensions with perfect and searing wit. "The Lovely Leave" and "The Game," which focus, as many of the stories do, on the lives of women, are especially worthwhile.

Ann Petry *The Street* (Virago/Houghton Mifflin). The story of a black woman's struggle to rise from the slums of Harlem in the 1940s. Convincingly bleak.

Dawn Powell *The Locusts Have No King* (Steerforth Press, US). A 1940s New York "comedy of manners" describing the high publishing society of the times.

Judith Rossner *Looking for Mr Goodbar* (Cape/Pocket Books). A disquieting book, tracing the progress – and eventual demise – of a woman teacher through volatile and permissive New York in the 1960s. Good on evoking the feel of the city in the 1960s era, but on the whole a depressing read.

Henry Roth *Call It Sleep* (Penguin/Avon). Roth's novel traces – presumably autobiographically – the awakening of a small immigrant child to the realities of life among the slums of the Jewish Lower East Side. Read more for the evocations of childhood than the social comment.

Paul Rudnick *Social Disease* (Penguin/Ballantine). Hilarious, often incredible, send-up of Manhattan night owls. Very New York, *very* funny.

Damon Runyon *First to Last* and *On Broadway* (Penguin); *Guys and Dolls* (River City) in the US. Collections of short stories drawn from the chatter of *Lindy's Bar* on Broadway and since made into the successful musical *Guys 'n' Dolls*.

J.D. Salinger *The Catcher in the Rye* (Penguin/Bantam). Salinger's gripping novel of adolescence, following Holden Caulfield's sardonic journey of discovery through the streets of New York. A classic.

Sarah Schulman *The Sophie Horowitz Story* (Naiad Press, US) and *After Delores* (Plume US, o/p). Lesbian detective stories set in contemporary New York: dry, downbeat and very funny. See also *Girls, Visions and Everything* (Seal Press, US), a stylish and, again, humorous study of the lives of Lower East Side lesbians.

Hubert Selby Jr. *Last Exit to Brooklyn* (Paladin/Grove Weidenfeld). When first published in Britain in 1966 this novel was tried on charges of obscenity and even now it's a disturbing read, evoking the sex, the immorality, the drugs, and the violence of downtown Brooklyn in the 1960s with fearsome clarity. An important book, but to use the words of David Shepherd at the obscenity trial, you will not be unscathed.

Betty Smith *A Tree Grows in Brooklyn* (Pan/HarperCollins). Something of a classic, and rightly so, in which a courageous Irish girl makes good against a vivid prewar Brooklyn backdrop. Totally absorbing.

Rex Stout *The Doorbell Rang* (Fontana/Bantam). Stout's Nero Wolfe is perhaps the most intrinsically "New York" of all the literary detectives based in the city, a larger-than-life character who, with the help of his dashing assistant, Archie Goodwin, solves crimes – in this story and others published by Fontana – from the comfort of his sumptuous midtown Manhattan brownstone. Compulsive reading, and wonderfully evocative of the city in the 1940s and 1950s.

Kay Thompson *Kay Thompson's Eloise* (Simon & Schuster, US). Renowned children's book that works just as well for adults. It details a day in the life of our heroine Eloise, who lives at the Plaza Hotel with her nanny.

Edith Wharton *Old New York* (Virago/Scribners). A collection of short novels on the manners and mores of New York in the mid-nineteenth century, written with Jamesian clarity and precision. Virago/Scribner also publish her *Hudson River Bracketed* and *The Mother's Recompense*, both of which center around the lives of women in nineteenth-century New York.

New York on film

With its dashing skyline and its rugged facades, its mean streets and its swanky avenues, its electric energy and its no-quarter attitude, New York City is a natural-born **movie star**. From the silent era with its cautionary tales of young lovers ground down by the big city, through the noirs of the 1940s shot on the real mean streets themselves, right through to the Lower East Side indies of the 1980s and 1990s, New York – a perfect setting for glitzy romances and nihilistic thrillers alike – has probably been the most filmed city on earth, or at least the one most instantly recognizable from the movies. And the city's visual pizzazz is matched by the vitality of its filmmaking, fostered by a tough, eccentric, and independent spirit that has created mavericks like John Cassavetes and Jim Jarmusch, Shirley Clarke and Spike Lee, as well as directors like Woody Allen and Sidney Lumet who hate to film anywhere else.

What follows is a selection not just of the best New York movies but the most *New York* of New York movies – movies that capture the city's atmosphere, its pulse and its style; movies that celebrate its diversity or revel in its misfortunes;

For more exact movie locations, get hold of *The Movie Lover's Guide to New York* by Richard Alleman (See "Books, p.459").

and movies that, if nothing else, give you a pretty good idea of what you're going to get before you get there.

Ten great New York movies

Breakfast at Tiffany's (Blake Edwards, 1961). This most charming and cherished of New York movie romances stars Audrey Hepburn as party girl Holly Golightly flitting through the glittering playground of the Upper East Side. Hepburn and George Peppard run up and down each other's fire-escapes and skip down Fifth Avenue taking in the New York Public Library and that jewelry store.

Do the Right Thing (Spike Lee, 1989). Set over 24 hours on the hottest day of the year in Brooklyn's Bed-Stuy section – a day on which the melting pot is reaching boiling point – Spike Lee's colorful, stylish masterpiece moves from comedy to tragedy to compose an epic song of New York that just looks better every time you see it.

King Kong (Merian C. Cooper and Ernest B. Schoedsack, 1933). Though half of it takes place on the tropical island from which the eponymous thirty-foot ape is kidnapped, *King Kong* paints a vivid picture of Depression-era Manhattan upon which Kong wreaks havoc, and gives us the city's most indelible movie image: King Kong straddling the Empire State Building and swatting at passing planes.

Lonesome (Paul Fejos, 1928). This recently rediscovered silent classic follows two lonely working-class New Yorkers through one eventful summer Saturday, culminating in an ebullient afternoon at a breathtakingly crowded Coney Island. For full effect, see this visually expressive masterpiece with the witty, thundering live accompaniment of the Alloy Orchestra.

Manhattan (Woody Allen, 1979). A black-and-white masterpiece of middle-class intellectuals' self-absorptions, lifestyles and romances, cued by a Gershwin soundtrack in what is probably the greatest eulogy to the city ever made.

On the Town (Gene Kelly, Stanley Donen, 1949). Three sailors get 24 hours' shore leave in NYC and fight over whether to do the sights or chase the girls. This exhilarating, landmark musical with Gene Kelly, Frank Sinatra, and Ann Miller flashing her gams in the Museum of Natural History was the first to take the musical out of the studios and onto the streets.

On the Waterfront (Elia Kazan, 1954). Few images of New York are as indelible as Marlon Brando's rooftop pigeon coop at dawn and those misty views of the New York harbour (actually shot just over the river in Hoboken), in this unforgettable story of long-suffering longshoreman and union racketeering.

Shadows (John Cassavetes, 1960). Cassavetes later headed West, but his debut is a New York movie par excellence: a New Wave melody about jazz musicians, young love and racial prejudice, shot with a be-bop verve and a jazzy passion in Central Park, Greenwich Village, and even the MoMA sculpture garden.

The Sweet Smell of Success (Alexander Mackendrick, 1957). Broadway as a nest of vipers. Gossip columnist Burt Lancaster and sleazy press agent Tony Curtis eat each other's tails in this jazzy, cynical study of showbiz corruption. Shot on location, and mostly at night, in steely black and white, Times Square and the Great White Way never looked so alluring.

Taxi Driver (Martin Scorsese, 1976). A long night's journey into day by the great chronicler of the dark side of the city – and New York's greatest filmmaker. Scorsese's New York is hallucinatorily seductive and thoroughly repellent in this superbly unsettling study of obsessive outsider Travis Bickle (Robert De Niro).

New York in the 1990s

All Over Me (Alex Sichel, 1997). A beautifully acted coming-of-age tale about a heavyset teenager who is patently but unspokenly in love with her baby doll best friend. Set during a humid Hell's Kitchen summer, this doomed romance is played out in cramped tenement bedrooms and sweltering neighborhood bars and set to a pounding riot grrrl score.

Bad Lieutenant (Abel Ferrara, 1992). Nearly every movie by Ferrara from *Driller Killer* to *The Funeral* deserves a place in a list of great New York movies, but this, above all, seems his own personal *Manhattan*: a journey through the circles of Hell with Harvey Keitel as a depraved Dante.

Jungle Fever (Spike Lee, 1991). Interracial romance in the 1990s seems as taboo as it ever was, and Harlem and Bensonhurst worlds apart, in Lee's ambitious, pessimistic and angry urban love story. With a career-making turn from Samuel L. Jackson as the crack-addicted Gator.

Kids (Larry Clark, 1995). The best New York summer movie since *Do the Right Thing*, and just as controversial. An overhyped but affecting portrait of a group of amoral, though supposedly typical, teenagers hanging out on the Upper East Side, in Washington Square Park, and in the Carmine Street swimming pool on one muggy, mad day.

Little Odessa (James Gray, 1995). Tim Roth plays the prodigal son returning to Brooklyn in this somber, beautifully shot story of the Russian Mafia in Brighton Beach and Coney Island. One of a spate of New York ethnic gangster films made in the 1990s, which, among others, portrayed Irish mobsters (*State of Grace*), Jewish hoodlums (*Amongst Friends*) and African-American gang-bangers (*New Jack City*).

Metropolitan (Whit Stillman, 1990). Away from all the racism, the crime and the homelessness, a group of debutantes and rich young men socialize on the Upper East Side one Christmas, tackling head-on such pressing issues as where to buy a good tuxedo, and behaving as if the 1980s, or the 1880s for that matter, had never ended.

Ransom (Ron Howard, 1996). The haves and the have-nots battle it out on the Upper East Side in this ludicrous Mel Gibson thriller about a millionaire airline magnate whose son is kidnapped by underworld thugs at the Bethesda Fountain in Central Park. Underpaid rogue cop Gary Sinise rails about the "Elois" and "Morlocks" of H.G. Wells' *The Time Machine* to describe the class divide underpinning the economy of 1990s New York.

The Saint of Fort Washington (Tim Hunter, 1992). Nearly invisible on film, the plight of the city's homeless, and of the "squeegee men" – who'll clean your car windshield for spare change and whom Mayor Giuliani decided to outlaw from the city – is portrayed in this heartfelt and sentimental tale of a schizophrenic (Matt Dillon) and a Vietnam vet (Danny Glover) who meet at the Fort Washington shelter in Washington Heights.

Six Degrees of Separation (Fred Schepisi, 1993). Brilliant, enthralling adaptation of John Guare's acclaimed play uses the story of a young black man (Will Smith) who turns up at a rich Upper East Side apartment claiming to be the son of Sidney Poitier as a springboard for an examination of the great social and racial divides of the city.

Smoke (Wayne Wang, 1995). A clever, beguiling film scripted by novelist Paul Auster, which connects a handful of stories revolving around Harvey Keitel's Brooklyn cigar store. Deals with the "beautiful mosaic" in a somewhat self-satisfied way, but, as a fairy-tale about how we might all be able to get along, it's just fine.

New York past

Across the Sea of Time (Stephen Low, 1995). Despite its shamelessly schmaltzy story about a Russian boy searching for long-lost relatives in New York, this film, viewable in the glory of 3-D Imax, is a vivid travelogue which contrasts old stereoscope photographs of the city at the turn of the century with their present-day locations. A perfect introduction to the city's past and present.

The Age of Innocence (Martin Scorsese, 1993). The upper echelons of New York society in the 1870s brought gloriously to life. Though Scorsese, by necessity, restricts most of the action to drawing rooms and ballrooms, look out for the breathtaking matte-shot of a then undeveloped Upper East Side.

The Crowd (King Vidor, 1928). "You've got to be good in that town if you want to beat the crowd." A young couple try to make it in the big city but are swallowed up and spat out by the capitalist machine. A bleak vision of New York in the 1920s, and one of the great silent films.

The Docks of New York (Josef von Sternberg, 1928). Opening with dramatic shots of New York's shoreline during its heyday as a great port, this story of a couple of sailors' shore leave in waterfront flop houses and gin-soaked bars is a far cry from *On the Town*; an ugly world beautifully filmed.

The Godfather Part II (Francis Ford Coppola, 1974). Flashing back to the early life of Vito Corleone, Coppola's great sequel re-created the Italian immigrant experience at the turn of the century, portraying Corleone quarantined at Ellis Island and growing up tough on the meticulously re-created streets of Little Italy.

Hallelujah, I'm a Bum (Lewis Milestone, 1933). Set during the Depression, this eccentric musical

comedy (written in rhyming dialogue) imagines Central Park as a benign haven for the homeless. Die-hard hobo Al Jolson travels north to spend the summer *en plein air* in New York but when he falls in love with a girl he meets in the park he has to take a job on Wall Street.

Hester Street (Joan Micklin Silver, 1975). Young, tradition-bound Russian-Jewish immigrant joins her husband in turn-of-the-century Lower East Side to find he's cast of old world ways. Simple but appealing tale with splendid period feeling. The tenements and markets of 1896 Hester Street were convincingly re-created on the quaint back-streets of the West Village.

Little Fugitive (Morris Engel and Ruth Orkin, 1953). A Brooklyn seven-year-old, tricked into believing he has killed his older brother, takes flight to Coney Island where he spends a day and a night indulging in all its previously forbidden pleasures. This beautifully photographed time capsule of 1950s Brooklyn influenced both the American indie scene and the French New Wave.

Radio Days (Woody Allen, 1987). Woody contrasts reminiscences of his loud, vulgar family in 1940s Rockaway with reveries of the golden days of radio, and the glamour of Times Square, with the same kind of cynical nostalgia with which, in *Bullets Over Broadway* (1994), he spins a yarn about gangsters and theater people in the 1920s.

Speedy (Ted Wilde, 1928). This silent Harold Lloyd comedy shot on location in the city is a priceless time capsule of New York in the 1920s, featuring a horse-drawn trolley chase through the Lower East Side, a visit to Yankee Stadium, and an unforgettably exuberant trip to Coney Island.

New York comedy and romance

An Affair to Remember (Leo McCarey, 1957). After a romance at sea, Cary Grant and Deborah Kerr dock in New York and plan to meet six months hence at the top of the Empire State Building if they can free themselves from prior engagements, and if playboy Grant can make it as a painter in Greenwich Village. A weepy romance canonized by *Sleepless in Seattle*, whose romantic denouement also hinged on an Empire State building meeting.

Annie Hall (Woody Allen, 1977). Oscar-winning autobiographical comic romance, which flits from reminiscences of Alvy Singer's childhood living beneath the Coney Island Cyclone, to life and love in uptown Manhattan (enlivened by endless cocktail parties and trips to see *The Sorrow and the Pity* at the Thalia), is a valentine both to ex-lover co-star Diane Keaton and to the city. Simultaneously clever, bourgeois and very winning.

Big (Penny Marshall, 1988). Tom Hanks grows up far too soon and has to move from New Jersey to the Big City while still at Junior High. A natural at a Madison Avenue toy firm where he finds work as a computer clerk, he impresses his boss with his unbridled enthusiasm for the *F.A.O. Schwarz* toy store, and relocates from a hellish Times Square dive to a to-die-for SoHo loft while trying to find a cure for the secret of his precocious yuppie success.

Crossing Delancey (Joan Micklin Silver, 1989). Lovely story of a Jewish woman (Amy Irving) who lives uptown but visits her grandmother south of Delancey each week. The grandmother and the local yenta hitch her up with a nice young pickle vendor when all she wants is a nasty famous novelist. An engaging view of contemporary life in the Jewish Lower East Side and the yuppie Upper West.

The Daytrippers (Greg Mottola, 1996). This sleeper hit follows a hilariously dysfunctional Long Island family on a Manhattan odyssey in search of their eldest daughter's errant husband, taking them from Park Avenue publishing houses to a startling denouement at a rooftop SoHo party.

Desperately Seeking Susan (Susan Seidelman, 1985). Bored New Jersey housewife Rosanna Arquette arrives in Manhattan on a mission: to find Madonna, or rather Susan, the mysterious subject of a number of cryptic personal ads. Infected with East Village élan, Arquette is transformed into a grungy Madonna clone and finds happiness in this charming paean to the joys of downtown.

Men in Black (Barry Sonnenfeld, 1997). One of the most wittily imaginative Manhattan movies in years portrays the city as a haven for a brave new wave of immigration, with Tommy Lee Jones and Will Smith keeping watch over an Ellis Island for extraterrestrials in the bowels of the Battery Tunnel, while aliens scamper up the side of the Guggenheim Museum, and the future of the universe hangs in the balance in a MacDougal Street jewelry store.

Miracle on 34th Street (George Seaton, 1947). The perfect antidote to all the nightmares and mean streets of New York films, *Miracle* opens during *Macy's* annual Christmas parade, where a kindly old gentleman with a white beard offers to replace the store's inebriated Santa.

The Seven Year Itch (Billy Wilder, 1955). When his wife and kid vacate humid Manhattan, Mitty-like pulp editor Tom Ewell is left guiltily leching over the innocent TV-toothpaste temptress upstairs – Marilyn Monroe, at her most wistfully comic. The sight of her pushing down her billowing skirt as she stands on a subway grating (at Lexington Ave and 52nd St) is one of the era's and the city's most resonant movie images.

Stranger than Paradise (Jim Jarmusch, 1984). Only the first third of this, the original slacker indie, is set in New York, but its portrayal of Lower East Side lethargy is hilariously spot-on and permeates the rest of the film in which a couple of hipster fish venture out of water in Ohio and Florida. And the film's downtown credentials – John Lurie is a jazz saxophonist with the Lounge Lizards, Richard Edson used to drum for Sonic Youth, and Jarmusch himself is an East Village celebrity – are impeccable.

New York nightmares

The Addiction (Abel Ferrara, 1995). A simple trip home from the college library turns into a living nightmare for Lili Taylor when she is bitten by a vampiric street-walker on Bleecker Street and transformed into a blood junkie cruising the East Village for fresh kill.

After Hours (Martin Scorsese, 1985). And if getting into town is difficult, how about trying to enjoy a pleasant evening in the city? Yuppie computer programmer Griffin Dunne tries just that but ends up on an overnight odyssey into the Hades of downtown New York.

Escape from New York (John Carpenter, 1981). In the not too distant future (1997!), society has given up trying to solve the problems of Manhattan and has walled it up as a lawless maximum-security prison from which Kurt Russell has to rescue the hijacked US president.

Jacob's Ladder (Adrian Lyne, 1990). Tim Robbins gets off the subway in Brooklyn but discovers himself locked inside a deserted station . . . and then his troubles begin as his Vietnam-induced hallucinations turn Manhattan into one hell of a house of horrors.

The Lost Weekend (Billy Wilder, 1945). Alcoholic Ray Milland is left alone in the city with no money and a desperate thirst. The film's most famous scene is his long trek up Third Avenue (shot on location) trying to hawk his typewriter to buy booze, only to find all the pawn shops closed for Yom Kippur.

Marathon Man (John Schlesinger, 1976). Innocent, bookish Dustin Hoffman runs for his life all over Manhattan after being dragged into a conspiracy involving old Nazis and being tortured with dental instruments. Shot memorably around the Central Park Reservoir and Zoo, Columbia University, the Diamond District, and Spanish Harlem.

The Out-of-Towners (Arthur Hiller, 1969). If you have any problems getting into town from the airport take solace from the fact that they can be nothing compared to those endured by Jack Lemmon and Sandy Dennis – for whom everything that can go wrong does go wrong – in Neil Simon's frantic comedy.

Rosemary's Baby (Roman Polanski, 1968). Mia Farrow and John Cassavetes move into their dream New York apartment in the Dakota Building (72nd and Central Park West, where John Lennon lived and died) and think their problems stop with nosy neighbors and thin walls until Farrow gets pregnant and hell, literally, breaks loose. Arguably the most terrifying film ever set in the city.

The Taking of Pelham One Two Three (Joseph Sargent, 1974). Just when you thought it was safe to get back on the subway. A gang of mercenary hoods hijacks a train on its way through Midtown and threatens to start killing the passengers at the rate of one a minute if their million-dollar ransom is not paid within the hour.

Wolfen (Michael Wadleigh, 1981). The sins of New York's founding fathers and venal property developers return to haunt the city in the form of vicious wolves in this beautiful and serious horror movie from the director of *Woodstock*(!), one of the very few films that touch on the city's Native American history, and one of the first to use the Steadicam to intelligent effect.

The mean streets

The Cool World (Shirley Clarke, 1964). A 1960s *Boyz'n'the Hood*, this radical, documentary-type study of a Harlem teenager who longs to be a gun-toting gang member proved Clarke to be the political conscience of New York's streets; as had *The Connection* (1962), her portrait of a group of addicts awaiting their pusher, and *Portrait of Jason* (1967), her record of the monologue of an aging black hustler.

Dead End (William Wyler, 1937). Highly entertaining, stage-derived tragedy of the Lower East Side's teeming poor, starring Humphrey Bogart as a mother-obsessed small-time gangster, and a pack of lippy adolescents who earned their own movie series as The Dead End Kids.

Fort Apache, The Bronx (Daniel Petrie, 1981). A film to confirm people's worst fears about the Bronx. Paul Newman stars as veteran cop based in the city's most crime-infested and corrupt precinct. Tense, entertaining and totally unbelievable.

The French Connection (William Friedkin, 1971). Plenty of heady Brooklyn atmosphere in this sensational Oscar-winning cop thriller starring Gene Hackman, whose classic car-and-subway chase takes place under the Bensonhurst Elevated Railroad.

Kiss of Death (Henry Hathaway, 1947; Barbet Schroeder, 1995). The 1947 **Kiss**, with squealing ex-con Victor Mature battling giggling psycho Richard Widmark, was one of the very first films to be shot entirely on real New York locations. Schroeder's remake retells the story in the brighter, tackier Queens of the 1990s, with squealing ex-con David Caruso battling dumb ox Nicolas Cage.

Madigan (Don Siegel, 1968). Opens with a jazzy montage of Manhattan skyscrapers and affluent avenues, then plunges rogue cop Richard Widmark into the mean streets of Spanish Harlem. *Madigan* is a vivid study of the inevitability of police corruption with Henry Fonda as the police commissioner struggling to live within the law.

Mean Streets (Martin Scorsese, 1973). Scorsese's brilliant breakthrough film breathlessly follows small-time hood Harvey Keitel and his volatile, harum-scarum buddy Robert de Niro around a vividly portrayed Little Italy before reaching its violent climax.

Midnight Cowboy (John Schlesinger, 1969) The love story between Jon Voight's naive hustler Buck and Dustin Hoffman's touching city creep Taso Rizzo is the core of this ground-breaking Oscar winner. The pair are superlative.

Naked City (Jules Dassin, 1948). A crime story that views the city with a documentarist's eye. Shot on actual locations, it follows a police manhunt for a ruthless killer all over town toward an unforgettable chase through the Lower East Side and a shoot-out on the Williamsburg Bridge.

Prince of the City (Sidney Lumet, 1981). Lumet is a diehard New York director, and his crime films, including *Serpico, Dog Day Afternoon, Q&A* and *Twelve Angry Men* are all superb New York movies, but this is his New York epic. A corrupt narcotics detective turns federal informer to assuage his guilt, and Lumet takes us from drug busts in Harlem, to the cops' suburban homes on Long Island, to federal agents' swanky pads overlooking Central Park.

Superfly (Gordon Parks Jr, 1972). Propelled by its ecstatic Curtis Mayfield score, this Blaxploitation classic about one smooth-looking drug dealer's ultimate score is best seen today for its mind-boggling fashion excess and its almost documentary-like look at the Harlem bars, streets, clubs and diners of twenty years ago.

New York song and dance

Fame (Alan Parker, 1980). Set in Manhattan's High School for the Performing Arts, the film that spawned the TV series may be a gawky musical, but in its haphazard, sentimental, ungainly way it still manages to capture some of the city's agony and ecstasy.

42nd Street (Lloyd Bacon, 1933). One of the best films ever made about Broadway – though the film rarely ventures outside the theater – this backstage Warner Bros musical stars Ruby Keeler as the young chorus girl who has to replace the ailing leading lady: she goes on stage an unknown and, well, you know the rest.

A Great Day in Harlem (Jean Bach, 1994). A unique jazz documentary that spins many tales around the famous Art Kane photograph for which the cream of New York's jazz world assemble on the steps of a Harlem brownstone one August morning in 1958. Using home-movie footage of the event and present-day interviews, Bach creates a wonderful portrait of a golden age.

Guys and Dolls (Joseph L. Mankiewicz, 1955). *The* great Broadway musical shot entirely on soundstages and giving as unlikely a picture of Times Square hoodlums (all colorfully suited sweetie-pies) as was ever seen. And a singing and dancing Marlon Brando to boot!

Hair (Milos Forman, 1979). Film version of the counter-culture musical turns Central Park into a hippy paradise for the hirsute Treat Williams and his fellow Aquarians. Choreography (including dancing police horses) by Twyla Tharp.

It's Always Fair Weather (Gene Kelly, Stanley Donen, 1955). *On the Town* gone sour. A trio of wartime buddies vow to reunite in the Apple ten years hence, only to discover that they loathe one other and their own lives. Smart, cynical, satirical musical with a bunch of terrific numbers, including a back-alley trash-can dance.

New York, New York (Martin Scorsese, 1977). Scorsese's homage to the grand musicals of postwar Hollywood, reimagined for the post-Vietnam era. His grand folly opens on V-J day in Times Square with sax player Robert de Niro picking up Liza Minnelli in a dance hall, and follows their career and romance together through the Big Band era. Unusually for Scorsese, but befitting the film, the eponymous city was stylishly re-created on studio soundstages.

Saturday Night Fever (John Badham, 1977). What everybody remembers is the tacky glamour of flared white pants-suits and mirror-balled discos, but *Saturday Night Fever* is actually a touching and believable portrayal of working-class youth in the 1970s (Travolta works in a paint store when he's not strutting the dance floor), Italian-American Brooklyn, and the road to Manhattan.

Sweet Charity (Bob Fosse, 1969). Shirley MacLaine's lovable prostitute Charity hoofs around Manhattan getting the short end of the stick at every turn. Mugged in Central Park *by her boyfriend,* Charity blithely wanders the city dancing on roof-tops and in swank uptown clubs, and ends up back in the Park rescued by a merry band of escapees from *Hair.*

West Side Story (Robert Wise, Jerome Robbins, 1961). Sex, singing and Shakespeare in an over-lauded hypercinematic Oscar-winning musical (via Broadway) about rival street gangs. Lincoln Center now stands where the Sharks and the Jets once rumbled and interracial romance ended in tragedy.

Yankee Doodle Dandy (Michael Curtiz, 1932). James Cagney's Oscar-winning performance as showbiz renaissance man George M. Cohan is a big-spirited biopic with music. Of its kind, probably the best ever (see also "New York people").

A glossary of New York terms and people

New York has a **jargon** all its own – some of it unintelligible to non-natives. Though the selection below is by no means a dictionary of New York, it is basic to an understanding of the city and this guide – containing a scattering of art/architecture terms used here. Also included, lastly, is a roll call of prominent New Yorkers, past and present.

New York terms and acronyms

Art Deco Style of decoration popular in the 1930s, characterized by geometrical shape and pattern.

Art Nouveau Art, architecture and design of the 1890s typified by stylized vegetable and plant forms.

Atrium Enclosed, covered pedestrian space usually forming the lobby of a corporate building.

Avenue of the Americas Recent and little-used name for Sixth Avenue.

Bag Lady Homeless woman who carries her possessions around in a bag.

Bathroom/Restroom/Washroom/Comfort Station Euphemisms for a toilet.

Beaux Arts Style of Neoclassical architecture taught at the Ecole des Beaux Arts in Paris at the end of the last century and widely adopted in New York City.

Big Apple New York City. Possibly from the slang of jazz musicians who referred to anything large as a "big apple" – and, for them, New York was the biggest apple of all.

Brownstone Originally a nineteenth-century terraced house with a facade of brownstone (a kind of sandstone); now any row or townhouse.

Clapboard House covered with overlapping timber boards.

Colonial Style of Neoclassical architecture popular in the seventeenth and eighteenth centuries.

Colonial Dames of America Patriotic organization of women descended from worthy ancestors who became American residents before 1750.

Condo Short for condominium, an individually owned apartment within a building.

Co-op The most popular form of apartment ownership in the city. A co-op differs from a condo in that you buy shares in the building in which the apartment is sited, rather than the apartment itself.

CUNY City Universtiy of New York.

Federal Hybrid of French and Roman domestic architecture common in the late eighteenth century and early nineteenth century.

Gotham Another name for New York City, introduced in these parts by Washington Irving.

Greek Revival Style of architecture that mimicked that of classical Greece. Highly popular for major banks and larger houses in the early nineteenth century.

Gridlock Traffic freeze – when cars get trapped in street and avenue intersections, preventing traffic on the cross streets passing through.

Historical District Official label for an area considered of historic interest or importance.

Lex Conversational shorthand for Lexington Avenue.

Loft Large open space at the top of an apartment block, popular with artists because of the direct lighting.

MTA *(Metropolitan Transit Authority)* Runs the city's buses and subway lines: the *IND* (Independent), *BMT* (Brooklyn-Manhattan Transit) and *IRT* (Interborough Rapid Transit).

PATH *(Port Authority Trans Hudson)* The agency that operates the commuter train, also known as the PATH, between Manhattan and New Jersey.

Plaza Wide, open space that acts as a pedestrian forecourt to a skyscraper – and that gives it a prestigious address (One So-and-So Plaza) that can lead to much confusion when you try to work out just where the building actually *is*. See also **Zoning Ordinances**.

Port Authority Conversational shorthand for the Port Authority Bus Terminal on Eighth Avenue and 41st Street.

Robber Barons Nineteenth-century magnates who made their fortunes at the expense and to the detriment of ordinary Americans.

Skyscraper The word comes from the highest sail on a sailing ship, and hence refers to any high building.

SRO Single-room occupancy hotel – most often lived in long term by those on welfare (state benefit).

Stoop Open platform, with steps leading up to it, at the entrance to a house.

SUNY State University of New York.

Tenement Large, nowadays often slummy, building divided into apartments.

Tri-State Area All-encompassing term for New York, New Jersey and Connecticut states.

Vest Pocket Park Tiny park or open space.

WPA (Works Project Administration) Agency begun by Roosevelt in 1935 to create employment. As well as construction work the **WPA** art projects produced many murals in public buildings and a renowned set of guidebooks to the country.

Zoning Ordinances Series of building regulations. The first, passed in 1915, stated that the floor space of a building could not be more than twelve times the area of its site, discouraging giant monoliths and leading to the setback or wedding cake style of skyscraper. A later ordinance allowed developers to build higher provided they supplied a public space at the foot of the building. Hence the **Plaza**.

New York people

ALLEN Woody Writer, director, comedian. Many people's clichéd idea of the neurotic Jewish Upper East Side Manhattanite. His clever, crafted films *Annie Hall*, *Manhattan*, *Broadway Danny Rose*, *Hannah and Her Sisters*, *Radio Days* and *Crimes and Misdemeanors* comment on, and have become part of, the New York myth. His fall from grace in 1993, accused of child abuse by Mia Farrow after he left her for his adopted daughter, caused the biggest storm of publicity seen in the city in years.

ASTOR John Jacob (1822–90) Robber baron, slum landlord and, when he died, the richest man in the world. Astor made his packet from exacting swingeing rents from those living in abject squalor in his many tenement buildings. By all accounts, a real bastard.

BEECHER Henry Ward (1813–87) Revivalist preacher famed for his support of women's suffrage, the abolition of slavery – and as the victim of a scandalous accusation of adultery that rocked nineteenth-century New York. His sister, Harriet Beecher Stowe, wrote the bestselling novel *Uncle Tom's Cabin*, which contributed greatly to the antislavery cause.

BRADY James ("Diamond Jim") (1856–1917) Financier, wide boy and bon vivant of the Gay Nineties. Famed for bespattering himself with diamonds – hence the nickname. One of the good guys of the era, he gave much money to philanthropic causes.

BRESLIN Jimmy Bitter, Brit-hating but often brilliant columnist for *New York Newsday*. Once ran for mayor on a Secessionist ticket (declaring New York City independent from the State) with Norman Mailer (q.v.) as running mate.

BRYANT William Cullen (1794–1878) Poet, newspaper editor and main mover for Central Park and the Metropolitan Museum. The small park that bears his name at 42nd Street and Fifth Avenue has been expertly cleaned up and is now a fitting memorial to this nineteenth-century Wunderkind.

BURR Aaron (1756–1836) Fascinating politician whose action-packed career included a stint as vice-president, a trial and acquittal for treason, and, most famously, the murder of Alexander Hamilton (q.v.) in a duel. His house, the Morris-Jumel Mansion, still stands.

CARNEGIE Andrew (1835–1919) Emigré Scottish industrialist who spent most of his life amassing a vast fortune and his final years giving it all away. Unlike most of his wealthy contemporaries he was not an ostentatious man – as his house, now the Cooper-Hewitt Museum, shows.

COHAN George M. (1878–1942) If you've seen the illustrious biopic *Yankee Doodle Dandy* you probably think this actor, dancer, composer, playwright and Broadway producer was a wonderful chap; in reality Cohan was a dislikable and disreputable wheeler-dealer who ruined others for his success.

CRISP Quentin Writer (*The Naked Civil Servant*) and celebrated apologist for NYC, living in self-imposed exile from his native England. Frequently to be found giving readings.

CUOMO Mario Former governor of New York State and once a suggested contender for the Democratic Party presidential nomination. A liberalish politician, Cuomo has increasingly taken a backseat to his son Andrew – a rising star in the Democratic Party.

DINKINS David First black mayor of New York City, elected in 1989 after a hard, mud-slinging mayoral battle against Republican Rudolph Giuliani. His term in office left him seeming ineffectual and weak: "Everything sticks to him but praise," said a pundit.

FRICK Henry Clay (1849–1919) John Jacob Astor (q.v.) minus the likable side. Frick's single contribution to civilization was to use his inestimable wealth to plunder some of the finest art treasures of Europe, now on show at his erstwhile home on Fifth Avenue.

FULTON Robert (1765–1815) Engineer, inventor and painter who got surburban commuting going with his ferry service to Brooklyn. The point where it landed now marks the beginning of Fulton Street. He did not, as you'll read everywhere else, invent the steamboat.

GARVEY Marcus (1887–1940) Activist who did much to raise the consciousness of blacks in the early part of the century (and is now a Rasta myth). When he started to become a credible political threat to the white-controlled government he was thrown in prison for fraud; pardoned but deported, he spent his last years in London.

GILBERT Cass (1859–1934) Architect of two of the city's most beguiling landmarks – the Woolworth Building and the Customs House.

GINSBERG Allen (1926-97) Revereed beatnik poet, activisit and hero of the Lower East Side.

GOULD Jay (1836–92) Robber baron extraordinaire. Using the telegraph network to be the first person in the know, Gould made his fortune during the Civil War, and went on to manipulate the stock market and make millions more. His most spectacular swindle cornered the gold market, netted him $11 million in a fortnight and provoked the "Black Friday" crash of 1869.

GREELEY Horace (1811–72) Campaigning founder-editor of the *New Yorker* magazine and *Tribune* newspaper who said, "Go West, young man!", but never did. An advocate of women's rights, union rights, the abolition of slavery and other worthy, liberal matters.

GIULIANI Rudolph Mayor. Former US district attorney who has carried his bulldog ways of prosecuting crimes to the mayor's office. Often derided for his "quality of life" laws, but gets the job done as a Republican leader in a Democrat-heavy city.

HAMILL Pete Newspaper editor, writer, broadcaster and expert on Manhattan and – especially – the Outer Boroughs. One of the best no-bullshit commentators around today, though recently forced from his chief position at *Daily News*.

HAMILTON Alexander (1755–1804) Brilliant Revolutionary propagandist, fighter (battlefield aide to Washington), political thinker (drafted sections of the Constitution) and statesman (first Secretary to the Treasury). Shot and killed in a duel by Aaron Burr (q.v.). His house, Hamilton Grange, is preserved at the edge of Harlem.

HARING Keith (1958–90) Big-name artist who used crude animal forms for decoration/patterning. Designed bits of *Palladium* nightclub, sleeve to Malcolm McLaren's *Buffalo Girls*, etc. His early death prematurely removed one of America's most promising artists and designers.

HELMSLEY Harry (1904–97) Property-owning tycoon who, like Donald Trump (q.v.), had a penchant for slapping his name on all that fell into his grasp. Hence many old hotels are now Helmsley Hotels, and, more offendingly, the New York Central Building on Park Avenue has become the Helmsley Building.

HELMSLEY Leona Widow of Harry, self-styled "Queen of New York" and major-domo of the *Helmsley Palace Hotel*. To the delight of many, the shit hit the fan for Leona in 1989, when she was found guilty of million-dollar tax evasion.

IRVING Washington (1783–1859) Satirist, biographer, short story writer (*The Legend of Sleepy Hollow*, *Rip Van Winkle*) and diplomat. His house, just outside the city at Tarrytown, is worth a visit.

JOHNSON Philip Architect. As henchman to Ludwig Mies Van der Rohe, high priest of the International Style glass box skyscraper, he designed the Seagram Building on Park Avenue. In later years he has moved from Modernism to postmodernism, with the AT&T Building on Third Avenue (passable), the Federal Reserve Plaza on Liberty Street (puerile) and the thing at 53rd

Street and Third (unspeakable). Other claims to fame: a brief stint as token intellectual for quasi-fascist senator Huey Long in the 1930s, and his personal founding of the thoroughly fascist *Youth and the Nation* organization.

KOCH Ed The most popular mayor of New York since Fiorello LaGuardia (q.v.). Elected by a slender majority in 1978, Koch won New Yorkers over by his straight-talking, no-bullshit approach – and by moving to appease the loudest liberal/ethnic groups when, and only when, it became politically necessary. After three terms in office, he lost the Democratic nomination in 1989 to David Dinkins (q.v.) following scandals involving other council officials and his insensitive handling of black social problems.

LAGUARDIA Fiorello (1882–1947) NYC mayor who replaced Jimmy Walker (q.v.) and who gained great popularity with his honest and down-to-earth administration.

MAILER Norman The old sexist slugger still breezes in from Brooklyn between novels.

MORGAN J. Pierpont (1837–1913) Top-of-the-pile industrialist and financier who bailed the country out of impending doom in 1907 and used a little of his spare cash to build the Morgan Library on Third Avenue. He created a financial empire that was bigger than the Gettys' and that enabled him to buy out Andrew Carnegie and Henry Frick.

MOSES Robert (1889–1981) Moses is perhaps more than anyone else responsible for the way the city looks today. Holder of all the key planning and building posts from the 1930s to the 1960s, his philosophy of urban development was to tear down whatever was old and in the way, and slap concrete over the green bits in between.

OLMSTED Fredrick (1822–1903) Landscape designer and writer. Central Park and many others were the fruits of his partnership with architect Calvert Vaux.

ONASSIS Jaqueline Kennedy (1929–94). The former First Lady spent most of her later years in the city, working as an editor for Doubleday. Long a byword in style and grace, by the time of her death she had regained much of the public favor lost after her unpopular marriage to the Greek shipping magnate.

O'NEILL Eugene (1888–1953) NYC's (and America's) most influential playwright. Many of the characters from plays like *Mourning Becomes Electra, The Iceman Cometh* and *Long Day's Journey into Night* are based on his drinking companions in *The Golden Swan* bar.

PARKER Dorothy (1893–1967) Playwright, essayist and acid wit. A founding member of the Round Table group at the Algonquin Hotel.

PATAKI George Governor of New York State, who surprisingly ousted Mario Cuomo (q.v) and has had standing feuds with Mayor Giuliani, his fellow Republican who did not back him in 1994.

REED Lou Guitarist, songwriter and poet, Reed was the front man of punk precursors and Warhol-disciples the Velvet Underground. He's still around, still writing and singing songs about life in the city, and his catalog of those is second to none.

RIIS Jacob (1849–1914) Photojournalist. His compassionate account of the poor and the horrors of slum dwelling, *How the Other Half Lives*, was instrumental in hastening the destruction of the worst tenements.

ROCKEFELLER John D. (1839–1937) Multimillionaire oil magnate and founder of the dynasty.

ROCKEFELLER John D. Jr (1874–1960) Unlike his tightfisted dad, Rockefeller Junior gave away tidy sums for philanthropic ventures in New York. The Cloisters Museum, The Museum of Modern Art, Lincoln Center, Riverside Church and most famously the Rockefeller Center were mostly his doing.

ROCKEFELLER Nelson (1908–1979) Politician son of John D. Jr. Elected governor of New York State in 1958, he held on to the post until 1974, when he turned to greater things and sought the Republican Party presidential nomination. He didn't get it, but before his death served briefly as vice-president under Gerald Ford.

RUBELL Steve (1946–89) Entrepreneur. Founder and former owner of *Studio 54*, his last venture (with business partner Ian Shrager) was *The Royalton* hotel, the last word in with-it luxury.

SEINFELD Jerry Comedian of the moment, whose long-running and immensely popular TV series (though filmed in LA) captures New Yorkers' neuroses better than anyone this side of Woody Allen.

SIMON Neil Playwright. With a record of Broadway/film hits as big as his bank balance (*Brighton Beach Memoirs* the latest), Simon can lay claim to being the most popular MOR playwright today.

STEINBRENNER George Baseball team owner/entrepreneur. Known as "The Boss," Steinbrenner runs the beloved Yankees, often with an iron fist, though generous pockets.

TRUMP Donald Property tycoon. When you shell out $70 for your shoebox room, reflect that Donald sits on top of a real estate empire worth, at its peak, $1.3 billion. His creations include the glammed-out Trump Tower on Fifth Avenue, Trump Plaza near Bloomingdale's and Trump's Casino in Atlantic City, NJ. The 1990s have been a rollercoaster: his financial empire took a massive drumming early on; there was a much-publicized divorce from his wife Ivana; then a new marriage and mid-decade comeback; and even more recently, another divorce.

TWEED William Marcy "Boss" (1823–78) Top banana of the NY Democratic Party who fiddled city funds to the tune of $200 million and gave Democratic Party headquarters Tammanny Hall its bad name.

VANDERBILT Cornelius "Commodore" (1794–1877) Builder and owner of much of the nation's railroads in the nineteenth century. At his death he was the wealthiest American ever.

VANDERBILT Cornelius (1843–99) Commodore's son and another hard-nosed capitalist. He doubled the family wealth between his father's death and his own – a fortune that kept (and keeps) successive generations of Vanderbilts in spare change.

WALKER Jimmy (1881–1946) Professional songwriter who turned politician and was elected NYC mayor at the height of the Jazz Age. As a dapperdressed man-about-town he reflected much of its fizz, but with the Depression he lost popularity and office.

WARHOL Andy (1926–87) Artist and media maneuverer. Instigator of Pop Art, The Velvet Underground, The Factory, *Interview* magazine and *Empire* – a 24-hour movie of the Empire State Building (no commentary, no gorillas, nothing but the building). Died, oddly enough, after a routine gallstone operation.

WHITE Stanford (1853–1906) Partner of the architectural firm McKim, Mead and White, which designed such Neoclassical piles as the General Post Office, Washington Square Arch, the Municipal Building and bits of Columbia University. Something of a *roué*, White's days were brought to an abrupt end with a bullet through the head from the gun of a cuckolded husband.

Index

Stay in touch with us!

ROUGH*NEWS* **is Rough Guides' free newsletter. In three issues a year we give you news, travel issues, music reviews, readers' letters and the latest dispatches from authors on the road.**

I would like to receive ROUGH*NEWS*: please put me on your free mailing list.

NAME . . . .

ADDRESS . . . .

Please clip or photocopy and send to: Rough Guides, 1 Mercer Street, London WC2H 9QJ, England or Rough Guides, 375 Hudson Street, New York, NY 10014, USA.

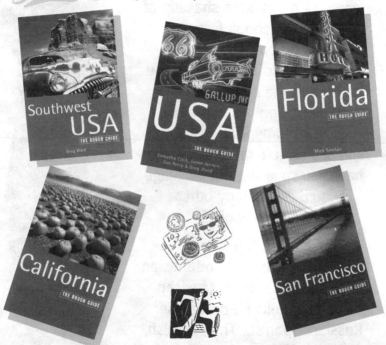

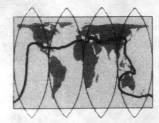

the perfect getaway vehicle

low-price holiday car rental.

rent a car from holiday autos and you'll give yourself real freedom to explore your holiday destination. with great-value, fully-inclusive rates in over 4,000 locations worldwide, wherever you're escaping to, we're there to make sure you get excellent prices and superb service.

what's more, you can book now with complete confidence. our £5 undercut* ensures that you are guaranteed the best value for money in holiday destinations right around the globe.

drive away with a great deal, call holiday autos now on **0990 300 400** and quote ref RG.

holiday autos miles ahead

*in the unlikely event that you should see a cheaper like for like pre-paid rental rate offered by any other independent uk car rental company before or after booking but prior to departure, holiday autos will undercut that price by a full £5. we truly believe we cannot be beaten on price.

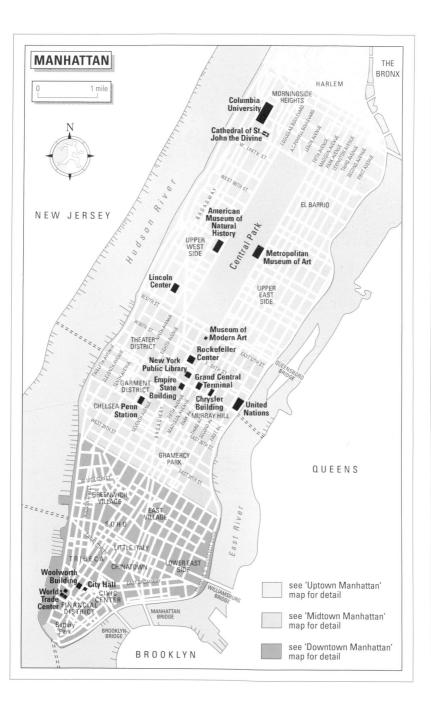

MANHATTAN

0   1 mile

N

THE BRONX

HARLEM

MORNINGSIDE
HEIGHTS

Columbia
University

Cathedral of St.
John the Divine

W. 106TH ST

WEST 96TH ST

NEW JERSEY

FREDERICK DOUGLAS BOULEVARD

A. C. POWELL BOULEVARD

LENOX AVENUE

FIFTH AVENUE

MADISON AVENUE

PARK AVENUE

LEXINGTON AVENUE

THIRD AVENUE

SECOND AVENUE

FIRST AVENUE

Hudson River

BROADWAY

EL BARRIO

American
Museum of
Natural
History

Central Park

UPPER
WEST
SIDE

Metropolitan
Museum of Art

Lincoln
Center

W. 57TH ST

UPPER
EAST
SIDE

W. 50TH ST

NINTH AVENUE

Museum of
Modern Art

THEATER
DISTRICT

EIGHTH AVENUE

Rockefeller
Center

EAST 57TH ST

New York
Public Library

E. 50TH ST

TWELFTH AVENUE

ELEVENTH AVENUE

TENTH AVENUE

Empire
State
Building

Grand Central
Terminal

GARMENT
DISTRICT

SEVENTH AVENUE

BROADWAY

FIFTH AVENUE

MADISON AVENUE

PARK AV.

Chrysler
Building

United
Nations

CHELSEA

Penn
Station

THIRD AVE.

SECOND AVE.

FIRST AV.

MURRAY HILL

WEST 20TH ST

EAST 30TH ST

QUEENSBORO
BRIDGE

QUEENS

GRAMERCY
PARK

EAST 20TH ST

W 10TH STREET

HUDSON STREET

GREENWICH
VILLAGE

EAST
VILLAGE

East River

SOHO

CANAL STREET

LITTLE ITALY

TRIBECA

CHINATOWN

LOWER EAST
SIDE

EAST BROADWAY

Woolworth
Building

City Hall

WILLIAMSBURG
BRIDGE

World
Trade
Center

CIVIC
CENTER

FINANCIAL
DISTRICT

MANHATTAN
BRIDGE

Battery
Park

BROOKLYN
BRIDGE

BROOKLYN

☐ see 'Uptown Manhattan'
map for detail

☐ see 'Midtown Manhattan'
map for detail

☐ see 'Downtown Manhattan'
map for detail

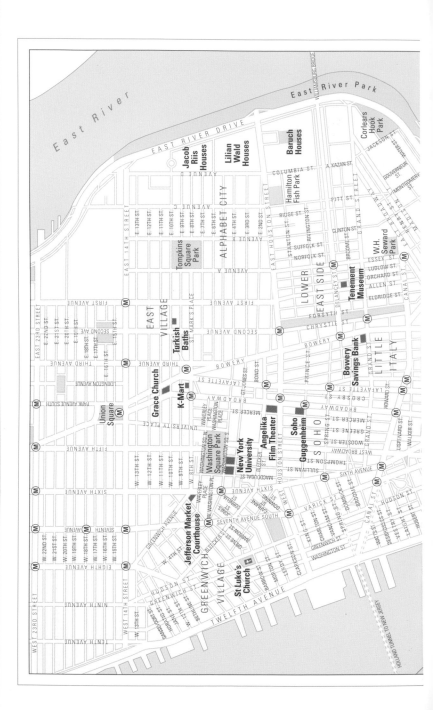

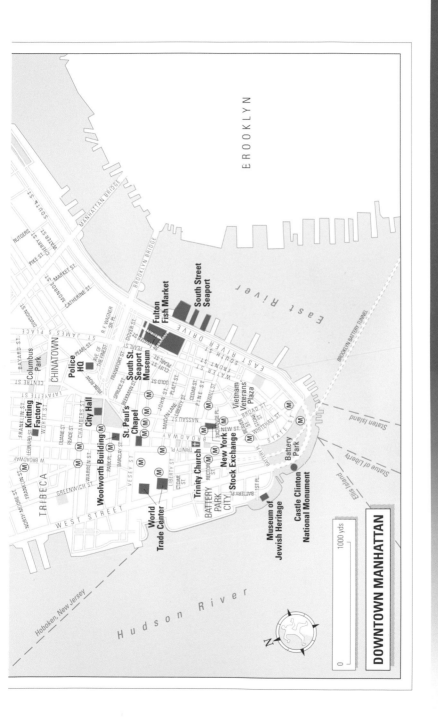

DOWNTOWN MANHATTAN

BROOKLYN

East River

Hudson River

Hoboken, New Jersey

Staten Island

Ellis Island

Statue of Liberty

Brooklyn Battery Tunnel

South Street Seaport

Fulton Fish Market

Manhattan Bridge

Brooklyn Bridge

SOUTH ST DRIVE

EAST RIVER DRIVE

CHINATOWN

Columbus Park

Police HQ

South St. Seaport Museum

Knitting Factory

City Hall

St. Paul's Chapel

Woolworth Building

World Trade Center

Trinity Church

New York Stock Exchange

Vietnam Veterans' Plaza

Battery Park

BATTERY PARK CITY

Museum of Jewish Heritage

Castle Clinton National Monument

TRIBECA

WEST STREET

N

0   1000 yds

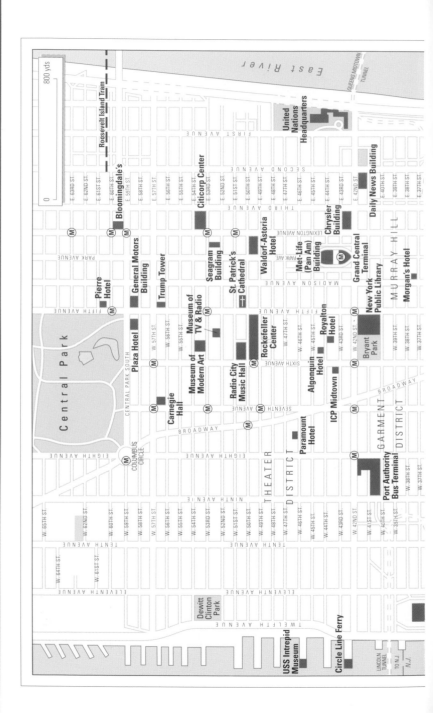

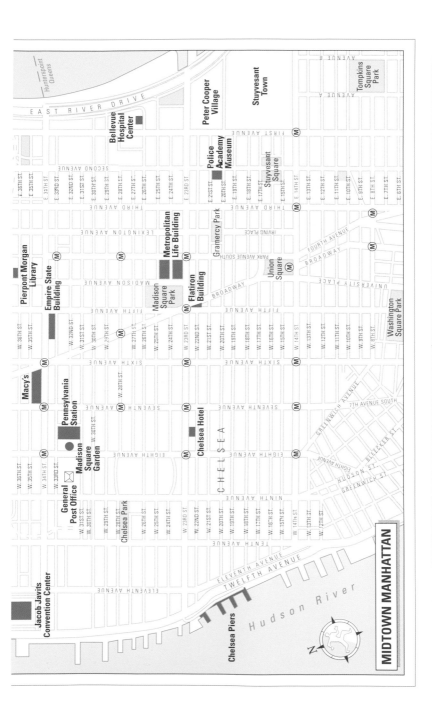

MIDTOWN MANHATTAN

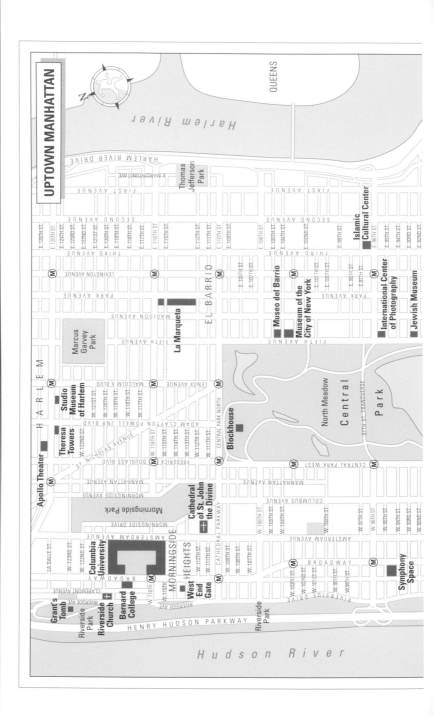

UPTOWN MANHATTAN

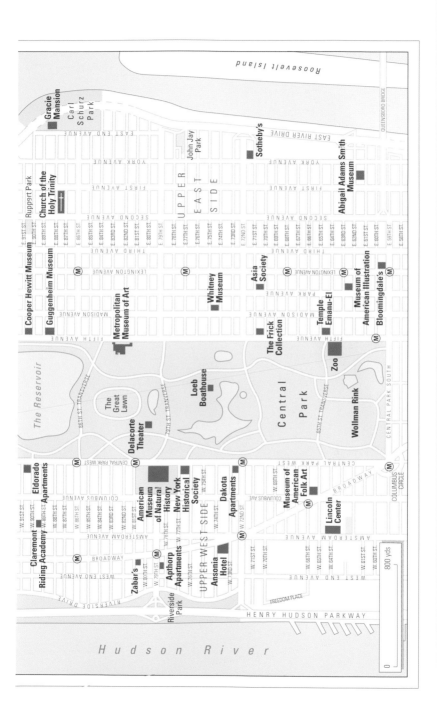

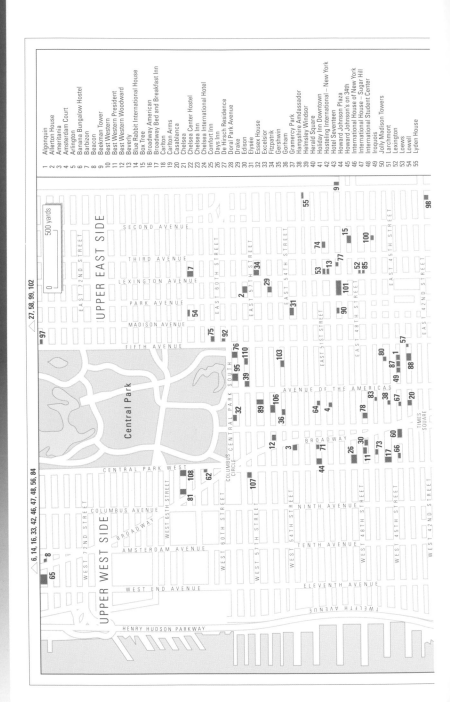

1 Algonquin
2 Allerton House
3 Ameritania
4 Amsterdam Court
5 Arlington
6 Banana Bungalow Hostel
7 Barbizon
8 Beacon
9 Beekman Tower
10 Best Western
11 Best Western President
12 Best Western Woodward
13 Beverly
14 Blue Rabbit International House
15 Box Tree
16 Broadway American
17 Broadway Bed and Breakfast Inn
18 Carlton
19 Carlton Arms
20 Casablanca
21 Chelsea
22 Chelsea Center Hostel
23 Chelsea Inn
24 Chelsea International Hotel
25 Comfort Inn
26 Days Inn
27 De Hirsch Residence
28 Doral Park Avenue
29 Drake
30 Edison
31 Elysée
32 Essex House
33 Excelsior
34 Fitzpatrik
35 Gershwin
36 Gorham
37 Gramercy Park
38 Hampshire Amdassador
39 Helmsley Windsor
40 Herald Square
41 Holiday Inn Downtown
42 Hosteling International – New York
43 Hotel Seventeen
44 Howard Johnson Plaza
45 Howard Johnson's on 34th
46 International House of New York
47 International House – Sugar Hill
48 International Student Center
49 Iroquois
50 Jolly Madison Towers
51 Larchmont
52 Lexington
53 Loews
54 Lowell
55 Lyden House

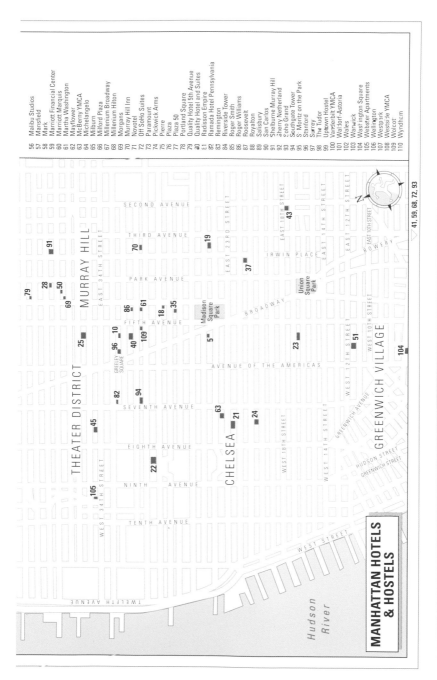

MANHATTAN HOTELS & HOSTELS

56 Malibu Studios
57 Mansfield
58 Mark
59 Marriott Financial Center
60 Marriott Marquis
61 Martha Washington
62 Mayflower
63 McBurny YMCA
64 Michelangelo
65 Milburn
66 Milford Plaza
67 Millenium Broadway
68 Millenium Hilton
69 Morgans
70 Murray Hill Inn
71 Novotel
72 Off SoHo Suites
73 Paramount
74 Pickwick Arms
75 Pierre
76 Plaza
77 Plaza 50
78 Portland Square
79 Quality Hotel 5th Avenue
40 Quality Hotel and Suites
L1 Radisson Empire
82 Ramada Hotel Pennsylvania
83 Remington
84 Riverside Tower
85 Roger Smith
86 Roger Williams
87 Roosevelt
88 Royalton
89 Salisbury
90 San Carlos
91 Shelburne Murray Hill
92 Sherry Netherland
93 Soho Grand
94 Southgate Tower
95 S. Moritz on the Park
96 Stanford
97 Surrey
98 The Tudor
99 Uptown Hostel
100 Vanderbilt YMCA
101 Waldorf-Astoria
102 Wales
103 Warwick
104 Washington Square
105 Webster Apartments
106 Wellington
107 Westpark
108 Westside YMCA
109 Wolcott
110 Wyndham

▷ 41, 59, 68, 72, 93

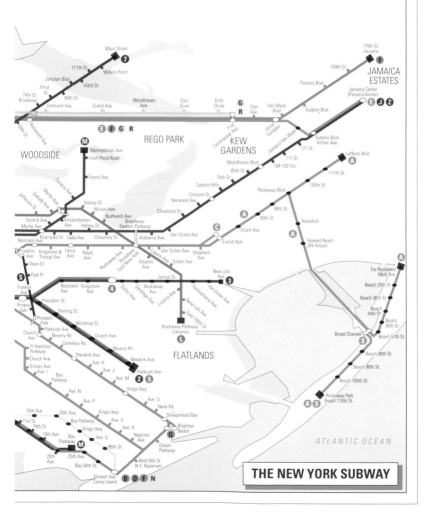

How to Use This Map

Transit Authority services operate 24 hours a day, but not all routes operate at all times. Train identification letters or numbers next to the station names on this map show the basic, seven-day-a-week service, from 6AM to midnight.

- ■ Terminal
- – Local Stop
- ● Express Stop
- ○ All trains stops
- Express and Local Stop (Free Transfer)

THE NEW YORK SUBWAY

ATLANTIC OCEAN

JAMAICA ESTATES

WOODSIDE

REGO PARK

KEW GARDENS

FLATLANDS

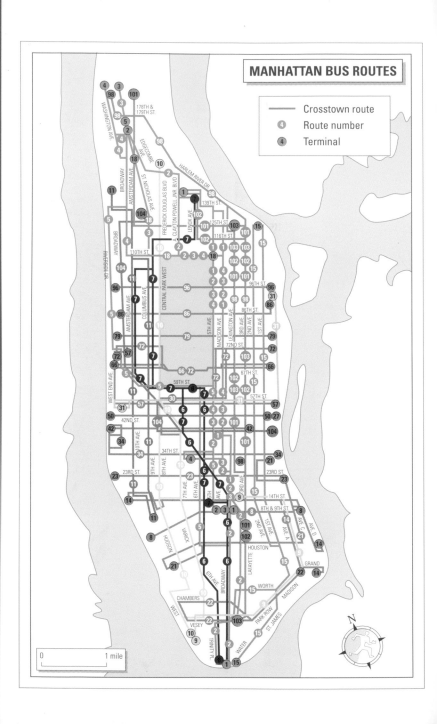

MANHATTAN BUS ROUTES

Crosstown route

④ Route number

④ Terminal